# POLITICS IN THE METROPOLIS

# POLITICS IN THE METROPOLIS

## A Reader in Conflict and Cooperation

### Second Edition

Edited by

## Thomas R. Dye
*Florida State University*

## Brett W. Hawkins
*The University of Wisconsin—Milwaukee*

Charles E. Merrill Publishing Company
*A Bell & Howell Company*
*Columbus, Ohio*

ISBN: 0–675–09252–3

Library of Congress Catalog Card Number: 79–139964

2 3 4 5 6 7 8 9—79 78 77 76 75 74

Printed in the United States of America

# PREFACE

Since the publication of the first edition of this volume in 1967, we have become even more convinced that the principle task of metropolitan government is the resolution of conflict. Recent events in the nation's cities have dramatized the seriousness of divisions among urban Americans. The emphasis in the first edition on conflict and conflict management turned out to be a realistic approach to urban political life.

In this edition we have continued the conflict management thesis, with many new insights and contributions, including: Presidential Advisor Daniel P. Moynihan's analysis of the failures of community action programs in the war on poverty; an examination of the history and growth of racial ghettos in America; a political analysis of the election of Carl Stokes as Mayor of Cleveland, the first black mayor of a large city; a vivid description of the urban riots, together with the recommendations of the President's Commission on Civil Disorder; a dramatic account of urban guerilla warfare, "Shoot-Out in Cleveland"; an analysis of the continuing flight of middle-class whites from the central city to the suburbs; a review of the many problems of big city schools; and an account of New York's attempt at school decentralization and the resulting teachers strike.

THOMAS R. DYE
Tallahassee, Florida

BRETT W. HAWKINS
Milwaukee, Wisconsin

# PREFACE TO THE FIRST EDITION

*Politics in the Metropolis: A Reader in Conflict and Cooperation* is a book of readings dealing with the major conflicts in urban society, and with the structures and processes that function to manage conflict and maintain order in the metropolis. Rather than emphasize the administrative or service problems of metropolitan government, these readings focus upon important conflicts in the metropolis and the way in which conflicts are managed.

Part One, "People and Politics in the Metropolis," describes the diversity of metropolitan life and suggests that conflict is a natural consequence of this diversity. Part Two, "Conflict in the Metropolis: Divisions, Differences, and Discontinuities" describes several specific sources of conflict that divide the metropolis—race, poverty, violence, partisanship, and city-suburban cleavages. Part Three, "Interdependence in the Metropolis: The Promise of Cooperation," focuses on the interdependence of parts of the metropolis as a basis for metropolitan-wide cooperation. It documents the promise of coordination in transportation, education, finance, planning, and public service. Part Four, "Managing Metropolitan Conflict: Structures of Power and Action in the Metropolis" describes the structures and processes available to resolve conflict and bring order to metropolitan areas. It presents readings dealing with both "machine" and "reform" models of city politics and with both "elite" and "pluralist" models of power and influence in urban communities. Finally, Part Five, "Metropolitan Cooperation: Reform and Reality," presents proposals for reform and reorganization of metropolitan government. Perhaps more importantly, it also presents articles which critically examine the obstacles to reorganization and realistically appraise the prospects for metropolitan integration.

Some of the readings in this volume are argumentative in character, while others are more analytic and objective. Some readings are written by the leading participants in urban affairs—John A. McCone, Martin Luther King, and Daniel P. Moynihan, for example—while others are authored by such outstanding urban scholars as Edward C. Banfield, Scott Greer, James Q. Wilson, Henry J. Schmandt, and Charles R. Adrian. The purpose of the editors is to provide both "a feel for" and "an understanding of" the principal conflicts in metropolitan society and the way in which government attempts to resolve these conflicts.

The editors are particularly indebted to Scott Greer, Edward C. Banfield, and James Q. Wilson whose previous scholarship provided the theoretical framework for organizing these selections and whose own writings appear in the volume. We also wish to thank Miss Jane Horowitz and Miss Candace Peltier who prepared the readings.

THOMAS R. DYE

BRETT W. HAWKINS

# CONTENTS

# INTRODUCTION

## Politics in the Metropolis:
## Conflict and Cooperation

**THOMAS R. DYE**

**BRETT W. HAWKINS**

### Politics as the Management of Conflict

It is appropriate that a reader on "metropolitan politics" focus on conflicts in metropolitan life and the way in which these conflicts are managed. For "politics arises out of conflicts, and it consists of the activities
—for example, reasonable discussion, impassioned oratory, balloting,
and street fighting—by which conflict is carried on." [1] The management
of conflict in society is one of the basic purposes of government. The
Founding Fathers were very much aware that the control of "faction"
was a principal function of government. They defined "faction" as a
number of citizens united by a common interest which is adverse to the
interests of a number of other citizens. James Madison thought that
regulating conflict among people with diverse interests was "the principal task of modern legislation." To paraphrase Madison, we think
that the management of conflict is the "principal task" of metropolitan
government.

For many years the literature on metropolitan government seemed
to ignore the insights of the Founding Fathers. Texts on local government overlooked the many conflicts in urban life and talked almost exclusively about the service functions of municipalities. It is true, of
course, that urban governments serve two functions: the "service"
function of providing certain goods and services—such as street paving
and fire protection—and the "political" function of managing conflict.
No one denies the importance of the administrative and technical aspects
of paving streets, fighting fires, directing traffic, removing trash, treating

---

[1] Edward C. Banfield and James Q. Wilson, *City Politics* (Boston: Harvard
University Press and The M.I.T. Press, 1963), p. 7.

1

sewage, and so on. But the really critical problems facing urban dwellers are problems which cannot be solved by administrative efficiency or technological invention. Poverty, racial hatred, violence, slum housing, crime, financial crisis, and transportation chaos are problems which cannot be solved by expertise alone. It is not for lack of technological know-how that these problems go unsolved. Nor is it because administrative arrangements are inadequate. The obstacles to the solution of these problems are primarily political. By that we mean that people have opposing ideas and differing interests regarding what should be done, or whether anything should be done at all. Only when everyone agrees on what should be done is there much to be said for leaving decisions to the technicians. In metropolitan areas there is rarely this agreement on fundamentals. Even if it is true that there is "only one way to pave a street," political questions remain: "Whose street shall be paved?" "Who will get the paving contract?" "Who will bear the cost?" or "Why not build a school gym instead of paving the street?"

But traditional books on urban government sought to eliminate "politics" from the legitimate scope of governmental study. Historically, this attitude arose in conjunction with the municipal reform movement of the progressive era. The reform movement involved a preference for non-partisan elections, city manager government, and an "antiseptic," "no-party" style of government devoid of the stigma of "politics." A city without politics appealed to many idealists who were disenchanted with "boss rule." Another incentive to banishing politics from urban life has been the distaste that many people feel for conflict. Conflict is psychologically discomforting; it arouses strong and unpleasant emotions. Many people feel that the world would be a much more desirable place to live if there were no conflicts among men. Often associated with these feelings is a belief that there is always a "right" answer to public questions, that conflict is unnecessary, and the "reasonable men" can arrive at this answer by thought and discussion. It is a belief that differences of opinion are not really legitimate, that the pursuit of "special interests" is immoral, that all men should devote themselves to the "public interest."

Interestingly enough, even though Madison shared this distaste for conflict, he had long ago given up the notion of eliminating "politics" from public life. He pointed out that this could be done only by "destroying liberty" or by "giving to every citizen the same opinions, the same passions, and the same interests." The former method he thought "unwise" and the latter "impracticable." We think that Madison was right about this.

What are the sources of conflict in metropolitan areas? One might again turn to Madison for insight into this question:

The latent causes of faction are thus sown in the nature of man; and we see them everywhere brought into different degrees of activity, according to the different circumstances of civil society. A zeal for different opinions concerning religion, concerning government, and many other points, as well of speculation as of practice; an attachment to different leaders ambitiously contending for pre-eminence and power; or to persons of other descriptions whose fortunes have been interesting to human passions, have in turn, divided mankind into parties, inflamed them to mutual animosity, and rendered them much more disposed to vex and oppress each other than to cooperate for their common good. So strong is this propensity of mankind to fall into mutual animosity, that where no substantial occasion presents itself, the most frivolous and fanciful distinctions have been sufficient to kindle their unfriendly passions and excite their most violent conflicts. But the most common and durable source of factions has been the various and unequal distribution of property. Those who hold and those who are without property have ever formed distinct interests in society. Those who are creditors, and those who are debtors, fall under a like discrimination. A landed interest, a manufacturing interest, a mercantile interest, a moneyed interest, with many lesser interests grow up of necessity in civilized nations, and divide them into different classes, actuated by different sentiments and views.

In short, a fundamental source of conflict is human diversity. Differences among men in the way they make their living, in their income and educational levels, in the color of their skin, in the way they worship, in their style of living, and so on, are at the roots of political life.

## Cleavages in the Metropolis

Madison's insight about diversity as a source of political conflict is important in understanding metropolitan politics. Urban sociologists tell us that the very definition of urban life involves large numbers of *different* kinds of people living closely together. Numbers, density, and heterogeneity are said to be the distinguishing characteristics of urban life. The concentration of large numbers of people in urban centers, together with technological advancements, has made possible a high degree of specialization. The modern economic system of the metropolis is based upon a highly specialized and complex division of labor. We are told that in the simple peasant village, a dozen occupations exhausted the job opportunities available to men. An agricultural economy meant homogeneous employment opportunities; that is to say, nearly everyone was a farmer or was closely connected to and dependent upon farming. But in the modern metropolis there are tens of thousands of different kinds of jobs, each of which is a distinct part of the economic system. There are wide differences between these many occupational worlds. It is on the basis of his job that the individual receives his income and his share of the goods and services available. Different jobs produce different levels of affluence, dress, and styles of living. The individual's job shapes the way he looks at the world and his evaluations of social and political events. In acquiring his job, he attains a certain level and type of education which also distinguishes him from individuals in other jobs with different educational requirements. Differences in educational level in turn produce a wide variety of differences in opinions, attitudes, and styles of living. Metropolitan living concentrates people with all of these different economic and occupational characteristics in a very few square miles. If Madison was right in saying that differences among men are the source of political conflict, the problem of regulating conflict and maintaining order in the heterogeneous metropolitan community assumes tremendous proportions.

Moreover, we know that differences based on income, occupation, and education are not the only kinds of human diversity in metropolitan areas. People are also differentiated by the color of their skin. In recent years, racial differences have threatened to tear America's cities apart—indeed, to burn them down. A few decades ago opportunities for human betterment in the cities attracted immigrants from Ireland, Germany, Italy, Poland, and Russia; and today the city attracts Negroes, Puerto Ricans, and rural families. These newcomers to the metropolis bring with them different needs, attitudes, and ways of life. The "melting pot" tends to reduce some of this diversity over time, but the pot does not "melt" people fast enough, and not all want to be "melted." Racial conflict remains the most critical problem facing American cities.

People also differ in where they live and how they live. There is a certain uniformity to rural living; day-to-day family life on the farm is remarkably similar from one county to the next. But urban dwellers may live in apartments in the central city or in single-family homes in the suburbs. Some urban dwellers choose a familistic style of life—raising two or more children in their own single-family house with the wife functioning as a homemaker. Others are less familistic—raising no children or a single child in a rented apartment with the wife holding down a job outside of the home. In addition to these economic, ethnic, and life-style differences, we always have with us—as Madison observed—"a zeal for different opinions," "an attachment to different leaders," and even "frivolous and fanciful distinctions."

The list of social, economic, and life-style differences among people in the metropolis is almost endless. Scott Greer writes, "The city is a maze, a social zoo, a mass of heterogeneous social types." Moreover, urban ecologists tell us that people with different social, economic, and life-style characteristics generally live in different parts of the metropolis. Physical separation of residences generally accompanies social and economic separation, and so there are "ghettos," "silk-stocking districts," "Little Italies," upper-class suburbs, and so on. This tends to emphasize and even reinforce differences among people.

The readings in this volume begin by describing the diversity of urban life and the consequences of this diversity for urban government. Part One, "People and Politics in the Metropolis," describes the character of urban living and the different kinds of people who reside in the metropolis. It also describes the formation of the nation's "black ghettos"—the most explosive sector of urban life.

Part Two, "Conflict in the Metropolis," describes a variety of important conflicts in urban life—racial discord, violence, antagonism over poverty and welfare, civil disobedience, friction between city and suburb, and competition between the parties. These conflicts are the divisive forces in the metropolis.

## Interdependence and Decentralization in the Metropolis

The task of governing the metropolis is complicated by another fundamental characteristic of metropolitan life—interdependence. Urban sociologists seem to agree that in addition to numbers, density, and heterogeneity, the interdependence of the inhabitants of the metropolis is a distinguishing characteristic of urban living. Rural living involves much less interdependence. Thus while the traditional family farm was not wholly self-sufficient, its members were much less dependent upon the larger community for employment, goods, and services than the modern urban dweller.

Urban dwellers are highly dependent upon one another in their daily economic and social activities. Suburbanites, for example, rely on the central city for food, clothing, newspapers, entertainment, hospitalization, and a host of other modern household needs. More importantly, they rely on the central city for employment opportunities. Conversely, the central city relies upon the suburbs to supply its labor and management forces. Downtown merchants look to the entire metropolitan area for consumers. This interdependence involves an intricate web of economic and social relationships, a high degree of communication, and a great deal of daily physical interchange among residents, groups, and firms. Just as specialization produces diversity among men, it also produces interdependence among men and the need for coordinated human activity.

If men are to depend upon one another, the behavior of large numbers of diverse individuals and groups must be organized and made predictable. Trains must pull in and out of the city, people must be fed, traffic must be kept moving, water must be made to flow from the taps, public safety must be maintained, epidemics must be avoided. In other words, integrating and coordinating mechanisms must be found to maintain order amid the extreme diversity of the metropolis. This is the first responsibility of metropolitan governments.

Yet even while diversity and heterogeneity require government to coordinate activity in the metropolis, these same forces encourage demands for decentralization and community autonomy. Governmental centralization promotes coordination, but decentralization allows socially homogeneous communities greater control over their own way of life. This means community control over police, schools, garbage collection, recreation, and so on. In the 1950's the cries for decentralization were loudest in the white suburbs, but today the same arguments for community control are being expressed in the ghettos. Governments must structure public programs to meet the requirements for coordination of metropolitan life, yet at the same time incorporate enough flexibility for meaningful community participation.

Part Three of this volume, "Interdependence and Decentralization in the Metropolis," describes some of the major public programs designed to deal with metropolitan life. It presents selections which document the interdependent character of life in the metropolis and which illustrate the need for coordination in education, transportation, housing, urban development, finance, and community action. But these selections also testify to the demands for decentralization and community control in these same programs.

## Structures of Power and Action in the Metropolis

How is order maintained in the metropolis? Certainly the behavior of individuals is regularized through their memberships in large-scale formal organizations—offices, plants, schools, banks, and stores. But how is order maintained among these organizations? How is order maintained in the interstices between organizations, in the public streets and thoroughfares? Values, morals, and "rules of the road" help. And in a private economy the market mechanism is a very potent organizing force. But the principal responsibility for regulating conflict among organizations and groups and maintaining order in the metropolitan community falls to government.

Government regulates conflict by establishing and enforcing general rules by which conflict is to be carried on, by arranging compromises and balancing interests, and by imposing settlements which the parties to the disputes must accept. In other words, government must lay down certain "rules of the game" in political activity; it must make decisions which allocate values among competing interests, and then it must see that these decisions are carried out.

Yet how can government really serve as a manager of conflict in the sense of a referee, arbitrator, and scorekeeper? For government is only men, men who are members of the community themselves and who have the same diversity of interests as their constituents. How can men act impartially on behalf of the public good? James Madison was aware of this paradox:

> No man is allowed to be a judge in his own cause, because his interest would certainly bias his judgment, and, not improbably, corrupt his integrity. With equal, nay with greater reason, a body of men are unfit to be both judges and parties at the same time; yet what are many of the most important acts of legislation, but so many judicial determinations, not indeed concerning the rights of single persons, but concerning the rights of large bodies of citizens? And what are the different classes of legislators but advocates and parties to the causes which they determine?

Thus another complication arises in attempting to find a way to manage conflict—the imperfect nature of government itself. Conflicts must be managed, but how can we devise a human institution which can stand above partisanship and resolve conflicts impartially?

Madison felt that the solution to maintaining order in a faction-ridden society lay in the "republican principle." By this he meant more than just the representation of diverse interests in the government itself. He also envisioned a pluralistic society with so many competing interests that it would be unlikely that any single interest could come to dominate public policy to the exclusion of all other interests. He implied that it might be easier to manage conflict in a large community encompassing many diverse interests than in a small community where "a single factious combination" can "more easily execute their plans of oppression." His real fear was that a single interest would achieve majority status and be able to "outnumber and oppress the rest." He therefore sought to place obstacles in the way of "an unjust and interested majority."

Many political scientists feel that metropolitan areas are today governed in much the same fashion that Madison envisioned. These "pluralists" feel that there are many competing interests and structures of power in the metropolis, that they often tend to balance each other, and that interests which exercise influence over some kinds of decisions do not necessarily exercise influence over other kinds of decisions. They contend that no single interest or elite dominates decision-making in all substantive areas, that there is considerable competition among interests, that the influentials in the community are not united by any common interests nor do they act in unison. In short, pluralistic thinking about metropolitan government stresses competition, fluidity, access, and equality in community political activity.

But many other social scientists are less optimistic about the way decisions are really made in the modern metropolis. They feel that power is concentrated in the hands of a very small proportion of the population. These "elitists" contend that community decision-makers are not typical or representative of the people at large, and that they possess unequal control over the resources of the community, particularly over economic resources. They argue that a single elite is influential in different kinds of decisions, that members of this elite share an interest in maintaining the community more or less as it is, and that this elite is not really subject to much control by the masses of people who are largely ill-informed and apathetic about public affairs. In short, elitist thinking about metropolitan government stresses the concentration of power in the hands of business leaders who influence political events in many subtle ways.

Both pluralist and elitist writers on metropolitan affairs claim to be "describing" the facts of community politics rather than "prescribing" the cures for its ills. But other writers have not hesitated to set forth recommendations about how government should be organized. Many of these writers contend that better local government institutions is the key to orderly government. Their program of reform includes non-partisan elections, municipal home rule, the short ballot, centralized municipal administration, and the professional manager. In addition, "good government" should be honest, impartial, and efficient and should be operated by professional administrators who are directly responsible to public-spirited citizens. Such reformers feel that the institutions of government can be manipulated to bring "good" people into control. They also deplore "boss rule," "machines," and partisan styles of politics.

Carried to its logical conclusion, these writers imply a government without politics, an "impractical" scheme in Madison's view. We have already implied, moreover, that "political" government is not necessarily pathological. The open and effective management of conflict serves an important social function by permitting the expression of competing interests and opinions and preventing their festering and later eruption into violence.

Many political scientists are coming to recognize the socially useful functions of "machine politics"; that is, tightly disciplined political organizations held together and motivated by a desire for tangible benefits rather than by principle or ideology. For a long time in America the machine was the major instrument for regulating conflict and maintaining order in the nation's cities. From a service point of view, of course, the machine was dishonest and inefficient, and yet it performed many vital social functions. There can be no doubt that America's cities thrived and prospered under "boss rule." The machine was like a large brokerage organization obtaining votes from the poor and the recent immigrants in return for social services, patronage, and petty favors. To get the money to pay for these votes it traded city contracts, protection, and privileges to business interests which paid off in cash. Of course, the machine ran an extremely inefficient welfare program, since so many middlemen came between the cash paid for a bribe and the turkey sent by the ward chairman to Widow O'Rourke. But it worked. The machine helped to centralize power; it could "get things done at city hall." It humanized and personalized assistance to the indigent. It facilitated matters for businessmen, including those engaged in illicit businesses. It was a source of upward social mobility for Irishmen, Italians, and other immigrants for whom upward mobility was denied in private enterprise.

In many ways the urban machine served the very rich and the very poor. The middle class was excluded, and much of the opposition to the machine came from the middle class. "Good government" was concerned with efficiency and economy and saving the tax dollars of the middle class; it offered very little to the low-income and low-status elements of the metropolis. But as the middle class grew in power in American cities some aspects of machine politics began to go out of style. Even today good government is more likely to be supported by the white middle-class voter than by Negroes or the poor.

Styles of black politics have been changing rapidly in recent years. In part these changes reflect the massive migration from the rural South into Northern metropolitan ghettos, but they also reflect the differing perspectives of successive generations of blacks. Disadvantaged Negro masses provided a pool of support for a machine style of politics which relied upon personal and material rewards. Even before World War II Negro political machines had emerged in large cities where the prevailing style of white politics was the machine style. Residential segregation which concentrated black voters, together with ward organizations and representation, strengthened the political role of blacks, particularly in the Democratic party. The importance of Negro voters to big city Democratic machines was not unrelated to the pro-civil rights stance of the Democratic party in national politics after World War II.

In recent years, the traditional machine style of politics in the ghettos has been challenged by newer militant "racial" politicians. In contrast to the organizational style of politics, the racial style emphasizes ideological values rather than material rewards. Appeals are made to principle, to lofty moral and racial goals, to the wishes and fears of black ghetto residents, and not to their material welfare. Black status and black power are the goal of the racial leader; petty favors and patronage are of secondary importance. Today black racial demands are placing strains on urban political and governmental organizations and on the coalition of black, labor, ethnic, and liberal groups which form the urban Democratic party.

Part Four of this volume, "Managing Metropolitan Conflict: Structures of Power and Action," presents readings which deal with all of these styles of urban government. The readings include both "pluralist" and "elitist" descriptions of urban power structures. They also include descriptions of "machine" and "reform" styles of politics. Some additional readings are provided on the special flavor of political life in suburbia. Finally, traditional and emerging styles of black politics are described, as well as the recent victories of black mayors in big cities.

## Metropolitan Cooperation: Structural Reform

A few years ago, many political scientists felt that the "metropolitan problem" was one of ridding the nation's metropolitan areas of "fragmented government" with its "ineffective, multiple local jurisdictions," and its "inefficiencies and duplication of services." Consolidation of governments in metropolitan areas was given high priority in their recommendations, but cooperative arrangements involving less disruption of the governmental status quo were also championed. Metropolitan reformers argued that governmental integration, or reorganization, would result in improved public services, increased coordination of governmental activities, elimination of tax and service inequalities, and increased ability to focus responsibility for metropolitan ills. In short, they felt that reorganization would better reflect the interdependent character of the metropolis and enable government to perform better its service functions.

Yet, despite these arguments, reorganization proposals have met with heavy opposition from voters and political leaders alike. Although such reforms as metropolitan authorities and functional consolidation have been approved occasionally by the voters, reform proposals generally are defeated at the polls more often than they are victorious. This lack of success suggests that metropolitan reorganization challenges some important values held by urban dwellers. It suggests that the divisive forces at work in the metropolis cannot easily be overcome, even when administrative and service requirements seem to dictate metropolitan consolidation.

Part Five of this volume, "Metropolitan Cooperation: Reform and Reality," deals with the several devices recommended to achieve metropolitan integration. But perhaps more importantly, it presents readings that describe the obstacles to metropolitan governmental reorganization. These readings set forth the conditions requisite for success in metropolitan "reform" and present a more realistic appraisal of the necessity and likelihood of metropolitan reorganization.

# People and Politics
# in the
# Metropolis

Part One develops the theme that urbanization concentrates large numbers of diverse people in a few square miles, separates them residentially, and generates conflict based on diversity. Urban ecologists emphasize and Scott Greer reiterates below that the dynamic forces producing the metropolis create great differences among urban people and sub-areas. Professor Greer describes these differences and considers how the resulting "vast array of behavior" is managed by local government.

The forces creating black ghettos are described by the President's Commission on Civil Disorder. Some of these forces, the Commission notes, are similar to those that produced segregation by national origin; but others are unique to blacks because of their race. The concentration and segregation of blacks imply special burdens on the conflict managing capacity of urban governments.

# The People of the Metropolis

## SCOTT GREER

The dynamic forces producing the metropolis have created great differences among urban people. Increase in scale, the process which built the organizational network in which the city is the "knot," has three major aspects, each of which results in greater social differences among the citizens. As scale increases, populations hitherto separated are united in one network of order; there is a vast proliferation in the number and kinds of tasks within the larger system; there is a consistent tendency for the work of the world to be performed by larger organizations, culminating in the world-spanning corporate giants. Each of these changes profoundly affects the everyday life and times of the citizen.

### Variation of Urban Lives: Ethnicity, Social Rank, and Life-Style

As the society expands, scattered and diverse groups are brought within one network of control. This comes about through the melding of nearby populations in the growing order (as occurred with the country towns on the outskirts of a city, or with the Sabines who lived near the city of Rome). It also comes about through migration, the movement of people from outside areas into the system. Both processes have been important in America. Close integration of the regions has brought the problems of race relations in Alabama into the northern home and classroom, while union-management relations in Chicago have become a topic in the South. Furthermore, closer integration of the national system has greatly encouraged the migration of people from one region to another. Thus Southerners, Negro and white, have moved in a steady

Reprinted from *Governing the Metropolis* (New York: John Wiley & Sons, Inc., 1962), pp. 23–41, by permission of the publisher.

stream from the Southeast towards St. Louis, Baltimore, Los Angeles. In New York's Harlem and Chicago's South Side, Negroes originally from the South have built massive cities within cities.

Equally important has been the growth of the national system and its cities through immigration. During the floodtide, as many as one million immigrants a year entered the United States. They came in stages. In the early days came the people from Great Britain, Ireland, Germany—in short, northern and western Europe. Then came those from Italy, Poland, Russia—southern and eastern Europe. Finally, in the past three decades, we have experienced a massive immigration of persons from Mexico and Puerto Rico.

Thus the city of a large-scale society is a polyglot mosaic of national and regional cultures. Every nationality of any size on earth is represented in New York City. Every language is spoken. These strangers, coming from the various tundras, savannahs, steppes, and heaths of the earth, bring with them distinct and unique histories, sacred symbols, ways of life. Their gods are different from those of the host society and from those of other newcomers. Furthermore, many of them come from a biological stock that varies from those who have already arrived and from fellow immigrants. Though mankind varies less biologically than does one subspecies of Spider Monkey, human beings in their narcissism are extremely self-conscious about minor variations in looks. So the growing population of the large-scale metropolis may seem as heterogeneous as the birds and beasts of the jungle. *This kind of social differentiation is known as ethnicity.*

The tremendous increase in the division of labor with expanding scale creates a society where citizenship is based upon "the job." In simple societies like that of the peasant village, a dozen occupations exhausted the opportunities a self-respecting man had to make a living. Even the America of Jefferson's day was not much more varied. In our society, estimates place the number of kinds of jobs at thirty-five thousand and up, each of them a distinct part of the necessary work in some social enterprise. Similarity of occupation and near-equality among a few broad classes of workers have given way to wide distances between many occupational worlds. The research physicist who lives near the advertising executive, the small business man, and the city councilman, can share with them an evening in the swimming pool; he cannot share his professional problems, or his professional code and folkways. Nor do they all share equal rewards. They are separated in these respects by social distance.

Upon the basis of the job a person receives his share of the social surplus, the economic goods and services available. In qualifying for his job, he reaches some level of skill and general expertise; he must be educated to some level. Furthermore, once he is within the world of the job he shares a way of looking at things, of conceptualizing and evaluating, which is unique to this kind of job and to no other. In other words physicists, advertising executives, small business men, politicians, develop little cultural worlds of their own, or subcultures. When, therefore, we say that the change in the nature of work affects the differences among men, we refer to three interconnected variations which all relate to the job. Putting them in the simplest everyday language, they are variations in occupation, education, and income. As a general kind of social differentiation, this is known as *social rank*.

The increasing importance of large-scale organizations in doing the world's work results in another kind of variation. With the rise of vast bureaucracies in the extraction, fabrication, and marketing of material goods, as well as in government and other areas of our common life, there has been a decline of the small enterprise. The latter was, in the past, often a family enterprise. Family farm and shop and store are disappearing today, leaving a labor force to be reorganized as factories in the fields (the term for the giant land companies of California), assembly-line manufacturing, or chain supermarkets. With the disappearance of family enterprise, however, we are separating completely two great organizational realms of human society; kinship and work.

The separation of the worlds of kinship and work has several major effects upon our lives. First, it means that we are free to live completely outside the boundaries of a kinship. In many small-scale societies membership in a large network of kinship was a person's only claim on the land and therefore on a living; to be outside the family was to die. In large-scale society we can disregard the relatives entirely, for we sell only our own actions to a large organization which cares not at all for our relatives. Second, this separation means that we need not even enter into conjugal family relations; even if we marry, we need not have children for there is no formal or informal constraint that forces it. Thus Americans range from those with large families to those without children and even without a marriage partner. A third major result is the separation of work place and residence; the sites for economic activity and family activity may lie on opposite sides of the metropolis. This means that the effects of one upon the other tend to be minimized, for the two kinds of relationships are insulated. A person works as an isolated, non-family individual.

The separation of work from kinship allows a wide latitude for individual choice. People at the same level of social rank, with similar jobs and resources, may choose to live in single bliss (or married without children, or with a single child), spending their leisure and economic surplus on the various avocations and amusements available in the city. They will have little need for large space, and they are likely to live near the center in the apartment house complexes. Theirs is an urbane mode of life. On the other hand, they may marry, cherish children, and therefore require private space, indoors and out. In this case they are likely to be found in single-family houses, and to care a great deal about owning their homes. Theirs is a familistic way of life. This kind of variation among a population has been called *life-style,* or variation along the *familism-urbanism* continuum.

We have discussed these three kinds of variations at some length because they are basic in understanding the urban residents who must be governed. We have taken each dimension separately, and indeed they are not necessarily connected. *Ethnicity, social rank,* and *life-style* may each vary independently of the remaining dimensions, just as length can vary independently of height, and thickness independently of either, in a sculpture, a building, or a cloud. Historically, however, they have been connected. In the period of most rapid proportional increase in the scale of American society, around 1900, all three dimensions tended to go together. This was because a great many people were coming into the urban centers from the small towns of the hinterlands and the small towns and villages of European nations. They came in without much experience of urban life, without much education (many foreign-born immigrants could not even speak English), and with ways of acting and life-styles developed in familistic rural society. Thus ethnicity, social rank, and life-style all went together among the newest migrants.

We might speak of two polar examples to clarify the point. At one extreme were the newer migrants, the first generation from southern and eastern Europe. They spoke strange languages and broken English, their religions (chiefly Judaism, Orthodox Christianity, or Catholicism), were different from English faiths, their national traditions were alien. With little formal education and few skills, they had to take the lowest-level jobs, which demanded little and paid little. And, tending to perpetuate their small town way of life, they centered much of their surplus time, energy, and money upon their family. In some cases this even included the extended family, uncles and aunts and "cousins by the dozens," for entire villages and clans moved intact from the old country to certain American cities. At the other extreme we might imagine the "Old American" family, originally from Great Britain, Protestant in religion, Anglo-Saxon in cultural background. Such families had been here longer; they tended to have better educations for the urban milieu, and consequently occupied the higher level jobs and received the better rewards.

In becoming acculturated to the city they left behind much of the countryman's concern with kin and kinder; their way of life was more urbane.

## Increasing Social Choice and Variations
## in Urban Lives

Such a picture is greatly oversimplified. However, it makes the important point that the three dimensions of variation were highly intercorrelated. They tended to go together. The more urban the population, the higher its social rank, the fewer its children; and the reverse was also true. In such a society the various subareas of the city were indeed, as Park calls them, "a mosaic of words which touch but do not interpenetrate." Moving from Little Sicily to the Polish Corridor, from Germantown to the Ghetto, from the Main Line or North Shore to the Bowery, was to move from one incapsullated and bounded subworld to another. Today, however, the three dimensions of urban differentiation are no longer so closely related. The *analytical separateness,* the logical distinctness between them which we noted earlier, has become a real separation: ethnicity, social rank, and life-style all vary in contemporary American cities, and each varies independently of the others.

The reasons are again implicit in the great processes of change involved when scale increases. The continued delegation of work to large-scale bureaucracies, utilizing new energy sources and machines, requires a continual improvement in the average job of the labor force. It becomes more demanding of thought and skill. The result is a decline in the demand for unskilled labor. At the same time free public education has greatly improved the average man's chance for a high school education. The economy has increased its productivity, and there are more rewards for all. Education, occupation, and income have all increased. The vast ethnic segments of the population have benefited from these trends. At the same time, the closing of immigration in the 1920's to most nationalities means that today those bearing the signs of foreign birth are about to disappear. Their children are not easily distinguishable from the other people of the city. In time newcomers to the city, from American small towns or from Italy and Poland, abandon their efforts to continue an older, familistic way of life. Automatic conformity to the old life-style gives way to a free choice along the continuum from urbanism to familism as ways of life.

Thus the contemporary population of the metropolis is less like a patchwork quilt, with sharp boundaries separating those who differ simultaneously on all three counts, and more like a single woven fabric. Though an individual's nationality of origin still makes a difference in the friends he has and the things he does, the differences are muted and softer. The grandchild of the Sicilian does not stand out, as his grandfather did, among his own age groups.

With higher education and income levels, even the blue collar worker differs less from the professional or manager than was the case a short while ago. Increasing social surplus, resulting from increase in scale, allows (1) more material goods and services, (2) more leisure time, and (3) more access to the flow of communication in the society through literacy and the mass media, for all of the occupational levels of the metropolis. In the process the more dramatic differences disappear. Thirty-five years ago the Lynd's describing a midwestern city, spoke of a six-day, sixty-hour work week for factory hands, without a vacation. Today the work week averages less than forty hours, and the annual vacation of two or three weeks is nearly universal. Heavy, unskilled labor is rapidly disappearing with the increase in mechanization. Off the job, it is frequently difficult to distinguish between executive, accountant, and machine operator. And during the summer, in the National Park, they park their trailers side by side and seem to enjoy similar experiences.

Such a blurring of class and nationality differences does not mean they have disappeared. Nobody who drives the length of a metropolitan area can fail to be impressed by the great differences in size and quality of housing, as well as style of dwelling unit. There remain substantial average differences in income for different occupational levels (or *strata* as they are called by analogy with geological layers), and these differences are translated into a major reward in our society, the family dwelling place. The family home, however, rarely stands out from its background: rich man, poor man, beggar man, and thief rarely live side by side. Houses are like their neighborhoods, and neighborhoods are, in turn, like the larger local communities within the metropolis. How does this come about?

*The Map of the Metropolis and the Division of Rewards*

The map of the contemporary urban area is a dramatic example of a geographical division of labor. A complex and enormous network of activity is separated into component parts and carried on at different spatial locations. The results are all coordinated. At the same time the major part of the space is allocated to the endless seas of houses, the residential areas of the city. It is probably true that no fact about a person will tell you as much about his general place in the world and his behavior as the single fact of his job. When Americans meet strangers, their first question is typically "What do you do?" After the job, however, the residential address is a strong candidate for second place.

Where you live tells those persons with information about a city such things as your general income level, the kind of people you live among, your probable prestige or social honor, and any number of less basic matters.

Of course it does not tell with precision much about your temperament or character. These are not social facts, whereas the permanent residential address is a social fact and highly correlated with other important social facts such as those noted above. It is produced by the housing market, the mechanism which allocates rewards in the shape of homes, in the metropolis. The importance of those rewards is evident in the sometimes violent struggles for different and better housing carried on by the Negroes and other ethnic groups. Their importance is also manifest in the fierce resistance to "invasion" of a neighborhood by a different kind of people. The family home is, in most cases, all that the average American ever achieves of private property; his attachment to it may be the basis for the popular sacredness of that concept. The home is both his score in the game of success and his most precious asset.

Neighborhoods tend to be inhabited by families of roughly similar social rank because they have the same price for the same kind of housing. This comes about since the site as a scene for human action lies a specific distance from given structures—workplaces, markets, and the like, including nuisances like heavy industry—and has a specific kind of topography. These are translated by bids for the ownership and use of the land (in other words, the market) into a given price level per lot. The price level in turn sets the limits within which housing is built.

We have already discussed briefly the building layout in the City of Steam. It is a settlement where workplaces lie near the rivers and the railroads, and near them are the houses of the workers. Such residential areas are not very attractive to most Americans for they tend to be in the lowlands near water, while nearby are the noisy, dirty, and odoriferous plants of heavy industry. They are, however, admirably suited to reducing the amount of time the worker spends in going to and from his job. As a person moves away from these centers of activity the land's altitude and prestige increase, and with these increases go larger and more expensive houses with carriage circles and gardened estates.

The ruins of this city still exist in the centers of our older urban complexes, but the changes brought about by increase in scale have greatly modified the values on which it was based. The increasing economic surplus has allowed millions of families more resources and greater choice of housing: a person who buys a new structure has more control over his residence than one who rents. At the same time, as social choice with respect to life-style has increased, a larger and larger proportion of urban dwellers have chosen a familistic way of life. Committed to home and children, they need private space indoors and out, and the row houses and crowded three-flat structures of the central city are obsolete. At the same time, the change in the space-time ratio brought about by widespread distribution of automobiles has meant that enormous new spaces on the peripheries of the city can be developed as neighborhoods.

## The Inherited City and the
## Changing Neighborhoods

Thus the contemporary metropolitan area differs greatly from center to periphery. The grid of housing opportunities shows decreasing density as we move outwards into the areas of new building. The suburban rings are typically dispersed, with neighborhoods composed entirely of detached single-family houses surrounded by yard and patio. Here live the grandchildren of the immigrants, the white-collar workers and factory workers, professionals and entrepreneurs, for the great expansion in available housing sites meant that familistic neighborhoods could be built for the different social ranks, from semiskilled workers on up. Here live all those who have chosen a familistic life-style, whatever their level of occupation, income, and education. The suburbs, once homes of the wealthy commuters, are today a broad slice of the middle and upper ranks of urban society. They have in common only a commitment to familism, to children, home, and neighborhood.

The older central city, however, is heavily committed to structures and uses inherited from the past. It remains the center of work. Most suburban residents still travel inwards to work, and this is particularly true of those with the highest social rank, the most skilled and honored jobs, the greatest rewards. The city is also still a center of the national organization and the metropolis-wide markets, though certain types of commercial activity are decentralizing rapidly, with the neighborhood shopping centers taking over the rich suburban market in family consumables.

The central city also retains a monopoly of the older, denser, residential neighborhoods. Because of the attraction of newer alternatives, the bright ranch-style houses of the peripheries, a wide band of urban population which once lived near the center now lives in the suburbs. Vast segments of the central city are termed "grey areas," they are not slums, either physically or socially, and they are not apt to be razed by the demand for space to house new developments. They are simply declining in market value. In these areas, halfway between the center and the peripheries, are found a large proportion of the manual workers of the city's labor force. And here also are found those ethnic minorities who, like the Mexican-Americans, are new to the city and therefore poorly equipped to cope in terms of social rank. Finally, in the grey areas and the slums,—in the black belt of Chicago, the Hill of Pittsburgh, Harlem in New York—are found the huge and growing population of ethnics segregated on the basis of skin color. Negroes and Puerto Ricans, whatever their social rank and acculturation to the ways of the city, cannot choose the familistic suburban neighborhood, for they are disbarred, legally and illegally, from the move outward. Consequently land values in the city are still high for such segregated groups.

On the outer edges of the old central city are many neighborhoods indistinguishable from those of the suburbs. They were the last to be built within the city's boundaries, and they were usually of upper social rank from their beginnings. Thus they have the qualities of private space and distance from workplaces which give them a suburban air. Here are populations of middle to high social rank, low ethnicity, and familistic life-styles. In fact there is little difference between the outlying city neighborhoods and the suburbs nearest the urban border.

Indeed, we must not think of the central city and the suburbs as absolute contrasts. To be sure, the central area tends to have a monopoly of the very poor and the ethnic populations, just as the suburbs have most of the wealthy residents of a metropolis. But these two extremes account for only a fraction of the total population in a giant metropolitan complex; the other two-thirds are the middle ranges of social rank, those who were once entirely within the central city's boundaries. The familistic neighborhoods are not all suburban, nor are most central city dwellers highly urban in their style of life. While the central city has a monopoly of the highly urban populations, the majority of its people are still family-centered, home-centered, child-rearing populations.

The suburbs are today predominantly at the familistic end of the life-style continuum. They are middle to upper social rank. They are the home of the great middle range of American society. Though many of their residents are from families that were originally ethnic, the process of acculturation has blurred these distinctions. Irish, Italian, Hungarian, and German—the names linger on, but they have a new meaning in the middle-rank, familistic neighborhoods of the suburban community. The central city may look radically different, but if we are careful to avoid literary stereotypes we will find that most central city people are just about the same as most suburbanites.

## *The Maintenance of Order in the Urban Community*

Lately some have argued that the metropolitan complex is in no meaningful sense a unity. They point out its loss of autonomy: it has no military or foreign relations, it is a creature of the State with little governmental freedom. The growth of the larger system has merged it in a set of relationships making it utterly dependent upon the entire nation. That growth has also meant that most of the important affairs of its citizens, most social tasks, are carried out by giant, specialized formal organizations. These do not involve many citizens of one city, but they span dozens of cities with organizational structures, and those committed to them as members and publics give only a subordinate loyalty to their local area. The organizations in turn have no reason to care about one specific city: they are natives of many, so transients in all.

As a consequence, so the argument runs, the urban area is simply a site. Upon this site, individuals with the most heterogeneous and disparate loyalties and concerns go their separate ways, with little concern for the common welfare or the fate of the city. For this reason there can be no community, no common order and common commitment to the area as a social whole. Interdependence is no longer a result of residence in any one place, nor is that structure of rights and duties called a normative order based upon living there. Consequently, the things that move and constrain men do not have their roots in any particular city; they result from the giant bureaucracies of large-scale society. Eighty per cent of our labor force works for such bureaucracies, and he who pays the piper calls the tune.

This argument is so plausible, and at so many points consistent with our argument from the nature of increasing scale, that one tends to ignore some of the assumptions involved. When the assumptions are questioned, however, a new definition of the city emerges. To see it, we must first consider what is meant by a social order, cease to take for granted all of the routine, predictable behavior of men, and all the efforts at accommodation and peaceful cooperation. Instead we ask: how does this order come about, and what keeps it alive?

## The City as a Problem of Social Order

The city is a maze, a social zoo, a mass of heterogeneous social types. They come from the four corners of the earth. Much of their behavior is completely beyond the understanding of any one actor, and they are related in a thousand different ways. Their city teems with conflict and hums with tension: Negroes fight for housing and jobs, landlords fight the housing inspectors and their tenants, gangs of adolescents terrify entire neighborhoods, men of violence terrify entire labor unions and industries.

To make the latent conflict sharp and clear, we have only to travel the few miles from the Negro ghetto (Harlem, the Chicago South Side) to the enclaves of the upper classes (Westchester County in New York, the North Shore suburbs in Chicago), keeping our eyes open to differences in social rank, honor, wealth, the accoutrements of life. It is a journey that thousands of Negro servants make every day. Or, from another perspective, look at the hundred thousand automobiles travelling an arterial throughway during the rush hour, or read statistics on the mountains of food and materials which must be moved into New York City every twenty-four hours. Here is a massive order maintained among enormous variation. To account for this order, we shall have to consider the urban complex as far more than a convenient resting together of many people in a small place.

### Solutions to the Problem of Order

Our impatience with the existing order, our hopes for a better one, may blind us to the magnitude of our achievements. Let us look at the metropolis and ask one question: how is this vast array of behavior among a heterogeneous mass organized and made predictable, so that trains pull into the city before dawn and the people are fed? First, and most easily, we can say that within the boundaries of clearly defined membership groups order is relatively explicable. Out of interdependence grows communication through a role system and norms. Jobs, morals, and rules of the road tell people what to do. This communication leads to an ordering of behavior, one that perpetuates the organization. Such an approach explains much about the internal order of a group—public school, corporation, household, or labor union. We have a growing theoretical understanding of the single organization looked at as a system.

Such understanding, however, is not enough. Order within groups tells us little about order between them. It is even possible that the greater the control within organizations the greater the chaos in their relationships with each other. (Look, for example, at the relationships between nation-states.) And intergroup order is crucial in the urban area for two reasons. First, some groups cannot perform their tasks at all without predictable cooperation from others—workers and managements, schools and families, businesses and customers. Second, external groups may easily block the activity crucial to the continuation of any one group's enterprise: the tannery and slaughterhouse can move into an area and destroy its value for the real estate firm, or the organized gang of teen-age hoodlums can make a playground unusable.

Order outside the bounds of the bureaucracies is required at another point. Cities are filled with spaces between groups. In places of public aggregation, in parks and playgrounds, on the city sidewalks and streets, we are not members of any known group. There is no prescribed communication system, and we have no way of sanctioning the actions of others. The city population is various, and many do not always agree with us about what is right and proper. Yet millions of us spend minutes or hours each day in such public places, outside the organizational walls of work or home where automatic order can be expected. In short, there is an inescapable area of social interaction with no social group to order it.

Two radically different types of organization are involved in that social order called the city. The first we have discussed: the large-scale, specialized, formal organizations which control segments of our behavior and do much of the world's work. They span cities, states, nations; they are completely responsible for none of these. They are exclusive, concerned with only some people in any city, and only some aspects of their behavior. Yet they must be established somewhere; they must have offices, plants, stores. And wherever they go they have neighbors, they have property to protect, and business contracts to enforce, and paths to walk down city streets at night. In short, they are dependent upon an order which they alone cannot maintain. That order is maintained by the second type of social organization.

## The Basis of Urban Order:
## The Local Political Community

The order of the local political community is the product of a *spatially inclusive* organization. Such an organization grows out of the interdependence among those persons committed to a given scene for human action. It establishes rights and duties in the areas crucial to the common life. It develops a basis for punishment in that same interdependence. And, on the basis of interdependence, such an organization develops formal agencies, mechanisms for maintaining the site. To the tasks of maintaining public order and the safety of persons by policing the organizational interstices and by arbitrating conflict between organized groups, are added the basic housekeeping duties of the city.

Some tasks growing out of the dense concentration of highly interdependent populations are inescapable. The transport system must have a certain speed, capacity, and predictability in circulating men, goods, and messages. (Without transport a city would be merely a scatteration of villages, unable to combine and therefore unable to achieve a division of labor.) The flow of water from its sources to the population must be guaranteed, as must the disposal of collective waste, a massive problem in any city. A minimal level of public health and protection against fire are closely associated with these tasks: sanitation is related to the first, water supply to the second. To these are added, in various amounts, other public facilities—parks, museums, theatres, and monuments—but the basic necessities for continual operation of the enterprise are those listed above.

Thus two sorts of tasks are carried out through the inclusive territorial organization: the maintenance of order beyond and outside the exclusive membership organization, and the maintenance of the plant, the common site. Both are chiefly the responsibility of local government in our metropolitan areas today. Public order between interdependent groups is maintained by the development of a role system at a higher level. In this system, groups and social categories are the actors. Their rights and duties are spelled out and sanctions are applied through the police power ordered by the courts. The safety of person and property is maintained by that peculiarly urban role system, the police force. In the anonymity of mass interaction in public aggregates there is no social group whose members, through punishments and rewards, or threats and promises, control each other's behavior. Yet a rough system of rights and duties is defined in the law. The police officer is the general substitute for that group: *our* rights become *his* duties, and our duties, his rights.

We have noted that the maintenance of the scene is not as clearly defined in scope as the maintenance of order. This is because many of the tasks traditionally assigned to government could probably be carried out by some other kind of organization *if the market would permit*. Early highways in America were private enterprises in many cases, paid for by users through a toll. Parks and playgrounds, as we know, need not be public. In short, the government as entrepreneur and developer, as an economic force maintaining the plant of the metropolis, is much less inescapable than it is in its role as guarantor and enforcer of order.

We cannot escape the political nature of the order in its latter role. The localized world of the metropolis could conceivably be administered by a proconsul from Washington, D.C., or the state capitol. It could not be operated by a private enterprise. Its function is the adjustment of conflict among the corporate citizens and social categories of the area. This conflict is real, the stakes may be very high, and the final question is no less than this: Who is a first class citizen, and whose interests shall prevail in this area? Such questions are not answered by simple administrative routine; they cannot be answered in a laboratory or with an electronic computer. They can be answered only through a political process which is accepted as legitimate, and which can make binding decisions enforceable by the police power and the public treasury of the society.

# The Formation of Racial Ghettos

## PRESIDENT'S COMMISSION ON CIVIL DISORDER

### Major Trends in Negro Population

Throughout the 20th century, and particularly in the last three decades, the Negro population of the United States has been steadily moving from rural areas to urban, from South to North and West.

In 1910, 2.7 million Negroes lived in American cities—28 percent of the nation's Negro population of 9.8 million. Today, about 15 million Negro Americans live in metropolitan areas, or 69 percent of the Negro population of 21.5 million. In 1910, 885,000 Negroes—9 percent— lived outside the South. Now, almost 10 million, about 45 percent, live in the North or West.

These shifts in population have resulted from three basic trends:

A rapid increase in the size of the Negro population.

A continuous flow of Negroes from Southern rural areas, partly to large cities in the South, but primarily to large cities in the North and West.

An increasing concentration of Negroes in large metropolitan areas within racially segregated neighborhoods.

Taken together, these trends have produced large and constantly growing concentrations of Negro population within big cities in all parts of the nation. Because most major civil disorders of recent years occurred in predominantly Negro neighborhoods, we have examined the causes of this concentration.

### The Growth Rate of the Negro Population

During the first half of this century, the white population of the United States grew at a slightly faster rate than the Negro population. Because

---

Reprinted from the President's Commission on Civil Disorder, *Report* (Washington, D.C.: U.S. Government Printing Office, 1968).

fertility rates [1] among Negro women were more than offset by death rates among Negroes and by large-scale immigration of whites from Europe, the proportion of Negroes in the country declined from 12 percent in 1900 to 10 percent in 1940.

By the end of World War II—and increasingly since then—major advances in medicine and medical care, together with the increasing youth of the Negro population resulting from higher fertility rates, caused death rates among Negroes to fall much faster than among whites. This is shown in the following table:

| | Death Rate/1,000 Population | | Ratio of Nonwhite Rate |
| Year | Whites | Nonwhites | to White Rate |
| --- | --- | --- | --- |
| 1900 | 17.0 | 25.0 | 1.47 |
| 1940 | 10.4 | 13.8 | 1.33 |
| 1965 | 9.4 | 9.6 | 1.02 |

In addition, white immigration from outside the United States dropped dramatically after stringent restrictions were adopted in the 1920's.

| Twenty-Year Period | Total Immigration (millions) |
| --- | --- |
| 1901–1920 | 14.5 |
| 1921–1940 | 4.6 |
| 1941–1960 | 3.6 |

Thus, by mid-century, both factors which previously had offset higher fertility rates among Negro women no longer were in effect.

While Negro fertility rates, after rising rapidly to 1957, have declined sharply in the past decade, white fertility rates have dropped even more, leaving Negro rates much higher in comparison.

| | Live Births Per 1,000 Women Aged 15–44 | | Ratio of Nonwhite |
| Year | White | Nonwhite | to White |
| --- | --- | --- | --- |
| 1940 | 77.1 | 102.4 | 1.33 |
| 1957 | 117.4 | 163.4 | 1.39 |
| 1965 | 91.4 | 133.9 | 1.46 |

The result is that Negro population is now growing significantly faster than white population. From 1940 to 1960, the white population rose 34.0 percent, but the Negro population rose 46.6 percent. From 1960 to 1966, the white population grew 7.6 percent; whereas Negro population jumped 14.4 percent, almost twice as much.

---

[1] The "fertility rate" is the number of live births per year per 1,000 women age 15 to 44 in the group concerned.

Consequently, the proportion of Negroes in the total population has risen from 10.0 percent in 1950 to 10.5 percent in 1960, and 11.1 percent in 1966.[2]

In 1950, at least one of every ten Americans was Negro; in 1966, one of nine. If this trend continues, one of every eight Americans will be Negro by 1972.

Another consequence of higher birth rates among Negroes is that the Negro population is considerably younger than the white population. In 1966, the median age among whites was 29.1 years, as compared to 21.1 among Negroes. About 35 percent of the white population was under 18 years of age, compared with 45 percent for Negroes. About one of every six children under five and one of every six new babies are Negro.

Negro-white fertility rates bear an interesting relationship to educational experience. Negro women with low levels of education have more children than white women with similar schooling, while Negro women with four years or more of college education have fewer children than white women similarly educated. The following table illustrates this:

| Educational Level Attained | Number of Children Ever Born to All Women (Married or Unmarried) 35–39 Years Old, by Level of Education (Based on 1960 Census) | |
|---|---|---|
| | Nonwhite | White |
| Completed elementary school | 3.0 | 2.8 |
| Four years of high school | 2.3 | 2.3 |
| Four years of college | 1.7 | 2.2 |
| Five years or more of college | 1.2 | 1.6 |

This suggests that the difference between Negro and white fertility rates may decline in the future if Negro educational attainment compares more closely with that of whites, and if a rising proportion of members of both groups complete college.

## The Migration of Negroes from the South

*The Magnitude of this Migration*

In 1910, 91 percent of the nation's 9.8 million Negroes lived in the South. Twenty-seven percent of American Negroes lived in cities of 2,500 persons or more, as compared to 49 percent of the nation's white population.

---

[2] These proportions are undoubtedly too low because the Census Bureau has consistently undercounted the number of Negroes in the U.S. by as much as 10 percent.

By 1966, the Negro population had increased to 21.5 million, and two significant geographic shifts had taken place. The proportion of Negroes living in the South had dropped to 55 percent and about 69 percent of all Negroes lived in metropolitan areas compared to 64 percent for whites. While the total Negro population more than doubled from 1910 to 1966, the number living in cities rose five-fold (from 2.7 million to 14.8 million) and the number outside the South rose eleven-fold (from 885,000 to 9.7 million).

Negro migration from the South began after the Civil War. By the turn of the century, sizeable Negro populations lived in many large Northern cities—Philadelphia, for example, had 63,400 Negro residents in 1900. The movement of Negroes out of the rural South accelerated during World War I, when floods and boll weevils hurt farming in the South, and the industrial demands of the war created thousands of new jobs for unskilled workers in the North. After the war, the shift to mechanized farming spurred the continuing movement of Negroes from rural Southern areas.

The Depression slowed this migratory flow, but World War II set it in motion again. More recently, continuing mechanization of agriculture and the expansion of industrial employment in Northern and Western cities have served to sustain the movement of Negroes out of the South, although at a slightly lower rate.

| Period | Net Negro Out-migration from the South | Annual Average Rate |
|---|---|---|
| 1910–1920 | 454,000 | 45,400 |
| 1920–1930 | 749,000 | 74,900 |
| 1930–1940 | 348,000 | 34,800 |
| 1940–1950 | 1,597,000 | 159,700 |
| 1950–1960 | 1,457,000 | 145,700 |
| 1960–1966 | 613,000 | 102,500 |

From 1960 to 1963, annual Negro out-migration actually dropped to 78,000 but then rose to over 125,000 from 1963 to 1966.

## Important Characteristics of this Migration

It is useful to recall that even the latest scale of Negro migration is relatively small when compared to the earlier waves of European immigrants. A total of 8.8 million immigrants entered the United States between 1901 and 1911, and another 5.7 million arrived during the following decade. Even during the years from 1960 through 1966, the 1.8 million immigrants from abroad were almost three times the 613,000 Negroes who departed the South. In these same six years, California alone gained over 1.5 million new residents from internal shifts of American population.

Three major routes of Negro migration from the South have developed. One runs north along the Atlantic Seaboard toward Boston, another north from Mississippi toward Chicago, and the third west from Texas and Louisiana toward California. Between 1955 and 1960, 50 percent of the nonwhite migrants to the New York metropolitan area came from North Carolina, South Carolina, Virginia, Georgia, and Alabama; North Carolina alone supplied 20 percent of all New York's nonwhite immigrants. During the same period, almost 60 percent of the nonwhite migrants to Chicago came from Mississippi, Tennessee, Arkansas, Alabama, and Louisana; Mississippi accounted for almost one-third. During these years, three-fourths of the nonwhite migrants to Los Angeles came from Texas, Louisiana, Mississippi, Arkansas, and Alabama.

The flow of Negroes from the South has caused the Negro population to grow more rapidly in the North and West, as indicated below.

*Total Negro Population Gains (millions)*

| Period | North & West | South | Percent of Gain in North & West |
|--------|--------------|-------|----------------------------------|
| 1940–1950 | 1.859 | 0.321 | 85.2% |
| 1950–1960 | 2.741 | 1.086 | 71.6% |
| 1960–1966 | 2.119 | 0.517 | 80.4% |

As a result, although a much higher proportion of Negroes still reside in the South, the distribution of Negroes throughout the United States is beginning to approximate that of whites, as the following tables show.

*Percent Distribution of the Population by Region—1950, 1960 and 1966*

| | Negro | | | White | | |
|---|------|------|------|-------|------|------|
| | 1950 | 1960 | 1966 | 1950 | 1960 | 1966 |
| United States | 100 | 100 | 100 | 100 | 100 | 100 |
| South | 68 | 60 | 55 | 27 | 27 | 28 |
| North | 28 | 34 | 37 | 59 | 56 | 55 |
| Northeast | 13 | 16 | 17 | 28 | 26 | 26 |
| North-central | 15 | 18 | 20 | 31 | 30 | 29 |
| West | 4 | 6 | 8 | 14 | 16 | 17 |

*Negroes as a Percentage of the Total Population in the United States and Each Region 1950, 1960, and 1966*

| | 1950 | 1960 | 1966 |
|---|------|------|------|
| United States | 10 | 11 | 11 |
| South | 22 | 21 | 20 |
| North | 5 | 7 | 8 |
| West | 3 | 4 | 5 |

Negroes in the North and West are now so numerous that natural increase rather than migration provides the greater part of Negro population gains there. And even though Negro migration has continued at a high level, it comprises a constantly declining proportion of Negro growth in these regions.

| Period | Percentage of Total North & West Negro Gain from Southern In-migration |
|---|---|
| 1940–1950 | 85.9% |
| 1950–1960 | 53.1% |
| 1960–1966 | 28.9% |

In other words, we have reached the point where the Negro populations of the North and West will continue to expand significantly even if migration from the South drops substantially.

*Future Migration*

Despite accelerating Negro migration from the South, the Negro population there has continued to rise.

| Date | Negro Population in the South (millions) | Change from Preceding Date Total | Annual Average |
|---|---|---|---|
| 1940 | 9.9 | — | — |
| 1950 | 10.2 | 321,000 | 32,100 |
| 1960 | 11.3 | 1,086,000 | 108,600 |
| 1966 | 11.8 | 517,000 | 86,200 |

Nor is it likely to halt. Negro birth rates in the South, as elsewhere, have fallen sharply since 1957, but so far, this decline has been offset by the rising Negro population base remaining in the South. From 1950 to 1960, Southern Negro births generated an average net increase of 254,000 per year, and from 1960 to 1966, an almost identical 188,000 per year. Even if Negro birth rates continue to fall, they are likely to remain high enough to support significant migration to other regions for some time to come.

The Negro population in the South is becoming increasingly urbanized. In 1950, there were 5.4 million Southern rural Negroes; by 1960, 4.8 million. But this decline has been more than offset by increases in the urban population. A rising proportion of inter-regional migration now consists of persons moving from one city to another. From 1960 to 1966, rural Negro population in the South was far below its peak, but the annual average migration of Negroes from the South was still substantial.

These facts demonstrate that Negro migration from the South, which has maintained a high rate for the past 60 years, will continue, unless economic conditions change dramatically in either the South or the North and West. This conclusion is reinforced by the fact that most Southern states in recent decades have also experienced outflows of white population. From 1950 to 1960, 11 of the 17 Southern states (including the District of Columbia) "exported" white population—as compared to 13 which "exported" Negro population. Excluding Florida's net gain by migration of 1.5 million, the other 16 Southern states together had a net loss by migration of 1.46 million whites.

## The Concentration of Negro Population in Large Cities

*Where Negro Urbanization Has Occurred*

Statistically, the Negro population in America has become more urbanized, and more metropolitan, than the white population. According to Census Bureau estimates, almost 70 percent of all Negroes in 1966 lived in metropolitan areas, compared to 64 percent of all whites. In the South, more than half the Negro population now lives in cities. Rural Negroes outnumber urban Negroes in only four states: Arkansas, Mississippi, North Carolina, and South Carolina.

Basic data concerning Negro urbanization trends, presented in tables at the conclusion of this chapter, indicate that:

Almost all Negro population growth is occurring within metropolitan areas, primarily within central cities. From 1950 to 1966, the U.S. Negro population rose 6.5 million. Over 98 percent of that increase took place in metropolitan areas—86 percent within central cities, 12 percent in the urban fringe.

The vast majority of white population growth is occurring in suburban portions of metropolitan areas. From 1950 to 1966, 77.8 percent of the white population increase of 35.6 million took place in the suburbs. Central cities received only 2.5 percent of this total white increase. Since 1960, white central-city population has actually declined by 1.3 million.

As a result, central cities are steadily becoming more heavily Negro, while the urban fringes around them remain almost entirely white. The proportion of Negroes in all central cities rose steadily from 12 percent in 1950, to 17 percent in 1960, to 20 percent in 1966. Meanwhile, metropolitan areas outside of central cities remained 95 percent white from 1950 to 1960, and became 96 percent white by 1966.

The Negro population is growing faster, both absolutely and relatively, in the larger metropolitan areas than in the smaller ones. From 1950 to 1966, the proportion of nonwhites in the central cities of metropolitan areas with one million or more persons doubled, reaching 26 percent, as compared with 20 percent in the central cities of metropolitan areas containing from 250,000 to one million persons, and 12 percent in the central cities of metropolitan areas containing under 250,000 persons.

The 12 largest central cities (New York, Chicago, Los Angeles, Philadelphia, Detroit, Baltimore, Houston, Cleveland, Washington, D.C.,

St. Louis, Milwaukee, and San Francisco) now contain over two-thirds of the Negro population outside the South, and one-third of the total in the United States. All these cities have experienced rapid increases in Negro population since 1950. In six (Chicago, Detroit, Cleveland, St. Louis, Milwaukee, and San Francisco), the proportion of Negroes at least doubled. In two others (New York and Los Angeles), it probably doubled. In 1968, seven of these cities are over 30 percent Negro, and one (Washington, D.C.) is two-thirds Negro.

## Factors Causing Residential Segregation in Metropolitan Areas

The early pattern of Negro settlement within each metropolitan area followed that of immigrant groups. Migrants converged on the older sections of the central city because the lowest cost housing was there, friends and relatives were likely to be there; and the older neighborhoods then often had good public transportation.

But the later phases of Negro settlement and expansion in metropolitan areas diverge sharply from those typical of white immigrants. As the whites were absorbed by the larger society, many left their predominantly ethnic neighborhoods and moved to outlying areas to obtain newer housing and better schools. Some scattered randomly over the suburban area. Others established new ethnic clusters in the suburbs, but even these rarely contained solely members of a single ethnic group. As a result, most middle-class neighborhoods—both in the suburbs and within central cities—have no distinctive ethnic character, except that they are white.

Nowhere has the expansion of America's urban Negro population followed this pattern of dispersal. Thousands of Negro families have attained incomes, living standards, and cultural levels matching or surpassing those of whites who have "upgraded" themselves from distinctly ethnic neighborhoods. Yet most Negro families have remained within predominantly Negro neighborhoods, primarily because they have been effectively excluded from white residential areas.

Their exclusion has been accomplished through various discriminatory practices, some obvious and overt, others subtle and hidden. Deliberate efforts are sometimes made to discourage Negro families from purchasing or renting homes in all-white neighborhoods. Intimidation and threats of violence have ranged from throwing garbage on lawns and making threatening phone calls to burning crosses in yards and even dynamiting property. More often, real estate agents simply refuse to show homes to Negro buyers.

Many middle-class Negro families, therefore, cease looking for homes beyond all-Negro areas or nearby "changing" neighborhoods. For them, trying to move into all-white neighborhoods is not worth the psychological efforts and costs required.

Another form of discrimination just as significant is white with-drawal from, or refusal to enter, neighborhoods where large numbers of Negroes are moving or already residing. Normal population turnover causes about 20 percent of the residents of average United States neigh-borhoods to move out every year because of income changes, job trans-fers, shifts in life-cycle position or deaths. This normal turnover rate is even higher in apartment areas. The refusal of whites to move into chang-ing areas when vacancies occur there from normal turnover means that most of these vacancies are eventually occupied by Negroes. An inexo-rable shift toward heavy Negro occupancy results.

Once this happens, the remaining whites seek to leave, thus con-firming the existing belief among whites that complete transformation of a neighborhood is inevitable once Negroes begin to enter. Since the belief itself is one of the major causes of the transformation, it becomes a self-fulfilling prophecy, which inhibits the development of racially integrated neighborhoods.

Thus, Negro settlements expand almost entirely through "massive racial transition" at the edges of existing all-Negro neighborhoods, rather than by a gradual dispersion of population throughout the metropolitan area.

Two points are particularly important:

"Massive transition" requires no panic or flight by the original white residents of a neighborhood into which Negroes begin moving. All it requires is the failure or refusal of other whites to fill the vacancies resulting from normal turnover.

Thus, efforts to stop massive transition by persuading present white residents to remain will ultimately fail unless whites outside the neighborhood can be persuaded to move in.

It is obviously true that some residential separation of whites and Negroes would occur even without discriminatory practices by whites. This would result from the desires of some Negroes to live in predomi-nantly Negro neighborhoods and from differences in meaningful social variables, such as income and educational levels. But these factors alone would not lead to the almost complete segregation of whites and Negroes which has developed in our metropolitan areas.

## The Exodus of Whites from Central Cities

The process of racial transition in central-city neighborhoods has beeen only one factor among many others causing millions of whites to move out of central cities as the Negro populations there expanded. More basic perhaps have been the rising mobility and affluence of middle-class families and the more attractive living conditions—particularly better schools —in the suburbs.

Whatever the reason, the result is clear. In 1950, 45.5 million whites lived in central cities. If this population had grown from 1950 to 1960 at the same rate as the nation's white population as a whole, it would have increased by eight million. It actually rose only 2.2 million, indicating an outflow of 5.8 million.[3]

From 1960 to 1966, the white outflow appears to have been even more rapid. White population of central cities declined 1.3 million instead of rising 3.6 million as it would if it had grown at the same rate as the entire white population. In theory, therefore, 4.9 million whites left central cities during these six years.

Statistics for all central cities as a group understate the relationship between Negro population growth and white outflow in individual central cities. The fact is, many cities with relatively few Negroes experienced rapid white-population growth, thereby obscuring the size of white out-migration that took place in cities having large increases in Negro population. For example, from 1950 to 1960, the 10 largest cities in the United States had a total Negro population increase of 1.6 million, or 55 percent, while the white population there declined 1.4 million. If we remove the two cities where the white population increased (Los Angeles and Houston), the nonwhite population in the remaining eight rose 1.4 million; whereas their white population declined 2.1 million. If the white population in these cities had increased at only half the rate of the white population in the United States as a whole from 1950 to 1960, it would have risen by 1.4 million. Thus, these eight cities actually experienced a white out-migration of at least 3.5 million, while gaining 1.4 million nonwhites.

## The Extent of Residential Segregation

The rapid expansion of all-Negro residential areas and large-scale white withdrawal have continued a pattern of residential segregation that has existed in American cities for decades. A recent study [4] reveals that this pattern is present to a high degree in every large city in America. The authors devised an index to measure the degree of residential segregation. The index indicates for each city the percentage of Negroes who would

---

[3] The outflow of whites may be somewhat smaller than the 5.8 million difference between these figures, because the ages of the whites in many central cities are higher than in the nation as a whole, and therefore the population would have grown somewhat more slowly.

[4] *Negroes in Cities,* Karl and Alma Taeuber, Aldine Publishing Co., Chicago (1965).

have to move from the blocks where they now live to other blocks in order to provide a perfectly proportional, unsegregated distribution of population.

According to their findings, the average segregation index for 207 of the largest United States cities was 86.2 in 1960. This means that an average of over 86 percent of all Negroes would have had to change blocks to create an unsegregated population distribution. Southern cities had a higher average index (90.9) than cities in the Northeast (79.2), the North Central (87.7), or the West (79.3). Only eight cities had index values below 70, whereas over 50 had values above 91.7.

The degree of residential segregation for all 207 cities has been relatively stable, averaging 85.2 in 1940, 87.3 in 1950, and 86.2 in 1960. Variations within individual regions were only slightly larger. However,

### PROPORTION OF NEGROES IN EACH OF THE 30 LARGEST CITIES, 1950, 1960, AND ESTIMATED 1965

|  | 1950 | 1960 | (Estimate) [a] 1965 |
|---|---|---|---|
| New York, N.Y. | 10 | 14 | 18 |
| Chicago, Ill. | 14 | 23 | 28 |
| Los Angeles, Calif. | 9 | 14 | 17 |
| Philadelphia, Pa. | 18 | 26 | 31 |
| Detroit, Michigan | 16 | 29 | 34 |
| Baltimore, Md. | 24 | 35 | 38 |
| Houston, Texas | 21 | 23 | 23 |
| Cleveland, Ohio | 16 | 29 | 34 |
| Washington, D.C. | 35 | 54 | 66 |
| St. Louis, Mo. | 18 | 29 | 36 |
| Milwaukee, Wis. | 3 | 8 | 11 |
| San Francisco, Calif. | 6 | 10 | 12 |
| Boston, Mass. | 5 | 9 | 13 |
| Dallas, Texas | 13 | 19 | 21 |
| New Orleans, La. | 32 | 37 | 41 |
| Pittsburgh, Pa. | 12 | 17 | 20 |
| San Antonio, Tex. | 7 | 7 | 8 |
| San Diego, Calif. | 5 | 6 | 7 |
| Seattle, Wash. | 3 | 5 | 7 |
| Buffalo, N.Y. | 6 | 13 | 17 |
| Cincinnati, Ohio | 16 | 22 | 24 |
| Memphis, Tenn. | 37 | 37 | 40 |
| Denver, Colo. | 4 | 6 | 9 |
| Atlanta, Ga. | 37 | 38 | 44 |
| Minneapolis, Minn. | 1 | 2 | 4 |
| Indianapolis, Ind. | 15 | 21 | 23 |
| Kansas City, Mo. | 12 | 18 | 22 |
| Columbus, Ohio | 12 | 16 | 18 |
| Phoenix, Ariz. | 5 | 5 | 5 |
| Newark, N.J. | 17 | 34 | 47 |

[a] Except for Cleveland, Buffalo, Memphis, and Phoenix, for which a special census has been made in recent years, these are very rough estimations computed on the basis of the change in relative proportions of Negro birth and deaths since 1960.

Source: U.S. Department of Commerce, Bureau of the Census, BLS Report No. 332, p. 11.

a recent Census Bureau study shows that in most of the 12 large cities where special censuses were taken in the mid-1960's, the proportions of Negroes living in neighborhoods of greatest Negro concentration had increased since 1960.

Residential segregation is generally more prevalent with respect to Negroes than for any other minority group, including Puerto Ricans, Orientals, and Mexican Americans. Moreover, it varies little between central city and suburb. This nearly universal pattern cannot be explained in terms of economic discrimination against all low-income groups. Analysis of 15 representative cities indicates that white upper- and middle-income households are far more segregated from Negro upper- and middle-income households than from white lower-income households.

In summary, the concentration of Negroes in central cities results from a combination of forces. Some of these forces, such as migration and initial settlement patterns in older neighborhoods, are similar to those which affected previous ethnic minorities. Others—particularly discrimination in employment and segregation in housing and schools—are a result of white attitudes based on race and color. These forces continue to shape the future of the central city.

**PART TWO**

# Conflict in the Metropolis: Divisions, Differences, and Discontinuities

The purpose of this section is to describe the major sources of conflict in the metropolis and to suggest some of their manifestations. As pointed out in Part One, the very process of metropolitan growth involves racial, ethnic, life-style, and class heterogeneities. Such heterogeneities, of course, imply divergent values and interests. They nourish political conflict and divide the metropolis.

The following are among the principal divisions in the metropolis: racial and ethnic differences, city-suburban differences, violence, partisan differences, and differences between haves and have-nots. These divisions are discussed in the readings below, which are introduced by a general look at "cleavages in urban politics."

In the section on race is the much-discussed "Moynihan Report" dealing with the harsh circumstances of the black family in America. Many blacks, especially militants, feel that the Moynihan Report blames the present condition of blacks on blacks ("Negroes have unstable families") rather than on whites where, in their view, it belongs. Stokely Carmichael's "Black Power" presents the militant's indictment of white society. "White America will not acknowledge that the ways in which this country sees itself are contradicted by being black—and always have been." Carmichael also presents the militant view on what blacks should do about this situation.

A related section on civil disobedience is introduced by philosophy professor Charles Frankel's discussion of the individual's moral right to disobey the law. Frankel contends that civil disobedience may sometimes be justified but is a "grave enterprise" that puts special moral burdens on its practitioners. Also in the civil disobedience section is the famous exchange of letters between a group of Alabama clergymen and Martin Luther King.

41

The section on haves and have-nots begins with an Office of Economic Opportunity picture of the lives of the poor. The President's Commission on Civil Disorder next presents some of the hard facts of nonwhite privation, unemployment, and social disorganization. It concludes that children growing up in these conditions make better candidates for crime and disorder than for jobs.

Violence in the streets—both a manifestation of metropolitan cleavages and a cause of them—is represented by the controversial report of the President's Commission on Civil Disorder, and by "Shoot-Out in Cleveland," a spellbinding account of the 1968 battle between Cleveland police and black snipers.

In the final selection Herbert J. Gans discusses racial and class "Polarization" between cities and suburbs. The adverse effects of this polarization are noted, and across-the-board residential integration and ghetto rebuilding (or enrichment) are recommended.

# Cleavages in Urban Politics

## EDWARD C. BANFIELD
## JAMES Q. WILSON

Issues arise out of, or at least are nourished from, the more lasting divisions in the society that we have called cleavages. These are conflicts that run from issue to issue, and which divide the community into "we" and "they."

In some communities there are few lines of cleavage and none that run very deep. There are many villages and small cities in the United States with extremely homogeneous populations; conflict occurs in these, of course, but the grouping of forces is *ad hoc.* It is necessary to choose up sides afresh for every conflict, because there are no lasting principles of division, or, to change the metaphor, no fault line along which a fissure opens when pressure is applied.

### The Urban-Rural Cleavage

Historically the principal division affecting city politics has not been *within* the city, but between the countryside and the city. This cleavage goes back to the very beginnings of our history; since colonial days, Americans have cherished the myth that the farmer is morally superior to the city dweller. The view of the city as the harlot bent on corrupting the simple, wholesome countryman has been accepted not only by countrymen, but, to a surprising extent, by city dwellers as well.

In turn, some city dwellers, particularly liberals, have in recent years viewed with increasing dismay the "backward" and "selfish" attitudes of rural people. In part this is a reaction to the success of rural areas in frustrating the attainment of urban liberal objectives;

Reprinted by permission of the publishers from Edward C. Banfield and James Q. Wilson, *City Politics.* Cambridge, Mass.: Harvard University Press, Copyright, 1963, by the President and Fellows of Harvard College and The Massachusetts Institute of Technology.

in part it springs from the contempt in which the city slicker has always held the "country bumpkin."

The long-standing antipathy of "upstate" or "downstate" to the big city is in some cases a reflection of original differences in culture. Chicago, for example, was settled by immigrants from Ohio and New York, whereas "downstate" Illinois was settled by immigrants from the border states and the South. When Chicago was hardly more than a village and contained no "foreigners" to speak of, it was actively disliked by the rural hinterland. The downstate Southerners could see even then that eventually the city—the Northerners—would dominate the state. Today traces of this old hostility remain. Cotton is still grown in Southern Illinois, and a lobbyist who speaks with a trace of a southern accent gets a better reception in Springfield, other things being equal, than one who does not.

Historically, alcohol was the issue over which the rural hinterland was most generally at odds with the city. Rural Protestants—Methodists and Baptists—were much affected in the nineteenth century by evangelical preachers for whom abstinence from alcohol was almost synonymous with virtue. The city was the place of the saloon, and the Methodists and Baptists loathed the Papists and Lutherans who drank whiskey and beer there.[1]

Although some of the old distrust of the country for the city still exists, the farm population is now so diminished in numbers as to make it politically unimportant in most places. In Wisconsin, the voters recently instituted daylight saving time, something farmers detest. This may be taken as a sign of the times: it is not farmers but rural nonfarm and small-town people who now hold the power upstate or downstate. Such people may accept some of the old mythology about rural goodness and urban badness, but the conditions of life in small towns are today not so different as they used to be from the conditions of life in the city, and this tends to make for understanding and collaboration. A city administrator in Cincinnati recently told an interviewer: "The legislature is rural-controlled, but the character of the representation from former rural areas is changing; where those areas are becoming part of a metropolitan community, they are beginning to have the same industrial urban problems that we have. Their point of view is changing."[2]

---

[1] D. W. Brogan, in *An Introduction to American Politics* (London: Hamish Hamilton, 1954), chap. v, describes the saloon struggle at the turn of the century.

[2] Kenneth Gray, *A Report on City Politics in Cincinnati* (Cambridge, Mass.: Joint Center for Urban Studies, 1959, mimeo).

The rural point of view is no doubt changing, but in many places it is still a good deal different from that of the city. By and large, the rural and small-town areas are unwilling to let the cities have high levels of public services even when it is the city taxpayer who will pay for them. Rural people are often inclined to think that the cities are spending more than they should for schools, police, and, especially, welfare services. The voters of upstate New York, for example, have repeatedly refused to allow New York City to increase its debt and to expand school and other such facilities.[3]

The cleavage between the hinterland and the city has probably tended (and probably still tends) to prevent mayors from rising to higher offices. Only a few mayors have been elected governor or senator;[4] and mayors—those from the largest cities least of all—are not seriously considered for the Presidency. Even La Guardia, who wanted the nomination very much, never had a chance of getting it, or for that matter of being nominated for governor or senator. To be President, a man must have some identification with the hinterland, or at any rate must not be too exclusively identified with the Big City. That city office is not a route to the great prize—the Presidency—must inevitably discourage some of the most able men from entering city politics. John F. Kennedy, for example, was too ambitious and too astute to begin his career by running for mayor of Boston.

## Urban Cleavages

Within the cities and metropolitan areas the most important cleavages are those between (1) haves and have-nots, (2) suburbanites and the central city, (3) ethnic and racial groups, and (4) political parties. These tend to cut across each other and, in general, to become one fundamental cleavage separating two opposed conceptions of the public interest.

### Haves and Have-Nots

Disparity in kinds and distribution of property, James Madison said, is the most fundamental cause of parties and factions in all ages and

---

[3] See Lyle C. Fitch, "Fiscal and Political Problems of Increasing Urbanization," *Political Science Quarterly,* vol. LXXI (1956), pp. 80–82.

[4] Governor David Lawrence of Pennsylvania had been mayor of Pittsburgh; Governor Michael DiSalle of Ohio had been mayor of Toledo; Governor and later Senator Frank Lausche of Ohio had been mayor of Cleveland; Senator Hubert Humphrey had been mayor of Minneapolis; Governor Murphy of Michigan had been mayor of Detroit.

places. In the city, it is useful to think in terms of three income groups—low, middle, and high. Surprising as it may seem to Marxists, the conflict is generally between an alliance of the low-income and high-income groups on the one side and the middle-income groups on the other. The reason is not hard to find. The poorest people in the city favor a high level of expenditure for welfare, housing, and sometimes schools, and rarely oppose expenditure for any purpose whatever. They favor expenditures even for services that they are not likely to use—municipal opera, for example—because they pay no local taxes, or hardly any. Upper-income people also favor a high level of expenditures. They want good public services for the same reason that they want good private ones—they can afford them. But they also want good, or at any rate adequate, services for others, and they willingly support—although no doubt at levels lower than the poor would like—welfare services which they themselves will never use.

The middle-income group generally wants a low level of public expenditures. It consists of people who are worrying about the mortgage on their bungalow and about keeping up the payments on the new car. Such people are not especially charitable, no doubt partly because they feel they cannot afford to be, but partly, also, perhaps, because they feel that if others are less well off than they it is mainly because the others have not put forth as much effort as they. Many of these people want to spend their money in status-giving ways, and obviously a new car is more status-giving than a new school or a better equipped police force.

The United Auto Workers has tried for years without success to take control of Detroit's nonpartisan government. Detroit is largely a one-industry and one-union town, and the UAW has been extraordinarily successful in state politics, as evidenced by the fact that G. Mennen Williams, the workingman's friend, was elected governor five times. Nevertheless, the mayor of Detroit for four terms was Albert E. Cobo, a conservative businessman who opposed public housing and favored economy and efficiency. Why did the working people who voted for Williams for governor vote for Cobo for mayor? The answer may be that Detroit is a predominantly lower middle-class homeowning town. In partisan state and national elections, a UAW member votes as a "liberal" because the costs of measures he supports will not be assessed against his bungalow. In nonpartisan city elections, however, he votes as a property owner and taxpayer, and in all probability (if he is white) as one who fears that a progressive city government might make it easier for Negroes to move into his neighborhood.

## Suburbanites and the Central City

The spectacular recent growth of the suburbs and the not unrelated deterioration of the central city have tended to deepen a long-standing line of cleavage between the city and its suburbs. Today many central cities find that their principal antagonist in the legislature is not the rural hinterland but an alliance of the hinterland and the suburbs.[5]

The suburbs are not all of one kind, of course; they are industrial as well as residential, lower-income as well as upper. Not very far from upper-class suburbs where garbage is collected in paper bags and put in fly-proof trucks and where high school teachers are paid as much as many Ivy League college professors, there may be communities (often unincorporated) in which most people cannot afford or else do not want even such basic amenities as sidewalks, police protection, and community sewage disposal. The upper-income suburbanite fears that by annexation or the creation of a metropolitan-area government he may be brought within the jurisdiction of the central city's government and receive a lower level of government service in consequence. The low-income suburbanite also fears being brought within the jurisdiction of the city, but for an opposite reason: it would insist upon providing him with—and taxing him for—services that he would rather do without.

This is not the only basis for the cleavage between city and suburb. Central-city residents often think that the city is being exploited by suburbanites, who use its facilities without paying taxes to it. Because the suburbanite comes to the city to work and shop, the city must spend more than it otherwise would for certain public services—traffic control and police protection, for example—but none of this extra expense, the city resident points out, can be charged against the suburbanite. To this, the suburbanite may reply that by coming to the city to work and shop he creates enough taxable values to make the city a net gainer. He may even assert that it is the suburbanite who is the victim of injustice since suburbs must provide expensive public facilities, particularly schools, even though most of the tax base created by suburbanite spending is in the city.[6] When central cities try to annex suburbs

---

[5] See David R. Derge, "Metropolitan and Outstate Alignments in Illinois and Missouri Legislative Delegations," *American Political Science Review,* December 1958, pp. 1062–1065.

[6] For some discussion of these claims by an economist, see Julius Margolis, "Metropolitan Finance Problems," in National Bureau of Economics Research, *Public Finances: Needs, Sources, and Utilization* (Princeton, N.J.: Princeton University Press, 1961), especially pp. 256–259.

or impose taxes upon the earnings of suburbanites who work in the cities, there is always a howl of protest and usually the effort fails.

### Ethnic and Racial Groups

Ethnic and racial differences have been, and still are, basic to much of the conflict in the city. Here it will be convenient to speak of three such lines of cleavage: that between native Protestant and all others, that among the various nationality groups of foreign stock, and that between the Negro and all others.

Although the largest waves of immigration ended long ago, some cities, such as New York and Boston, still have a sizable number of persons of foreign stock. Other cities, such as Dallas, have scarcely been touched by immigration at all.

Until the latter part of the last century, native Protestant industrialists and businessmen ran most cities. Then, in the Northern cities, when the tide of immigration swelled, the newly arrived ethnic groups began to challenge the natives for political control. For a time there was a sharp conflict, but in most cities the natives soon retired from the scene, or, more precisely, they transferred their activity from one sector of the scene to another.

In Boston, for example, the Irish were able to command a majority beginning about 1890 and the native Protestants thereafter ran the city from the state house. Boston's police commissioner was appointed by the governor and so was its licensing board; a finance commission, also appointed by the governor, was set up to make continuing investigations of the city's affairs and was given the power of subpoena. Much of the interference of the legislatures in the affairs of other large cities at this time and afterward reflected the same cleavage between the outnumbered native Protestants and what Mayor James M. Curley of Boston used to call the "newer races."

In a good many cities, where several new ethnic groups competed for control, the old native Protestant elite might conceivably have retained its control by serving—as the Irish so often have—as a neutral force on which all elements of the ethnic struggle could agree. But the elite was incapacitated for this role by its distaste for the political culture of the new immigrant, a distaste that it did not try to conceal. As Peter and Alice Rossi have shown in an unpublished paper on "Bay City," Massachusetts, local politics, which was a source of prestige for the local industrialists until the immigrants became numerous, was "dirty business" afterwards. Accordingly, the old elite turned from elective office and took up instead the control of a relatively new set of institutions, the community service organizations. The local hospital,

Red Cross chapter, Community Chest, and Family Welfare Society became the arenas in which the "old families," who of course now asserted that there was no prestige in public office, carried on their public activities.[7]

One can see today in many places elements of informal government that have been produced by this cleavage between the "old family" Protestants and the "newer races." A study in 1947 indicated that in "Jonesville," Illinois, the Rotary Club was handpicking the members of the school board.[8] The interviewer was told: "This school board around here has been looked upon as the private property of the Rotary Club for about twenty-five years. The fact is, the school board has been kind of a closed corporation. . . . The boys decide who they want to run. The fact is, they invite them to run." For at least fifteen years prior to 1947, all members of the "Jonesville" school board were Protestant Republicans; only twice in that period did candidates for the board face any opposition.

The Rossis, who are sociologists, in their report on "Bay City" interpret the change in the character of the old elite's public service as a redirection of its drive for status and recognition. Unwilling to play the status game in the same set with the immigrant, the old elite (according to the Rossis) set up its own game and in effect said that henceforth that was to be *the* game.

We prefer a different explanation. The native middle-class Protestant inherited from his Anglo-Saxon ancestors a political ethos very different from that which the new immigrants brought with them. The ethos of the native could not mix with that of the immigrant, and therefore the natives, who were in the minority, retired to a sphere in which they could conduct public affairs in the manner their culture prescribed.

Richard Hofstadter described the difference of ethos very well in *The Age of Reform:*

> Out of the clash between the needs of the immigrants and the sentiments of the natives there emerged two thoroughly different systems of political ethics. . . . One, founded upon the indigenous Yankee-Protestant political traditions, and upon middle class life, assumed and demanded the constant, disinterested activity of the citizen in public affairs, argued that political life ought to be run, to a greater degree than it was, in accordance with general principles and abstract

---

[7] Peter H. and Alice S. Rossi, "An Historical Perspective on Local Politics," paper delivered at the 1956 meeting of the American Sociological Association (mimeo).

[8] Joseph Rosenstein, "Small-Town Party Politics," unpublished dissertation, Department of Sociology, University of Chicago, 1950.

laws apart from and superior to personal needs, and expressed a common feeling that government should be in good part an effort to moralize the lives of individuals while economic life should be intimately related to the stimulation and development of individual character. The other system, founded upon the European background of the immigrants, upon their unfamiliarity with independent political action, their familiarity with hierarchy and authority and upon the urgent needs that so often grew out of their migration, took for granted that the political life of the individual would arise out of family needs, interpreted political and civic relations chiefly in terms of personal obligations, and placed strong personal loyalties above allegiance to abstract codes of law or morals.[9]

The Anglo-Saxon Protestant middle-class style of politics, with its emphasis upon the obligation of the individual to participate in public affairs and to seek the good of the community "as a whole" (which implies, among other things, the necessity of honesty, impartiality, and efficiency) was fundamentally incompatible with the immigrants' style of politics, which took no account of the community.

The native elite withdrew to the community service organizations because these constituted the only sphere in which their political style could prevail. The boards of these organizations were self-perpetuating; they could not be "crashed" by "outsiders." Because of the nature of their political ethos, Protestants and Jews have been in the vanguard of every fight for municipal reform. In Worcester, Massachusetts, for example, according to Robert Binstock:

> Yankees are the cultural, business, and social leaders—in short, "the first families of Worcester." They are not numerous enough to control the governmental apparatus of the city, yet by forming an alliance with the Scandinavians, they manage to place two representatives on the City Council. The influence of the Yankee within the city government is limited, but participation in a strong and active citizens association, the CEA, enables this group to enlarge its role in the political process.
>
> The Jews, more often than not, are political allies of the Yankees and Scandinavians. . . .[10]

Conflict as between one immigrant ethnic group and another has tended to be over "recognition"—the prestige that accrues to a nationality group when one of its members is elected to public office. Since

---

[9] Richard Hofstadter, *The Age of Reform* (New York: Alfred A. Knopf, 1955), p. 9.

[10] Robert H. Binstock, *A Report on Politics in Worcester, Mass.* (Cambridge, Mass.: Joint Center for Urban Studies, 1961, mimeo), part V, p. 2.

in the nature of the case there cannot be enough recognition to go around (if all were equally recognized, none would be recognized at all), the question of which groups are to get it must inevitably lead to conflict. The avidity of the "newer" ethnic groups to see their kind in office has been, and still is, of great importance, both as a motive force in the political system and because of certain incidental effects.

When one recalls the contempt with which "micks," "wops," and "polacks" were once—and to some extent still are—treated by some other Americans, no further explanation of the appeal of ethnic "recognition" is needed. But an additional reason is that ethnic politics, like sports, entertainment, and crime, provided a route of social mobility to people who were to a large extent excluded from power in business and industry. Mayor Daley of Chicago was born behind the stockyards. John E. Powers, the president of the Massachusetts Senate, began life as a clam digger.

One would expect that as the "newer" ethnic groups became assimilated to the middle class, they would become assimilated to the Anglo-Saxon Protestant political ethos as well, and that their interest in ethnic politics would decline accordingly. This seems to be happening, but at different rates among different groups. Jews, particularly those in the reform tradition, seem to acquire the Protestant political ethos very readily.[11] It is interesting that the Jews have not sought ethnic "recognition" in city politics to the extent that other groups have. It may be that they have never doubted their worth as a group, and therefore have not felt any need for public reassurance. More likely, however, their political ethos is such that a politics of ethnic appeal strikes them, as it does the Anglo-Saxon Protestant, as uninteresting and even immoral.

Other ethnic groups also seem to be taking on the middle-class political ethos, but to be doing it more slowly. Third-generation Poles, for example, usually show a decided preference for Polish candidates, and third-generation Italians usually prefer Italian candidates. Middle-class Irish Catholics who seem entirely to have shed the mentality that

---

[11] Compare the findings of Edgar Litt: "Jewish Ethno-Religious Involvement and Political Liberalism," *Social Forces,* May 1961, pp. 328–332; "Ethnic Status and Political Perspectives," *Midwest Journal of Political Science,* August 1961, pp. 276–283; and "Status, Ethnicity, and Patterns of Jewish Voting Behavior in Baltimore," *Jewish Social Studies,* July 1960, pp. 159–164. Litt argues that the basis of Jewish identification with the Democratic party varies with socio-economic status: upper-class Jews are Democratic because they see the party as an instrument of "social justice" on national and international issues; lower-class Jews are Democratic because they see it as a source of material benefits and economic welfare. These findings are broadly consistent with our argument about political ethos.

caused the immigrant to vote on the basis of personal loyalty to a ward politician are nevertheless rarely found in the ranks of the civic reformers; these are almost all Protestants and Jews.

Where the taste for ethnic recognition persists, it is for a special kind of recognition, however. The candidate must not be *too* Polish, *too* Italian, or *too* Irish in the old style. The following description of Jewish candidates in Worcester suggests the trend:

> Israel Katz, like Casdin, is a Jewish Democrat now serving his fourth term on the Worcester City Council. Although he is much more identifiably Jewish than Casdin, he gets little ethnic support at the polls; there is a lack of rapport between him and the Jewish voter. The voter apparently wants to transcend many features of his ethnic identification and therefore rejects candidates who fit the stereotype of the Jew too well. Casdin is an assimilated Jew in Ivy-League clothes; Katz, by contrast, is old world rather than new, clannish rather than civic-minded, and penny-pinching rather than liberal. Non-Jews call Katz a "character," Casdin a "leader." It is not too much to say that the Jews, like other minorities, want a flattering, not an unflattering mirror held up to them.[12]

Apparently, nowadays, the nationality-minded voter prefers candidates who represent the ethnic group but at the same time display the attributes of the generally admired Anglo-Saxon model. The perfect candidate, then, is of Jewish, Polish, Italian or Irish extraction and has the speech, dress, manner, and the public virtues—honesty, impartiality, and devotion to the public interest—of the upper-class Anglo-Saxon.

The cleavage between white and Negro is pervasive in city politics. Until World War II, few Northern cities had many Negroes. As we have already seen, the Negro population of most Northern cities now is growing at a very rapid rate, partly from natural increase and partly from migration from the rural South. The new arrivals go into the Negro slum, which almost everywhere is the oldest part of the central city, where housing has been swept by successive waves of low-status and low-income migrants. For many years restrictive covenants, written into deeds and prohibiting sale of property to Negroes, made it difficult or impossible for Negroes to buy in districts that were not already Negro; their districts therefore became more and more crowded. But after 1948, when the Supreme Court declared such covenants to be unenforceable in the courts, the Negro community began to spread more rapidly.[13]

---

[12] Binstock, part II, pp. 33–34.

[13] *Shelley v. Kraemer,* 334 U.S. 1 (1948).

In many Northern cities, the question of where Negroes are to live lies behind almost every proposal for civic action. Will locating a major highway here prevent them from "invading" that white neighborhood? And where will those Negroes who are displaced by an urban renewal project resettle? If a school or a hospital is placed here or there, will it bring Negroes to the neighborhood? And if it does, will the neighborhood eventually "tip" and become all Negro?

Many whites have fled to the suburbs to get away from the Negroes. One reason why many suburbanites want to remain politically separate from the central city is that they think this will make it easier for them to resist "invasion" by Negroes.

In all this, upper-class Negroes exhibit much the same attitude as do whites. Everything that we have said of the reaction of whites to Negroes can also be said of the reaction of upper-class Negroes to lower-class ones.

## Political Parties

The central cities are almost all heavily Democratic; the suburbs tend to be heavily Republican, although there are many exceptions, and their Republicanism is nowhere near as solid or stable as the Democracy of the central cities.

The Democratic ascendancy is so great in most central cities that cleavage along party lines within the cities is not of great practical importance. Party cleavage is important, however, in matters that involve both the central city and the area which lies outside of it.

About 60 percent of all cities (but fewer large ones) are nonpartisan, which means that candidates are not chosen in party primaries and are not identified by party on the ballot. In some places, there are purely local parties—the "blues" and the "yellows," so to speak—and in other places local politics is carried on without anything that could properly be called a party (it is "unorganized"). Some cities are nominally nonpartisan and actually partisan (Chicago is an example) and others are nominally partisan and actually nonpartisan in the sense of having no connection with the *national* parties (La Guardia, for example, was a nominal Republican who ran on a Fusion ticket, and so was in this sense nonpartisan).

The most interesting thing about party, with respect to the present analysis, is that it is an *artificially-created* cleavage which cuts across all other cleavages and often supersedes them in importance: party "regularity" requires that the voter ignore all cleavages except the party one. The party cleavage *has* to cut across others because in the nature of things there are no general organizing principles under which all cleavages can be subsumed. The nearest thing to general organizing principles, perhaps, are "conservatism" and "liberalism." But the cleavages in the city do not fall logically into this or any other pattern; each side of each cleavage stands by itself and ought, in logic, to have its own party. The attachment to party, then, *must* cut across issues. If people were divided into fat men and lean (or Guelfs and Ghibellines, as in medieval Florence) and party feeling were then whipped up, the result would be not unlike the American political party. Indeed, in Salt Lake City the party division is said to have been formed in a way as arbitrary as this. The Mormon hierarchy, obliged to liquidate its church political party when it was admitted to the Union, is said to have told people on one side of the street to vote Republican and those on the other side to vote Democratic. Their descendants, some people insist, still vote the same way.

M. I. Ostrogorski wrote on the development of American parties:

> The problems preoccupying public opinion being numerous and varied, it was necessary, instead of grouping the men in accordance with the issues, to adapt the issues to fixed groups of men. With this object confusion of the questions of the day was erected into a system; they were huddled together into "omnibus" programmes; they were put one on top of another; they were shuffled like a pack of cards, some being played at one time and some at another; at a pinch those which caused irreconcilable divergencies were made away with.[14]

This suggests something about the social function of cleavage in general. If cleavages run across each other (so to speak), they may serve to moderate conflict and to prevent "irreconcilable divergencies," because those who are enemies with respect to cleavage *a* are close allies with respect to cleavage *b* and indifferent (and therefore in a position to mediate) with respect to cleavage *c*. The "artificial" cleavage represented by party is especially functional in this respect because it cuts across *all* other cleavages. What Ostrogorski regarded as defects may therefore be great virtues.

Although logically all of these cleavages—between the haves and have-nots, the suburbanites and the central city, the natives and the immigrants, and the major political parties—are separate and often crosscutting, there is a tendency for them to coalesce into two opposed patterns. These patterns reflect two conceptions of the public interest that are widely held. The first, which derives from the middle-class ethos, favors what the municipal reform movement has always defined as "good

---

[14] M. I. Ostrogorski, *Democracy and the Organization of Political Parties* (New York, 1902), II, 618.

government"—namely efficiency, impartiality, honesty, planning, strong executives, no favoritism, model legal codes, and strict enforcement of laws against gambling and vice. The other conception of the public interest (one never explicitly formulated as such, but one all the same) derives from the "immigrant ethos." This is the conception of those people who identify with the ward or neighborhood rather than the city "as a whole," who look to politicians for "help" and "favors," who regard gambling and vice as, at worst, necessary evils, and who are far less interested in the efficiency, impartiality, and honesty of local government than in its readiness to confer material benefits of one sort or another upon them. In the largest, most heterogeneous of our cities, these two mentalities stand forth as distinctly as did those which, in another context, caused Disraeli to write of "The Two Nations."

# A. RACE

## The Roots of the Negro Problem

### DANIEL P. MOYNIHAN

### Slavery

The most perplexing question about American slavery, which has never been altogether explained, and which indeed most Americans hardly know exists, has been stated by Nathan Glazer as follows: "Why was American slavery the most awful the world has ever known?" The only thing that can be said with certainty is that this is true: it was.

American slavery was profoundly different from, and in its lasting effects on individuals and their children, indescribably worse than, any recorded servitude, ancient or modern. The peculiar nature of American slavery was noted by Alexis de Tocqueville and others, but it was not until 1948 that Frank Tannenbaum, a South American specialist, pointed to the striking differences between Brazilian and American slavery. The feudal, Catholic society of Brazil had a legal and religious tradition which accorded the slave a place as a human being in the hierarchy of society—a luckless, miserable place, to be sure, but a place withal. In contrast, there was nothing in the tradition of English law or Protestant theology which could accommodate to the fact of human bondage—the slaves were therefore reduced to the status of chattels—often, no doubt, well cared for, even privileged chattels, but chattels nevertheless.

Glazer, also focusing on the Brazil–United States comparison, continues.

> In Brazil, the slave had many more rights than in the United States: he could legally marry, he could, indeed had to, be baptized and become a member of the Catholic Church, his family could not be broken up for sale, and he had many days on which he could either rest or earn

Reprinted from *The Negro Family: The Case for National Action* (Washington: Government Printing Office, 1965), pp. 15–23. Footnotes in original text omitted.

money to buy his freedom. The Government encouraged manumission, and the freedom of infants could often be purchased for a small sum at the baptismal font. In short: the Brazilian slave knew he was a man, and that he differed in degree, not in kind, from his master.

[In the United States,] the slave was totally removed from the protection of organized society (compare the elaborate provisions for the protection of slaves in the Bible), his existence as a human being was given no recognition by any religious or secular agency, he was totally ignorant of and completely cut off from his past, and he was offered absolutely no hope for the future. His children could be sold, his marriage was not recognized, his wife could be violated or sold (there was something comic about calling the woman with whom the master permitted him to live a "wife"), and he could also be subject, without redress, to frightful barbarities—there were presumably as many sadists among slaveowners, men and women, as there are in other groups. The slave could not, by law, be taught to read or write; he could not practice any religion without the permission of his master, and could never meet with his fellows, for religious or any other purposes, except in the presence of a white; and finally, if a master wished to free him, every legal obstacle was used to thwart such action. This was not what slavery meant in the ancient world, in medieval and early modern Europe, or in Brazil and the West Indies.

More important, American slavery was also awful in its effects. If we compared the present situation of the American Negro with that of, let us say, Brazilian Negroes (who were slaves 20 years longer), we begin to suspect that the differences are the result of very different patterns of slavery. Today the Brazilian Negroes are Brazilians; though most are poor and do the hard and dirty work of the country, as Negroes do in the United States, they are not cut off from society. They reach into its highest strata, merging there—in smaller and smaller numbers, it is true, but with complete acceptance—with other Brazilians of all kinds. The relations between Negroes and whites in Brazil show nothing of the mass irrationality that prevails in this country.

Stanley M. Elkins, drawing on the aberrant behavior of the prisoners in Nazi concentration camps, drew an elaborate parallel between the two institutions. This thesis has been summarized as follows by Thomas F. Pettigrew:

Both were closed systems, with little chance of manumission, emphasis on survival and a single, omnipresent authority. The profound personality change created by Nazi internment, as independently reported by a number of psychologists and psychiatrists who survived, was toward childishness and total acceptance of the SS guards as father-figures—a syndrome strikingly similar to the "Sambo" caricature of the Southern slave. Nineteenth-century racists readily believed that the

"Sambo" personality was simply an inborn racial type. Yet no African anthropological data have ever shown any personality type resembling Sambo; and the concentration camps molded the equivalent personality pattern in a wide variety of Caucasian prisoners. Nor was Sambo merely a product of "slavery" in the abstract, for the less devastating Latin American system never developed such a type.

Extending this line of reasoning, psychologists point out that slavery in all its forms sharply lowered the need for achievement in slaves . . . Negroes in bondage, stripped of their African heritage, were placed in a completely dependent role. All of their rewards came, not from individual initiative and enterprise, but from absolute obedience—a situation that severely depresses the need for achievement among all peoples. Most important of all, slavery vitiated family life. . . . Since many slaveowners neither fostered Christian marriage among their slave couples nor hesitated to separate them on the auction block, the slave household often developed a fatherless matrifocal (mother-centered) pattern.

## The Reconstruction

With the emancipation of the slaves, the Negro American family began to form in the United States on a widespread scale. But it did so in an atmosphere markedly different from that which has produced the white American family.

The Negro was given liberty, but not equality. Life remained hazardous and marginal. Of the greatest importance, the Negro male, particularly in the South, became an object of intense hostility, an attitude unquestionably based in some measure on fear.

When Jim Crow made its appearance towards the end of the 19th century, it may be speculated that it was the Negro male who was most humiliated thereby; the male was more likely to use public facilities, which rapidly became segregated once the process began, and just as important, segregation, and the submissiveness it exacts, is surely more destructive to the male than to the female personality. Keeping the Negro "in his place" can be translated as keeping the Negro male in his place: the female was not a threat to anyone.

Unquestionably, these events worked against the emergence of a strong father figure. The very essence of the male animal, from the bantam rooster to the four-star general, is to strut. Indeed, in 19th century America, a particular type of exaggerated male boastfulness became almost a national style. Not for the Negro male. The "sassy nigger" was lynched.

In this situation, the Negro family made but little progress toward the middle-class pattern of the present time. Margaret Mead has pointed out that while "In every known human society, everywhere in the world, the young male learns that when he grows up one of the things which he must do in order to be a full member of society is to provide food for some female and her young." This pattern is not immutable, however: it can be broken, even though it has always eventually reasserted itself.

> Within the family, each new generation of young males learn the appropriate nurturing behavior and superimpose upon their biologically given maleness this learned parental role. When the family breaks down —as it does under slavery, under certain forms of indentured labor and serfdom, in periods of extreme social unrest during wars, revolutions, famines, and epidemics, or in periods of abrupt transition from one type of economy to another—this delicate line of transmission is broken. Men may flounder badly in these periods, during which the primary unit may again become mother and child, the biologically given, and the special conditions under which man has held his social traditions in trust are violated and distorted.

E. Franklin Frazier makes clear that at any time of emancipation Negro women were already "accustomed to playing the dominant role in family and marriage relations" and that this role persisted in the decades of rural life that followed.

## Urbanization

Country life and city life are profoundly different. The gradual shift of American society from a rural to an urban basis over the past century and a half has caused abundant strains, many of which are still much in evidence. When this shift occurs suddenly, drastically, in one or two generations, the effect is immensely disruptive of traditional social patterns.

It was this abrupt transition that produced the wild Irish slums of the 19th Century Northeast. Drunkenness, crime, corruption, discrimination, family disorganization, juvenile delinquency were the routine of that era. In our own time, the same sudden transition has produced the Negro slum—different from, but hardly better than its predecessors, and fundamentally the result of the same process.

Negroes are now more urbanized than whites.

Negro families in the cities are more frequently headed by a woman than those in the country. The difference between the white and Negro proportions of families headed by a woman is greater in the city than in the country.

The promise of the city has so far been denied the majority of the Negro migrants, and most particularly the Negro family.

In 1939, E. Franklin Frazier described its plight movingly in that part of *The Negro Family* entitled "In the City of Destruction":

> The impact of hundreds of thousands of rural southern Negroes upon northern metropolitan communities presents a bewildering spectacle. Striking contrasts in levels of civilization and economic well-being among these newcomers to modern civilization seem to baffle any attempt to discover order and direction in their mode of life.
>
> In many cases, of course, the dissolution of the simple family organization has begun before the family reaches the northern city. But, if these families have managed to preserve their integrity until they reach the northern city, poverty, ignorance, and color forces them to seek homes in deteriorated slum areas from which practically all institutional life has disappeared. Hence, at the same time that these simple rural families are losing their internal cohesions, they are being freed from the controlling force of public opinion and communal institutions. Family desertion among Negroes in cities appears, then, to be one of the inevitable consequences of the impact of urban life on the simple family organization and folk culture which the Negro has evolved in the rural South. The distribution of desertions in relation to the general economic and cultural organization of Negro communities that have grown up in our American cities shows in a striking manner the influence of selective factors in the process of adjustment to the urban environment.

In every index of family pathology—divorce, separation, and desertion, female family head, children in broken homes, and illegitimacy —the contrast between the urban and rural environment for Negro families is unmistakable.

Harlem, into which Negroes began to move early in this century, is the center and symbol of the urban life of the Negro American. Conditions in Harlem are not worse, they are probably better than in most Negro ghettos. The social disorganization of central Harlem, comprising ten health areas, was thoroughly documented by the HARYOU report, save for the illegitimacy rates. These have now been made available to the Labor Department by the New York City Department of Health. There could hardly be a more dramatic demonstration of the crumbling —the breaking—of the family structure on the urban frontier.

## Unemployment and Poverty

The impact of unemployment on the Negro family, and particularly on the Negro male, is the least understood of all the developments that have contributed to the present crisis. There is little analysis because there has been almost no inquiry. Unemployment, for whites and nonwhites alike, has on the whole been treated as an economic phenomenon, with almost no attention paid for at least a quarter-century to social and personal consequences.

In 1940, Edward Wight Bakke described the effects of unemployment on family structure in terms of six stages of adjustment. Although the families studied were white, the pattern would clearly seem to be a general one, and apply to Negro families as well.

The first two stages end with the exhaustion of credit and the entry of the wife into the labor force. The father is no longer the provider and the elder children become resentful.

The third stage is the critical one of commencing a new day-to-day existence. At this point two women are in charge:

Consider the fact that relief investigators or case workers are normally women and deal with the housewife. Already suffering a loss in prestige and authority in the family because of his failure to be the chief bread winner, the male head of the family feels deeply this obvious transfer of planning for the family's well-being to two women, one of them an outsider. His role is reduced to that of errand boy to and from the relief office.

If the family makes it through this stage Bakke finds that it is likely to survive, and the rest of the process is one of adjustment. *The critical element of adjustment was not welfare payments, but work.*

Having observed our families under conditions of unemployment with no public help, or with that help coming from direct [sic] and from work relief, we are convinced that after the exhaustion of self-produced resources, work relief is the only type of assistance which can restore the strained bonds of family relationship in a way which promises the continued functioning of that family in meeting the responsibilities imposed upon it by our culture.

Work is precisely the one thing the Negro family head in such circumstances has not received over the past generation.

The fundamental, overwhelming fact is that *Negro unemployment,* with the exception of a few years during World War II and the Korean War, *has continued at disaster levels for 35 years.*

Once again, this is particularly the case in the northern urban areas to which the Negro population has been moving.

The 1930 Census (taken in the spring, before the depression was in full swing) showed Negro unemployment at 6.1 percent, as against

6.6 percent for whites. But taking out the South reversed the relationship: white 7.4 percent, nonwhite 11.5 percent.

By 1940, the 2 to 1 white-Negro unemployment relationship that persists to this day had clearly emerged. Taking out the South again, whites were 14.8 percent, nonwhites 29.7 percent.

Since 1929, the Negro worker has been tremendously affected by the movements of the business cycle and of employment. He has been hit worse by declines than whites, and proportionately helped more by recoveries.

From 1951 to 1963, the level of Negro male unemployment was on a long-run rising trend, while at the same time following the short-run ups and downs of the business cycle. During the same period, the number of broken families in the Negro world was also on a long-run rise, with intermediate ups and downs.

Divorce is expensive: those without money resort to separation or desertion. While divorce is not a desirable goal for a society, it recognizes the importance of marriage and family, and for children some family continuity and support is more likely when the institution of the family has been so recognized.

The conclusion from these and similar data is difficult to avoid: During times when jobs were reasonably plentiful (although at no time during this period, save perhaps the first 2 years, did the unemployment rate for Negro males drop to anything like a reasonable level) the Negro family became stronger and more stable. As jobs became more and more difficult to find, the stability of the family became more and more difficult to maintain.

This relation is clearly seen in terms of the illegitimacy rates of census tracts in the District of Columbia compared with male unemployment rates in the same neighborhoods.

In 1963, a prosperous year, 29.2 percent of all Negro men in the labor force were unemployed at some time during the year. Almost half of these men were out of work 15 weeks or more.

The impact of poverty on Negro family structure is no less obvious, although again it may not be widely acknowledged. There would seem to be an American tradition, agrarian in its origins but reinforced by attitudes of urban immigrant groups, to the effect that family morality and stability decline as income and social position rise. Over the years this may have provided some consolation to the poor, but there is little evidence that it is true. On the contrary, higher family incomes are unmistakably associated with greater family stability—which comes first may be a matter for conjecture, but the conjunction of the two characteristics is unmistakable.

The Negro family is no exception. In the District of Columbia, for example, census tracts with median incomes over $8,000 had an illegitimacy rate one-third that of tracts in the category under $4,000.

## The Wage System

The American wage system is conspicuous in the degree to which it provides high incomes for individuals, but is rarely adjusted to insure that family, as well as individual needs are met. Almost without exception, the social welfare and social insurance systems of other industrial democracies provide for some adjustment or supplement of a worker's income to provide for the extra expenses of those with families. American arrangements do not, save for income tax deductions.

The Federal minimum wage of $1.25 per hour provides a basic income for an individual, but an income well below the poverty line for a couple, much less a family with children.

The 1965 Economic Report of the President revised the data on the number of persons living in poverty in the United States to take account of the varying needs of families of different sizes, rather than using a flat cut off at the $3,000 income level. The resulting revision illustrates the significance of family size. Using these criteria, the number of poor families is smaller, but the number of large families who are poor increases, and the number of children in poverty rises by more than one-third—from 11 million to 15 million. This means that one-fourth of the Nation's children live in families that are poor.

A third of these children belong to families in which the father was not only present, but was employed the year round. In overall terms, median family income is lower for large families than for small families. Families of six or more children have median incomes 24 percent below families with three. (It may be added that 47 percent of young men who fail the Selective Service education test come from families of six or more.)

During the 1950–60 decade of heavy Negro migration to the cities of the North and West, the ratio of nonwhite to white family income in cities increased from 57 to 63 percent. Corresponding declines in the ratio in the rural nonfarm and farm areas kept the national ratio virtually unchanged. But between 1960 and 1963, median nonwhite family income slipped from 55 percent to 53 percent of white income. The drop occurred in three regions, with only the South, where a larger portion of Negro families have more than one earner, showing a slight improvement.

Because in general terms Negro families have the largest number of children and the lowest incomes, many Negro fathers literally cannot

RATIO OF NONWHITE TO WHITE FAMILY MEDIAN INCOME,
UNITED STATES AND REGIONS, 1960–63

| Region | 1960 | 1961 | 1962 | 1963 |
|---|---|---|---|---|
| United States | 55 | 53 | 53 | 53 |
| Northeast | 68 | 67 | 66 | 65 |
| North Central | 74 | 72 | 68 | 73 |
| South | 43 | 43 | 47 | 45 |
| West | 81 | 87 | 73 | 76 |

support their families. Because the father is either not present, is unemployed, or makes such a low wage, the Negro woman goes to work. Fifty-six percent of Negro women, age 25 to 64, are in the work force, against 42 percent of white women. This dependence on the mother's income undermines the position of the father and deprives the children of the kind of attention, particularly in school matters, which is now a standard feature of middle-class upbringing.

## The Dimensions Grow

The dimensions of the problems of Negro Americans are compounded by the present extraordinary growth in Negro population. At the founding of the nation, and into the first decade of the 19th century, 1 American in 5 was a Negro. The proportion declined steadily until it was only 1 in 10 by 1920, where it held until the 1950's, when it began to rise. Since 1950, the Negro population has grown at a rate of 2.4 percent per year compared with 1.7 percent for the total population. If this rate continues, in seven years 1 American in 8 will be nonwhite.

These changes are the result of a declining Negro death rate, now approaching that of the nation generally, and a fertility rate that grew steadily during the postwar period. By 1959, the ratio of white to nonwhite fertility rates reached 1:1.42. Both the white and nonwhite fertility rates have declined since 1959, but the differential has not narrowed.

Family size increased among nonwhite families between 1950 and 1960—as much for those without father as for those with fathers. Average family size changed little among white families, with a slight increase in the size of husband-wife families balanced by a decline in the size of families without fathers.

Negro women not only have more children, but have them earlier. Thus in 1960, there were 1,247 children ever born per thousand evermarried nonwhite women 15 to 19 years of age, as against only 725 among white women, a ratio of 1.7:1. The Negro fertility rate overall is now 1.4 times the white, but what might be called the generation rate is 1.7 times the white.

This population growth must inevitably lead to an unconcealable crisis in Negro unemployment. The most conspicuous failure of the American social system in the past 10 years has been its inadequacy in providing jobs for Negro youth. Thus, in January 1965 the unemployment rate for Negro teenagers stood at 29 percent. This problem will now become steadily more serious.

During the rest of the 1960's the nonwhite civilian population 14 years of age and over will increase by 20 percent—more than double the white rate. The nonwhite labor force will correspondingly increase 20 percent in the next 6 years, double the rate of increase in the nonwhite labor force of the past decade.

As with the population as a whole, there is much evidence that children are being born most rapidly in those Negro families with the least financial resources. This is an ancient pattern, but because the needs of children are greater today it is very possible that the education and opportunity gap between the offspring of these families and those of stable middle-class unions is not closing, but is growing wider.

A cycle is at work; too many children too early make it most difficult for the parents to finish school. (In February, 1963, 38 percent of the white girls who dropped out of school did so because of marriage or pregnancy, as against 49 percent of nonwhite girls.) An Urban League study in New York reported that 44 percent of girl dropouts left school because of pregnancy.

Low education levels in turn produce low income levels, which deprive children of many opportunities, and so the cycle repeats itself.

# Black Power

## STOKELY CARMICHAEL

One of the tragedies of the struggle against racism is that up to now there has been no national organization which could speak to the growing militancy of young black people in the urban ghetto. There has been only a civil rights movement, whose tone of voice was adapted to an audience of liberal whites. It served as a sort of buffer zone between them and angry young blacks. None of its so-called leaders could go into a rioting community and be listened to. In a sense, I blame ourselves—together with the mass media—for what has happened in Watts, Harlem, Chicago, Cleveland, Omaha. Each time the people in those cities saw Martin Luther King get slapped, they became angry; when they saw four little black girls bombed to death, they were angrier; and when nothing happened, they were steaming. We had nothing to offer that they could see, except to go out and be beaten again. We helped to build their frustration.

For too many years, black Americans marched and had their heads broken and got shot. They were saying to the country, "Look, you guys are supposed to be nice guys and we are only going to do what we are supposed to do—why do you beat us up, why don't you give us what we ask, why don't you straighten yourselves out?" After years of this, we are at almost the same point—because we demonstrated from a position of weakness. We cannot be expected any longer to march and have our heads broken in order to say to whites: Come on, you're nice guys. For you are not nice guys. We have found you out.

An organization which claims to speak for the needs of a community—as does the Student Nonviolent Coordinating Committee—must speak in the tone of that community, not as somebody else's buffer zone.

From a public statement by Stokely Carmichael, Executive Director, Student Nonviolent Coordinating Committee, 1966.

This is the significance of black power as a slogan. For once, black people are going to use the words they want to use—not just the words whites want to hear. And they will do this no matter how often the press tries to stop the use of the slogan by equating it with racism and separatism.

An organization which claims to be working for the needs of a community—as SNCC does—must work to provide that community with a position of strength from which to make its voice heard. This is the significance of black power beyond the slogan.

Black power can be clearly defined for those who do not attach the fears of white America to their questions about it. We should begin with the basic fact that black Americans have two problems: they are poor and they are black. All other problems arise from this two-sided reality: lack of education, the so-called apathy of black men. Any program to end racism must address itself to that double reality.

Almost from its beginning, SNCC sought to address itself to both conditions with a program aimed at winning political power for impoverished southern blacks. We had to begin with politics because black Americans are a propertyless people in a country where property is valued above all. We had to work for power, because this country does not function by morality, love, and nonviolence, but by power. Thus we determined to win political power, with the idea of moving on from there into activity that would have economic effects. With power, the masses could *make or participate in making* the decisions which govern their destinies, and thus create basic change in their day-to-day lives.

But if political power seemed to be the key to self-determination, it was also obvious that the key had been thrown down a deep well many years earlier. Disenfranchisement, maintained by racist terror, made it impossible to talk about organizing for political power in 1960. The right to vote had to be won, and SNCC workers devoted their energies to this from 1961 to 1965. They set up voter registration drives in the Deep South. They created pressure for the vote by holding mock elections in Mississippi in 1963 and by helping to establish the Mississippi Freedom Democratic Party (MFDP) in 1964. That struggle was eased, though not won, with the passage of the 1965 Voting Rights Act. SNCC workers could then address themselves to the question: "Who can we vote for, to have our needs met—how do we make our vote meaningful?"

SNCC had already gone to Atlantic City for recognition of the Mississippi Freedom Democratic Party by the Democratic convention and been rejected; it had gone with the MFDP to Washington for recognition by Congress and been rejected. In Arkansas, SNCC helped thirty Negroes to run for school board elections; all but one were defeated, and there was evidence of fraud and intimidation sufficient to cause their defeat. In Atlanta, Julian Bond ran for the state legislature and was elected—twice—and unseated—twice. In several states, black farmers ran in elections for agricultural committees which make crucial decisions concerning land use, loans, etc. Although they won places on a number of committees, they never gained the majorities needed to control them.

All of the efforts were attempts to win black power. Then, in Alabama, the opportunity came to see how blacks could be organized on an independent party basis. An unusual Alabama law provides that any group of citizens can nominate candidates for county office and, if they win 20 per cent of the vote, may be recognized as a county political party. The same then applies on a state level. SNCC went to organize in several counties such as Lowndes, where black people—who form 80 per cent of the population and have an average annual income of $943 —felt they could accomplish nothing within the framework of the Alabama Democratic party because of its racism and because the qualifying fee for this year's elections was raised from $50 to $500 in order to prevent most Negroes from becoming candidates. On May 3, five new county "freedom organizations" convened and nominated candidates for the offices of sheriff, tax assessor, members of the school boards. These men and women are up for election in November—if they live until then. Their ballot symbol is the black panther: a bold, beautiful animal, representing the strength and dignity of black demands today. A man needs a black panther on his side when he and his family must endure —as hundreds of Alabamians have endured—loss of job, eviction, starvation, and sometimes death, for political activity. He may also need a gun and SNCC reaffirms the right of black men everywhere to defend themselves when threatened or attacked. As for initiating the use of violence, we hope that such programs as ours will make that unnecessary; but it is not for us to tell black communities whether they can or cannot use any particular form of action to resolve their problems. Responsibility for the use of violence by black men, whether in self-defense or initiated by them, lies with the white community.

This is the specific historical experience from which SNCC's call for "black power" emerged on the Mississippi march last July. But the concept of "black power" is not a recent or isolated phenomenon: It has grown out of the ferment of agitation and activity by different people and organizations in many black communities over the years. Our last year of work in Alabama added a new concrete possibility. In Lowndes county, for example, black power will mean that if a Negro is elected sheriff, he can end police brutality. If a black man is elected tax assessor, he can collect and channel funds for the building of better roads and schools serving black people—thus advancing the move from political power into the economic arena. In such areas as Lowndes, where black men have a majority, they will attempt to use it to exercise control. This is what they seek: control. Where Negroes lack a majority, black power means proper representation and sharing of control. It means the creation of power bases from which black people can work to change state-wide or nationwide patterns of oppression through pressure from strength—instead of weakness. Politically, black power means what it has always meant to SNCC: the coming together of black people to elect representatives and *to force those representatives to speak to their needs.* It does not mean merely putting black faces into office. A man or women who is black and from the slums cannot be automatically expected to speak to the needs of the black people. Most of the black politicians we see around the country today are not what SNCC means by black power. The power must be that of a community, and emanate from there.

SNCC today is working in both North and South on programs of voter registration and independent political organizing. In some places, such as Alabama, Los Angeles, New York, Philadelphia, and New Jersey, independent organizing under the black panther symbol is in progress. The creation of a national "black panther party" must come about: It will take time to build, and it is much too early to predict its success. We have no infallible master plan and we make no claim to exclusive knowledge of how to end racism; different groups will work in their own different ways. SNCC cannot spell out the full logistics of self-determination but it can address itself to the problem by helping black communities define their needs, realize their strength, and go into action along a variety of lines which they must choose for themselves. Without knowing all the answers, it can address itself to the basic problem of poverty—to the fact that in Lowndes county, 86 white families own 90 per cent of the land. What are black people in that county going to do for jobs, where are they going to get money? There must be reallocation of land, of money.

Ultimately, the economic foundations of this country must be shaken if black people are to control their lives. The colonies of the United States—and this includes the black ghettos within its borders, north and south—must be liberated. For a century, this nation has been like an octopus of exploitation, its tentacles stretching from Mississippi and Harlem to South America, the Middle East, southern Africa, and Vietnam; the form of exploitation varies from area to area but the essential result has been the same—a powerful few have been maintained and enriched at the expense of the poor and voiceless colored masses. This pattern must be broken. As its grip loosens here and there around the world, the hopes of black Americans become more realistic. For racism to die, a totally different America must be born.

This is what the white society does not wish to face; this is why that society prefers to talk about integration. But integration speaks not at all to the problem of poverty, only to the problem of blackness. Integration today means the man who "makes it," leaves his black brothers behind in the ghetto as fast as his new sports car will take him. It has no relevance to the Harlem wino or to the cottonpicker making three dollars a day. As a lady I know in Alabama once said, "the food that Ralph Bunche eats doesn't fill my stomach."

Integration, moreover, speaks to the problem of blackness in a despicable way. As a goal, it has been based on complete acceptance of the fact that *in order to have* a decent house or education, blacks must move into a white neighborhood or send their children to a white school. This reinforces, among both black and white, the idea that "white" is automatically better and "black" is by definition inferior. This is why integration is a subterfuge for the maintenance of white supremacy. It allows the nation to focus on a handful of southern children who get into white schools, at great price, and to ignore the 94 per cent who are left behind in unimproved all-black schools. Such situations will not change until black people have power—to control their own school boards, in this case. Then Negroes become equal in a way that means something, and integration ceases to be a one-way street. Then integration doesn't mean draining skills and energies from the ghetto into white neighborhoods; then it can mean white people moving from Beverly Hills into Watts, white people joining the Lowndes County Freedom Organization. Then integration becomes relevant.

Last April, before the furor over black power, Christopher Jencks wrote in a *New Republic* article on white Mississippi's manipulation of the antipoverty program:

> The War on Poverty has been predicated on the notion that there is such a thing as *a community* which can be defined geographically and mobilized for a collective effort to help the poor. This theory has no relationship to reality in the Deep South. In every Mississippi county there are *two* communities. Despite all the pious platitudes of the moderates on both sides, these two communities habitually see their interests in terms of conflict rather than cooperation. Only when the Negro community can muster enough political, economic, and professional strength to compete on somewhat equal terms, will Negroes believe in the possibility of true cooperation and whites accept its necessity. En route to integration, the Negro community needs to

develop greater independence—a chance to run its own affairs and not cave in whenever "the man" barks. . . . Or so it seems to me, and to most of the knowledgeable people with whom I talked in Mississippi. To OEO, this judgment may sound like black nationalism. . . .

Mr. Jencks, a white reporter, perceived the reason why America's anti-poverty program has been a sick farce in both North and South. In the South, it is clearly racism which prevents the poor from running their own programs; in the North, it more often seems to be politicking and bureaucracy. But the results are not so different: In the North, nonwhites make up 42 per cent of all families in metropolitan "poverty areas" and only 6 per cent of families in areas classified as not poor. SNCC has been working with local residents in Arkansas, Alabama, and Mississippi to achieve control by the poor of the program and its funds; it has also been working with groups in the North, and the struggle is no less difficult. Behind it all is a federal government which cares far more about winning the war on the Vietnamese than the War on Poverty; which has put the poverty program in the hands of self-serving politicians and bureaucrats rather than [in the hands of] the poor themselves; which is unwilling to curb the misuse of white power but quick to condemn black power.

To most whites, black power seems to mean that the Mau Mau are coming to the suburbs at night. The Mau Mau are coming, and whites must stop them. Articles appear about plots to "get Whitey," creating an atmosphere in which "law and order must be maintained." Once again, responsibility is shifted from the oppressor to the oppressed. Other whites chide, "Don't forget—you're only 10 per cent of the population; if you get too smart, we'll wipe you out." If they are liberals they complain, "What about me?—don't you want my help any more?" These are people supposedly concerned about black Americans, but today they think first of themselves, or their feelings of rejection. Or they admonish, "You can't get anywhere without coalitions," without considering the problems of coalition with whom, on what terms (coalition from weakness can mean absorption, betrayal), when? Or they accuse us of "polarizing the races" by our calls for black unity, when the true responsibility for polarization lies with whites who will not accept their responsibility as the majority power for making the democratic process work.

White America will not face the problem of color, the reality of it. The well-intended say: "We're all human, everybody is really decent, we must forget color." But color cannot be "forgotten" until its weight is recognized and dealt with. White America will not acknowledge that the ways in which this country sees itself are contradicted by being black—and always have been. Whereas most of the people who settled this country came here for freedom or for economic opportunity, blacks were brought here to be slaves. When the Lowndes County Freedom Organization chose the black panther as its symbol, it was christened by the press "the Black Panther party"—but the Alabama Democratic party, whose symbol is a rooster, has never been called the White Cock party. No one ever talked about "white power" because power in this country *is* white. All this adds up to more than merely identifying a group phenomenon by some catchy name or adjective. The furor over that black panther reveals the problems that white America has with color and sex; the furor over "black power" reveals how deep racism runs and the great fear which is attached to it.

Whites will not see that I, for example, as a person oppressed because of my blackness, have common cause with other blacks who are oppressed because of blackness. This is not to say that there are no white people who see things as I do, but that it is black people I must speak to first. It must be the oppressed to whom SNCC addresses itself primarily, not to friends from the oppressing group.

From birth, black people are told a set of lies about themselves. We are told that we are lazy—yet I drive through the Delta area of Mississippi and watch black people picking cotton in the hot sun for fourteen hours. We are told, "If you work hard, you'll succeed"—but if that were true, black people would own this country. We are oppressed because we are black—not because we are ignorant, not because we are lazy, not because we're stupid (and got good rhythm), but because we're black.

I remember that when I was a boy, I used to go to see Tarzan movies on Saturday. White Tarzan used to beat up the black natives. I would sit there yelling, "Kill the beasts, kill the savages, kill 'em!" I was saying: Kill *me*. It was as if a Jewish boy watched Nazis taking Jews off to concentration camps and cheered them on. Today, I want the chief to beat hell out of Tarzan and send him back to Europe. But it takes time to become free of the lies and their shaming effect on black minds. It takes time to reject the most important lie: that black people inherently can't do the same things white people can do, unless white people help them.

The need for psychological equality is the reason why SNCC today believes that blacks must organize in the black community. Only black people can convey the revolutionary idea that black people are able to do things themselves. Only they can create in the community an aroused and continuing black consciousness that will provide the basis for political strength. In the past, white allies have furthered white supremacy without the whites involved realizing it—or wanting it, I think. Black people must do things for themselves; they must get poverty money they will control and spend themselves, they must conduct tutorial programs themselves so that black children can identify with black people. This is one reason Africa has such importance: The reality of black men ruling their own nations gives blacks elsewhere a sense of possibility, of power, which they do not now have.

This does not mean we don't welcome help, or friends. But we want the right to decide whether anyone is, in fact, our friend. In the past, black Americans have been almost the only people whom everybody and his momma could jump up and call their friends. We have been tokens, symbols, objects—as I was in high school to many young whites, who like having "a Negro friend." We want to decide who is our friend, and we will not accept someone who comes to us and says: "If you do X, Y, and Z, then I'll help you." We will not be told whom we should choose as allies. We will not be isolated from any group or nation except by our own choice. We cannot have the oppressors telling the oppressed how to rid themselves of the oppressor.

I have said that most liberal whites react to "black power" with the question, What about me?, rather than saying: Tell me what you want me to do and I'll see if I can do it. There are answers to the right question. One of the most disturbing things about almost all white supporters of the movement has been that they are afraid to go into their own communities—which is where the racism exists—and work to get rid of it. They want to run from Berkeley to tell us what to do in Mississippi; let them look instead at Berkeley. They admonish blacks to be nonviolent; let them preach nonviolence in the white community. They come to teach me Negro history; let them go to the suburbs and open up freedom schools for whites. Let them work to stop America's racist foreign policy; let them press this government to cease supporting the economy of South Africa.

There is a vital job to be done among poor whites. We hope to see, eventually, a coalition between poor blacks and poor whites. That is the only coalition which seems acceptable to us, and we see such a coalition as the major internal instrument of change in American society. SNCC has tried several times to organize poor whites; we are trying again now, with an initial training program in Tennessee. It is purely academic today to talk about bringing poor blacks and whites together, but the job of creating a poor-white power bloc must be attempted. The main responsibility for it falls upon whites. Black and white can work together in the white community where possible; it is not possible, however, to go into a poor southern town and talk about integration. Poor whites everywhere are becoming more hostile—not less—partly because they see the nation's attention focused on black poverty and nobody coming to them. Too many young middle-class Americans, like some sort of Pepsi generation, have wanted to come alive through the black community; they've wanted to be where the action is—and the action has been in the black community.

Black people do not want to "take over" this country. They don't want to "get whitey"; they just want to get him off their backs, as the saying goes. It was for example the exploitation by Jewish landlords and merchants which first created black resentment toward Jews—not Judaism. The white man is irrelevant to blacks, except as an oppressive force. Blacks want to be in his place, yes, but not in order to terrorize and lynch and starve him. They want to be in his place because that is where a decent life can be had.

But our vision is not merely of a society in which all black men have enough to buy the good things of life. When we urge that black money go into black pockets, we mean the communal pocket. We want to see money go back into the community and used to benefit it. We want to see the cooperative concept applied in business and banking. We want to see black ghetto residents demand that an exploiting landlord or storekeeper sell them, at minimal cost, a building or a shop that they will own and improve cooperatively; they can back their demand with a rent strike, or a boycott, and a community so unified behind them that no one else will move into the building or buy at the store. The society we seek to build among black people, then, is not a capitalist one. It is a society in which the spirit of community and humanistic love prevail. The word love is suspect; black expectations of what it might produce have been betrayed too often. But those were expectations of a response from the white community, which failed us. The love we seek to encourage is within the black community, the only American community where men call each other "brother" when they meet. We can build a community of love only where we have the ability and power to do so: among blacks.

As for white America, perhaps, it can stop crying out against "black supremacy," "black nationalism," "racism in reverse," and begin facing reality. The reality is that this nation, from top to bottom, is racist; that racism is not primarily a problem of "human relations" but of an exploitation maintained—either actively or through silence—by the society as a whole. Camus and Sartre have asked, can a man condemn himself? Can whites, particularly liberal whites, condemn themselves? Can they stop blaming us, and blame their own system? Are they capable of the shame which might become a revolutionary emotion?

We have found that they usually cannot condemn themselves, and so we have done it. But the rebuilding of this society, if at all possible, is basically the responsibility of whites—not blacks. We won't fight to save the present society, in Vietnam or anywhere else. We are just going to work, in the way *we* see fit, and on goals *we* define, not for civil rights but for all our human rights.

# B. CIVIL DISOBEDIENCE

## *Is It Ever Right to Break the Law?*

### CHARLES FRANKEL

During recent months, public events have repeatedly dramatized an old and troublesome problem. A group of students defies the State Department's ban on travel to Cuba; a teachers' union threatens a strike even though a state law prohibits strikes by public employees; advocates of civil rights employ mass demonstrations of disobedience to the law to advance their cause; the Governor of a Southern state deliberately obstructs the enforcement of Federal laws, and declares himself thoroughly within his rights in doing so. . . .

When is it justified for the citizen to act as his own legislator, and to decide that he will or will not obey a given law?

An answer that covers all the issues this question raises cannot be given here, nor can a set of principles be proposed that will allow anyone to make automatic and infallible judgments concerning the legitimacy or illegitimacy of specific acts of civil disobedience. Such judgments require detailed knowledge of the facts of specific cases, and such knowledge is often unavailable to the outsider. Nevertheless, it is possible to indicate some of the principal issues that are raised by civil disobedience, some of the more common mistakes that are made in thinking about these issues, and, at least in outline, the approach that one man would take toward such issues.

We can begin, it seems to me, by rejecting one extreme position. This is the view that disobedience to the law can never be justified in any circumstances. To take this position is to say one of two things: either every law that exists is a just law, or a greater wrong is always done by breaking the law. The first statement is plainly false. The second is highly doubtful. If it is true, then the signers of the Declaration of Independence, and those Germans who refused to carry out Hitler's orders, committed acts of injustice.

It is possible, however, to take a much more moderate and plausible version of this position, and many quite reasonable people do. Such people concede that disobedience to the law can sometimes be legitimate and necessary under a despotic regime. They argue, however, that civil disobedience can never be justified in a democratic society, because such a society provides its members with legal instruments for the redress of their grievances.

This is one of the standard arguments that is made, often quite sincerely, against the activities of people like supporters of the Congress of Racial Equality, who set about changing laws they find objectionable by dramatically breaking them. Such groups are often condemned for risking disorder and for spreading disrespect for the law when, so it is maintained, they could accomplish their goals a great deal more fairly and patriotically by staying within the law, and confining themselves to the courts and to methods of peaceful persuasion.

Now it is perfectly true, I believe, that there is a stronger case for obedience to the law, including bad law, in a democracy than in a dictatorship. The people who must abide by the law have presumably been consulted, and they have legal channels through which to express their protests and to work for reform. One way to define democracy is to say that it is a system whose aim is to provide alternatives to civil disobedience. Nevertheless, when applied to the kind of situation faced, say, by CORE, these generalizations, it seems to me, become cruelly abstract.

The basic fallacy in the proposition that, in a democracy, civil disobedience can never be justified, is that is confuses the *ideals* or *aims* of democracy with the inevitably less than perfect accomplishments of democracy at any given moment. In accordance with democratic ideals, the laws of a democracy may give rights and powers to individuals which, in theory, enable them to work legally for the elimination of injustices.

In actual fact, however, these rights and powers may be empty. The police may be hostile, the courts biased, the elections rigged—and the legal remedies available to the individual may be unavailing against these evils.

Worse still, the majority may have demonstrated, in a series of free and honest elections, that it is unwavering in its support of what the minority regards as an unspeakable evil. This is obviously the case today in many parts of the South, where the white majority is either opposed to desegregation or not so impatient to get on with it as is the Negro minority. Are we prepared to say that majorities never err? If not, there is no absolutely conclusive reason why we must invariably give the results of an election greater weight than considerations of elementary justice.

It is true, of course, that one swallow does not make a summer, and that the test of legal democratic processes is not this or that particular success or failure, but rather the general direction in which these processes move over the long run. Still, the position that violation of the law is never justifiable so long as there are legal alternatives overstates this important truth. It fails to face at least three important exceptions to it.

In the first place, dramatic disobedience to the law by a minority may be the only effective way of catching the attention or winning the support of the majority. Most classic cases of civil disobedience, from the early Christians to Gandhi and his supporters, exemplify this truth. Civil disobedience, like almost no other technique, can shame a majority and make it ask itself just how far it is willing to go, just how seriously it really is committed to defending the status quo.

Second, there is the simple but painful factor of time. If a man is holding you down on a bed of nails, it is all very well for a bystander to say that you live in a great country in which there are legal remedies for your condition, and that you ought, therefore, to be patient and wait for these remedies to take effect. But your willingness to listen to this counsel will depend, quite properly, on the nature of the injury you are suffering.

Third, it is baseless prejudice to assume that observance of the laws is *always* conducive to strengthening a democratic system while disobedience to the law can never have a salutary effect. A majority's complacent acquiescence in bad laws can undermine the faith of a minority in the power of democratic methods to rectify manifest evils; yet a vigorous democracy depends on the existence of minorities holding just such a faith.

Disobedience to bad laws can sometimes jolt democratic processes into motion. Which strengthens one's hope for democracy more—the behavior of the Negroes in Birmingham who broke municipal ordinances when they staged their protest marches, or the behavior of the police, using dogs and fire hoses to assert their legal authority?

Another factor should also be taken into account. In our Federal system, there are often legitimate doubts concerning the legal validity, under our Constitution, of various state or local ordinances. Disobedience to these laws is in many cases simply a practical, though painful, way of testing their legality. But even where no thought of such a test is involved, there is often present a moral issue which no one can easily dodge—least of all the man whose personal dignity and self-respect are caught up in the issue.

A citizen caught in a conflict between local laws and what he thinks will be upheld as the superior Federal law can sometimes afford to wait until the courts have determined the issue for him. But often he cannot afford to wait, or must take a stand in order to force a decision. This is the situation of many Negro citizens in Southern states as they confront the conflict between local and Federal laws.

Yet there is another side to the story. It would be a mistake to conclude from what has been said that civil disobedience is justified, provided only that it is disobedience in the name of higher principles. Strong moral conviction is not all that is required to turn breaking the law into service to society.

Civil disobedience is not simply like other acts in which men stand up courageously for their principles. It involves violation of the law. And the law can make no provision for its violation except to hold the offender liable to punishment. This is why President Kennedy was in such a delicate position last spring at the time of the Negro demonstrations in Birmingham. He gave many signs that, as an individual, he was in sympathy with the goals of the demonstrators. As a political leader, he probably realized that these goals could not be attained without dramatic actions that crossed the line into illegality. But as Chief Executive he could not give permission or approval to such actions.

We may admire a man like Martin Luther King, who is prepared to defy the authorities in the name of a principle, and we may think that he is entirely in the right; just the same, his right to break the law cannot be officially recognized. No society, whether free or tyrannical, can give its citizens the right to break its laws: To ask it to do so is to ask it to proclaim, as a matter of law, that its laws are not laws.

In short, if anybody ever has a right to break the law, this cannot be a legal right under the law. It has to be a moral right against the law. And this moral right is not an unlimited right to disobey any law which one regards as unjust. It is a right that is hedged about, it seems to me, with important restrictions.

First of all, the exercise of this right is subject to standards of just and fair behavior. I may be correct, for example, in thinking that an ordinance against jaywalking is an unnecessary infringement of my rights. This does not make it reasonable, however, for me to organize a giant sit-down strike in the streets which holds up traffic for a week. Conformity to the concept of justice requires that there be some *proportion* between the importance of the end one desires to attain and the power of the means one employs to attain it.

When applied to civil disobedience, this principle constitutes a very large restriction. Civil disobedience is an effort to change the law by making it impossible to enforce the law, or by making the price of such enforcement extremely high. It is a case, as it were, of holding the legal system to ransom. It can arouse extreme passions on one side or the other, excite and provoke the unbalanced, and make disrespect for the law a commonplace and popular attitude.

Although violence may be no part of the intention of those who practice civil disobedience, the risks of violence are present, and are part of what must be taken into account when a program of civil disobedience is being contemplated.

In short, civil disobedience is a grave enterprise. It may sometimes be justified, but the provocation for it has to be equally grave. Basic principles have to be at issue. The evils being combated have to be serious evils that are likely to endure unless they are fought. There should be reasonable grounds to believe that legal methods of fighting them are likely to be insufficient by themselves.

Nor is this the only limitation on the individual's moral right to disobey the law. The most important limitation is that his cause must be a just one. It was right for General de Gaulle to disobey Marshal Pétain; it was wrong for the commanders of the French Army in Algeria, 20 years later, to disobey General de Gaulle.

Similarly, if it is absolutely necessary, and if the consequences have been properly weighed, then it is right to break the law in order to eliminate inequalities based on race. But it can never be necessary, and no weighing of consequences can ever make it right, to break the law in the name of Nazi principles.

In sum, the goals of those who disobey the law have to lie at the very heart of what we regard as morality before we can say that they have a moral right to do what they are doing.

But who is to make these difficult decisions? Who is to say that one man's moral principles are right and another man's wrong? We come here to the special function that civil disobedience serves in a society. The man who breaks the law on the ground that the law is immoral asks the rest of us, in effect, to trust him, or to trust those he trusts, in preference to the established conventions and authorities of our society.

He has taken a large and visible chance, and implicitly asked us to join him in taking that chance; on the probity of his personal moral judgment. In doing so, he has put it to us whether we are willing to take a similar chance on the probity of our own judgment.

Thomas Hobbes, who knew the trouble that rebels and dissenters convinced of their rectitude can cause, once remarked that a man may be convinced that God has commanded him to act as he has, but that God, after all, does not command other men to believe that this is so. The man who chooses to disobey the law on grounds of principle may be a saint, but he may also be a madman. He may be a courageous and lonely individualist, but he may also merely be taking orders and following his own crowd. Whatever he may be, however, his existence tends to make us painfully aware that we too are implicitly making choices, and must bear responsibility for the ones we make.

This, indeed, may be the most important function of those who practice civil disobedience. They remind us that the man who obeys the law has as much of an obligation to look into the morality of his acts and the rationality of his society as does the man who breaks the law. The occurrence of civil disobedience can never be a happy phenomenon; when it is justified, something is seriously wrong with the society in which it takes place.

But the man who puts his conscience above the law, though he may be right or he may be wrong, does take personal moral responsibility for the social arrangements under which he lives. And so he dramatizes the fascinating and fearful possibility that those who obey the law might do the same. They might obey the law and support what exists, not out of habit or fear, but because they have freely chosen to do so, and are prepared to live with their consciences after having made that choice.

# Letter to Martin Luther King, Jr.

## A GROUP OF ALABAMA CLERGYMEN

*Following is the text of the public statement on Negro demonstrations directed to Dr. Martin Luther King, Jr. by eight Alabama clergymen.*

April 12, 1963

We clergymen are among those who, in January, issued "An Appeal for Law and Order and Common Sense," in dealing with racial problems in Alabama. We expressed understanding that honest convictions in racial matters could properly be pursued in the courts, but urged that decisions of those courts should in the meantime be peacefully obeyed.

Since that time there has been some evidence of increased forbearance and a willingness to face facts. Responsible citizens have undertaken to work on various problems which cause racial friction and unrest. In Birmingham, recent public events have given indication that we all have opportunity for a new constructive and realistic approach to racial problems.

However, we are now confronted by a series of demonstrations by some of our Negro citizens, directed and led in part by outsiders. We recognize the natural impatience of people who feel that their hopes are slow in being realized. But we are convinced that these demonstrations are unwise and untimely.

We agree rather with certain local Negro leadership which has called for honest and open negotiation of racial issues in our area. And we believe this kind of facing of issues can best be accomplished by citizens of our own metropolitan area, white and Negro, meeting with their knowledge and experience of the local situation. All of us need to face that responsibility and find proper channels for its accomplishment.

Just as we formerly pointed out that "hatred and violence have no sanction in our religious and political traditions," we also point out that such actions as incite to hatred and violence, however technically peaceful those actions may be, have not contributed to the resolution of our local problems. We do not believe that these days of new hope are days when extreme measures are justified in Birmingham.

We commend the community as a whole, and the local news media and law enforcement officials in particular, on the calm manner in which these demonstrations have been handled. We urge the public to continue to show restraint should the demonstrations continue, and the law enforcement officials to remain calm and continue to protect our city from violence.

We further strongly urge our own Negro community to withdraw support from these demonstrations, and to unite locally in working peacefully for a better Birmingham. When rights are consistently denied, a cause should be pressed in the courts and in negotiations among local leaders, and not in the streets. We appeal to both our white and Negro citizenry to observe the principles of law and order and common sense.

*Signed by:*

C. C. J. CARPENTER, D.D, LL.D., *Bishop of Alabama*

JOSEPH A. DURICK, D.D., *Auxiliary Bishop, Diocese of Mobile-Birmingham*

Rabbi MILTON L. GRAFMAN, *Temple Emanu-El, Birmingham, Alabama*

Bishop PAUL HARDIN, *Bishop of the Alabama-West Florida Conference of the Methodist Church*

Bishop NOLAN B. HARMON, *Bishop of the North Alabama Conference of the Methodist Church*

GEORGE M. MURRAY, D.D., LL.D., *Bishop Coadjutor, Episcopal Diocese of Alabama*

EDWARD V. RAMAGE, *Moderator, Synod of the Alabama Presbyterian Church in the United States*

EARL STALLINGS, *Pastor, First Baptist Church, Birmingham, Alabama*

# Letter from Birmingham City Jail

## MARTIN LUTHER KING, JR.

April 16, 1963

My Dear Fellow Clergymen,

While confined here in the Birmingham City Jail, I came across your recent statement calling our present activities "unwise and untimely." Seldom, if ever, do I pause to answer criticism of my work and ideas. . . . But since I feel that you are men of genuine good will and your criticisms are sincerely set forth, I would like to answer your statement in what I hope will be patient and reasonable terms. . . .

I am in Birmingham because injustice is here. Just as the 8th century prophets left their little villages and carried their "thus saith the Lord" far beyond the boundaries of their home town, and just as the Apostle Paul left his little village of Tarsus and carried the gospel of Jesus Christ to practically every hamlet and city of the Graeco-Roman world, I too am compelled to carry the gospel of freedom beyond my particular home town. Like Paul, I must constantly respond to the Macedonian call for aid.

Moreover, I am cognizant of the interrelatedness of all communities and states. I cannot sit idly by in Atlanta and not be concerned about what happens in Birmingham. Injustice anywhere is a threat to justice everywhere. We are caught in an inescapable network of mutuality tied in a single garment of destiny. Whatever affects one directly affects all indirectly. Never again can we afford to live with the narrow, provincial "outside agitator" idea. Anyone who lives inside the United States can never be considered an outsider anywhere in this country.

You deplore the demonstrations that are presently taking place in Birmingham. But I am sorry that your statement did not express a similar concern for the conditions that brought the demonstrations into being. I am sure that each of you would want to go far beyond the superficial social analyst who looks merely at effects, and does not grapple with underlying causes. I would not hesitate to say that it is unfortunate that so-called demonstrations are taking place in Birmingham at this time, but I would say in more emphatic terms that it is even more unfortunate that the white power structure of this city left the Negro community with no other alternative.

In any nonviolent campaign there are four basic steps: 1) collection of the facts to determine whether injustices are alive; 2) negotiation; 3) self-purification; and 4) direct action. We have gone through all of these steps in Birmingham. There can be no gainsaying of the fact that racial injustice engulfs this community. Birmingham is probably the most thoroughly segregated city in the United States. Its ugly record of police brutality is known in every section of this country. Its unjust treatment of Negroes in the courts is a notorious reality. There have been more unsolved bombings of Negro homes and churches in Birmingham than any city in this nation. These are the hard, brutal, and unbelievable facts. On the basis of these conditions Negro leaders sought to negotiate with the city fathers. But the political leaders consistently refused to engage in good faith negotiation. . . .

As in so many experiences of the past, we were confronted with blasted hopes, and the dark shadow of a deep disappointment settled upon us. So we had no alternative except that of preparing for direct action, whereby we would present our very bodies as a means of laying our case before the conscience of the local and national community. We were not unmindful of the difficulties involved. So we decided to go through a process of self-purification. We started having workshops on nonviolence and repeatedly asked ourselves the questions, "Are you able to accept blows without retaliating?" "Are you able to endure the ordeals of jail?" . . .

You may well ask, "Why direct action? Why sit-ins, marches, etc.? Isn't negotiation a better path?" You are exactly right in your call for negotiation. Indeed, this is the purpose of direct action. Nonviolent direct action seeks to create such a crisis and establish such creative tension that a community that has constantly refused to negotiate is forced to confront the issue. It seeks so to dramatize the issue that it can no longer be ignored.

I just referred to the creation of tension as a part of the work of the nonviolent resister. This may sound rather shocking. But I must confess that I am not afraid of the word tension. I have earnestly worked and preached against violent tension, but there is a type of constructive nonviolent tension that is necessary for growth. Just as Socrates felt that it was necessary to create a tension in the mind so that individuals could rise from the bondage of myths and half-truths to the unfettered realm of creative analysis and objective appraisal, we must see the need of having nonviolent gadflies to create the kind of tension in society that will help men rise from the dark depths of prejudice and racism to the majestic heights of understanding and brotherhood. So the purpose of the direct action is to create a situation so crisis-packed that it will inevitably open the door to negotiation. We, therefore, concur with you in your call for negotiation. Too long has our beloved Southland been bogged down in the tragic attempt to live in monologue rather than dialogue. . . .

My friends, I must say to you that we have not made a single gain in civil rights without determined legal and nonviolent pressure. History is the long and tragic story of the fact that privileged groups seldom give up their privileges voluntarily. Individuals may see the moral light and voluntarily give up their unjust posture; but as Reinhold Niebuhr has reminded us, groups are more immoral than individuals.

We know through painful experience that freedom is never voluntarily given by the oppressor; it must be demanded by the oppressed. Frankly I have never yet engaged in a direct action movement that was "well timed," according to the timetable of those who have not suffered unduly from the disease of segregation. For years now I have heard the word "Wait!" It rings in the ear of every Negro with a piercing familiarity. This "wait" has almost always meant "never." It has been a tranquilizing Thalidomide, relieving the emotional stress for a moment, only to give birth to an ill-formed infant of frustration. We must come to see with the distinguished jurist of yesterday that "justice too long delayed is justice denied." We have waited for more than 340 years for our constitutional and God-given rights. The nations of Asia and Africa are moving with jet-like speed toward the goal of political independence, and we still creep at horse and buggy pace toward the gaining of a cup of coffee at a lunch counter.

I guess it is easy for those who have never felt the stinging darts of segregation to say wait. But when you have seen vicious mobs lynch your mothers and fathers at will and drown your sisters and brothers at whim; when you have seen hate-filled policemen curse, kick, brutalize, and even kill your black brothers and sisters with impunity; when you see the vast majority of your 20 million Negro brothers smothering in an air-tight cage of poverty in the midst of an affluent society; when you suddenly find your tongue twisted and your speech stammering as you seek to explain to your six-year-old daughter why she can't go to the public amusement park that has just been advertised on television, and see tears welling up in her little eyes when she is told that Funtown is closed to colored children, and see the depressing clouds of inferiority begin to form in her little mental sky, and see her begin to distort her little personality by unconsciously developing a bitterness toward white people; when you have to concoct an answer for a five-year-old son asking in agonizing pathos: "Daddy, why do white people treat colored people so mean?"; when you take a cross country drive and find it necessary to sleep night after night in the uncomfortable corners of your automobile because no motel will accept you; when you are humiliated day in and day out by nagging signs reading "white" men and "colored"; when you first name becomes "nigger" and your middle name becomes "boy" (however old you are) and your last name becomes "John," and when your wife and mother are never given the respected title "Mrs."; when you are harried by day and haunted by night by the fact that you are a Negro, living constantly at tip-toe stance never quite knowing what to expect next, and plagued with inner fears and outer resentments; when you are forever fighting a degenerating sense of "nobodiness"—then you will understand why we find it difficult to wait. There comes a time when the cup of endurance runs over, and men are no longer willing to be plunged into an abyss of injustice where they experience the bleakness of corroding despair. I hope, sirs, you can understand our legitimate and unavoidable impatience.

You express a great deal of anxiety over our willingness to break laws. This is certainly a legitimate concern. Since we so diligently urge people to obey the Supreme Court's decision of 1954 outlawing segregation in the public schools, it is rather strange and paradoxical to find us consciously breaking laws. One may well ask, "How can you advocate breaking some laws and obeying others?" The answer is found in the fact that there are two types of laws: There are *just* laws and there are *unjust* laws. I would be the first to advocate obeying just laws. One has not only a legal but a moral responsibility to obey just laws. Conversely, one has a moral responsibility to disobey unjust laws. I would agree with Saint Augustine that "An unjust law is no law at all."

Now what is the difference between the two? How does one determine when a law is just or unjust? A just law is a man-made code that squares with the moral law or the law of God. An unjust law is a mode that is out of harmony with the moral law. To put it in the terms of Saint Thomas Aquinas, an unjust law is a human law that is not rooted in eternal and natural law. Any law that uplifts human personality is just. Any law that degrades human personality is unjust.

All segregation statutes are unjust because segregation distorts the soul and damages the personality. It gives the segregator a false sense of superiority and the segregated a false sense of inferiority. To use the words of Martin Buber, the great Jewish philosopher, segregation substitutes an "I-it" relationship for the "I-thou" relationship, and ends up

relegating persons to the status of things. So segregation is not only politically, economically, and sociologically unsound, but it is morally
wrong and sinful. Paul Tillich has said that sin is separation. Isn't segregation an existential expression of man's tragic separation, an expression of his awful estrangement, his terrible sinfulness? So I can urge men
to obey the 1954 decision of the Supreme Court because it is morally
right, and I can urge them to disobey segregation ordinances because
they are morally wrong.

Let me give another example of just and unjust laws. An unjust
law is a code that a majority inflicts on a minority that is not binding on
itself. This is *difference* made legal. On the other hand a just law is a
code that a majority compels a minority to follow that it is willing to
follow itself. This is *sameness* made legal.

Let us give another explanation. An unjust law is a code inflicted
upon a minority which that minority had no part in enacting or creating
because they did not have the unhampered right to vote. Who can say
the legislature of Alabama which set up the segregation laws was democratically elected? Throughout the state of Alabama all types of conniv-
ing methods are used to prevent Negroes from becoming registered
voters and there are some counties without a single Negro registered to
vote despite the fact that the Negro constitutes a majority of the population. Can any law set up in such a state be considered democratically
structured?

These are just a few examples of unjust and just laws. There are
some instances when a law is just in its face but unjust in its application.
For instance, I was arrested Friday on a charge of parading without a
permit. Now there is nothing wrong with an ordinance which requires
a permit for a parade, but when the ordinance is used to preserve segregation and to deny citizens the First Amendment privilege of peaceful
assembly and peaceful protest, then it becomes unjust.

I hope you can see the distinction I am trying to point out. In no
sense do I advocate evading or defying the law as the rabid segregationist would do. This would lead to anarchy. One who breaks an unjust
law must do it *openly, lovingly* (not hatefully as the white mothers did
in New Orleans when they were seen on television screaming "nigger,
nigger, nigger") and with a willingness to accept the penalty. I submit
that an individual who breaks a law that conscience tells him is unjust,
and willingly accepts the penalty by staying in jail to arouse the conscience of the community over its injustice, is in reality expressing the
very highest respect for law.

Of course there is nothing new about this kind of civil disobedience.
It was seen sublimely in the refusal of Shadrach, Meshach, and Abed-

nego to obey the laws of Nebuchadnezzar because a higher moral law was involved. It was practiced superbly by the early Christians who were willing to face hungry lions and the excruciating pain of chopping blocks before submitting to certain unjust laws of the Roman Empire. To a degree academic freedom is a reality today because Socrates practiced civil disobedience.

We can never forget that everything Hitler did in Germany was "legal" and everything the Hungarian freedom fighters did in Hungary was "illegal." It was "illegal" to aid and comfort a Jew in Hitler's Germany. But I am sure that, if I had lived in Germany during that time, I would have aided and comforted my Jewish brothers even though it was illegal. If I lived in a Communist country today where certain principles dear to the Christian faith are suppressed, I believe I would openly advocate disobeying these anti-religious laws. . . .

In your statement you asserted that our actions, even though peaceful, must be condemned because they precipitate violence. But can this assertion be logically made? Isn't this like condemning the robbed man because his possession of money precipitated the evil act of robbery? Isn't this like condemning Socrates because his unswerving commitment to truth and his philosophical delvings precipitated the misguided popular mind to make him drink the hemlock? Isn't this like condemning Jesus because His unique God consciousness and never-ceasing devotion to His will precipitated the evil act of crucifixon? We must come to see, as Federal courts have consistently affirmed, that it is immoral to urge an individual to withdraw his efforts to gain his basic constitutional rights because the quest precipitates violence. Society must protect the robbed and punish the robber.

I had also hoped that the white moderate would reject the myth of time. I received a letter this morning from a white brother in Texas which said: "All Christians know that the colored people will receive equal rights eventually, but is it possible that you are in too great of a religious hurry? It has taken Christianity almost 2,000 years to accomplish what it has. The teachings of Christ take time to come to earth." All that is said here grows out of a tragic misconception of time. It is the strangely irrational notion that there is something in the very flow of time that will inevitably cure all ills. Actually time is neutral. It can be used either destructively or constructively. I am coming to feel that the people of ill will have used time much more effectively than the people of good will.

We will have to repent in this generation not merely for the vitriolic words and actions of the bad people, but for the appalling silence of the good people. We must come to see that human progress never rolls in on wheels of inevitability. It comes through the tireless efforts and persistent work of men willing to be co-workers with God, and without this hard work time itself becomes an ally of the forces of social stagnation.

We must use time creatively, and forever realize that the time is always ripe to do right. Now is the time to make real the promise of democracy, and transform our pending national elegy into a creative psalm of brotherhood. Now is the time to lift our national policy from the quicksand of raciàl injustice to the solid rock of human dignity.

You spoke of our activity in Birmingham as extreme. At first I was rather disappointed that fellow clergymen would see my nonviolent efforts as those of the extremist. I started thinking about the fact that I stand in the middle of two opposing forces in the Negro community. One is a force of complacency made up of Negroes who, as a result of long years of oppression, have been so completely drained of self-respect and a sense of "somebodiness" that they have adjusted to segregation, and of a few Negroes in the middle class who, because of a degree of academic and economic security, and because at points they profit by segregation, have unconsciously become insensitive to the problems of the masses. The other force is one of bitterness and hatred and comes perilously close to advocating violence. It is expressed in the various black nationalist groups that are springing up over the nation, the largest and best known being Elijah Muhammad's Muslim movement. This movement is nourished by the contemporary frustration over the continued existence of racial discrimination. It is made up of people who have lost faith in America, who have absolutely repudiated Christianity, and who have concluded that the white man is an incurable "devil."

I have tried to stand between these two forces saying that we need not follow the "do-nothingism" of the complacent or the hatred and despair of the black nationalist. There is the more excellent way of love and nonviolent protest. I'm grateful to God that, through the Negro church, the dimension of nonviolence entered our struggle. If this philosophy had not emerged I am convinced that by now many streets of the South would be flowing with floods of blood. And I am further convinced that if our white brothers dismiss us as "rabble rousers" and "outside agitators"—those of us who are working through the channels of nonviolent direct action—and refuse to support our nonviolent efforts, millions of Negroes, out of frustration and despair, will seek solace and security in black nationalist ideologies, a development that will lead inevitably to a frightening racial nightmare.

Oppressed people cannot remain oppressed forever. The urge for freedom will eventually come. This is what has happened to the American Negro. Something within has reminded him of his birthright of freedom; something without has reminded him that he can gain it. Consciously and unconsciously, he has been swept in by what the Germans call the *Zeitgeist,* and with his black brothers of Africa, and his brown and yellow brothers of Asia, South America, and the Caribbean, he is moving with a sense of cosmic urgency toward the promised land of racial justice. Recognizing this vital urge that has engulfed the Negro community, one should readily understand public demonstrations.

The Negro has many pent-up resentments and latent frustrations. He has to get them out. So let him march sometime; let him have his prayer pilgrimages to the city hall; understand why he must have sit-ins and freedom rides. If his repressed emotions do not come out in these nonviolent ways, they will come out in ominous expressions of violence. This is not a threat; it is a fact of history. So I have not said to my people, "Get rid of your discontent." But I have tried to say that this normal and healthy discontent can be channeled through the creative outlet of nonviolent direct action. Now this approach is being dismissed as extremist. I must admit that I was initially disappointed in being so categorized.

But as I continued to think about the matter I gradually gained a bit of satisfaction from being considered an extremist. Was not Jesus an extremist in love? "Love your enemies, bless them that curse you, pray for them that despitefully use you." Was not Amos an extremist for justice—"Let justice roll down like waters and righteousness like a mighty stream." Was not Paul an extremist for the gospel of Jesus Christ —"I bear in my body the marks of the Lord Jesus." Was not Martin Luther an extremist—"Here I stand; I can do none other so help me God." Was not John Bunyan an extremist—"I will stay in jail to the end of my days before I make a butchery of my conscience." Was not Abraham Lincoln an extremist—"This nation cannot survive half slave and half free." Was not Thomas Jefferson an extremist—"We hold these truths to be self evident that all men are created equal."

So the question is not whether we will be extremist but what kind of extremist will we be. Will we be extremists for hate or will we be extremists for love? Will we be extremists for the preservation of injustice —or will we be extremists for the cause of justice? In that dramatic scene on Calvary's hill three men were crucified. We must never forget that all three were crucified for the same crime—the crime of extremism. Two were extremists for immorality, and thus fell below their environment. The other, Jesus Christ, was an extremist for love, truth, and goodness, and thereby rose above His environment. So, after all, maybe the South, the nation, and the world are in dire need of creative extremists. . . .

I hope the Church as a whole will meet the challenge of this decisive hour. But even if the Church does not come to the aid of justice, I have no despair about the future. I have no fear about the outcome of our struggle in Birmingham, even if our motives are presently misunderstood. We will reach the goal of freedom in Birmingham and all over the nation, because the goal of America is freedom. Abused and scorned though we may be, our destiny is tied up with the destiny of America.

Before the pilgrims landed at Plymouth, we were here. Before the pen of Jefferson etched across the pages of history the majestic words of the Declaration of Independence, we were here. For more than two centuries our foreparents labored in this country without wages; they made cotton "king"; and they built the homes of their masters in the midst of brutal injustice and shameful humiliation—and yet out of a bottomless vitality they continued to thrive and develop. If the inexpressible cruelties of slavery could not stop us, the opposition we now face will surely fail. We will win our freedom because the sacred heritage of our nation and the eternal will of God are embodied in our echoing demands.

I must close now. But before closing I am impelled to mention one other point in your statement that troubled me profoundly. You warmly commended the Birmingham police force for keeping "order" and "preventing violence." I don't believe you would have so warmly commended the police force if you had seen its angry violent dogs literally biting six unarmed, nonviolent Negroes. I don't believe you would so quickly commend the policemen if you would observe their ugly and inhuman treatment of Negroes here in the city jail; if you would watch them push and curse old Negro women and young Negro girls; if you would see them slap and kick old Negro men and young Negro boys; if you will observe them, as they did on two occasions, refuse to give us food because we wanted to sing our grace together. I'm sorry that I can't join you in your praise for the police department. . . .

It is true that they have been rather disciplined in their public handling of the demonstrators. In this sense they have been rather publicly "nonviolent." But for what purpose? To preserve the evil system of segregation. Over the last few years I have consistently preached that nonviolence demands that the means we use must be as pure as the ends we seek. So I have tried to make it clear that it is wrong to use immoral means to attain moral ends. But now I must affirm that it is just as wrong, or even more so, to use moral means to preserve immoral ends. . . . T. S. Eliot has said that there is no greater treason than to do the right deed for the wrong reason.

I wish you had commended the Negro sit-inners and demonstrators of Birmingham for their sublime courage, their willingness to suffer, and their amazing discipline in the midst of the most inhuman provocation. One day the south will recognize its real heroes. They will be the James Merediths, courageously and with a majestic sense of purpose, facing jeering and hostile mobs and the agonizing loneliness that characterizes the life of the pioneer. They will be old, oppressed, battered Negro women, symbolized in a 72-year-old woman of Montgomery, Alabama, who rose up with a sense of dignity and with her people decided not to ride the segregated buses, and responded to one who inquired about her tiredness with ungrammatical profundity: "My feets is tired, but my soul is rested." They will be young high school and college students, young ministers of the gospel and a host of the elders, courageously and nonviolently sitting in at lunch counters and willingly going to jail for conscience sake. One day the South will know that when these disinherited children of God sat down at lunch counters they were in reality standing up for the best in the American dream and the most sacred values in our Judeo-Christian heritage, and thus carrying our whole nation back to great wells of democracy which were dug deep by the founding fathers in the formulation of the Constitution and the Declaration of Independence.

*Yours for the cause of Peace and Brotherhood*

M. L. KING JR.

# C. HAVES AND
# HAVE NOTS

## The American Poor and How They Live

### OFFICE OF ECONOMIC OPPORTUNITY

Prosperity has been kind to most Americans. Despite higher price levels, real income—the buying power of aggregate dollars available to most of us—has risen sharply. A cursory look at our cities, suburbs, highways and countryside reveals a land almost of conspicuous consumption.

A closer look, both at the countryside and our inner cities, would show clearly that prosperity has passed millions of us by. Rural and Urban poverty afflict these millions who view the affluent society from the outside.

The poor live in a world unrecognizable to the majority of the nation. That world has been eloquently described by authors and newspapermen who have dared to enter it—if only for a close-up glance. They have found a land where the inhabitants are isolated from the mainstream of American economic, political and social life. It is a world where the major concern is survival for today, where even a minor illness can become a major tragedy, where privacy is almost unknown, where the American dream is hollow and unreal, where the poverty of the father is visited upon the next generation.

Americans are not poor in the way that poverty afflicts millions of the world's under-developed nations. But domestic poverty is possibly more cruel since it co-exists with abundance. As author Michael Harrington has pointed out, "tens of millions of Americans are, at this very moment, maimed in body and spirit, existing at levels beneath those necessary for human decency. If these people are not starving, they are hungry, and sometimes fat with hunger, for that is what cheap foods do. They are without adequate housing and education and medical care."

Reprinted from the Office of Economic Opportunity, *Selected Readings about the President's War on Poverty Program,* Program Support Division, Community Action Program, Office of Economic Opportunity, Washington, D.C., 1965.

Significant progress has been made in reducing poverty in the United States. Between 1947 and 1956, unemployment rates were low and incomes grew at a relatively rapid rate. The number of poor families declined from 11.9 to 9.9 million at a time of rapid population growth. In 1947, the poor accounted for 32 percent of American families. By 1956, some 23 percent remained in poverty.

Between 1957 and 1962, the rate of decline slowed significantly. Economic growth slowed and the unemployment rate rose and remained high. The number of families remaining in poverty declined only from 9.9 to 9.3 million, about a fifth of the 47 million family units in the nation.

Arbitrary income cut-off points cannot be used to delimit poverty, since a family of eight with $4,000 annually may suffer greater want than an aged couple with $2,500. But poverty and affluence are still best determined with an income measuring stick.

In 1962, the Social Security Administration defined a low-cost budget for a nonfarm family of four, and put the income requirement at $3,955. It also defined an "economy-plan" budget which it reported would cost $3,165. On balance, it has been determined that a family of four must have at least $3,000 a year to burst the bonds of poverty.

Low income family budgets assume that a third of family income will go for food, about $20 per week for a family of four. Of the $2,000 remaining to a family at the poverty line, about $800 would be allowed for housing. The remaining $1,200—less than $25 weekly —would go for clothing, transportation, medical care, education, recreation, insurance, personal care, etc.

The 9.3 million families with incomes below $3,000 comprise 30 million persons. Of these, 11 million—about one-sixth of America's young—are children. Condemned to deprivation, inadequate educational opportunity and cultural alienation, far too many of these children will inherit poverty for their entire lives and, in turn, pass it on to their children.

More than 5.4 million of the nation's impoverished families have incomes below $2,000 a year. More than a million children of very large families—six or more in the family unit—live in these circumstances.

A minimum income of $1,500 annually—less than $30 a week— has been found necessary to support an unattached individual above the poverty line. Some 45 percent of all unattached individuals—a total of five million—lived below the poverty level in 1962. Of these, more than three million had incomes of a thousand dollars or less.

Hard-core poverty can be eliminated in the foreseeable future only through an active program striking at the roots of want and deprivation. Should present trends continue, about 13 percent of all families would still be poor in 1980. In view of the nature of today's poverty, there is reason to believe that even reduction to this level would not be achieved if nothing were done about the problem.

Poverty exacts a frightening social and economic cost. Just by lifting our impoverished families to the $3,000 mark, $11 billion annually would be added to the wealth of the nation. The costs in needless ignorance, crime delinquency, health deterioration, unemployment, and wasted lives is incalculable. Since abuse and misuse of human resources represents tragic social and economic waste, America will never reach her full potential while massive poverty is tolerated.

Of all nations, America can most readily afford the costs of combatting poverty. Present programs, stressing education, training and social services, seek to break the poverty cycle. They represent an important beginning in the only war this nation seeks—the war against needless want.

## Ethnic Composition

About 45 percent of nonwhite families had incomes under $3,000 annually in 1962, compared with 17 percent of white families. And while the incomes of both white and nonwhite families have risen in the post-war period, the relative position of the nonwhite has not improved. Data of the Census Bureau, on the contrary, suggests that the relative position of nonwhite families may have deteriorated.

Nearly half of Negro families—49 percent—had incomes below $3,000 annually (in 1962 dollars) in 1960 and 54 percent of American Indian families were in the poverty category. But only 11 percent of Japanese and 16 percent of Chinese families had low incomes. About 35 percent of persons with Spanish surnames—Mexican-Americans —in the Southwest were poor, and 32 percent of Puerto Rican families were in this category.

Of the two million Negro poor families in the United States (incomes below $3,000 in 1959), nearly three-fourths lived in the South. About 23 percent lived in the North, but only four percent in the West.

Of the 1.4 million poor Negro families living in the South, 53 percent were found to reside in urban areas, 32 percent were rural nonfarm and 15 percent were on the farm. Nearly all of the Negro poor in the North and West—about 95 percent—lived in urban areas.

Of the 700,000 families with Spanish surnames living in the Southwest, 240,000 were poor. About 57 percent of the poor lived in Texas, 24 percent in California and the remainder in Arizona, Colorado and New Mexico.

Nearly all of the 200,000 Puerto Rican families in continental United States lived in urban areas in 1960. About 73 percent of these lived in the New York metropolitan area. About 76 percent of the 80,000 impoverished Puerto Rican families lived in the New York area.

White poverty is less concentrated by geography. About two-fifths of the nation's poor white families are in the South and another 29 percent are in the North Central area.

Among white families, there is a direct relationship between poverty and age. A third of poor white families are headed by persons over age 65. Among nonwhites, only 17 percent of impoverished families are headed by elderly persons.

Lack of education is a deeply rooted cause of poverty which respects no racial boundaries. About 70 percent of nonwhite poor families and 60 percent of white poor families are headed by persons with less than a grade school education.

Many more of nonwhite poor families are headed by wage workers than is the case with whites. About 36 percent of nonwhite family heads are employed in the services or as laborers, a proportion three times as great as among white families. Proportionately, on the other hand, twice as many of the white poor are farmers (12 percent against six).

Nonwhite poor families have more and younger children; 67 percent of the former families include at least one child under 18 while only 45 percent of whites are so characterized. About 43 percent of nonwhite poor families include children under six, as compared with 23 percent of whites. Nearly a fourth of the nonwhite poor have four or more children but only eight percent of whites were so situated.

Nonwhite poor families are much larger than white families in similar economic circumstances. Over half of white families of low income are two person units, compared with only a third of nonwhites.

## Urban Poor Neighborhoods

The poor are a minority in most urban complexes, but the greatest concentrations of poverty lie within these centers. Over half of all poor families—4.9 million—live in cities of a quarter of a million or more. Nonwhite low income families are highly concentrated in these big cities which house half of all poor white families and 63 percent of the nonwhite poor.

New York City's poor make up an eighth of its total population. This meant that the central city housed 371,000 families with incomes below the $3,000 level in 1960.

Certain Chicago areas illustrate the deterioration of poor neighborhoods. Changes in Chicago over recent years appear to be typical of those in other major urban concentrations. The population of the inner city decreased by two percent during the fifties. In the same decade, Negro population increased by 65 percent. As the sixties began, Negroes accounted for 23 percent of Chicago's total population.

In the Chicago neighborhoods cited here, at least one-fourth of all families had incomes below $3,000 annually in 1959. Unemployment rates were far higher than the national average; the population suffered serious educational deficiencies; slum housing was common or predominant; median family income was significantly lower than that of the metropolitan area. The neighborhoods now are predominantly Negro, but they are not the sum total of Negro neighborhoods in the city.

East Garfield Park, in Central Chicago, is bounded by industrial areas and railroad tracks. Almost 30 percent of the housing is substandard and there has been little residential construction since the early thirties. As the fifties began, the neighborhood was predominantly white. Today, it is about three-fifths Negro. During the fifties total population declined by five percent, but Negro population increased by 250 percent. Nearly 80 percent of today's East Garfield housing is multiple dwelling and there is almost no individual home ownership.

The Near West Side has long housed waves of new immigrants, and since 1930 has been predominantly populated by persons of Italian extraction. Beginning with 1930, Mexican migrants began to move in and were soon joined by Southern Negroes seeking employment in the big city. Together, the Mexican and Negro population now is the second largest group to inhabit the Near West Side. As the newcomers came, older groups—Germans, Irish, Russian-Jews, and Poles—moved out. Newcomers included Puerto Ricans who, in 1960, numbered 19 percent of all Puerto Ricans in the city.

An increasing part of the Near West Side is becoming industrial. Industry is located on the borders of the neighborhood, close to the railroad tracks and in the northeastern section. The eastern portion of the area is marked by light industry, and wholesale houses. Madison

Street, in the heart of the area, has become a big city "skid row," complete with cheap saloons and flophouses.

The Near West Side is a multiple-housing community where, in 1960, thirty percent of the dwellings contained 10 or more rental units and 46 percent more contained three to nine units. Large single-home units on Ashland Avenue, long ago occupied by the wealthy and near-wealthy, today house cheap boarding-houses and small businesses. Only 10 percent of the area's housing is owner occupied.

An influx of Negro population in the forties reversed a population decline in the Near South Side but outflow exceeded intake again in the fifties. Negroes now make up about 77 percent of the area's population. While the percentage of Negroes increased during the fifties, there was only a small absolute increase in numbers. The higher percentage of Negroes was chiefly attributable to an outflow of whites.

New housing construction in the Near South Side was virtually nonexistent until 1955 when the Chicago Housing Authority completed the Harold L. Ickes Homes with 803 units.

Industrial and commercial development has increased and less land is being used for residential purposes. Substandard conditions and overcrowding prevail in deteriorating housing generally sandwiched in between industrial and commercial establishments. Warehousing and industrial uses predominate in the area west of the Illinois Central tracks. Wholesale establishments and auto agencies dominate along Michigan Boulevard.

Negroes started to move into the Kenwood area in the middle forties, and by 1960 the neighborhood was 84 percent Negro. The remaining whites in Kenwood are concentrated in new high rise apartment houses in the southeastern corner of the area. Most whites are of the German and Russian-Jewish stock who once were the preponderant majority. The Japanese population of the area has dwindled.

The southern half of Kenwood has been included in the Hyde Park–Kenwood conservation area established by the Chicago Community Conservation Board in 1956. In 1962, ground was broken for 1,949 residential units. In the same year, work was begun by the Chicago Dwellings Association on a nine-story structure which will contain 103 rental units for elderly middle-income families.

### How They Live

Nowhere does poverty manifest itself with greater impact than in housing. Housing for the poor often lacks adequate plumbing and heating facilities, is in woeful disrepair, is vermin infested and constitutes a threat to the health and safety of the occupants.

More than any other group, the poor live in rental housing. About half of the poor are renters, while in the over $6,000 group 74 percent are home-owners.

Nearly half of the 8.5 million housing units found dilapidated or lacking some or all plumbing in the census report of 1960 was occupied by households with incomes below $2,000 a year, and 1.3 million more units were occupied by families with incomes between $2,000 and $3,000.

Large families with six, seven or eight children are poor even when incomes are significantly above $3,000. It is not surprising, therefore, to find such families living in substandard housing even when incomes are in the $4,000–$5,000 range.

While poor housing is usually a hallmark of poverty, good or relatively good housing may hide want and privation. The 1960 census found that five million families with incomes under $2,000 and another three million with incomes between $2,000 and $3,000 lived in adequate housing. Good housing occupied by owners tends to be more common than that occupied by renters among the poor.

Relatively good housing among the poor is accounted for by such factors as acquisition before retirement, inheritance and periods of relative affluence. The incidence of elderly couples with low incomes among the better housed poor explains why there is considerably less crowding among households with annual incomes below $3,000 than at any other point on the income scale. With children gone, these couples often have a whole house to themselves, although it was originally intended for families of three, four or more.

Overcrowding often afflicts the urban poor families who are renters. The worst condition prevails in the $2,000 to $3,000 income group where one in five renters have an average density of more than one person to a room. While there is less overcrowding in rural areas, a significant amount prevails, especially in the dilapidated shacks that dot depressed areas.

The statistics show poor home-owners are less mobile than those of higher income groups. Some 60 percent of these families with less than $2,000, and more than half those with incomes between $2,000 and $3,000, had been living in the same unit since 1949 at the time of the 1960 census. In contrast, only 30 percent of owners with incomes of $6,000 or more had remained in the same house.

This is not the case with renters. Only 20 percent of those with incomes below $2,000 had not moved since 1949.

The 11 million children living in poverty stricken families are most victimized by squalid housing. Large families are especially handicapped by lack of adequate housing. Large units are often in short supply, and are almost always expensive.

The drab existence forced upon the children of the poor by inadequate housing, "often in the worst slums and frequently completely lacking in play areas and open space, cannot help but exert a stultifying influence upon them. ... It is small wonder that there is such a high correlation between the incidence of substandard housing, and such things as juvenile delinquency, school dropouts, and health problems ... ," the House report stressed.

Almost 70 percent of family heads over age 65 were home-owners, although poverty afflicts about half the households of senior citizens. A fifth of all housing units occupied by families headed by senior citizens, or in which senior citizens live, are substandard. These units, whether owner occupied, or rental, have been classified as dilapidated or lacking in essential plumbing facilities.

While there is relatively little crowding in households headed by poor persons over age 65, this often is not the case where the elderly live in a family headed by a person under age 60. Overcrowding in households of this type reflects the moving in of parents with children in city or suburban homes not built to accommodate extra persons.

The condition of housing among the nonwhite poor is worse than among the impoverished whites. Only 38 percent of nonwhites own their own homes. About half the nonwhite renters and two-fifths of home-owners live in substandard housing. Housing for nonwhites is worst in the South. For renters it is best in the West. For owners, it is best in the North.

Racial bias, as well as poverty, contributes to substandard minority housing. Among nonwhite families with incomes of $5,000 or more, 16 percent lived in substandard housing in 1960. Among whites, the figure was 4.9 percent.

Overcrowding is three times greater among nonwhite than among whites, with conditions poorest in the South. Nonwhites live in older buildings and generally are forced to take the leavings of the housing market. This is particularly true among the nonwhite poor.

Three major Federal housing programs are concerned with low income families. The major program is that of the Public Housing Administration which administers loans and grants assisting local housing authorities. A total of 550,000 public housing units have been constructed, but the great majority of the poor have not been affected. Public housing, particularly the huge high-rise buildings of our cities, has been criticized for creating a new kind of ghetto in which the poor lose neighborhood roots and become further alienated.

The general view, however, is that despite its faults, public housing creates better living than the housing it has replaced.

An FHA program conducted under Sec. 221 of the Housing Act has made it possible to produce some housing within the reach of low income families. Under this program, interest rates below the going market rate are charged. Some 35,000 rental units have been constructed since the program began in 1961.

Urban renewal programs have eliminated more than a quarter of a million substandard housing units occupied for the most part by the poor. Three-fourths of those displaced by these programs are reported to have been relocated—or will be relocated—in decent housing.

Three special senior citizen programs involving public housing, mortgage insurance and long term direct loans had resulted in the construction of 46,000 units by the end of 1963. At that time, another 87,000 units were reported to be under construction.

Housing remains one of the pressing unmet needs of the poor despite current and anticipated government programs. Millions of housing units are substandard, and other millions are deteriorating. Housing is a legitimate area of concern for Community Action Programs. Much can be done through proper enforcement of local building codes.

# The Magnitude of Poverty in Disadvantaged Neighborhoods

## PRESIDENT'S COMMISSION ON CIVIL DISORDER

The chronic unemployment problems in the central city, aggravated by the constant arrival of new unemployed migrants, is the fundamental cause of the persistent poverty in disadvantaged Negro areas.

"Poverty" in the affluent society is more than absolute deprivation. Many of the poor in the United States would be well-off in other societies. Relative deprivation—inequality—is a more useful concept of poverty with respect to the Negro in America because it encompasses social and political exclusion as well as economic inequality. Because of the lack of data of this type, we have had to focus our analysis on a measure of poverty which is both economic and absolute—the Social Security Administration's "poverty level" [1] concept. It is clear, however, that broader measures of poverty would substantiate the conclusions that follow.

In 1966 there were 29.7 million persons in the United States— 15.3 percent of the nation's population—with incomes below the "poverty level," as defined by the Social Security Administration. Of these, 20.3 million were white (68.3 percent), and 9.3 million nonwhite (31.7 percent). Thus, about 11.9 percent of the nation's whites and 40.6 percent of its nonwhites were poor under the Social Security definition.

The location of the nation's poor is best shown from 1964 data as indicated by the following table:

---

Reprinted from the President's Commission on Civil Disorder, *Report* (Washington, D.C.: U.S. Government Printing Office, 1968).

[1] $3335 per year for an urban family of four.

*Percentage of Those in Poverty in*
*Each Group Living in:*

| Group | Metropolitan Areas In Central Cities | Outside Central Cities | Other Areas | Total |
|---|---|---|---|---|
| Whites | 23.8% | 21.8% | 54.4% | 100% |
| Nonwhites | 41.7 | 10.8 | 47.5 | 100 |
| Total | 29.4 | 18.4 | 52.2 | 100 |

Source: Social Security Administration

The following facts concerning poverty are relevant to an under-standing of the problems faced by people living in disadvantaged neighborhoods.[2]

In central cities 30.7 percent of nonwhite families of two or more persons lived in poverty compared to only 8.8 percent of whites.

Of the 10.1 million poor persons in central cities in 1964, about 4.4 million of these (43.6 percent) were nonwhites, and 5.7 million (56.4 percent) were whites. The poor whites were much older on the average than the poor nonwhites. The proportion of poor persons 65 years old or older was 23.2 percent among whites, but only 6.8 percent among nonwhites.

Poverty was more than twice as prevalent among nonwhite families with female heads than among those with male heads, 57 percent compared to 21 percent. In central cities, 26 percent of all nonwhite families of two or more persons had female heads, as compared to 12 percent of white families.

Among nonwhite families headed by a female, and having children under 6, the incidence of poverty was 81.0 percent. Moreover, there were 243,000 such families living in poverty in central cities—or over 9 percent of all nonwhite families in those cities.

Among all children living in poverty within central cities, nonwhites outnumbered whites by over 400,000. The number of poor nonwhite children equalled or surpassed the number of white poor children in every age group.

*Number of Children Living in Poverty (millions)*

| Age Group | White | Nonwhite | Percent of Total Nonwhite |
|---|---|---|---|
| Under 6 | 0.9 | 1.0 | 53% |
| 6–15 | 1.0 | 1.3 | 57 |
| 16–21 | 0.4 | 0.4 | 50 |
| Total | 2.3 | 2.7 | 54% |

[2] Source: Social Security Administration; based on 1964 data.

Two stark facts emerge:

54 percent of all poor children in central cities in 1964 were nonwhites;

Of the 4.4 million nonwhites living in poverty within central cities in 1964, 52 percent were children under 16, and 61 percent were under 21.

Since 1964, the number of nonwhite families living in poverty within central cities has remained about the same; hence, these poverty conditions are probably still prevalent in central cities in terms of absolute numbers of persons, although the proportion of persons in poverty may have dropped slightly.[3]

## The Social Impact of Employment Problems in Disadvantaged Negro Areas

*Unemployment and the Family*

The high rates of unemployment and underemployment in racial ghettos are evidence, in part, that many men living in these areas are seeking but cannot obtain jobs which will support a family. Perhaps equally important, most jobs they can get are at the low end of the occupational scale, and often lack the necessary status to sustain a worker's self-respect, or the respect of his family and friends. These same men are also constantly confronted with the message of discrimination: "You are inferior because of a trait you did not cause and cannot change." This message reinforces feelings of inadequacy arising from repeated failure to obtain and keep decent jobs.

Wives of these men are forced to work, and usually produce more money. If men stay at home without working, their inadequacies constantly confront them and tensions arise between them and their wives and children. Under these pressures, it is not surprising that many of these men flee their responsibilities as husbands and fathers, leaving home, and drifting from city to city, or adopting the style of "street corner men."

Statistical evidence tends to document this. A close correlation exists between the number of nonwhite married women separated from

---

[3] For the nation as a whole, the proportion of nonwhite families living in poverty dropped from 39 percent to 35 percent from 1964 to 1966 (defining "family" somewhat differently from the definition used in the data above). The number of such families declined from 1.9 million to 1.7 million. However, the number and proportion of all nonwhites living in central cities rose in the same period. As a result, the number of nonwhite families living in so-called "poverty areas" of large cities actually rose from 1,561,000 in 1960 to 1,588,000 in 1966.

their husbands each year and the unemployment rate among nonwhite males 20 years old and over. Similarly, from 1948 to 1962, the number of new Aid to Families with Dependent Children cases rose and fell with the nonwhite male unemployment rate. Since 1963, however, the number of new cases—most of them Negro children—has steadily increased even though the unemployment rate among nonwhite males has declined. The impact of marital status on employment among Negroes is shown by the fact that in 1967 the proportion of married men either divorced or separated from their wives was more than twice as high among unemployed nonwhite men as among employed nonwhite men. Moreover, among those participating in the labor force, there was a higher proportion of married men with wives present than with wives absent.

*Unemployment Rate and Participation in Total Labor Force, 25 to 54–Year-Old Nonwhite Men, by Marital Status, March, 1967*

|  | Unemployment Rate Nonwhite | Labor Force Participation (%) Nonwhite |
|---|---|---|
| Married, Wife Present | 3.7 | 96.7 |
| Other (Separated, Divorced, Widowed) | 8.7 | 77.6 |

## Fatherless Families

The abandonment of the home by many Negro males affects a great many children growing up in the racial ghetto. As previously indicated, most American Negro families are headed by men, just like most other American families. Yet the proportion of families with female heads is much greater among Negroes than among whites at all income levels, and has been rising in recent years.

*Proportion of Families of Various Types*

| Date | Husband-Wife White | Nonwhite | Female Head White | Nonwhite |
|---|---|---|---|---|
| 1950 | 88.0% | 77.7% | 8.5% | 17.6% |
| 1960 | 88.7 | 73.6 | 8.7 | 22.4 |
| 1966 | 88.8 | 72.7 | 8.9 | 23.7 |

This disparity between white and nonwhite families is far greater among the lowest income families—those most likely to reside in disadvantaged big-city neighborhoods—than among higher income families. Among families with incomes under $3,000 in 1966, the proportion with female heads was 42 percent for Negroes but only 23 percent for whites. In contrast, among families with incomes of $7,000 or more, 8 percent of Negro families had female heads compared to 4 percent of whites.

The problems of "fatherlessness" are aggravated by the tendency of the poor to have large families. The average poor, urban nonwhite family contains 4.8 persons, as compared with 3.7 for the average poor, urban white family. This is one of the primary factors in the poverty status of nonwhite households in large cities.

The proportion of fatherless families appears to be increasing in the poorest Negro neighborhoods. In the Hough section of Cleveland, the proportion of families with female heads rose from 23 to 32 percent from 1960 to 1965. In the Watts section of Los Angeles it rose from 36 to 39 percent during the same period.

The handicap imposed on children growing up without fathers, in an atmosphere of poverty and deprivation, is increased because many mothers must work to provide support. The following table illustrates disparity between the proportion of nonwhite women in the child-rearing ages who are in the labor force and the comparable proportion of white women:

|  | Percentage of Women in the Labor Force | |
| --- | --- | --- |
| Age Group | Nonwhite | White |
| 20–24 | 55% | 51% |
| 25–34 | 55 | 38 |
| 35–44 | 61 | 45 |

With the father absent and the mother working, many ghetto children spend the bulk of their time on the streets—the streets of a crime-ridden, violence-prone and poverty-stricken world. The image of success in this world is not that of the "solid citizen," the responsible husband and father, but rather that of the "hustler" who promotes his own interests by exploiting others. The dope sellers and the numbers runners are the "successful" men because their earnings far outstrip those men who try to climb the economic ladder in honest ways.

Young people in the ghetto are acutely conscious of a system which appears to offer rewards to those who illegally exploit others, and failure to those who struggle under traditional responsibilities. Under these circumstances, many adopt exploitation and the "hustle" as a way of life, disclaiming both work and marriage in favor of casual and temporary liaisons. This pattern reinforces itself from one generation to the next, creating a "culture of poverty" and an ingrained cynicism about society and its institutions.

### The "Jungle"

The culture of poverty that results from unemployment and family disorganization generates a system of ruthless, exploitative relationships within the ghetto. Prostitution, dope addiction, casual sexual affairs, and crime create an environmental jungle characterized by personal insecurity and tension. The effects of this development are stark:

The rate of illegitimate births among nonwhite women has risen sharply in the past two decades. In 1940, 16.8 percent of all nonwhite births were illegitimate. By 1950 this proportion was 18 percent; by 1960, 21.6 percent; by 1966, 26.3 percent. In the ghettos of many large cities, illegitimacy rates exceed 50 percent.

The rate of illegitimacy among nonwhite women is closely related to low income and high unemployment. In Washington, D.C., for example, an analysis of 1960 census tracts shows that in tracts with unemployment rates of 12 percent or more among nonwhite men, illegitimacy was over 40 percent. But in tracts with unemployment rates of 2.9 percent and below among nonwhite men, reported illegitimacy was under 20 percent. A similar contrast existed between tracts in which median nonwhite income was under $4,000 (where illegitimacy was 38 percent) and those in which it was $8,000 and over (where illegitimacy was 11 percent).

Narcotics addiction is also heavily concentrated in low-income Negro neighborhoods, particularly in New York City. Of the 59,720 addicts known to the U.S. Bureau of Narcotics at the end of 1966, just over 50 percent were Negroes. Over 52 percent of all known addicts lived within New York State, mostly in Harlem and other Negro neighborhoods. These figures undoubtedly greatly understate the actual number of persons using narcotics regularly—especially those under 21.

Not surprisingly, at every age from 6 through 19, the proportion of children from homes with both parents present who actually attend school is higher than the proportion of children from homes with only one parent or neither present.

Social Distress—Major Predominantly Negro
Neighborhoods in New York City and the City as a Whole

| | Juvenile Delinquency [4] | Venereal Disease [5] | ADC [6] | Public Assistance [7] |
|---|---|---|---|---|
| Brownsville | 125.3 | 609.9 | 459.0 | 265.8 |
| East New York | 98.6 | 207.5 | 148.6 | 71.8 |
| Bedford-Stuyvesant | 115.2 | 771.3 | 337.1 | 197.2 |
| Harlem | 110.8 | 1,603.5 | 265.7 | 138.1 |
| South Bronx | 84.4 | 308.3 | 278.5 | 165.5 |
| New York City | 52.2 | 269.1 | 120.7 | 60.8 |

[4] Number of offenses per 1,000 persons 7–20 years (1965).

[5] Number of cases per 100,000 persons under 21 years (1964).

[6] Number of children in Aid to Dependent Children cases per 1,000 under 18 years, using 1960 population as base (1965).

[7] Welfare assistance recipients per 1,000 persons, using 1960 population as base (1965).

Rates of juvenile delinquency, venereal disease, dependency upon AFDC support, and use of public assistance in general are much higher in disadvantaged Negro areas than in other parts of large cities. Data taken from New York City contrasting predominantly Negro neighborhoods with the city as a whole clearly illustrate this fact.

In conclusion: in 1965, 1.2 million nonwhite children under 16 lived in central city families headed by a woman under 65. The great majority of these children were growing up in poverty under conditions that make them better candidates for crime and civil disorder than for jobs providing an entry into American society.

# D. VIOLENCE IN THE STREETS

## Patterns of Disorder and What Can Be Done

### PRESIDENT'S COMMISSION ON CIVIL DISORDER

#### Introduction

The summer of 1967 again brought racial disorders to American cities, and with them shock, fear and bewilderment to the nation.

The worst came during a two-week period in July, first in Newark and then in Detroit. Each set off a chain reaction in neighboring communities.

On July 28, 1967, the President of the United States established this Commission and directed us to answer three basic questions:

What happened?

Why did it happen?

What can be done to prevent it from happening again?

To respond to these questions, we have undertaken a broad range of studies and investigations. We have visited the riot cities; we have heard many witnesses; we have sought the counsel of experts across the country.

This is our basic conclusion: Our nation is moving toward two societies, one black, one white—separate and unequal.

Reaction to last summer's disorders has quickened the movement and deepened the division. Discrimination and segregation have long permeated much of American life; they now threaten the future of every American.

This deepening racial division is not inevitable. The movement apart can be reversed. Choice is still possible. Our principal task is to define that choice and to press for a national resolution.

To pursue our present course will involve the continuing polarization of the American community and, ultimately, the destruction of basic democratic values.

Reprinted from the President's Commission on Civil Disorder, *Report* (Washington, D.C.: U.S. Government Printing Office, 1968).

The alternative is not blind repression or capitulation to lawlessness. It is the realization of common opportunities for all within a single society.

This alternative will require a commitment to national action—compassionate, massive and sustained, backed by the resources of the most powerful and the richest nation on this earth. From every American it will require new attitudes, new understanding, and, above all, new will.

The vital needs of the nation must be met; hard choices must be made, and, if necessary, new taxes enacted.

Violence cannot build a better society. Disruption and disorder nourish repression, not justice. They strike at the freedom of every citizen. The community cannot—it will not—tolerate coercion and mob rule.

Violence and destruction must be ended—in the streets of the ghetto and in the lives of people.

Segregation and poverty have created in the racial ghetto a destructive environment totally unknown to most white Americans.

What white Americans have never fully understood—but what the Negro can never forget—is that white society is deeply implicated in the ghetto. White institutions created it, white institutions maintain it, and white society condones it.

It is time now to turn with all the purpose at our command to the major unfinished business of this nation. It is time to adopt strategies for action that will produce quick and visible progress. It is time to make good the promises of American democracy to all citizens—urban and rural, white and black, Spanish-surname, American Indian, and every minority group.

Our recommendations embrace three basic principles:

To mount programs on a scale equal to the dimension of the problems;

To aim these programs for high impact in the immediate future in order to close the gap between promise and performance;

To undertake new initiatives and experiments that can change the system of failure and frustration that now dominates the ghetto and weakens our society.

These programs will require unprecedented levels of funding and performance, but they neither probe deeper nor demand more than the problems which called them forth. There can be no higher priority for national action and no higher claim on the nation's conscience.

We issue this Report now, five months before the date called for by the President. Much remain that can be learned. Continued study is essential.

As Commissioners we have worked together with a sense of the greatest urgency and have sought to compose whatever differences exist among us. Some differences remain. But the gravity of the problem and the pressing need for action are too clear to allow further delay in the issuance of this Report.

## Part I—What Happened?

*Chapter 1—Profiles of Disorder*

The report contains profiles of a selection of the disorders that took place during the summer of 1967. These profiles are designed to indicate how the disorders happened, who participated in them, and how local officials, police forces, and the National Guard responded. Illustrative excerpts follow:

NEWARK

. . . It was decided to attempt to channel the energies of the people into a nonviolent protest. While Lofton promised the crowd that a full investigation would be made of the Smith incident, the other Negro leaders began urging those on the scene to form a line of march toward the city hall.

Some persons joined the line of march. Others milled about in the narrow street. From the dark grounds of the housing project came a barrage of rocks. Some of them fell among the crowd. Others hit persons in the line of march. Many smashed the windows of the police station. The rock throwing, it was believed, was the work of youngsters; approximately 2,500 children lived in the housing project.

Almost at the same time, an old car was set afire in a parking lot. The line of march began to disintegrate. The police, their heads protected by World War I-type helmets, sallied forth to disperse the crowd. A fire engine, arriving on the scene, was pelted with rocks. As police drove people away from the station, they scattered in all directions.

A few minutes later a nearby liquor store was broken into. Some persons, seeing a caravan of cabs appear at city hall to protest Smith's arrest, interpreted this as evidence that the disturbance had been organized, and generated rumors to that effect.

However, only a few stores were looted. Within a short period of time, the disorder appeared to have run its course.

\*        \*        \*

. . . On Saturday, July 15, [Director of Police Dominick] Spina received a report of snipers in a housing project. When he arrived he saw approximately 100 National Guardsmen and police officers crouching behind vehicles, hiding in corners and lying on the ground around the edge of the courtyard.

Since everything appeared quiet and it was broad daylight, Spina walked directly down the middle of the street. Nothing happened. As he came to the last building of the complex, he heard a shot. All around him the troopers jumped, believing themselves to be under sniper fire. A moment later a young Guardsman ran from behind a building.

The Director of Police went over and asked him if he had fired the shot. The soldier said yes, he had fired to scare a man away from a window; that his orders were to keep everyone away from windows.

Spina said he told the soldier: "Do you know what you just did? You have now created a state of hysteria. Every Guardsman up and down this street and every state policeman and every city policeman that is present thinks that somebody just fired a shot and that it is probably a sniper."

A short time later more "gunshots" were heard. Investigating, Spina came upon a Puerto Rican sitting on a wall. In reply to a question as to whether he knew "where the firing is coming from?" the man said:

"That's no firing. That's fireworks. If you look up to the fourth floor, you will see the people who are throwing down these cherry bombs."

By this time four truckloads of National Guardsmen had arrived and troopers and policemen were again crouched everywhere looking for a sniper. The Director of Police remained at the scene for three hours, and the only shot fired was the one by the Guardsman.

Nevertheless, at six o'clock that evening two columns of National Guardsmen and state troopers were directing mass fire at the Hayes Housing Project in response to what they believed were snipers. . . .

DETROIT

. . . A spirit of carefree nihilism was taking hold. To riot and destroy appeared more and more to become ends in themselves. Late Sunday afternoon it appeared to one observer that the young people were "dancing amidst the flames."

A Negro plainclothes officer was standing at an intersection when a man threw a Molotov cocktail into a business establishment at the corner. In the heat of the afternoon, fanned by the 20 to 25 m.p.h. winds of both Sunday and Monday, the fire reached the home next door within minutes. As residents uselessly sprayed the flames with garden hoses, the fire jumped from roof to roof of adjacent two- and three-story buildings. Within the hour the entire block was in flames. The ninth house in the burning row belonged to the arsonist who had thrown the Molotov cocktail. . . .

*     *     *

. . . Employed as a private guard, 55-year-old Julius L. Dorsey, a Negro, was standing in front of a market when accosted by two Negro men and a woman. They demanded he permit them to loot the market. He ignored their demands. They began to berate him. He asked a neighbor to call the police. As the argument grew more heated, Dorsey fired three shots from his pistol into the air.

The police radio reported: "Looters, they have rifles." A patrol car driven by a police officer and carrying three Naitonal Guardsmen arrived. As the looters fled, the law enforcement personnel opened fire. When the firing ceased, one person lay dead.

He was Julius L. Dorsey . . .

*    *    *

. . . As the riot alternately waxed and waned, one area of the ghetto remained insulated. On the northeast side the residents of some 150 square blocks inhabited by 21,000 persons had, in 1966, banded together in the Positive Neighborhood Action Committee (PNAC). With professional help from the Institute of Urban Dynamics, they had organized block clubs and made plans for the improvement of the neighborhood. . . .

When the riot broke out, the residents, through the block clubs, were able to organize quickly. Youngsters, agreeing to stay in the neighborhood, participated in detouring traffic. While many persons reportedly sympathized with the idea of a rebellion against the "system," only two small fires were set—one in an empty building.

*    *    *

. . . According to Lt. Gen. Throckmorton and Col. Bolling, the city, at this time, was saturated with fear. The National Guardsmen were afraid, the citizens were afraid, and the police were afraid. Numerous persons, the majority of them Negroes, were being injured by gunshots of undetermined origin. The general and his staff felt that the major task of the troops was to reduce the fear and restore an air of normalcy.

In order to accomplish this, every effort was made to establish contact and rapport between the troops and the residents. The soldiers —20 percent of whom were Negro—began helping to clean up the streets, collect garbage, and trace persons who had disappeared in the confusion. Residents in the neighborhoods responded with soup and sandwiches for the troops. In areas where the National Guard tried to establish rapport with the citizens, there was a similar response.

NEW BRUNSWICK

. . . A short time later, elements of the crowd—an older and rougher one than the night before—appeared in front of the police station. The participants wanted to see the mayor.

Mayor [Patricia] Sheehan went out onto the steps of the station. Using a bullhorn, she talked to the people and asked that she be given an opportunity to correct conditions. The crowd was boisterous. Some persons challenged the mayor. But, finally, the opinion, "She's new! Give her a chance!" prevailed.

A demand was issued by people in the crowd that all persons arrested the previous night be released. Told that this already had been done, the people were suspicious. They asked to be allowed to inspect the jail cells.

It was agreed to permit representatives of the people to look in the cells to satisfy themselves that everyone had been released.

The crowd dispersed. The New Brunswick riot had failed to materialize.

## Chapter 2—*Patterns of Disorder*

The "typical" riot did not take place. The disorders of 1967 were unusual, irregular, complex and unpredictable social processes. Like most human events, they did not unfold in an orderly sequence. However, an analysis of our survey information leads to some conclusions about the riot process.

In general:

The civil disorders of 1967 involved Negroes acting against local symbols of white American society, authority and property in Negro neighborhoods—rather than against white persons.

Of 164 disorders reported during the first nine months of 1967, eight (5 percent) were major in terms of violence and damage; 33 (20 percent) were serious but not major; 123 (75 percent) were minor and undoubtedly would not have received national attention as riots had the nation not been sensitized by the more serious outbreaks.

In the 75 disorders studied by a Senate subcommittee, 83 deaths were reported. Eighty-two percent of the deaths and more than half the injuries occurred in Newark and Detroit. About 10 percent of the dead and 38 percent of the injured were public employees, primarily law officers and firemen. The overwhelming majority of the persons killed or injured in all the disorders were Negro civilians.

Initial damage estimates were greatly exaggerated. In Detroit, newspaper damage estimates at first ranged from $200 million to $500 million; the highest recent estimate is $45 million. In Newark, early estimates ranged from $15 to $25 million. A month later damage was estimated at $10.2 million, 80 percent in inventory losses.

In the 24 disorders in 23 cities which we surveyed:

The final incident before the outbreak of disorder, and the initial violence itself, generally took place in the evening or at night at a place in which it was normal for many people to be on the streets.

Violence usually occurred almost immediately following the occurrence of the final precipitating incident, and then escalated rapidly.

With but few exceptions, violence subsided during the day, and flared rapidly again at night. The night-day cycles continued through the early period of the major disorders.

Disorder generally began with rock and bottle throwing and window breaking. Once store windows were broken, looting usually followed.

Disorder did not erupt as a result of a single "triggering" or "precipitating" incident. Instead, it was generated out of an increasingly disturbed social atmosphere, in which typically a series of tension-heightening incidents over a period of weeks or months became linked in the minds of many in the Negro community with a reservoir of underlying grievances. At some point in the mounting tension, a further incident—in itself often routine or trivial—became the breaking point and the tension spilled over into violence.

"Prior" incidents, which increased tensions and ultimately led to violence, were police actions in almost half the cases; police actions were "final" incidents before the outbreak of violence in 12 of the 24 surveyed disorders.

No particular control tactic was successful in every situation. The varied effectiveness of control techniques emphasizes the need for advance training, planning, adequate intelligence systems, and knowledge of the ghetto community.

Negotiations between Negroes—including young militants as well as older Negro leaders—and white officials concerning "terms of peace" occurred during virtually all the disorders surveyed. In many cases, these negotiations involved discussion of underlying grievances as well as the handling of the disorder by control authorities.

The typical rioter was a teenager or young adult, a lifelong resident of the city in which he rioted, a high school dropout; he was, nevertheless, somewhat better educated than his nonrioting Negro neighbor, and was usually underemployed or employed in a menial job. He was proud of his race, extremely hostile to both whites and middle-class Negroes and, although informed about politics, highly distrustful of the political system.

A Detroit survey revealed that approximately 11 percent of the total residents of two riot areas admitted participation in the rioting, 20 to 25 percent identified themselves as "bystanders," over 16 percent identified themselves as "counter-rioters" who urged rioters to "cool it," and the remaining 48 to 53 percent said they were at home or elsewhere and did not participate. In a survey of Negro males between the ages of 15 and 35 residing in the disturbance area in Newark, about 45 percent identified themselves as rioters, and about 55 percent as "noninvolved."

Most rioters were young Negro males. Nearly 53 percent of arrestees were between 15 and 24 years of age; nearly 81 percent between 15 and 35.

In Detroit and Newark about 74 percent of the rioters were brought up in the North. In contrast, of the noninvolved, 36 percent in Detroit and 52 percent in Newark were brought up in the North.

What the rioters appeared to be seeking was fuller participation in the social order and the material benefits enjoyed by the majority of American citizens. Rather than rejecting the American system, they were anxious to obtain a place for themselves in it.

Numerous Negro counter-rioters walked the streets urging rioters to "cool it." The typical counter-rioter was better educated and had higher income than either the rioter or the noninvolved.

The proportion of Negroes in local government was substantially smaller than the Negro proportion of population. Only three of the 20 cities studied had more than one Negro legislator; none had ever had a Negro mayor or city manager. In only four cities did Negroes hold other important policy-making positions or serve as heads of municipal departments.

Although almost all cities had some sort of formal grievance mechanism for handling citizen complaints, this typically was regarded by Negroes as ineffective and was generally ignored.

Although specific grievances varied from city to city, at least 12 deeply held grievances can be identified and ranked into three levels of relative intensity:

*First Level of Intensity*

1. Police practices
2. Unemployment and underemployment
3. Inadequate housing

*Second Level of Intensity*

4. Inadequate education
5. Poor recreation facilities and programs
6. Ineffectiveness of the political structure and grievance mechanisms

*Third Level of Intensity*

7. Disrespectful white attitudes
8. Discriminatory administration of justice
9. Inadequacy of federal programs
10. Inadequacy of municipal services
11. Discriminatory consumer and credit practices
12. Inadequate welfare programs

The results of a three-city survey of various federal programs—manpower, education, housing, welfare and community action—indicate that, despite substantial expenditures, the number of persons assisted constituted only a fraction of those in need.

The background of disorder is often as complex and difficult to analyze as the disorder itself. But we find that certain general conclusions can be drawn:

Social and economic conditions in the riot cities constituted a clear pattern of severe disadvantage for Negroes compared with whites, whether the Negroes lived in the area where the riot took place or outside it. Negroes had completed fewer years of education and fewer had attended high school. Negroes were twice as likely to be unemployed and three times as likely to be in unskilled and service jobs. Negroes averaged 70 percent of the income earned by whites and were more than twice as likely to be living in poverty. Although housing cost Negroes relatively more, they had worse housing—three times as likely to be overcrowded and substandard. When compared to white suburbs, the relative disadvantage is even more pronounced.

A study of the aftermath of disorder leads to disturbing conclusions. We find that, despite the institution of some post-riot programs:

Little basic change in the conditions underlying the outbreak of disorder has taken place. Actions to ameliorate Negro grievances have been limited and sporadic; with but few exceptions, they have not significantly reduced tensions.

In several cities, the principal official response has been to train and equip the police with more sophisticated weapons.

In several cities, increasing polarization is evident, with continuing breakdown of inter-racial communication, and growth of white segregationist or black separatist groups.

*Chapter 3—Organized Activity*

The President directed the Commission to investigate "to what extent, if any, there has been planning or organization in any of the riots."

To carry out this part of the President's charge, the Commission established a special investigative staff supplementing the field teams that made the general examination of the riots in 23 cities. The unit examined data collected by federal agencies and congressional committees, including thousands of documents supplied by the Federal Bureau of Investigation, gathered and evaluated information from local and state law enforcement agencies and officials, and conducted its own field investigation in selected cities.

On the basis of all the information collected, the Commission concludes that:

The urban disorders of the summer of 1967 were not caused by, nor were they the consequence of, any organized plan or "conspiracy."

Specifically, the Commission has found no evidence that all or any of the disorders or the incidents that led to them were planned or directed by any organization or group, international, national or local.

Militant organizations, local and national, and individual agitators, who repeatedly forecast and called for violence, were active in the spring and summer of 1967. We believe that they sought to encourage violence, and that they helped to create an atmosphere that contributed to the outbreak of disorder.

We recognize that the continuation of disorders and the polarization of the races would provide fertile ground for organized exploitation in the future.

Investigations of organized activity are continuing at all levels of government, including committees of Congress. These investigations relate not only to the disorders of 1967 but also to the actions of groups and individuals, particularly in schools and colleges, during this last fall and winter. The Commission has cooperated in these investigations. They should continue.

## Part II—Why Did It Happen?

*Chapter 4—The Basic Causes*

In addressing the question "Why did it happen?" we shift our focus from the local to the national scene, from the particular events of the summer of 1967 to the factors within the society at large that created a mood of violence among many urban Negroes.

These factors are complex and interacting; they vary significantly in their effect from city to city and from year to year; and the consequences of one disorder, generating new grievances and new demands, become the causes of the next. Thus was created the "thicket of tension, conflicting evidence and extreme opinions" cited by the President.

Despite these complexities, certain fundamental matters are clear. Of these, the most fundamental is the racial attitude and behavior of white Americans toward black Americans.

Race prejudice has shaped our history decisively; it now threatens to affect our future.

White racism is essentially responsible for the explosive mixture which has been accumulating in our cities since the end of World War II. Among the ingredients of this mixture are:

*Pervasive discrimination and segregation* in employment, education, and housing, which have resulted in the continuing exclusion of great numbers of Negroes from the benefits of economic progress.

*Black in-migration and white exodus,* which have produced the massive and growing concentrations of impoverished Negroes in our major cities, creating a growing crisis of deteriorating facilities and services and unmet human needs.

*The black ghettos* where segregation and poverty converge on the young to destroy opportunity and enforce failure. Crime, drug addiction, dependency on welfare, and bitterness and resentment against society in general and white society in particular are the result.

At the same time, most whites and some Negroes outside the ghetto have prospered to a degree unparalleled in the history of civilization. Through television and other media, this affluence has been flaunted before the eyes of the Negro poor and the jobless ghetto youth.

Yet these facts alone cannot be said to have caused the disorders. Recently, other powerful ingredients have begun to catalyze the mixture:

*Frustrated hopes* are the residue of the unfulfilled expectations aroused by the great judicial and legislative victories of the Civil Rights Movement and the dramatic struggle for equal rights in the South.

*A climate that tends toward approval and encouragement of violence* as a form of protest has been created by white terrorism directed against nonviolent protest; by the open defiance of law and federal authority by state and local officials resisting desegregation; and by some protest groups engaging in civil disobedience who turn their backs on nonviolence, go beyond the constitutionally protected rights of petition and free assembly, and resort to violence to attempt to compel alteration of laws and policies with which they disagree.

*The frustrations of powerlessness* have led some Negroes to the conviction that there is no effective alternative to violence as a means of achieving redress of grievances, and of "moving the system." These frustrations are reflected in alienation and hostility toward the institutions of law and government and the white society which controls them, and in the reach toward racial consciousness and solidarity reflected in the slogan "Black Power."

*A new mood* has sprung up among Negroes, particularly among the young, in which self-esteem and enhanced racial pride are replacing apathy and submission to "the system."

*The police are not merely a "spark" factor.* To some Negroes police have come to symbolize white power, white racism and white repression. And the fact is that many police do reflect and express these white attitudes. The atmosphere of hostility and cynicism is reinforced by a widespread belief among Negroes in the existence of police brutality and in a "double standard" of justice and protection—one for Negroes and one for whites.

\* \* \*

To this point, we have attempted to identify the prime components of the "explosive mixture." In the chapters that follow we seek to analyze them in the perspective of history. Their meaning, however, is clear:

In the summer of 1967, we have seen in our cities a chain reaction of racial violence. If we are heedless, none of us shall escape the consequences.

\* \* \*

## Part III—What Can Be Done?

*Chapter 10—The Community Response*

Our investigation of the 1967 riot cities establishes that virtually every major episode of violence was foreshadowed by an accumulation of unresolved grievances and by widespread dissatisfaction among Negroes with the unwillingness or inability of local government to respond.

Overcoming these conditions is essential for community support of law enforcement and civil order. City governments need new and more vital channels of communication to the residents of the ghetto; they need to improve their capacity to respond effectively to community needs before they become community grievances; and they need to provide opportunity for meaningful involvement of ghetto residents in shaping policies and programs which affect the community.

The Commission recommends that local governments:

Develop Neighborhood Action Task Forces as joint community-government efforts through which more effective communication can be achieved, and the delivery of city services to ghetto residents improved.

Establish comprehensive grievance-response mechanisms in order to bring all public agencies under public scrutiny.

Bring the institutions of local government closer to the people they serve by establishing neighborhood outlets for local, state and federal administrative and public service agencies.

Expand opportunities for ghetto residents to participate in the formulation of public policy and the implementation of programs affecting them through improved political representation, creation of institutional channels for community action, expansion of legal services, and legislative hearings on ghetto problems.

In this effort, city governments will require state and federal support.

The Commission recommends:

State and federal financial assistance for mayors and city councils to support the research, consultants, staff and other resources needed to respond effectively to federal program initiatives.

State cooperation in providing municipalities with the jurisdictional tools needed to deal with their problems; a fuller measure of financial aid to urban areas; and the focusing of the interests of suburban communities on the physical, social and cultural environment of the central city.

## *Chapter 11—Police and the Community*

The abrasive relationship between the police and the minority communities has been a major—and explosive—source of grievance, tension and disorder. The blame must be shared by the total society.

The police are faced with demands for increased protection and service in the ghetto. Yet the aggressive patrol practices thought necessary to meet these demands themselves create tension and hostility. The resulting grievances have been further aggravated by the lack of effective mechanisms for handling complaints against the police. Special programs for bettering police-community relations have been instituted, but these alone are not enough. Police administrators, with the guidance of public officials, and the support of the entire community, must take vigorous action to improve law enforcement and to decrease the potential for disorder.

The Commission recommends that city government and police authorities:

Review police operations in the ghetto to ensure proper conduct by police officers, and eliminate abrasive practices.

Provide more adequate police protection to ghetto residents to eliminate their high sense of insecurity, and the belief in the existence of a dual standard of law enforcement.

Establish fair and effective mechanisms for the redress of grievances against the police, and other municipal employees.

Develop and adopt policy guidelines to assist officers in making critical decisions in areas where police conduct can create tension.

Develop and use innovative programs to ensure widespread community support for law enforcement.

Recruit more Negroes into the regular police force, and review promotion policies to ensure fair promotion for Negro officers.

Establish a "Community Service Officer" program to attract ghetto youths between the ages of 17 and 21 to police work. These junior officers would perform duties in ghetto neighborhoods, but would not have full police authority. The federal government should provide support equal to 90 percent of the costs of employing CSOs on the basis of one for every ten regular officers.

## Chapter 12—Control of Disorder

Preserving civil peace is the first responsibility of government. Unless the rule of law prevails, our society will lack not only order but also the environment essential to social and economic progress.

The maintenance of civil order cannot be left to the police alone. The police need guidance, as well as support, from mayors and other public officials. It is the responsibility of public officials to determine proper police policies, support adequate police standards for personnel and performance, and participate in planning for the control of disorders.

To maintain control of incidents which could lead to disorders, the Commission recommends that local officials:

Assign seasoned, well-trained policemen and supervisory officers to patrol ghetto areas, and to respond to disturbances.

Develop plans which will quickly muster maximum police manpower and highly qualified senior commanders at the outbreak of disorders.

Provide special training in the prevention of disorders, and prepare police for riot control and for operation in units, with adequate command and control and field communication for proper discipline and effectiveness.

Develop guidelines governing the use of control equipment and provide alternatives to the use of lethal weapons. Federal support for research in this area is needed.

Establish an intelligence system to provide police and other public officials with reliable information that may help to prevent the outbreak of a disorder and to institute effective control measures in the event a riot erupts.

Develop continuing contacts with ghetto residents to make use of the forces for order which exist within the community.

Establish machinery for neutralizing rumors, and enabling Negro leaders and residents to obtain the facts. Create special rumor details to collect, evaluate, and dispel rumors that may lead to a civil disorder.

The Commission believes there is a grave danger that some communities may resort to the indiscriminate and excessive use of force. The harmful effects of overreaction are incalculable. The Commission condemns moves to equip police departments with mass destruction weapons, such as automatic rifles, machine guns and tanks. Weapons which are designed to destroy, not to control, have no place in densely populated urban communities.

The Commission recommends that the federal government share in the financing of programs for improvement of police forces, both in their normal law enforcement activities as well as in their response to civil disorders.

To assist government authorities in planning their response to civil disorder, this report contains a Supplement on Control of Disorder. It deals with specific problems encountered during riot-control operations, and includes:

> Assessment of the present capabilities of police, National Guard and Army forces to control major riots, and recommendations for improvement;

> Recommended means by which the control operations of those forces may be coordinated with the response of other agencies, such as fire departments, and with the community at large;

> Recommendations for review and revision of federal, state and local laws needed to provide the framework for control efforts and for the call-up and interrelated action of public safety forces.

*Chapter 13—The Administration of Justice Under Emergency Conditions*

In many of the cities which experienced disorders last summer, there were recurring breakdowns in the mechanisms for processing, prosecuting and protecting arrested persons. These resulted mainly from long-standing structural deficiencies in criminal court systems, and from the failure of communities to anticipate and plan for the emergency demands of civil disorders.

In part, because of this, there were few successful prosecutions for serious crimes committed during the riots. In those cities where mass arrests occurred many arrestees were deprived of basic legal rights.

The Commission recommends that the cities and states:

> Undertake reform of the lower courts so as to improve the quality of justice rendered under normal conditions.

> Plan comprehensive measures by which the criminal justice system may be supplemented during civil disorders so that its deliberative functions are protected, and the quality of justice is maintained.

Such emergency plans require broad community participation and dedicated leadership by the bench and bar. They should include:

Laws sufficient to deter and punish riot conduct.

Additional judges, bail and probation officers, and clerical staff.

Arrangements for volunteer lawyers to help prosecutors and to represent riot defendants at every stage of proceedings.

Policies to ensure proper and individual bail, arraignment, pre-trial, trial and sentencing proceedings.

Adequate emergency processing and detention facilities.

## Chapter 14—Damages: Repair and Compensation

The Commission recommends that the federal government:

Amend the Federal Disaster Act—which now applies only to natural disasters—to permit federal emergency food and medical assistance to cities during major civil disorders, and provide long-term economic assistance afterwards.

With the cooperation of the states, create incentives for the private insurance industry to provide more adequate property-insurance coverage in inner-city areas.

The Commission endorses the report of the National Advisory Panel on Insurance in Riot-Affected Areas: "Meeting the Insurance Crisis of our Cities."

## Chapter 15—The News Media and the Disorders

In his charge to the Commission, the President asked: "What effect do the mass media have on the riots?"

The Commission determined that the answer to the President's question did not lie solely in the performance of the press and broadcasters in reporting the riots. Our analysis had to consider also the overall treatment by the media of the Negro ghettos, community relations, racial attitudes, and poverty—day by day and month by month, year in and year out.

A wide range of interviews with government officials, law enforcement authorities, media personnel and other citizens, including ghetto residents, as well as a quantitative analysis of riot coverage and a special conference with industry representatives, leads us to conclude that:

Despite instances of sensationalism, inaccuracy and distortion, newspapers, radio and television tried on the whole to give a balanced, factual account of the 1967 disorders.

Elements of the news media failed to portray accurately the scale and character of the violence that occurred last summer. The overall effect was, we believe, an exaggeration of both mood and event.

Important segments of the media failed to report adequately on the causes and consequences of civil disorders and on the underlying problems of race relations. They have not communicated to the majority of their audience—which is white—a sense of the degradation, misery and hopelessness of life in the ghetto.

These failings must be corrected, and the improvement must come from within the industry. Freedom of the press is not the issue. Any effort to impose governmental restrictions would be inconsistent with fundamental constitutional precepts.

We have seen evidence that the news media are becoming aware of and concerned about their performance in this field. As that concern grows, coverage will improve. But much more must be done, and it must be done soon.

The Commission recommends that the media:

Expand coverage of the Negro community and of race problems through permanent assignment of reporters familiar with urban and racial affairs, and through establishment of more and better links with the Negro community.

Integrate Negroes and Negro activities into all aspects of coverage and content, including newspaper articles and television programming. The news media must publish newspapers and produce programs that recognize the existence and activities of Negroes as a group within the community and as a part of the larger community.

Recruit more Negroes into journalism and broadcasting and promote those who are qualified to positions of significant responsibility. Recruitment should begin in high schools and continue through college; where necessary, aid for training should be provided.

Improve coordination with police in reporting riot news through advance planning, and cooperate with the police in the designation of police information officers, establishment of information centers, and development of mutually acceptable guidelines for riot reporting and the conduct of media personnel.

Accelerate efforts to ensure accurate and responsible reporting of riot and racial news, through adoption by all news gathering organizations of stringent internal staff guidelines.

Cooperate in the establishment of a privately organized and funded Institute of Urban Communications to train and educate journalists in urban affairs, recruit and train more Negro journalists, develop methods for improving police-press relations, review coverage of riots and racial issues, and support continuing research in the urban field.

*Chapter 16—The Future of the Cities*

By 1985, the Negro population in central cities is expected to increase by 68 percent to approximately 20.3 million. Coupled with the continued exodus of white families to the suburbs, this growth will produce majority Negro populations in many of the nation's largest cities.

The future of these cities, and of their burgeoning Negro populations, is grim. Most new employment opportunities are being created in suburbs and outlying areas. This trend will continue unless important changes in public policy are made.

In prospect, therefore, is further deterioration of already inadequate municipal tax bases in the face of increasing demands for public services, and continuing unemployment and poverty among the urban Negro population:

Three choices are open to the nation:

We can maintain present policies, continuing both the proportion of the nation's resources now allocated to programs for the unemployed and the disadvantaged, and the inadequate and failing effort to achieve an integrated society.

We can adopt a policy of "enrichment" aimed at improving dramatically the quality of ghetto life while abandoning integration as a goal.

We can pursue integration by combining ghetto "enrichment" with policies which will encourage Negro movement out of central city areas.

The first choice, continuance of present policies, has ominous consequences for our society. The share of the nation's resources now allocated to programs for the disadvantaged is insufficient to arrest the deterioration of life in central city ghettos. Under such conditions, a rising proportion of Negroes may come to see in the deprivation and segregation they experience, a justification for violent protest, or for extending support to now isolated extremists who advocate civil disruption. Large-scale and continuing violence could result, followed by white retaliation, and, ultimately, the separation of the two communities in a garrison state.

Even if violence does not occur, the consequences are unacceptable. Development of a racially integrated society, extraordinarily difficult today, will be virtually impossible when the present black central city population of 12.1 million has grown to almost 21 million.

To continue present policies is to make permanent the division of our country into two societies; one, largely Negro and poor, located in the central cities; the other, predominantly white and affluent, located in the suburbs and in outlying areas.

The second choice, ghetto enrichment coupled with abandonment of integration, is also unacceptable. It is another way of choosing a permanently divided country. Moreover, equality cannot be achieved under conditions of nearly complete separation. In a country where the economy, and particularly the resources of employment, are predominantly white, a policy of separation can only relegate Negroes to a permanently inferior economic status.

We believe that the only possible choice for America is the third— a policy which combines ghetto enrichment with programs designed to encourage integration of substantial numbers of Negroes into the society outside the ghetto.

Enrichment must be an important adjunct to integration, for no matter how ambitious or energetic the program, few Negroes now living in central cities can be quickly integrated. In the meantime, large-scale improvement in the quality of ghetto life is essential.

But this can be no more than an interim strategy. Programs must be developed which will permit substantial Negro movement out of the ghettos. The primary goal must be a single society, in which every citizen will be free to live and work according to his capabilities and desires, not his color.

*Chapter 17—Recommendations for National Action*

INTRODUCTION

No American—white or black—can escape the consequences of the continuing social and economic decay of our major cities.

Only a commitment to national action on an unprecedented scale can shape a future compatible with the historic ideals of American society.

The great productivity of our economy, and a federal revenue system which is highly responsive to economic growth, can provide the resources.

The major need is to generate new will—the will to tax ourselves to the extent necessary to meet the vital needs of the nation.

We have set forth goals and proposed strategies to reach those goals. We discuss and recommend programs not to commit each of us to specific parts of such programs but to illustrate the type and dimension of action needed.

The major goal is the creation of a true union—a single society and a single American identity. Toward that goal, we propose the following objectives for national action:

Opening up opportunities to those who are restricted by racial segregation and discrimination, and eliminating all barriers to their choice of jobs, education and housing.

Removing the frustration of powerlessness among the disadvantaged by providing the means for them to deal with the problems that affect their own lives and by increasing the capacity of our public and private institutions to respond to these problems.

Increasing communication across racial lines to destroy stereotypes, to halt polarization, end distrust and hostility, and create common ground for efforts toward public order and social justice.

We propose these aims to fulfill our pledge of equality and to meet the fundamental needs of a democratic and civilized society—domestic peace and social justice.

## EMPLOYMENT

Pervasive unemployment and underemployment are the most persistent and serious grievances in minority areas. They are inextricably linked to the problem of civil disorder.

Despite growing federal expenditures for manpower development and training programs, and sustained general economic prosperity and increasing demands for skilled workers, about two million—white and nonwhite—are permanently unemployed. About ten million are underemployed, of whom 6.5 million work full time for wages below the poverty line.

The 500,000 "hard-core" unemployed in the central cities who lack a basic education and are unable to hold a steady job are made up in large part of Negro males between the ages of 18 and 25. In the riot cities which we surveyed, Negroes were three times as likely as whites to hold unskilled jobs, which are often part time, seasonal, low-paying and "dead end."

Negro males between the ages of 15 and 25 predominated among the rioters. More than 20 percent of the rioters were unemployed, and many who were employed held intermittent, low status, unskilled jobs which they regarded as below their education and ability.

The Commission recommends that the federal government:

Undertake joint efforts with cities and states to consolidate existing manpower programs to avoid fragmentation and duplication.

Take immediate action to create 2,000,000 new jobs over the next three years—one million in the public sector and one million in the private sector—to absorb the hard-core unemployed and materially reduce the level of underemployment for all workers, black and white. We propose 250,000 public sector and 300,000 private sector jobs in the first year.

Provide on-the-job training by both public and private employers with reimbursement to private employers for the extra costs of training the hard-core unemployed, by contract or by tax credits.

Provide tax and other incentives to investment in rural as well as urban poverty areas in order to offer to the rural poor an alternative to migration to urban centers.

Take new and vigorous action to remove artificial barriers to employment and promotion, including not only racial discrimination but, in certain cases, arrest records or lack of a high school diploma. Strengthen those agencies such as the Equal Employment Opportunity Commission, charged with eliminating discriminatory practices, and provide full support for Title VI of the 1964 Civil Rights Act allowing federal grant-in-aid funds to be withheld from activities which discriminate on grounds of color or race.

The Commission commends the recent public commitment of the National Council of the Building and Construction Trades Unions, AFL-CIO, to encourage and recruit Negro membership in apprenticeship programs. This commitment should be intensified and implemented.

EDUCATION

Education in a democratic society must equip children to develop their potential and to participate fully in American life. For the community at large, the schools have discharged this responsibility well. But for many minorities, and particularly for the children of the ghetto, the schools have failed to provide the educational experience which could overcome the effects of discrimination and deprivation.

This failure is one of the persistent sources of grievance and resentment within the Negro community. The hostility of Negro parents and students toward the school system is generating increasing conflict and causing disruption within many city school districts. But the most dramatic evidence of the relationship between educational practices and civil disorders lies in the high incidence of riot participation by ghetto youth who have not completed high school.

The bleak record of public education for ghetto children is growing worse. In the critical skills—verbal and reading ability—Negro students are falling further behind whites with each year of school completed. The high unemployment and underemployment rate for Negro youth is evidence, in part, of the growing educational crisis.

We support integration as the priority education strategy; it is essential to the future of American society. In this last summer's disorders we have seen the consequences of racial isolation at all levels, and of attitudes toward race, on both sides, produced by three centuries of myth, ignorance and bias. It is indispensable that opportunities for interaction between the races be expanded.

We recognize that the growing dominance of pupils from disadvantaged minorities in city school populations will not soon be reversed. No matter how great the effort toward desegregation, many children of the ghetto will not, within their school careers, attend integrated schools.

If existing disadvantages are not to be perpetuated, we must drastically improve the quality of ghetto education. Equality of results with all-white schools must be the goal.

To implement these strategies, the Commission recommends:

Sharply increased efforts to eliminate de facto segregation in our schools through substantial federal aid to school systems seeking to desegregate either within the system or in cooperation with neighboring school systems.

Elimination of racial discrimination in Northern as well as Southern schools by vigorous application of Title VI of the Civil Rights Act of 1964.

Extension of quality early childhood education to every disadvantaged child in the country.

Efforts to improve dramatically schools serving disadvantaged children through substantial federal funding of year-round compensatory education programs, improved teaching, and expanded experimentation and research.

Elimination of illiteracy through greater federal support for adult basic education.

Enlarged opportunities for parent and community participation in the public schools.

Reoriented vocational education emphasizing work-experience training and the involvement of business and industry.

Expanded opportunities for higher education through increased federal assistance to disadvantaged students.

Revision of state aid fomulas to assure more per student aid to districts having a high proportion of disadvantaged school-age children.

## THE WELFARE SYSTEM

Our present system of public welfare is designed to save money instead of people, and tragically ends up doing neither. This system has two critical deficiencies:

First, it excludes large numbers of persons who are in great need, and who, if provided a decent level of support, might be able to become more productive and self-sufficient. No federal funds are available for millions of unemployed and underemployed men and women who are needy but neither aged, handicapped nor the parents of minor children.

Second, for those included, the system provides assistance well below the minimum necessary for a decent level of existence, and imposes restrictions that encourage continued dependency on welfare and undermine self-respect.

A welter of statutory requirements and administrative practices and regulations operate to remind recipients that they are considered untrustworthy, promiscuous and lazy. Residence requirements prevent assistance to people in need who are newly arrived in the state. Searches of recipients' homes violate privacy. Inadequate social services compound the problems.

The Commission recommends that the federal government, acting with state and local governments where necessary, reform the existing welfare system to:

Establish, for recipients in existing welfare categories, uniform national standards of assistance at least as high as the annual "poverty level" of income, now set by the Social Security Administration at $3,335 per year for an urban family of four.

Require that all states receiving federal welfare contributions participate in the Aid to Families with Dependent Children—Unemployed Parents program (AFDC-UP) that permits assistance to families with both father and mother in the home, thus aiding the family while it is still intact.

Bear a substantially greater portion of all welfare costs—at least 90 percent of total payments.

Increase incentives for seeking employment and job training, but remove restrictions recently enacted by the Congress that would compel mothers of young children to work.

Provide more adequate social services through neighborhood centers and family-planning programs.

Remove the freeze placed by the 1967 welfare amendments on the percentage of children in a state that can be covered by federal assistance.

Eliminate residence requirements.

As a long-range goal, the Commission recommends that the federal government seek to develop a national system of income supplementation based strictly on need with two broad and basic purposes:

To provide, for those who can work or who do work, any necessary supplements in such a way as to develop incentives for fuller employment;

To provide, for those who cannot work and for mothers who decide to remain with their children, a minimum standard of decent living, and to aid in the saving of children from the prison of poverty that has held their parents.

A broad system of supplementation would involve substantially greater federal expenditures than anything now contemplated. The cost will range widely depending on the standard of need accepted as the "basic allowance" to individuals and families, and on the rate at which additional income above this level is taxed. Yet if the deepening cycle of poverty and dependence on welfare can be broken, if the children of the poor can be given the opportunity to scale the wall that now separates them from the rest of society, the return on this investment will be great indeed.

HOUSING

After more than three decades of fragmented and grossly underfunded federal housing programs, nearly six million substandard housing units remain occupied in the United States.

The housing problem is particularly acute in the minority ghettos. Nearly two-thirds of all non-white families living in the central cities today live in neighborhoods marked with substandard housing and general urban blight. Two major factors are responsible.

First: Many ghetto residents simply cannot pay the rent necessary to support decent housing. In Detroit, for example, over 40 percent of the non-white occupied units in 1960 required rent of over 35 percent of the tenants' income.

Second: Discrimination prevents access to many non-slum areas, particularly where good housing exists. In addition, by creating a "back pressure" in the racial ghettos, it makes it possible for landlords to break up apartments for denser occupancy, and keeps prices and rents of deteriorated ghetto housing higher than they would be in a truly free market.

To date, federal programs have been able to do comparatively little to provide housing for the disadvantaged. In the 31-year history of subsidized federal housing, only about 800,000 units have been constructed, with recent production averaging about 50,000 units a year. By comparison, over a period of three years longer, FHA insurance guarantees have made possible the construction of over ten million middle and upper-income units.

Two points are fundamental to the Commission's recommendations:

First: Federal housing programs must be given a new thrust aimed at overcoming the prevailing patterns of racial segregation. If this is not done, those programs will continue to concentrate the most impoverished and dependent segments of the population into the central-city ghettos where there is already a critical gap between the needs of the population and the public resources to deal with them.

Second: The private sector must be brought into the production and financing of low and moderate rental housing to supply the capabilities and capital necessary to meet the housing needs of the nation.

The Commission recommends that the federal government:

Enact a comprehensive and enforceable federal open housing law to cover the sale or rental of all housing, including single family homes.

Reorient federal housing programs to place more low and moderate income housing outside of ghetto areas.

Bring within the reach of low and moderate income families within the next five years six million new and existing units of decent housing, beginning with 600,000 units in the next year.

To reach this goal we recommend:

Expansion and modification of the rent supplement program to permit use of supplements for existing housing, thus greatly increasing the reach of the program.

Expansion and modification of the below-market interest rate program to enlarge the interest subsidy to all sponsors and provide interest-free loans to nonprofit sponsors to cover pre-construction costs, and permit sale of projects to nonprofit corporations, cooperatives, or condominiums.

Creation of an ownership supplement program similar to present rent supplements, to make home ownership possible for low-income families.

Federal writedown of interest rates on loans to private builders constructing moderate-rent housing.

Expansion of the public housing program, with emphasis on small units on scattered sites, and leasing and "turnkey" programs.

Expansion of the Model Cities program.

Expansion and reorientation of the urban renewal program to give priority to projects directly assisting low-income households to obtain adequate housing.

CONCLUSION

One of the first witnesses to be invited to appear before this Commission was Dr. Kenneth B. Clark, a distinguished and perceptive scholar. Referring to the reports of earlier riot commissions, he said:

> I read that report ... of the 1919 riot in Chicago, and it is as if I were reading the report of the investigating committee on the Harlem riot of '35, the report of the investigating committee on the Harlem riot of '43, the report of the McCone Commission on the Watts riot.
>
> I must again in candor say to you members of this Commission— it is a kind of Alice in Wonderland—with the same moving picture reshown over and over again, the same analysis, the same recommendations, and the same inaction.

These words come to our minds as we conclude this report.

We have provided an honest beginning. We have learned much. But we have uncovered no startling truths, no unique insights, no simple solutions. The destruction and the bitterness of racial disorder, the harsh polemics of black revolt and white repression have been seen and heard before in this country.

It is time now to end the destruction and the violence, not only in the streets of the ghetto but in the lives of people.

# Shoot-Out in Cleveland

## LOUIS H. MASOTTI
## JEROME R. CORSI

### Introduction

On the evening of July 23, 1968, shots rang out on a narrow street in Cleveland's racially troubled East Side. Within minutes, a full-scale gun battle was raging between Cleveland police and black snipers. An hour and a half later, seven people lay dead; fifteen others were wounded. Fifteen of the casualties were policemen.

For the next five days, violence flared in Glenville and other East Side neighborhoods. Arsonists heaved fire bombs into buildings; teenagers smashed store windows and led mobs in looting. The police lashed back, sometimes in blind fury. In the smoldering aftermath, sixty-three business establishments were counted damaged or destroyed. Property losses exceeded two million dollars.

In human and dollar costs, the Glenville incident was not the most serious event in the recent tide of racial violence in America. But it differed sharply from the current pattern of violence in significant, instructive ways. Indeed, it established a new theme and an apparent escalation in the level of racial conflict in America.

Racial clashes have produced bloodshed and property damage before. Most recent outbreaks, like the Detroit riot of 1967, were initiated by blacks—itself a deviation from earlier patterns—but the hostility was directed toward property, not persons. (Sporadic sniper fire—less of it than originally believed—occurred during major disorders in 1967, but long after the violence had expressed itself in property damage.) The Glenville incident was different; it began as person-oriented violence, black and whites shooting at each other, snipers against cops. And ap-

Reprinted from a Report to the President's Commission on the Causes and Prevention of Violence, 1969.

parently alone among major outbreaks of racial violence in American history, it ended in more white casualties than black.

Moreover, the Glenville incident occurred in the first major American city to have elected a Negro mayor and in a city that had been spared serious disorders during the volatile summer of 1967. Because of Carl B. Stokes' success in preventing violence after the assassination of Martin Luther King in April, 1968, Clevelanders looked upon him as a positive guarantee against future racial disturbances in their city. Yet the violence occurred, and the Glenville incident raised disturbing questions for other American cities with increasing Negro populations that can expect to have Negro-led governments in the future.

Lastly, Mayor Stokes introduced a new technique for quenching the violence. At the urging of black leaders, he placed control of the troubled neighborhoods in their hands, barring white policemen, National Guardsmen, and white non-residents from the area. After one night's trial, the policy was altered; police and National Guardsmen were brought into the area, chiefly to protect property. Born in controversy, carried out under complicating circumstances and with only partial success, the technique of "community control" during riots is still a matter of dispute as to its effectiveness.

Why did it happen, especially in Cleveland? Was the Glenville incident the result of a vast conspiracy to "get Whitey" or the sudden, unpremeditated act of a few individuals? Who is to blame? Will it happen again—in Cleveland or elsewhere?

## A Midsummer's Nightmare

Glenville, lying near the northeast corner of Cleveland, is a neighborhood of two- and three-story houses with broad front porches and small front lawns. In the 1940's, Glenville was a largely Jewish area; today it is very predominantly Negro. Except for pockets of deterioration, it stands in tidy contrast to the Hough area, lying to the west.

For Patrolman William Kehoe, performing traffic duty on the East Side, July 23, 1968, was a slow day. Shortly after noon he called headquarters for a possible assignment. Lt. Edward Anderson, traffic coordinator for the Cleveland Police Department, assigned him to check an abandoned automobile in the Glenville area. Anderson had received a telephone call about the car not long before. "It was just a routine call of an abandoned auto," he later recalled. "I told the gentleman we'd get to it as soon as possible. I couldn't promise action that day." Following standard procedure, Anderson did not ask the caller's name.

The car, a 1958 Cadillac, was on Beulah Avenue, between East 123rd Street and Lakeview. The left front tire was flat; to Patrolman Kehoe, it appeared the car was a "junk car" that had not been driven for some time. Neighbors confirmed that the car had been there many days; none had any idea who owned it. At 1:25 p.m., Kehoe placed a parking ticket on the abandoned car, then filled out a routine report for the tow-truck division of the Police Department.

Kehoe expected that the car would be towed away before the evening rush hour. But William McMillan and Roy Benslay, operating Tow Truck #58, had other assignments that kept them from the pick-up in Glenville until dusk. They arrived on Beulah Avenue in their uniforms, which resemble standard police uniforms except that the jackets are of the Eisenhower type. Clevelanders commonly assume that the tow-truck operators are policemen, but in fact they are civilian employees and carry no weapons.

What happened next has been recounted by McMillan. After Benslay backed the truck up to the Cadillac, McMillan emerged from the cab to check the license plate number against the assignment card. "The next thing I knew I was shot in the back. I turned around and saw a man with a shotgun firing from the side of a house on the corner of Lakeview."

McMillan ran to the front of the tow truck to take cover. A second shot hit him in the right side. "Another sniper was firing from the bushes just in front of the truck." Benslay, crouching in the cab of the truck, radioed for help. Then the shooting stopped.

"A Negro with a carbine in his hand walked up the sidewalk and stopped just across from me," McMillan told a reporter several days later.

"Are you one of the sons of bitches stealing cars?" the Negro asked him. McMillan pleaded that he was unarmed and rose from the street to show that he had no weapon. The Negro raised the carbine to his shoulder and took aim. McMillan ran toward 123rd Street. As he turned the corner, another bullet hit him in the right side. McMillan kept running.

Halfway along the block a Negro woman shouted to McMillan and offered him refuge. Inside the house he telephoned the Police Department, but the lines were busy. When he heard sirens, McMillan left the house and walked northward on 123rd Street. After turning right on Oakland Avenue he spotted a squad car, which rushed him to a hospital.

McMillan identified the Negro with the carbine as Fred (Ahmed) Evans.

He also offered an explanation of the event. "The snipers set up the ambush and used the tow truck as a decoy to bring the police in," he said. "They had their crossfire all planned. We all were sitting ducks."

McMillan's ambush theory found ready acceptance. Many Clevelanders, and at least two national news magazines, accepted it unquestioningly. But other events of that grim Tuesday, and the accounts of other eyewitnesses, cast doubts upon the ambush theory.

Ahmed lived in an apartment in a two-story, red brick house at 12312 Auburndale, a block and a half from the scene of the tow-truck shooting. On the evening of July 23, shortly before the tow-truck incident, he had visitors: George Forbes, the City Councilman from Ahmed's area, and Walter Beach, a former halfback for the Cleveland Browns, who was the director of the Mayor's Council on Youth Opportunities. According to a summary of events, issued later by the Mayor's office, the meeting lasted from 7:50 p.m. to 8:05 p.m.

Forbes and Beach had come from a meeting at City Hall where Ahmed had been the subject of anxious discussion. The meeting, which began at 2:30 that afternoon, had been called by Inspector Lewis Coffey of the Cleveland Police Department. Coffey had intelligence reports, which the Police Department had obtained chiefly through the Federal Bureau of Investigation, that warned of an outbreak of violence planned for Cleveland the next morning, July 24, at 8:00 a.m. The central figures in the outbreak would be Ahmed and his group, the Black Nationalists of New Libya.

Ahmed's group, according to the reports, had been assembling an arsenal of hand guns and carbines and stashing them in Ahmed's apartment. Some of the group had gone to Pittsburgh, Detroit, and Akron on Sunday night to collect semi-automatic weapons; a further trip to Detroit was planned for Tuesday evening, July 23. In addition to the Wednesday morning outbreak, the reports added, there was the possibility of simultaneous outbreaks in other Northern cities.

*        *        *

Who shot first? And at whom? Various accounts of where, how, and why the shooting started have appeared. Even after extensive investigation, questions remain unanswered.

Accounts of the activities of the surveillance teams, and of what they observed, have been provided by the policemen in the surveillance cars. Three patrolmen—O'Malley, Sweeney, and Gallagher—were in the unmarked car at 124th and Auburndale, facing westward toward Ahmed's house. When they arrived about 6:00 p.m., about a dozen

Negroes, including women and children, were on the porch at 12312 Auburndale. About half were dressed in Afro garb, the others conventionally. The policemen kept watch through binoculars. Later in the evening, shortly before Councilman Forbes and Walter Beach arrived at the apartment, they saw Ahmed himself arrive in a red Volkswagen. Evidently no one was on the porch at this time.

Shortly after Beach and Forbes left, according to James O'Malley, a Negro carrying a carbine came out of 12312 Auburndale and stood guard. Ahmed came out a short while later, followed by about sixteen others carrying arms and wearing bandoliers. The man who had come out first crossed the street, dropped to his knees, and pointed his rifle toward the surveillance car. O'Malley radioed for instructions and was told to get out of the area immediately. The time, he recalls, was 8:20 p.m.

Patrolman Gallagher, driving the surveillance car, turned left onto 124th Street to escape from the area. As they were leaving, O'Malley saw two men get into a Ford station wagon and set off in pursuit of the surveillance car. The policemen heard a shot; it did not hit their car. Moments later the station wagon halted the pursuit, turned around, and headed back toward Auburndale.

Patrolmen Thomas Gerrity and Thomas Horgan were in the other surveillance car parked at the corner of Lakeview and Moulton, facing Ahmed's house from the opposite direction. They, too, observed the people on the porch, the later arrival of Ahmed in the red Volkswagen, and the arrival and departure of Councilman Forbes and Walter Beach. When Ahmed's group came out of the house, according to Horgan, several of the men headed toward their surveillance car. The surveillance car turned left onto Lakeview, heading northward toward Superior Avenue, to escape. A green Chevrolet followed them; Gerrity and Horgan heard several shots, but none hit their car. Horgan broadcast a warning to other police cars to stay out of the area. As their car headed west on Superior Avenue, Horgan heard a broadcast about the tow-truck operator being fired upon. Gerrity and Horgan turned southward, back toward the scene of trouble. When they arrived within view of the tow truck, says Horgan, they saw the tow-truck operator running with his hands up and an armed black nationalist chasing him. Then the surveillance car was struck by fire coming from 123rd and Beulah. Bullets hit the windshield and the hood and demolished the grille. Gerrity and Horgan returned the fire, shooting toward two snipers hiding behind the tow truck, until their ammunition was exhausted. Then they sought escape northward on 123rd Street. By the time they were back on Superior, all four tires of their surveillance car were flat. When Gerrity returned to the police station, a colleague recalled, the 28-year-old patrol-man was "dry-vomiting and shaking so hard he put his hand on the letter basket and the whole table shook."

According to Lieutenant Burt Miller, who had been assigned by the Police Department to reconstruct the history of the events of July 23, other police cars were on the scene when Gerrity and Horgan ap-proached the tow truck. "They engaged with other cars that were ar-riving in a fire fight with males that were carrying weapons," he told a City Press conference on August 9. Thus, police cars had converged on the scene and the full-scale shoot-out had begun. Three males, according to Lt. Miller, were firing at police from two corners of Lakeview and Beulah; a fourth lay, wounded or dead, on the sidewalk at 123rd and Beulah.

*  *  *

Against theories of an ambush or well-planned conspiracy stands the evidence that on Tuesday evening Ahmed was annoyed and appre-hensive about the police surveillance. He expressed such sentiments to Walter Beach and George Forbes. He had memories of police violence in Akron. "So we armed ourselves. And what followed was chaos."

In an interview published in the *Cleveland Press,* August 2, Ahmed offered his version of his movements after leaving the house:

> I was heading for the Lakeview Tavern [at the corner of Auburndale and Lakeview] when I heard some shots coming from the end of the street. Then one of the brothers passed me running. Some policemen in a blue detective's car opened up with a machine gun and he was dead. So I ran into a yard and I began trading shots with a policeman behind a parked car. I couldn't hit him. I wasn't coming anywhere close to him. And then my carbine jammed.

According to Ahmed, he then hid in bushes and tried to fix the carbine, but without success.

In an interview for this study, Ahmed said that he had rounded the corner and was walking on Lakeview when he heard the first shot. When he went to investigate, he saw the tow-truck operator running along Beulah. Then, he said, he heard what sounded like a submachine gun blast; he later concluded that this was the fire that killed Amir Iber Katir, one of his followers. (The account by Lt. Miller and the observations of a radio operator who arrived at the scene support the conclusion that the first person killed was a black nationalist. The coroner's autopsy re-vealed four bullet wounds: the right chest, right thigh, left leg, and left thigh.) Ahmed has concluded: "We were ambushed, not the police."

An eyewitness recalled that Ahmed came down the street very coolly. By the time he got to Beulah, the shooting had begun. Ahmed, said the witness, was carrying an automatic weapon, and when he reached the corner he started firing.

> Ahmed himself, he came down later. On his side, and when he came down with the automatic rifle or machine gun, whichever it be, his rifle drowned all the other guns. . . . He came down peacefully. He came down the left side of the street and when he turned the corner, that's when all hell broke loose.

Ahmed has admitted that he did not have total control of the situation. There were many nationalists involved and he was only one. "I had come to be the leader. But the night of the 23rd, there was no leader. After we got our guns, it was every man for himself."

In the one-hour period between 8:30 p.m. and 9:30 p.m. on Tuesday evening, at least twenty-two people were killed or injured in the raging gun battle between police and snipers. The major shooting occurred along Lakeview Avenue between Beulah Avenue and Auburndale, a distance of less than three hundred yards, and ranged no more than a block each way on side streets.

The area is no place to hold a shoot-out. Lakeview itself is narrow. The side streets are even narrower, and some of them jut at odd angles. Houses are close together, sometimes separated by narrow passageways. There is little room to maneuver.

When a radio call for assistance went out about 8:30 p.m., it was an "all units" call; any available unit in the city could respond. Police throughout the city left their regular patrols and rushed to the scene, anxious to help their comrades in trouble. A radio newsman estimated there were forty to fifty police officers when he arrived at 8:45 p.m. Later there were "several hundred officers," according to the *Cleveland Press*. Nearby streets accumulated long lines of abandoned patrol cars as police parked their cars close to the shooting as possible, grabbed their weapons, and ran to lend assistance.*

The battle that ensued was a combination of confusion and panic. Police enthusiastically rushed into the area without knowing precisely, or even generally, what they were rushing into. The response had largely been personal initiative rather than planned reaction and an orderly show

---

* The abandoned police cars were vulnerable to one of the tactics of urban guerrilla warfare. At 12:46 a.m. (then Wednesday morning) the following alert was broadcast over the police radio: "All Cars—Check all abandoned police cars for bombs prior to moving them."

of controlled force. Each officer grabbed his gun and did what he could. "Perhaps some snipers were shot and killed," a policeman recalled of his experience. "I fired, mostly at shadows." No one assumed command. There was no orderly way to report to headquarters and no way for headquarters to issue directives. Police had largely abandoned their radios when they left their cars.

After the initial shooting the violence clustered around three locations: East 123rd and Beulah (location of the tow truck); two adjoining houses on Lakeview (1391 and 1395); and, the Lakeview Tavern and 12312 Auburndale (Ahmed's residence).

Among the first to respond to the call for assistance were Patrolmen Joseph McManamon and Chester Szukalski in Car 591. They approached the area from the south, driving up 123rd Street. "I didn't see any people, any children or anyone playing," Szukalski recalls. "All I could see was the yellow tow truck parked on the northeast corner of 123rd and Beulah."

As McManamon pulled in front of the tow truck, shots hit the patrol car on the passenger side where Szukalski was sitting. Both men crawled out the driver's side, but Szukalski was hit before he escaped.

> I got hit in the right forearm first, but I couldn't see where the shots were coming from. I just knew they were coming from my right and from a higher elevation. As I tried to crawl to safety, I was hit in the right thigh. It was the third shot that hit me that really wrecked me. That one hit my right calf, causing a compound fracture of my right leg, then hit my left calf. By then I could hardly crawl. The pain was awful. I crawled about thirty or forty feet to a building, waiting for help. We [Szukalski and McManamon] could see other policemen in the area, but they couldn't get to us because the gunfire was so intense and constant. We waited about fifteen minutes for our buddies to get us out.

McManamon was slightly wounded by fragments from the bullet that broke Szukalski's leg.

As Amir Iber Katir lay dying on the sidewalk and more police cars converged on the scene, the snipers on Beulah Avenue retreated across Lakeview into the narrow alley that is an extension of Beulah. With police in pursuit they turned right into the alley parallel to Lakeview and began exchanging fire with police from between the houses. Some forced their way into the two-and-a-half-story frame house at 1395 Lakeview and occupied the second floor. Beatrice Flagg was watching television in her first-floor apartment when the shooting started.

> They started shooting and I was afraid to look out. I told my kids to get down on the ground and pray. I looked out and there was an army

of police there. I could hear a lot of loud swearing upstairs. I begged the police to stop shooting but they wouldn't listen. I barred the door because I didn't want anybody to get in and then I just got back down on the ground.

Mrs. Flagg and her children escaped from the house after tear gas began to fill her living room. Mrs. Henry Perryman, on the second floor with her 9-month-old baby, also managed to escape.*

Police then occupied the first floor of the house next door (1391 Lakeview). In the area between the two buildings, Patrolman Louis E. Golonka was shot and killed. Police, firing at armed men in the alley from windows of 1391 Lakeview, killed Sidney Curtis Taylor (Malik Ali Bey) and wounded Lathan Donald (Londue). From nearby bushes a man rose and tried to fire at police. Picking up Patrolman Golonka's shotgun, a policeman fatally shot the man, who was Bernard Donald (Nondu Bey), brother of Lathan Donald. The bodies of the three black nationalists—two dead, one severely injured—lay in the alley amid carbines and bandolers until after midnight.

Another gun battle was raging at the intersection of Auburndale and Lakeview. Patrolman Kenneth Gibbons and Willard Wolff, in Car 505, had responded to the call for assistance and reportedly were the first to arrive at the intersection. Another policeman was on the scene, however: an unidentified plainclothesman struggling with a "young punk" near Ahmed's house. As they left the car to assist, a high-powered bullet hit the motor and the car exploded. Gibbons was shot and seriously injured; Wolff was killed.

Sergeants Sam Levy and Bill Moran also were among the first to arrive at Auburndale and Lakeview. They heard shots coming from back yards. Levy describes their response:

We dodged through the yards and crawled along to the back of the Lakeview Tavern, where I saw shells on the ground. I got to the northeast corner of Auburndale and Lakeview and I saw some empty ammunition clips in the driveway behind the bar. I started up the driveway and I must have gone about three steps when I was hit. . . . I dove into the gutter and tried to get behind a car parked near the intersec-

---

* Mrs. Perryman denies newspaper quotations attributed to her that would indicate snipers barged into her apartment while she was there. According to her husband, who was away at the time, the first activity of which Mrs. Perryman and Mrs. Flagg were aware was the shooting by police, without warning, of tear gas shells and bullets into the house.

The *Call & Post,* on July 27, gave this version of the sequence of events: "Police ordered the Perryman home evacuated . . . to protect the occupants and to get vantage points from which they could flush out the snipers. The snipers later entered the abandoned Perryman home and used it as a sniper's [sic] post."

tion. They kept shooting and I was hit again. They shot at anybody who moved.

Levy took refuge under the parked car. He was stranded for nearly an hour before help could reach him.

Lieutenant Elmer Joseph entered Auburndale from Lakeview about the same time that Sgt. Levy was wounded. He was on the sidewalk when he was hit; he managed to get himself to cover. Lt. Joseph was also stranded for almost an hour. Henry Orange, a 50-year-old civilian, was wounded at about the same time, allegedly while assisting police. Patrolman Richard Hart was shot in the back, apparently by a sniper hiding in a dark doorway, then hit several more times as he writhed in the middle of Lakeview.

Lieutenant Leroy Jones and Sergeant Gentile stopped at Sixth District headquarters to "pick up extra weapons" after they heard the call for assistance. They entered the battleground area from East 124th Street, thus approaching Auburndale from the east. They parked and continued to Auburndale on foot. As Lt. Jones turned the corner onto Auburndale, Sgt. Gentile, behind him, heard heavy fire. Gentile hurried around the corner, only to see Jones fall to the sidewalk in the middle of the block. Gentile attempted to approach Jones, but the heavy fire kept him from reaching his wounded partner.

Patrolmen Angelo Santa Maria and Steve Sopko also rushed to the scene. By the time they got there, so many police cars were in the area that they had to park two blocks away. While Sopko headed in another direction, Santa Maria ran behind the houses on Auburndale. From there he could see a police officer lying on the sidewalk. "I yelled to other police under cover across the street, 'Who is it'? They yelled back, 'Lieutenant Jones.' "

Then, says Santa Maria, he talked to several Negro bystanders, asking for a volunteer to drive a car alongside Lt. Jones so that Santa Maria could drag him into it. Several offered help; Santa Maria chose a man whom police later identified as James E. Chapman, a 22-year-old filing clerk who lived next door to the Lakeview Tavern. Santa Maria got into Chapman's car.

> I told him to drive up parallel to Jones and throw himself on the floor and I would try to drag Jones in. But cars were parked bumper to bumper. We both got out and separated, trying to get around them. On the sidewalk a sergeant met me. We decided to throw a smoke bomb for cover.

Then, according to the *Cleveland Press,* "the sergeant opened up with his submachine gun to protect Santa Maria, who went into the smoke to get Jones." (Cleveland police are not issued automatic weapons, and it is against regulations to possess them.) Santa Maria describes the rescue:

> I grabbed his legs and started to drag him out when I was hit in the back. I tried to crawl but I didn't get very far. Some policeman [later identified as Patrolman Steven Marencky] dragged me, then threw me over his shoulder and put me in a police car.

Santa Maria did not know the identity of the Negro who was helping him nor what happened to him next. From newspaper accounts and the coroner's report it is apparent that James E. Chapman died from a massive head wound, fired from an automatic weapon from a direction to his right and above him. The identification of Chapman as Santa Maria's helper was first made by police in a *Cleveland Press* article eight days after the event. Chapman was proclaimed a hero, and Bluecoats, Inc., an organization that helps widows of policemen, departed from standard policy to present a thousand-dollar check to Chapman's widow.

Two patrolmen made an attempt to rescue Sgt. Levy and Lt. Joseph, who lay wounded on the street, pinned there by sniper fire. Thomas Smith ran to Lt. Joseph, dragged him across the street to safety, then ran to Sgt. Levy, who was lying under a car. He dragged Levy from under the car, started to pick him up, and was shot in the right shoulder. "I spun around and then I was struck by crossfire and fell to the ground." Patrolman Ernest Rowell had joined in the attempt to rescue Levy.

> Smith was hit. I was hit as I dropped to the ground near Levy. Smith was still exposed. I managed to pull him near us. I couldn't get him under the car. So I put my legs over his head. He was moaning that he couldn't move his legs. I loosened Levy's shirt and partially stopped the bleeding. We kept assuring each other help would reach us.... Finally—it must have been an hour later—a tear gas cannister was accidentally triggered by another policeman. But that cloud was a welcome sight, even though it was burning our eyes. As the cloud covered the car, I jumped up and ran towards Lakeview Road. The gunfire was rat-tat-tat-ing in spurts. It was now or never.

Two other patrolmen, William Traine and James Herron, took advantage of the tear gas and headed toward the car protecting Levy and Smith. With the help of other policemen they got them placed on stretchers and rolled to an ambulance about twenty feet away.

Patrolman Leonard Szalkiewicz was wounded on Lakeview, near the intersection of Auburndale, as he was pushing a patrol car blocking the street. "At first I wasn't sure whether I was shot or whether I was cut by flying glass." Another patrolman, Anthony Sherbinski, was wounded about 9:30 p.m. as he shot at snipers from the second floor of the Lakeview tavern. A civilian, John Pegues, was shot in the leg about the same time.

By 9:45 the shooting had died down, and police were able to move into 12312 and 12314 Auburndale to search for suspects. A reporter at the scene counted seventeen men and women, presumably all the occupants of the two houses, brought out, loaded into patrol cars, and taken to district headquarters for questioning. Fred (Ahmed) Evans was not among them. No casualties were found in the two houses. Four rifles and a number of boxes of ammunition were recovered from the houses, another rifle from a car parked nearby.

\* \* \*

At 11:11 p.m., before the fire in the Perryman house started, a call went out over the police radio: "1384 Lakeview: front door open, man wants to give himself up, wants [to surrender to] Negro policemen." A similar message went out at 12:24 p.m. This time, three white policemen, Sergeant Ronald Heinz, Patrolmen David Hicks, and John Cullen, approached 1384 Lakeview to apprehend the man who wished to surrender. Fred (Ahmed) Evans emerged from the house, shirtless, wearing slacks and sandals.

The house from which Ahmed came was across the street from the Perryman house. The only times that 1384 Lakeview appeared in official police chronologies and records were the two broadcasts offering Ahmed's surrender.\*

When Ahmed emerged, he was reported to have asked: "How are my people?" Told that at least three had been killed, he replied: "They died for a worthy cause." Ahmed said he had seventeen in his group.

When police asked Ahmed where his weapon was, he pointed to the bushes in front of the house. The police found a toga, a loaded carbine, five boxes of ammunition, and a first-aid kit. Ahmed explained: "If my carbine hadn't jammed I would have killed you three. I had you in my sights when my rifle jammed." Before taking him to central head-

---

\* Detectives who later investigated the attic of 1384 Lakeview, where Ahmed had been, found cigaret butts and bullets but no spent shells. According to Joseph Turpin, a workhouse guard who lives at 1384, Ahmed broke in the house about the time the tow-truck shooting took place. (Turpin, who had been watching the tow-truck incident, insists that Ahmed did no shooting.) Ahmed went to the attic and, at least three times during the evening, yelled to Turpin that he wanted to stop the battle by surrendering. Turpin says he called the police in Ahmed's behalf at least five times.

quarters, one of the policemen asked Ahmed: "Why did you start all this?" He replied, "You police have bothered us too long." *

Though the battle between police and snipers waged past midnight, the casualties of that battle occurred within the first hour of the shooting.

A chronology of events, issued by the Mayor's office on August 9, lists the following casualties:

*Around E. 123rd St. and Beulah*

| | | |
|---|---|---|
| William McMillan | | |
| (tow-truck operator) | wounded at | 8:25 p.m. |
| Ptl. Chester Szukalski | wounded | 8:30 |
| Ptl. Joseph McManamon | wounded | 8:30 |
| Leroy Mansfield Williams (suspect) | killed at | 9:26 (?) |

*Around 1391 and 1395 Lakeview*

| | | |
|---|---|---|
| Ptl. Louis Golonka | killed at | 8:35 p.m. |
| Sidney Taylor Curtis (suspect) | killed | 8:40 |
| Bernard Donald (suspect) | killed | 8:40 |
| Lathan Donald (suspect) | wounded | 8:45 |

*Around the Lakeview Tavern, 12312 and 12314 Auburndale*

a. at Lakeview and Auburndale:

| | | |
|---|---|---|
| Ptl. Willard Wolff | killed at | 8:30 p.m. |
| Ptl. Kenneth Gibbons | wounded | 8:30 |
| Sgt. Samuel Levy | wounded | 8:45 |
| Henry Orange (civilian) | wounded | 8:45 |
| Lt. Elmer Joseph | wounded | 8:45 |
| Ptl. Richard Hart | wounded at | 9:30 p.m. |
| Ptl. Leonard Szalkiewicz | wounded | 8:55 |
| Ptl. Ernest Rowell | wounded | 9:30 |
| Ptl. Thomas Smith | wounded | 9:30 |

b. at the Lakeview Tavern:

| | | |
|---|---|---|
| Ptl. Anthony Sherbinski | wounded | 9:30 |
| John Pegues (civilian) | wounded | 9:30 |

---

* These statements attributed to Ahmed and published in Cleveland newspapers are the substance of what police told reporters Ahmed said at the time. At the beginning of his murder trial in March, 1969, Ahmed's lawyers were denied a motion to have these statements suppressed.

c. in the vicinity of 12312 and 12314 Auburndale:

| | | |
|---|---|---|
| Lt. Leroy Jones | killed | 8:45 |
| Ptl. Angelo Santa Maria | wounded | 9:00 |
| James E. Chapman (civilian) | killed | 9:00 |

Thus, by 9:30 p.m., the official casualty list read: three police killed, twelve injured (counting McMillan, the tow-truck operator); three suspects killed, one wounded; one civilian killed, two injured. The count shows seven lives lost and fifteen individuals wounded: a total of twenty-two casualties.*

---

* There is evidence that some individuals who received injuries, mostly minor, were not included on the official casualty list. It is probable that snipers escaped from the scene, and some of these may have been injured. Injured or dead snipers may have been borne to hiding places by friends. Two policemen said they saw a sniper fall from the roof of an Auburndale house; then four people dragged him to a panel truck and drove away. Randel T. Osburn, Cleveland Director of the Southern Christian Leadership Conference, says he saw a number of men running near Lakeview and Beulah and heading toward Superior: "One guy was running into an alley and he had been shot and he was holding his shoulder, all bloody. Two other fellows were carrying a second guy that we never heard anything else about, so I guess they made a clean getaway."

# E. CITIES AGAINST SUBURBS

## The White Exodus to Suburbia Steps Up

### HERBERT J. GANS

In this unpredictable world, nothing can be predicted quite so easily as the continued proliferation of suburbia. Not only have American cities stopped growing for more than a generation, while the metropolitan areas of which they are a part were continuing to expand lustily, but there is incontrovertible evidence that another huge wave of suburban home building can be expected in the coming decade.

Between 1947 and about 1960, the country experienced the greatest baby boom ever, ending the slow-down in marriages and childbirths created first by the Depression and then by World War II. Today, the earliest arrivals of that baby boom are themselves old enough to marry, and many are now setting up housekeeping in urban or suburban apartments. In a few years, however, when their first child is 2 to 3 years old, and the second is about to appear, many young parents will decide to buy suburban homes. Only simple addition is necessary to see that by the mid-seventies, they will be fashioning another massive suburban building boom, provided of course that the country is affluent and not engaged in World War III.

The new suburbia may not look much different from the old; there will, however, be an increase in the class and racial polarization that has been developing between the suburbs and the cities for several generations now. The suburbs will be home for an ever larger proportion of working-class, middle-class and upper-class whites; the cities, for an ever larger proportion of poor and nonwhite people. The continuation of this trend means that, by the nineteen-seventies, a greater number of cities will be 40 to 50 percent nonwhite in population, with

From *The New York Times Magazine,* January 7, 1968, pp. 25+. © 1968 by The New York Times Company. Reprinted by permission of the author and the publisher.

more and larger ghettos and greater municipal poverty on the one hand, and stronger suburban opposition to open housing and related policies to solve the city's problems on the other hand. The urban crisis will worsen, and although there is no shortage of rational solutions, nothing much will be done about the crisis unless white America permits a radical change of public policy and undergoes a miraculous change of attitude toward its cities and their populations.

Another wave of suburban building would develop even if there had been no post-World War II baby boom, for American cities have always grown at the edges, like trees, adding new rings of residential development every generation as the beneficiaries of affluence and young families sought more modern housing and "better" neighborhoods. At first, the new rings were added inside the city limits, but ever since the last half of the 19th century, they have more often sprung up in the suburbs.

Although these trends may not be so apparent to New Yorkers, who live in a world capital rather than in a typical American city, both urban and suburban growth have almost always taken the form of single family houses, first on large lots and later, as less affluent city dwellers could afford to move out, on smaller lots. Even inside most American cities— again, other than New York and a few others—the majority of people live in single family homes.

Moreover, studies of housing preferences indicate that the majority of Americans, including those now living in the city, want a suburban single family house once they have children, and want to remain in that house when their children have grown up. This urge for suburban life is not limited to the middle class or just to America; the poor would leave the city as well if they could afford to go, and so would many Europeans.

The only people who clearly do not want to live in the suburbs are the single and some of the childless couples, and that handful of urban middle-class professionals and intellectuals living in New York and a few other cosmopolitan cities. For everyone else, suburbia means more housing space at less cost, a backyard and an up-to-date community— all of which make raising children significantly easier for the mother, more compatible neighbors, cleaner air, a chance to leave the dirt and congestion behind and, in recent years, a chance also to escape the expansion of Negro and poor neighborhoods. Even some of the dedicated urbanites move to the suburbs when their children are young, although they—but only they—miss the cultural facilities of the big city and are often unhappy in suburbia.

Obviously, the popular antisuburban literature, which falsely accuses the suburbs of causing conformity, matriarchy, adultery, divorce, alcoholism and other standard American pathologies, has not kept any-one from moving to the suburbs, and even the current predictions of land shortages, longer commuting and urban congestion in the suburbs will not discourage the next generation of home buyers. Most, if not all, metropolitan areas still have plenty of rural land available for suburban housing. Moreover, with industry and offices now moving to the suburbs, new areas previously outside commuting range become ripe for resi-dential development to house their employes. Thus, for several years now, more than half the suburbanites of Nassau County have been com-muting to jobs inside Nassau County; in the next decade, they will probably be joined by new commuters living in Suffolk County. Of course, all this leads to increasing suburban congestion, but most sub-urbanites do not mind it. They do not leave the city for a rural existence, as the folklore has it; they want a half acre or more of land and all their favorite urban facilities within a short driving distance from the house.

In some metropolitan areas, or in parts of them, land may indeed be too scarce and thus too expensive to permit another round of old-style suburbanization. There, people will move into "townhouses" and semidetached houses, which have less privacy than single family houses, but still provide private yards and a feeling of separateness from the next-door neighbors. The recent failure of Reston, Va., the much praised new town near Washington, D.C., suggests, however, that the exquisitely designed communal recreational areas cannot substitute for private space. Most home buyers do not seem to want that much togetherness, and Reston's townhouses, which lacked front or backyards, sold too slowly.

It goes without saying that almost all the new suburbanites—and the developments built for them—will be white and middle-income, for, barring miracles in the housing industry and in Federal subsidies, the subdivisions of the seventies will be too expensive for any family earning less than about $7,500 (in 1967 dollars). Thus, even if suburbia were to be racially integrated, cost alone would exclude most nonwhites. Today, less than 5 per cent of New York State's suburban inhabitants are non-white, and many of them live in ghettos and slums in the small towns around which suburbia has developed.

Nevertheless, the minuscule proportion of nonwhite suburbanites will increase somewhat in the future, for, if the current affluence con-tinues, it will benefit a small percentage of Negroes and Puerto Ricans. Some of them will be able to move into integrated suburban communi-ties, but the majority will probably wind up in existing and new middle-class ghettos.

If urban employment is available, or if the ongoing industrialization of the South pushes more people off the land, poverty-stricken Negroes will continue to come to the cities, overcrowding and eventually enlarging the inner-city ghettos. Some of the better-off residents of these areas will move to "outer-city" ghettos, which can now be found in most American cities; for example, in Queens. And older suburbs like Yonkers and Mount Vernon will continue to lose some of their present residents and attract less affluent newcomers, as their housing, schools and other facilities age. As a result of this process, which affects suburbs as inevitably as city neighborhoods, some of their new inhabitants may be almost as poor as inner-city ghetto residents, so that more and more of the older suburbs will face problems of poverty and social pathology now thought to be distinctive to the city.

That further suburban growth is practically inevitable does not mean it is necessarily desirable, however. Many objections have been raised, some to suburbia itself, others to its consequences for the city. For example, ever since the rise of the postwar suburbs, cities have charged that suburban life is culturally and psychologically harmful for its residents, although many sociological studies, including my own, have shown that most suburbanites are happier and emotionally healthier than when they lived in the city. In addition, the critics have charged that suburbia desecrates valuable farm and recreation land, and that it results in "suburban" sprawl.

Suburbia undoubtedly reduces the supply of farm acreage, but America has long suffered from an oversupply of farmland, and I have never understood why allowing people to raise children where other people once raised potatoes or tomatoes desecrates the land. Usually, the criticism is directed to "ugly, mass-produced, look-alike little boxes," adding a class bias to the charges, as if people who can only afford mass-produced housing are not entitled to live where they please, or should stay in the city.

Suburban developments sometimes also rise on recreational land, although state and Federal funds are now available to save such land for public leisure-time use. Even so, I find it difficult to believe that child raising and the at-home recreation that goes on in a suburban house is a less worthy use of land than parks, which people only visit during part of the year. Furthermore, there is no reason why we cannot have both suburbia *and* parks, the latter built further out, with high-speed expressways and mass transit to bring them closer to visitors.

Suburban sprawl scatters residential developments over large areas because single-family houses take up so much more acreage than multiple dwellings. As a result, highways, transit systems, utility lines and sewers must be longer and therefore more expensive. These added costs are not a steep price for affluent suburbanites; they want low-density housing more than economy, and they do not care that sprawl looks ugly to the trained eye of the architect. There may even be somewhat less sprawl in the future, partly because of townhouse developments, partly because high land costs at the far edges of the suburbs may induce builders to fill up vacant land left in the existing suburban rings during earlier periods of residential construction. Moreover, the next wave of suburbia may finally generate sufficient political support for the building of high-speed mass transit systems, now languishing on the planners' drawing boards, to connect the parts of the sprawling area.

The harmful effects of suburbia on the city are a more important criticism. One charge, made ever since the beginning of suburbanization in the 19th century, is that the suburbs rob the city of its tax paying, civic-minded and culture-loving middle class. Actually, however, middle-class families are often a tax liability for the city; they demand and receive more services, particularly more schools, than their taxes pay for. Nor is there any evidence that they are more civic minded than their non-middle-class neighbors; they may be more enthusiastic joiners of civic organizations, but these tend to defend middle-class interests and not necessarily the public interest. Moreover, many people who live in the suburbs still exert considerable political influence in the city because of their work or their property holdings and see to it that urban power structures still put middle-class interests first, as slum organizations, whose demands for more antipoverty funds or public housing are regularly turned down by city hall, can testify.

The alleged effect of the suburbs on urban culture is belied by the vast cultural revival in the city which occurred at the same time the suburban exodus was in full swing. Actually, most suburbanites rarely used the city's cultural facilities even when they lived in the city, and the minority which did, continues to do so, commuting in without difficulty. Indeed, I suspect that over half the ticket buyers for plays, art movies, concerts and museums, particularly outside New York, are— and have long been—suburbanites. Besides, there is no reason why cultural institutions cannot, like banks, build branches in the suburbs, as they are beginning to do now. Culture is no less culture by being outside the city.

A much more valid criticism of suburbanization is its effect on class and racial segregation, for the fact that the suburbs have effectively zoned out the poor and the nonwhites is resulting in an ever-increasing class and racial polarization of city and suburb. In one sense, however, the familiar data about the increasing polarization are slightly misleading. In years past, when urban census statistics showed Negroes and whites living side by side, they were actually quite polarized socially. On New York's Upper West Side, for example, the big apartment buildings are *de facto* segregated for whites, while the rotting brownstones between them are inhabited by Negroes and Puerto Ricans. These blocks are integrated statistically or geographically, but not socially, particularly if white parents send their children to private schools.

Nor is suburbanization the sole cause of class and racial polarization; it is itself an effect of trends that have gone on inside the city as well, and not only in America. When people become more affluent and can choose where they want to live, they choose to live with people like themselves. What has happened in the last generation or two is that the opportunity of home buyers to live among compatible neighbors, an opportunity previously available only to the rich, has been extended to people in the middle- and lower-middle-income brackets. This fact does not justify either class or racial segregation, but it does suggest that the polarization resulting from affluence would have occurred even without suburbanization.

Class and racial polarization are harmful because they restrict freedom of housing choice to many people, but also because of the financial consequences for the city. For one thing, affluent suburbia exploits the financially bankrupt city; even when payroll taxes are levied, suburbanites do not pay their fair share of the city's cost in providing them with places of work, shopping areas and cultural facilities and with streets and utilities, maintenance, garbage removal and police protection for these facilities.

More important, suburbanites live in vest-pocket principalities where they can, in effect, vote to keep out the poor and the nonwhites and even the not very affluent whites.

As a result, the cities are in a traumatic financial squeeze. Their ever more numerous low-income residents pay fewer taxes but need costly municipal services, yet cities are taking in less in property taxes all the time, particularly as the firms that employ suburbanites and the shops that cater to them also move to the suburbs. Consequently, city costs rise at the same time as city income declines. To compound the injustice state and Federal politicians from suburban areas often vote against antipoverty efforts and other Federal funding activities that would relieve the city's financial troubles, and they also vote to prevent residential integration.

These trends are not likely to change in the years to come. In fact, if the present white affluence continues, the economic gap between the urban have-nots and the suburban haves will only increase, resulting on the one hand in greater suburban opposition to integration and to solving the city's problems, and on the other hand to greater discontent and more ghetto rebellions in the city. This in turn could result in a new white exodus from the city, which, unlike the earlier exodus, will be based almost entirely on racial fear, making suburbanites out of the middle-aged and older middle-class families who are normally reluctant to change communities at this age and working-class whites who cannot really afford a suburban house. Many of them will, however, stay put and oppose all efforts toward desegregation, as indicated even now by their violent reaction to integration marches in Milwaukee and Chicago, and to scattered-site public housing schemes which would locate projects in middle-income areas in New York and elsewhere.

Ultimately, these trends could create a vicious spiral, with more ghetto protest leading to more white demands, urban and suburban, for repression, resulting in yet more intense ghetto protests, and culminating eventually in a massive exodus of urban whites. If this spiral were allowed to escalate, it might well hasten the coming of the predominantly Negro city.

Today, the predominantly Negro city is still far off in the future, and the all-Negro city is unlikely. Although Washington, D.C.'s population is already about 60 per cent Negro, and several other cities, including Newark, Gary and Richmond, hover around the 50 per cent mark, recent estimates by the Center for Research in marketing suggest that only five of the country's 25 largest cities and 10 of the 130 cities with over 100,000 population will be 40 per cent or more Negro by 1970. (New York's Negro population was estimated at 18 per cent in 1964, although in Manhattan, the proportion of Negroes was 27 per cent and of Negroes and Puerto Ricans, 39 per cent.)

Moreover, these statistics only count the nighttime residential population, but who lives in the city is, economically and politically, a less relevant statistic than who works there, and the daytime working population of most cities is today, and will long remain, heavily and even predominantly white.

Still, to a suburbanite who may someday have to work in a downtown surrounded by a black city, the future may seem threatening. A century ago, native-born WASP's must have felt similarly, when a majority of the urban population consisted of foreign-born Catholics and Jews, to whom they attributed the same pejorative racial characteristics now attributed to Negroes. The city and the WASP's survived, of course, as the immigrants were incorporated into the American economy, and suburban whites would also survive.

Today's nonwhite poor play a more marginal role in the urban economy, however, raising the possibility that if the city became predominantly Negro, many private firms and institutions, which hire relatively few Negroes, would leave to build a new downtown elsewhere, a phenomenon already developing on a small scale in Arlington, Va., just outside Washington, D.C., and in Clayton, Mo., just outside St. Louis. If this trend became widespread, someday in the distant future only public agencies and low-wage industries, which boast integrated work forces, would remain in the present downtown area.

Many white suburbanites might welcome this development, for it would cut their remaining ties to the city altogether. Some Negroes might also prefer a predominantly black city, partly because they would be able to move into the good housing left by whites, and partly because they would take over political control of the city, thus promising the rank-and-file ghetto resident more sympathetic if not necessarily better treatment than he now gets from the white incumbents of city hall.

Nevertheless, the predominantly black city is undesirable, not only because it would create apartheid on a metropolitan scale, but because it would be a yet poorer city, less able to provide the needed public services to its low-income population and less likely to get the funds it would need from a predominantly white Federal Government.

Unfortunately, present governmental policies, local, state and Federal, are doing little to reverse the mounting class and racial polarization of city and suburb. Admittedly, the strong economic and cultural forces that send the middle classes into the suburbs and bring poor nonwhite people from the rural areas into the city in ever larger numbers are difficult to reverse even by the wisest government action.

Still, governmental policies have not been especially wise. The major efforts to slow down class and racial polarization have been these: legislation to achieve racial integration; programs to woo the white middle class back to the city; plans to establish unified metropolitan governments, encompassing both urban and suburban governmental units. All three have failed. None of the open housing and other integration laws now on the books have been enforced sufficiently to permit more than a handful of Negroes to live in the suburbs, and the more recent attempt to prevent the coming of the predominantly black city by enticing the white middle class back has not worked either.

The main technique used for this last purpose has been urban renewal, but there is no evidence—and, in fact, there have been no studies —to show that it has brought back a significant number of middle-class people. Most likely, it has only helped confirmed urbanites find better housing in the city. The attractions of suburbia are simply too persuasive for urban renewal or any other governmental program to succeed in bringing the middle class back to the city.

Even most older couples, whose children have left the suburban house empty, will not return; they have just paid off the mortgage and are not likely to give up a cheap and familiar house for an expensive city apartment, not to mention their gardens, or the friends they have made in the suburbs. At best, some may move to suburban apartments, but most American cities other than New York have too few downtown attractions to lure a sizable number of people back to the center.

Metropolitan government is, in theory, a good solution, for it would require the suburbs to contribute to solving the city's problems, but it has long been opposed by the suburbs for just this reason. They have felt that the improvements and economies in public services that could be obtained by organizing them on a metropolitan basis would be offset by what suburbanites saw as major disadvantages, principally the reduction of political autonomy and the loss of power to keep out the poor and the nonwhites.

The cities, which have in the past advocated metropolitan government, may become less enthusiastic as Negroes obtain greater political power. Since the metropolitan area is so predominantly white, urban Negroes would be outvoted every time in any kind of metropolitan government. Some metropolitanization may nevertheless be brought about by Federal planning requirements, for as Frances Piven and Richard Cloward point out in a recent New Republic article, several Federal grant programs, particularly for housing and community facilities, now require a metropolitan plan as a prerequisite for funding. Piven and Cloward suggest that these requirements could disfranchise the urban Negro, and it is of course always possible that a white urban-suburban coalition in favor of metropolitan government could be put together deliberately for precisely this purpose. Under such conditions, however, metropolitan government would only increase racial conflict and polarization.

What, then, can be done to eliminate this polarization? One partial solution is to reduce the dependence of both urban and suburban governments on the property tax, which reduces city income as the population becomes poorer, and forces suburbs to exclude low-income residents because their housing does not bring in enough tax money. If urban and suburban governments could obtain more funds from other sources, including perhaps the Federal income tax, parts of the proceeds of which would be returned to them by Washington, urban property owners would bear a smaller burden in supporting the city and might be less opposed to higher spending. Suburbanites would also worry less about their tax rate, and might not feel so impelled to bar less affluent newcomers, or to object to paying their share of the cost of using city services.

Class polarization can be reduced by rent- or price-supplement programs which would enable less affluent urbanites to pay the price of suburban living and would reduce the building and financing costs of housing. But such measures would not persuade the suburbs to let in Negroes; ultimately, the only solution is still across-the-board residential integration.

The outlook for early and enforceable legislation toward this end, however, is dim. Although election results have shown time and again that Northern white majorities will not vote for segregation, they will not vote for integration either. I cannot imagine many political bodies, Federal or otherwise, passing or enforcing laws that would result in significant amounts of suburban integration; they would be punished summarily at the next election.

For example, proposals have often been made that state and Federal governments should withdraw all subsidies to suburban communities and builders practicing *de facto* segregation, thus depriving the former of at least half their school operating funds, and the latter of Federal Housing Authority (F.H.A.) insurance on which their building plans depend. However desirable such legislation is, the chance that it would be passed is almost nil. One can also argue that Washington should offer grants-in-aid to suburban governments which admit low-income residents, but these grants would often be turned down. Many suburban municipalities would rather starve their public services instead, and the voters would support them all the way.

The best hope now is for judicial action. The New Jersey Supreme Court ruled some years back that builders relying on F.H.A. insurance had to sell to Negroes, and many suburban subdivisions in that state now have some Negro residents. The United States Supreme Court has just decided that it will rule on whether racial discrimination by large suburban developers is unconstitutional. If the answer turns out to be yes, the long, slow process of implementing the Court's decisions can at least begin.*

In the meantime, solutions that need not be tested at the ballot box must be advanced. One possibility is new towns, built for integrated populations with Federal support, or even by the Federal Government alone,

---

* EDITORS' NOTE: On June 18, 1968, the U.S. Supreme Court by a 7–2 vote ruled that an 1866 civil rights law barred racial discrimination in all sales and rentals of property. This ruling was handed down in the case, *Jones, et al.* v. *Mayer, et al.* See the New York *Times,* June 18, 1968, p. 1.

on land now vacant. Although hope springs eternal in American society that the problems of old towns can be avoided by starting from scratch, these problems seep easily across the borders of the new community. Even if rural governments can be persuaded to accept new towns in their bailiwicks and white residents could be attracted, such towns would be viable only if Federal grants and powers were used to obtain industries—and of a kind that would hire and train poorly skilled workers.

Greater emphasis should be placed on eliminating job discrimination in suburban work places, particularly in industries which are crying for workers, so that unions are less impelled to keep out nonwhite applicants. Mass transit systems should be built to enable city dwellers, black and white, to obtain suburban jobs without necessarily living in the suburbs.

Another and equally important solution is more school integration —for example, through urban-suburban educational parks that will build up integrated student enrollment by providing high-quality schooling to attract suburban whites, and through expansion of the busing programs that send ghetto children into suburban schools. Although white suburban parents have strenuously opposed busing their children into the city, several suburban communities have accepted Negro students who are bused in from the ghetto; for example, in the Boston area and in Westchester County.

And while the Supreme Court is deliberating, it would be worthwhile to persuade frightened suburbanites that, as all the studies so far have indicated, open housing would not mean a massive invasion of slum dwellers, but only the gradual arrival of a relatively small number of Negroes, most of them as middle-class as the whitest suburbanite. A massive suburban invasion by slum dwellers of any color is sheer fantasy. Economic studies have shown the sad fact that only a tiny proportion of ghetto residents can even afford to live in the suburbs. Moreover, as long as Negro workers lack substantial job security, they need to live near the center of the urban transportation system so that they can travel to jobs all over the city.

In addition, there are probably many ghetto residents who do not even want suburban integration now; they want the same freedom of housing choice as whites, but they do not want to be "dispersed" to the suburbs involuntarily. Unfortunately, no reliable studies exist to tell us where ghetto residents do want to live, but should they have freedom of choice, I suspect many would leave the slums for better housing and better neighborhoods outside the present ghetto. Not many would now choose predominantly white areas, however, at least not until living among whites is psychologically and socially less taxing, and until integration means more than just assimilation to white middle-class ways.

Because of the meager success of past integration efforts, many civil-rights leaders have given up on integration and are now demanding the rebuilding of the ghetto. They argue persuasively that residential integration has so far and will in the future benefit only a small number of affluent Negroes, and that if the poverty-stricken ghetto residents are to be helped soon, that help must be located in the ghetto. The advocates of integration are strongly opposed. They demand that all future housing must be built outside the ghetto, for anything else would just perpetuate segregation. In recent months, the debate between the two positions has become bitter, each side claiming only its solution has merit.

Actually there is partial truth on both sides. The integrationists are correct about the long-term dangers of rebuilding the ghetto; the ghetto rebuilders (or separatists) are correct about the short-term failure of integration. But if there is little likelihood that the integrationists' demands will be carried out soon, their high idealism in effect sentences ghetto residents to remaining in slum poverty.

Moreover, there is no need to choose between integration and rebuilding, for both policies can be carried out simultaneously. The struggle for integration must continue, but if the immediate prospects for success on a large scale are dim, the ghetto must be rebuilt in the meantime.

The primary aim of rebuilding, however, should not be to rehabilitate houses or clear slums, but to raise the standard of living of ghetto residents. The highest priority must be a massive antipoverty program which will, through the creation of jobs, more effective job-training schemes, the negative income tax, children's allowances and other measures, raise ghetto families to the middle-income level, using outside resources from government and private enterprise and inside participation in the planning and decision-making. Also needed are a concerted effort at quality compensatory education for children who cannot attend integrated schools; federally funded efforts to improve the quality of ghetto housing, as well as public services; some municipal decentralization to give ghetto residents the ability to plan their own communities and their own lives, and political power so that the ghetto can exert more influence in behalf of its demands.

If such programs could extend the middle-income standard of living to the ghetto in the years to come, residential integration might well be achieved in subsequent generations. Much of the white opposition to integration is based on stereotypes of Negro behavior—some true, some false—that stem from poverty rather than from color, and many of the fears about Negro neighbors reflect the traditional American belief that poor people will not live up to middle-class standards. Moreover, even lack of enthusiasm for integration among ghetto residents is a result of poverty; they feel, rightly or not, that they must solve their economic problems before they can even think about integration.

If ghetto poverty were eliminated, the white fears—and the Negro ones—would begin to disappear, as did the pejorative stereotypes which earlier Americans held about the "inferior races"—a favorite 19th-century term for the European immigrants—until they achieved affluence. Because attitudes based on color differences are harder to overcome than those based on cultural differences, the disappearance of anti-Negro stereotypes will be slower than that of anti-immigrant stereotypes. Still, once color is no longer an index of poverty and lower-class status, it will cease to arouse white fears, so that open-housing laws can be enforced more easily and eventually may even be unnecessary. White suburbanites will not exclude Negroes to protect their status or their property values, and many, although not necessarily all, Negroes will choose to leave the ghetto.

Morally speaking, any solution that does not promise immediate integration is repugnant, but moral dicta will neither persuade suburbanites to admit low-income Negroes into their communities, nor entice urbane suburbanites to live near low-income Negroes in the city. Instead of seeking to increase their middle-income population by importing suburban whites, cities must instead make their poor residents middle-income. The practical solution, then, is to continue to press for residential integration, but also to eliminate ghetto poverty immediately, in order to achieve integration in the future, substituting government anti-poverty programs for the private economy which once created the jobs and incomes that helped poorer groups escape the slums in past generations. Such a policy will not only reduce many of the problems of the city, which are ultimately caused by the poverty of its inhabitants, but it will assure the ultimate disappearance of the class and racial polarization of cities and suburbs.

There is only one hitch: This policy is not likely to be adopted. Although white voters and their elected officials are probably more favorable to ghetto rebuilding than to integration, they are, at the moment, not inclined or impelled to support even the former. They lack inclination to rebuild the ghetto because they do not want to pay the taxes that would raise ghetto incomes; they are not so impelled because neither the problems of the ghetto nor even its rebellions touch their lives directly and intimately. So far, most of them still experience the ghetto only on television. Until many white Americans are directly affected by what goes on in the ghetto, they will probably support nothing more than a minuscule antipoverty program and a token effort toward racial integration.

# PART THREE

# Interdependence and Decentralization in the Metropolis

Parts One and Two described the metropolis as a collection of conflicts and potential conflicts based on social heterogeneity. Also stressed was the fact that areas, as well as individuals, are differentiated and specialized. Here two implications of specialization and differentiation are considered: demands for cooperative and area-wide approaches to urban ills, based on the interdependence of people and sub-areas, and demands for autonomy based on differences among people and sub-areas. That urbanization means differentiation, and differentiation means pressures for *both* centralization and decentralization, has not been sufficiently emphasized by students of the metropolis.

Interdependence and differentiation are opposite sides of the same coin. No elaborate argument is needed to demonstrate this point. Entire sections of the city and suburbs are devoted to particular industrial and commercial activities. Whole neighborhoods are populated by one racial, ethnic, or class group. Residential suburbs provide part of the central city's work force; the suburbs rely on the city for many of life's necessities; the central business district relies on the entire region for customers; and a massive transfer of persons for work, play, and shopping is a daily occurrence.

Looking at differentiation leads some observers to stress interdependence and the "metropolitan-wide" character of problems. Because such problems as planning, transportation, and clean water are common problems that cross local governmental boundaries, they suggest common, metropolitan-wide solutions. Since the components of the metropolis are interdependent everyone has a stake in urban ills—including the fate of the core city. If the core city sinks, the argument goes, the whole metropolis will be swamped.

However, many people are not interested in cooperative efforts to save core cities, or in metropolitan-wide solutions to problems. They are interested in preserving their own style of life by separating them-selves from other people. They value separatist enclaves and seek to maintain and enhance them. Often they are heard giving voice to the political and social values threatened by centralization, such as local self-government, popular participation, living with one's own kind, keeping up property values, and living one's own life style.

Of course, many suburbanites already enjoy governmentally au-tonomous, socially homogeneous communities. Few city residents do. Still fewer central city blacks do. The papers below indicate that city blacks also value community autonomy, and—like white suburbanites—are especially concerned about schools. Furthermore, they invoke the same symbols of local control, freedom, and popular rule.

Given the heterogeneity and diversity of the metropolis, it may be that conflict can only be managed by allowing and encouraging de-centralization—in central cities as well as suburbs, among blacks as well as whites, poor as well as affluent. Perhaps government will have to allow city residents a certain amount of autonomy. The growing power of ghetto blacks—if only to embarrass and disrupt—may never match the power of white suburbanites; but it may be sufficient to wrest a large measure of autonomy from white government. Decentralization within cities, not just outside, may be the only way to manage conflict in the increasingly diverse metropolis.

This section is introduced by a general discussion of metropolitan problems, social and economic as well as governmental. Also noted is the interdependence of people in an urban setting. The next two papers illustrate the metropolitan-wide approach to problem-solving. The first stresses area-wide tax administration, and the second details efforts to get area-wide transportation facilities in Baltimore and Seattle.

The next two articles illustrate interdependence in a different way. President Johnson's message to Congress recommending the Demon-stration Cities Program is based on the view that a lot of people, besides those who live there, have a stake in the future of central cities. As the cities decay, we all suffer, and because we do we should support govern-mental spending to rescue the cities, especially in housing. James Q. Wilson's "The War on Cities" critically evaluates the Demonstration Cities Program. Wilson suggests that the problem is more people than physical structures, and that therefore government should emphasize education, health, and police protection.

The last four papers illustrate the growing pressures for decen-tralization within cities, and the resistance to those pressures. Moyni-han's well-known "Maximum Feasible Misunderstanding" shows that OEO community action programs designed to ensure the participation of the poor have led to retaliation by the white community and government. The Sexton and Schrag papers present the case against existing schools for their class bias and suggest the urgent need for schools that are relevant to the poor and black. In a similar vein Marilyn Gittel recounts the struggle for community control of schools in a black section of New York City and makes the case for community control.

# The Web of Metropolitan Problems

## JOHN C. BOLLENS
## HENRY J. SCHMANDT

Contemporary middle-aged Americans have successively witnessed the New Deal of the Roosevelt era, the Fair Deal of the Eisenhower period, the New Frontier of the Kennedy days, and more recently the Great Society of the Johnson presidency. Although the rhetoric of promise has far exceeded the attainment, they have seen notable strides made in social legislation and in the enlargement of the opportunity structure for many in the society. At the same time, however, they have also witnessed rank discrimination in housing and employment on the basis of race, civil disturbances and riots, deep internal divisions and even violence over United States military involvment in Vietnam, a growing unrest among the youth, the poor, and the racial minorities, and an intensification of urban problems in general. They have listened to optimistic prophecies but increasingly they have heard warnings that the nation's large cities and metropolises are on the verge of catastrophe and doomed, as Thomas Hobbes' man in the state of nature, to a "poor, nasty, brutish and short life" unless immediate and massive action is taken to redeem them.

Current events, the outbreaks of violence in particular, have awakened some concern among the citizenry, but blessed with unprecedented prosperity—as a majority are—they are reluctant to believe that major change is necessary or desirable or that the problems are as bad as portrayed. To many of them, only simplistic solutions—better law enforcement, for example—are required to eliminate the most obvious difficulties. Whether the problems are as alarming as some would have us believe or a natural and inevitable by-product of a technological society is not the question. Problems of major import do exist—no one denies this fact—and they are affecting in important ways the quality and potential of urban life and the environment in which man pursues his daily tasks. The individual who wants to behave like a metropolitan ostrich will find little sand in which to bury his head. Even the most callous city dweller cannot fail to sense the changes that are sweeping over and around him, impinging upon numerous aspects of his life, affecting his activities and goals, and conditioning his behavior.

Problems are an integral part of this environment, the common lot of men everywhere and at all times and the inevitable concomitants of living together. These problems, moreover, are continually changing just as the community itself is constantly, if slowly, evolving into new forms. What constitutes a minor source of irritation today may be a major issue tomorrow. Nothing is more certain than that if we solve one troublesome difficulty, another will soon appear in its stead. Thus we may drain a swamp to get rid of the mosquitos only to find that the water table drops because rain is no longer being absorbed into the earth. Or we may speed up production by automating the factories only to discover that we have an unemployment problem on our hands. Or we may build massive expressways or freeways to move people swiftly in and out of the central business district only to learn that we have created a severe parking crisis. We cannot expect to find the total answer for our rapidly urbanizing communities, for the future is never finished. Nor can we ever expect to have enough resources and enough agreement on goals to make everybody happy. Yet we can and must act vigorously in seeking solutions to our most pressing problems and in correcting the inequities and injustices which exist in the society.

## The Web of Problems

Until the civil disturbances of the mid-1960s came as a rude awakening, most political scientists, planners, and community influentials tended to limit the discussion of metropolitan problems to those of a service nature. Written in large print in their catalogue were such items as water supply, sewage disposal, air pollution, and traffic control. This emphasis on the service role of the metropolis finds expression in the notion that local government is a business institution to be structured and administered like a private corporation. Such being the case, the most important metropolitan task to many people was to organize the bureaucratic machinery so that it could furnish the necessary services in an efficient, economical, and apolitical manner.

Accompanying this preoccupation with service problems was a heavy emphasis on the city as a physical plant. Paul Ylvisaker, then director of the Ford Foundation's public affairs division, called attention to this fact when he said:

> Examine the literature on the city and the substance of action programs and you will find them dominated by a concern with physical plant. The going criteria of urban success are the beauty and solvency of the city's real properties, not the condition of the people who flow through them. As a result, the civilizing and ennobling function of the city, mainly its job of turning second-class newcomers into first-class citizens, is downgraded into pious pronouncements and last-place priorities. We despair of our wasting city property, and count the costs of urban renewal in building values. These are nothing compared to the wasting resources of the human beings who get trapped in these aging buildings, and the value of their lost contribution to their own and the world's society.[1]

The problems of service and of physical development are not to be minimized. Nor is the efficient and economical operation of the governmental machinery to be denied as a desirable goal. What is to be avoided, whether by central city or suburban residents, is the tendency to regard such matters as exhausting the list of locally relevant issues or as occupying first priority on the civic agenda. We can put water in the taps, dispose of the waste, develop an outstanding fire department, build countless miles of expressway to accommodate the automobile, and bulldoze slums, yet leave untouched some of the most critical issues facing the urban complex. What can be done to provide adequate housing and equal opportunities for all members of the metropolitan community? How can racial strife be mitigated and minority groups, particularly the Negro, be assimilated fully into the life of the city and its environs? What changes can be made in the educational system to make it more relevant to the needs of modern urban society?

One might argue that social and economic problems of this nature and magnitude lie outside the sphere of local government and cannot be solved by action at the municipal or metropolitan level. Some of the more conservative would even maintain that their resolution lies primarily in private hands, by business, labor unions, social agencies, property owners, and people acting individually and through their voluntary associations. Arguments of this kind are valid up to a point. Obviously, a problem such as poverty or discrimination is national in scope and cannot be effectively dealt with solely by local means. Even the control of crime and delinquency, while basically a community func-

---

[1] Address to the World Traffic Engineering Conference, Washington, D.C., August 21, 1961.

tion, is affected by national conditions such as poverty, unemployment, and general societal attitudes.

But whether these problems are "national" or not, their location is principally in the metropolis. Local government cannot possibly escape involvement with them, for they are part and parcel of the community environment. Urban renewal is a case in point. Even though the national government furnishes the lion's share of the money, it is local authorities which must design and initiate the project, resolve the differences among competing interests, and administer the program. The same is true of race relations. Constitutional and statutory provisions at the national and state levels may bar racial segregation in public schools and discrimination in housing and employment, but the full enforcement of these rights will depend upon the active cooperation of local officials and private groups.

## Whose Responsibility?

Some myopic defenders of suburbia go so far as to say that the major socioeconomic problems of urban society are problems of the central city, not those of the total metropolitan community. Where but within the boundaries of the core city, they ask, does one find an abundance of racial strife, crime, blighted housing, and welfare recipients? Superficially, their logic may seem sound since they are correct about the prevelant spatial location of these maladies. Although crime and other social problems exist in suburbia, their magnitude and extent are substantially less than in the central city. But why in an interdependent metropolitan community should the responsibility of suburbanites be any less than that of the central city dwellers? Certainly no one would think of contending that residents of higher income neighborhoods within the corporate limits of the city should be exempt from responsibility for its less fortunate districts. What logic then is there in believing that neighborhoods on the other side of a legal line can wash their hands of social disorders in these sections?

Low-income areas are unfortunately a part of every large urban complex. Without the workers that these neighborhoods house, industrial production would be curtailed and the service trades seriously crippled. It was not too long ago, for example, that factories in the northern cities were conducting active recruiting campaigns for low-income southern workers. Automation may be reducing this demand, but it has not stopped the migration of dispossessed rural dwellers, also victims of the new technology, into our urban centers. In fact, it would be difficult to find any industrial community that did not have its concentrations of the poor and underprivileged. These concentrations most often happen to be in the central city simply because it is here that cheap and available housing is located. Were the reverse true, as it is in some smaller metropolitan areas, these groups would be found in the suburban ring. No large community can hope to reap the benefits of industrialization and urbanization and yet escape their less desirable by-products. The suburbanite and the central city resident share responsibility for the total community and its problems. Neither can run fast enough to escape involvement.

## The "Deteriorating" City

In 1953, economist Miles Colean wrote a book for the Twentieth Century Fund which he titled *Renewing Our Cities*. The term "urban renewal" caught on and became the symbolic designation for the efforts of public agencies and private groups to eliminate slums and curb the spread of blight in American cities. Urban renewal is not a modern invention; only its technical aspects are. Man has been engaged in the construction and reconstruction of cities since antiquity. Athens, for example, was rebuilt under Pericles, Rome under Augustus, and Paris under Napoleon III, and one might even say with tongue in cheek, New York City under Moses—that is, Robert Moses. Renewal, however, is not always so spectacular or dramatic, yet it is constantly taking place in one fashion or another regardless of whether we are aware of the fact. The city we live in today, if not destroyed or abandoned in the interim, will be completely rebuilt—renewed if you please—for better or worse within the next 100 years.

A city or a metropolitan area is not like frozen sculpture. It is forever undergoing change, being added to and subtracted from, shaped and reshaped like pliable clay, sometimes with deliberate intent, more often without conscious design. The visitor to any major American city today—and many of lesser size, such as New Haven, Connecticut—is invariably amazed at the physical transformations that are taking place. In New York, Chicago, Philadelphia, St. Louis, Detroit—and the list could go on—large sections of the community have been razed. This planned destruction is being followed by rebuilding, in a few cases at a feverish pace, in the others more slowly and even hesitantly.

Governmental efforts at urban renewal in the United States have been subjected to a barrage of criticism in recent years from both conservative and liberal sources. Economists have questioned the economic arguments advanced in behalf of the program, and one of their number has even called for its abolition on the grounds that the private market could eliminate the nation's housing problem and clear its slums at less social cost.[2] Other critics charge that redevelopment authorities have been more responsive to the desires of central business district interests than the housing needs of low-income groups and have thus created new slums by uprooting families from old ones without providing adequate relocation. Still others object to the disruption of "viable" although poor neighborhoods in the name of redevelopment. Joined to these voices of protest are those of individuals and groups who have become alarmed at the "human impact" of renewal projects and the emphasis on physical rehabilitation to the seeming exclusion of social consequences. Finally, increasing resistance has come from those most affected, the residents of the neighborhoods slated for renewal, who rightfully feel they should have a voice in the determination of their fate.

*Housing*

The extent of substandard housing in metropolitan areas has been the subject of considerable dispute. Martin Anderson, author of the highly controversial *Federal Bulldozer,* uses census data to show that such housing in central cities of over 100,000 declined from 19 percent to 11 percent during the decade of the 1950s and can be expected to drop to 4 percent by 1970.[3] In attacking these findings, a staff member of the National Association of Housing and Redevelopment Officials charged Anderson with distorting the figures by failing to take into account definitional changes and post-census enumerations which reveal that no significant reduction in the amount of substandard dwellings took place over the decade.[4] Other observers point out that while the overall proportion of inadequate units in SMSAs has declined due to the large amount of new suburban construction, at least one-sixth to one-quarter of the population in most of the large central cities is inadequately housed.[5] Regardless of who is right in this numbers game, a great many American families, disproportionately nonwhite, still reside in substandard dwelling units or unsuitable living environments despite the nation's much publicized opulence.

Universally condemned as slums, the areas where most of this housing is located serve as the home of the poor and the deprived, those

---

[2] Martin Anderson, *The Federal Bulldozer: A Critical Analysis of Urban Renewal, 1949–1962* (Cambridge: The M.I.T. Press, 1964).

[3] "Fiasco of Urban Renewal," *Harvard Business Review,* 43 (January–February, 1965), 6–21.

[4] Robert P. Groberg, "Urban Renewal Realistically Reappraised," *Law and Contemporary Problems,* XXX (Winter, 1965), 212–229.

[5] See, for example, William Grigsby, *Housing Markets and Public Policy* (Philadelphia: University of Pennsylvania Press, 1963).

not integrated into the mainstream of community life because of lack of equal educational and employment opportunities, color barriers, and social problems. Slums, however, are nothing new; they have been with us ever since the middle-class families abandoned the task of rebuilding the original areas of settlement and moved outward in search of better neighborhoods and better homes. Boston, Chicago, New York, San Francisco, St. Louis, and other large communities had their slums long before the wave of southern migrants began to enter the industrial cities of the North and West.

Blight and substandard housing went unrecognized in public policy until the 1930s when interest was generated in a wide range of social legislation. The first efforts of the national government in this field embodied the curious combination of goals—economic pump-priming and social amelioration—that characterized many of the New Deal programs. To stimulate the home building industry and at the same time clear away some of the worst slums, Congress enacted the Housing Act of 1937 authorizing loans and subsidies to local agencies for construction of public housing. The law required cities as a condition of the grant to eliminate dilapidated dwelling units equal in number to those constructed with federal aid. This was a cautious beginning, but the severe housing shortage which followed World War II fanned wider public interest in the problem and led to the passage of the more comprehensive Housing Act of 1949.[6]

In passing the new legislation, Congress made explicit its purpose: "a decent home and a suitable living environment for every American family." To accomplish this objective, two major components were included in the act, one pertaining to slum clearance or renewal, the other to public housing. The first (the famous Title I) provided for grants to local redevelopment agencies covering two-thirds of the loss involved in acquiring, clearing, and disposing of blighted areas at a marked-down price for public or private purposes; the second authorized aid to localities for the construction of 810,000 low-rent housing units. Despite strong opposition to the latter program, the bill passed largely because the various interests, like the blind men feeling the elephant, made entirely different assumptions about the purpose of the legislation.[7] Welfare

---

[6] The history of urban renewal legislation is outlined in Ashley A. Foard and Hilbert Fefferman, "Federal Urban Renewal Legislation," *Law and Contemporary Problems*, XXV Autumn, 1960), 635–684. A perceptive analysis of the program is found in Scott Greer, *Urban Renewal and American Cities* (Indianapolis: Bobbs-Merrill, 1965).

[7] See in this connection Catherine Bauer Wurster, "Redevelopment: A Misfit in the Fifties," in Coleman Woodbury (ed.), *The Future of Cities and Urban Redevelopment* (Chicago: University of Chicago Press, 1953), pp. 7–25.

groups viewed it as an enlargement of the power to get rid of bad living conditions. Businessmen saw it as a means of bolstering waning property values in central areas. Central city officials looked upon it as a device for bolstering the tax base and luring back some of the expatriates, the consumers and taxpayers of substance who had fled to the greener pastures of suburbia.

Two trends have been discernible in the evolution of the housing and renewal program since the enactment of the 1949 act, one relating to philosophy, the other to emphasis. At the time of its passage, Senator Robert Taft and other sponsors of the bill made it clear that the program should be housing-oriented as distinguished from the betterment of cities and urban life in general. This concept was vigorously questioned by representatives of the planning profession who argued that the major objective should be redevelopment in accord with a general plan for the entire community. In such a plan, slums would be treated as but one important phase of urban blight and housing as but one important segment of renewal. Objections to the housing orientation of the act also came from economic interests and city officials who wanted primary emphasis placed on the reconstruction of blighted business and industrial properties rather than the dwelling needs of the poor.

In reality, subsequent congressional and local action has moved in both of these directions despite the continued reaffirmation of a decent home for every American family as the principal goal of urban renewal. The 1954 revision of the Housing Act, for example, embodied the philosophy of the planners by requiring cities, as a condition of federal aid, to formulate a workable program or plan of action for meeting the overall problems of slums and of community development generally. The 1959 legislation went a step further by authorizing funds for the preparation of long-range community renewal programs (CRP) with respect to all of the urban renewal needs of a city. Along with these modifications, the provision in the original act limiting aid to residential projects only was amended in 1954 to permit 10 percent of federal capital grant funds to be used for nonresidential projects, a proportion that was later tripled. These trends are not necessarily undesirable; in fact, the increasing attention to overall planning and the economic base of the community makes sense in terms of general city development. The misfortune is that, amid all of this, the housing needs of low-income families somehow or other became lost in the shuffle.

## Urban Renewal

Although the arguments for urban renewal are not necessarily compatible, they reflect the different assumptions on which the program was originally inaugurated. If the principal objective is to bolster the tax base of the community, efforts should be directed toward developing the cleared land at its highest income-producing use. The fate of the people who are to be relocated becomes secondary in this case. If, on the other hand, the primary and overriding purpose is to provide better housing for the low-income and underprivileged classes, the economic argument must give way to the social. In most communities, the former goal has prevailed. Private investors are seldom interested in building low-income housing on renewal sites since the land is too expensive, even with the federal and local write-down.

Whatever the motives of those who have promoted urban renewal, the economic rather than the social or moral appeal has sustained the program. Given this emphasis, it is understandable that the plight of low-income families has not been of high priority in the renewal plans of municipalities. Solving the housing problems of the poor does little to solve the financial problems of the cities while redevelopment for other purposes presumably does. Blighted areas have thus generally been re-built for new occupants and not for the slum dwellers themselves. Only a small fraction of the total construction on renewal sites has been de-voted to public housing. Most of the new buildings are high-rise apart-ments for upper-income families. This fact has prompted the charge that the program has actually made housing conditions worse for the poorer residents of cities by destroying more low-cost dwelling units than it has created.

Growing public resistance to large-scale residential demolition has caused the emphasis in urban renewal to shift from wholesale clearance to the rehabilitation and conservation of existing structures and neigh-borhoods. The underlying philosophy of this approach is to help the residents of affected areas help themselves through a combination of governmental action and private effort. Local governments are to use their powers in upgrading and stabilizing the neighborhood environment through public improvements, creating additional new open space, re-ducing heavy traffic on residential streets, providing new playgrounds and other recreation facilities, and stepping up enforcement of minimum housing standards and zoning. At the same time individual owners are to be encouraged to improve their property by making liberal govern-ment-insured financing available to them.

Rehabilitation and conservation are obviously applicable only in neighborhoods where a majority of the buildings are still structurally sound even though shabby and in need of repairs. They cannot work ef-fectively in areas where poverty and social disorganization are rampant or where the residents are contemplating flight because of threatened invasion by racial minorities or evicted slum dwellers. More basically, these devices are not the answers to the housing needs of low-income families. For if successful, they raise the price of the property and its rental value in many cases to a point beyond the resources of the poorer members of the community. Rent supplements for the latter in which government pays a portion of the rent can be particularly helpful in bringing rehabilitated housing within the means of this group. Congress enacted such a law in 1965 but the appropriation accompanying it was minuscule. Lack of public support for any form of shelter subsidy to low-income families remains an obstacle to anything beyond token action in this direction.[8]

By the end of 1968, approximately 1550 urban renewal projects in over 1000 communities had been approved for execution by the Department of Housing and Urban Development (HUD) and its predecessor agencies. Less than $3 billion in federal funds had actually been disbursed since the inception of the program in 1949, with another $4.5 billion committed for projects under way or in the planning stage. This is a remarkably small amount for the national government to invest in the redevelopment of cities, particularly in comparison to the $24 billion spent on the lunar program.

*Relocation*

A strongly criticized aspect of urban renewal has been the relocation of families uprooted by slum clearance projects. For the most part, relocation was initially ignored or not considered a problem by local authorities. It was assumed that many of the displaced would be able to upgrade their shelter through the filtering-down process as higher income families vacated older properties for the new construction in redevelopment sites. And for the remainder, a minimum of public housing could be provided. The question of how relocated families make out in meeting their shelter needs is difficult to answer. According to the periodic reports of the Urban Renewal Administration, a high proportion of them end up in "locally certified standard housing," but these figures are contradicted by several studies which indicate that most move to neighborhoods similar

---

[8] According to the rent supplement program authorized by the Housing and Urban Development Act of 1965, those eligible are required to pay 25 percent of their income for rent. The difference between this amount and the full market rent for the dwelling unit represents the amount of the supplement. It is well to keep in mind that many of the problems which have plagued public housing generally, such as increasing nonwhite occupancy, site selection, and segregation of low-income families, are also applicable to the rent supplement program. See in this connection Irving H. Welfeld, "Rent Supplements and the Subsidy Dilemma," *Law and Contemporary Problems,* XXXII (Summer, 1967), 465–481.

to those from which they were cleared, usually on the fringe of renewal projects. One study in the early 1960s, for example, revealed that roughly 60 percent of the relocated families in the forty-one cities examined were still living in substandard conditions.[9] A Bureau of the Census survey in 1964, on the other hand, lent support to the URA statistics by showing that 94 percent of the families displaced during the summer of that year found standard housing. This, however, was a single survey and its findings have also been disputed.[10]

Whatever the validity of these various figures, relocation has been one of the weak features of the renewal program, a fact acknowledged by federal officials.[11] There is general agreement in the studies that those families which have succeeded in moving to better housing have done so at the cost of substantially higher rent.[12] Many of the poor, however, cannot afford such an additional expenditure. If the nation is to assure standard housing for low-income families displaced by renewal projects or living in slums, it must follow one of two paths (or a combination of them). The first is to provide the disadvantaged with sufficient income—in the form of family allowances, minimum income guarantees, rent supplements, or similar aids—to enable them to compete for housing in the private market; the other is to make sufficient public housing available to them. Up to the present the former course (with the exception of the timid beginning in rent subsidization) has been rejected and the latter followed but in a totally inadequate fashion. At the end of 1968, nearly two decades after the passage of the 1949 act, only about 700,000 public housing units were in operation and another 50,000 under construction.

Aside from the question of low income, one need not search far to find the major impediment to relocation. Over 70 percent of the people

---

[9] Harry W. Reynolds, Jr., "Population Displacement in Urban Renewal," *American Journal of Economics and Sociology,* XXII (January, 1963), 113–128. See also Peter Marris, "The Social Implications of Urban Redevelopment," *Journal of the American Institute of Planners,* XXVIII (August, 1962), 180–186; and Alvin L. Schorr, *Slums and Social Insecurity* (Washington: U.S. Government Printing Office, 1963).

[10] The census survey is reported in Housing and Home Finance Agency, *The Housing of Relocated Families* (Washington: March, 1965). The findings of this survey are questioned by Chester Hartman in a commentary in *Journal of the American Institute of Planners,* XXXI (November, 1965), 340–344.

[11] For example, Robert Weaver, former Secretary of the Department of Housing and Urban Development, frankly acknowledged the weaknesses of the relocation program, pointing out, however, that much of the criticism relates to conditions which the government has moved to correct. See his *Dilemmas of Urban Renewal* (Cambridge: Harvard University Press, 1965).

[12] Nathaniel Lichfield, "Relocation: The Impact on Housing Welfare," *Journal of the American Institute of Planners,* XXVII (August, 1961), 199–203.

who have been forced out of their homes by Title I clearance projects have been nonwhites. Racial discrimination has greatly complicated the task of finding satisfactory dwelling units for the displaced blacks in the private market and has significantly curtailed the expansion of public housing.[13] The latter is well demonstrated by the eagerness with which local officials have embraced federally-subsidized housing for the aged, authorized by Congress in 1961, while showing a distinct coolness toward projects for low-income families generally.[14] (In 1968, for example, over 100,000 low-rent units for senior citizens were under construction.) As one observer trenchantly explains it: "Housing for the elderly taps the only remaining reservoir of poor people who are also white, orderly, and middle-class in behavior. Neighborhoods which will not tolerate a ten-story tower packed with Negro mothers on AFDC [aid to families with dependent children] might tolerate a tower of sweet but impoverished old folks." [15]

*Recent Trends*

In signing the 1968 Housing and Urban Redevelopment Act, President Lyndon Johnson called it "the most farsighted, the most comprehensive, the most massive housing program in all American history." The act, obviously a reflection of the concern over the disturbances in many of the nation's cities, reaffirmed the place of housing as the major component in urban redevelopment and gave the highest priority to meeting the shelter needs of the underprivileged. It set a ten-year goal of 6 million new and rehabilitated homes for those in this category, specifying that a majority of the units provided in future urban renewal projects for residential purposes must be for low- and moderate-income families.

The act contains a number of interesting features which constitute at least a partial answer to some of the criticism directed at earlier programs. These include: (1) subsidies to reduce mortgage interest rates for lower-income families to assist them in purchasing homes; (2) credit assistance for low- and moderate-income families who do not qualify for FHA mortgage insurance; (3) a relaxation of mortgage insurance re-

---

[13] For a refutation of the myth that the entrance of Negroes into a neighborhood lowers property values—an obstacle to relocation as well as to the solution of the Negro housing problem generally—see Luigi Laurenti, *Property Values and Race* (Berkeley and Los Angeles: University of California Press, 1960).

[14] For a review of public housing and the controversy over it, see William H. Ledbetter, Jr., "Public Housing: A Social Experiment Seeks Acceptance," *Law and Contemporary Problems,* XXXII (Summer, 1967), 490–527.

[15] Laurence M. Friedman, "Public Housing and the Poor: An Overview," *California Law Review,* 54 (May, 1966), 654.

quirements for housing in older, declining neighborhoods; (4) grants to local housing agencies to furnish tenant services (such as counseling on household and money management, housekeeping, and child care; and advice as to resources for job training and placement, education, welfare, and health) with preference to be given to programs providing for maximum tenant participation in the development and operation of such services; (5) a bar on the construction of high-rise public housing projects for families with children unless no practical alternative exists; and (6) creation of a government-chartered nonprofit corporation, known as the National Home Ownership Foundation, to assist public and private organizations in initiating, developing, and conducting programs to expand home ownership and housing opportunities for lower-income families.

The 1968 law, in short, embodies several key concepts indicating changes in the direction of federal housing policy. First of all, it enlarges opportunities for the less affluent members of society to own homes by modifying the traditional business-management and banking philosophy which has long dominated such governmental finance agencies as the Federal Housing Administration and the Federal National Mortgage Association. Second, it specifically espouses the concept of citizen involvement initially enunciated in the anti-poverty legislation by making it clear that lower-income families are to be involved as participants as well as recipients in housing assistance programs. Third, it lends further support to the "total approach" philosophy to slum-area needs first embodied in the Model Cities law.[16] Finally, the 1968 act, for the first time in the country's history, makes housing an element of national economic planning, requiring the President to report annually on progress in this field and establishing a National Advisory Commission on Low Income Housing.

Housing, of course, is only one aspect of a much larger picture. Many of the families in blighted or slum areas are plagued by other problems besides poor living quarters. Merely moving the residents of these neighborhoods into better dwelling units will not cure the other social and physical ills which beset them. Much of the disillusionment over public housing has been caused by the failure to recognize that a change in dwelling status does not automatically lead to changes in the attitudes or behavior of low-income families or inculcate them with middle-class values. Some empirical findings, in fact, question the relationship be-

---

[16] The Model Cities Act of 1966 provides for technical and financial assistance to enable communities to carry out comprehensive attacks on the total range of urban problems—social, economic, and physical—in selected disadvantaged areas of the city through coordinated federal, state, local, and private efforts.

tween poor housing and social or physical maladies.[17] Yet whatever this association may be, decent housing is at minimum critical to providing a proper setting for an attack on the other related problems of poverty and deprivation.

## The Problem of Race

Many of the most acute social problems of metropolitan areas including housing, poverty, unemployment, and education revolve around the racial question. By virtually every socioeconomic indicator, the wellbeing of urban nonwhites ranks substantially below that of whites. Compared to the latter, they have on the average lower incomes, more substandard dwellings, greater unemployment, less education and training, and more families on welfare. The last two decades have brought material gains to minority people but they have not narrowed significantly the gap between black and white or eliminated the crippling discrimination based on the color of one's skin.

The Negro—and in lesser numbers the Puerto Rican and Mexican-American—is the latest ethnic migrant to the cities. Earlier groups of ethnic newcomers, such as the Irish, Polish, and Italians, achieved the goals of better housing, improved neighborhoods, adequate schools, and occupational mobility once they had demonstrated adherence to the dominant culture and secured the economic rewards offered by the system. The case has been far different for the Negro. Even when he has succeeded in attaining middle-class status, as a minority of blacks has done, discriminatory practices by the white-dominated society have continued to deny him the acceptance and social recognition to which his income and behavior qualify him. The attitudes and actions of the majoritarian society toward Negroes as a whole have left the nation with a legacy of unredressed grievances, bitter frustrations, and deep alienation in the black ghettos of the metropolises. And for a disproportionate number of nonwhites they have created almost insurmountable barriers to the development of individual abilities that would enable them to escape from their inferior status.

### Racial Disturbances

The decade spanned by the school desegregation decision of 1954 (*Brown* v. *Board of Education*) and the Civil Rights Act of 1964 was

---

[17] See, for example, Daniel M. Wilner and Rosabelle P. Wakely, "The Effects of Housing on Health and Performance," in Leonard J. Duhl (ed.), *The Urban Condition* (New York: Basic Books, 1963), pp. 215–228.

the period in which the legal foundations of racial discrimination were destroyed. As described by Bayard Rustin, a leading Negro intellectual, the civil rights movement is now concerned "not merely with removing the barriers to full opportunities but with achieving the fact of equality." [18] Voting guarantees, school desegregation, fair employment acts, and similar legal remedies, the chief thrust of the movement during the 1950s, do not of and by themselves solve the problems of poor housing, inadequate educational resources, and unemployment or provide the institutional means through which the disadvantaged can develop their potential. Rustin's words were echoed a short time later by President Johnson in his famous Howard University speech of June, 1965.[19] In the President's words, we must seek "not just freedom but opportunity— not just equality as a right and a theory but equality as a fact and a result." This, he said, is the next stage of the battle for civil rights.

Two months later, as if to underscore the President's remarks, a large-scale riot erupted in the Watts area, a predominantly Negro section located largely within the city of Los Angeles, resulting in thirty-four deaths, hundreds of injuries, and $35 million in property damage. The earlier disturbances had been confined largely to the South, but Watts signalled the beginning of a long series of violent disorders in cities in other parts of the nation during the course of the next two years. Some observers began to refer to urban communities with large racial concentrations as "tinder-boxes." The riots came as a shock to most white Americans who had assumed that progress was being made in solving the race problem. They also dramatized the inadequacy of the response, in all regions and by all levels of government, to the needs of the racial minorities and the poor. "Tokenism" could no longer serve as a substitute for basic change.

The wave of disorders led President Johnson, in July, 1967, to establish the National Advisory Commission on Civil Disorders with the charge to seek answers to the questions: "What happened? Why did it happen? What can prevent it from happening again and again?" The Commission in its widely-heralded report found racial prejudice ("white racism" as it was termed) essentially responsible for the explosive situation that has been developing in the cities since the end of World War

---

[18] "From Protest to Politics: The Future of the Civil Rights Movement," *Commentary,* 39 (February, 1965), 27.

[19] The text of the President's speech and an account of the events surrounding it are found in Lee Rainwater and William L. Yancey, *The Moynihan Report and the Politics of Controversy* (Cambridge: The M.I.T. Press, 1967).

II.[20] Striking a basic theme in its indictment of the majoritarian society, the Commission reminded the nation: "What white Americans have never fully understood—but what the Negro can never forget—is that white society is deeply implicated in the ghetto. White institutions created it, white institutions maintain it, and white society condones it." [21]

The inability on the part of most white Americans to comprehend the nature and depth of Negro grievances is itself an important facet of the racial problem. The following exchange between Senator John McClellan, chairman of a Congressional subcommittee which investigated the riots, and Harvey Judkins, a Negro councilman of Plainfield, New Jersey, illustrates in a disturbing fashion how this lack of comprehension is not confined to the poorly educated white.

CHAIRMAN:        You spoke about recreational facilities. I think the record already reflects, and I don't recall exactly, what recreational facilities your city has. What does it have?

MR. JUDKINS:     We have several playgrounds.

CHAIRMAN:        How many?

MR. JUDKINS:     I would say roughly maybe about 10. . . .

CHAIRMAN:        Counsel reminds me there are about 13.

MR. JUDKINS:     I could be wrong about three playgrounds.

CHAIRMAN:        Of course, I was just trying to get as near the facts as we could. What kind of playgrounds are they? Are they large, small, enough to accommodate substantial groups?

MR. JUDKINS:     Some are small. The majority of them are small. We have three major size playgrounds which don't offer too much for, I would say, the age group of 15 to 20 years old. There isn't any type of planned program for the type of youth we are talking about, who were basically involved in the riots that we had.

CHAIRMAN:        You have a city of 50,000 population and you have 13 playgrounds, 13 public recreational places. How many

---

[20] The term "racism" has different meanings for different people. Many whites define it in terms of overt, intentional hostility, or the expression of attitudes of superiority toward Negroes. But for many blacks it goes beyond such patent manifestations; to them it means a form of prejudice so ingrained in the feelings of whites that it is often subtle and even unwitting, yet always sensed by the nonwhite.

[21] *Report of the National Advisory Commission on Civil Disorders* (New York: Bantam Books, 1968), p. 2.

|  |  |
|---|---|
|  | more do you think it would take to satisfy them? How many more do they want? |
| MR. JUDKINS: | It is not the point of satisfying anyone, as far as this is concerned. It is the point of a program, I stipulated a program, a planned program. |
| CHAIRMAN: | It wasn't facilities but lack of a program? |
| MR. JUDKINS: | That is correct. |
| CHAIRMAN: | It wasn't inadequate facilities? |
| MR. JUDKINS: | That is correct. |
| CHAIRMAN: | That is what I was trying to determine. I thought they were complaining about facilities. What kind of program did they want? |
| MR. JUDKINS: | A program that offered them some type of athletic opportunities, to maybe let off steam if we want to speak in that term; something constructive. |
| CHAIRMAN: | Was there anything to keep the young people from organizing and having their own ball games and so forth and playing? . . . I never did have anybody plan a baseball game for me when I was young. . . . Is that the reason they gave for this rioting, that there wasn't anybody there to organize and plan recreation for them? |
| MR. JUDKINS: | I said that was one of the reasons. I didn't say it was the primary reason. . . . |
| CHAIRMAN: | What is the other one? |
| MR. JUDKINS: | The other one was the Vietnam situation. |
| CHAIRMAN: | How could they blame the mayor for the Vietnam situation or blame you as a councilman for it? . . . What else was the rioting about? |
| MR. JUDKINS: | The dethroning of Cassius Clay. |
| CHAIRMAN: | Because of Cassius Clay? |
| MR. JUDKINS: | Dethroning him. |
| CHAIRMAN: | Did you have anything to do with that? |
| MR. JUDKINS: | No. |
| CHAIRMAN: | Neither did I.[22] |

The vast gulf between the perceptions of the racial problem held by whites and Negroes is strikingly evident in their views toward the riots. Studies show that most blacks saw the disorders partly or wholly as spontaneous protests against unfair conditions and economic depriva-

---

[22] U.S. Senate, Committee on Government Operations, Permanent Subcommittee on Investigations, *Riots, Civil and Criminal Disorders,* part 4 (Washington: 1967), pp. 1080–1085.

tions. Only a very small percentage defined the disturbances as criminal acts to be suppressed forcibly by the police. A majority of the white population, on the other hand, viewed the riots as criminal or conspiratorial acts precipitated by riffraff, hoodlums, and outside agitators. Numerous surveys have documented the existence of this perceptual gap across a wide range of issues and events. A Harris poll taken in August, 1967, for example, revealed that two-thirds of the Negroes attributed the riots to police brutality while whites rejected this proposition by 8 to 1.[23]

Contrary to popular impression, the riots were not the work primarily of criminal types or those lowest on the socioeconomic status scale. Surveys made by the Commission on Civil Disorders disclosed that the typical rioter was a young adult with somewhat more education than the average inner-city black, employed, and a long-time resident of the area. In Detroit, more than two-thirds of the men arrested during the 1967 disorders were fully and gainfully employed. And in Watts, support for the disturbances was found to be as great among the better educated and economically advantaged persons in the riot area as among the poorly educated and economically disadvantaged.[24] These and similar facts run counter to the conventional wisdom concerning the racial problem and show the utter incongruity of the type of questioning observed in the McClellan hearings.

## The Racial Paradox

"Our nation is moving toward two societies, one black, one white—separate and unequal." This conclusion of the Commission on Civil Disorders is reinforced by the white "backlash" and the growing separatist movement among the blacks. To most liberals, these latter developments represent critical threats to the goal of a fully integrated society in which

---

[23] On the question of attitudes generally, see William Brink and Louis Harris, *Black and White: A Study of U.S. Racial Attitudes Today* (New York: Simon and Schuster, 1967) and the National Advisory Commission on Civil Disorders, *The Supplemental Studies for the National Advisory Commission on Civil Disorders* (Washington: 1968). The insupportability of the "riffraff" hypothesis is shown in James Geschwinder, "Civil Right Protests and Riots," *Social Science Quarterly,* 49 (December, 1968), 474–484.

[24] Nathan E. Cohen, *Los Angeles Riot Study: Summary and Implications for Policy* (Los Angeles: University of California Institute of Government and Public Affairs, 1967). See also William McCord and John Howard, "Negro Opinion in Three Riot Cities," *American Behavioral Scientist,* 11 (March–April, 1968), 24–27, showing that the better-educated Negroes tended to express greater concern about the speed of integration, claimed to have participated in civil rights activities more often, and condemned police behavior with greater vehemence than those lower on the socioeconomic scale.

whites and blacks live together harmoniously and in which an individual's race is not an important factor in determining public or private action. To others, however, separatism is regarded as the only path to the attainment of this ideal. These divergent views have resulted in two fundamentally different strategies or approaches to the racial problem. On the one hand, a majority of white liberals and older Negro leaders call for the massive upgrading of efforts and programs designed to facilitate integration and improve the socioeconomic status of the disadvantaged. On the other hand, many of the younger black leaders advocate the deferment of integration efforts and the development of "black power." Each course has different policy and tactical implications although the ultimate objective of each is presumably the same.

Until the mid-1960s, the whole spectrum of civil rights efforts was concentrated on the goal of integration. The strategy was to desegregate the schools, disperse black families in white neighborhoods, end discrimination in employment practices, and improve the social conditions of the nonwhites. As expectations rose but progress toward equality in fact proved distressingly slow, black leaders turned to direct action to speed up the process: sit-ins, demonstrations, rent strikes, economic boycotts, poverty marches, and similar forms of pressure. Integrationists urged the nation to respond to these developments by increasing the rate of material and social advance. The report of the Commission on Civil Disorders is a brief for this position. It calls both for stepping up the pace of programs like Model Cities, the War on Poverty, and manpower training, and for creating strong incentives to facilitate Negro movement out of central city ghettos.

The second and more recent approach to the racial problem rests on the assumption that equality cannot be achieved through integration efforts because of implacable white resistance. As Kenneth Clark describes it: "The hopes of the Negroes that racial equality and democracy could be obtained through legislation, executive action, and negotiation, and through strong alliances with various white liberal groups were supplanted by disillusionment, bitterness and anger which erupted under the cry of 'Black Power.'. . ."[25] Those who advocate black power often have little more in common than the desire to redress the historical pattern of black subordination to white society.[26] The term, in fact, has many meanings ranging from ideological commitment to violence and the creation of a separate black nation within the United States ("black

---

[25] "The Present Dilemma of the Negro," *Journal of Negro History,* LIII (January, 1968), 5.

[26] See in this connection Martin Kilson, "Black Power: Anatomy of a Paradox," *Harvard Journal of Negro Affairs,* 2 (1968), 30–35.

nationalism") to the development of political and economic strength within the ghetto.

The argument for black power, as defined in the latter sense, states that the Negro population must first overcome its feelings of powerlessness and lack of self respect and develop pride in its color and ethnicity before it can function effectively in the larger society. For this purpose, it must have control over decisions which directly affect its members. Implicit here is the creation of some form of neighborhood government and the promotion of "black capitalism" within the confines of the ghetto. These developments would be accomplished by what some refer to as "ghetto enrichment," or attempts to improve dramatically the quality of life for residents of the area.

Defined in this way, black power is difficult to fault since it is based on the proposition that the nonwhite minority must achieve a position of strength through solidarity if it hopes to bargain effectively with the rest of society—the majority is far more likely to make concessions to power than to justice of conscience.[27] It is also hard to deny the justice of the argument for more self-government in areas of the large central city when suburban villages can have their own school systems and police forces. At the same time, however, it is unrealistic to believe that "black capitalism" can successfully compete in a white-controlled economy or that local political and educational institutions can be manned solely by blacks. The wide range of skills and resources necessary for these complex tasks is simply not available in sufficient quantity among the nonwhites.

The manner in which the majoritarian society responds to the separatist movement and the aspirations it represents will do much to determine the fate of the nation's metropolitan areas. Such a response can take several forms. First, the white-dominated institutions of the community, public and private, can resist the movement by insisting on the retention of full control over the formulation and administration of programs in the nonwhite enclaves, thereby seeking to perpetuate the dependency relationship which the blacks desperately and rightfully want to sever. Two, they can use the demand for autonomy as an excuse for abdicating their responsibility to the black community (other than providing financial subsidization) and in this way encourage the maintenance of a segregated society. Or three, they can demonstrate a genuine rather than rhetorical commitment to the philosophy of maximum feasible participation of the disadvantaged by permitting a devolution of limited governmental powers to the neighborhoods and by significantly enlarging

---

[27] Martin Duberman, "Black Power in America," *Partisan Review*, XXXV (Winter, 1968), 34–48.

the opportunity structure for the nonwhites in such areas as housing, employment, and education so that alternatives would be open to them.

The first two courses would be disastrous since they would further dichotomize urban communities and strengthen the appeal of the black extremists who maintain there is no effective way of "moving the system" short of violence—"patience got us nowhere." (Unfortunately, the record of community response to the needs of the nonwhites shows that the militants have a point here.) The third course offers the only realistic alternative for both whites and blacks. It can succeed, however, only if the latter are permitted to develop the same kind of power base enjoyed by other groups in the society and if the more moderate Negro leaders are afforded the opportunity and means of demonstrating that they can bring about changes in the intolerable conditions of the nonwhite minority. No matter which path is taken, neither the Negro nor white can, in Kenneth Clark's words, "be free of the other."

## Urban Education

The major problem of urban education today is not curriculum or instruction but the challenge of upgrading the educational achievement of the disadvantaged who are concentrated in the nation's metropolitan areas. Since the majority in this category are nonwhite, the racial dimensions of the problem overshadow its other aspects and dominate the debate over solutions. In seventy-five of the most populous cities, for example, three of every four Negro children in the elementary grades now attend schools with enrollments of 90 percent or more black. Moreover, it is estimated that by 1975, assuming current practices and trends continue, 80 percent of all Negro students in the twenty largest cities—which contain nearly one-half the nation's black population—will be attending schools 90 percent to 100 percent nonwhite.

The Brown decision in 1954 outlawed segregation imposed or recognized by law (*de jure*) but its effect on segregation resulting from residential patterns (*de facto*) has been negligible. If anything, color lines—and therefore socioeconomic lines—have sharpened significantly, with more pupils today attending totally segregated schools in all regions than at the time of the decision. In the District of Columbia, to cite one instance, 55 percent of the enrollment in the public schools in 1954 was white; today this proportion is less than 10 percent, as most of the white families have either fled to suburbia or placed their children in private or parochial schools.

*Equality of Opportunity*

After surveying the public school systems of ten major metropolitan areas in 1961, James B. Conant warned: "We are allowing social dynamite to accumulate in our large cities." [28] Citing the high dropout rate and the generally lower levels of educational achievement of slum area youth, he commented that the large differential between funds available to schools in the wealthier suburbs and those in the core cities "jolts one's notion of the meaning of equality of opportunity." Conant's statement strikes at the heart of the urban school issue. As a nation, we are dedicated to the principle of equal opportunity whether in education, housing, employment, or other basic areas of human living. But while there is wide societal acceptance of this goal, there is considerable disagreement over its meaning when it comes to the matter of specific application.

Equality, as the concept relates to public education, may be evaluated in several ways. It may be measured in terms of the community input to the schools, such as expenditures per pupil. Or it may be assessed on the basis of the racial composition of the student body in light of the Supreme Court's holding that segregated schooling is by its very nature inferior. Or it may be defined in terms of the outputs or effects schools have on their students. [29] On all three of these counts, substantial inequality is found among metropolitan educational systems. Those in the suburbs spend more on the average than their counterparts in the central city; *de facto* racial segregation is the common pattern; and the academic achievement of students in schools of predominantly middle-class composition exceeds by a wide margin that of pupils in lower-income schools.

Comparison of achievement in verbal skills by Negro and white students in the urban Northeast shows the two groups beginning far apart in the first grade and remaining about the same distance from each other through the twelfth year. In other words, the gap did not narrow; instead, the average Negro pupil was left at about the same level of academic accomplishment relative to whites as existed at the beginning of his school career. The contrast between whites and blacks in the rural South is even sharper. The two groups begin far apart and the distance widens considerably over the years of schooling to the disadvantage of the Negro.

## Integration or Separatism?

School integration has been one of the prime targets of civil rights advocates, both black and white, for more than three decades. Following the invalidation of the "separate but equal clause," they turned their attention to the elimination of *de facto* segregation in urban areas outside

---

28 *Slums and Suburbs* (New York: McGraw-Hill, 1961), p. 2.

29 For a discussion of this question, see James S. Coleman, "The Concept of Equality of Educational Opportunity," *Harvard Educational Review,* 38 (Winter, 1968), 7–22.

the South as well as in southern cities. Since this form of racial and social-class segregation is the normal consequence of providing school facilities as close as possible to the pupil's home (the widely-publicized "neighborhood school" concept), whites have been able to draw on this traditional practice as justification for their resistance to integration. The obstacles to school integration, moreover, have multiplied with the growing concentration of nonwhite minorities in the core cities. Such remedies as the busing of pupils, adopting open enrollment or voluntary transfer policies, redrawing school district boundaries to cut across racial and socioeconomic population lines, and even establishing educational parks (the concentration of a set of schools in a limited spatial area, thus permitting joint use of common facilities) no longer offer meaningful solutions in many of the large urban centers. The only possible way of effecting integration in cities where the nonwhite school population far exceeds that of the whites—Washington, D.C., Newark, Baltimore, and St. Louis are examples—is through a metropolitan-wide plan involving the suburbs. Such a solution is presently beyond the realm of political feasibility.

Just as the years prior to 1954 were devoted to the legal war against *de jure* segregation and the succeeding decade to attacking the *de facto* variety, the period since the middle 1960s has been characterized by increasing emphasis on upgrading the quality of Negro schools. This emphasis takes many forms but basically it falls into two categories, one pragmatic, the other philosophical, both of which are prompted by the persistent failure of integration attempts. The first reasons that, given the present strong resistance to integration, efforts should be mobilized and directed toward obtaining the highest quality education for Negro pupils regardless of the racial composition of the school they attend. Stress would be placed on compensatory education (measures designed to overcome shortcomings in the learner) and would include such programs as Project Headstart and Follow Through. This approach, espoused by many of the moderate black leaders, represents a shift in tactics and strategy, not an abandonment of the larger goal of racially integrated schools.

The second category places primary emphasis on the attainment of power and control by Negro and other racial-minority parents over the schools their children attend.[30] Those who support this course argue that families in the deprived neighborhoods have been through the whole

---

[30] There is also a third approach known as "parallel systems." It rests on the rationale that if the disadvantaged cannot reform the public education system they should be afforded options to it. One version is to give tuition grants to parents who would then be able to purchase education from competing private schools. In view of the many constitutional, political, fiscal, and philosophical questions involved, this alternative is not likely to receive serious consideration in the foreseeable future.

range of educational challenges and responses, from desegregation to compensatory schooling, without witnessing significant improvements in either the achievement levels of their children or in the opportunities open to those who graduate. Since, as they have come to conclude, the white-dominated and centralized school bureaucracies are really not interested in improving the educational lot of the disadvantaged minority, the latter should be permitted to operate their own systems. The underlying rationale, an outgrowth of the general philosophy of black power, is that after the nonwhites attain a higher educational level under their own aegis, they will then be in a position to integrate with white society on a basis of parity rather than deficiency.

Decentralization of control over the schools as a solution to the urban educational problem has won some political support although it is regarded with skepticism and even downright hostility by many officials and educators, including administrators and teachers. The first comprehensive decentralization plan for a large city was proposed in 1967 by an advisory panel appointed by Mayor John Lindsay and headed by McGeorge Bundy, president of the Ford Foundation.[31] Under the panel's recommendations, the New York city school system would be reorganized into a federation of 30 to 60 units, each governed by an 11-member board (6 elected by the parents and 5 appointed by the Mayor from a list prepared by the central educational authority). Each of these local boards would be vested with power to hire and fire personnel, make curriculum adaptations, and control its budget (funds would be allocated to it by the central authorities on the basis of a need formula). As is evident, the Bundy plan embodies the principle of community or neighborhood control; it does not, however, go as far as ghetto leaders want because of the Mayor's appointive authority over part of the governing board and the retention of certain veto powers over local decisions by the central board of education. These latter requirements were designed to provide broader perspective in the administration of the community schools and prevent arbitrary localism from jeopardizing the educational goals of the total city. The reorganization proposals, on the other hand, went much too far in the eyes of the teachers' union which fears a diminution of its powers in a decentralized system and the loss of job security for its white members in black-dominated districts.[32]

---

[31] Mayor's Advisory Panel on Decentralization of the New York City Schools, *Reconnection for Learning: A Community School System for New York City* (New York, 1967).

[32] Several experimental districts have been set up, the one in the Ocean Hill–Brownsville area of New York City being the best known because of the controversy it precipitated between the local governing board and the teachers' union. For an account of this struggle, see Agee Ward, *The Center Forum,* 3 (November 13, 1968), 1–10.

## The Coleman Report

*Equality of Educational Opportunity,* known as the Coleman report, appeared at a time (1966) when the thrust of the civil rights movement in the field of education was turning from the quest for racial integration to the establishment of black control over the public schools serving black children.[33] Carried out under a mandate in the Civil Rights Act of 1964 and based on a nationwide statistical survey of integrated and segregated public schools, the report represents the most far-reaching study of educational inequality yet conducted in the United States. Although the findings have been challenged as well as variously interpreted, they have been described by Daniel Moynihan and others as the most powerful social science case for school integration yet made.

According to the study, organizational efforts at educational improvement, such as reduced class size, account for little, if any, of the difference in pupil achievement when other variables are held constant—a finding which casts doubt on the efficacy of special or compensatory programs. The central thesis of the study is essentially a substantiation of the rationale in the Brown decision: the major favorable influence on the academic attainment of minority group students is the presence in the classroom of the more motivated and higher-achieving pupils from more advantaged backgrounds. In the words of the report: "If a minority pupil from a home without much educational strength is put with schoolmates with strong educational backgrounds, his achievement is likely to increase." [34] The question of whether this improvement is an effect of racial or social-class integration is for the most part academic since there are proportionately so few middle-class Negroes that the social integration of black children—and the same would be true for other nonwhite minorities—could not be accomplished without racial desegregation.[35]

The Coleman findings, in short, suggest that the mere improvement of school facilities exercises little independent effect on pupil achievement when family background variables are controlled. At the same time, however, the data also lend support to those who argue for community or neighborhood control of the schools. They indicate, for example, that in the case of minority group students a sense of control over one's environment is more highly related to academic accomplishment than

---

[33] James S. Coleman et al., *Equality of Educational Opportunity* (Washington: 1968).

[34] *Ibid.,* p. 22.

[35] See in this respect David K. Cohen, "Policy for the Public Schools: Compensation and Integration," *Harvard Educational Review,* 38 (Winter, 1968), 114–137; also U.S. Commission on Civil Rights, *Racial Isolation in the Public Schools* (Washington: 1967).

any other single variable measured in the study. This suggests the possibility of enhancing achievement by vesting more control over the schools in the parents and pupils in the disadvantaged neighborhoods— a key concept in the black power philosophy. Subsequent analyses of the Coleman data also indicate that the educational attainment levels of Negro children are particularly sensitive to the quality and attitudes of the teaching staffs assigned to them. Presumably local control over the hiring of teachers and administrators (accompanied by adequate financing) could better assure this quality and compatibility.[36] At any rate, the movement for parental control is likely to increase in cities with serious racial problems. In others, the status quo of appointed or elected boards composed of businessmen and professionals may be expected to continue.

## Educational Responsibility

When Sputnik I launched the space age in 1957, it set off a barrage of criticism directed against the "weaknesses" of the American educational system and led to major reforms in the teaching of the sciences and mathematics. Were the United States in a similar race with the Soviet Union to eliminate the inequities in educational opportunities, Americans might also be willing to invest similar efforts in bringing about the necessary social changes. As it is, the nation's response to the growing demands for equality in the field of education have been woefully disproportionate to the challenge. This situation is hardly surprising since the sources of inequality are deeply embedded in the structure of metropolitan areas and their school systems. To achieve the goal of equal opportunity would require changes in the distribution of power; and rarely does any group or institution relinquish power without a struggle, as the New York city school controversy demonstrates so dramatically.

Education obviously cannot be treated separately from the problems of housing, welfare, and employment. To raise the academic attainment levels of Negro students but leave them with inappropriate job opportunities and restricted housing choices would only compound the bitterness and frustration which now exist. The attack must come on a broad front and involve the total range of public and private agencies, such as is envisaged in the Model Cities program. The educational system, nevertheless, is an important instrumentality in combatting the critical problems facing urban communities even though many of these difficulties are rooted in poverty and social disadvantage. It cannot

---

[36] Samuel Bowles, "Toward Equality of Educational Opportunity," *Harvard Educational Review,* 38 (Winter, 1968), 89–99.

absolve itself from this responsibility, as it has sometimes tended to do, by citing the failure of other institutions in the society. The easy answer in school integration, for example, has been to point to the segregated housing patterns as justification for inaction. Yet if the public school establishment is to remain relevant to the needs of the modern metropolitan community, it must deliberately use its skills and resources to promote social change in the interest of equality of opportunity.

### The Good Life

The growth of the metropolitan economic and social system has brought expanded opportunities for millions of Americans in the form of better jobs, improved educational and cultural facilities, and greater social mobility. At the same time it has also brought problems of far greater magnitude than those experienced by less complex societies. We have discussed some of these difficulties in this chapter and others. We have also observed that burgeoning urbanization and its accompanying features have decreased the self-sufficiency of individual metropolitan areas and made their economy and well-being more dependent than ever before on national and even international events and trends. Whether a particular metropolis thrives can be affected only partially by what its local institutions do or fail to do. Greater forces are at work than the zeal and resources of local leaders and officials. Nevertheless, within these circumscribed limits, achievement of the good life for the city or the metropolis can be fostered or deterred by the spirit and acts of the local citizenry and its public and private agencies.

For some urban dwellers the "good life" or its approximation has become a reality. The goal seems within the grasp of many others. For the economically and culturally deprived whites and a majority of nonwhites, the American dream appears a hollow mockery. Throughout a century in which the Negro enjoyed freedom from legal servitude, equality remained for him little more than a vague dream and an unattainable ideal. All this has been changed with the events of the 1960s. Equality has ceased to be an abstraction for him and has now become directly related to the house in which he lives, to the job opportunities available to him, to the schools where he sends his children, and to the public and private accommodations open to him. He no longer wants just the right to sit anywhere in the same bus or live in the same neighborhood with whites or go to the same school with them, but to own a car and a home and have his children receive quality education.

Nonwhites who were formerly apathetic and resigned to their lot in life have now been drawn into a massive campaign of social action.

Embittered by the seeming intransigency of the white-dominated institutions and sparked by a growing sense of pride in their race, American Negroes have turned from the regular channels of democratic decision-making to the strategy of confrontation politics, crisis precipitation, and direct action. The transformation has been traumatic for the officials and administrators who man the urban bureaucratic structures. Accustomed to operate in a basically consensual milieu governed by middle-class norms and practices, they now find their intentions and objectives questioned, their expertise challenged, and their policies resisted by groups traditionally excluded from the power arrangements. Refusing to believe that the script has been changed, they have often reacted in ways which have served to aggravate social tension and unrest. Their ability to adjust to the new urban and metropolitan world is critical for the future.

# A. FINANCE

## Metropolitan Financial Problems

### LYLE C. FITCH

Continued urban growth, economic development, and rise of living standards almost certainly will require maintaining, and probably increasing, the share of the national product taken in the form of urban government services. The evidence of current trends and existing unmet needs indicates the strength of the pressures for more and better services.

Expenditures of large cities rose by approximately 75 per cent between 1948 and 1956, and total local government expenditures in the corresponding metropolitan areas doubtless increased considerably more.*

Developed central cities and mushrooming suburbs have faced, and will continue to face, peculiar needs. The central cities have had to meet demands arising from population shifts within their own boundaries—shifts which are economic and social as well as geographic. The larger cities are tending to become concentration points of low-income groups and require disproportionately large outlays for welfare and social development. Many cities are increasingly impressed with the necessity for large-scale physical rehabilitation and redevelopment if they are to compete with the suburbs as places to live and do business, and if they are to avoid untimely obsolescence of private and public investment in their central areas. In the suburbs, rapid expansion requires enormous amounts of new capital facilities in the form of streets, schools, recreational facilities, and the like.

---

Reprinted from Lyle C. Fitch, *Annals of the American Academy of Social and Political Science: Metropolis in Ferment* (Philadelphia: November, 1957), pp. 66–73, with the permission of the publisher.

* Reference is to the forty-one cities with populations exceeding 250,000 in 1950.

The advent of the metropolitan age and the concomitant development of modern urban culture are creating new demands for many government services and increasing standards of other services. Many of the emergent needs can be supplied only by new governmental agencies designed to operate on a metropolitan scale.

This is the root of the metropolitan financial problem: how to divert a larger share of resources to government use, or, more simply, how to get more funds than existing revenue systems will produce, without unduly impinging on private production. (The last qualifying clause is added because one main objective of urban government should be to increase productivity of private firms by providing them with better-educated and healthier workers, better transportation facilities, and so on.) Solutions, even partial solutions, require better fiscal machinery and broader fiscal powers, as well as organizational innovations, at the local government level. Above all, they require public education and political leadership. Most of these requirements are outside the scope of this paper. Other articles [have considered] the task of organization of the metropolitan community for effective action; this discussion is concerned with equipping it with improved fiscal tools.

## Deficiencies of Metropolitan Fiscal Machinery

Metropolitan financial problems arise primarily from the lack of adequate machinery rather than from any lack of capacity. Presumptively, today's large urban communities, being typically the focal points of wealth and income, have the resources to meet their urban needs.

The following deficiencies in the fiscal machinery characteristic of metropolitan areas seem to the writer to be the most important and the ones whose rectification will have greatest importance for the future.

1. Existing revenue-producing machinery is generally inadequate for the task of financing local government functions; this is true of functions appropriate for the conventional (submetropolitan) local government and functions which can best be handled by metropolitan jurisdictions.

2. The extension of activities across jurisdictional boundary lines makes it more and more difficult to relate benefits and taxes at the local government level. In the modern metropolitan community, a family may reside in one jurisdiction, earn its living in one or more others, send the children to school in another, and shop and seek recreation in still others. But to a considerable extent, the American local financial system still reflects the presumption that these various activities are concentrated in one governmental jurisdiction.

3. In many areas there are great discrepancies in the capacities of local government jurisdictions to provide needed governmental services. At one extreme are the communities which have not sufficient taxable capacity for essential services. The most common case is the bedroom community or low- and middle-income workers which has little industry or commerce. At the other extreme are the wealthy tax colonies, zoned to keep out low-income residents.[1]

Three main types of decisions must be made in setting up and financing functions on an areawide scale. They concern:

The services and benefits which should be provided on an areawide basis.

The question of whether services should be financed by taxes or charges.

The type and rate of tax or charge which should be imposed.

Some services and benefits, like health protection and air pollution control, can be provided efficiently only if they extend over a wide area and their administration is integrated; some, like hospitals and tax administration, are more economical if handled on a large scale; * and some, like intrametropolitan transportation, can be controlled satisfactorily only by a central authority with powers to establish areawide standards and policies and to resolve intra-area conflicts.

## Taxes and Charges

This discussion distinguishes mainly between general taxes bearing no direct relation to benefits of expenditures, like sales and income taxes, and charges, or public prices, which vary directly with the amount of the service provided, like bridge tolls, subway fares, and metered charges for water.

General taxes and public prices are at the opposite ends of the revenue spectrum. In between are benefit taxes, which are imposed on beneficiaries of a related service, with the proceeds being devoted largely

---

* Results of two recent, as yet unpublished, studies indicate that the unit costs of government services may be less affected by the scale of operations than has been popularly supposed. Harvey Brazer's study (sponsored by the National Bureau of Economic Research) of general government expenditures in larger cities, the group exceeding 25,000 in 1950, finds little correlation between per capita costs of local government functions and city size. Werner Hirsch's study of municipal expenditures in St. Louis County, for the St. Louis Metropolitan Survey, shows similar results for some 80 municipalities, most of them under 25,000 population.

[1] See Julius Margolis, "Municipal Fiscal Structure in a Metropolitan Region," *Journal of Political Economy,* 55 (June, 1957).

or entirely to financing the service. Gasoline taxes used for financing highways are a familiar example; the real estate tax is at least in part a benefit tax where it pays for services which benefit the taxed properties.

## Local Taxes

Local governments, within the generally narrow confines of state-imposed restrictions, have shown considerable ingenuity in tapping pools of potential revenue, however small; few things on land, sea, or in the air, from pleasures and palaces to loaves and fishes, escape taxation somewhere. However, most of the principal local taxes used today are loosely enforced or expensive to administer and dubious in their economic effect. Even the property tax is not exempt from this indictment, although its praises have long been sung and its vices excused on the ground that it is the only tax which can be administered successfully even by the smallest local government. The fact is that it has generally not been successfully administered at all, according to most criteria of equity and efficiency. It is capricious and inequitable even in what it purports to do best.

Part of the typical difficulties of local taxation arise from smallness, both in size of jurisdiction and scale of administrative organization. These, of course, may be obviated by metropolitan areawide administration. Efficient collection of most types of revenues requires an organization large enough to afford trained personnel, costly equipment, and professional direction and research. Geographically, the taxing area must be large enough and isolated enough to discourage avoidance of taxes by persons who move their residences or business establishments over boundary lines or who go outside the jurisdiction to shop. When imposed by several neighboring local governments, many taxes involve issues of intergovernmental jurisdiction and allocation of tax bases.

Where taxes are imposed on an areawide basis, one issue of metropolitan area finance—allocation of government service costs among communities—is resolved; allocation is a function of the type of tax imposed. Areawide taxes also eliminate tax competition within the area; however this may not be an unmitigated blessing if competition by offering better services also is eliminated.

To date, the principal revenue sources of areawide public agencies have been property taxes and user charges, although some metropolitan counties in New York and California, for instance, impose sales taxes and occasionally other nonproperty taxes. The problems of granting taxing powers to metropolitan jurisdictions which extend over several counties remain largely unexplored. A bill introduced in the 1957 session of the California legislature to establish a multi-county San

Francisco Bay area rapid transit district went further in this direction than most legislative proposals by giving the proposed district power to impose both a property and a sales tax. The sales tax authority was eliminated in the version of the bill finally adopted.*

The difficulties of working out harmonious tax arrangements between metropolitan jurisdictions and state and already existing local governments have been great enough when only one state was involved to block all but the feeblest beginnings beyond the one-county level. They have thus far been considered insuperable where interstate arrangements are involved. For some time to come, interstate functions probably will be financed by user charges, supplemented where necessary by contributions from the state or local governments involved.

In the almost perfect metropolitan area, we would expect to see metropolitan real estate taxes assessed by an areawide agency,** with metropolitan levies for such metropolitan services as were deemed to be of particular benefit to property and additional local levies for local government activities. Only metropolitan jurisdictions would be authorized to impose nonproperty taxes. In general, the permissible nonproperty taxes would include general sales and amusements taxes and a levy on personal income. Business firms might be taxed, if at all, by some simple form of value-added tax.

The following are among the taxes not used at the local level in the almost perfect metropolitan area: gross receipts taxes and taxes on utility services, because of their excessively deleterious economic effect; and corporate income taxes and such selective excises as gasoline, alcoholic beverages, and tobacco taxes, because they can be much better administered at the state level.

Along with several others, the revenue sources mentioned above are now being used by municipalities with two exceptions: the value-added tax and the general income tax. The so-called municipal income taxes now imposed in Pennsylvania, Ohio, and a few other states rest largely on wages and salaries. Considerations of equity manifestly require a broader tax base, and the need for administrative simplicity suggests a supplemental rate on an existing base where this is practicable.[2]

---

* Tax revenues of the proposed district would be used mainly for service of debt incurred in building a rapid transit system and to meet expenses of the district board.

** Personal property, with the possible exception of depreciable business assets, would not be taxed in the almost perfect metropolitan area.

[2] See Harold M. Groves, "New Sources of Light on Intergovernmental Fiscal Relations," *National Tax Journal,* 5:3 (September, 1952).

## The Real Estate Tax

The principal justification for the real estate tax, aside from tradition, convenience, and expediency, is that by financing beneficial services, it benefits property. Another logical function, which it performs very inadequately, is to capture at least part of the unearned increments to land values accruing by reason of urban developments. Special assessments have been widely used to recoup at least part of land values accruing from public improvements,† but no means has been devised, at least at the local level, of recapturing land values not attributable to specific public improvements.

The enormous increases of land values which typically occur as land is converted from rural to urban use and from less to more intensive urban use constitute a pool of resources which can be appropriately utilized to meet the social costs of urban development, if taxes can be devised to tap the pool. Such land value increases, however, seem characteristically to be concentrated in the expanding sections, mostly the suburbs. Available evidence suggests that land values in many core cities have lagged far behind general price levels and in some cities have not even regained levels reached in the 1920's.* In such cases, urban redevelopment, unlike the initial urban development, cannot count on pools of expanding land values; on the contrary land costs often must be written down at government expense if redevelopment is to be economically feasible.**

Clearly the real estate tax must be adapted to the dynamic characteristics of the urban economy. The tax in its present form gives equal weight to the incremental values resulting from urban development, the values of land already developed, and the values of improvements. Several possible new features should be explored. Some of them are: a local capital gains tax on land value increments, special levies on property values accruing after the announcement of public improvements which benefit the whole community, and a differential tax on land values. Of these three possibilities, the last seems most promising, if only because the basic concept is familiar; it has been used in Australia,

---

† As an alternative to the special assessment device, developers in many instances are required to provide for streets, sewers, water mains, and similar improvements which otherwise would be provided by public funds.

* Such tendencies, however, do not necessarily reflect an absolute economic declining of the core.

** In the long run, of course, one test of urban redevelopment programs is whether they increase land and other property values, relative to the value that would otherwise have obtained.

Canada, and elsewhere abroad, but by only a few cities in the United States.

## The Role of User Charges

There is a case for charging for a service instead of financing it by general taxation if the following conditions are met:

1. The charge must be administratively feasible. Among the other requirements, the service must be divisible into units whose use by the beneficiary can be measured, like kilowatts, gallons of water, trips across a bridge, or miles traveled on a turnpike.

2. The immediate benefits of the service should go mainly to the person paying for it. This condition, not always easy to apply, means that if a person refrains from using the service because of the charge, the rest of the community suffers relatively little loss. For example, the community is ordinarily not much damaged if a person uses less electricity or makes fewer long-distance telephone calls. In some cases, an additional use by a few individuals may greatly inconvenience many others; for example, a few additional vehicles on a roadway may produce traffic congestion.

3. The charge should encourage economical use of resources. Metered charges, for instance, encourage consumers to conserve water and electricity by turning off faucets and lights.

One of the most important functions of charges is to balance demand and supply in cases where excess demand produces undesirable results. If the number of curb parking spaces is less than the number of would-be parkers, the space will be allocated on a first-come first-served basis, in the absence of any better device, and there is no way of assuring that space will go to those who need it most. In such cases, a charge may be the most efficient way of rationing space. This is frequently attempted by use of parking meters, although nearly always in a crude fashion. Meter systems could be much improved if the elementary principles of charges were better understood.

Conversely, a charge—or the increase of an already existing charge —is not justified if it results in the underutilization or waste of resources. For example, as an immediate result of the increase of the New York subway fare from ten to fifteen cents in 1953, passenger traffic declined at least 120 million rides per year, the bulk of the drop being concentrated in nonrush hours and holidays when subways have excess capacity. Not only did the community lose 120 million rides per year, which could be provided at little additional cost, but traffic congestion increased because former subway riders switched to private passenger cars and taxis, and downtown shopping and amusement centers suffered to an undetermined extent.[3]

The peripatetic propensities of metropolitan man and the fact that he may consume services in several jurisdictions while voting in only one have disjointed local government fiscal structures in several places. First, the separation of workshops and bedrooms may create disparities between taxable capacities and service needs. Second, the separation of political jurisdictions in which individuals are taxed and in which they require services handicaps the budget-making process; it makes more difficult a rational determination of how much of the community's product should take the form of government services. Third, the necessity of providing services to outsiders, particularly commuters, creates pressure for taxation without representation.

These considerations argue for a policy of structuring metropolitan governmental organizations in order to allow as much freedom as possible to the play of market forces in determining the kinds and quantities of government services to be supplied, subject to the general principles previously noted (section on the role of user charges).*

The market system can operate at two levels: that of the individual or firm purchasing services or goods from a government enterprise and that of the group—for example, the smaller governmental jurisdiction—purchasing goods or services from a larger jurisdiction. The second level is exemplified by the city of Lakewood, California, and several other cities which purchase their municipal services from Los Angeles County.**

One of the principal decisions respecting any government service is the quantity to be furnished. The important distinction between ordinary government services and services provided under enterprise principles lies in the nature of the decision-making process. Budgetary decisions affecting regular government services are political decisions, reflecting judgments of legislatures regarding how much of the services are needed by the community and how much the taxpayers are willing

---

* We can go this far without agreeing with Calvin Coolidge that legislatures should make it their business to discover natural economic laws and enact them into legislation.

** Another way of relating charges on particular areas to services rendered is the establishment of special service districts within a metropolitan jurisdiction which pay differential taxes for special services.

[3] For a general discussion see William Vickrey, *Revision of Rapid Transit Fares in the City of New York,* Mayor's Committee on Management Survey, Finance Project Publication, item No. 8, Technical Monograph No. 3 (New York, 1952); Lyle C. Fitch, "Pricing Transportation in a Metropolitan Area," *Proceedings of the National Tax Association* (New York: The Association, 1955).

to pay. Not infrequently, decisions are referred directly to voters. The amount of service to be provided under enterprise principles is dictated by consumers, by the usual market test of how much individuals or firms in the aggregate will buy at cost-of-production prices.† In other words, the question of how much is decided by following the simple rule that where demand exceeds supply, the service should be expanded, and vice versa.

## Price-Market Test

The price-market test of resource allocation greatly simplifies the problem of citizen participation in the governmental process. Where services and goods are bought by individuals, each consumer takes part in the decision-making process by determining how much of the service he will buy.

Where purchases are by groups, decisions as to how much to spend must be political ones; but the issue of citizen participation can be simplified in several ways as compared with the situation where budgetary decisions are made by large political units. If the purchasing group is more homogeneous than the whole community, any decision is more wholly satisfactory to a larger percentage of the members. Even if the small group is no more homogeneous than the large, individuals may participate more effectively in small-group decisions.*

Although user charges and the demand-supply rule can simplify the budgetary problem, they do not divorce public enterprise operations from the political process; political participation in many decisions is essential, including the crucial decisions respecting organizational form, investment policies, and integrating the particular function with other community services. For instance, the quantity of services to be supplied by a basically enterprise type of operation may be extended by public decision and public subsidy beyond the amounts which could be made available at cost-of-production prices.** In some cases, public subsidies may be necessary to avoid waste of an already existing resource. Public prices too often are fixed to achieve narrow objectives, such as meeting debt service on construction bonds, without regard for their over-all economic effect.

---

† The question of price cannot be disposed of by the simple qualification "cost-of-production," but that question need not be considered here.

* This statement rests on the not uncomplicated assumption that the opportunity of participating in decisions of a smaller group is a positive value.

** Even more basic is the question, not considered here, of whether enterprises in particular instances should be private or public.

Some of the most urgent areawide needs are appropriately financed partly or wholly by charges. They include the services which are frequently provided by private regulated utilities such as gas and electricity, water, and mass transportation and other transportation facilities, port development, waste disposal, many recreational services, and hospital services.[4]

## Balancing Costs and Taxable Capacity

There have been few studies of the over-all relationship of costs and taxable capacity in metropolitan areas—although endless attention has been lavished on particular functions, notably education—and the subject still abounds with unsettled questions. Brazer's analyses indicate that the relative size of the suburban population is an important determinant of local government expenditures in large cities, a finding consistent with the hypothesis that cities assume considerable expense in providing services to suburban residents. Both Brazer's and Hirsch's studies indicate, moreover, that per capita expenditures on some functions—police, for instance—typically increase with population density; this may in part result from the tendency of low-income groups to congregate in central cities. On the other hand, the worst cases of fiscal undernourishment appear to be in the suburbs.

This article has space only for several generalizations which may serve to indicate directions for further analysis:

1. Costs of essential services may be "equalized" over a metropolitan area, either by areawide administration and financing, or by grants to local jurisdictions financed at least in part by areawide taxes. Experience with state and federal subventions indicates that the subvention is a clumsy tool. On the other hand, putting services on an areawide basis may deprive local communities of the privilege of determining the amount of resources to be allocated to specific services.

2. In many cases, the remedy for fiscal undernourishment may lie in areawide planning and zoning; fiscal measures as such may strike only at symptoms rather than underlying difficulties.

---

[4] A recent study of metropolitan government in the Sacramento area recommended that the capital and operating costs of water, sewage service, garbage pickup and disposal, and transit "be metered and charged to the new areas receiving them." Public Administration Service, *The Government of Metropolitan Sacramento* (Chicago: Public Administration Service, 1957), p. 144.

For discussions of transportation pricing see Vickrey and Fitch, *op. cit.;* also Fitch, "Financing Urban Roadways," in *Highway Financing,* Tax Institute Symposium (Princeton: 1957); and Wilfred Owen, *The Metropolitan Transportation Problem* (Washington, D.C.: Brookings Institution, 1956), Chap. 7.

3. Fiscal stress in the modern American community is often more psychological than economic. A common case is that of the former city apartment dweller who buys his own house in the suburbs and for the first time in his life is confronted with a property tax bill. It is not strange that he should resist taxes while demanding municipal services of a level to which he has been accustomed in the city, nor that he should seek outside assistance in meeting his unaccustomed burden.

4. The point has been made that intercommunity variations in the levels of services should allow metropolitan residents to satisfy their preferences as to levels of local government services and taxes and hence promote the general satisfactions of the entire community.[5] Although the argument may be valid within limits, the limits are narrow; they may extend, for instance, to the quality of refuse collection, but not air and water pollution control.

5. Services rendered to individuals in their capacity of workers, shoppers, and other economic functionaries may in some instances be properly treated as a charge upon the business firm involved rather than upon the individual. Suburbanites, like other persons, create real property values wherever they work, shop, or play.[6] This fact refutes the case for a general tax on commuters, although it does not damage the case for user charges where these would improve the allocation of resources. On the other hand, the maintenance of minimal service levels in poor communities and care for the economically stranded, wherever located, are the responsibility of the entire community.

---

[5] See Charles Tiebout, "The Pure Theory of Local Government Expenditures," *Journal of Political Economy*, 64:5 (October, 1956).

[6] Margolis, *op. cit.:* "A priori, there is no reason to believe that the increment in the tax receipts of the central city accompanying the commuter is less than it costs the city to attract and service him."

# B. TRANSPORTATION

## Decision-Making and Transportation Policy: A Comparative Analysis

### FRANK C. COLCORD, JR.

The purpose of this paper is to formulate some generalizations about the way political decisions are made with respect to the transportation problems of large urban areas.

The movement of people and goods has been a major public issue in America's large urban areas since the Second World War.[1] It has absorbed increasing amounts of the attention of political actors—both public and private—and increasing amounts of the nation's financial resources. Transportation problems have been the product of continuing urbanization, rapid decentralization and a steady growth of motor vehicle ownership and use.

The characteristic response to the "transportation crisis" during most of the post-war period has been the construction of more and more highways (best demonstrated by the passage in 1956 of the Federal Interstate and Defense Highway Act, which provided 90 per cent federal financing for the major expressway system, much of which was intended for urban areas). Until recently, alternatives to this response were not seriously considered.

---

Reprinted with permission from *The Southwestern Social Science Quarterly,* XLVIII (December 1967), 383–97.

[1] The major literature treating the general problem includes: Wilfred Owen, *The Metropolitan Transportation Problem* (Washington, D.C.: The Brookings Institution, 1956, revised 1966); Lyle C. Fitch, *et al., Urban Transportation and Public Policy* (San Francisco: Chandler Publishing Company, 1964); J. R. Meyer, J. F. Kain, and M. Wohl, *The Urban Transportation Problem* (Cambridge: Harvard University Press, 1965); and Committee for Economic Development, *Developing Transportation Policies: A Guide for Local Leadership* (April, 1965). Also, see The Editors of *Fortune, The Exploding Metropolis* (Garden City: Doubleday Anchor Books, 1957, 1958), pp 32–61; Lewis Mumford, *The Highway and the City* (New York: Harcourt, Brace and World, Inc., 1963), pp. 234–246; and The Scientific American, *Cities* (New York: Alfred A. Knopf, 1965), pp. 133- 155.

However, as more and more highways were actually completed, an increasingly vocal skepticism has developed among significant public officials and influential private citizens and organizations in many larger cities. This first became audible late in the 1950's in the handful of cities with large rapid transit systems and/or commuter railroads (New York, Philadelphia, Chicago and Boston). These facilities had been allowed to languish, and their financial difficulties and declining patronage raised them to the status of a major public issue. The dependence of large segments of the population on these facilities made their discontinuance unimaginable, and the first response of the cities and their states was to adopt various stop-gap measures (tax exemptions, subsidies, loans, etc.) to prevent their demise.[2] However, by the early 1960's serious efforts at finding long-range solutions were being pressed. By 1967 significant programs to extend and improve the rail systems, involving major capital investments, were underway in all of these urban areas. In large part because of pressures from these cities and states,[3] Congress in 1961 and 1964 passed two measures to provide new programs of assistance to transit and commuter systems. Also, by the mid-1960's, both the San Francisco and Washington, D.C., areas had committed themselves to the construction of new and expensive mass-transit networks.

Less obvious than these cases have been the later but similar responses of many other large urban areas in the United States which lack rapid transit or commuter rail facilities. Indeed, there appears to be a major reconsideration of urban transportation policy underway in most of our larger centers throughout the country, including Seattle, Baltimore, Denver, Detroit, Pittsburgh, Atlanta, and even Miami, Los Angeles and Houston.

Urban transportation has become a matter of *public* policy in all large urban areas, and is a case of *metropolitan* political decision-making in every area because of the very nature of the function. Since the federal government has now chosen to intervene in all aspects of the field, it

---

[2] For a full treatment of the response in the New York area to these problems see Jameson W. Doig, *Metropolitan Transportation Politics and the New York Region* (New York: Columbia University Press, 1966). Also, see Robert C. Wood, *1400 Governments* (Cambridge: Harvard University Press, 1961), particularly pp. 123–143. For Boston, see Frank C. Colcord, Jr., *Metropolitan Transportation Politics,* unpublished Ph.D. dissertation, MIT, 1964. A portion of the Chicago story is told in Edward Banfield, *Political Influence* (Glencoe, Illinois: Free Press, 1961), pp. 91–125. Unfortunately, the activities in the Philadelphia area, which were the earliest and most extensive, have not been the subject of any research literature.

[3] Michael N. Danielson, *Federal-Metropolitan Politics and the Commuter Crisis* (New York: Columbia University Press, 1965).

has also become the subject of one of the numerous recent experiments in the "new federalism." Thus its study explores some rather new territory which will unquestionably be illustrative of other urban public problems lying before us. Because of the many political actors involved and the absence of a government with sole responsibility for the problem, it is an extremely complex case in political decision-making.

Urban transportation decisions can be divided into several subcategories, all of which must be explored to comprehend the totality. Broadly, these include decisions relating to (1) the structure of government for transportation, (2) transportation planning, and (3) financing, construction and operation of facilities. Included in all of these are (4) decisions concerning the extent to which transportation will be handled comprehensively or piecemeal. Furthermore, transportation decisions are not made in a vacuum. Other closely related decisions bearing directly on transportation include those concerning (5) the general structure of metropolitan government, (6) metropolitan land-use planning, (7) home rule, and the distribution of powers between state and local government, and (8) financing and taxes.

Transportation policy-making in all large U.S. urban areas occurs in the same objective context. Relevant federal legislation applies to all, including the several highway acts, the 1958 Transportation Act (relating to Federal regulation of intra-state common carriers), the 1961 amendments to the Housing Act (providing for demonstration grants and loans to urban transit), the Urban Mass Transportation Act of 1964 (which authorized $375 million in matching grants for urban transit), as well as other relevant sections of the Housing Act providing for urban renewal, planning grants, community-facilities grants, *etc.* Also, all states have the same basic constitutional powers; everywhere the states have the primary responsibility for planning and building major highways, and have agencies for the regulation of common carriers. And everywhere, with rare exceptions, there exists no true metropolitan government.[4]

Given these uniformities and the universal requirement of providing facilities for movement of persons and goods within large urban regions, and armed with some scattered and limited information about transportation politics in a few urban areas,[5] several hypotheses were constructed. (1) The "dynamics" of transportation politics will be similar in all large urban areas—*i.e.,* roughly the same public and private political actors (see definition below) will be involved in the decision-

---

[4] The *only* exception among the larger urban areas is Miami-Dade County (Fla.).

[5] Refer to footnote 2, above.

making process; they will take roughly the same positions on issues, and much the same political alliances will be forming. (2) The outcome of the political process (*i.e.,* the decisions) will depend upon (a) the extent of influence of the alliances and their members, (b) the degree of cohesiveness among the members of the alliances, and (c) the degree of intensity with which these members view the actual or potential impact of transportation policies on their own interests.[6] (3) The major membership of the alliance seeking alternatives to the prevailing "highways only" policy will be heavily concentrated in the central city, with some assistance from "metropolitan" organizations, where they exist. (4) Because of the absence of metropolitan government, the primary arena in which political controversies will be fought will be the state political system, since state officials control the roads program and must approve most other metropolitan transportation decisions.

## Method of Investigation

This article represents a preliminary report of a larger study of transportation policy in seven large U.S. metropolitan areas. Baltimore and Seattle were the first two studied and were thus chosen for discussion herein. The study is being made possible by a grant to M.I.T. by the General Motors Corporation.[7]

The basic research method involves open-ended interviews with all significant "political actors" (or their staffs) concerned with urban transportation policy. These are defined as: (1) the general policymakers (governors, mayors, county commissioners, selected suburban executives and relevant state legislators and city councilmen), (2) public officials directly or indirectly concerned with transportation policy (*e.g.,* city, county and state public works directors, planning heads, and police chiefs, state motor vehicle and traffic safety directors, city urban

---

[6] This hypothesis is an adaptation of a theory advanced by Edward C. Banfield and James Q. Wilson in *City Politics* (Cambridge: Harvard University Press, 1963), pp. 272–276.

[7] The other areas included in the study are Boston, St. Louis, Kansas City, Houston, and San Francisco Bay. The seven areas were selected to provide a regional distribution, a distribution by size (ranging from one million to almost three million) and by stage of development of their present and planned local transportation systems. In this study we have avoided the "urban giants" (New York, Los Angeles, and Chicago) because of a fear they might be atypical, or at least that such a charge could be made. In fact, however, the literature regarding New York and the limited information available on Chicago and Los Angeles suggest that they may not differ significantly from the urban areas studied. Metropolitan areas below one million were omitted because we believed the character of most of their transportation problems is significantly different.

renewal, traffic management and transit chiefs, metropolitan agency directors, locally based federal officials, *etc.*), and (3) private organizations and individuals actively interested in transportation policy (*e.g.,* newspapers, chambers of commerce, labor unions, downtown business groups, transit operating companies, Negro organizations, Leagues of Women Voters, planning associations, automobile clubs, associations of contractors, truckers, *etc.*). The private actors were initially chosen from a standardized list of "transportation interests" but were expanded from information received from respondents. These interviews were augmented by interviews with knowledgeable academics and newspapermen, and by review of newspaper clipping files, published documents and papers, as well as historical and political literature relating to each urban area and its state (or states).

## Baltimore and Seattle: A Profile

*The History and the Economy.* Baltimore became a major city in the early nineteenth century, Seattle in the early twentieth. In both cases, the initial spur to growth was the port: in both the port remains an important aspect of the economy, but manufacturing has become the major growing point.[8] Industry is highly diversified in the Baltimore area, and largely absentee-owned; in Seattle, there is a heavy concentration in aircraft manufacture, with Boeing employing over half the total industrial workers of the region. Both areas have experienced substantial industrial expansion in the past few decades.

Population, industry and commerce have been steadily decentralizing since World War II, in accord with the national pattern. In both places, the central city now has approximately half the total metropolitan population, but still employs around two thirds of the total metropolitan work-force. However, the central business districts (CBD) have experienced absolute declines. In the case of Baltimore, this decline was rather precipitous until 1963, when a major downtown renewal program began to take effect and the decline was arrested and later reversed. It appears to have stabilized in Seattle as well, although urban renewal has not been a major factor there. Employees working in the CBD in both places now constitute less than 20 per cent of the total area employment figure.

Both areas have experienced substantial population growth since World War II, although the central city remained stable in the decade

---

[8] Hamilton Owens, *Baltimore on the Chesapeake* (Garden City: Doubleday, 1941), pp. 33–41.

of the 1950's.[9] There are major differences in the socioeconomic characteristics of the two areas. Baltimore is typical of cities in the eastern half of the nation, in that its central city population exhibits distinctly lower socioeconomic status characteristics than the suburban areas. Population size has remained stable, but the city has lost heavily in white population and gained many Negroes. In 1960 the latter constituted 33 per cent of the total, and their numbers have grown substantially since. The Seattle area, on the other hand, is remarkably homogeneous. Socioeconomic measures show little difference between city and surrounding suburban areas. Negroes constituted less than 5 per cent of the total in 1960, although they were also concentrated in the central city. Also, the Seattle area population is substantially richer and better educated than that of the Baltimore area, with the differences, of course, most extreme between the two central cities. For example, 1960 median family income in the Seattle Standard Metropolitan Statistical Area (SMSA) was 11 per cent higher, and in the city 23 per cent higher, than in Baltimore.

*Government.* There are major differences both in the structure of government and in the character of the politics of the two urban areas. Structurally, the Baltimore area is probably the simplest in the continental United States. The urban population lives in only four jurisdictions: Baltimore City, Annapolis (the state capital) and two counties (Baltimore County and Anne Arundel). Baltimore City is actually a city-county, and is totally separated from Baltimore County. There are no other municipalities in the urban area.[10] Seattle, on the other hand, lies within King County, and the SMSA spreads into a second county, Snohomish. Including Seattle, there are 48 municipalities in the SMSA, as well as literally hundreds of special districts, many of them with their own taxing powers. The counties have relatively little authority over the incorporated municipalities. In both places, the states have rather strong powers relative to the local jurisdictions; most major decisions must be approved by the state legislatures, particularly decisions of a metropolitan nature. In addition to the counties and municipalities, the two areas have a number of metropolitan agencies relevant to transportation (see below).

---

[9] The Baltimore SMSA grew from 1.4 in 1950 to 1.7 million in 1960, a 22.9% increase. The Seattle SMSA grew from 844,000 in 1950 to 1,107,000 in 1960, a 31.1% increase. By 1960 the Baltimore SMSA constituted 56% of Maryland's total population, while that of Seattle was 39% of Washington's. Seattle's population growth from 1950–1960 is largely attributed to an annexation which took place during the decade (Source: U.S. Census materials).

[10] The Baltimore SMSA consists of two additional counties, Howard and Carroll, containing a total of only 5% of the SMSA population. Carroll County contains one small municipality: Westminster.

The character of politics in the two areas differs significantly. Although an attempt at a brief summary within the constraints of this paper risks oversimplification and thus inaccuracy, nonetheless it is impossible to understand transportation policy-making without some appreciation of the nature of the political system and character of the political culture. Baltimore and Maryland politics are partisan and professional, demonstrating an odd admixture of Southern rural and Northern urban styles.[11] Despite the fact that the state and all the local governments of the Baltimore region are overwhelmingly Democratic, Republicans now occupy the governor's and mayor's chairs,[11a] as well as that of county executive of Anne Arundel County. Democrats control Baltimore County and the legislative bodies of the city, the state and Anne Arundel County. The two counties seem to be in something of a state of transition from the old-fashioned machine government typical of Maryland's rural counties to modernized urban systems; they have been reformed in structure, but the transition is not yet complete. The city still has vestiges of localized political machines within it, but there has not been a city-wide machine for several decades. In the city, the mayors D'Alesandro and McKeldin— who have dominated that office for many years—have worked effectively and cooperatively with the major business organizations in developing city programs.

The political systems of Seattle and the State of Washington provide a strong contrast to the Maryland systems. They tend to be highly "service-oriented." Evidence of corruption is rare, but both governments tend to be weak and disinclined to activism. Indeed, both governments are structured in such a way as to make political leadership exceedingly difficult. The city has a "weak-mayor" system with non-partisan voting, large numbers of commissions, and a strong merit system (thus limiting the mayor's appointment powers). The governor is similarly limited; particularly in the field of transportation, there is a long-standing tradition of highway commission independence. Major program changes in both city and state must generally go before the voters in referenda, which has meant that program leadership originates with citizens' groups. The county governments are traditional in form and politics; they do not have merit systems, and generally lack the service-orientation of the city and state. Their structure and traditions are not conducive to pro-

---

[11] John H. Fenton, *Politics in the Border States* (New Orleans: The Hauser Press, 1957), pp. 171–221; Jean E. Spencer, *Contemporary Local Government in Maryland* (College Park: University of Maryland, 1965).

[11a] As a result of the 1967 city election, in which the incumbent Republican mayor (Theodore McKeldin) did not seek re-election, the city returned to "normal" with the overwhelming victory of Thomas D'Alesandro III, a Democrat.

gram innovation, and they are poorly equipped to carry on urban functions. In general, the Washington political systems are far more "open" than those of Maryland; they are less dominated by professional politicians, which has allowed more direct intervention by individual citizens and organized groups. This type of system carries with it the disadvantage of extreme difficulty in accomplishing change, a problem which is less severe in the Maryland-Baltimore system.[12]

### Transportation Decisions in Baltimore and Seattle

Baltimore and Seattle are currently in an almost identical stage of development in their transportation planning. In this respect, they are well behind San Francisco and Washington (D.C.), which have made the crucial financing decisions, and are proceeding with construction. But they are well ahead of any other cities which do not now have rapid transit.

*Structural decisions.* Because metropolitan government does not exist in most U.S. urban areas, an important decision that must be made prior to the development of a transportation program is to establish the structure through which the program can be planned, developed and carried out. Baltimore and Seattle have both developed rather elaborate arrangements to accomplish these purposes. As they entered the postwar era, both were equipped with only the traditional agencies for transportation: state roads commissions and regulatory agencies for utilities, city departments of public works and planning boards, as well as bus transit operators. It was not until the late 1950's that new institutions began to develop.

In the Baltimore area, the first major development was the creation in 1958 of the Baltimore Regional Planning Council as a semi-autonomous unit within the State Planning Council. This was later (1963) established as an official representative body separate from the state unit, with its own assured financing from state and local sources. In 1961 the Maryland General Assembly created the Metropolitan Transit Authority with regulatory powers over all Baltimore area public carriers, a directive to prepare a long-range master plan, and authority to purchase the private bus lines. In 1966 two additional organizations were established: the Metropolitan Area Council, which is a voluntary intergovernmental coordinating body of local public officials, and a special organization (ACCORD) of similar makeup created to meet the 1962 requirement of the federal highway act that all transportation planning be based upon

---

[12] Edward C. Banfield, *Big City Politics* (New York: Random House, 1965), pp. 133–146; Donald H. Webster, Ernest H. Campbell, George D. Smith, *Washington State Government* (Seattle: University of Washington Press, 1962).

comprehensive regional plans. In 1967 a "Governor's Steering Committee for Mass Transit," composed of representatives of the state and local governments, was created to spearhead the planning for rapid transit. Within the city, a Department of Traffic and Transit and the Baltimore Urban Renewal and Housing Authority were established in the mid-1950's.

The mid-50's also saw the establishment of a number of private organizations of importance to transportation planning. The chief of these are the Committee for Downtown, Inc., and the Greater Baltimore Committee (both businessmen's groups primarily concerned with the renewal of the downtown), the Citizens Planning and Housing Association and Baltimore Heritage, Inc. The last named is concerned particularly with preservation of historic areas and buildings.

In the Seattle area, the first major post-war step was the authorization by the state legislature in 1957 of the Municipality of Metropolitan Seattle, with a wide variety of permissive "metropolitan" functions, including transportation planning and transit. Establishment of the agency, and the decision as to which functions would be performed, were made subject to approval of the voters through referenda. Only the function of sewage disposal was approved in the 1958 election. Also in 1957, five counties in the Seattle-Tacoma region agreed to establish the Puget Sound Governmental Conference, a voluntary coordinating committee, which has evolved into a regional planning agency with its own staff. Within the city, Mayor Braman has established an advisory committee for rapid transit, which is spearheading efforts to gain public support and working with interested private groups. In 1967 at the request of the governor, the Washington legislature approved a bill to authorize the Municipality of Metropolitan Seattle to assume responsibility for planning a rapid transit system for King County; that body has in turn established a rapid transit committee.

During the 1950's and 1960's, a number of private organizations relevant to transportation were established: the Central Association, a businessmen's group concerned with the downtown area, the Citizen's Planning Council, Allied Arts, the Washington Roadside Council, and Design for Washington. All of these groups are concerned with aspects of planning, including aesthetics. Finally, in 1966, a new group called Forward Thrust was established with a broad membership representing most elements in the metropolitan area, whose objective is to raise funds through a major bond issue for necessary capital investments in the region (including rapid transit).

Thus, by 1967 both areas had developed, with the cooperation of their states, a whole array of new metropolitan and regional agencies with at least the theoretical capability of planning, constructing and operating transportation facilities on a comprehensive, metropolitan basis.

*Planning decisions.* Before transportation programs can become operable, there must be a plan of action agreed to by the effective decision-makers. In the case of major highways, in most states this is the state highway commission, with advice (but rarely a veto) from the local jurisdictions, varying amounts of influence from the governor and legislature, and final approval by the Federal Bureau of Public Roads. This is an accurate description in the Seattle area, but Baltimore has an almost unique situation. The city builds and maintains all roads itself, except Federal Interstate Highways, and has an effective veto over the latter.

Since 1962 the Federal Highway Act has contained language requiring that urban highway plans be consistent with a comprehensive plan for the region. This has been interpreted to mean, among other things, that all transportation planning (roads and public transportation) must be done in an integrated fashion. Baltimore's present highway "master plan" was completed in 1961 [13] before this requirement took effect, and thus did not fully consider mass transportation requirements. It is based on land-use projections developed by the Regional Planning Council.[14] Following creation of the MTA, that agency engaged a consulting firm to prepare a long-range transit plan, and required that it use the same land-use projections as well as assume that the total highway plan would be built. The firm concluded that Baltimore needed a rapid transit system, but was forced to limit it to filling the interstices between the proposed highways. The result is a plan calling for a "downtown loop" (a subway) and two suburban legs. The plan was presented to the MTA in 1965, and endorsed in principle by that body in 1966.[15]

The Seattle-Tacoma area went through a rather similar process, although the first plan was intended to be comprehensive in compliance with the 1962 amendment. Unlike the Baltimore case, this plan was developed "in-house" by a special staff attached to the Puget Sound Governmental Conference (PSGC), whose director was borrowed from the State Highway Commission. The report, published in 1966, proposed a highway network for the region, but concluded that a rapid

---

[13] *Baltimore Metropolitan Area Transportation Study,* 1964 (prepared by Wilbur Smith & Associates for the Maryland State Roads Commission).

[14] Baltimore Regional Planning Council, *Technical Report No. 9,* "A Projection of Planning Factors for Land Use and Transportation," March, 1963.

[15] *Baltimore Area Mass Transportation Plan: Phase II—Long Range Program,* Oct., 1965.

transit system would not be necessary for the foreseeable future.[16] Because of dissatisfaction with this latter finding, the City of Seattle persuaded the PSGC to sponsor a special transit study. This was completed in 1966 by the consultants, who proposed a "two-leg" rapid transit system meeting in a downtown subway line. "Metro" in Seattle and The Governor's Steering Committee in Baltimore have now engaged consultants to prepare comprehensive plans for the two transit networks.

*Financing.* Federal Interstate Highways are financed with 90 per cent federal participation, the funds for both federal and state shares coming largely from gasoline taxes. While these are never sufficient to meet all demands for highways, nonetheless highway officials have a steady and dependable income for their programs, which is raised relatively painlessly. Such is not the case for public transit needs. Although modest federal assistance has been available since 1964,[17] most of the costs must come from local and state sources, usually the property tax or other general revenue. Thus, decisions to engage in major capital programs for transit are much more difficult and controversial.

These decisions are all the more difficult because many persons, including transportation experts, express serious doubts about the viability of rail rapid transit in highly decentralized urban regions, such as Baltimore and Seattle.[18] The proposals for these two regions, both providing for minimal systems, involve the expenditure of hundreds of millions of dollars. In both places, the question will undoubtedly have to be presented to the voters for their approval.[18a] In neither case has the

---

[16] *Puget Sound Regional Transportation Study: A Summary Report,* Seattle (undated).

[17] The Urban Mass Transportation Act of 1964 (P.L. 88–365) authorizes $375 million for three years for grants-in-aid for transit capital expenditures on a ⅔ federal, ⅓ local matching basis.

[18] In the conclusions of their exhaustive study of the subject, Meyer, Kain, and Wohl state,

Rail transit remains economically attractive for the line-haul only where population densities are extremely high, facilities are to be constructed underground, or rail roadbed structures are already on hand and can be regarded as sunk costs. *It is therefore significant that most American cities with enough population density to support a rail transit operation, or even with prospects of having enough, usually possess rail transit already* (emphasis added) (Meyer, Kain, and Wohl, *Urban Transportation Problem,* p. 364).

Wilfred Owen similarly states, "The inflexibility of rail operations, ... indicates that rail rapid transit and railroad commutation services will not be greatly expanded beyond facilities now in use" (Owen, *Metropolitan Transportation Problem,* p. 214).

[18a] In February 1968, the voters of the "Metro District" of Seattle voted on a bond proposal of $385 million for rapid transit construction. It received a 50.7% favorable vote, but was defeated because the constitutional requirement is a 60% majority. It must be assumed at this point that the battle is not yet over.

state made any commitment to participate in the construction cost, so the non-federal share may have to come entirely from the local jurisdictions.

Thus, while significant steps have been taken in both places toward the development of a "balanced" transportation system, these have all been relatively inexpensive steps, largely financed by the federal government. It will remain to be seen whether such "auto-oriented" populations will be willing to assume such a major financial burden.

Meanwhile, despite noisy objections from private planning and aesthetically oriented groups to various aspects of the program, highway construction is proceeding apace in the Seattle area. In Baltimore, after many years of delay, agreement has been reached on routes for two major interstate highways through the city. The major elements of the suburban highway networks are now complete.

## The Politics of Transportation

The events in the Baltimore and Seattle areas have not yet resulted in commitments to build rapid transit systems, but they do represent rather dramatic changes in the political system for transportation decision-making. Whether transit comes or not, the cast of characters involved in the political process has changed radically since the early 1950's, and the transportation decisions that are made will be different as a result. The mere relation of these events is of relatively little interest, however; what does interest us is how they occurred. What were the forces which influenced these political decisions? A few preliminary conclusions can be suggested on the basis of our study of these two large urban areas, which may outline the typical metropolitan political process in this age of the "new federalism."

*First, federal policy has clearly been a major influence.* In 1954 the Federal Housing Act was broadened in two important ways relevant to transportation: Section 701 was added, providing federal grants for metropolitan planning, and sections relating to urban renewal programs were liberalized. Metropolitan planning programs of the Baltimore Regional Planning Council and the Puget Sound Governmental Conference were almost wholly supported by 701 grants during their early years, thus giving impetus to the first major efforts at metropolitan planning in both areas. After demonstrating their usefulness, these two agencies were able to attract local funds to add to this source, and both now have full-time staffs and are statutorily more secure. Furthermore, 701 funds were the major component of both transit studies.

Liberalization of federal urban renewal legislation was instrumental in assuring the success of Baltimore's downtown reconstruction program. The imposing Charles Center project—the first downtown program—has reversed the downward trend of the central business district, and given new strength and confidence to its business leadership. It and later CBD projects have played a major role in bringing a strong sense of cohesiveness to the business groups and the city's political leadership. These groups have devoted much of their new-found political strength to metropolitan planning and transportation issues as well.

The Federal Interstate and Defense Highway Act of 1956 gave great impetus in both metropolitan areas to their highway construction programs. The regional highway master plans, developed largely with federal funds, have identified more clearly the program issues and provided the grist for appropriate debate among the interested actors. Actual progress on construction of these roads has even more dramatically raised these issues by their very visibility. In both cities, the secondary effects of highway construction on social units, the economy of the downtown, historic sites and aesthetic considerations, have become the subject of active debate, and have fostered the establishment of new civic organizations.

The 1962 amendment to the Federal Highway Act requiring comprehensive planning has had mixed results, but has at least forced recognition by some in both communities of the desirability of this approach and provided ammunition to the opponents of the "roads only" approach. In Seattle the transportation study was in large part a product of this amendment and the study has been found by the Bureau of Public Roads, if not by some of its local critics, to be in compliance with it. In Baltimore the amendment had the direct effect of causing the establishment of a new metropolitan institution. While this organization (ACCORD) has never gotten off the ground, the amendment has given added strength to other metropolitan institutions with more direct action responsibilities in their negotiations with the State Highway Commission.

Finally, the Urban Mass Transportation Act of 1964 has offered the first glimmer of hope to mass transit enthusiasts for a feasible and dramatic change in the mass transit arrangements for the regions. While the funds are still limited, the proponents in the two areas are obviously relying on the hope that appropriations will be increased in the future, and the local share thus reduced to manageable proportions. The sharp imbalance of federal aid between alternative transportation programs, however, continues to distort the local decision-making process.

*Second, the local stimulus for a rethinking of existing policy and for innovative action in the field of transportation has come almost entirely from central city actors.* Prior to the mid-1950's, there was relatively little concern for public transportation and there existed a broad consensus in both regions favorable to the highways approach, including the downtown. In 1955 and 1958 the City of Baltimore made two studies of its languishing bus transit system; the major recommendation of each was the creation of a metropolitan transit authority. Following a third study, this time by the state legislature, which reached the same conclusion, legislation was introduced to establish the MTA.[19] The evidence indicates clearly that this bill and the bill to establish a permanent, independent Regional Planning Council, as well as a third bill to create a study commission to study the metropolitan governmental structure and tax problems, were all results of initiatives from the central city's public officials and private organizations. More recently (winter 1966–1967), this type of initiative was demonstrated again by the joint efforts of the mayor and the Greater Baltimore Committee to get rapid transit planning off dead center, where it had been since the 1965 publication of the consultants' report. Through their initiative, agreement was reached with the two suburban counties and the governor (a) to alter the plan to make it more politically feasible,[20] (b) to obtain a state contribution for the costs of the detailed engineering studies, and (c) to remove the planning function from the MTA and place it in the new Governor's Steering Committee, working with the Regional Planning Council and the MTA. The state contribution was approved by the General Assembly, and a proposal has been sent to Washington for a federal contribution.

Transportation policy-making in the Seattle area has exhibited very similar characteristics, although differing in detail. From the mid-1950's until about 1965, a Seattle attorney carried on almost single-handedly a crusade for rapid transit. He was the leading figure in the unsuccessful effort of 1958 to gain voter approval for inclusion of rapid transit as a function of the new "Metro" organization, and participated in a second unsuccessful effort in 1962. In 1965, however, he gained a major ally, the new mayor, who then appointed him chairman of his special committee on rapid transit. The mayor and his committee were largely responsible for persuading the PSGC to sponsor a transit study, and for gaining approval of the detailed engineering studies which have just begun. The same attorney is one of the organizers of Forward Thrust, which is expected to take the leadership in creating a favorable public

---

[19] *Report,* Baltimore Metropolitan Area Mass Transit Legislative Commission, Oct., 1960.

[20] The original plan proposed by the consultants, based on economic, demographic, and engineering considerations, proposed that the two suburban "legs" extend into Baltimore County. Under the new tentative plan, one of these legs will go to Anne Arundel County.

opinion for a major 1968 bond issue referendum to include capital costs for the transit program.

In both areas, political action regarding highways has taken a different course, and the role of central city actors has been less concerted. One generalization about both can be made: the business and political communities of the central cities favor "balanced transportation." What this means for highway construction, however, is a matter of controversy. In Baltimore, the CBD businessmen and the mayor have publicly supported new highways, but they have not exerted themselves strongly. Support has come chiefly from such groups as the local automobile clubs and bureaucrats responsible for roads and traffic. Opposition seldom takes the form of negativism on roads in general, but rather on particular routes—from city councilmen, neighborhood organizations, public and private planning groups, historic societies, *etc*. But, since the key decisions have to be made within the city, this particularistic opposition has been crucial; Baltimore's highway program is hardly off the ground. Now, thanks to pressure from the state and federal roads agencies and leadership from a few city councilmen, the impasse seems to be ending, and two major roads should be under construction in the near future. In the suburban counties, no such obstruction has occurred or been feasible since they have no veto.

In Seattle similar opposition has arisen to particular roads on social, aesthetic, and economic grounds, but, lacking a veto, city groups have not effectively stopped construction. Two other factors may explain the difference between the two cities: (1) traffic congestion is patently worse in Seattle than in Baltimore, in part because of the topography of the city, but also because Baltimore in the late 1950's employed Mr. Henry Barnes [21] and invested substantial sums (and continues to do so) to establish the latest in traffic management techniques; and (2) auto ownership in the city of Seattle is substantially greater than in Baltimore. [22]

*Third, it seems clear from our own study of these two areas that the creation of new metropolitan institutions has resulted in new allies for the central city proponents of "balanced transportation."* It is a cardinal tenet of the planners' catechism that transportation planning should be

---

[21] Mr. Barnes [was] probably the nation's most famous traffic director. He established his reputation in Denver, whence he came to Baltimore; he [last held] this position in New York City. His reputation [was] based on a combination of traffic engineering skills and public relations techniques. There is a general agreement in Baltimore that he "worked a miracle" with that city traffic, the effects of which are still decidedly being felt. [Mr. Barnes died in 1968.]

[22] In the latter city, 41% of the housing units in 1960 had no automobile, whereas the comparable figure for Seattle was 26%. The figures for the two suburban areas were 11% and 8% respectively (Source: U.S. Census of 1960).

"comprehensive" and should serve general land-use objectives.[23] Since metropolitan planning agencies and commissions are the only metropolitan actors in any position to identify these objectives, they naturally seek to play an influential role in determining transportation policy, so that those objectives can be better served. Traditional highway planning methods contradict these tenets and thus tend to be opposed by regional and metropolitan planners. It is thus not surprising that these new regional agencies—or at least their professional staffs—have developed alliances with the central city interests promoting "balanced" transportation. While they have little formal power in either urban area, their influence derives from their professional skill and their position as spokesmen for the whole metropolitan region. Federal policy, if not always practice, also supports these views, adding greater weight to the argument.[24]

The evidence of the above two sections tends to demonstrate the validity of our third hypothesis. Another factor which tends to effectuate this position is the fact that, despite the declining proportion of the SMSA represented by the central city, it remains the most highly organized jurisdiction politically, and contains (either as employees or residents) the major portion of the area's professional skills relevant to transportation and planning.

*Fourth, there is considerable evidence in these two states that the governor's office is becoming a more important source of initiative for innovations in transportation planning and programming.* In largely urban states, the governors have little choice but to at least appear to be responsive to urban needs. We have observed in this study two Maryland governors and one in Washington. The incumbent governor in Maryland at the time of our interviews (1966), J. Millard Tawes, was a product of pre-reapportionment Maryland. He was from a rural district, but like all Maryland governors, he could not ignore the city of Baltimore, which is a major center of Democratic political strength. It was during his term of office that most of the new metropolitan agencies were created. The [former] governor, Spiro T. Agnew, a Republican from Baltimore County, . . . demonstrated his responsiveness to the needs of the

---

[23] "An effective solution to the urban transportation problem . . . should . . . be functionally comprehensive . . . should be comprehensive geographically . . . , (and) . . . should be comprehensive from a planning standpoint by assuring that transportation is used to promote community goals, and that community plans make satisfactory transportation possible" Owen, *Metropolitan Transportation Problem,* p. 224. It is interesting to note that it is almost exactly his prescription that was added to the Federal Highway Act by the 1962 amendment.

[24] Federal Highway Act of 1962; Section 701 of the Housing Act of 1954.

central city, as expressed by the business community and its Republican mayor, by supporting state assistance to transportation planning and by strongly and successfully promoting a tax reform program beneficial to urban areas. In Washington, Republican Governor Evans, who comes from Seattle, was instrumental in staging a major conference soon after his election, called "Design for Washington," which laid great stress on the importance of improving the quality of the environment, particularly in urban areas. Both Governor Agnew and Governor Evans have urged the establishment of Departments of Transportation at the state level, in order to achieve better coordination of transportation planning, an objective which is only meaningful in urban areas. In March 1967, at Governor Evans' request, the Washington legislature approved establishment of a new "Planning and Community Affairs Agency." [25]

The wide variety of legislation approved in recent years relevant to metropolitan transportation and the increasingly active role of the governors suggests the validity of our fourth hypothesis. Most of this activity to date, however, has been "instrumental" rather than creative or participatory. Specifically, so far there has been little in the way of financial participation. Whether this will develop in these two highly urban states will no doubt depend on the fruits of reapportionment, the character of which it is too early to tell.

## Conclusions

Transportation policy-making in these two areas has experienced major and important changes in the past decade. Numerous new actors are now on the scene, both public and private, both central city and metropolitan, thus creating essentially an entirely new bargaining system. Concepts of metropolitan planning have been accepted in theory, by practically all actors, even those who oppose it in practice. The central cities have demonstrated their substantial influence in affecting metropolitan decision-making. The issues relating to transportation have been more clearly delineated, and, whether or not either area ever builds a rapid transit system, a new awareness of the need for making "metropolitan" and "comprehensive" decisions and new mechanisms for accomplishing these have been created.

Despite the many changes in the last decade or so, the highway agencies have not lost their power, nor are they likely to in the near future. Their programs serve a vital and ever-growing need to meet the

---

[25] "Washington Creates Local Affairs Agency," *Metropolitan Area Digest,* 10:3 (May–June 1967), p. 4.

demands of the motoring public, which is the vast majority of the population. They are very strongly supported by many powerful interests and by the driving public. However, particularly within the central cities, their power is being modified. Those responsible for decisions in these cities are taking vigorous actions, both locally and in the state and national political arenas, to find ways of making the cities more viable and attractive. Through the devices suggested above, they have already succeeded in improving their chances of accomplishing this. While more roads will no doubt be built in these cities, they are now more likely to be built in a manner consistent with these general objectives.

# C. HOUSING AND URBAN DEVELOPMENT

## The Demonstration Cities Program

### LYNDON B. JOHNSON

To the Congress of the United States:

Nineteen hundred and sixty-six can be the year of rebirth for American cities. This Congress, and this people, can set in motion forces of change in great urban areas that will make them the masterpieces of our civilization. Fifty years from now our population will reach that of today's India. Our grandchildren will inhabit a world as different from ours as ours is from the world of Jefferson.

None can predict the shape of his life with any certainty. Yet one thing is sure. It will be lived in cities. By the year 2000, four out of five Americans will live and work in a metropolitan area. We are not strangers to an urban world. We began our national life gathered in towns along the Atlantic seaboard. We built new commercial centers around the Great Lakes and in the Midwest, to serve our westward expansion. Forty million came from Europe to fuel our economy and enrich our community life. This century has seen the steady and rapid migration of farm families—seeking jobs and the promise of the city.

From this rich experience we have learned much. We know that cities can stimulate the best in man, and aggravate the worst. We know the convenience of city life, and its paralysis. We know its promise, and its dark foreboding. What we may only dimly perceive is the gravity of the choice before us. Shall we make our cities livable for ourselves and our posterity? Or shall we by timidity and neglect damn them to fester and decay?

If we permit our cities to grow without rational design; if we stand passively by, while the center of each becomes a hive of deprivation, crime, and hopelessness; if we devour the countryside as though it were

Message from the President to the Congress, transmitting recommendations for City Demonstration Programs, January 26, 1966. Reprinted from H.R. Doc. No. 368, 89th Congress, 2nd session.

limitless, while our ruins—millions of tenement apartments and dilapidated houses—go unredeemed; if we become two people, the suburban affluent and the urban poor, each filled with mistrust and fear one for the other—if this is our desire and policy as a people, then we shall effectively cripple each generation to come. We shall as well condemn our own generation to a bitter paradox: an educated, wealthy, progressive people, who would not give their thoughts, their resources, or their wills to provide for their common well-being.

I do not believe such a fate is either necessary or inevitable. But I believe this will come to pass—unless we commit ourselves now to the planning, the building, the teaching, and the caring that alone can forestall it. That is why I am recommending a massive demonstration cities program. I recommend that both the public and private sectors of our economy join to build in our cities and towns an environment for man equal to the dignity of his aspirations. I recommend an effort larger in scope, more comprehensive, more concentrated, than any that has gone before.

# I

## The Work of the Past

I know the work of the past three decades. I have shared in the forging of our Federal housing and renewal programs. I know what they have done for millions of urban Americans:

8 million single-family dwellings assisted by the Federal Housing Administration.

An additional 6.7 million assisted by the Veterans Administration.

1.1 million multiple units created.

605,000 families moved out of decayed and unsanitary dwellings into decent public housing.

300,000 dwelling units supported under urban renewal.

Without these programs, the goal I recommend today would be impossible to achieve. Because Federal sponsorship is so effective a part of our system of homebuilding, we can conceive a far larger purpose than it has yet fulfilled. We must make use of every established housing program—and of social, educational, and economic instruments as well—if the demonstration cities program is to succeed.

## The Problem Today

Our housing programs have built a platform, from which we may see how far away is the reborn city we desire. For there still remain:

Some four million urban families living in homes of such disrepair as to violate decent housing standards.

The need to provide over 30 per cent more housing annually than we are currently building.

Our chronic inability to provide sufficient low- and moderate-income housing, of adequate quality, at a reasonable price.

The special problem of the poor and the Negro, unable to move freely from their ghettoes, exploited in the quest for the necessities of life.

Increasing pressures on municipal budgets, with large city per capita expenditures rising 36 per cent in the three years after 1960.

The high human costs: crime, delinquency, welfare loads, disease, and health hazards. This is man's fate in those broken neighborhoods where he can "feel the enclosure of the flaking walls and see through the window the blackened reflection of the tenement across the street that blocks out the world beyond."

The tragic waste, and indeed, the chaos, that threatens where children are born into the stifling air of overcrowded rooms, and destined for a poor diet, inadequate schools, streets of fear and sordid temptation, joblessness, and the gray anxiety of the ill prepared.

And the flight to the suburbs of more fortunate men and women who might have provided the leadership and the means for reversing this human decline.

## The Inadequate Response

Since 1949, the urban renewal program has been our chief instrument in the struggle for a decent urban environment. Over 800 cities are participating in urban renewal programs. Undertaken and designed by the cities themselves, these efforts have had an increasing influence on the use of urban land. Last year the Congress wisely extended the authorization for urban renewal at a higher level than before.

Years of experience with urban renewal have taught us much about its strengths and weaknesses. Since 1961 we have made major alterations in its administration. We have made it more responsive to human needs. We have more vigorously enforced the requirement of a workable program for the entire community. Within the limits of current law, we have achieved considerable progress toward these goals.

Nevertheless, the social and psychological effects of relocating the poor have not always been treated as what they are. They are the unavoidable consequences of slum clearance, demanding as much concern as physical redevelopment.

The size and scale of urban assistance have been too small, and too widely dispersed. Present programs are often prisoners of archaic and wasteful building practices. They have inhibited the use of modern technology. They have inflated the cost of rebuilding.

The benefits and efficiencies that can come from metropolitan planning are still unrealized in most urban regions. Insufficient resources cause extensive delays in many projects. The result is growing blight and overcrowding that thwart our best efforts to resist them.

The goals of major Federal programs have often lacked cohesiveness. Some work for the revitalization of the central city. Some accelerate suburban growth. Some unite urban communities. Some disrupt them.

## Urban Dilemmas

Virtually every forward step we have taken has had its severe limitations. Each of those steps has involved a public choice, and created a public dilemma:

> Major clearance and reconstruction, with its attendant hardships of relocation.
>
> Relieving traffic congestion, thereby widening the gulf between the affluence of suburbia and the poverty of the city.
>
> Involving urban residents in redeveloping their own areas, hence lengthening the time and increasing the cost of the job.
>
> Preserving the autonomy of local agencies, thus crippling our efforts to attack regional problems on a regional basis.

These dilemmas cannot be completely resolved by any single program, no matter how well designed. The prize—cities of spacious beauty and lively promise, where men are truly free to determine how they will live—is too rich to be lost because the problems are complex.

Let there be debate over means and priorities. Let there be experiment with a dozen approaches, or a hundred. But let there be commitment to that goal.

## II

## What Is Required

From the experience of three decades, it is clear to me that American cities require a program that will—

> Concentrate our available resources—in planning tools, in housing construction, in job training, in health facilities, in recreation, in welfare programs, in education—to improve the conditions of life in urban areas. Join together all available talent and skills in a coordinated effort.

Mobilize local leadership and private initiative, so that local citizens will determine the shape of their new city—freed from the constraints that have handicapped their past efforts and inflated their costs.

## A Demonstration Cities Program

*I propose* a demonstration cities program that will offer qualifying cities of all sizes the promise of a new life for their people.

*I propose* that we make massive additions to the supply of low- and moderate-cost housing.

*I propose* that we combine physical reconstruction and rehabilitation with effective social programs throughout the rebuilding process.

*I propose* that we achieve new flexibility in administrative procedures.

*I propose* that we focus all the techniques and talents within our society on the crisis of the American city.

It will not be simple to qualify for such a program. We have neither the means nor the desire to invest public funds in an expensive program whose net effects will be marginal, wasteful, or visible only after protracted delay. We intend to help only those cities who help themselves. I propose these guidelines for determining a city's qualifications for the benefits—and achievements—of this program.

1. The demonstration should be of sufficient magnitude both in its physical and social dimensions to arrest blight and decay in entire neighborhoods. It must make a substantial impact within the coming few years on the development of the entire city.

2. The demonstration should bring about a change in the total environment of the area affected. It must provide schools, parks, playgrounds, community centers, and access to all necessary community facilities.

3. The demonstration—from its beginning—should make use of every available social program. The human cost of reconstruction and relocation must be reduced. New opportunities for work and training must be offered.

4. The demonstration should contribute to narrowing the housing gap between the deprived and the rest of the community. Major additions must be made to the supply of sound dwellings. Equal opportunity in the choice of housing must be assured to every race.

5. The demonstration should offer maximum occasions for employing residents of the demonstration area in all phases of the program.

6. The demonstration should foster the development of local and private initiative and widespread citizen participation—especially from the demonstration area—in the planning and execution of the program.

7. The demonstration should take advantage of modern cost-reducing technologies without reducing the quality of the work. Neither the structure of real estate taxation, cumbersome building codes, nor inefficient building practices should deter rehabilitation or inflate project costs.

8. The demonstration should make major improvements in the quality of the environment. There must be a high quality of design in new buildings, and attention to man's need for open spaces and attractive landscaping.

9. The demonstration should make relocation housing available at costs commensurate with the incomes of those displaced by the project. Counseling services, moving expenses, and small business loans should be provided, together with assistance in job placement and re-training.

10. The demonstration should be managed in each demonstration city by a single authority with adequate powers to carry out and coordinate all phases of the program. There must be a serious commitment to the project on the part of local, and, where appropriate, State authorities. Where required to carry out the plan, agreements should be reached with neighboring communities.

11. The demonstration proposal should offer proof that adequate municipal appropriations and services are available and will be sustained throughout the demonstration period.

12. The demonstration should maintain or establish a residential character in the area.

13. The demonstration should be consistent with existing development plans for the metropolitan areas involved. Transportation plans should coordinate every appropriate mode of city and regional transportation.

14. The demonstration should extend for an initial six-year period. It should maintain a schedule for the expeditious completion of the project.

These guidelines will demand the full cooperation of government at every level and of private citizens in each area. I believe our Federal system is creative enough to inspire that cooperative effort. I know it must be creative if it is to prosper and flourish.

## Size of the Program

The program I recommend is intended to eliminate blight in the entire demonstration area. Through efficient rebuilding it must replace that blight with attractive and economic housing, social services, and community facilities.

There are many ways by which this can be done, once the commitment has been made to do it. Total clearance and reconstruction; partial clearance and rehabilitation; rehabilitation alone—any of these methods may be chosen by local citizens. Whatever approach is selected, however, must be comprehensive enough to be effective and economic.

There are few cities or towns in America which could not participate in the demonstration cities program. We shall take special care to see that urban communities of all sizes are included. For each such community, the impact of the program will be significant, involving as much as 15 to 20 per cent of the existing substandard structures.

For the largest qualifying cities, a relatively modest program could provide decent housing for approximately 5,000 families now living in substandard dwelling units. It could rehabilitate other marginal housing sufficient to affect 50,000 people. A typical program could well involve a total of 35,000 units or 100,000 people.

For cities of approximately 100,000 people, 1,000 families could be rehoused and 3,000 units rehabilitated, affecting a total of 10,000 people.

### Benefits of the Program

I recommend that participating cities receive two types of Federal assistance:

First, *the complete array of all available grants and urban aids* in the fields of housing, renewal, transportation, education, welfare, economic opportunity, and related programs.

Second, *special grants amounting to 80 per cent of the non-Federal cost of our grant-in-aid programs included in the demonstration.* These grants are to supplement the efforts of local communities. They are not to be substituted for those efforts.

In every qualifying city, a Federal coordinator would be assigned to assist local officials in bringing together all the relevant Federal resources.

Once authorized, the supplemental funds would be made available in a common account. They would be drawn at the discretion of the community to support the program. They would be certified by the Federal coordinator.

It is vital that incentives be granted for cost reductions achieved during the performance of the program.

At least as vital as the dollar commitment for rebuilding and rehabilitation is the social program commitment. We must link our concern for the total welfare of the person with our desire to improve the physical city in which he lives. For the first time, social and construction agencies would be joined in a massive common effort, responsive to a common local authority.

There is another benefit—not measurable in dollars, or even in the extended range of social services—that qualifying cities would secure by participating in this program.

It is a sense of hope—

> That the city is not beyond reach of redemption by men of good will. That through wise planning, cooperation, hard work, and the sacrifice of those outmoded codes and practices that make widespread renewal impossibly expensive today, it *is* possible to reverse the city's decline.

That knowledge, that confidence, that hope can make all the difference in the decade ahead.

## III

### Federal Cost

Funds are required in the first year to assist our cities in the preparation of demonstration plans. We should not underestimate the problems involved in achieving such a plan. The very scale of the demonstration— its widespread and profound effects on the social and physical structure of the city—calls for marshaling the city's planning and administrative resources on an unprecedented scale.

I estimate the appropriate Federal contribution to this planning effort at $12 million. For the supplemental demonstration grants I will recommend appropriations, over a six-year period, totaling over $2.3 billion, or an average of some $400 million per year.

It is impossible to estimate exactly—but it is necessary to consider —the rising cost of welfare services, crime prevention, unemployment, and declining property values which will plague all governments, local, State, and Federal, if we do not move quickly to heal and revitalize our cities.

### Metropolitan Planning

The success of each demonstration will depend on the quality of its planning, and the degree of cooperation it elicits from the various governmental bodies concerned, as well as from private interests.

Most metropolitan areas conduct some degree of metropolitan planning now. The Federal Government has made funds available throughout the country so that State and local planning agencies might devise— many for the first time—comprehensive plans for metropolitan areas.

I recommend improvements and extensions of this program. The Congress enacted it recognizing that the problems of growth, transportation, housing, and public services cannot be considered by one entity of government alone.

The absence of cooperation between contiguous areas is wasteful. It is also blind to the reality of urban life. What happens in the central city, or the suburb, is certain to affect the quality of life in the other.

The widespread demand for these funds has resulted in their being spread thinly across the 50 States. Thus, the benefits of a truly coordinated attack on metropolitan problems have not generally been realized.

## Incentives to Orderly Metropolitan Development

Over the past five years, the Congress has authorized Federal grants for urban mass transportation, open space, and sewer and water facilities. The Congress has required that such projects be consistent with comprehensive planning for an entire urban or metropolitan area. The Federal Government has thus not only helped our localities to provide the facilities they need; it has also stimulated cooperation and joint planning among neighboring jurisdictions.

But more remains to be done. The powerful forces of urban growth threaten to overwhelm efforts to achieve orderly development. A metropolitan plan should be an instrument for shaping sound urban growth— not a neglected document.

I now propose a new incentive to help assure that metropolitan plans achieve their potential.

The Federal Government should bear a larger share of the total cost of related Federal aid programs. This share would be borne where local jurisdictions show that they are ready to be guided by their own plans in working out the patterns of their own development and where they establish the joint institutional arrangements necessary to carry out those plans.

## Demonstrations of Effective Planning

I propose that a series of demonstrations in effective metropolitan planning be undertaken promptly.

Metropolitan areas would be selected to return the broadest possible data and experience to Federal, State, and local governments. They should therefore be of varying size and environment, in widely separated locations. They would be selected to assure that their benefits reach small communities surrounding the large cities.

Advanced techniques and approaches should be employed. There must be—

Balanced consideration of physical and human development programs.

Coordinated treatment of the regional transportation network.

Technical innovations, such as metropolitan data banks and systems analysis.

New educational and training programs.

New arrangements for coordinating decisions of the various local governments involved.

I estimate the cost of the demonstrations at $6,500,000.

I shall impose on the new Department of Housing and Urban Development the continuing responsibility to stimulate effective planning. If local governments do not plan for inevitable urban growth cooperatively and sufficiently in advance, even adequate funds and an aggressive determination to improve our cities cannot succeed.

## IV

### Housing for All

The programs I have proposed—in rebuilding large areas of our cities, and in metropolitan planning—are essential for the rebirth of urban America.

Yet at the center of the cities' housing problem lies racial discrimination. Crowded miles of inadequate dwellings—poorly maintained and frequently overpriced—are the lot of most Negro Americans in many of our cities. Their avenue of escape to a more attractive neighborhood is often closed because of their color.

The Negro suffers from this, as do his children. So does the community at large. Where housing is poor, schools are generally poor. Unemployment is widespread. Family life is threatened. The community's welfare burden is steadily magnified. These are the links in the chain of racial discrimination.

This administration is working to break that chain—through aid to education, medical care, community action programs, job retraining, and the maintenance of a vigorous economy.

The time has come when we should break one of its strongest links —the often subtle but always effective force of housing discrimination. The impacted racial ghetto will become a thing of the past only when the Negro American can move his family wherever he can afford to do so.

I shall, therefore, present to the Congress at an early date legislation to bar racial discrimination in the sale or rental of housing.

## New Communities

Our existing urban centers, however revitalized, cannot accommodate all the urban Americans of the next generation.

Three million new residents are added each year to our present urban population. The growth of new communities is inevitable. Unless they are to be casual parts of a general urban sprawl, a new approach to their design is required.

We must—

Enlarge the entire scale of the building process.
Make possible new efficiencies in construction, land development, and municipal services.
Relieve population densities.
Offer a variety of homes to a wide range of incomes.

These communities must also provide an environment harmonious to man's needs. They must offer adequate transportation systems, attractive community buildings, and open spaces free from pollution. They must retain much of the natural beauty of the landscape.

The private sector must continue its prominent role in new community development. As I recommended to the Congress last year, mortgage insurance should be made available for sites and community facilities for entire new communities.

It is apparent that new communities will spring into being near an increasing number of major metropolitan areas. Some, already in existence, promise dramatic efficiencies through size and new construction techniques, without sacrificing beauty. Obviously such a development should be encouraged. I recommend that the Congress provide the means of doing so.

## Rent Supplement Program

Rarely has a new housing program evoked such a dramatic and positive response as the rent supplement program. The Department of Housing and Urban Affairs has already received preliminary proposals from sponsors to construct nearly 70,000 low-income units under this program as soon as funds become available. The proposals involve 424 projects in 265 localities in 43 States, the District of Columbia, and Puerto Rico. The sponsors have already selected sites for some 40,000 of these units. The interested groups are about equally divided between nonprofit organizations and private limited-dividend developers.

The need for this program is obvious. It is the need of the poor and the disadvantaged. The demand for the means to meet this need by private enterprise is demonstrated by the figures I have just cited.

I strongly urge the Congress to pass a supplementary appropriation to fund the rent supplement program at the $30 million level it has authorized in the Housing and Urban Development Act of 1965.

## Mass Transportation Program

We must continue to help our communities meet their increasing needs for mass transportation facilities. For this purpose, I propose an additional one-year authorization for the urban mass transportation program.

## The New Department

No Federal program can be effective unless the agency that administers it is efficient. This is even more crucial for programs that call for comprehensive approaches at both the Federal and local level.

Progress was made after 1961 toward unifying the Housing and Home Finance Agency. But the very nature of that Agency limited the extent to which its several parts could be welded into a truly unified whole. Its Administrator lacked the statutory basis for gaining full control over partially independent agencies.

With this in mind, I requested—and you enacted—legislation to create a Department of Housing and Urban Development. As a result, the Secretary of the new Department now has the authority and the machinery for implementing the new programs I have asked for. I see five ways by which he can do this:

1. He can organize the Department so that its emphasis will be upon meeting modern urban needs—rather than fitting new programs into old and outgrown patterns.

2. He can strengthen the regional structure so that more decisions can be made in the field.

3. He can assert effective leadership throughout the Department.

4. He can mesh together all our social and physical efforts to improve urban living.

5. He can assume leadership among intergovernmental agencies dealing with urban problems.

Such a Department, and such leadership, will be worthy of the program that I recommend you adopt.

## A Year of Rebirth

The evidence is all about us that to be complacent about the American city is to invite, at best, inconvenience; at worst, a divided nation.

The programs I have proposed in this message will require a determined commitment of our energy and a substantial commitment of our funds. Yet these programs are well within our resources. Nor do they compare in cost with the ugliness, hostility, and hopelessness of unlivable cities. What would it mean to begin now, and to bring about the rebirth of our cities?

It would mean—

A more tolerable and a more hopeful life for millions of Americans.

The possibility of retaining middle-income families in the city, and even attracting some to return.

Improving the cities' tax base at a time of heavy strain on city budgets.

Ultimately reducing welfare costs.

Avoiding the unnecessary waste of human resources.

Giving to both urban and suburban families the freedom to choose where they will live.

A clean room and a patch of sky for every person, a chance to live near an open space, and to reach it on a safe street.

As Thomas Wolfe wrote, "to every man his chance—to every man, regardless of his birth, his shining, golden opportunity—to every man the right to live, to work, to be himself, and to become whatever thing his manhood and his vision can combine to make him—this . . . is the promise of America."

I believe these are among the most profound aspirations of our people. I want to make them part of our destiny.

I urge the Congress promptly to adopt the Demonstration Cities Act of 1966. If we begin now the planning from which action will flow, the hopes of the twentieth century will become the realities of the twenty-first.

Lyndon B. Johnson

The White House, January 26, 1966.

# The War on Cities

## JAMES Q. WILSON

President Johnson's 1966 special message to Congress on improving the nation's cities was a notable document, both for what it said and for what it did not. It was, in many respects, the sanest and most thoughtful presidential statement on "the urban problem" ever issued. It avoided most of those rhetorical absurdities which link the future of Western civilization with the maintenance of the downtown business district; it stressed the primacy of human and social problems over purely physical ones; and it conceded with great candor the dilemmas, contradictions, and inadequacies of past and present federal programs. (Indeed, the first third of the message could easily have been written by any one of several critics of federal urban renewal and public housing programs.) Many of the proposals made by the President were entirely in keeping with a concern for the problems of disadvantaged people living in cities. Thus, legislation to bar racial discrimination in the sale or rental of housing, and appropriations to implement the rent supplement program (whereby through direct subsidy the poor are given a better chance to acquire decent housing on the private market) were requested.

As reasonable and humane as were this message and the subsequent Model Cities Bill passed by Congress, they both leave unanswered some fundamental questions. While it is refreshing to hear a President admit that present policies have produced some "urban dilemmas," listing the dilemmas is no substitute for resolving them. In fact, far from being resolved, these dilemmas are accentuated by having added to them those of a new program, devised in part by academic critics of the urban renewal program, which will, on a "demonstration" basis try to add to the supply of low and moderate cost housing (while the urban

---

Reprinted from *The Public Interest* © 1966 by National Affairs, Inc., by permission of the author and publisher.

renewal program continues reducing that supply) and to serve "poor and disadvantaged people" (while existing programs presumably go on serving other people). No cohesive policy is suggested—only the co-ordination at the *local* level of existing policies. This will not be easy since the programs to be co-ordinated are run by separate bureaucracies with different and often competing sources of political support at the federal as well as local level.

Indeed, it is striking that an agency—the Housing and Home Finance Agency, now renamed the Department of Housing and Urban Development—which has been so often criticized in the past for allowing almost unfettered discretion to local communities in their use of federal urban renewal funds should, partly in response to these criticisms, have a new program for "demonstration" or "model" cities which continues to rely on local initiative and local objectives in formulating plans.

The Model Cities Bill nowhere says *what* will be done. The difference between it and the older urban renewal program is that now local proposals must conform to "guidelines" laid down by HUD. Presumably these guidelines and the good intentions of the new leadership of HUD will insure that a "model" city is something more than—or at least something different from—an urban renewal city. But the debate on the program suggests that Congress is far from clear as to what that difference is to be; everything depends on administrative decisions, and so far there have not been many.

**I**

The fundamental problem afflicting federal policy in this area—the problem which this message and bill suggest but do not face—is that *we do not know what we are trying to accomplish.* We have neither concrete goals nor clear priorities; as a result, not only are federal programs productive of dilemmas, but the dilemmas are each year becoming more expensive and more obvious. Do we seek to raise standards of living, maximize housing choices, revitalize the commercial centers of our cities, end suburban sprawl, eliminate discrimination, reduce traffic congestion, improve the quality of urban design, check crime and delinquency, strengthen the effectiveness of local planning, increase citizen participation in local government? All these objectives sound attractive—in part, because they are rather vague—but unfortunately they are in many cases incompatible.

Improving urban design is made harder by efforts to find housing for the poor, for well-designed housing almost always costs more than the poor can afford. A "revitalized" downtown business district not only implies, *it requires* traffic congestion—an "uncongested" Broadway or State Street would be no Broadway or State Street at all. Effective local planning requires *less,* not more, citizen participation—the more views represented, the less the possibility of agreement on any single (especially any single comprehensive) view. Maximum housing choices, unconstrained by discriminatory practices, and reinforced by higher incomes, will give more people the opportunity to join the movement to the suburbs.

American political life has a proven and oft-remarked genius for surviving and even prospering on dilemmas and contradictions. Government maintains the support of potentially hostile groups by letting different federal agencies serve incompatible goals and by encouraging local communities to follow competing policies at federal expense. The new Department of Housing and Urban Development stands squarely in this tradition. Under its previous name (the Housing and Home Finance Agency), it subsidized the flight to the suburbs with FHA mortgage insurance, while trying to lure suburbanites back to the central city with subsidies provided by the Urban Renewal Administration. The Public Housing Administration built low-rent units for the poor while urban renewal was tearing them down. Furthermore, the goals for most programs—especially urban renewal—were determined at the local level. This meant that urban renewal, in itself simply a tool, was used for very different purposes in different cities—in some places to get Negroes out of white neighborhoods, in others to bring middle-class people closer to downtown department stores, in still other places to build dramatic civic monuments, and in a few places to rehabilitate declining neighborhoods and add to the supply of moderately priced housing. Throughout its life, HHFA could have the best of both worlds —in Washington, its leaders could make broad policy statements which were intended to satisfy whatever critics of the program the administration was most sensitive to; meanwhile, in the hundreds of communities where the actual purposes of our housing programs were determined by the decisions of local governing bodies, many objectives which bore only the loosest relationship to federal policy statements were being pursued.

One can admire a system which so neatly accommodates the tensions of political reality without approving of all its consequences. And these consequences stem, in my view, from the fact that, in thinking about solutions to the "urban problem," we have committed ourselves to certain means before we have made a commitment to any goals. The means have been federally subsidized alterations in the housing stock and in certain other physical equipment (mass transportation, community facilities, and the like). The *a priori* commitment to this program has the result that alternative tactics to reach certain goals are not systematically considered, or are considered only as afterthoughts. Surely few would ever have disagreed that the two greatest causes of inadequate housing have been the fact that some people have not been able to afford good housing and that some have, because of race, been denied an opportunity to bid freely for such housing as exists. Yet it was not until last year that HHFA requested of Congress a program that would improve the purchasing power of poor families by direct income subsidies and it was not until this year that legislation was proposed by the President to bar discrimination in the sale or rental of housing (an executive order by President Kennedy had previously barred discrimination in federally assisted housing, which is about one-fifth of the total).

In the meantime—and continuing right down to the present—local communities are allowed great latitude in deciding how federal funds will be spent on the bread-and-butter programs: urban renewal and public housing. If the Main Street merchants are in power, they can use renewal funds to tear down low-cost housing and put up luxury apartments near the department stores—in effect redistributing income from the poor to the well-to-do while reducing the stock of low-cost housing. If more generous souls are in power, the worst housing is torn down to make room for middle- or lower-middle-income housing; the income transfer from poor to not-so-poor is much less, but it is still in the wrong direction. And if the mayor simply is seeking funds with which to run his city in the face of a declining tax base, he discovers that he must join with those who want one of these urban renewal programs because that is about the only way he can get large-scale federal money into his city. He discovers, in short, that he has to hurt his poorest and weakest citizens in order to provide for the general welfare; his only option is to try to do it as humanely as possible. Under any or all of these conditions, urban renewal may or may not produce attractive, well-designed new structures; that is a separate issue. The point is that for almost any legitimate community objective—improving the supply of housing, strengthening the tax base, etc.—urban renewal has in most cases proved to be an unwieldy and costly tool.

We have recently been making some improvements in that tool at the federal level; and in communities which elect to use the improved version of urban renewal, the human costs are reduced and the incidence of those costs is made more equitable. Rehabilitation of existing structures reduces displacement (it does not eliminate it—you can drive out

a low-income family as easily by raising its rent as by tearing down
its apartment); below-the-market interest rates make it possible to bring
the cost of new construction down to what "moderate" income families
can afford (which is usually a lot more than poor families can afford);
public housing can be better designed and built on scattered sites (though
the cost of an apartment in many public housing projects is still more
than what it would take to build a brand new suburban home for the
family). No one can object to the sentiments and intentions represented
by these changes. But now that a new department has come into being,
perhaps it is time to ask whether a new approach to the "urban problem"
is conceivable.

*     *     *

## III

Federal policies have moved only recently in a direction that
acknowledges that the "urban problem" is not primarily, or even significantly, a housing problem. The rent supplement program is a recognition
of the need to deal directly with the cause of slum housing—i.e., the fact
that there are people who cannot afford non-slum housing. The call for
legislation to bar discrimination in the housing market is a recognition
of the need to reduce the inflated prices of Negro housing by giving
Negroes access to the entire housing market. (Although the principle is
sound, not much is likely to happen as a result of such a statute; open
occupancy laws already on the books in many states and cities have
not broken up the Negro enclaves, partly because housing outside such
enclaves sometimes costs more than housing inside them.)

But for the present, these and other modifications are largely frost-
ing on a tasteless cake. The major thrust of federal policy is now, and
always has been, a commitment to maintain and enhance the physical
shells of existing American cities—adding, where appropriate, a few
new towns to handle the overflow. The desire to make all American
cities "livable" not only exaggerates the extent to which cities are now
"unlivable," but it thoughtlessly lumps together all cities—whether or
not they continue to serve any functions, whether or not there is any
rational ground for conserving them at public expense, and even whether
or not the local leadership conceives of urban conservation as driving
the poor across the city line into somebody else's city.

It was long argued that urban interests deserved a cabinet department, just as agricultural interests had one. It is a disturbing analogy.
For thirty years the Department of Agriculture has, in effect, been committed to the preservation of farms regardless of how inefficient or

economically unsound they became. Now there are signs that pressure from mayors and downtown business interests may move the Department of Housing and Urban Development even farther toward a policy of guaranteeing the perpetual existence of the central business district of every American city, no matter how inefficient or economically unsound they may become.

There is nothing sacrosanct about the present patterns or functions of urban life; cities, like people, pass through life cycles during which their values and functions change. Cities sometimes die, and for good cause. But the implicit commitment of our new Department to physical structures, rather than to concrete human needs, makes it almost impossible for it to distinguish between cities which need help and cities which do not; any city "needs" help if it says it does. The result is that while the rhetoric of the "urban crisis" is aimed at the great national and regional centers of commerce, culture, education, and government—Washington, New York, Philadelphia, Boston, Los Angeles—the reality of federal programs can be found in Barre, Vermont, and Wink, Texas. *Over half of all cities with urban renewal projects have populations of less than 25,000.* (In this respect, HUD is more democratic than the Department of Agriculture; whereas the latter was of more help to the big than to the small farmer, the former is subsidizing the smaller as well as the larger cities.)

There is an alternative policy which could direct federal activities. It would require, not the scrapping of existing federal programs, but only their redirection. Such a policy would begin with a recognition of the different kinds of "urban problems"—some of which, like poverty, are as much rural as urban problems, and others of which, like the gap between expectations and achievements, are not problems that government can do anything about. Such a policy would, I suggest, contain the following elements:

First, the federal government would assume responsibility for placing a floor under the capacity of Americans to acquire a minimally satisfactory level of personal and family amenities—housing, food, clothing, medical care. Where possible, guaranteeing such resources to every family would be done by combining aggregate fiscal policies which produce full employment with direct income transfers—in the form, say, of a negative income tax, family allowances, or rent subsidies—so that each family has a maximum free choice as to the type and location of its housing. Some conservatives will of course object that this is a "dole," productive of moral debilitation. I submit that, unless we are willing to tolerate privation, we of necessity must have some sort of dole; the real question is whether it will be one which minimizes choice and maximizes bureaucratic intervention in private lives (as is the case with public housing projects and many welfare programs) or one with the opposite characteristics.

I am under no illusion that the problems of the central-city poor, white and Negro, will vanish because we adopt an income maintenance strategy. All I am suggesting is that whatever else must be done to cope with poverty, there will be little progress unless the one indisputable component of poverty—low incomes—is dealt with by methods more effective and less debasing than those which require husbands to desert their wives and children before these latter can apply for welfare.

Second, public power and public funds would be used to provide those common benefits (or, as the economists say, collective goods) which are enjoyed, and thus must be paid for, by everybody. Fresh air, pure water, open spaces, parkland, and police protection are the most common examples of indivisible benefits whose achievement requires the exercise of public powers. Ironically, it is in this area (where even in the days of Adam Smith it was agreed that public intervention was required) that federal action has been the slowest in developing. The reason, of course, is understandable enough; most collective goods require control over those aspects of community life—the education of the young, the policing of the city, and the use of land—which Americans have long insisted be kept in local hands. So long as most of us lived and worked in the same place—i.e., the central city—purely local control of these matters may have made sense. What services we used as we traveled to and from work we also paid for through taxes. Upper-middle-class citizens with a strong interest in (and a healthy capacity to pay for) common benefits, such as parks and the like, lived in—and often governed—the central city. With the exodus to the suburbs, and our self-segregation into radically different kinds of communities on the periphery, differences in preferences and income which used to co-exist within a single taxing authority now are separated by political boundaries. If the incidence of costs and benefits of various collective goods is to be equalized throughout the metropolitan area, some higher taxing authority must assume responsibility for transfer payments. There are only two such authorities—the state and the federal government.

Third, where possible, central cities facing a fiscal crisis ought to receive block grants from state or federal governments in order to help defray the cost of servicing the poor, providing decent education and police protection, etc. At the present time, cities must commit themselves to a whole range of federally conceived programs in order to get money they urgently need, even though many of these programs may be either irrelevant or harmful to the interests of parts of the city's population. Cities with an eroding tax base seize upon urban renewal as the only way to get federal support for that tax base, even though it is a clumsy and inefficient way—it requires destroying homes or businesses, allowing land to lie vacant for long periods of time, and pushing people who consume high levels of local services into neighboring cities where they cause the whole dreary cycle to be repeated. The already-enacted federal aid to education program is a step in the right direction, though the amounts will surely have to be increased.

Even if one were to accept the dubious proposition that the cities could be rebuilt to retain or lure back the middle classes—a proposition that lies at the bottom of much of the urban renewal strategy—any but the most blind partisans ought to concede that what drives the middle classes out of the city in the first place may have much less to do with the physical condition of the buildings than with the quality of the public schools and the level of public safety. Subsidizing these institutions, rather than the rents the middle classes have to pay, strikes me as both fairer (since it will help the poor as well as the better off) and more likely to produce desirable results.

Fourth, the federal government, through special incentives, ought to encourage cities to experiment with various user charges as a way of making certain that non-residents pay their fair share of the services they use in the cities where they work or shop, and that residents have a more precise and personal way than voting for or against the mayor to indicate how much of a particular local service they really desire for themselves. At the present time, large groups of people get something for nothing—non-residents who park on the city's streets, for example, or residents who, owning no taxable property, enthusiastically vote for more and more free public facilities. The whole burden is thrown on the property-tax payer, and he cannot sustain it.

Fifth, urban renewal and other land clearance programs can be used as a tool to aid in providing collective goods (by assembling land and financing good design for public buildings, schools, and the like), and as a way of eliminating hazardous or unsalvageable structures. If renewal is to do more than this, then to insure against the excesses of the past it ought to be hedged about with the most explicit restrictions. If decent low-cost housing is to be torn down for high-cost housing, then it should be done only when either a clear collective benefit (e.g., a new school or park) will result or when *surplus* low-cost housing can be removed. The latter would require a prior showing that the vacancy rate among low-cost housing units in that city or area is high enough to make possible the absorption of displaced families without serious economic loss, and that a close study of the social structure of the affected neighborhood reveals it to be primarily a place with high transiency rates where strong family life and neighborhood ties have not developed. And if a subsidy is conferred on the developer and his new upper-income tenants, then provision ought to be made to recapture that subsidy over time—perhaps by making the federal contribution a long-term loan rather than a grant (this was actually proposed when the original legislation was first debated in Congress), or by allowing the city to adopt special tax measures to recover the subsidy for itself.

## IV

It is possible to conceive of a rational policy for dealing with so-called "urban" problems, once one begins to realize that the word "urban" is less relevant than the word "human." And perhaps this is implied in the Model Cities Program now getting underway, though the details are still sufficiently vague to make its real significance unclear. Leaving aside the obvious contradictions in the "guidelines" for determining whether a city is qualified to participate (for example, the incompatibility between maximum "co-ordination" achieved by a "single authority with adequate powers" and "widespread citizen participation" in the demonstration area), one may take the optimistic view that the Model Cities Program is simply a fancy way of describing a new federal effort to impose federal standards on the local use of renewal money, so that renewal projects are more likely to serve legitimate national objectives than whatever purposes, good or bad, local leaders cook up.

The demand for more local "co-ordination" and "planning" may be a tactic for creating an organized local constituency for HUD. A good case can be made for such intentions, but it is doubtful that a Congress sensitive to local interests and pressures is going to let HUD or anyone else get away with it entirely. And this, of course, should provide a good political reason for shifting federal efforts more in the direction of universalistic programs (maintaining the incomes of all poor, and subsidizing services—like education—which provide general benefits) and away from particularistic programs (tearing down some buildings and subsidizing others). So long as programs are designed to achieve particular effects in particular places, they will frequently be used by local groups to the disadvantage of the poor and powerless, or to produce effects that the federal taxpayer should not be required to pay for. And so long as HUD has no consistent federal policy, Congress will be able to insist that policies be set at the local level.

There is a bureaucratic as well as political reason for favoring universalistic programs—large bureaucracies are not very good at performing complex tasks requiring the exercise of a great deal of co-ordination over disparate activities, the accomplishments of which cannot be easily measured or evaluated. Direct income transfers, block grants to local governments, and increased reliance on individual choice are ways of reducing the impossible burdens on government agencies, most of which are (necessarily) staffed by men of average attainments.

Making full allowance for the good intentions behind the Model Cities Program, its central problem—apart from (though related to) the obscurity as to its goals and the mystery as to its means—is that it is an effort to improve on old programs, not by changing them or by substituting a wholly new strategy, but by creating a new apparatus to show how by "co-ordination" (i.e., more administration) the job can be done better. But the failures of the past sixteen years have been precisely the failures of administration—of seeking inappropriate or incompatible goals, or of being unable to attain given goals, or of failing to take into account the consequences of working toward these goals. Overcoming the weaknesses of administration by providing more administration is likely to succeed only if extraordinary men do the administering. There are such men, but not many; hoping that enough of them wind up in HUD strikes me as, to say the least, imprudent.

For almost two decades we have been "attacking" the problems of the city—almost literally—by mounting successive assaults against various real and imagined difficulties. Each assault force has had its own leadership and ideology, and the weaknesses of each have been the signal for a new assault, under different leadership and with a new ideology. First came public housing, then urban redevelopment, then urban renewal, and now the Model Cities Program. The old assaults, of course, never vanished, they just moved over a bit (not without complaints) to let the newcomers in. The common objective is to capture and hold central-city real estate; the differences in tactics concern the number of fronts on which the fighting is to proceed. In general, each successive assault has had broader objectives—the current President's message calls for a change in the "total environment." The motto is, "more is better." Perhaps it will all work out, if humane weapons are used and we evacuate the wounded. But I suspect that in the confusion the real enemies—poverty, ignorance, despair—may slip away, to live and strike again in another place.

# D. COMMUNITY ACTION

## *Maximum Feasible Misunderstanding*

### DANIEL P. MOYNIHAN

The 1964 election passed, the war on poverty began. By the end of January, 1966, more than nine hundred grants had been made for the establishment or planning of Community Action Programs in some one thousand counties. All of the fifty largest cities in the country had CAP's. Although the richest counties had been ahead of the poorest in getting started, the latter gradually caught up. If the object had been to "cover" as many of the poor as possible with a local "umbrella" agency, the planners and administrators at OEO had done a remarkable job. Shriver's strong point was getting into position fast: no small matter in combat.

But the CAP program was not, from the point of view of its sponsors, a success. From the outset, it was in trouble. If MFY had sent out road companies (as in a sense it did), the drama could hardly have been more faithfully re-enacted in city after city across the land. There was even an extended run in rural Mississippi. This at least is an impression easily acquired.

The history of these early programs has not been written. It must be. Almost certainly a careful, detailed enquiry will turn up a great number and wide variety of innovations, changes, improvements that took place as a result of the community efforts stimulated by the Economic Opportunity Act. Some of the programs involved—Head Start, Neighborhood Legal Services—have become so familiar and popular as no longer particularly to be associated with community action, or even the war on poverty! In the manner that American advertising can transform a household appliance from a luxury to a necessity in a matter of years, almost in a matter of months OEO made preschool education

Reprinted from Daniel P. Moynihan, *Maximum Feasible Misunderstanding* (New York: Free Press, 1969), Chapter Seven, by permission of the publisher.

a standard feature of an up-to-date community, such that any without it could properly consider themselves badly governed, deprived, or whatever. Very possibly, the most important long run impact of the community action programs of the 1960's will prove to have been the formation of an urban Negro leadership echelon at just the time when the Negro masses and other minorities were verging towards extensive commitments to urban politics. Tammany at its best (or worst) would have envied the political apprenticeship provided by the neighborhood coordinators of the antipoverty program. Wofford reports that in the period 1964–66 between 25 per cent and 35 per cent of the field representatives recruited for the community action program were Negro, Puerto Rican, or Mexican American. It was, he continues, "probably the ablest and largest group of minority group *professionals* ever assembled in one government program." [1] Kenneth E. Marshall, one of the planners with Kenneth B. Clark and Cyril Tyson of HARYOU, and subsequently head of the Paterson, New Jersey, community action program agrees: "The major immediate beneficiaries of these programs," he stated in 1967, "have been non-poor persons who have been afforded the opportunity of executive, technical and professional positions in the program." [2] Saul Alinsky was more blunt, referring early in 1965 to the "vast network of sergeants drawing general's pay" in the poverty program, and noting also the speed with which apparently quite lucrative consulting firms spring up to help the indigenous disadvantaged prepare requests for grants from OEO. Even the *Wall Street Journal* took note of this new business opportunity.

The future is never to be predicted, but it would be surprising if a Namier-like history of American politics in the coming generation did not record in some detail the influence of the community action programs of the war on poverty on the personal and ideological formation of a significant number of urban political leaders. But as for the utterly disparate, but simultaneously entertained goals of program coordination and political activism, neither occurred, and in the process of not occurring, all hell broke loose all over the place.

With no detailed history available, it is hardly possible to develop a typology of the CAP's which varied considerably: some were citywide and run by City Hall; some neighborhood based and run from, if not by the neighborhood; still others took in large areas yet were relatively inde-

---

[1] Wofford, *op. cit.*, p. 11. It may be noted that earlier in the same paragraph he states, "We were looking for the bright generalist with an ability to negotiate, to review budgets, to know his own limitations, and to ask the right questions." But this becomes a "professional role."

[2] *Nation's Business*, October 1967.

pendent. In the first year of operation three-quarters of the community action agencies that began operations were newly established non-profit bodies, although actual control within these organizations varied. Although all manner of groups were represented, it would appear that by and large, in large cities, community action came to be primarily associated with the cause of Negro betterment.

At the risk of oversimplification, it might be said that the CAP's most closely controlled by City Hall were disappointing, and that the ones most antagonistic were destroyed. There was a large area in between, but it tended to receive little attention. For the most militant agencies, something like a four-stage sequence seems to have been followed. First, a period of organizing, with much publicity and great expectations everywhere. Second, the beginning of operations, with the onset of conflict between the agency and local government institutions, with even greater publicity. Third, a period of counterattack from local government, not infrequently accompanied by conflict and difficulties, including accounting troubles, within the agency itself. Fourth, victory for the established institutions, or at best, stalemate, accompanied by bitterness and charges of betrayal. Whatever else had occurred, the quest for community had failed.

The nub of the difficulty was that the program was nominally designed to bring about institutional cooperation, but in fact, in the words of John G. Wofford, staff assistant to the Deputy Director of the Community Action Program, the "key—and often unstated—objective of the Community Action Program [was] institutional change."[3] Chazen puts it even more bluntly: "section 202(a)(3) . . . has been commonly interpreted as a mandate for federal assistance in the effort to create political organizations for the poor."[4] Michael Harrington, whose influence among poverty workers was very considerable at this time, or so would be the impression, argued in one forum after another that the Economic Opportunity Act would—should—mean for the organization of the poor in the 1960's what the Wagner Act had meant for the organization of the industrial workers in the 1930's. That is to say, the Federal government would not do the job, but had made it much easier for others to do, not least by lending its moral authority to the enterprise. These various objectives were incompatible and proved such.

The drama was excruciatingly played out in Syracuse, New York. With the enactment of the antipoverty program, an organization origi-

---

[3] John G. Wofford, "Community Action; the Original Purpose," *Social Sciences Forum*, Adams House, Harvard University, Fall–Winter 1966–67.

[4] *Op. cit.,* p. 599.

nally established by the President's Committee on Juvenile Delinquency was promptly transformed into the Syracuse Crusade For Opportunity and promptly undertook to serve as an umbrella agency in the best Ylvisaker/Hackett formulation. In a city of 222,000 inhabitants, with only 16,000 Negroes, the Crusade began with a white majority on its board. Simultaneously, however, OEO gave a grant to Syracuse University to establish a Community Action Training Center to experiment with new approaches for enabling the poor to participate in the management of programs such as that of the Crusade For Opportunity. In no time, tensions were rising. As one Federal official put it to a Wall Street Journal reporter: "The community leaders felt the University was training agents provocateurs—and of course, it was." Systematic agitation began among the Negro poor, demanding that Negroes take over Crusade For Opportunity. Early in 1966 the white, Jewish executive director resigned the $19,000 job and was replaced by a militant Negro, James Tillman, Jr., who had been associate director of the University's Community Action Training Center. A year later, Negroes acquired a majority on the Board itself, and a Negro board chairman was chosen. Crusade For Opportunity "went black." It also became more and more abrasive. "How else do you gain power for the poor?" asked the new executive director. Remedial reading manuals informed their struggling "functional illiterates": "No ends are accomplished without the use of force. . . . Squeamishness about force is the mark not of idealistic, but moonstruck morals." The local NAACP charged that such materials were "geared to rioting," and called for the resignation of the new director. Militants joined the chapter and packed a meeting to denounce *its* head as a "house nigger." The turbulence steadily mounted.

This might have been well enough had there been any results to show of the kind that would justify the abrasiveness or enable the new organization to defend itself when attacked. But this would seem not to be the case. Repeated efforts to start job training programs apparently came to little. The official in charge of the program confessed in mid-1967 that it had been "a dismal failure." Nor were there any political payoffs for advocates of social change. The Republican Mayor was easily re-elected in 1965, not only in spite of but, in the view of local observers, largely *because* of the intense opposition, even harassment, directed against him by the various poverty groups. Nor does there appear to have been any very great deal of actual participation by the poor in the operation of the poverty agency. Those who got hold of it seem to have been secretive and jealous of power. And then finances became a scandal. To the doubtless immense satisfaction of the conservative Irish, Italian, and German working-class groups of the city, the Negroes turned out to have been running Crusade For Opportunity with all the concern for niceties of a Reconstruction legislature. Of some $8 million expended by mid-1967, about $7 million had gone for salaries. Just what the poor got out of it was hard to see. In July, 1967, for the first time anywhere, OEO placed the Syracuse community action program in trusteeship. Two white and one Negro trustees were appointed.

Later that year, in the crucial November debates in the House of Representatives over the future of OEO, Rep. James M. Hanley, a Syracuse Democrat elected in the Johnson sweep in 1964 spoke on the floor of the importance of greater local government involvement in poverty programs. A sensible and sensitive representative of the long (and decidedly mixed) tradition of Irish politics in the city, all he asked of the poverty program was what the PCJD and the Ford Foundation had promised. Speaking of Crusade For Opportunity, he said: [5]

> The Crusade did not assume the responsibility to effectively and efficiently manage and administer the program grants awarded by the OEO. But most of all, the old community action agency *failed to mobilize all of the resources of the community* to wage an effective war on poverty. Many battles were fought, but few were against poverty. [My italics.]

This was a recurrent theme of not unsympathetic observers of big city community action programs elsewhere in the nation. In June, 1965, in an article entitled "More Shouting than Shooting," Paul Weeks of the *Los Angeles Times* (June 13, 1965) described the situation in that city weeks before the great riot:

> Nowhere . . . has the turn in the war from fighting the enemy to fighting over who is going to run the war been more evident than in the Los Angeles area. . . . The frontal assault on deprivation has been reduced to sporadic fire while a showdown rages behind the lines over who are going to be generals and who will be the privates.

Seemingly it comes to this. Over and again, the attempt by official and quasi-official agencies (such as the Ford Foundation) to organize poor communities led first to the radicalization of the middle-class persons who began the effort; next to a certain amount of stirring among the poor, but accompanied by heightened racial antagonism *on the part of the poor* if they happened to be black; next to retaliation from the larger white community; whereupon it would emerge that the community action agency, which had talked so much, been so much in the headlines, promised so much in the way of change in the fundamentals

---

[5] *Syracuse Post-Standard,* November 9, 1967. My italics.

of things, was powerless. A creature of a Washington bureaucracy, subject to discontinuation without notice. Finally, much bitterness all around. Just possibly, the philanthropists and socially concerned intellectuals never took seriously enough their talk about the "power structure." Certainly, they seemed repeatedly to assume that those who had power would let it be taken away a lot easier than could possibly be the case if what was involved was *power*. Dismissed from his post, sitting at home surrounded by African artifacts, James Tillman, Jr., may have spoken more truly than he knew in describing what had happened to him. Speaking of himself in the third person, he put it thus: [6]

> Tillman happens to be a social engineer, and understands fear. Only real patricians can give up power easily, while nouveau riche resent any inroads on their authority. There obviously aren't any patricians in Syracuse.

Technically he was wrong. Decision-making in Syracuse is as diffuse a process as in most medium American cities, yet to a pronounced degree events there are influenced by a fairly small number of men in banks and law firms whose names are not generally known, who do not run for Congress, who do not run for mayor. It may be that Tillman had not met them; he would not in that event describe them as especially nouveau, but neither would he have concluded they were patricians. They were and remain the tough power brokers of an American city, and they can outwait a black "agent provocateur" anytime *if* that individual is dependent on the House of Representatives and the General Accounting Office to stay in business.

In a number of instances the demise of the community action organization has been prevented by a transfer of leadership from political or racial militants to social welfare professionals. This happened at MFY, and also at HARYOU. But the results were not necessarily different as to social change, nor were the difficulties of simply running a large organization avoided. Early in 1968, Kenneth E. Marshall, speaking of HARYOU, charged before the Community Council of Greater New York that "none of it worked." Charles H. King, a 47-year-old social worker who had been appointed director of the program early in 1967, agreed that the indices of "social pathology" which had been laid out in 1964 as a measure of the social situation were still worsening in Central Harlem. He insisted, however, and correctly, that HARYOU had never got the funding it anticipated. Even so, the question was to be asked what had it done with what it had got. In July 1968 the presi-

---

[6] *Wall Street Journal,* August 25, 1967.

dent of the HARYOU board, Marshall England announced that he
would ask for a Federal investigation of the agency. The clear implication of his statement was that funds were being misused. At a 12-hour
board meeting preceding his statement, a pistol and tear gas were discharged. Returning to his own office, England received a telephone call
warning him to "stay out of the HARYOU office or you'll be killed." [7]
The conclusion seems unavoidable: the programs were at once too big,
and not big enough, and where Negro communities were involved, constituted a devastating form of what had by then come to be known as
"white colonialist imperialism."

It may be that the poor are never "ready" to assume power in an
advanced society: the exercise of power in an effective manner is an
ability acquired through apprenticeship and seasoning. Thrust on an
individual or a group, the results are often painful to observe, and when
what in fact conveyed is not power, but a kind of playacting at power,
the results can be absurd. The devise of holding elections among the
poor to choose representatives for the CAP governing boards made the
program look absurd. The turnouts in effect declared that the poor
weren't interested: in Philadelphia 2.7 per cent; Los Angeles 0.7 per
cent; Boston 2.4 per cent; Cleveland 4.2 per cent; Kansas City, Mo.
5.0 per cent.[8] Smaller communities sometimes got larger turnouts, but
never anything nearly approaching that of a listless off-year election.
(If theory held the poor to be apathetic, why proceed as if this were not
so? In the Democratic primary election of 1968, with the election of the
first Negro Congressman from Brooklyn at issue, a mere 11,825 votes
were cast in the 12th Congressional district, comprising the Bedford
Stuyvesant area, compared to 43,940 in the adjacent 13th district.)
Once elected or chosen, the representatives do not seem to have been
especially effective. Rubin, a wholly sympathetic observer, writes: "The
Boards have been rent by endless quarrels, born of a basic lack of understanding of the differentiation between policy-making and administrative functions." [9] As Negroes grew more militant, the impression would be
that more and more white executives were forced out of the programs,
but this only precipitated intensive struggles for place among blacks.
Community action salaries were often extraordinarily high in terms of
what was otherwise available to the Negro middle class, and the struggle
was often bitter, with all the accoutrement of charge, countercharge, and
scandal. In Harlem, for example, it was the local Negro newspaper that

---

[7] *New York Times,* February 21, July 3, 1968.

[8] Cited in Rubin, *op. cit.,* p. 12.

[9] *Ibid.,* p. 11.

led the campaign against the executive salary structure in HARYOU-ACT. Irony: patronage, which was the source of stability in the original ethnic neighborhood political organization, became a source of instability in the contrived organizations created to fill the gap left by the destruction of the real thing.

A final verdict *must* be withheld. But interim ones are available, and by and large they have been negative. Bayard Rustin, for example, speaks of the "bedlam of community action programs" and clearly suggests they have made organized "ghetto" political activity more difficult, not less. S. M. Miller and Pamela Roby, of the Ford Foundation, conclude that OEO, far from creating a constituency and bringing about institutional change, has in fact brought about little change, produced few supporters, and has brought on "enormous dissatisfaction." All the result of "maximum feasible participation" for which "civil rights and other groups were not effectively organized" despite the best efforts of OEO.[10]

Within CAP's the struggle for control frequently acquired bitter ideological and generation aspects. Thus in 1966 the executive director and three high staff members of the $8 million Youth in Action program in New York's Bedford-Stuyvesant area resigned in fury, charging the board of directors with being "middle class oriented," shaking the organization very considerably.[11] That Cloward and Ohlin would have hoped for nothing better than a middle-class oriented local board giving youth opportunities was a detail long since obscured. In a city such as New York where the poor are not so exclusively Negro, the potential for ethnic conflict for control over the CAP's, especially within the framework of the election of poor representatives, provided plentiful opportunities for ethnic hostility. Negro–Puerto Rican battles raged within New York City's antipoverty program. Under the administration of John V. Lindsay, Mitchell Sviridoff who had headed the community action program in New Haven, was brought in to run New York's program. Ethnic conflict was immediate. In 1967, Herman Badillo, the Puerto Rican-born Borough President of the Bronx declared of the local election scheme: [12]

> In effect, they are taking the poverty program and making it like a political campaign with winner take all. When you say that whoever

---

[10] S. M. Miller and Pamela Roby, "The War on Poverty Reconsidered," to be published in Irving Howe and Jeremy Larner, *Poverty: Views from the Left* (New York: Morrill Publications, 1968).

[11] *New York Times*, September 24, 1966.

[12] *New York Times*, October 8, 1967.

gets 51 per cent is going to control the program, you put a premium on groups vying for control, and that's not going to lead to people working together.

At his side, Percy Sutton, the Negro Borough President of Manhattan, nodded assent. Two unusually gifted and successful elected officials, working in the tradition of New York ethnic politics, their shared view, contrasting as they do with those of the professional reformers is to be noted.

Before long, ideological, generational, and ethnic problems were compounded by the familiar ones of bureaucracy. An administrative study of OEO is much needed, especially with respect to the degree to which under the banner of community control, the essential decisions about local affairs came increasingly to be made in Washington via the direct CAP-OEO line of communication and funding. But rigidities of the more familiar kind early made their appearance. In 1967, Wofford asked whether the one thousand community action agencies around the country were becoming a new bureaucracy that would "stifle change" and have to be superceded. The following year George Nicolau, stepping down after running for 18 months the largest community action agency in the nation, declared himself "a victim of that process which in the space of three short years created and has almost been overwhelmed by its own complexities and its own bureaucracy." [13]

A final irony, and in its many ramifications a fateful one, is that the Federal antipoverty warriors, for all their desperately good intentions, got precious little thanks. Each local conflict solved seemed to bear the seeds of the next one. Wofford describes the process: a mayor undertakes to step up a community action program under his own control; a pressure group, the "***Committee for a More Effective Community Action Program" is formed to demand that the poor be given greater participation; the Mayor forms a new community action agency and makes the head of the pressure group the executive director; the new director is denounced for having sold out to the white power structure; the "***Committee for an Even More Effective Community Action Program" is formed. [14]

With militancy the mark of merit and increasingly measured in terms of the ability to be sufficiently outrageous to obtain press and television coverage—or so one is forced to conclude from the behavior of those involved—more and more the antipoverty program came to be

---

[13] George Nicolau, Address to the National Association for Community Development, Atlanta, April 8, 1968, mimeographed.

[14] Wofford, *op. cit.,* p. 18.

associated with the kind of bad manners and arrogance that are more the mark of the rich than the poor, or perhaps more accurately, the too-common attributes of the radical right and left. Shriver's experience with the Citizens Crusade Against Poverty is not unrepresentative. Early on, the need for a constituency for OEO became evident. Further, Reuther by 1965 was more and more attracted by the possibility of organizing "community unions," freeing the labor movement from its confines of work place and craft, "providing the poor with their own self-sufficient economic organization in their community." With a $1 million pledge from the UAW, 125 organizations were brought together in November, 1965, and the Citizens Crusade Against Poverty was founded, ostensibly to give OEO support, possibly to create an atmosphere for an organizing campaign. (Bayard Rustin's vision of a coalition of labor, liberal, and civil rights forces was much in mind.) Boone left OEO to become executive director. A prestigious board was assembled, complete with bona fide representatives of the poor. In 1966 a great meeting was held in Washington. Shriver appeared, but far from receiving support, he was hooted, booed, jostled, and verbally attacked. The predominantly Negro audience remained passive while a militant minority raged at the director of OEO. "He hasn't done anything for us," cried one delegate, "Where do the poor have an opportunity?" "It's just a big publicity deal," shouted another. "We aren't being heard because we don't have the money." "The poverty program is a laugh," declared a mother of six from Watts. "When all the money is spent, the rich will get richer and I will still be receiving a welfare check." [15]

Seven months later, on December 22nd, a busload of what the *New York Times* called "the vocal poor and their representatives" made their way to Timberlawn, Shriver's home in suburban Washington, where much of the antipoverty program had been planned, and where he and his family were gathered for the Christmas holidays. Carols were sung:

> Hark the Herald Angels sing
> Glory to the newborn king.
> Sing of peace forever more,
> While the poor finance the war.
> Shriver go to L.B.J.
> Tell him what the poor folk say.
> Charity begins at home.
> We want gigs to call our own.
> Young adults are on the roam
> Soon we'll have a war at home.

[15] *New York Herald-Tribune,* April 15, 1966.

O come all ye poor folk,
Soulful and together
Come ye, O come ye to Shriver's house.
Come and behold him, politicians' puppet.
O come and let us move him,
O come and sock it to him,
And send him on his way to L.B.J.

Keep the money in the kitty,
   Fa la la la la la la la la
Let's get down to nitty gritty
   Fa la la la la la la la la
Put us poor folks in the cold,
   Fa la la la la la la la la
Shriver you ain't got no soul,
   Fa la la la la la la la la

The painful quality about these demonstrations, and their counterparts in city after city across the land, is that at base they depend on the power of the weak: the power to disrupt, to embarrass, to provoke, to goad to punitive rage, but banking (usually) on the inhibitions, personal or collective, of those goaded. A gentleman does not strike a lady. But neither does the heart grow fonder in consequence of the restraint imposed by the unequal contest that would ensue. What all this told the White House was that the antipoverty program was becoming a political liability. It patently had few friends among mayors, few among congressmen, and now with the seemingly inexorable logic of conflict stimulation, few among the poor. A few months after the episode at Timberlawn, President Johnson confided to a member of the Senate Committee on Labor and Public Welfare that it was hardly his favorite program. He need not have been so cautious: the fact was painfully evident throughout Washington.

# E. SCHOOLS

# *City Schools*

## PATRICIA CAYO SEXTON

To talk about urban education is to talk about an old fallen phrase in such disrepute during two postwar decades that it has hidden out from scholarly journals like a furtive sex criminal. The phrase "class struggle" now appears in black tie and softened aliases as "slum and suburb," "inequalities," problems of the "disadvantaged," of the "culturally deprived," of "integration." However Americanized or blurred the new image may appear, the basic fact seems simple enough: a remarkable "class struggle" now rattles our nation's schools and the scene of sharpest conflict is the city. Southern cities—and New York—were the scenes of first eruptions, but now almost every northern city, and many suburbs, are feeling the new tremors.

A high-ranking official in New Rochelle, New York put it in these words: "It's not just race in our schools . . . it's class warfare!" Class conflict, of course, is not the only issue in city schools. There is ethnic conflict and the special status of Negroes—and of Puerto Ricans and other identifiable groups—at the bottom end of the ladder and the special Rickover pressure-cooked conformism and prestige-college frenzy at the upper end.[1] Nor are the sides in the conflict always clearly formed. But, usually, when the chaff and wheat are separated, what is left is the "haves" in one pile and "have-nots" in another, with some impurities in each—middle-class white "liberals," for example, who support some Negro demands and white have-nots who oppose them. Banfield and Wilson claim four important cleavages in city politics: (1) haves and have-nots, (2) suburbanites and the central city, (3)

---

Reprinted from *Annals of the American Academy of Political and Social Science,* vol. 352 (March 1964), 95–106, by permission of the publisher.

[1] Rickover supporters in the Council on Basic Education voice some misgivings about the Admiral's program to restrict higher education to an elite.

ethnic and racial groups, (4) political parties.[2] A reduction to more
basic outlines might show that the first category would, with some
slippage, cover the other three. Indeed, the authors acknowledge as
much when they say: "These tend to cut across each other and, in
general, to become one fundamental cleavage separating two opposed
conceptions of the public interest." [3] When they refer to "... The
fundamental cleavage between the public-regarding Anglo-Saxon Protestant, middle-class ethos and the private-regarding lower-class, immigrant
ethos," they seem to refer, though the phrase is unspoken, to one aspect
of the class struggle.[4]

Other major urban school issues exist—finances, bureaucracy, and
the unionization of teachers, among others—and may seem, on the
surface, unrelated to class conflict. At second glance, the shortage of
school funds can be seen as a product of the antitax ideology of haves.
The behemoth bureaucracies may be seen everywhere as more accessible
to and influenced by haves, and the decentralization of administration—
to which New York's Superintendent Gross and others have devoted
themselves—may be seen as a partial response to the growing arousal
of have-not groups. The unionization of city teachers may be seen as
a response to the hitherto rather rigid conservative control of school
systems and the new thrust of liberalism in the cities and the schools,
released by have-not votes and agitation, as well as a defense against
the difficult conditions in have-not schools.[5]

## Levels of Conflict

The class struggle in the schools and the struggle for power which is
part of it are carried on at many levels. In some cases, it seems least

---

   [2] Edward C. Banfield and James Q. Wilson, *City Politics* (Cambridge, Mass.:
Harvard University Press and MIT Press, 1963).

   [3] *Ibid.,* p. 35.

   [4] *Ibid.,* p. 329. Their ascription of a "public-regarding" ethos to the middle
class and a "private-regarding" one to the "lower class" seems an extraordinary
and questionable reversal of the usual association of the middle class with private
efforts and the lower class with public efforts. It is most puzzling when contrasted
with their summary statement: "If in the old days [of lower class ward politics]
specific material inducements were illegally given as bribes to favored individuals,
now much bigger ones are legally given to a different class of favored individuals . . ." (p. 340).

   [5] In New York and Chicago especially, the popular political issues of "boss-
ism" and "machine politics" have been referred to the school arena. In New York,
110 Livingston Street (the Board of Education headquarters) has appeared to
many as the school equivalent of "city hall," the one place you "can't beat" and
with which you often cannot even communicate. Now a proposal is being considered to divide the city schools into several fairly autonomous geographic units in
order to scatter the shots at "city hall" and provide easier access.

visible under the spotlight—on the school boards. Through liberal and have-not activity, some city school boards are now composed of middle-class moderates who are more inclined to represent the educational interests of have-nots than were their more conservative predecessors. Some big-city boards, as New York's, seem exemplary public servants, superior in purpose and competence to higher political bodies. Their efforts on behalf of have-nots are limited by several personal as well as external characteristics: they are haves, a quality that usually though not invariably limits zeal and identity with have-nots; they are moderates in contrast to those leading the more militant have-not groups. Among the limits set by school systems are: (1) the traditional conservative reluctance of boards to interfere in the operations of the bureaucracy; (2) the inertia and resistance of the bureaucracy to pressure from the board; (3) the usual tendency to become defensive of "their system" and to take criticisms of the system as personal affronts; (4) influences from middle-class interests which are usually more insistent and weighty than have-not pressure; (5) interference from outside groups—such as the unprecedented threat of the Northcentral Association to withdraw accreditation from the Chicago schools if the school board insisted on a step which forced Superintendent Willis into further desegregation. The external limits on the situation, however, seem more determining: (1) the difficulty of the job to be done, (2) the lack of sufficient money to do the job.

Services to have-nots within the city system, therefore, are limited by these conservative factors: (1) the moderate position of most liberal board members and the insufficiency of zeal or identification to drive home the grievances of have-nots; (2) conservatism and resistance within the bureaucracy; (3) conservative influence which acts to shut off funds to the schools.

In the movement of the class struggle from one end of the continuum, where a small elite holds total power, to the other extreme, where have-nots share proportionate influence, there are many points of compromise, and public officials tend to pursue ever more liberal ends and means. The white liberals who sit on some city boards may begin to push for more rapid change or may be replaced soon by representatives who will.

The claim that the city and its school system are so constrained by outside conservatism, especially at the state level, that they can do little seems largely true, though partially exaggerated. Too often outside interference is made an excuse for inertia. City schools have not given adequate service to have-nots largely because the have-nots were underrepresented in decision-making positions. As cities go, New

York's school board seems unusually enlightened, appointed as it is by a relatively responsive mayor and served by two unusually alert citizen groups—the Public Education Association and the United Parents Association. Yet a nine-member board includes only one Negro and no Puerto Rican, although these groups together compose 40 per cent of the city's public school enrollment. Nor is there any blue-collar worker or person of modest means or position on the board, but, then, such individuals are rare specimens on city boards. One trade unionist, himself a university graduate and member of a professional union, sits on the board. Of some 777 top officials in the system—board members, superintendents, and principals—it appears that only six are Negroes, 0.8 per cent of the total.[6]

Although it is sometimes asserted that the interest-group identity of board members does not affect their decision-making, what may be more nearly the case, given present knowledge of group dynamics, is that the group interests of the lone have-not representative may be submerged in a board's moderate consensus.

Perhaps the "equality lag" within city systems may be more directly attributable to deficiencies in have-not organization than to lack of good faith among liberals and board members. Many cities could nearly be "possessed" by Negroes who approach a majority in some cases, but Negroes do not vote their numerical strength and may be evicted from the city limits by urban renewal before they catch up with their potential. Nor do labor unions use their full authority in school affairs. A major weakness of have-nots is their limited understanding of power, who has it and how to get it; they also lack the time, money, and organization often needed to purchase it.[7]

## Beyond the City Limits

Local class conflict seems only a dim reflection of a larger conflict. The main drama of class conflict and thrust of conservatism are seen in full

---

[6] Daniel Griffiths and Others, *Teacher Mobility in New York City* (New York, 1963).

[7] Banfield and Wilson, *op. cit.*, p. 282: "Organized labor—even if it includes in its ranks the majority of all the adult citizens in the community—is generally regarded as a 'special interest' which must be 'represented'; businessmen, on the other hand, are often regarded, not as 'representing business' as a 'special interest,' but as serving the community as a whole. Businessmen, in Peter Clark's term, often are viewed as 'symbols of civic legitimacy.' Labor leaders rarely have this symbolic quality, but must contend with whatever stigma attaches to being from a lower-class background and associated with a special-interest group. . . . Labor is handicapped not only by having imputed to it less civic virtue but also by a shortage of money and organizational skills."

dimension in a larger arena—at the federal and state levels. The national scene cannot be ignored in any consideration of the city school situation. Only at this level does there appear a possibility of releasing the funds needed to support high-quality education and the high-level job opportunity that goes with it. The claim that federal aid to education is the *only* school issue and that other concerns are simply distractions is given substantial support by any cursory study of city school budgets and revenue limitations.[8]

Nationally, the conflict seems shaped by at least two major factors:

(1) The congressional system is biased against have-nots and their representatives. The bias results from at least two forms of conservative manipulation: (a) manipulation of rural and small-town interests, North and South, and, through them, congressional apportionment and votes; (b) the additional manipulation of southern rural conservatism—which is given unusual congressional power by the committee seniority system—through the exchange of votes on the race issue.

The superior effective power of haves at this top level serves to block federal legislation in general but specifically those measures that might ensure rapid economic growth through federal expenditures, full employment, and the extension of power to have-nots—measures that would give significant relief to the city's distress. More directly relevant, it has blocked any substantial aid to urban areas and held up the transfer of political power from rural to urban areas.[9]

Moreover, largely by the manipulation of conflicting religious interests, this coalition has prevented the passage of the federal aid that seems indispensable to urban schools. At the same time, it has continued, through extension programs, copious aid to rural education.

(2) Seriously deprived have-nots have failed to enter their full power into the political arena.

## The State

If direct federal aid seems distant and the aid formula unlikely to provide much assistance to the cities, fiscal aid from the state may be closer

---

[8] This seems to suggest that social scientists could much more profitably study the political mechanisms by which such aid could be released rather than the often esoteric and "academic" studies of culture, personality, and the like which now tend overly to occupy many who are concerned with have-nots.

[9] The assumption that a proper apportioning of representatives, giving a proper share to the city's suburban areas, will result in an accretion of power to haves may not be warranted inasmuch as have-nots are also being rapidly suburbanized yet, contrary to expectation, seem to be maintaining their political identity.

at hand, depending upon how quickly reapportionment will be enforced in the states. New York City received $197 in school aid for each student in its public schools in 1961–1962, while the average in the rest of the state was $314. Miami, Florida paid $47 million in state taxes in one recent year and got back only $1.5 million in grants-in-aid. With sympathetic legislatures, cities may be able to call on other revenues, including an income tax on suburbanites working in the city such as has been adopted in Philadelphia and Detroit.

### Inequalities

The consequences of local, state, and national class conflict are seen in the school inequalities and class-biased training given to children even within the most liberal city systems. Only in the past few years has the concern of some unionists, academicians, liberals, and many Negroes brought the full range of inequities to public attention. The "spoils" of the city school, limited as they are by outside controls, are usually divided according to the crude formula "them as has gets." Only now in some cities is there any insistence on the more radical "compensatory" formula—"to each according to need."

Documentary evidence about class inequalities, past and present, is now weighty. My own study of one large city school system, *Education and Income,* describes the various forms of class inequities within one system.[10] I will refer here only to a few facts about Chicago and New York (not the cities of my study). In 1955, following Dr. Kenneth Clark's demand for attention to Negro schools, an "outside" study found that Negro and Puerto Rican schools in New York City were generally inferior to "Other" schools.[11] In a group of Negro and Puerto Rican schools (the $X$ Group), 50.3 per cent of teachers were on tenure, compared to 78.2 per cent in the "Other" group (the $Y$ Group); 18.1 per cent in the $X$ group and only 8.3 per cent in the $Y$ group were "permanent substitutes." On the average, facilities in Group $X$ schools were older, less adequate, and more poorly maintained than $Y$ schools. The costs of operating $Y$ schools were higher than costs in $X$ schools. Though the New York Board of Education now claims that Negro and Puerto Rican schools are equal or superior to "Other" schools, Dr. Kenneth Clark still says Harlem schools reflect "a consistent pattern of criminal neglect."

---

[10] Patricia Cayo Sexton, *Education and Income* (New York: Viking Press, 1961).

[11] *The Status of the Public School Education of Negro and Puerto Rican Children in New York City,* October, 1955.

In the absence of cost-accounting, comparative expenditures in have and have-not schools in New York cannot be checked. Certainly efforts are being made by New York schools to provide better education for deprived minorities, especially in "certain" schools where extra services tend to be over-concentrated, but the schools still do not seem to approach full equality, and the cost estimates do not measure the *full* cost of education—the differences in nursery and kindergarten education, the last two years of high school missed by the low-income dropout, and the costs of higher education—not to mention the low-quality and segregated "ability" tracks into which have-not children are often placed.

Though New York permitted an outside study of school inequalities in 1954, the Chicago Superintendent of Schools, Benjamin Willis, has only in the past year agreed to a three-man study committee of which he will be a member. In 1962, John E. Coons, Northwestern University law professor, prepared for the United States Commission on Civil Rights a report on segregated schools in Chicago.[12] Ten schools in each of three groups were selected—white, integrated, Negro—and the findings were as follows:

| 1961–1962 | White | Inte-grated | Negro |
|---|---|---|---|
| Number of pupils per classroom | 30.95 | 34.95 | 46.8 |
| Appropriation per pupil | $342 | $320 | $269 |
| Number of uncertified teachers | 12% | 23% | 27% |
| Average number of books per pupil | 5.0 | 3.5 | 2.5 |

In 1963 a *Handbook of Chicago School Segregation* claimed that 1961 appropriations for school operating expenses were almost 25 per cent greater per pupil in white than in Negro schools, that teacher salaries were 18 per cent higher, that nonteaching operating expenses—clerical and maintenance, salaries, supplies, textbooks—were 50 per cent higher, and that only 3 per cent of Chicago's Negro population finishes college.[13]

The reluctance of Chicago schools to move as far as New York on the race issue seems to derive from at least these sources: (1) the centralization of power in the Chicago system, parallel to the centralization of civic power in the person of the mayor; (2) the praise of Dr. Conant—probably the most influential person in American education—for Mr. Willis and the Chicago method and his concurrent criticism of the New York method; (3) the presence in New York of large numbers

---

[12] John E. Coons, *Civil Rights USA, Chicago, 1962,* A Report to the United States Commission on Civil Rights.

[13] *Handbook of Chicago School Segregation, 1963,* compiled and edited by the Education Committee, Coordinating Council of Community Organizations, August 1963.

of unusually concerned and articulate white middle-class liberals; (4) the inordinate influence in Chicago schools and civic affairs of State Street, tax-conscious financial interests; (5) the past failures of have-not organization in Chicago.

An example of influential conservatism in relation to have-nots and the schools is seen in this passage from the Chicago *Tribune:* "Let's Throw the Slobs out of School": [14]

> The ignoramuses have had their chance. It is time to make them responsible for their actions. . . . Sweep through the school house with a fiery broom. Remove the deadwood, the troublemakers, the nogoods, the thugs. . . .
>
> [The teacher can tell on the first day] which students are the dissatisfied, the misfits, the illitarates [*sic*], undeserving, *non compos* nincompoops.
>
> We have become the victims of the great transcendental fraud, a deceit put upon us by a generation of psychiatrists, guidance counselors, and psychologists, none of whom spends any more time in the classroom dealing with these apes than he has to.

Despite the fact that median income in Chicago is higher than in New York, Chicago in one recent year spent $410 per pupil while New York spent $761.52.[15]

Inequalities and the compensatory formula now being advocated —reverse inequality—produce only one kind of conflict, one which may be more easily resolved than other disputes because it involves simply the redistribution of money. The "concept" of equality itself seems far less susceptible to change—the notion that, with proper attention, the abilities of have-not children may prove roughly equal to those of haves and that, therefore, they should not be separated, sent off at an early age on different tracks, or given disproportionate access to higher education.

In New York City, fiscal inequality, segregation, and the "concept" of inequality resulted in the following racial distribution of recent graduating classes in New York's special high schools for "gifted children" drawn from the whole city:

---

[14] Reprint from *Chicago Tribune Magazine,* "Let's Throw the Slobs out of School," as it appears in *Human Events,* September 21, 1963, a weekly magazine distributed to social-studies classes in schools throughout the nation.

[15] While 21.3 per cent of Chicago's population have incomes over $10,000 annually, only 18.5 per cent of New Yorkers are in this category. In Chicago, 26.3 per cent of whites are in this bracket and only 8.7 per cent of Negroes; at the same time, 9.9 per cent of whites and 28.4 per cent of Negroes have incomes less than $3,000 per year.

|  | Negroes | Puerto Ricans | Others |
|---|---|---|---|
| Bronx High School of Science | 14 | 2 | 863 |
| Stuyvesant High School | 23 | 2 | 629 |
| High School of Music and Art | 45 | 12 | 638 |
| Brooklyn Technical School | 22 | 6 | 907 |

In one recent year, Negroes and Puerto Ricans were about 14 per cent of the graduating class in the city's academic high schools and about 50 per cent in the city's vocational high schools. In the vocational schools, Negroes and Puerto Ricans tend to be heavily concentrated in inferior manual trade schools and seriously underrepresented in the technical schools. For example, in a class of 361 in the aviation school (a high-level technical school), 26 were Negroes, 51 were Puerto Ricans, 284 were "Others." In the class at the New York printing school, 4 were Negroes, 16 were Puerto Ricans, and 183 were "Others." At the Clara Barton school for hospital workers, Negroes were a clear majority. Vocational schools have been "tightening standards" recently and sending minorities to "academic" schools where, if neglected, they may be no better off.

### Higher Education

A developing conflict centers on higher education. Though ethnic records are not kept, one expert estimate is that about 2 per cent of students at the University of the City of New York (formerly the city's free colleges) are Negro. One branch of the University is located at the edge of Harlem and is more integrated and accessible to Negroes than other branches, yet less than 5 per cent Negro enrollment is reported there.

In New York, Negroes tend to fall between the free city colleges and the dominant and expensive private universities (New York University, Columbia, and their like). They can neither qualify for the former nor afford the latter. Needs tests are not applied to city-college admissions, and free tuition is extended to the affluent with an 85 high school average and denied the impoverished with an 84 average; enrollments are reported to be now predominantly middle class.[16]

Some critics now say that the only equitable system of tuition charges, in all types of institutions, is a sliding scale based on ability to pay. New York does not have a single state university; what is called the University of the State of New York is simply a scattered collection, mainly in nonurban areas, of teachers colleges, agricultural schools, a

---

[16] A recent admissions change at the city university from sole reliance on high school averages to inclusion of college boards scores is expected further to lighten the skin of enrollees. The Board of Higher Education, however, is now discussing a change of admissions standards to accommodate more Negroes.

few technical schools.[17] Recently, the state gave a 40 per cent subsidy to New York's city colleges, converted by some graduate offerings into the University of the City of New York. The importance of federal funds to education is seen in federal research and development investments in California and the pervading effect such funds have had in underwriting and stimulating growth of educational institutions there.

New York City's effort through the years to provide free college education and to compensate for the void at the state level has been extraordinary. No other city appears to have made any comparable effort. Still the city seems not to have deployed its college resources equitably, and the gathering debate over the city colleges suggests a conflict of view—or interest—between the city's have-nots and its numerous liberal middle class.[18]

The compilation and release of information about ethnic and social class enrollments in institutions of higher education as well as the post-secondary experiences of students, appear to be the first step out of the college inequities which have, in turn, imposed inequities on lower educational levels. Equality of opportunity in higher education will probably come only through a national network of community colleges—low in cost and located within easy commuting distance—and available to all "average"-or-above students who want further education.[19] Perhaps Britain's proposed experiment with televised university instruction will provide an alternative, or supplementary model, to the community college.

## Class and Ethnic Roles

Within the city itself, at least these elements seem to have some separate, though often overlapping, identity: (1) Negroes; (2) labor unions;

---

[17] California spent $33 million on community and junior colleges in 1961–1962 and $214 million on other types of higher education. New York State spent $5.7 million on community and junior colleges and $111 million on other types of higher education. M. M. Chambers, Joint Office of Institutional Research, "Appropriations of State Funds for Operating Expenses of Higher Education, 1961–62," Washington, D.C., January 1962.

[18] None of the New York Board of Education's three community colleges (where admissions standards are such that Negroes can, and often do, qualify) are located in Negro areas. One is now scheduled for Manhattan, but the tentative location is between 23rd and 42nd streets, a white area—one of the few in Manhattan. One high ranking public-school official is quoted as saying "the municipal colleges are not equipped to operate vestibule courses for students who have to be civilized."

[19] The so-called "Russell Report" (Columbia Teachers College) to the Michigan legislature reported that the college enrollments by area rose and fell in proportion to the distance from the state's colleges.

(3) white have-nots; (4) white liberals; (5) the Jewish community; (6) the Catholic community; (7) business organizations and their allies in city silk-stocking areas.

The roles and activities of these groups in relation to the schools have never been adequately defined, but impressionistic observation seems to indicate the following outlines: The main white support for civil rights in the past several decades has unquestionably come from the leadership within the labor and Jewish communities—with some major assists from middle-class liberal and church groups, particularly in the last several years. The rank-and-file within the labor-union and Jewish communities, more personally threatened by Negroes, have tended to lag some distance behind on civil rights.[20]

In the schools, the class and ethnic lines are distinct, even though less clearly drawn than in the larger community. Some political allies of Negroes have been largely outside the school conflict: unions and large numbers of white have-nots, notably the Poles, Italians, and Irish who have tended to use parochial schools. Some feel it is fortunate that these have-not groups have tended to be outside the public school controversy; others feel that the parochial-public school separation has worked hardships on the public schools and delayed a crisis that would, in the long run, be beneficial to the public schools. Union leaders have been less involved in the schools than in other political affairs because of what seems to be a rather basic alienation from the schools and frequently because of their own parochial background. They have, however, supported school expansion, improvement, financing, and their organized political power, as in New York, has given important direct assistance to the schools and to the claims of Negroes on the schools.

The organized business community has traditionally opposed tax increases for public education, the leadership in these groups usually residing in the suburbs where they have provided ample funds for good schools. Powerful real-estate groups have opposed property taxes as well as school and housing integration. The "swing" group has been the Jewish community and, to some extent, the white liberal. The Jewish community, even middle and upper income, has consistently given solid

---

[20] On general political and economic issues, class lines seem quite clearly drawn: Negroes, unions, white have-nots, and a preponderance of the Jewish community appear on the have-not side, and the organized business, middle-class, and upper-class groups on the have side. Strangely, perhaps, and to some large extent understandably, Negroes chose two groups closest to them politically for their first-line offense: unions and the Jewish community. Both were vulnerable, having made continuing proclamations, accompanied by considerable effort, on behalf of equality and brotherhood, yet having done much less than their best to provide equality for Negroes within their own jurisdictions.

support to the public schools,[21] but its own heavy stress on education and the fact that it is one of the largest remaining white middle-class groups within many cities have produced some ambivalence in its role and some conflict in unexpected places. The confrontation of these two allies in the city public schools is a source of growing distress to both groups. Because the Jewish community has tended to remain in the city and to use the public schools, it is generally contiguous, geographically and emphatically, with the Negro community and located in the middle of the integration cross fire.[22] Negroes point to Jewish predominance in the "better" high schools, the top "ability" groups, the free city colleges, and in public school administration. In many of the "integrating" areas of the city, the two groups have joined in open conflict, though in other areas they have integrated without friction. Thus, the Jewish community, because it has not fled like others from the city, often finds itself in the same situation as the labor movement with regard to Negroes: competition within a family of mutual interest for a scarcity of opportunities —in the schools in one case and in the job market in the other.[23] Perhaps for this reason, among others, the International Ladies Garment Workers Union has been a particularly sensitive target.[24]

## Acculturation and Integration

The urban schools now confront the most difficult task they have attempted. Never before has a major *racial* minority been integrated into

---

[21] In Detroit, a recent school-tax election was won, informed observers report, by majorities rolled up in the Negro and Jewish precincts.

[22] If the Jewish community is represented in the schools in proportion to its numbers in the population (one quarter of the New York population), then together with Negroes and Puerto Ricans (40 per cent) it would represent at least 65 per cent of public school enrollments.

[23] On the nine-man New York City school board, three representatives are traditionally selected for each of the three religious communities: Catholic, Protestant, Jewish. Though the Jewish community is represented by three board members, plus a Jewish-Unitarian superintendent of schools, the Negro and Puerto Rican communities, who constitute 40 per cent of the public school population, have only one representative (a Negro) on the board.

[24] The Negro struggle seems to have an interacting effect on other have-not groups. In Detroit, the civil-rights movement is supported by the auto workers' union. In battle-torn Chicago, where the class struggle appears in its more primitive form, unembellished by righteous platitudes, the school board seems to have had two lone dissenters on equality and class issues: a steelworker representative (the only unionist on the board) and a Negro (another Negro member has consistently voted with the more conservative majority). The civil-rights drive, however, comes at a time when white workers feel insecure about jobs and their place in society and fear Negro competition in an already glutted job market. In areas of the nation where white have-nots are not organized (as in the South) and therefore do not have this broad view, racial conflict among have-nots is maximum.

a nation's school or society. In fact, such integration within a dominantly non-Latin European population is unprecedented in history, the Soviets having settled their racial affairs by geographic separation.

The urban school, whose heavy job has always been the acculturation of immigrant and foreign-speaking ethnic groups, is now taking its first large bite of racial acculturation, as a giant reptile tries to swallow a whole animal. The city is accustomed to educating the immigrant: In New York City in 1960, 48.6 per cent of the population was either foreign-born or had at least one foreign-born parent; in Chicago, the figure was 35.9; in Detroit, 32.2; in San Francisco, 43.5. But the Negro group is unique in these respects: (1) it is the largest "immigrant" group of low-income, public-school-using Protestants (many other recent immigrations having skirted the public schools); (2) it is the first large racial minority to come to the city schools and the first large group with non-Western origins; (3) it has had a unique history of educational and social deprivation.

The active demand of Negro parents for integration perhaps cannot be fully appeased. Negro—and Puerto Rican—students are approaching a majority in many city public schools and any demand for total, one-for-one integration—which few would make—may be impossible in view of the increasing shortage of white public school students. Rather large-scale integration seems possible, however, as New York City is now beginning to demonstrate. Perhaps the issue will finally be settled by integrated urban renewal, or by setting up superschools and superservices in Negro areas—such as the Amidon school in Washington, D.C.—that will attract white students into Negro areas. Mainly, the urban school integration movement has served the latent function of calling attention to Negro education and arousing concern over the quality of Negro schools. The hope is held by many that, if Negro schools are improved, Negroes will not be so eager to integrate.

Among the newer racial demands in urban schools are: (1) compensatory treatment to balance past inequities; (2) "reverse" integration of schools and the busing of whites into Negro schools in order to "equalize" sacrifice (in New York, the demand has been for compulsory busing of both groups; on this most controversial point, Dr. Kenneth Clark has objected that Harlem schools are not fit either for Negroes or for whites and that busing should be "out" only); (3) heterogeneous grouping to scatter Negroes throughout the school population in any given school, rather than segregating them into slow-moving, homogeneous "ability" groups. In New York City and elsewhere, homogeneous grouping has proceeded so far that children in some places are "ability grouped" in kindergarten, based on whether or not they have been to nursery school; these groups, starting almost in the cradle, tend to perpetuate themselves throughout the child's school life.

## Some Ways Out

In this author's view, major breakthroughs in urban education may come via any or all of the numerous possible routes.

Outside the school, the possibilities include: (1) a political breakthrough of have-nots at the congressional and state legislative levels; (2) increasing civil-rights activity and pressure; (3) organization of have-nots at the following levels: political community, ethnic (civil rights), on the job (union), out of a job (unemployed); (4) federal aid programs—either through direct federal aid or around this bottleneck and through special funds, job retraining, Health, Education, and Welfare funds, urban-renewal domestic peace corps, vocational education; (5) massive infusions of voluntary aid to the schools and assistance from private foundations.

Inside the schools, the break-through might come from such sources as: (1) massive enlargement of college opportunities through the introduction of new funds or new methods of teaching; (2) technological innovation in public school, especially educational television; (3) the unionization of teachers and the arousal of the professional group with the greatest stake in improved schools (organized teachers, it has been demonstrated in New York City, can have an electric effect on the schools, attracting qualified teachers through improved salaries and working conditions, reduced class size, improved curriculum, and quality of school administration and instruction); (4) decentralization of city school systems to encourage greater participation of have-nots and clearer and closer channels of communication.[25]

Recent months have seen a spectacular burst of citizen interest in the schools, perhaps unparalleled by anything in the history of public education. Women's clubs, youth groups, civil-rights organizations, settlement houses, churches, local government, private funds, and foundations have taken up "tutorials" in deprived areas, and the more imaginative and energetic groups have moved out from there into community organization. The intrusion of nonschool groups into the learning process has injected some new excited spirit into the institutional drabness.

---

[25] In New York, the new community school boards, serving as advisory groups, have already geometrically increased the flow of new ideas, spirit, and activity into the schools from the local communities and cleared the clogged lines of communication.

Accompanying this new citizen concern with the "disadvantaged" is a new wave of interest among educators, writers, and scholars in the problems of poverty and equality, a current that has in recent months washed over previous concentration on the "gifted" and almost swept the word out of the educator's vocabulary.

Another source of backdoor assistance to the schools will be the decongestion of cities—a desperate need of New York especially—by: (1) the natural attrition of a suburban-bound, affluent population, and a Negro population pushing ever outward; (2) the forced decentralization of urban renewal, thinning out populations and bringing back into central areas a more taxable balance of middle and lower income groups. Renewal, intelligently, humanely, and artfully carried on, has the potential, of course, to remake urban life—by decentralizing, rebuilding, rehabilitating, and creating a truly heterogeneous class and ethnic community.

# Why Our Schools Have Failed

## PETER SCHRAG

In the context of traditional American belief, Section 402 of the Civil Rights Act of 1964 is one of the simplest, most unambiguous directives ever issued to a government agency. It instructs the U.S. Commissioner of Education to carry out a survey "concerning the lack of availability of equal educational opportunities for individuals by reason of race, color, religion, or national origin in educational institutions" in the United States and its possessions. Presumably, the wording of Section 402 merely pointed toward an examination of the effects of overt racial discrimination in American schools. What it produced instead was a 737-page document that demonstrated not only the ineffectiveness of schools in overcoming the handicaps of poverty and deprivation, but also the fact that no one knows what the phrase "equal educational opportunities" means and that, given the conditions of contemporary American society, it can have no meaning. Education in America is patently unequal, it is structured to be unequal, and it can only define its successes by its failures. On the dark side of every conception of "opportunity" lies an equal measure of exclusion and rejection.

No one needs another set of statistics to prove that American Negro children—and many others—are being miseducated, that they are behind in the elementary grades, and that they fall further behind as they move through school. In the twelfth grade more than 85 per cent of Negro children score below the average white on standardized tests of achievement, their dropout rates are higher, and their self-esteem is lower. We can dispute the validity of the tests as indicators of intelligence, but there is not the slightest doubt that, if they measure educa-

Reprinted from *Commentary*, XLV (March 1968), 31–38, by permission of the author and the publisher. Copyright © 1968 by the American Jewish Committee.

tional achievement and if they predict future success in school and college (as they do), then the children of the poor minorities in America perform well below average. What the new statistics do provide is solid evidence for the repeated assertion by civil rights leaders and others that what children learn in school are the rules and attitudes of second-class citizenship, and that the school is a highly effective mechanism not only for advancement but for selecting people out.

Historically, "equality of educational opportunity" simply demanded that all individuals were to have access to similar resources in similar public schools; where children failed, it was because of their own limitations, their lack of ambition and intelligence, not because of the inadequacies of the schools or the society. If the schools were found to favor a particular race or economic group (as they were in many of the desegregation cases), one could rectify the inequities through application of relatively simple standards: the appropriation of equal resources to the education of children of all races, the integration of schools, or the reassignment of teachers. The definition never contemplated the difficulties children might bring from home or the fact that even the best teachers and resources, according to the conventional standards, were keyed to middle-class experience, motivation, and attitude. More important, it never contemplated genuine integration. What it presumed was that only the white middle-class society offered ideals and standards of value and that whatever the ghetto offered, or what minority children brought with them, was to be disregarded, deflated, or denied. The traditional melting pot was stirred by Protestant hands with a white ladle.

It will be years before the sociologists and statisticians get through with the data in the government's report, *Equality of Educational Opportunity,* that was prompted by Section 402. The study, headed by Professor James S. Coleman, of The Johns Hopkins University, was eighteen months in the making, cost $2 million to produce, and included data on 600,000 children and 60,000 teachers in 4,000 schools. It is written, as Christopher Jencks said, "in the workmanlike prose of an Agriculture Department bulletin on fertilizer," and it is so thoroughly crammed with tables, regression coefficients, and standard deviations as to make all but the most passionate statisticians shudder. (Ultimately, it turned out, even some of the statisticians began to shudder.) Nonetheless, the Coleman Report has probably become the most influential educational study of the decade. It formed the basis of the recent report of the U.S. Civil Rights Commission, *Racial Isolation in the Public Schools,* it provided ammunition for a federal-court opinion on segregation in the Washington schools, it is the topic of conferences and seminars, it is endlessly quoted at meetings, and it became the subject of a year-long study at Harvard under the direction of Daniel P. Moynihan and Thomas Pettigrew (who also wrote the Civil Rights Commission Report). It may be a measure of the times that, where forty years ago we produced educational philosophy and ideology, we are now producing statistics.

The Coleman Report comes to two central conclusions:

1. That the most significant determinant of educational success (as measured by standardized tests of mathematical and verbal performance) is the social and economic background of the individual student, that formal instructional inputs—which are not as unequally distributed between races as supposed—make relatively little difference, and that the social and economic composition of fellow students, not materials or libraries, is the most important in-school resource.

2. That children from disadvantaged backgrounds (regardless of race) benefit from integration with advantaged kids (regardless of race), but that the latter are not harmed by such integration. Proper integration mixes rich and poor and produces a general social gain: The poor learn more; the performance of the rich does not go down.

The Coleman conclusions substantiate propositions that have been gaining currency in the last few years. If racial integration is pedagogically desirable, then clearly social and economic integration, and the interplay of cultural styles, are even more important. Poor blacks and whites can learn from each other, but rich and poor—under the proper conditions—can benefit even more. The report's conclusions on the impact of teachers are not entirely clear, but they do indicate that good teachers and effective educational environments are more important to the disadvantaged than to those who have access (in the home, for example) to other resources. Even so, teachers, libraries, laboratories, and other formal inputs are not as important as fellow students.

Carried to its ultimate, the Coleman Report seems to indicate that schools make relatively little difference, except as a place where kids learn from each other, and that money spent in improving them is likely, at best, to yield marginal results. The first temptation, of course, is to dismiss that assertion as an absurdity: We take it as an article of faith that the public school has always been the great American social instrument, the device that converted the raw material of immigration into an endless stream of social success. Now, oddly enough, the school seems to be failing in the very functions on which its reputation has always been based. It does not seem to be able to bring the most indigenous and American of all "immigrants" into the mainstream or even to give them the educational qualifications that life in the mainstream requires. Given the insights of recent experience, we might now properly ask whether the school was ever as successful or important in the process of Americanization and education as the history textbooks sentimentally picture it. With the possible exception of the Jews, did the school ever become a major avenue of entry for the ethnic minorities of the urban centers? How effective was it for the Irish, the Italians, the Poles? Was it the school or the street that acculturated our immigrants? What about such Americanizing institutions as the political ward, the shop, and the small town? A half century ago American society provided alternatives to formal education, and no one became officially distressed about dropouts and slow readers. Now the school has become *the* gatekeeper to advancement, and, while it is being blamed for obvious failures, it may actually be doing better than it ever did before.

And yet, despite the accumulation of studies and statistics, we still don't know how much difference formal instruction makes, except to amplify characteristics that have already been determined somewhere else. The Coleman *conclusions* indicate that it doesn't make much difference, but here semantic problems and statistical difficulties begin to get in the way. What the Coleman group did was, in essence, to take schools with students of similar backgrounds and try to determine how much difference varying inputs seemed to make. (E.g., given two all-Negro schools, did children in the school where teachers had better training, higher degrees, for example, perform better than those in the other school?) In controlling for student background, however, Coleman and his colleagues may have underestimated the crucial fact that almost all schools are internally harmonious systems and that, where children come from disadvantaged backgrounds, their teachers are also likely, in some respects, to be disadvantaged. Two economists, Samuel Bowles of Harvard and Henry M. Levin of The Brookings Institution, point out in the *Journal of Human Resources* [1] that if the methodology of the study had been reversed, so would the conclusions; that is, if Coleman had controlled for such educational inputs as teacher training, the social background of the students would have appeared to make little difference. They point out, moreover, that the Coleman Report, despite the vast sample, was unavoidably biased through the refusal of many school systems to furnish data; suburban systems were statistically overrepresented while big cities, which have the most severe problems, were underrepresented. The most vicious attribute of urban school systems, until recently, has not been their consistent failure with the dis-

---

[1] Samuel Bowles and Henry M. Levin, "The Determinants of Scholastic Achievement—An Appraisal of Some Recent Evidence," *Journal of Human Resources* (Winter, 1968).

advantaged, but their refusal to produce honest data on that failure. In case after case, they pretended (perhaps because of the historical definition of "equality") that, despite statistical evidence to the contrary, it was individual children, not schools, that failed. Bowles and Levin contend, moreover, that the Coleman Report's conclusion that teachers' traits (verbal facility, educational level, etc.) are relatively unimportant is not supported by the data, which suggest exactly the opposite; that the report's data on the importance of class size are useless; and that its conclusions about the effect of integration are questionable, since "the processes of residential and academic selection imply that those Negroes who attend predominantly white schools are drawn largely from higher social strata." In brief, integration is educationally effective among those who are already educationally and socially "advantaged."

The most significant difficulty, however, is one that the Coleman Report did not create and cannot solve. What does equality mean in education? Does it mean that the average Negro should be doing as well as the average white, and that the resources devoted to his education should be improved until he does? Or does it point to some sort of parity in resources? Or to something else? Coleman himself said that the focus of his report was not on "what resources go into education, but on what product comes out." He then goes on to say (in an article in *The Public Interest* [2]) that "equality of educational opportunity implies not merely 'equal' schools but equally effective schools, whose influences will overcome the differences in starting point of children from different social groups."

Pedagogically and politically, Coleman's suggestion is pleasant, impossible, and probably undesirable—pleasant because it has a nice democratic ring; impossible because the haves in the society won't allow it to happen; undesirable because it assumes that all social and cultural differences should be equalized away, that Negro children (or Chinese or Jews) have nothing to offer *as Negroes* except problems and disadvantage, and that their culture (or perhaps even their genes) gives them nothing special that might be socially, educationally, or personally valuable. A Negro in this context is nothing but a disadvantaged white.

Since we are now beginning to discover the crucial importance of the very early years of childhood, it is likely that we can achieve a greater measure of equality—to narrow the gap between the advantaged and the disadvantaged. More effective preschool programs, and a general extension of the social responsibility of the school for children from deprived

---

[2] James S. Coleman, "Toward Open Schools," *The Public Interest* (Fall, 1968).

homes, may make the classroom more effective. But the matter of achieving genuine equality is another question.

As to the politics: the most effective way that a middle-class parent can endow his children is by buying them a superior education—by giving them the head start his advantages can provide—and he is not likely to run slower to let the poor catch up. Given Coleman's standards, the only way to determine whether schools "overcome the differences in starting point of children from different social groups" is when Negro children from Harlem do as well in College Board scores or reading achievement as do whites from Scarsdale. Yet, when that happens, Scarsdale will have lost its reason to exist. Is the average white afraid of integration or "equality" only because the Negroes would, as he often says, "drag down the standards" or also because, ultimately, they might succeed? What would happen if the prep schools and suburban high schools, let alone the Ivy League universities, were no longer a guarantee of advantage and ultimate success? What if the game were genuinely open? It has often been said that American economic viability depended in part on the existence of a class of individuals who were available for the dirty jobs that the society requires (try the suggestion that we guarantee everyone a living wage, and listen to the prophecies of economic doom), but is it not equally conceivable that, for many, self-esteem and success are themselves defined by the failures of others? We can assert that technology is taking us to some sort of economic nirvana in which menial work is superfluous and we will no longer require Negroes to do it. And yet, doesn't the psychology of success always require a class of failures, and aren't the black, by virtue of their cultural inheritance, always the best candidates? Can we ever maintain a middle class without a lower class, or does it thrive, like Alcoholics Anonymous, on the continued presence of a group of people who, it is assumed, need reform and from whose failures the successful can draw esteem? Even if we dismiss that as the bleakest kind of cynicism, we are still confronted by the difficulty of a system where cash and power are convertible into educational assets; where educational assets are, in turn, the major qualifications for entry into the life and prerogatives of the middle class; and where the poor have neither. No governmental program is likely to alleviate the inequities.

As to the pedagogy: Coleman's assumption in talking about the different starting points of children "from different social groups" is that all talent is equally distributed through the population, and that inequities are generated only by social, rather than ethnic or cultural, characteristics. The current evidence seems to make the assumption doubtful; it points, indeed, to a very different course of action from the one Coleman advocates. For years there was a lot of condescending talk about the attributes and activities of different ethnic groups (all Jews were tailors, the Chinese ran laundries, the Negro had "rhythm"), and we properly reacted with egalitarian indignity when we decided how silly and pernicious that talk had become. Are we now going overboard the other way by suggesting that all talents and interests, of whatever kind, are distributed absolutely equally through the different ethnic sectors of the population? In establishing criteria for academic success—indeed, for social success generally—are we emphasizing certain skills and measures at the expense of others that may be equally valuable not only to the individual's personality and self-esteem but to the society generally? In a recent article in the *Harvard Educational Review*,[3] Susan S. Stodolsky and Gerald Lesser report on research that indicates that the relative strengths and weaknesses in different attributes remain constant for various ethnic groups, regardless of whether they are middle or lower class. Jews, for example, score higher, relative to the general population, in verbal ability than they do in space conceptualization. For Chinese children, the relative strengths and weaknesses in verbal ability and space conceptualization are reversed. (Similarly, Negroes seem to perform somewhat better in arithmetic skills and space conceptualization than they do in verbal tests; for Puerto-Ricans, the pattern is almost the reverse.) Although middle-class children score higher in *all categories,* the relative ethnic differences are not eliminated. To Lesser and Stodolsky, these findings suggest new distinctions, definitions, and a new course of action. To Coleman's call for equalization, they want to add what they consider the equally important objective of diversification, of trading on the strengths of different ethnic groups and helping them to develop those strengths to the maximum. "Beyond deploying all necessary resources to achieve minimal equality in essential goals, further development of students may well be diverse," they write. "Following our principle of matching instruction and ability we incidentally may enhance the initial strengths which each group possesses. For example, through the incidental enhancement of the space-conceptualization skills of the Chinese children, we may produce proportionally more Chinese than Jewish architects and engineers. Conversely, through incidental enhancement of verbal skills of the Jewish children, we may produce proportionally more Jewish than Chinese authors or lawyers." There is no suggestion here about producing a Jewish or a Chinese curriculum; what they do propose is tailoring the mode and techniques of instruction to the strengths of particular children.

---

[3] Susan S. Stodolsky and Gerald Lesser, "Learning Patterns in the Disadvantaged," *Harvard Educational Review* (Fall, 1967).

Studies like this are a long way from producing comprehensive solutions, but they demonstrate how complex the problem has become, how little we know about learning, and how ineffective most current remedial programs seem to be. One of the difficulties, indeed, is determining just what the problem really is. The Coleman Report, whatever its weaknesses, has made the definitional problem painfully clear. When we talk about the education of Negroes, or urban schools, or the ghetto, are we talking about ethnic minorities, a social class, or simply the universal difficulties of operating effective schools, no matter who their pupils happen to be? Clearly, there is validity in the charge that some teachers are racially and socially biased, and that the phrase "cultural disadvantage" can be used, like assertions about Negro inferiority, as an excuse for failure, a cop-out for bad teachers. The psychologist Kenneth B. Clark has often pointed out that statements about uneducable children tend to become self-fulfilling prophecies, and that teachers who talk this way don't belong in the classroom. At the same time, it's hard to believe that the same attitudes don't operate in classrooms full of lower-class Italians or Appalachian mountaineers, or that the Protestant schoolmarms of the year 1900 were altogether open-minded about the Jews and the Catholics.

Before anyone comes back with the declaration that "we made it on our own, why can't they?" let's quickly add that the economy that permitted "making it" on one's own is dead and gone, and that, when it comes to many contemporary school systems, *all children* tend to be disadvantaged. What I'm suggesting is that many schools are not educational but sociological devices which destroy learning and curiosity and deny differences as often as they encourage them, and which value managerial order above initiative, good behavior above originality, and mediocrity above engagement. (Yes, of course, there are exceptions.) All too often, they demand styles of behavior antithetical not only to social and ethnic minorities but also to most other original or "difficult" children, no matter what their background. They are instruments of social selection and, as such, they screen out misfits for the middle class, regardless of race, color, or national origin. In performing this function, every guidance counselor becomes an immigration officer and every examination a petition for a passport. Lower-class youngsters, wrote Edgar Z. Friedenberg in *The Vanishing Adolescent,* "are handy with their fists and worse; but they are helpless in the meshes of middle-class administrative procedure and are rapidly neutralized and eliminated by it. . . . They quickly learn that the most terrifying creatures are those whose bite passes unnoticed at the time and later swells, festers, and paralyzes; they cannot defend themselves against the covert, lingering hostility of teachers and school administrators." This hostility, says

Friedenberg, is generated by a reaction to the personal intensity of young men and women who resist personal repression offered in the name of adjustment. "Any individual through whom subjective intensity may intrude into the processes of bureaucratic equilibrium is extremely threatening to our society." The school, in short, is not an instrument of pluralism, but of conformity. It turns out shoddy goods for the dime-store trade; its teachers are not professionals but petty civil servants who teach children to deny their own instincts and honesty, teach them little tricks of evasion, and reject those who are not acceptable for the mold. While the deviants of the upper class may have access to special schools in the suburbs or the hills of New England, the poor have no choice: The law *requires* them to go to one particular school in one community which, as often as not, treats them as inmates. The school in this instance becomes a sort of colonial outpost manned by a collection of sahibs from downtown. Their idea of community relations is telling parents to encourage their kids to stay in school, help them with their homework, and live the life of Dick and Jane. As a result, the neighborhood school is in, but not of or by, the neighborhood.

Given these conditions and the failures of the ghetto schools, the current demands for decentralization and community control are hardly surprising. There is nothing radical about them, except in the view of school personnel who have been trained to suspect community pressure and who regard any overt mixture of politics and education as the ultimate evil. The advocates of decentralization, who feel that ghetto parents should have as much control over the education of their children as the parents of the small suburb, see political action as the only way to make the school effective and responsible: The issue is not a black principal or a black curriculum for their own sake, but making the schools accountable, and developing the sense of participation that is expected to come with it. If parents are involved, they may provide the interest and support that the education of their children requires. The schools will then become *their* schools, the teachers *their* teachers. A principal working for parents is going to try harder than one who is responsible only to bureaucrats downtown.

For many militants, the appeal of decentralization—as an essential component of community power (read Black Power, if preferred)—is extremely powerful. At the same time, the concept of decentralization suffers from some serious ambiguities. There are people like Roy Innis, a leader in CORE, who favor a single Negro school district in Harlem, a system as distinct from that of New York City as the schools of Buffalo. For most others, including white liberals, the model is a collection of small districts, each hopefully resembling those of the suburbs or the small town, each immediately accessible to the parents and the community. The difference between the two is as large as the difference between Thomas Jefferson and John C. Calhoun: One visualizes a thoroughgoing decentralization—educational federalism; the other calls forth the ghost of the doctrine of the concurrent majority. It is based on the presumption that the Negro community is as distinct from the mainstream as the peculiar institution which helped give it birth and on which Calhoun founded his brand of separatism more than a century ago. Both suffer from what may be an excessive belief in the power of formal education and a conviction that racism and bad intentions, rather than educational incompetence, are the major sources of educational inadequacy.

Yet if this were the whole problem—if teachers and schools were guilty of nothing more than middle-class bias or political irresponsibility toward the poor—the situation would not be as difficult as it is. Even if one grants the possibility of effective decentralization as a *political* solution (assuming that parents can run schools without turning them into political battlegrounds or hothouses of nepotism), what of the educational solutions? The pressure for decentralization does not stem from some specific educational program that large systems refuse to adopt and which the militants consider appropriate to the problems of their neighborhoods and children. Indeed, if the Coleman Report has any validity—and there is little reason to doubt that children from different social backgrounds do learn from each other—then decentralization, which will help institutionalize segregation, is a step backward. Thus, the Bundy Report, which outlines a plan of decentralization for New York City, and the Coleman Report, one might think, were composed on different planets.

The great possibility of decentralization (in New York, the proposal is to establish between thirty and sixty semi-autonomous districts) is not some large educational breakthrough, but no more, and no less, than the immediate objective itself: giving the community a greater sense of participation and voice in the management of one of its institutions. (In this respect, it is no different from increasing community control over planning, street-cleaning, or the administration of the local precinct of the police.) It is thus a revolt against the "professionals"—the people who took charge, in the name of reform and good government, and apparently failed to deliver the goods. In its unwillingness to trust the experts, the demand for decentralization is frontier populism come to the city, a rejection of outside planning and expertise. Parents whose children attend decentralized schools may (with luck) learn more about political action and school management than their children learn about reading or mathematics; so far, at any rate, the chances for the first outweigh those of the second. The mystery of power is, for the moment, more fascinating than the problems of instruction.

The fact is that no one, in the ghetto or out, has yet developed a vision of what the ghetto schools ought to do, how they should operate, or what an educated Negro child ought to be if he is to be something different from a dark-skinned middle-class white. The existing ghetto schools fail Negroes not so much because they are different from all other schools—as the integrationists once assumed—but because they are too much like them. Local control may introduce diversity and few alternative models to the existing public school program. The current talk about relevance in Negro education—about more Afro-American-ism in the curriculum, about Negro history, about urban problems—and the peripheral efforts to use the arts (painting, the dance, music) as ways of engaging children's interests have not taken us very far toward genuine educational integration, toward the point, that is, where ghetto children have the skills to compete effectively in the larger world. It has been said again and again that conventional instruction in formalized academic skills is difficult for children whose lives provide few examples of the value of formal education and little reinforcement for work that might pay off in some vague abstract future. Middle-class kids are, in some measure, to the manner born, and they find plenty of reinforce-ment around them: They often succeed regardless of school. For many ghetto children, instruction, to be successful, has to be immediately attractive or interesting. (There are, to be sure, many ghetto children from families whose ambitions are identical to those of the middle class.) Whether or not "enjoyment," as someone said, "is a prerequisite to competence," it is plain that skills for the larger world may appear only remotely valuable in the immediate life of a child. The humanity of children may be very distant from the problems of negotiating the economy. The problem is how to get from one to the other.

The proposals for solving the problem are endless and, as might be expected, they are often contradictory. There is no consistent Negro demand in education, any more than there is a white one. Some Negro parents are as committed to authoritarian teachers and rote learning as the village schoolmarm; others regard them as racially repressive and pedagogically useless. (Most Negro parents are probably as conservative about education as any others.) I suspect that part of the anger and frustration in all racial school disputes stems from the inability of the parties to be entirely clear about what they want. Should the schools be more middle class, more white than white, turning out suburban doctors and lawyers, or should they be training men and women who can cope with the outside world but whose energies are directed to the black community and whose loyalties remain in the ghetto? (The controversy is similar to a conventional school debate between advocates of vocational training and college preparation, but the race aspect charges it with explosive overtones.) Whatever the position, the issue is clear: Almost inevitably it revolves around the problem of moving the child from where he is to the larger world—resolving the inconsistencies between the attitudes and experience of poverty and the formalized skills and motivation that the world demands.

There is no disagreement anywhere that there is a common culture that demands certain levels of verbal and social ability. The question slowly emerging from the current debates, however, is whether that ability must become a universal virtue. Should we be concerned only with the preparation of economic functionaries and the development of conventional academic skills, or also with the growth of human beings whose dignity is not necessarily dependent on middle-class standards of success? Is an understanding of algebraic functions any more desirable than the ability to paint or dance? (The mandated requirements for many jobs—nursing, for example—include verbal abilities that are higher than those the jobs actually require; the stipulated credentials are not necessarily related to the characteristics the jobs demand.) Are we establishing norms that tend to undervalue characteristics that all of society could well use, and for which certain children might be especially well prepared, or do we have to make *all* children into replicas of the middle class?

For the next several years we are likely to hear more and more along this line. In its most extreme form, the argument says that not only is the American school an instrument of the white middle class, but that the overriding emphasis—in school and out—on high verbal and cognitive skills is itself a form of racial and social bias. The rational mind, with its emphasis on a high degree of verbal and analytical facility, is, in a manner of speaking, our thing. We invented and perfected it, and for the last fifteen years most curricular reform has been directed to the task of putting a larger and more powerful dose of it into the classroom. Thus we have, even more thoroughly than before, arranged education to separate the sheep of privilege from the goats of deprivation. Increasingly, we will now have to confront questions about what has been excluded. Are we missing something more intuitive, personal, and intangible? Is it possible to extend the Lesser-Stodolsky kind of analysis to include—along with assessments of verbal and mathematical characteristics and the ability to conceptualize space—things like affective and intuitive qualities, creativity, and some general feeling for the poetic, the visual, the musical?

Because these things are difficult to test, and because their cash value has usually been remote, the schools tend to disregard them, or to assign them to a secondary level of importance. Of all the things that make life rich—the arts, the various elements of literary and personal sensitivity, social and political involvement, philosophy, religion—very few have even a minimal place (except as lip service) in the public school program. One may not be able to mandate such activities in a large compulsory school system, but it is possible to offer them as alternatives to the public school, and one can conceive of all sorts of programs for doing so. The issue here is not to turn every ghetto school into an academy of the arts, but to offer diversity—teaching the skills of a trade or of an art with as much of a sense of importance as we teach mathematics or history. The objective, in each instance, is to draw upon the experiences and interests of the kids, to give them a sense of motion and relevance, and to provide choices, not only as to school and school control, but also as to style of learning. We have, with the single public system, and the instruction it offers, created a single standard of success and failure (and the large hippie element seems to indicate that the standard is not acceptable even to some of those who might meet it). Perhaps we have to recognize the principle of pluralism not only in a cultural context but in an educational one as well. A few years ago such suggestions would have been regarded as racist slurs, but it is now the black militant who regards Swahili as desirable for Negroes as Latin.

Carried to its extreme, the argument leads to a romantic trap, a wishful attempt to arm the weakest members of a technological society with the least effective weapons for dealing with it. It may be nice to think that there are dishwashers with the souls of poets (or even with the skills of poets), but that thought provides no foundation on which to base an educational system. There are, in our culture, a variety of important and rewarding functions that require no extensive verbal or mathematical skills (despite the exclusionist tendency of certain trades and professions to impose arbitrary educational standards for membership). Nonetheless, there remain certain levels of verbal ability without which few people can survive, except in the most menial situations. In our ambiguity and guilt about middle-class life, many of us hold a corresponding ambiguity about those who are left outside the mainstream: the happy hillbilly, the engagement and passion of the ghetto, the uninhibited poor. What we disregard is that, given the choice, most of them would elect to live like us; because of educational deficiencies, they do not have the choice. There is, said a Negro sociologist, only one way out of the ghetto, "and that's out." The reason, finally, that so few of them make it has little to do with differences in culture, or the fact that teachers and administrators are ignorant about the lives of the children assigned to them; it is because they still don't know how to teach. Negro schools are bad because all schools are bad. We simply don't know very much about how children learn. This is, in the end, what the Coleman Report proved. It may also be the greatest single contribution of the civil rights movement.

But to say that greater diversity, the provision of educational options, and a new emphasis on intuitive learning can be carried to extremes is not to deny the validity of the idea, either in the ghetto or anywhere else. For the past decade we masculinized the schools with mathematics, physics, and with a variety of new tough-minded curriculums. Educational criticism in the next decade may well concern itself more with the soft side of things—with noncognitive approaches, and with a reaffirmation of Deweyan ideas. There are a number of people who are talking seriously about a "curriculum of concerns," educational programs that begin with the interests and experience of kids, not with predetermined sets of skills to be learned. Most of the ghetto experiments that seem to have potential are pure Dewey: letting children talk their own stories and developing vocabulary and writing skills from them; trips to factories, galleries, and museums; stories and poems about the streets of the city and even about addicts and junkies. These things, too, can be carried to undisciplined extremes. None is a cure-all, but nothing in education ever is. The very nature of the enterprise is unsettling and troublesome. Education and maturation mean change, and that, in turn, means dealing with new problems, new elements every day. Equality is relatively easy to define in employment, in housing, or in medicine. It is impossible to define in education because the very nature of the enterprise demands distinctions and produces diversity.

Are we then to abandon integration and concentrate exclusively on the problems of the classroom? Plainly, the answer is no—no, because it still seems, at least to some of us, morally important; no, because, lacking better tools, it still appears to be an effective technique for education; no, because any alternative to integration is, despite immediate attractions to the contrary, unthinkable. Yet, if integration is to have any meaning, it must be a two-way street—integration not only *between* races, going both ways, but also between the school and the community, school and job, culture and culture. If equality of educational opportunity means merely an effort to improve the chances of the disadvantaged to run the race on our terms, things will never be equal and whatever they have to offer will be lost. Are we really courageous enough to provide a broad range of educational options and not to worry about who's at what level in which track? Are we really interested in education or merely in grades, credits, and diplomas? In the structure of the existing school system, segregation, repression, competition, and failure are all essential parts. Every class has a bottom half, and it tends to include, numerically, as many whites as blacks. Until we are ready to stop selecting people out, almost any conception of education is going to involve some sort of segregation. Our democratic professions might be vindicated if the ranks of the successful were as well integrated as the ranks of the failures, but would that solve the problem of education? What would we do with the failures if they were a statistically average shade of tan? The fundamental issue is not the equality of Negro schools, but the lives of all young men and women, no matter what their category or stigma. "If urban educators are failing," says Robert Dentler, the director of the Center for Urban Education, "they are failing where the newly emergent culture of the urban society itself has failed to specify either ends or means for the educator or his clientele. . . . We are in a period when the place of all children in this culture is in transition." What the problem of Negro education has done, or should be doing, is to alert us to a far larger range of social and educational questions, and to the fact that the goal of maximizing human potential is still a long way off.

# School Decentralization: The Ocean Hill-Brownsville Dispute

## MARILYN GITTELL

While political scientists and sociologists research who has power, we tend to ignore the powerless. While we study decision-making, we are reluctant to expose nondecision-making. Satisfied to rationalize a multiple-elite structure as pluralism,[1] we depreciate the relevance of public participation in the political process.[2] The scope of our research and concerns is reflected in our limited views of institutional and social change in the cities.[3]

---

This is a revised and expanded version of "Community Control of Education," reprinted with the author's permission from *Urban Riots: Violence and Social Change*, Proceedings of The Academy of Political Science, Vol. XXIX, No. 1 (1968).

[1] Robert A. Dahl, *Who Governs? Democracy and Power in an American City* (New Haven: Yale University Press, 1961); Edward C. Banfield, *Political Influence* (New York: The Free Press of Glencoe, 1961); Wallace S. Sayre and Herbert Kaufman, *Governing New York City: Politics in the Metropolis* (New York: Russell Sage Foundation, 1960); and Nelson W. Polsby, *Community Power and Political Theory* (New Haven: Yale University Press, 1963).

[2] Lester W. Milbrath, *Political Participation: How and Why Do People Get Involved in Politics* (Chicago: Rand McNally Co., 1965); Gabriel A. Almond and Sidney Verba, *The Civic Culture: Political Attitudes and Democracy in Five Nations* (Boston: Little, Brown & Co., 1963); and Robert E. Lane, *Political Life: Why and How People Get Involved in Politics* (Glencoe, Ill.: The Free Press, 1959), particularly chap. vi. The data in these studies are generally supportive of the correlation between Socio-Economic-Status and participation, concluding that middle-class, educated people are more likely to participate. Participation is largely defined as voting and there are only limited surveys of other types of participation and/or differences among such culture groups under different circumstances. The general assumption that moderate or low participation indicates consensus has undoubtedly conditioned the character and limited scope of research on participation.

[3] The critics of the democratic elitist theories have thus far been notably unsuccessful in their efforts to undermine the rationalization for replacing concepts of participatory democracy. There are obvious reasons for that failure; most important is that they have not developed empirical data to support their position. The

The ghetto community, in the meantime, has exposed the insulation of the political system and challenged its irrelevance to their demands for "a piece of the action." These communities are struggling daily with a political structure in the cities that combines two oppressive elements: bureaucratic centralization and specialization, and professionalism. In the face of these obstacles, ghetto leaders are necessarily concerned with restructuring to form a participatory system. They are forced to consider, and force all of us to consider, new mechanisms for increasing public participation. Unless they and we can find the channels for such participation, our political system may be in serious difficulty. The city school system is one of the battlegrounds and, in many respects, it reflects the larger problem of microcosm.

## City Schools and Public Education

There are those who suggest that educational institutions cannot correct the maladies of the society that reflect larger social problems. In the 1930's, when educators similarly rejected George Counts's plea for using education as a vehicle for social change, they presaged a period of thirty years of insulation of the school system from social needs.[4] It should by now be evident that educational systems are a vital component of the constructive adjustment of urban institutions to the changing needs of our society.

---

bulk of the studies in political behavior are oriented to the reinforcement of the newly defined concepts of pluralism, as reflected in multiple-elite structure. Political scientists have generally avoided research on participation. The democratic elitists, after all, structured their defense of a new definition of pluralism on findings from the most current behavioral research. Such studies, from voting-behavior analysis to decision-making indicated an increasingly limited role for public participants. How then could one justify a traditional concept of participatory democracy in the face of a declining participatory system. The democratic elitists have stressed simplistic pluralistic elements in the system, i.e., the existence of many elites within a political system and the lack of overlapping of these groups. In addition, they have stressed the varied sources of recruitment of elites and the potential ability of anyone to enter those elites. Few have addressed themselves to the issue of the effects of increasing noninvolvement. Certainly the cities are a significant laboratory for gathering supportive empirical evidence to begin to challenge the democratic elitist theories. See Peter Bachrach, *The Theory of Democratic Elitism* (Boston: Little, Brown & Co., 1967); Jack L. Walker, "A Critique of the Elitist Theory of Democracy," in Chapter I, above; and Robert A. Dahl, "Further Reflections on 'The Elitist Theory of Democracy,'" *American Political Science Review,* LX (June, 1966), 296–305.

4 George Counts, *Decision-Making and American Values in School Administration* (New York: Teachers College, Columbia University, 1954). Published for the Cooperative Program in Educational Administration, Middle Atlantic Region, by the Bureau of Publications.

The public education systems in our large cities are paralyzed. Their failure is political as well as educational. The educational failure is relatively easy to substantiate: There is sufficient hard data in test scores, dropout rates, the number of academic diplomas produced, and so forth, to establish the nature of that failure. Rationales developed to relate the cause of this failure to the problems of a disadvantaged community, while they may be valid, do not in any way negate the responsibility of the school system to educate its clientele. The inability of school professionals to cope with this problem must still be labeled an educational failure.[5]

It is unfortunate that we do not have enough reliable information to measure comparatively the success or failure of the school systems in meeting the needs of immigrant populations over the years. Too often it is assumed that the education of the disadvantaged in previous decades was somehow successful. Nonetheless, while the data are limited, there is some evidence to suggest that educational institutions in large cities have traditionally been unable to meet the needs of the ghetto community. The difference in the current problem is that dropouts in the black community are unemployable because of racial barriers and automation, whereas earlier dropouts were hidden in an expanding work force.

## The Political Failure of City School Systems

The political failure of the school system cannot be measured quantitatively except in the sense that educational failings can be traced to the environment of the total system. From my own research, I am convinced that the political failure of the school system is fundamental.[6] It can best be described in terms of the development within the city of a political subsystem whose policy process is wholly controlled by a small professional elite at headquarters. The policies emanating from this elite support an educational establishment that maintains a status quo orientation in all areas of education policy.

The lack of innovation in city school systems, except as periodically stimulated by outside funding, is indicative of this status quo orientation.

---

[5] Peter Schrag, "Boston: Education's Last Hurrah," in Chapter III, above; Herbert Kohl, *36 Children* (N.Y.: New American Library, 1967); Peter Schrag, *Village School Downtown* (Boston: Beacon Press, 1967); Jonathan Kozol, *Death at an Early Age: The Destruction of the Hearts and Minds of Negro Children in the Boston Public Schools* (Boston: Houghton Mifflin Co., 1967); and Bel Kaufman, *Up the Down Staircase* (Englewood Cliffs, N.J.: Prentice-Hall, 1964).

[6] Marilyn Gittell, *Participants and Participation* (New York: Frederick A. Praeger, 1967); and Marilyn Gittell and T. Edward Hollander, *Six Urban School Districts* (New York: Frederick A. Praeger, 1967).

Over the last sixty years, city school systems have experienced a high degree of professionalization combined with extensive centralization of the educational bureaucracy. In every large city, an inbred bureaucratic supervisory staff sits at headquarters offices holding a tight rein on educational policy. Their vested interests are clear: Any major shift in educational policy might well challenge their control of the system. Perhaps the only new agent to enter the domain of school affairs in recent years is the teacher organization or union. Unfortunately, these groups have concentrated their attention on salary and related issues; on all other questions, they have supported establishment policies.[7] Additionally, we have seen the abdication of responsibility for education by civic groups, businessmen, labor unions, and parents. The result is a closed political system, which, if measured against our ideological commitments to public participation, falls far short of any standards for a pluralistic society.

## The Rationale for Community Control

The initial thrust that followed on the *Brown v. Board of Education* decision in 1954 was directed at achieving quality integrated education. It met not only with public opposition to change but also with bureaucratic inaction. In every large city, school segregation has increased in the last decade. Residential patterns explain part of the problem, but, beyond this, many plans for integration have simply been sidetracked. The integration movement, however, provided the ghetto community with insights into their exclusion from the school decision-making process. It was the struggle for integration that spotlighted the political failure of large-city school systems. How could the ghetto communities be assured of quality education and a participatory role in the system? The response has been clear. Those who now control the schools have been unable to produce results; they have excluded the public from its rightful role in the policy process; the structure, therefore, must be adjusted to give the community a measure of control over educational institutions. Participation in itself provides an involvement with the system that can not only diminish attitudes of alienation but also serve to stimulate educational change. This new role for the community is not conceived of as an abandonment of professionalism but, rather, as an effort to achieve a proper balance between professionalism and public involvement in the policy process. The definition of community includes

---

[7] Marilyn Gittell, "Teacher Power and Its Implications for Urban Education," *Theory Into Practice* (April, 1968).

parents of school children, as well as those segments of the public that have been excluded from a role in public education. Hence, community control implies a redistribution of power within the educational subsystem.[8] It is directed toward achieving a modern mechanism for participatory democracy. It attempts to answer the political failure in education systems, and, as regards the educational failure, community control is intended to create an environment in which more meaningful educational policies can be developed and a wide variety of alternative solutions and techniques can be tested. It seems plausible to assume that a school system devoted to community needs and serving as an agent of community interests will provide an environment more conducive to learning.

## Community Control as an Instrument for Social Change

Support for community participation is voiced by the educational establishment and the professionals, but their concept of community participation is more closely related to the traditional parent-association concept and has nothing to do with community control of decision-making. It is essential that community control be defined in clear and precise terms. As one critic has noted, "participation without power is a ritual." Community control of the schools must involve local control over key policy decisions in four critical areas: (1) personnel, (2) budget, (3) curriculum, and (4) pupil policy. Local governing bodies must be locally selected, and mechanisms for encouraging broader community participation must be thoughtfully developed.

Properly instituted, community control is an instrument of social change. The redistribution of power is in itself an aspect of that change. If adequate provision is made for giving the community the technical resources to carry out this new role, community control has the potential for offering new insights into our concept of professionalism and our general theories of educational expertise. If community boards have the resources to engage a variety of professionals and nonprofessionals in the policy process, institutional changes of all kinds can be anticipated. The business community as well as university faculties and research centers may become more actively involved in the schools. Flexible staffing policies and innovative institutional arrangements are more

---

[8] The redistribution of power is an important element in social change. The further enhancement of new power sources in a political system in turn provides the opportunity for achieving other changes in the system and related institutions. See Marilyn Gittell, "A Typology of Power for Measuring Social Change," *American Behavioral Scientist,* IX (April, 1966), 23–28.

likely to be developed. The scope of other community resources will be greatly expanded as well.

## Demonstration School Projects in New York City

The three demonstration projects established in New York City, in July, 1967, to experiment with community participation offer some experience on which to base predictions. Although these three demonstration districts (Ocean Hill–Brownsville, Two Bridges, and the 201 complex) suffer from an almost total lack of delegated power and resources, they have already proved that community involvement can and does expand the scope of professional and public participation. Teacher and administrative recruitment in these districts has been innovative even within the constraints of established central procedures and the union contract. In Ocean Hill–Brownsville, seven new principals were appointed by the Local Governing Board, drawing on people from outside the regular bureaucratic hierarchy. For the first time, a Puerto Rican and a Chinese principal were appointed to head local schools.[9] A unit administrator (equivalent to a district superintendent) appointed by another of the local boards is trained in public administration rather than in the traditional professional education area. His insights and approach differ markedly from the usual school administrator. Another district, in the process of recruiting a unit administrator, established community orientation as a *sine qua non* for the candidates. Each of the districts is seriously discussing teacher-training programs to be developed jointly with universities; it is hoped that such programs will be more realistic and more constructive in recruiting and preparing teachers for ghetto schools. The districts have, in their short history, drawn on the expertise of professionals in fields not previously involved in the schools; anthropologists, political scientists, and sociologists have been used. In addition, community people have been viewed as a new and special kind of resource.

The implications of community control as an instrument of social change are reflected in the obvious threat they present to the holders of power in the system and to the public in general. The press and propaganda reports describe only the difficulties that these communities have encountered. Charges of racism have been played up, but no effort has been made to discuss constructive changes in the districts. The United Federation of Teachers (UFT) and the Council of Supervisory Associations (CSA) regularly proclaim the extremist character of governing

---

[9] A recent court action has held that these appointments were illegal since they were made in violation of state law. The case is presently on appeal.

board members or those who control them. Actually, the governing boards include a representative cross-section of ethnic groups in the communities, and these attacks are often motivated by a refusal to accept the political and educational goals and interests of the boards. Members of the local boards are, largely, parents of school children in the district; many are from lower-income groups and their involvement in community affairs began in poverty programs; several had never been involved in school affairs prior to the creation of the demonstration districts.

Unfortunately, the three districts have been spending a great deal of their time and effort struggling with the Board of Education to secure the powers that would justify labeling them experiments in community control; a more reliable test of their viability awaits the conclusion of that negotiation.

### The Bundy Plan

The most significant general proposal for community control to date is the Bundy Plan, presented to the mayor of New York City in the autumn of 1967.[10] The plan calls for city-wide decentralization and rather extensive community control. It suggests a city-wide education structure for special schools, for establishing minimum standards, for control of capital construction, and for provision of voluntary services at the request of local districts. By its provision for local selection of a majority of the member of local school boards and for community control of the expense budget, student policy, curriculum, and personnel, the Bundy Plan meets the test of redistributing power in the system. Perhaps the plan's obvious commitment to community control explains the opposition to it. The outcry surrounding the Bundy Plan suggests the general alignment of forces to be faced by any proposal for decentralization and increased community control in cities throughout the country. It also reflects the current education power structure and its failure to respond to the pressing demands of the community.

Those who, for a decade, have resisted school integration and eschewed the plight of the ghetto schools now draw on these very arguments to denigrate the Bundy Plan. Local school board members who have resisted efforts at integration in their own areas for over a decade are now defenders of city-wide integration—or, at least, they oppose plans for decentralization and community control because such plans

---

[10] Mayor's Advisory Panel on Decentralization of the New York City Schools, *Reconnection for Learning: A Community School System for New York City* (November, 1967), excerpts of which appear in Chapter IV, above.

presumably would deny the possibility of achieving integration. The UFT, which, in the last decade, successfully staved off several mandatory teacher transfer plans (designed to ensure adequate staffing for ghetto schools), now expresses great concern with the effect that the Bundy Plan might have on integrated staffing of ghetto schools. The CSA, which has regularly impeded the progress of plans developed to effect integration and, over the years, has shown minimum interest in programs to improve ghetto schools (in one effort, it acted as plaintiff in a court action—which is rumored to have cost $1 million—against the three ghetto school demonstration projects and the Bundy Plan) now rationalizes its opposition to the Bundy Plan by arguing that the ghetto areas will suffer if decentralization is implemented. Political leaders who, in the past, have ignored school issues—except to support local community efforts to resist the various integration plans that have periodically been mounted, announced, and cancelled—are now also champions of integration for the ghetto community.

Viewing the decentralization controversy as it has developed around the Bundy Plan and the experimental demonstration districts, it is possible to mark out three phases. In the first phase, a rhetoric related to the concept of community control was developed to defeat the Bundy Plan. The Board of Education, initially reticent about the development of the three school demonstration projects (in effect, they were charmed by Ford Foundation funding into accepting them), began to claim the projects as proof of their own commitment to evolutionary decentralization and as evidence of their faith in community participation. Apparently, however, their faith fell short of giving those districts control of budget and personnel, the essential elements of local power. The UFT, in order to maintain a proper image, indicated its strong support for community control while simultaneously waging a continuing struggle against ghetto parents. It supported the court action of the CSA against the demonstration projects and directed that its members boycott local school board elections. (It should be noted that the directive was ignored by a sizable group of teachers in elections in the I.S. 201 and Two Bridges projects.) The UFT has, at different times, been on both sides of the demonstration project issue. It originally participated in the creation of the projects and insisted on representation in their planning and governance. In fact, each of the project plans embodied requirements for teacher representation on local boards. The UFT supported representation by chapter chairmen to assure UFT, as distinguished from teacher, involvement. Almost as soon as the UFT recognized that it could not control the enterprise, it withdrew support and prepared to battle community interests. The UFT leadership reinforced their opposition to the projects after their September, 1967, strike action. They could not forgive the ghetto parents who had violated their picket lines. The growing conflict between the UFT and ghetto parents was reflected in the fact that, in the demonstration project areas, all schools remained opened during the strike. (Ghetto parents, particularly in the project areas, see the UFT's contract as a major restriction on their power to engage in the development of educational policy; accordingly, if the More Effective Schools program pushed by the union were to be expanded, they believe that it should be a policy decision made by the community or, minimally, with the community.)

The CSA apparently never had any conflict about community control; they have consistently opposed it and they readily defend unadulterated professionalism as a primary need of any school system. Parent and community control, they continue to suggest, will result only in a return to corruption, patronage, and chaos. Either they have no compunction in shedding the Deweyan theories and ideology of education in a democracy or they have become far more concerned with power than with ideology. The CSA battle is not one of rhetoric alone. They have lobbied local and state legislators and party leaders and they have mustered all their strength for what they consider a life and death battle. They feel themselves deeply threatened by parent and community power.

An evaluation of the first phase of the school-reform movement and the attempt to secure community control in New York City cannot ignore the role of the mayor and the white community. The Bundy Plan was developed by a mayor's panel and, although the mayor's revised plan reduced community control somewhat, his general support of the concept has been a source of its strength. Professionals in the system and in the Board of Education have not been reluctant to label the mayor's interest and involvement as "political interference." The white community, on the other hand, has been decidedly split on the Bundy Plan. Large segments of the educated middle class are so committed to professionalism that they vigorously reject community control by questioning their own qualifications to participate in school decision-making. While the adage of "let George do it" aroused the ire of the old-style reformer, the new reform movement has to face a tougher trend of "let George, the professional, do it."

The first phase in the controversy culminated in the spring of 1968 in a concerted attempt by opponents of decentralization to prevent legislative action. The thrust of the attempt was directed against the Regents' bill that had been introduced into the State Legislature during that spring. Neither the union nor its new-found ally, the CSA, spared any expense in trying to defeat the passage of this decentralization bill, which had been based on the Bundy Plan. The UFT reportedly spent upward of $500,000 in a public relations campaign that included hundreds of school meetings, newspaper ads, and radio spots; the CSA assessed its members nearly $1 million for a war chest, though it actually spent less money and expended less effort than did the UFT.

The pro-decentralization forces, lacking tight organizational direction and unlimited funds, were hampered in their attempts to press for a meaningful bill. The two most influential civic educational organizations, for example, the United Parents Association and the Public Education Association, in presenting their own drafts of a decentralization bill, departed significantly from the Bundy model. The net effect of the various ideological differences among black and reform white groups was to enfeeble their collective strength. A loose umbrella coalition was finally formed in the early spring of 1968, under the chairmanship of RCA President Robert Sarnoff, to lobby for the mayor's amended version of the Bundy Plan. At the same time, it appears that the mayor did not play as forceful a role as he could have in pushing for passage of the bill. It has been said that the mayor did not feel the white community, already divided in its support, backed his efforts sufficiently to enable him to push harder.

In the attempt to set up an effective decentralization plan, a compromise bill was worked out by State Commissioner of Education Allen and the New York State Board of Regents; it renewed hope that the legislature would pass a strong measure. The bill had the support of the mayor, the governor, and leaders of the legislature. While the governor, the state commissioner of education, and the Regents supported a more moderate plan for decentralization, there was nonetheless only a minimum of legislative backing for it. The more liberal, or reform, city democrats in the legislature and the few black legislators were a small coalition operating for passage. Most of the members were ill-informed on the matter and were especially susceptible to pressure from the various groups lobbying in the capital.

The UFT successfully coupled a threat of political vengeance with the fear of extremism over the involuntary transfer of nineteen educators from the Ocean Hill–Brownsville experimental district. As a result, the legislators, all up for re-election in the fall, merely postponed action for a year, empowering a hostile city school board to draw up another decentralization plan. In order to placate the pro-decentralization forces, the legislature increased the membership of the nine-member city board to thirteen. Although the legislative battle was postponed to the 1969 session, a new campaign was begun by the UFT in the fall of 1968.

The defeat of both the Bundy Plan and the Regents Plan ended the first phase of the political decentralization struggle. The escalation of the Ocean Hill–Brownsville controversy by the UFT into a city-wide strike marked the beginning of the second phase, which pitted white and black against each other in a racial confrontation.

The opening thrust was a not-too-subtle CSA–UFT campaign that charged the Ocean Hill–Brownsville district with encouraging racial extremism and anti-Semitism; it proved very successful. The Jewish community in the city became supportive and grew increasingly militant in its demands for redress. Leaflets and flyers, distributed throughout the city by the UFT and the CSA, quoted from materials purported to have been circulating in the Ocean Hill–Brownsville district. Some of the material was later proven to have been falsified; none of it was ever proven to have come from the district. Mass circulation of this propaganda fed existing fears and latent racism, as the atmosphere in the city became more charged with the passing of each day of the strike.

Although the mayor attempted to balance the interests of both sides during the strike, he was committed to the preservation of the Ocean Hill–Brownsville district and of decentralization, and this pitted him against the UFT–CSA, creating a political stalemate. The solid alignment of labor in support of the UFT was a major element in the controversy. The Central Labor Council threatened a general strike and forced the mayor to make a series of concessions to the union. The mayor appeared to have no political leverage in dealing with the union and was unable to use any of his normal political powers to de-escalate the union's demands or to force a settlement. Additionally, new efforts to develop institutional muscle for decentralization through the Committee to Save Decentralization and Community Control were slow in getting off the ground, although several sources of support, particularly church groups, were successfully tapped.

The future of school decentralization in the State Legislature this year will mark the third phase of the dispute. Legislators who were merely ill-informed in 1968 are now solidly opposed to decentralization. The New York City Democrats have largely been supportive of the union and would like nothing better than to pin the mayor's ears back. The governor, while publicly in favor of decentralization, is also not anxious to stick his neck out or to enhance in any way the career of John Lindsay.

## Reformism and Community Control

It is apparent from this brief rundown of the politics of community control in New York City that traditional reform concepts developed in the first half of the twentieth century are a source of much of the opposition rhetoric. The failure of neoreformers to challenge these outdated concepts has allowed their opposition to use the rhetoric of reform against them. These traditional concepts are reflected in the professionals' defense of their role and in the white middle-class reactions to community control. Historically, the reform movement distrusted machine politics. The movement was a reaction to widespread corruption in government, and professionalism was the panacea that it developed to replace "political" or public decision-making. Citizen participation was to be satisfied by public voting in referenda and the creation of watchdog civic groups. Consequently, any challenge to professionalism, or any attempt to strengthen community control, would be an anathema to middle-class and professional attitudes. Neoreformers in the city have not been emphatic enough in arguing that much has happened in the last two decades to prove that the traditional reform mechanisms and battle lines are no longer meaningful. Because of the radical changes in the character of large-city populations and the ever increasing expansion of city functions and responsibilities, with a concurrent growth in city bureaucracy, reform must take on a new character. We cannot ignore the fact that increasingly large segments of our city population are alienated from formal policy-makers as well as from old-style civic reformers. Consequently, they have been unable to use the traditional and limited mechanisms for public participation and influence.

## The Ghetto and Community Control

The ghetto communities and their leaders are not "hung-up" on professionalism. They have adequate proof that the school system and the professionals who run it have failed. In fact, the frustrations engendered by the unwillingness of the educators to yield power within the system has led to more broad-based demands for fundamental change. In two recent conferences, the Five State Organizing Committee for Community Control reaffirmed as one of its objectives absolute community control of school administrative and fiscal policies.[11] It rejected the idea of a subsystem within the city school system; such a subsystem would be a violation of self-determination because "basic control remains with the white establishment." Harlem CORE has been working on a proposal,

---

[11] Five State Organizing Committee for Community Control to the Office of Metropolitan Educational Sub-systems, *Position Statement* (January 25, 1968), p. 3.

which is gathering increased support, for a Harlem school district under state aegis. Its characterization of the present system states: "The present structure of the New York City school system as it manifests itself in Harlem does not allow the utilization of positive factors and rich resources in the Harlem community as a lever in the education of Harlem children." [12] It is their contention that only a wholly independent district can draw on community resources and engage the public in meaningful participation. The kinds of social change they seek can evolve only from effective community control.

## Opposition to the Concept

The arguments against community control tend to center around two themes—the parochialism that might result from neighborhood districts' controlling the schools and the lack of qualifications of community people and their inability to cope with the highly technical problems in education.

The concern with the dangers of parochialism usually relates to fears of the emergence of black racism and separatism. State legislation and administrative regulations now prescribe certain limitations, but it is possible that new protective controls will prove necessary; these could be worked out as the need suggests. The concern with black racism is more often a misinterpretation of the movement toward creating a sense of community identity; it is evidence of a lack of understanding of the ghetto community's desire to increase the number of black teachers and administrators in local schools. In fact, there is no evidence in any of the three demonstration projects that there is any unusual stress in this area.

Local rivalries and ethnic conflicts may be intensified by local control and this should be anticipated. However, the ability to deal with, and resolve or compromise, these conflicts locally may well be an important part of the participatory process. Conflict does not necessarily have to be viewed as dangerous; rather, it may stimulate increased public and group participation in the affairs of the community. The advantages to be gained from encouraging community identity and consciousness, particularly in the ghetto, may well outweigh any negative aspects of parochialism. There is empirical evidence that participation and involvement increase when group identity is stronger: Alinsky identified greater worker participation in a worker-identified community; the ex-

---

[12] New York Harlem CORE, *Questions and Answers Regarding the Autonomous Harlem School System* (1967), p. 2.

perience in Norway with a workers' party showed similar results.[13] The group identity factor probably supersedes Socio-Economic-Status (SES) and racial background as an influence on the kind and extent of community participation. In fact, from the reactions and responses in the three demonstration school projects, it appears that community control has already stimulated wider local participation. Election returns in governing-board elections, although somewhat influenced by lack of publicity, inability to attain registration lists from the Board of Education, and absence of experience in conducting political campaigns, are higher than the responses in other local political elections in the same districts. Estimates of eligible parent voters who participated in the three districts were, approximately, 20 per cent in the 201 complex, 30 per cent in Ocean Hill–Brownsville, and 50 per cent in the Two Bridges district. There are also indications of wider parent interest and involvement in school meetings and school organizations in these three communities. The background of governing-board members suggests that low SES has not deterred extensive participation in the policy process—when the group can exercise power. This experience may offer important evidence to suggest that low participation by level of income or SES reflects the failure of our political system to provide either the means for participation or the direct power to lower-class groups. Given both a political structure with which the ghetto resident can identify and a delegation of effective power in decision-making, his involvement is substantially increased.

Participation should be defined in two general categories: first, as involvement or expressed interest, as reflected in attendance at meetings or voting; second, as direct engagement in the policy-making process and in the exercise of power. The latter experience should provide the basis for testing the effect of community control as a mechanism for achieving social and institutional change in the system. The limited evidence in the three demonstration projects strongly supports the hypothesis that community control in the ghetto is a source of social change.

Serious opposition to community control stems from a lack of confidence in the ability of community people to make decisions that may

---

[13] Lane, *op. cit.* A Norwegian study indicated higher turnout in elections where socio-economic status of an area is more homogeneous; see Stein Rokkan, "The Comparative Study of Political Participation: Notes Toward a Perspective on Current Research," in Austin Ranney (ed.), *Essays on the Behavioral Study of Politics* (Urbana, Ill.: University of Illinois Press, 1962), pp. 47–90. See also Herbert J. Gans, *The Urban Villagers. Group and Class in the Life of Italian Americans* (New York: The Free Press of Glencoe, 1965), pp. 106–10.

require some technical competence. A corollary to that position is the fear that community control denies or negates professionalism. In fact, public attitudes often attribute far too much to the ability of the professionals to come up with answers to problems. Community control must embody decision-making power vested in community representatives. Those representatives, however, must, to some extent, still rely on both professionals and nonprofessionals for inputs into the policy process.

In addition, technical resources must be made readily available to the community, to be used at its discretion. Such resources should be integral to any projected plan for community control. It should also be noted that there is advantage to injecting the dimension of community nonprofessional experience and expertise, which is now excluded from the policy process; in many ways, the parents of school children have insights into needs and values that can contribute significantly to a more viable educational program.[14] A broader concept of education, one that goes beyond the four-walls classroom concept and extends into the larger community, can gain particularly from that experience.

Again, the experience of the three demonstration projects suggests that community control does not deny professional involvement; rather, it broadens it, tapping new professional resources. However, achieving the proper balance between a professional and a public role is a continuing process that can only be defined in a practical setting.

Community control of education is only one aspect of the general movement toward expanded community involvement. Underlying the effort toward this goal is the desire to guarantee a meaningful redistribution of power in our cities. Although the community-at-large has suffered from the insulation of the policy process in the bureaucratic structure, it is the ghetto population that has recognized the problem and pressed for change. The ends that they seek and the thrust of their actions may benefit the political system and the larger community as a whole.

---

[14] Curriculum experts now suggest the value of wider participation in the development of school curriculum; see George A. Beauchamp, *Planning the Elementary School Curriculum* (Englewood Cliffs, N.J.: Allyn and Bacon, 1956), p. 10.

# PART FOUR

# Managing Metropolitan Conflict: Structures of Power and Action

The purpose of this section is to describe the formal and informal structures by which metropolitan decisions are made and conflict managed. By formal structures we refer to government and politics—to official policy makers—and by informal structures we refer to influential groups and persons outside of formal government—to unofficial policy makers. Both formal and informal structures function to overcome the metropolitan area's internal divisiveness and make concerted public action possible. They provide the means for making policy in the metropolis.

One common focus in the analysis of policy making and conflict management is the operation of formal governmental institutions. Governmental institutions, of course, are cooperative arrangements that imply some basis of agreement. In this section three categories of governmental institutions are discussed: the city "machine" model, the city "reform" model, and suburban style institutions.

Also stressed here is the operation of extragovernmental structures of influence. Extragovernmental structures are considered under two headings: the elitist model, which depicts cities as subject to the manipulation of economic notables, and the pluralist model, which more optimistically suggests a balancing-off of competing groups.

The first article on the machine model of city government, "How to Get a Political Following," is a turn-of-the-century original that the student should find engaging as well as informative. The second article examines the operation and decline of the classic city machine. It also considers the implications of the "new immigration" of Negroes and Puerto Ricans.

The articles dealing with the reform model of city government focus on the actual operation of reformed institutions rather than on their theory. "Governmental Structure and Political Environment: A Statistical Note About American Cities" is a systematic treatment of environmental conditions associated with the three major forms of city government. Kessel finds that the manager form—the favorite of reformers—is typically found in medium sized and rapidly growing cities, and in cities with concentrations of local businessmen. Phillips Cutright's "Non-partisan Electoral Systems in American Cities" is a systematic treatment of conditions associated with nonpartisan elections. Class and religious cleavages are among the environmental conditions investigated by Cutright, and his conclusions are of special interest in terms of the relationship between urban environment and governmental forms. Charles R. Adrian's article is an analysis of policy leadership in three council-manager cities. Adrian examines the policy-making role of interest groups, mayors, and councils as well as of the manager and his administration. "Reformism and Public Policy in American Cities" focuses on relationships among city (1) political system characteristics (classified into reformed and unreformed institutions) (2) socioeconomic cleavages and (3) taxes and expenditures. The main question is whether reformed and unreformed institutions differ in their responsiveness (in taxing and spending) to community cleavages. The data show that "the more reformed the city the less responsive it is to socioeconomic cleavages." This, the authors note, is exactly what the reformers wanted.

Under "Governing the Suburbs," Robert C. Wood's treatment of the grass roots democracy concept is presented. Wood questions the view that suburbia is the legitimate heir to the small democracy ideal; but he recognizes that the proliferation of governmental units, so distressing to metropolitan reformers, has developed in the name of that ideal. Wood also notes the suburbs' resistance to governmental reorganization; and he chides metropolitan reformers for not launching a full-scale attack on the grass roots ideology.

The section on urban power structures is introduced by Floyd Hunter's pioneering study of "regional city's" domination by a small group of men having exceptional economic resources. In contrast Aaron Wildavsky's "Why American Cities Are Pluralist" takes issue with the entire elitist thesis. Finally, "Two Faces of Power" develops the argument that the divergent findings of elitist and pluralist researchers are the product of differences in their assumptions and methods. "Two Faces of Power" also offers some suggestions for a fresh approach to the study of community power, with special emphasis on the way a community's pervasive biases determine which issues become public.

Banfield and Wilson's "Public-Regardingness as a Value Premise in Voting Behavior" is presented in the section on electoral systems. In it the authors examine the "admittedly implausible" hypothesis that the voter always tries to maximize his family income. Voting data on proposals for public expenditure in Cleveland and Chicago show that in fact some voters, especially in the upper income groups, vote against their self-interest narrowly conceived. Banfield and Wilson's explanation is that some income and ethnic groups have a "public-regarding" outlook, while others are "private-regarding." "The Making of Negro Mayors 1967" details the impressive victories of Carl B. Stokes in Cleveland and Richard D. Hatcher in Gary, Indiana.

# A. CITY GOVERNMENT— MACHINE STYLE

## How to Get a Political Following

### GEORGE WASHINGTON PLUNKITT

"There's thousands of young men in this city who will go to the polls for the first time next November. Among them will be many who have watched the careers of successful men in politics, and who are longin' to make names and fortunes for themselves at the same game. It is to these youths that I want to give advice. First, let me say that I am in a position to give what the courts call expert testimony on the subject. I don't think you can easily find a better example than I am of success in politics. After forty years' experience at the game I am—well, I'm George Washington Plunkitt. Everybody knows what figure I cut in the greatest organization on earth, and if you hear people say that I've laid away a million or so since I was a butcher's boy in Washington Market, don't come to me for an indignant denial. I'm pretty comfortable, thank you.

"Now, havin' qualified as an expert, as the lawyers say, I am goin' to give advice free to the young men who are goin' to cast their first votes, and who are lookin' forward to political glory and lots of cash. Some young men think they can learn how to be successful in politics from books, and they cram their heads with all sorts of college rot. They couldn't make a bigger mistake. Now, understand me, I ain't sayin' nothin' against colleges. I guess they'll have to exist as long as there's bookworms, and I suppose they do some good in a certain way, but they don't count in politics. In fact, a young man who has gone through the college course is handicapped at the outset. He may succeed in politics, but the chances are 100 to 1 against him.

"Another mistake; some young men think that the best way to prepare for the political game is to practise speakin' and becomin'

Reprinted from William L. Riordan, *Plunkitt of Tammany Hall* (New York: McClure Philips & Co., 1905), pp. 11–18 and 46–53.

orators. That's all wrong. We've got some orators in Tammany Hall, but they're chiefly ornamental. You never heard of Charlie Murphy delivering a speech, did you? Or Richard Croker, or John Kelly, or any other man who has been a real power in the organization? Look at the thirty-six district leaders of Tammany Hall to-day. How many of them travel on their tongues? Maybe one or two, and they don't count when business is doin' at Tammany Hall. The men who rule have practised keepin' their tongues still, not exercisin' them. So you want to drop the orator idea unless you mean to go into politics just to perform the sky-rocket act.

"Now, I've told you what not to do; I guess I can explain best what to do to succeed in politics by tellin' you what I did. After goin' through the apprenticeship of the business while I was a boy by workin' around the district headquarters and hustlin' about the polls on election day, I set out when I cast my first vote to win fame and money in New York city politics. Did I offer my services to the district leader as a stump speaker? Not much. The woods are always full of speakers. Did I get up a book on municipal government and show it to the leader? I wasn't such a fool. What I did was to get some marketable goods before goin' to the leaders. What do I mean by marketable goods? Let me tell you: I had a cousin, a young man who didn't take any particular interest in politics. I went to him and said: 'Tommy, I'm goin' to be a politician, and I want to get a followin'; can I count on you?' He said: 'Sure, George.' That's how I started in business. I got a marketable commodity—one vote. Then I went to the district leader and told him I could command two votes on election day, Tommy's and my own. He smiled on me and told me to go ahead. If I had offered him a speech or a bookful of learnin', he would have said, 'Oh, forget it!'

"That was beginnin' business in a small way, wasn't it? But that is the only way to become a real lastin' statesman. I soon branched out. Two young men in the flat next to mine were school friends. I went to them, just as I went to Tommy, and they agreed to stand by me. Then I had a followin' of three voters and I began to get a bit chesty. Whenever I dropped into district headquarters, everybody shook hands with me, and the leader one day honored me by lightin' a match for my cigar. And so it went on like a snowball rollin' down a hill. I worked the flat-house that I lived in from the basement to the top floor, and I got about a dozen young men to follow me. Then I tackled the next house and so on down the block and around the corner. Before long I had sixty men back of me, and formed the George Washington Plunkitt Association.

"What did the district leader say when I called at headquarters? I didn't have to call at headquarters. He came after me and said: 'George, what do you want? If you don't see what you want, ask for it. Wouldn't you like to have a job or two in the departments for your friends?' I said: 'I'll think it over; I haven't yet decided what the George Washington Plunkitt Association will do in the next campaign.' You ought to have seen how I was courted and petted then by the leaders of the rival organizations. I had market-able goods and there was bids for them from all sides, and I was a risin' man in politics. As time went on, and my association grew, I thought I would like to go to the Assembly. I just had to hint at what I wanted, and three different organizations offered me the nomi-nation. Afterwards, I went to the Board of Aldermen, then to the State Senate, then became leader of the district, and so on up and up till I became a statesman.

"That is the way and the only way to make a lastin' success in politics. If you are goin' to cast your first vote next November and want to go into politics, do as I did. Get a followin', if it's only one man, and then go to the district leader and say: 'I want to join the organization. I've got one man who'll follow me through thick and thin.' The leader won't laugh at your one-man followin'. He'll shake your hand warmly, offer to propose you for membership in his club, take you down to the corner for a drink and ask you to call again. But go to him and say: 'I took first prize at college in Aristotle; I can recite all Shakespeare forwards and backwards; there ain't nothin' in science that ain't as familiar to me as blockades on the elevated roads and I'm the real thing in the way of silver-tongued orators.' What will he answer? He'll probably say: 'I guess you are not to blame for your misfortunes, but we have no use for you here.' "

## To Hold Your District—
## Study Human Nature and Act Accordin'

"There's only one way to hold a district; you must study human nature and act accordin'. You can't study human nature in books. Books is a hindrance more than anything else. If you have been to college, so much the worse for you. You'll have to unlearn all you learned before you can get right down to human nature, and un-learnin' takes a lot of time. Some men can never forget what they learned at college. Such men may get to be district leaders by a fluke, but they never last.

"To learn real human nature you have to go among the people, see them and be seen. I know every man, woman, and child in the

Fifteenth District, except them that's been born this summer—and I know some of them, too. I know what they like and what they don't like, what they are strong at and what they are weak in, and I reach them by approachin' at the right side.

"For instance, here's how I gather in the young men. I hear of a young feller that's proud of his voice, thinks that he can sing fine. I ask him to come around to Washington Hall and join our Glee Club. He comes and sings, and he's a follower of Plunkitt for life. Another young feller gains a reputation as a base-ball player in a vacant lot. I bring him into our baseball club. That fixes him. You'll find him workin' for my ticket at the polls next election day. Then there's the feller that likes rowin' on the river, the young feller that makes a name as a waltzer on his block, the young feller that's handy with his dukes—I rope them all in by givin' them opportunities to show themselves off. I don't trouble them with political arguments. I just study human nature and act accordin'.

"But you may say this game won't work with the high-toned fellers, the fellers that go through college and then join the Citizens' Union. Of course it wouldn't work. I have a special treatment for them. I ain't like the patent medicine man that gives the same medicine for all diseases. The Citizens' Union kind of a young man! I love him! He's the daintiest morsel of the lot, and he don't often escape me.

"Before telling you how I catch him, let me mention that before the election last year, the Citizens' Union said they had four hundred or five hunderd enrolled voters in my district. They had a lovely headquarters, too, beautiful roll-top desks and the cutest rugs in the world. If I was accused of havin' contributed to fix up the nest for them, I wouldn't deny it under oath. What do I mean by that? Never mind. You can guess from the sequel, if you're sharp.

"Well, election day came. The Citizens' Union's candidate for Senator, who ran against me, just polled five votes in the district, while I polled something more than 14,000 votes. What became of the 400 or 500 Citizens' Union enrolled voters in my district? Some people guessed that many of them were good Plunkitt men all along and worked with the Cits just to bring them into the Plunkitt camp by election day. You can guess that way, too, if you want to. I never contradict stories about me, especially in hot weather. I just call your attention to the fact that on last election day 395 Citizens' Union enrolled voters in my district were missin' and unaccounted for.

"I tell you frankly, though, how I have captured some of the Citizens' Union's young men. I have a plan that never fails. I watch the

City Record to see when there's civil service examinations for good things. Then I take my young Cit in hand, tell him all about the good thing and get him worked up till he goes and takes an examination. I don't bother about him any more. It's a cinch that he comes back to me in a few days and asks to join Tammany Hall. Come over to Washington Hall some night and I'll show you a list of names on our rolls marked 'C.S.' which means, 'bucked up against civil service.'

"As to the older voters, I reach them, too. No, I don't send them campaign literature. That's rot. People can get all the political stuff they want to read—and a good deal more, too—in the papers. Who reads speeches, nowadays, anyhow? It's bad enough to listen to them. You ain't goin' to gain any votes by stuffin' the letter boxes with campaign documents. Like as not you'll lose votes, for there's nothin' a man hates more than to hear the letter-carrier ring his bell and go to the letter box expectin' to find a letter he was lookin' for, and find only a lot of printed politics. I met a man this very mornin' who told me he voted the Democratic State ticket last year just because the Republicans kept crammin' his letter-box with campaign documents.

"What tells in holdin' your grip on your district is to go right down among the poor families and help them in the different ways they need help. I've got a regular system for this. If there's a fire in Ninth, Tenth, or Eleventh Avenue, for example, any hour of the day or night, I'm usually there with some of my election district captains as soon as the fire-engines. If a family is burned out I don't ask whether they are Republicans or Democrats, and I don't refer them to the Charity Organization Society, which would investigate their case in a month or two and decide they were worthy of help about the time they are dead from starvation. I just get quarters for them, buy clothes for them if their clothes were burned up, and fix them up till they get things runnin' again. It's philanthropy, but it's politics, too—mighty good politics. Who can tell how many votes one of these fires bring me? The poor are the most grateful people in the world, and, let me tell you, they have more friends in their neighborhoods than the rich have in theirs.

"If there's a family in my district in want I know it before the charitable societies do, and me and my men are first on the ground. I have a special corps to look up such cases. The consequence is that the poor look up to George W. Plunkitt as a father, come to him in trouble —and don't forget him on election day.

"Another thing, I can always get a job for a deservin' man. I make it a point to keep on the track of jobs and it seldom happens that I don't have a few up my sleeve ready for use. I know every big employer in the district and in the whole city, for that matter, and they ain't in the habit of sayin' no to me when I ask them for a job.

"And the children—the little roses of the district! Do I forget them? Oh, no! They know me, every one of them, and they know that a sight of Uncle George and candy means the same thing. Some of them are the best kind of vote-getters. I'll tell you a case. Last year a little Eleventh Avenue rosebud whose father is a Republican, caught hold of his whiskers on election day and said she wouldn't let go till he'd promise to vote for me. And she didn't."

# Bosses, Machines, and Ethinc Groups

## ELMER E. CORNWELL, JR.

Though the direction of the causal relationship may be difficult to estab-lish, the classic urban machine and the century of immigration which ended in the 1920's were intimately intertwined phenomena. This fact is not always recognized as fully as it should be. Much of the literature on bosses and machines, beginning with the muckrakers, but not ex-cluding more recent studies with less overt moralistic flavor, carries the implication that such factors as the dispersal of power in urban govern-ment—under weak mayor charters and through rivalries among state, county, city and special district authorities, all plowing the same field but none with full responsibility for its cultivation—invited the ma-chine's extralegal reconcentration of power. It is also true that attitudes engendered by a business society whose prime movers characteristically had their eye on the "main chance"—and specifically on traction fran-chises and the like—also fostered the growth of the essentially entrepre-neurial role and amoral attitude of the boss.

### Relation of Machine to Immigration

When all this has been said, however, the fact still remains that the classic machine would probably not have been possible, and certainly would not have been so prominent a feature of the American political landscape, without the immigrant. Essentially, any disciplined grass-roots political organization rests upon a docile mass base which has in some manner been rendered dependable, predictable, and manipulable. The rank and file of the Soviet Communist party is disciplined by a com-bination of ideological allegiance, fear, and hope of reward. The average party supporter in a liberal-democratic society cannot be so disciplined under ordinary circumstances, at least not for long. The newly arrived

Reprinted from *Annals of the American Academy of Political and Social Science* (May 1964), pp. 27–39, by permission of the publisher.

immigrant was a special case, however. He was characteristically insecure, culturally and often linguistically alien, confused, and often in actual want. Thus, even if he had valued the franchise thrust upon him by his new political mentors, its careful exercise would have taken a low priority in his daily struggle for existence. In most cases, he did not value or even understand the political role into which he was being pushed.

Thus, it was the succeeding waves of immigrants that gave the urban political organizations the manipulable mass bases without which they could not have functioned as they did. And, until immigration dried up to a trickle in the 1920's, as one generation of newcomers began to espouse traditional American values of political independence, there was always a new group, often from a different country of origin, to which the machine could turn. As long as this continued to be possible, machines persisted, and once the immigrant base finally began to disappear, so did most of the bosses of the classic model. In a very real sense, then, the one phenomenon was dependent on the other.

The argument can be made that there were other machines that clearly were not immigrant-based in this sense. All generalizations, especially those in the social sciences, are but proximate truths. At the same time, machines based on white, Protestant, "old stock" clienteles were not wholly unrelated in their motivation and operation to the factor of immigration. Platt's smooth-functioning organization in New York State [1] and Blind Boss Brayton's contemporary operation in Rhode Island [2] were both based, in the immediate sense, on what Lincoln Steffens called "the good old American stock out in the country." [3] And yet recall that both of these states were highly urbanized even in the 1890's and early 1900's when these two worthies flourished and had ingested disproportionate numbers of immigrants. As of 1920, when 38 per cent of the total United States population was foreign born or of foreign parentage, the corresponding percentages for New York and Rhode Island were 64 and 71. [4] These facts alone suggest what the political history of both makes clear: these rural "old stock" machines existed largely as means of political defense against the newcomers and doubtless would not have existed had there been no immigrants.

---

[1] See Harold F. Gosnell, *Boss Platt and His New York Machine* (Chicago: University of Chicago Press, 1924).

[2] See Lincoln Steffens, "Rhode Island: A State for Sale," *McClure's Magazine*, Vol. 24 (February 1905), pp. 337–353.

[3] Lincoln Steffens, *Autobiography* (New York: Literary Guild, 1931), p. 367.

[4] E. P. Hutchinson, *Immigrants and Their Children* (New York: John Wiley, 1956), p. 27.

The point, then, is that, whereas in the cities the immigrants sold their political independence for the familiar currency of favors and aid, their rural native cousins were sometimes prompted to do the same, in part out of desire for cultural-religious as well as political, and perhaps at times economic, self-protection. Recollection of the Know-Nothing era of militant nativist activity a half-century earlier suggests that this kind of cultural-religious antagonism can be a very potent political force indeed. An analogous explanation could even be offered for the existence of machines in the South like that of Harry Byrd in Virginia, by simply substituting the perceived Negro threat for the danger of engulfment by foreigners in the North. And, curiously enough, the two examples of reasonably thoroughgoing machine-like organizations that flourished in the otherwise inhospitable English soil—Joseph Chamberlain's Birmingham caucus [5] and Archibald Salvidge's "machine" in Liverpool [6]—also were at least indirectly related to the problem of Irish home rule, and, in Liverpool, to actual rivalry with Irish immigrants over religion and jobs.

In short, whatever else may be said about the conditions and forces that spawned the classic machine, this kind of disciplined political entity must rest at bottom on a clientele which has felt it necessary to exchange political independence—its votes, in a word—for something seen as more essential to its well-being and security. In general, such a group will be the product of some kind of socio-economic disequilibrium or cultural tension which finds its members in an insecure or seriously disadvantaged situation. Thus, the immigrant was willing to submit to the boss in exchange for aid—real or imagined—in gaining his foothold in the new environment, and the old-stock machine supporters, North or South, submitted in part for protection against swarming aliens or a potential Negro threat to white dominance.

### The Classic Machine in Operation

It cannot be assumed that the process of machine exploitation of succeeding groups of newcomers was a smooth and simple operation. Any formal organization, political or otherwise, must maintain a continuing balance among a series of often contradictory forces.[7] Its very existence

---

[5] See J. L. Garvin, *The Life of Joseph Chamberlain* (3 vols.; London: Macmillan, 1932–34).

[6] Stanley Salvidge, *Salvidge of Liverpool* (London: Hodder and Stoughton, 1934).

[7] For an elaboration of this approach to the internal dynamics of the machine, see James Q. Wilson, "The Economy of Patronage," *Journal of Political Economy*, Vol. 69, pp. 369–380.

rests on the success with which it achieves its objective—in the case of a political party, the winning of elections and, thus, power. In the long run, this success depends on the organization's continuing ability to tap fresh sources of support as time goes on and old reliances dwindle and may at times depend on keeping newly available resources away from its rival or rivals. For the machine, this has meant wooing each new ethnic contingent. Yet this process of growth and renewal will inevitably threaten the very position of many of the proprietors of the organization itself by recruiting rivals for their roles. Any organizational entity must not only achieve its corporate goals but, to survive, it must also satisfy the needs and desires of its members as individuals. If it fails in this, its supporters will vanish and its own objectives remain unattainable. Specifically, for the machine, this fact of organizational life often tempered missionary zeal and tempted its members to protect even an eroding *status quo*.

Usually the machine did yield in the long run to the political imperative that all groups of potential supporters must be wooed, if for no other reason than to keep them from the enemy. The short-term risk to the present leadership often must have appeared minimal. The plight of the newcomers was so pitiful, their needs so elemental, and their prospects of achieving security and independence so problematical in the foreseeable future that they must have appeared like a windfall to the machine proprietors. Thus, after initial hesitancy, the Irish were taken into Tammany and found their way into the ranks of the clientele of other big city party organizations.

The ways in which immigrant political support was purchased are familiar and need no elaborate review here. They had at least three kinds of needs which the ward heeler could fill on behalf of the party leadership. Above all, they needed the means of physical existence: jobs, loans, rent money, contributions of food or fuel to tide them over, and the like. Secondly, they needed a buffer against an unfamiliar state and its legal minions: help when they or their offspring got in trouble with the police, help in dealing with inspectors, in seeking pushcart licenses, or in other relations with the public bureaucracy. Finally, they needed the intangibles of friendship, sympathy, and social intercourse. These were available, variously, through contact with the precinct captain, the hospitality of the political clubhouse, the attendance of the neighborhood boss at wakes and weddings, and the annual ward outing.[8]

---

[8] One of the most readable depictions of these machine functions is to be found in Edwin ●'Connor's novel *The Last Hurrah* (Boston: Little, Brown, 1956).

As has often been noted, these kinds of services were not available, as they are today, at the hands of "United Fund" agencies, city welfare departments with their platoons of social workers, or through federal social security legislation. The sporadic and quite inadequate aid rendered by the boss and his lieutenants thus filled a vacuum. Their only rivals were the self-help associations which did spring up within each ethnic group as soon as available resources allowed a meager surplus to support burial societies and the like. The fact that the politicians acted from self-serving motives in distributing their largess, expecting and receiving a *quid pro quo,* is obvious but not wholly relevant. At least it was not relevant in judging the social importance of the services rendered. It was highly relevant, of course, in terms of the political power base thus acquired.

Some of the later arrivals following the pioneering Irish were in at least as great need of aid. The Irish did speak English and had had some experience with political action and representative institutions at home. This, plus the fact that they got here first, doubtless accounts for their rapid rise in their chosen party, the Democracy. The groups that followed, however, usually did not know English and bore the additional burden of a cultural heritage that had less in common with the American patterns they encountered than had been the case with the Irish. And, too, almost all groups, the Sons of Erin included, differed religiously from the basic Protestant consensus of their Anglo-Saxon predecessors.

As group followed group—not only into the country but into the rickety tenements and "river wards" reserved, as it were, for the latest arrivals—the processes of absorption became more complex. The Irish ward politicians doubtless had, if anything, more difficulty bridging the cultural and language gap to meet the newcomers than the "Yankees" had had in dealing with themselves some decades earlier. Also, while it may well be that the Yankees gave up their party committee posts fairly willingly to the Irish, because politics was not essential to their well-being either economically or psychologically, the Irish were in a rather different position when their turn came to move over and make room.[9] They had not fully outgrown their dependence on politics for financial and psychic security. Thus, the conflicting demands of the machine for new sources of support versus the reluctance of the incumbents to encourage rivalry for their own positions, produced tension. In the long run, however, most of the new ethnic groups found their

---

[9] See the author's "Some Occupational Patterns in Party Committee Membership," *Rhode Island History,* Vol. 20 (July 1961), pp. 87–96.

place in the party system. In some cases, as with the Italians, the Republicans, generally less skillful in these arts, won support by default when the Irish were especially inhospitable.

## The Machine as Social Integration

There is another side to the coin of machine dependence on the continuing flow of immigrants. The "invisible hand"—to use an analogy with Adam Smith's economics—which operated to produce social benefits out of the *quid pro quo* which the ward heelers exchanged for votes was at work in other ways, too. Henry Jones Ford noted in the 1890's, while discussing the role of party: [10]

> This nationalizing influence continues to produce results of the greatest social value, for in co-ordinating the various elements of the population for political purposes, party organization at the same time tends to fuse them into one mass of citizenship, pervaded by a common order of ideas and sentiments, and actuated by the same class of motives. This is probably the secret of the powerful solvent influence which American civilization exerts upon the enormous deposits of alien population thrown upon this country by the torrent of emigration.

Again, in other words, the selfish quest by the politician for electoral support and power was transmuted by the "invisible hand" into the major force integrating the immigrant into the community.

This process has had several facets. In the first place, the mere seeking out of the immigrants in quest of their support, the assistance rendered in getting them naturalized (when it was necessary to observe these legal niceties), and so forth were of considerable importance in laying the foundation for their more meaningful political participation later. In addition, the parties have progressively drawn into their own hierarchies and committee offices representatives of the various ethnic groups. The mechanics of this process were varied. In some cases, there doubtless emerged leaders of a particular group in one ward or neighborhood who, if given official party status, would automatically bring their followings along with them.[11] On other occasions, new ethnic enclaves may have sought or even demanded representation in exchange for support. Perhaps prior to either of these, the machine sought to co-opt individuals who could speak the language and act as a cultural bridge between the party and the newcomers. Depending on the situation, it

---

[10] *The Rise and Growth of American Politics* (New York: Macmillan, 1911), p. 306.

[11] *Ibid,* p. 307.

probably was essential to do this and impossible for precinct captains of a different background to develop adequate rapport. It is at this point that ethnic group rivalry in the organization becomes difficult. Gratitude to the boss for initial admission into the lower ranks of the hierarchy would be bound to change in time into demands, of growing insistence, for further recognition of the individual and his group.

These general patterns can to some extent be documented, at least illustratively. The tendency for the urban machines to reap the Irish vote and later much of the vote of more recent arrivals is well known. The process of infiltration by group representatives into party structure is harder to identify precisely. With this in mind, the author did a study of the members of party ward committees in Providence, Rhode Island, the findings of which may reflect trends elsewhere.[12] Analysis of committee membership lists or their equivalent going back to the 1860's and 1870's showed initial overwhelming Anglo-Saxon majorities. For the Democrats, however, this majority gave way, between the 1880's and 1900, to a roughly 75 per cent Irish preponderance, while the Republican committees stayed "Yankee" until after the First World War. Then, in the 1920's, both parties simultaneously recruited Italian committeemen to replace some of the Irish and white Protestants, respectively. Today, both have varied, and roughly similar, proportions of all major groups in the city population. In other cities, the timing of shifts and the ethnic groups involved will have differed, but the general process and its relation to local patterns of immigration were doubtless similar.

It is incredible, viewed now with hindsight, how reckless the American republic was in its unpremeditated policy of the open door and the implied assumption that somehow, without any governmental or even organized private assistance, hundreds of thousands of immigrants from dozens of diverse cultures would fit themselves smoothly and automatically into a native culture which had its own share of ethnocentrism. The fact of the matter was that the process did not operate smoothly or particularly effectively. There were tensions and incidents which accentuated cultural differences and engendered bitterness. These ranged, chronologically, all the way from the abuses of the more militant Know-Nothings to the Ku Klux Klan activity of the 1920's.

Economically, most occupational doors that did not lead to manual labor jobs were closed to the Irish and later arrivals and were only gradually pried open after much time had passed and many lasting intergroup enmities had been engendered. Here again, the party organizations represented one of the few mechanisms, public or private, that lubricated

---

[12] "Party Absorption of Ethnic Groups," *Social Forces,* Vol. 38 (March 1960), pp. 205–210.

a process of integration which, in its very nature, was bound to generate enormous amounts of friction. Besides drawing group representatives into its councils, party work also was one of the few career ladders available to the immigrant and his ambitious sons. Here, status could be achieved, as well as a comfortable income, one way or another, when few other routes were open. This became not just status for the individual but a measure of recognition and acceptance for the group as a whole through the individual's success. In fact, not only did the newcomer use this alternative career ladder, but he carried over into the political sphere some of the "Horatio Alger" quest for success and other aspects of an essentially pragmatic, materialistic American culture as well.

Politics for the machine politician never was an ideological enterprise or a matter of beliefs and principles. As someone once said, the boss had only seven principles, five loaves and two fishes. Rather, politics was an entrepreneurial vocation like any other business. Banfield and Wilson have written: "A political machine is a business organization in a particular field of business—getting votes and winning elections. As a Chicago machine boss once said . . . it is 'just like any sales organization trying to sell its product.' " [13] The politician's aim was and is so to invest his supply of capital—jobs, favors, and the like—as to earn a profit, some of which he will take as "income" and the rest reinvest in quest of larger returns. In other words, the immigrant political leader took the one vocation open to him, politics, and made it into as close an approximation as he could of the more valued business callings in the society, from which he was effectively barred. He acted out the American success story in the only way open to him.

Obviously, the foregoing is not designed to portray the machine as a knight-errant rescuing American society from its willful folly. In the first place, the folly was not willful, and perhaps not folly. In the second, the boss's contribution toward making the melting pot melt should not be overrated. At the same time, many have testified—as does the record itself—to the almost unique ability of party as organization to bring people together across cultural and similar barriers. As Glazer and Moynihan have written of New York City: [14]

> . . . political life itself emphasizes the ethnic character of the city, with its balanced tickets and its social appeals. . . . For those in the field itself, there is more contact across the ethnic lines, and the ethnic lines themselves mean less, than in other areas of the city's life.

---

[13] Edward Banfield and James Q. Wilson, *City Politics* (Cambridge: Harvard and M.I.T. Presses, 1963), p. 115.

[14] Nathan Glazer and Daniel Patrick Moynihan, *Beyond the Melting Pot* (Cambridge: Harvard and M.I.T. Presses, 1963), p. 20.

Ticket-balancing, or United Nations politics, as it is sometimes called, is perhaps symbolic of the ultimate step in the process of granting group recognition and confirming the fact that something approaching inter-group equality has been achieved. Either, as with the Manhattan Borough presidency and the Negro group, certain prescriptive rights become established to a particular office or to one place on a city-wide ticket or ethnic allocation is made using the background of the head of the ticket as point of departure.

In short, the classic urban machine rested upon the immigrants, while at the same time it fostered their integration into American life. It also made, in the process, a major contribution to the over-all American political style. It is true that politics as a pragmatic entrepreneurial vocation owes much in America to the contributions of Burr, Van Buren, Weed, Marcy (to the victor belong the spoils), and, in a sense, to Andrew Jackson himself. Thus, Richard Hofstadter's attribution of one of the two central systems of political ethics in America to the immigrants is only partially valid.[15] He is clearly correct, however, in suggesting that a political style which stressed "personal obligations, and placed strong personal loyalties above allegiance to abstract codes of law or morals" [16] was congenial to the machine politicians and their followers, and they made it their own, developing its full implications in the process. At the same time, the immigrant versus old stock cultural cleavage prompted the latter to espouse the more vigorously the typically middle-class, reformist style which stresses honesty, impartiality, and efficiency. These two styles or ethics, since the late nineteenth century, have, by their interaction, shaped both the evolution of urban politics and the machinery of urban government.

## The Decline of the Machine

The decline and fall of the boss as a political phenomenon has often been chronicled and explained. It is argued, *inter alia,* that reforms like the direct primary, nonpartisan systems of election, voting machines and tightened registration requirements, and city-manager schemes often deal crippling blows. In the aggregate, they doubtless did, though many exceptions can be found to prove the rule. One particular contribution of the reformers which has had unquestioned importance—though circumvention has not proven impossible—was the elimination of patronage with the installation of civil service based on the merit principle.

---

[15] Richard Hofstadter, *The Age of Reform* (New York: Knopf, 1955), pp. 8 ff.

[16] *Ibid.,* p. 9.

And, generally, educational levels have risen, and occupational levels and incomes have risen as well. Even where patronage remains available, the latter development has rendered it less attractive, and to fewer people. Finally, and most often cited, there was the impact of the New Deal. Its installation of publicly sponsored welfare programs eliminated many of the rough-and-ready welfare functions of the precinct captain, though the more imaginative recouped part of their loss by helping to steer constituents through the bureaucratic maze, claiming credit for the benefits thus obtained.

Granting the importance of all these developments, in the long run, the decline of immigration doubtless proved the most important blow to the traditional machine operation. New arrivals had been entering the country at a rate in excess of four million each half decade up to the First World War. The rate averaged barely more than one third of that between 1915 and 1930 and dropped to a mere trickle for most of the period down to the present. Sharply restrictive legislation passed in 1921 and 1924 was responsible. Obviously, the impact on the machines came in the form of a delayed reaction, but most of them gradually withered. The few that survived did so through shrewd adaptation to changed conditions, specifically through judicious, self-administered doses of reformism, as, for example, with the Daley organization in Chicago.

Thus ended an era. Immigration may not have called the boss into being, but the two in most cases were closely linked. Two questions remain to be dealt with. What contemporary counterparts are there, if any, of the immigrant influx of yesteryear and how are the parties dealing with them? And what can be said of the current political behavior of the children and grandchildren of the former immigrants?

## The Parties and the New Immigration

There are, of course, two major groups that do represent close parallels with the earlier influx and at the same time carry important differences. These are the Negroes who have been migrating in increasing numbers from the South to northern urban centers since the First World War and the Puerto Ricans who began coming to New York City, for the most part, after the Second World War.[17] Both resemble their alien predecessors in the magnitude of their numbers, their basic and important cultural differences from the population into whose midst they

---

[17] Two recent books are especially useful discussions of these groups: Glazer and Moynihan, *op. cit.*; and Oscar Handlin, *The Newcomers: Negroes and Puerto Ricans in a Changing Metropolis* (Cambridge: Harvard Press, 1959).

are moving, an almost invariable need of assistance in adjusting to a new environment, and their potential impact on the political balance of forces.

The major points of difference are also worth noting. Both come bearing the credentials of American citizenship, which was not the case with the earlier groups. Though this factor should make for easier adjustment, other group characteristics operate to make acceptance more difficult. For the Negro, there is the fundamental problem of color, coupled with cultural characteristics which, though acquired ostensibly in the American environment, operate to make assimilation more difficult. These include all the long deposit of servitude and enforced inferior status: loose marital ties and correspondingly weak family ties generally, a poverty of leadership potential, low literacy and skill levels, and the like. For the Puerto Ricans, there is language, plus differences of culture, and a partial color barrier which operates to cause at least some Spanish Americans to be classified—against their will—as Negroes. On balance, it is probably true that, so far as these two groups are concerned as groups, they face higher barriers to integration into American life than almost any earlier group save, possibly, the orientals.

But the society itself has changed enormously from the society to which the Irish, Italians, and Jews sought entrance. Urban areas are now equipped with facilities to which the newcomer can turn for aid that counterbalance to some degree the particular hostilities which members of these two groups arouse. There are now elaborate public welfare programs, there is Aid to Dependent Children for the many fatherless families, there are numerous private agencies and charities which stand ready to help, and, in case of the Puerto Ricans, their land of origin has taken a unique interest in the welfare of its emigrants. There have even been legislative efforts to ban the discrimination in housing or employment which they encounter.

Though these facilities stand ready to ease aspects of the economic and social integration of these latest immigrants, there still remains the question of political absorption. Here, too, the situation today sharply differs from the past. The political parties now have neither the incentive nor the means with which to perform the functions they performed for the earlier immigrants. The machine in most affected areas is gone beyond recall, and there remain in its place party organizations that are hollow shells of their former strength and vigor. Party in general, given the proliferation of both public bureaucracies and the mass entertainment industry, has been pushed to the fringes of the average citizen's attention span and often to the fringes of the governing process itself. The debilitating impact of reform legislation contributed to the same end, needless to say. Thus, in general, the new immigrants can look to the parties for little of the former assistance they once provided in gaining entrance and leverage in the political processes of their new homes.

There are partial exceptions here, as there are to all the foregoing generalizations. Mayor Daley's modern Chicago version of the old-style machine has been mentioned earlier. Within his over-all Cook County Democratic organization, there is the "sub-machine" comprising the Negro followers of Representative William E. Dawson.[18] Dawson, a former maverick Republican, shifted parties in 1939 and joined forces with Mayor-boss Kelly. Some twenty years later, he had put together a combination, under his leadership, of five or six Negro wards. This "organization within an organization" appears to bargain as a unit through Dawson and his lieutenants for patronage and other kinds of preferment in the gift of Mayor Daley and in turn tends to exert a moderating influence on the more aggressive elements in the Negro community. Trends suggest that this is not destined to be a permanent arrangement. The population of the Dawson-controlled wards has been declining as the more prosperous Negroes manage to settle in more desirable locations, and, as Dawson and his associates grow older, they become more conservative. Whether or not this latter is partly an illusion produced by the rapid rise in Negro militancy since 1954 would be hard to say. It is probably true that leaders of the Dawson type will get more "out of phase" with the civil rights movement as that movement gains further momentum.

New York City, almost by traditional right, *the* locale for the study of the behavior of American parties in relation to the immigrant. The 1960 census reported just over a million Negroes in New York City and somewhat more than 600,000 Puerto Ricans. In broad terms, it can be said that, since the days of Al Smith and Boss Murphy, New York politics have been long on confusion and fragmentation and short on centralized, disciplined organization. There was, therefore, little possibility that a relationship such as Representative Dawson worked out with his Negro clientele on the one hand and the leaders of the Cook County Democracy on the other could be developed in New York. Especially in Manhattan—which we shall take for analysis—one finds exemplified the more typical contemporary party situation: no dominating borough-wide authority save that in the hands of the mayor himself, hence a series of local feudal chiefs who are rarely willing to exchange their relative independence for the rather meager supplies of

---

[18] This discussion of the Dawson organization draws particularly on James Q. Wilson, *Negro Politics* (Glencoe, Ill.: Free Press, 1960), pp. 50 ff. and *passim*.

patronage available, and the whole system, wracked periodically by factional feuding.

The Negro in New York, in apparent contrast to the Chicago situation, has been more fragmented in his political organization, has found little borough-wide structure with which to associate, but has made more spectacular symbolic gains in the party and city government. Representative Adam Clayton Powell, the rather erratic champion of the city's nonwhites, reaps vastly more national publicity for his espoused cause than the publicity-shy Congressman Dawson.[19] How much this means in concrete benefits would be hard to determine. More significant is the fact that in 1953 a Negro, Hulan Jack, was elected for the first time to a major office in the city, that of Borough President of Manhattan. Powell had a major role in this, though he later broke with Jack. Since then, this position has become an accepted Negro prerogative. Other high positions have been filled by Negroes in the city administration in recent years.

## Representation on Party Committees

A somewhat more useful basis for judging the reality of ethnic or racial group political absorption and power position than possession of some of these "commanding heights" (in Lenin's phrase) would be an analysis of the extent to which they had gained footholds in the lower and intermediate levels of the party organization. The ethnic proportions among Providence ward committee members cited above are a relatively accurate reflection of the nationality power relationships in city politics. For example, the fact that the Irish Democrats have held onto about half of the ward committee seats after yielding some places to Italians reflects the fact that they still have the dominant voice in the party. The rise of the Italians on the Republican side to the status of the largest single ethnic group also reflects their growing power.[20]

Table 1 shows the approximate percentages of ethnic/racial representation in the total New York City population and, in the second column, the background of the Manhattan Democratic Assembly district leaders and coleaders insofar as these could be determined.[21]

There are sixteen Assembly districts, but most are divided into two or three parts with a leader and coleader for each. There were some

---

19 A useful source on Powell is David Hapgood, *The Purge that Failed: Tammany v. Powell* (New York: Holt, 1959).

20 "Party Absorption of Ethnic Groups," *op. cit.*

21 Thanks are due the author's former student, Edwin Cohen, now active in Manhattan politics, and to George Osborne, himself a district leader, for tracking down the leadership data used.

**TABLE 1**

COMPARISON OF ETHNIC PROPORTIONS IN POPULATION WITH
DEMOCRATIC DISTRICT LEADERS IN MANHATTAN

| | Approximate Percentage of New York City 1960 Population [a] | Percentage of Democratic Assembly District Leaders (N = 66) |
|---|---|---|
| Negroes | 14 | 21 |
| Puerto Ricans | 8 | 6 |
| Jews | 25± | 38 |
| Italians | 17± | 11 |
| Irish | 10± | 9 |
| Others | 26± | 15 [b] |
| | 100 | 100 |

[a] Population percentage estimates are from Nathan Glazer and D. P. Moynihan, *Beyond the Melting Pot* (Cambridge: Massachusetts Institute of Technology and Harvard Press, 1963). Only figures for Negroes and Puerto Ricans were given in the 1960 census. It was impossible to get ethnic group percentages for Manhattan alone.

[b] Includes Anglo-Saxon Protestants and others of unidentified background.

vacancies at the time the data were obtained. It can be seen that the Negro has done quite well by this measure of political integration in that the group has considerably more than the share of district leadership positions it would be entitled to on a strict population basis. The bulk of these Negroes preside over districts in or around Harlem, as might be expected—the 11th, 12th, 13th, 14th, and 16th Assembly districts. Of the eighteen occupied positions in these five Assembly districts, they hold twelve. There are two Negroes, one each in the 5th and 10th, to the west and east of Central Park, respectively, but none to the south of the Park at all.

In passing it might be noted that the other groups on the Table each have something approximating their proportionate share of the leaderships. The Jewish contingent is disproportionately large, due in considerable measure to the fact that three-fifths of all the anti-Tammany "reform" leaders come from that part of the city population. True to what one knows about their situation in other cities, the Italians appear to be underrepresented. The Irish, however, even in view of the extreme difficulty in guessing their share of the city population, have far fewer positions than the prevailing myth of continuing Irish dominance of urban Democratic politics would suggest.

Turning now to the Puerto Ricans, they offer the best opportunity for assessing the ability of at least the Manhattan Democratic organization to absorb a genuinely new ethnic group. In Table 2, the backgrounds of the district leaders in the areas of heaviest Puerto Rican population are tabulated. Also included, in the last two columns, are figures on the personnel of the lowest level of "grass-roots" party organization, the election district captains. Out of the twelve district leader positions occupied at the time the data were obtained, four were held by Puerto Ricans, giving that group representation in three of the six most heavily Puerto Rican districts. Though only firsthand knowledge would indicate how effective these individuals are in representing their ethnic group and bargaining on its behalf, there is indication here of rather significant infiltration into the party structure. The figures for election district captains, where these could be obtained, point to the same conclusion. Except for the lower east side, where the proportion is smaller, roughly half of these captains are also Puerto Rican, casting further doubt on common assumptions that the party in Manhattan is lagging seriously in making room for this latest group to arrive.

**TABLE 2**

*AREAS OF HEAVY PUERTO RICAN POPULATION*

| Area | Assembly District | District Leaders | Election District Captains | |
| --- | --- | --- | --- | --- |
| | | | Total | Puerto Ricans |
| Lower East Side | 4th, South | 2 Jewish | 29 | 7 |
| East Harlem | 10th, North | 1 Puerto Rican and 1 Negro | 16 | 9 |
| | 14th, South | 2 Puerto Ricans | 17 | 8 |
| | 14th, North | 2 Negroes | —[b] | —[b] |
| | 16th, South | 1 Italian and 1 Puerto Rican | —[b] | —[b] |
| Upper West Side | 13th, South | 1 Italian and 1 Negro | 52 | 23 |

[a] Puerto Rican location population was determined by plotting location of census tracts with at least 15 per cent Puerto Ricans and coloring these in according to density. There are scatterings in a few other parts of Manhattan as well.

[b] Data could not be obtained.

In general, both Table 1 and Table 2 suggest that the Puerto Ricans have secured, in the relatively short time since their arrival in large numbers, party offices roughly commensurate with their share of the population over-all and in areas of high concentration. In addition, there are three state assemblymen from this group (two from East Harlem and one from the Bronx) and four or five with high positions in the city administration.[22]

[22] Layhmond Robinson, "Voting Gain Made by Puerto Ricans," *New York Times,* November 23, 1963.

These achievements, obviously, as well as the district leaderships themselves and election district captaincies, can only be taken as rough indicators of the political progress of the group as a whole and are doubtless far less significant than they could have been viewed in the political setting of forty or fifty years ago when parties were central to the governing process and urban life generally. At the same time, they must be evaluated in light of the fact that New York State will not accept literacy in a language other than English (such as Spanish) as qualification to vote, and, thus, only some 150,000 to 175,000 of the total Puerto Rican group are on the rolls.

Returning for a moment to the current status of descendants of earlier immigrants, the assumption that significant cultural distinctions and tendencies toward common political attitude and behavior would disappear in two or three generations has proven erroneous. Ticket-balancing, for example, in ethnic or religious terms is as prevalent, perhaps, as it ever was and shows few signs of disappearing in the immediate future. The election of an Irish Catholic President in 1960, if anything, enhanced the importance of such balancing tactics, as the discussion in early 1964 of Democratic vice-presidential candidates indicated. In psychoanalysis, it is well recognized that problems have to be clearly recognized and frankly made explicit before they can be eliminated. The same may in a sense be true of ethnic factors in American politics. Only the frank recognition of the once-potent barrier to a Catholic in the White House paved the way for the Kennedy election. At the state and local level, it is probably also true that only after various groups have achieved and enjoyed the recognition they feel they are entitled to and have done so for a long enough period to transform a privilege into a quasi right will it become possible, gradually, to choose candidates without these criteria in mind. The unfortunate thing is that American parties have decayed as organizations to the point that they can make far less contribution to this process of adjustment than they could and did in the past.

# B. CITY GOVERNMENT
# —REFORM STYLE

## Governmental Structure and Political
## Environment: A Statistical Note
## about American Cities

### JOHN H. KESSEL

The commission plan and the city manager plan—new forms of city government launched during the early years of this century—were both devised in response to local circumstances, but were soon being heralded as improvements over the then universal mayor-council system. Enthusiasts for both of these new governmental structures claimed many advantages for them. The hopes for the city manager plan seem to have been somewhat better founded, but the passage of time has shown that both plans had limitations which the reformers did not foresee.

Almost all of the early discussion about the relative merits of the three plans neglected the role of political environment. Proponents of the different systems deduced their arguments from "the principles" on which the plans were based. A three-year study of the actual operation of manager government in the late 1930s called attention to the importance of varying local conditions. "The tremendous variety of local political conditions and administrative habits apparent in the fifty cities covered by this survey," the authors concluded, "makes it impossible to [give general answers to] many questions about the city manager plan." [1]

A more explicit concern with the effects of the political environment was shown in two important papers published in the early 1950s.[2] Specific questions were raised about the affinity between the city manager system and medium-size cities, and the apparent fact that the

---

Reprinted from *American Political Science Review,* Vol. 56 (September 1962), 615–20, by permission of the publisher.

[1] Harold A. Stone, Don K. Price, and Kathryn H. Stone, *City Manager Government in the United States* (Chicago: Public Administration Service, 1940), p. 258.

[2] Wallace S. Sayre, "The General Manager Idea for Large Cities," *Public Administration Review,* 1954, pp. 253–258; and Inter-University Summer Seminar on Political Behavior, "Research in Political Behavior," this REVIEW, Vol. 46 (December 1952), pp. 1003–1032.

manager plan was more frequently adopted by cities which were either growing or declining in size. The authors also noted the concentration of manager adoptions in one-party states, and suggested that this plan had a depressing effect on the level of party activity. And they thought it significant that business groups generally supported introduction of the manager system while labor often opposed it.

1960 census data show that the city manager form now has been adopted by a majority of the medium-size cities. Though the majority is a bare one, 1960 is the first census year which has found the city manager plan the most common in any size-class of cities. The mayor-council system continues to dominate in the very large cities and in the

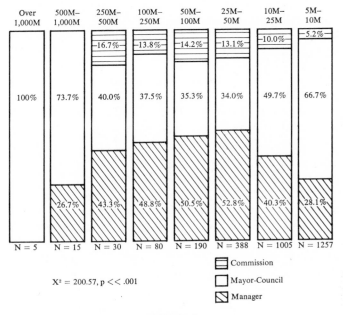

**FIGURE 1**

*GOVERNMENTAL FORM AND COMMUNITY SIZE*

small towns. The distribution of the three plans in cities between 250,000 and 500,000 and in those between 10,000 and 25,000 is very close to that which would occur normally. Therefore it is now possible to speak of three significant groups of cities in this context with dividing lines slightly above 250,000 and slightly below 25,000.

The failure of large cities to abandon the mayor-council plan has been much discussed in the literature. The most common explanation is that the political environment is so complex—there are so many competing interests—that a premium is placed on political leadership which can arbitrate the contest for the stakes of power in the city, and be held responsible by the electorate for its success or failure in doing so. Less has been done in analyzing the politics of the small towns. It would be consistent with our knowledge of small communities to argue that a well-defined structure of socio-economic power, and widely shared norms of behavior, are usually decisive elements in the political en-

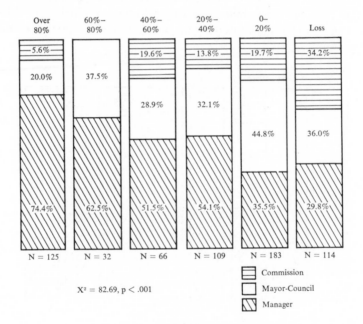

**FIGURE 2**

*GOVERNMENTAL FORM AND CITY GROWTH RATE, 1950–60*

vironment of a small town. The "natives" ordinarily are well aware of the nature of this power structure and the content of these norms. Thus a local resident would probably reach decisions which would accord with local folkways in most situations, and wait for a "sense of the community" to crystallize when a novel problem came along. A city manager who accepted his cues about correct behavior from outside professional sources would be much more likely to act so as to upset the social equilibrium or violate certain local norms.

These speculations about the dominance of the mayor-council form in large cities and small towns are consistent with each other. They could be summarized by stating that a frankly political form of government is often found where there are interests which must be deferred to, or whose claims must be arbitrated, before a policy decision is made. This would imply that when the reverse is true, that when there is no one who can claim deference, or when there is a single dominant group which is disposed to cooperate with the policy maker, then viable conditions exist for a professional administrator. The question is simply whether negotiating skill or professional expertise is more important in any given situation. We have reason to suspect that political aptitudes are necessary in a small town or big city. In the medium-size city, therefore, we should look for conditions which do not call for a special talent for judicious compromise, but which do present problems beyond a layman's grasp, that can be analyzed by one with a manager's technical training.

It is possible to test these hypotheses, at least in a preliminary fashion, by inspecting certain characteristics of the medium-size cities. (Note in Figure 1, that the frequencies of use of each of the three plans are almost constant for this group of cities.) Figure 2 shows a very strong relationship between the growth rate of these communities and the structure of their governments. There is a high probability that a rapidly growing community will have adopted the city manager system. The mayor-council form is closely associated with cities having relatively stable populations. And the commission form, in the single category in which it appears to be related to the political environment, is found with striking frequency in cities which lost population in the last decade.

These findings modify earlier speculation that the manager plan is associated with growth *or* decline in population, but are compatible with our ideas about the political and administrative conditions appropriate to each system. A rapidly growing city faces many administrative problems in the course of providing the streets, sewers, and other services required by the expanding population. Since so many new people are arriving the political patterns tend to be rather amorphous. A professional administrator is less likely to face organized opposition. In cities with stable populations, on the other hand, political pressures are apt to be well defined and persistent. Solutions to novel problems are not called for so often as the ability to appease long-standing rivalries. This situation would call for the political responsiveness of the mayor-council system. The concentration of commission governments in declining cities is also of interest. Unless these cities *want* to reduce their populations, it would seem that the commissioners are unable to respond to difficult conditions or that the influential persons in these communities lack the ability to initiate a switch to another form of government.

The states having the highest percentages of medium-size cities with manager plans are Virginia, North Carolina, California, Texas, and Florida. States with marked concentrations of mayor-council cities in the 25,000-to-250,000 range are Indiana, Connecticut, and Ohio. The manager cities, as has been noted frequently, are either in one-party states or in states in which the formal party organization is rather weak. The mayor-council cities are more often found in competitive two-party states. This, in itself, is an insufficient basis for concluding that the introduction of the manager plan depresses party activity. Competitive two-party systems, after all, were not to be found in Virginia, North Carolina, California, Texas, or Florida before the spread of the manager system. But the survival of strong party organizations in Connecticut, Indiana, and Ohio is suggestive. If we are correct in assuming that the mayor-council system flourishes best in environments which require political skills, then it would follow that these same skills could contribute to vigorous party organizations.

Another way of testing our hypotheses is to look for the presence of some group in the community which would be especially dependent on political activity because of its exclusion from alternative agencies of community integration. We therefore computed the percentage of foreign-born in the population over twenty-one for each city which had a population between 25,000 and 250,000 in 1950.[3] This percentage was chosen to isolate within the potential electorate a group which had arrived too recently for successful assimilation. As Figure 3 shows, the higher the percentage of foreign-born in a city, the more likely it is that the city will have a mayor-council form of government. The city manager plan, on the other hand, has been adopted most often by cities composed almost entirely of native-born residents.

We see here an association between the mayor-council form of government and the presence of a sizeable group which lacks social and economic opportunity. Newcomers are rarely offered invitations to long-established men's clubs or seats on the board of directors of a leading bank. As they lack opportunity to express their opinions through social and economic channels, they must voice them through political institutions if they are to be heard at all. And it is precisely in the communities

---

[3] These data, and those on the percentage of the labor force in a given occupational category, were not available for 1960 at the time this study was made. Therefore we are dealing with a different, and smaller, group of cities. The reader will also note some minor differences in the number of medium-size cities between Figures 1 and 2 and between Figures 3 and 4. These are caused by variations in the availability of data.

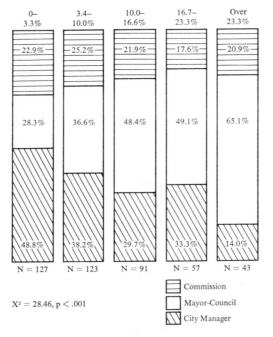

|            |            |            |            |            |
|------------|------------|------------|------------|------------|
| 0–<br>3.3% | 3.4–<br>10.0% | 10.0–<br>16.6% | 16.7–<br>23.3% | Over<br>23.3% |

22.9%    25.2%    21.9%    17.6%    20.9%

28.3%    36.6%    48.4%    49.1%    65.1%

48.8%    38.2%    29.7%    33.3%    14.0%

N = 127    N = 123    N = 91    N = 57    N = 43

$X^2 = 28.46$, p < .001

Commission
Mayor-Council
City Manager

**FIGURE 3**

*GOVERNMENTAL FORM AND MINORITY GROUPS: PERCENTAGE
OF OVER 21 FOREIGN BORN IN THE CITY POPULATION*

where there is such a need for political opportunities for community participation that the mayor-council form has been most frequently retained. We also see that the manager plan has been adopted most frequently when most of the residents grew up in an American culture. It is possible that the values in such a community would be not only homogeneous, but would also correspond to those of a professional manager.

If we turn from the ethnic composition of the city to its economic organization, we can do more than simply infer the existence of an important group whose values correspond to those of a professional manager. An analysis of the governmental forms used by cities having differing economic characteristics can be derived from Howard J. Nelson's "Service Classification" of cities.[4] Nelson computed the mean

---

[4] Howard J. Nelson, "A Service Classification of American Cities," *Economic Geography*, Vol. 31 (July, 1955), pp. 180–210. This classification was similar to the "functional classification" of the *Municipal Year Book* except that the latter is based on arbitrary cutting points. The functional classification did not permit identification of any correspondence between economic organization and governmental form.

percentage of the labor force engaged in given occupations in some eight hundred and ninety-seven urbanized areas. He then calculated the standard deviation from each of these means. He was thereby able to classify a city as, for example, "manufacturing" if the percentage of the labor force so engaged was more than one standard deviation above the mean percentage employed in manufacturing in all urbanized areas. In the case of manufacturing, to continue the same example, his calculations led to the conclusion that at least 43.1 per cent of the work force should be employed in manufacturing for an urban area to be so classified. Similar calculations enabled him to identify unusual concentrations of the labor force in personal service, retail trade, finance, the professions, public administration, wholesale trade, transportation, and mining. If an urbanized area had no unusual concentration of the labor force in any of these categories, Nelson designated it a diversified area.

Figure 4 indicates a decreasing use of the manager plan by medium-size cities if they are arranged in this order: personal service, retail, finance, professional, public administration, wholesale, transportation, diversified, manufacturing. This is suggestive for three reasons. First of all, this ranking seems to be directly related to the size of the area within which business is conducted. In the four "manager-type" classifications—personal service, retail, finance, and professional—there exist significant concentrations of businessmen whose principal market is to be found within and immediately around their own city. Diversified cities, by definition, lack any abnormal concentration of businessmen, and the industrialists in manufacturing cities are likely to be concerned with regional and national markets. A second reason for the suggestiveness of this ranking is the probability that a retail store or an establishment rendering some kind of personal service will be locally owned. A factory, on the other hand, is much more likely to be owned by stockholders and to have its main offices in some distant commercial center. Thus we see that the manager cities tend to have concentrations of local businessmen whose interests are directly related to their own communities. The mayor-council cities either lack such concentrations of businessmen, in the case of the diversified cities, or are neglected by absentee owners who are often preoccupied with national affairs. It is not implausible to assume that the small businessmen in the manager cities supply the consensus which enables the manager to concentrate on administrative problems.

A third implication of this economic classification concerns the nature of the labor force employed in these occupations. The white collar employees in retail stores and financial establishments, to say nothing of the professionals, are prone to regard themselves as self-sufficient. Industrial laborers, on the other hand, are likely to suffer the same kinds of socio-economic handicaps mentioned earlier in connection with ethnic groups. They need political channels for expression, channels which the mayor-council system is more likely to provide.

There are, of course, limits to this kind of statistical analysis. The most important is that the whole argument rests on an assumption that, given the adoptions and abandonments of the past fifty years, each governmental form will be most frequently found in that environment which is congenial to it. There are many reasons for the adoption of one system or another which have little to do with the suitability of the political environment. State laws may encourage one form and prohibit another. Local interests may advocate a different plan from the one

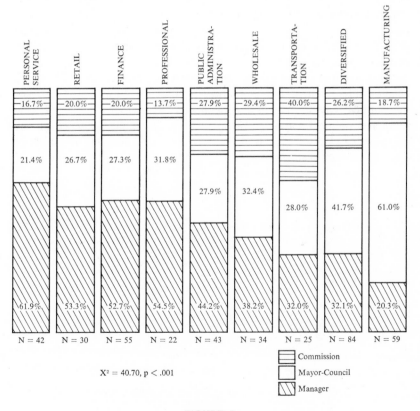

X² = 40.70, p < .001

Commission
Mayor-Council
Manager

**FIGURE 4**

*GOVERNMENTAL FORM AND ECONOMIC BASE: INCIDENCE OF
THREE SYSTEMS IN DIFFERENT TYPES OF CITIES*

they have, simply because they perceive some tactical advantage in changing the ground rules in their favor. A community often imitates the legal structure favored in a neighboring city. A small town frequently lacks the budget to hire a manager. And interia often causes the retention of a governmental system long after it has ceased to function effectively.

The reader must judge for himself whether this evidence is sufficient to support the hypotheses which have been suggested. But whether we have correctly identified certain linkages between the political environment and governmental structure or not, it should be clear that some sorts of linkages do exist. We should sweep away the lingering traces of disciplinary parochialism which still contaminate the study of urban affairs. A few students of public administration still hold that a given form of government is intrinsically superior to any other. Some latter-day Marxists still insist that industrial captains exercise the real power in any community. And certain sociologists would have us believe that "upper-upper" families are able to manipulate affairs because of their status and prestige. If the data we have reviewed are valid, then none of these arguments are correct. Neither a study of organization charts nor an identification of socio-economic elites is, in itself, a sufficient explanation of urban politics. Neither the formal structure nor the political environment is independent of the other. Studies of legal form and political setting must take into account the influence of one on the other. Only in this way will we be able to unravel the puzzle of the relationships between them.

# Nonpartisan Electoral Systems in American Cities*

## PHILLIPS CUTRIGHT

At regular intervals in the United States political parties conduct campaigns, the purpose of which is to elect their chosen candidates to public office. Each party seeks political power, guided in this pursuit by a complex set of election laws which spell out in detail the rights and duties of the parties. The electoral process is the mechanism by which power is maintained within a party or transferred to a competing party. The legitimate right of one party to take power from another when the people so elect is enforced. The ideal image of the American political system in action reflects two parties struggling to maximize the interests of their constituents in the hope of maximizing votes in the next election. Out of this struggle the rights of the people are preserved.

In contrast to this ideal image, one of the most startling features of the real political system of American cities is that in two out of three cities the same political parties on which we rely for maintaining our state and national democratic order are legally barred from participating in the election of local political leaders. In 66 per cent of the cities with over 25,000 inhabitants *neither* party has the legitimate right to take power from the other when the people so desire; the party system is forbidden and in its place the nonpartisan ballot has been substituted.[1]

---

Reprinted from *Comparative Studies in Society and History* (January 1963), 212–26. Reprinted by permission.

* My thanks to Peter H. Rossi, Duncan MacRae Jr., and Robert A. Dentler for a number of important suggestions. The help of the Department of Sociology of Washington State University and the Computing Center of that University is gratefully acknowledged. This paper is a revised version of one presented to the American Sociological Association in St. Louis, September 1961.

[1] Nonpartisan elections refer specifically to councilmanic offices only, but in cities with nonpartisan elections for the city council the office of the mayor and other city officers are usually nonpartisan as well. See Eugene C. Lee, *The Politics of Nonpartisanship: A Study of California City Elections* (Berkeley and Los Angeles: University of California Press, 1960), p. 25. A historical account of the

Under a nonpartisan system men continue to be elected by the people to public office, but these political leaders are not openly attached to either political party. The names of the Democratic and Republican party cannot be associated with any candidate on the ballot. When this is the case we have a nonpartisan ballot and a nonpartisan electoral system.[2]

In this paper we examine four structural conditions that are powerfully associated with the existence of the nonpartisan ballot. This approach cannot go to the level of analysis demanded of the case study of "how a community makes up its mind" to replace the partisan ballot with a nonpartisan ballot. This is not a study of individual community decision making but a study of the structural conditions that are associated with the distribution of partisan and nonpartisan ballots in the larger cities of the United States.

Two major classes of structural variables will be examined. The first class refers to state-wide political characteristics. The state political system may be characterized as Republican, Democratic or competitive, depending upon the balance of voting strength. It may also be classified according to how loyal its voters are to the major parties. Do the voters readily turn to third party candidates or do they resist the temptation to bolt and stay with the Democrats or Republicans? Considerable variation among the states exists on this characteristic.

The second class of structural variables concerns the individual community. Social class and religious composition are important structural characteristics in the American community. We classified cities into those with high or low social class or religious cleavage. Class and religious community cleavage form the second set of structural variables.

---

spread of nonpartisanship is given in this work. See also: Harold A. Stone, et al., *City Manager Government in the United States: A Review after Twenty-Five Years,* Chicago: Public Administration Service, 1940. *The Municipal Year Book, 1958* (Chicago: International City Managers' Association, 1958), is the data source used for electoral rules in the cities studied in this paper.

[2] Research on the consequences of the nonpartisan system of election rules may be found in: Charles R. Adrian, "Some General Characteristics of Nonpartisan Elections," *American Political Science Review,* XLVI (September, 1952), pp. 766–776. A later and more comprehensive work on the effects of nonpartisan elections may be found in Charlotte Frank, "Politics in the Non-partisan City," unpublished Masters Thesis, University of Chicago, 1957/58. For additional data on the consequences of nonpartisanship see Lee, *op. cit.,* Oliver P. Williams and Charles R. Adrian, "The Insulation of Local Politics under the Nonpartisan Ballot," *American Political Science Review,* LIII (December, 1959), pp. 1052–63, and J. Leiper Freeman, "Local Party Systems: Theoretical Considerations and a Case Analysis," *American Journal of Sociology,* LXIV (November, 1958), 282–289.

In a final section of the paper we will reexamine our classification of states into one and two party systems and show that Republican states are more likely to have turned to minority party candidates since 1950 than Democratic states. We then discuss the possible impact of the differences in community economic and religious structures between Democratic and Republican one-party states for the return of these areas to competitive state politics.

We will first examine the relationship of state political characteristics and community cleavage characteristics to the distribution of partisan or nonpartisan ballots in the larger American cities.

### The Role of the State Political System: Two-Party Competition

A great deal of political behavior within states goes on without the guidance or direction of forces from outside the state.[3] Investigation of the operation of state political systems indicates that our political parties are state-based and remain autonomous from national control. Examination of a city's political system may be more fruitful if we first examine the larger political system of which the city is a part.

The electoral base of either party is of prime importance in maintaining active political party organizations as well as permitting a "real" choice between parties for the voters in general elections. If the intensity of two-party competition rests upon the balance of voting strength in a state then we should be able to predict that a partisan election ballot will be retained in cities located in states that have competitive politics.[4] The parties will be active and may successfully resist attempts to remove traditional party functions.

Table 1 tests this hypothesis. When we compare states with competitive two-party politics against states that are attached to a single

---

[3] See E. E. Schattschneider, *Party Government,* New York: Farrar and Rinehart, 1942; H. F. Gosnell, *Grass Roots Politics,* Washington, D.C.: American Council on Public Affairs, 1942, V. O. Key, Jr., *Southern Politics,* New York: Alfred Knopf, 1949, and V. O. Key, Jr., *American State Politics:* An Introduction, New York: Alfred Knopf, 1956.

[4] We used the average of the vote for U.S. Representatives in the state as a whole for all Congressional elections from 1944 through 1950 as our indicator of the condition of the parties in each state. The data were taken from George Gallup, *The Political Almanac,* New York: B. C. Forbes & Sons, 1952. These statistics give us the classification of the 48 states listed in Table 1. Reliable data are not available for the electoral system changes before 1940 and in view of the *continuing change* in the direction of nonpartisan balloting it seemed reasonable to use the post-war vote as an indicator of the long term competitive status of a

## TABLE 1

### STATE PARTISANSHIP AND URBAN ELECTORAL SYSTEMS

| State Party partisanship [1] | Percent with partisan elections | Number of cities [2] |
|---|---|---|
| Competitive states | 44% | 280 |
| Democratic states | 26 | 115 |
| Republican states | 14 | 85 |
| Total | 35 | 480 |

$X^2$ (2 df) = 31.0 p < .001

[1] The average state-wide vote for U.S. Representatives in Competitive states was between 46 and 56 per cent Democratic.
The names of the states in each classification are:
Competitive: Calif., Colo., Conn., Del., Ill., Ind., Ky., Mass., Idaho, Mich., Md., Mont., Mo., N.M., N.Y., Nev., Ohio, Penn., Ut., Wash., W.Va., Wy.
Democratic: Ala., Ariz., Ark., Fla., Ga., La., Miss., N.C., Okla., R.I., S.C., Tenn., Tex., Va.
Republican: Ia., Kan., Me., Minn., Nebr., N.Dak., N.H., N.J., Ore., S.Dak., Vt., Wisc.

[2] This Table includes all incorporated cities with more than 25,000 inhabitants in 1950. These same 480 cities provide us with the data analyzed in the remaining tables.

party, we see that cities in the competitive states are more than twice as likely to have retained partisan ballots than cities in non-competitive states. Forty-four per cent of the cities in competitive states had retained partisan elections compared to 26 per cent in Democratic states and 14 per cent in Republican states. These differences are significant at the .001 level. State two-party competition is significantly related to the type of ballot adopted by cities within the states.

We can, at this point, ask the question of whether nonpartisan elections, once established, act to maintain (or even create) the one-party condition, or whether the one-party condition acts to generate conditions that facilitate the removal of partisan party politics from municipal elections. If a causal interpretation is suggested it is

---

state. Careful examination of the states in each category should persuade the reader that with the exception of Rhode Island the 14 democratic states have been one-party states since the Civil War. The 12 Republican states have long term histories as Republican strongholds. V. O. Key has a useful list of the average vote for Governor from around 1910 to around 1952 for 21 non-Southern states and *all* of the states he includes as having *less* than 45 per cent Democratic voters during that period are included in my Republican category. His listing would exclude only New Jersey placing it in the competitive group. See V. O. Key Jr., *American State Politics, op. cit.* p. 99. Any criteria will necessarily define the results of a classification; in the present case I assumed that a post-depression, post-war vote covering four elections at two-year intervals would reflect the long term predispositions of the state. We will see in a later section that some "Republican" states have developed two-party politics since 1950. This later development does not mean that the original classification is false, only that state political systems are subject to changes (given the appropriate types of social structures, as we will point out).

because of the following argument: the one-party condition precedes the adoption of nonpartisan elections. This is certainly clear for the Democratic one-party states. The first nonpartisan city ballot was introduced to Dallas in 1907 and by 1940 we count 299 nonpartisan cities among our 480 cities. In 1958 the number had increased to 314. Unfortunately reliable data are not available which would enable us to reconstruct the spread of nonpartisan ballots from 1907 to the present day. We do know that the first cities with Commission and city manager forms of government (and the accompanying non-partisan ballot) were concentrated in the South. It would appear that nonpartisanship followed one party rule. A causal relationship is not thereby proved, nor is it claimed that the one-party condition was either a necessary or a sufficient cause of this change in urban electoral rules. What we do claim is that the power of the association of the two variables makes it difficult to talk about this ballot change without discussion of the state political system within which the changes were taking place. In the absence of direct measures of the inter-vening variables a statement of a simple causal relationship would be premature.

We can maintain that the nonpartisan ballot does *not* contribute heavily to the long term survival of the one-party condition since our data indicate that the one-party condition precedes the introduc-tion of the nonpartisan ballot. In the last section of this paper we also note that states we have termed Republican one-party areas with few partisan ballots in their 85 cities have shown definite signs of returning to two-party politics. The urban areas of a state may be overwhelmingly nonpartisan without noticeably affecting the move-ment from the one to the two-party condition. We should also bear in mind the fact that 56 per cent of the cities in competitive states have nonpartisan ballots, and yet they seem to remain competitive.

## The Role of the State Political System: Voter Party Loyalty

The strength of voter attachment with either major political party may also play a role in the willingness with which communities abandon a partisan ballot for the nonpartisan ballot. Our second structural variable operating at the level of the state political system is a measure of voter attachment to the parties. States with loyal party voters should be more likely to have cities that have retained partisan elections. Our measure of party loyalty is the average of the third party vote in the 1912 and 1924 Presidential elections.[5] If a state gave more than 30 per cent of its vote to the "third party" then it is classified as "low" on party loyalty. If it gave less than 30 per cent of its total vote to the "third party" then it is "high" on its loyalty to the two traditional parties. Our hypothesis is that partisan elections will be retained in areas whose voters have high party loyalty as compared to areas whose voters are low on party loyalty. Table 2 tests this hypothesis. It reveals that when we differentiate high from low loyalty states we observe that 38 per cent of the cities in high-loyalty states have partisan elections compared to 28 per cent of the cities in low-loyalty states. This difference is significant at the .05 level. An inspection of the listing of states at the bottom of the table further reveals that while both competitive and Republican areas have a number of low-loyalty states, Democratic one-party states contain only high-loyalty voters.

**TABLE 2**

*VOTER LOYALTY AND URBAN ELECTORAL SYSTEMS* [1]

| State voter loyalty | Percent with partisan elections | Number of cities |
|---|---|---|
| High party loyalty | 38% | 335 |
| Low party loyalty | 28% | 145 |

$X^2$ (1 df) $= 4.4$ p $<.05$

[1] The names of the states by party competition and voter loyalty follow:
Democratic: High loyal: Ala., Ariz., Ark., Fla., Ga., La., Miss., N.C., Okla., R.I., S.C., Tenn., Tex., Va.
Competitive: High loyal: Colo., Conn., Del., Ind., Ky., Md., Mass., Mich., Mo., N.M., N.Y., Ohio, Ut., W.Va.
Low Loyal: Calif., Ida., Ill., Mont., Nev., Penn., Wash., Wy.
Republican: High loyal: Kan. Me., Nebr., N.H., N.J., Vt.
Low loyal: Ia., Minn., N. Dak., Wisc.

In Table 1 we have already observed that 26 per cent of the cities in Democratic states had partisan elections compared to only 14 per cent in Republican states. Because some Republican states are low on voter loyalty but no Democratic states are low on this characteristic we are curious as to the possible effect of the low loyalty factor as a source of explanation of the differences in the electoral rules between cities in Democratic and Republican one-party areas.

---

[5] Data on voting in these elections were taken from Edgar E. Robinson, *The Presidential Vote, 1896–1932*, Stanford: Stanford University Press, 1934. It is interesting to note that present day "ticket-splitting" by voters is often found in the same states we have called "low-loyalty" states. Ticket splitting may also be an indicator of low party loyalty. A separate indicator of differences among southern states in party loyalty was not available to this writer. Further analysis of party loyalty differences among southern states and the effect of these differences would be desirable.

Table 3 reveals that when we control for loyalty in Republican states, cities in those states with high loyalty have exactly the same rate (26 per cent) of partisan ballots as do their high-loyalty one-party Democratic counterparts. A second striking feature in the table is the difference in the impact of low voter loyalty in states with competitive politics and in one-party states. In competitive states the cities

**TABLE 3**

*STATE VOTER LOYALTY AND URBAN ELECTORAL SYSTEMS IN COMPETITIVE AND REPUBLICAN STATES*

Percent with Partisan Elections

| State voter loyalty | Competitive States | Numbers | Republican States | Numbers |
|---|---|---|---|---|
| High | 48% | 178 | 26% | 42 |
| Low | 38% | 102 | 2% | 43 |
| | $X^2$ (1 df) $= 2.4$ p $< .20$ | | $X^2$ (1 df) $= 10.1$ p $< .005$ | |

located in high-loyalty states are not significantly different from cities in low-loyalty states. In Republican states 26 per cent of the cities in high-loyalty states retained partisan elections compared to only 2 per cent of the cities in low-loyalty states. This difference is significant at the .005 level. This table would indicate that the two-party competitive condition tends to over-ride the effects of low party loyalty. On the other hand, low voter party loyalty seems to be strongly related to the nonpartisan ballot when a competitive party condition does not exist in the state. In the one-party Republican states the added factor of low voter loyalty increases the impact of the one-party condition. Where both a one-party system and the low voter loyalty condition prevail, only one of the 43 states has retained partisan elections. The combined attributes are overwhelmingly associated with nonpartisan election rules.

In the next section of the paper we will examine the relationship of two types of community cleavage to partisan or nonpartisan electoral rules.

## Community Cleavage and Election Rules

Our treatment of social class and religious cleavage is based on the assumption that community-wide cleavage provides political parties with the social basis necessary for effective organization and sufficient activity necessary for survival as a community force. Two-party organization is difficult to sustain in homogeneous communities. The theory underlying this view of the positive functions of social cleavage and conflict is given by Lipset and Kornhauser in recent publications.[6] While most writers seem to agree that conflict and cleavage is necessary for a democratic order they also stress the necessity for the political order to maintain consensus and legitimacy. It is difficult to make empirical predictions from such formulations, but they can be used as a guide to research nonetheless. Of specific relevance to this study are studies of community conflict and power structure that have examined the American community in some detail.

The social processes that accompany community controversy have been examined in detail by Coleman [7] in his monograph *Community Conflict.* Of particular interest to this paper are the factors that Coleman identifies as important "conditions" which inhibit or enhance the chances that a spark may ignite a full blown conflagration within a community. Differences in the economic structures of the community, the extent of class cleavage, social cleavages based on ethnic, cultural or religious differences serve to guide citizens in the position they will take on issues that affect their community. It is unnecessary to describe again here the intricate and varied ways in which these factors combine with other pressures to affect community decision making on particular types of issues, but it is appropriate to emphasize the important role assigned by community researchers to the role of social class and religious cleavage in the organization of community life.

A survey of sociological research of community power structures has also devoted considerable attention to the relationship of class and religious ethnic cleavage to the organization of power and leadership within the American community.[8] Variation in a community's social structure and its effect on "public" power structures is what concerns us in this paper. With regard to the part played by the electorate in community political organization, Rossi points out the importance of 1) political homogeneity and 2) "... the extent to which lines of

---

[6] S. M. Lipset, *Political Man,* New York: Doubleday, 1960, chapter 1, and William Kornhauser, *The Politics of Mass Society,* Glencoe, Illinois, The Free Press, 1959.

[7] James Coleman, *Community Conflict,* Glencoe, Illinois: The Free Press, 1957.

[8] Peter H. Rossi, "Theory and Method in the Study of Power in the Local Community," a paper presented at the 1960 Annual Meeting of the American Sociological Association (New York, 1960). Case studies of conflict over the form of government that a community adopts also support the idea that movements to return to a partisan political system stem from working class organizations. On this point see Edwin O. Stone and George K. Floro, *Abandonments of the Manager Plan,* Lawrence, Kansas: University of Kansas Publications, 1953.

political cleavages within the community coincide with its major social structural features. In this connection, important social structural features are class and status . . ." [9]

If we assume that political cleavage will be more likely to follow the lines of class and religion in communities that are high on class and religious cleavage, then the following hypothesis concerning the acceptance or rejection of the nonpartisan ballot can be made: where class and religious cleavage is high, political party organization will be strong. The community basis for party organization will be strong because each party will have a solid base from which to mobilize organized activities. This base can depend on either class or religion or both. Where party activity is strong, partisan elections will more likely be contained by the community.

Our consideration of the positive role of community cleavage in maintaining partisan elections and active political organization in a community has omitted one important factor: the community cannot be politically noncompetitive for too great a period of time. If the minority party has no opportunity for victory, social cleavage will not operate. It is one thing to have the social basis for two-party party activity and it is another to have also the prospect of victory as a result of such activity by a minority party. For an attribute of the political system such as the nature of the election rules we would predict that if high social cleavage is associated with partisan elections it will be more clearly associated in competitive states than in one-party states. A severe one-party condition may effectively obliterate the potential political activities of social groups unless a politically relevant crisis situation develops.

## Two Types of Community Cleavage

The first type of cleavage is economic class cleavage. We assume that in communities that are primarily engaged in manufacturing activities, the lines of association within the white and blue collar ranks will be such as to link members of each stratum more closely to homogeneous class-based organizations (such as unions or neighborhood groups). In short, there will be greater class homogeneity so far as organizational memberships and informal associations are concerned. Cleavages between economic classes should, therefore, be greater in industrial centers than in either homogeneous suburbs or cities in which diversified economic activities tend to narrow the organization base of the working class.

[9] Rossi, *ibid.*, p. 30.

The proportion of the total labor force that was employed in manufacturing activities in 1950 was dichotomized at 50 per cent; cities with 50 per cent or more of the labor force employed in manufacturing are classified as "high." [10]

Table 4 reveals that some 44 per cent of the high manufacturing cities retained partisan elections compared to 27 per cent of the low manufacturing cities. Cities high on manufacturing employment have significantly more partisan elections than cities low on manufacturing employment. The difference is significant at the 001. level and our hypothesis is sustained.

### TABLE 4

*MANUFACTURING LEVELS AND URBAN ELECTORAL SYSTEMS*

| City Manufacturing employment level | Per cent with partisan elections | Number of cities |
|---|---|---|
| High | 44% | 218 |
| Low | 27% | 262 |

$X^2$ (1 df) = 15.7 p < .001

The second type of cleavage focuses upon Catholic-Protestant cleavage. We assume that in communities with less than 20 per cent Catholic inhabitants the possibility for politically effective cleavage is small. (The intensity of in-group and out-group feeling may be great, but the possibility of doing something about it is not). Because of the repeated findings of religious cleavage in American communities we simply will assume that communities with more than 20 per cent Catholic population are "high" on religious cleavage.

Table 5 reveals identical percentage values with those in Table 4. Forty-four per cent of "high" Catholic cities have retained partisan elections compared to 27 per cent of the low Catholic cities.[11] The chi-square value is, again, significant at the .001 level. Tables 4 and 5 both tend to confirm the assumption that the social organization of

---

[10] This corresponds to the economic classification of cities as "industrial" and "manufacturing" as opposed to all other types of cities. These data were taken from *The Municipal Year Book, 1953, op. cit.* Data on union organization and political action in manufacturing as opposed to nonmanufacturing cities would possibly clarify this relationship.

[11] Religious data are taken from the U.S. Department of Commerce, *Religious Bodies, 1936,* Vol. 1, Washington: U.S. Government Printing Office, 1941. The number of Roman Catholics and Greek Orthodox Catholics as the percent of the total city population is used if the city had 25,000 inhabitants at the time of the 1930 census. If the city's population was less, we necessarily used similar data from the county in which the city was located as the best available estimate of the city's Catholic population.

**TABLE 5**

RELIGIOUS COMPOSITION AND URBAN ELECTORAL SYSTEMS

| Proportion Catholic | Per cent with partisan elections | Number of cities |
|---|---|---|
| High | 44% | 225 |
| Low | 27% | 255 |

$X^2$ (1 df) = 15.1 p $<$ .001

the community is related to the adoption of nonpartisan elections. We have now to specify the conditions under which this "community effect" takes hold.

## Community Cleavage in Two-Party Areas

We have, on the basis of our analysis of the effect of state political system variables on partisan elections, grouped cities into competitive and Republican or Democratic one-party states and into low or high voter loyalty states as well. We have seen that Democratic one-Party states were all high on voter loyalty, and that voter loyalties were not significant in their relationship to partisan electoral systems in competitive states, but were clearly related to partisan elections in the only one-party areas where such comparisons were possible, Republican areas.

In the competitive situation we have said that community class and religious differences should discriminate between cities with nonpartisan or partisan election rules. The greatest difference should exist between cities that are high on both class and religious cleavage and cities that are low on both religious and class cleavage. Table 6

**TABLE 6**

MANUFACTURING LEVEL, RELIGIOUS COMPOSITION AND URBAN ELECTORAL SYSTEMS: COMPETITIVE STATES ONLY

| Religious composition | Manufacturing level | Partisan elections | Numbers |
|---|---|---|---|
| High Catholic | High | 56% | 93 |
| Low Catholic | Low | 23% | 70 |

$X^2$ (1 df) = 17.9 p $<$ .001

reveals that a very large difference does exist between these extreme city types. Fifty-six per cent of the cities in competitive states which are high on both community attributes have retained partisan elections, while only 23 per cent of the cities that have neither community attribute have retained partisan ballots. To appreciate this difference (significant at the .001 level) the reader may recall that a larger proportion of cities in the one-party Democratic states had retained partisan elections (26 per cent) than those in cities in competitive states which lack both community cleavage attributes. Further, a larger proportion (26 per cent) of one-party Republican cities in high loyalty areas had retained partisan elections as well. In view of the strong positive relationship between state party competition and partisan elections (Table 1) we can see that community attributes play a very important role in determining the form of election rules of cities in competitive states.

Table 7 demonstrates that each of these community attributes plays an important role in the *absence* of the other. We do not have to have both attributes present or absent to reveal a significant difference between high and low religious or class cleavage as we did in Table 6. Table 7 reveals that the difference between the proportion of cities retaining partisan elections in high and low manufacturing cities is significant only when the effect of high religious cleavage is removed.

This can be seen by inspection of the column differences in the table. In cities with a low proportion of Catholics, a significant difference between high and low manufacturing levels is observed, while in cities with a high proportion of Catholics the difference is not statistically significant.

The row differences of Table 7 reveal that the difference between high and low Catholic cities in retaining partisan ballots is not signifi-

### TABLE 7

MANUFACTURING LEVELS, RELIGIOUS COMPOSITION AND
URBAN ELECTORAL SYSTEMS: COMPETITIVE
STATES ONLY

Percent with Partisan Elections

| Manufacturing levels | High Catholic only | Numbers | Low Catholic only | Numbers | Row differences |
|---|---|---|---|---|---|
| High | 56% | 93 | 48% | 60 | $X^2$ (1 df) = 0.8 $p < .50$ |
| Low | 47% | 57 | 23% | 70 | $X^2$ (1 df) = 8.4 $p < .005$ |
| Columns differences | $X^2$ (1 df) = 1.0 < .40 | | $X^2$ (1 df) = 9.1 $p < .005$ | | |

cant where high manufacturing levels are in effect. A statistically significant difference between high and low Catholic cities exists where manufacturing levels are low. Thus, if we accept our assumption concerning the relationship of manufacturing cities to high class cleavage, we can say that where class cleavage is absent religious cleavage plays a significant role in maintaining partisan local elections.

## Community Cleavage in One-Party Areas

The role of community cleavage in one-party areas is less clear. In competitive areas both types of community cleavage had equal weight and, further, the greatest impact upon the local electoral system occurred when both attributes were present or when both were absent. We further noted that statistically significant relationships between partisan and nonpartisan elections and either religious or class cleavage occurred when we compared cities in which both attributes were present against cities in which both were absent or when we compared high and low cleavage cities on one attribute against cities that were low (but not high) on the other attribute. This suggests that the attributes are additive in their effects upon the local political system.

In one-party areas this is not the case, although some weak trends in the direction of the relationships reported for competitive areas do exist. One conclusion to be drawn from the absence of an impact of community attributes on election rules in one-party areas is simply this: our assumption that the competitive balance of the state political system was of overriding importance seems to have been confirmed.

## From One-Party to Two-Party Politics

Community attributes operate with greatest effect within the competitive political system. Where the social basis for political party organization was present we also found the centers of partisan local political systems, given a compatible state-party system.

The distribution of the marginals shown in the basic data of Table 9 are arranged in Table 8. Here we examine the possible effects of the distribution of community attributes in states with two- and one-party systems. We might assume that if all the communities with favorable community attributes were located in competitive party areas, then our lack of relationship between community attributes and partisan elections in one party states would simply be an artifact of this unhappy distribution. Table 8 shows that this is not the case; in fact more cities

### TABLE 8

*COMMUNITY CLEAVAGE AND TWO PARTY COMPETITION*

| State party partisanship | Both cleavage present | One cleavage present | Neither cleavage present | Number of cases |
|---|---|---|---|---|
| Competitive | 33% | 41% | 26% | 280 |
| Republican | 41 | 36 | 23 | 85 |
| Democratic | 4 | 27 | 69 | 115 |

$X^2$ (2 df) Democratic vs. competitive $= 75.2$ p. $< .001$
$X^2$ (2 df) Republican vs. competitive $= 1.8$ p $< .20$

in Republican states had both favorable attributes (high class and religious cleavage) than cities in competitive areas. The greatest departure from a uniform distribution is in Democratic areas as compared to competitive or Republican areas. Chi-square with 2 degrees of freedom is significant at the .001 level when we compare the distribution of community attributes of Democratic against competitive states or Democratic against Republican states. There is no significant chi-square at the .05 level when we compare competitive and Republican areas.

This finding is of more than passing interest for it may help to explain the extremely durable one-party loyalty of the solid south. Inspection of the states contained in the Democratic group (see Table 1) shows us that the solid south is the region that contributes virtually all of the cities to this category. An examination of the states we have called Republican may cause the reader to wonder if they are properly classified, for we are well aware of the fact that New Jersey, Iowa, Minnesota, Oregon, Kansas and Wisconsin have regularly elected Democratic governors and senators during the past ten years. Even Maine and Vermont have elected Democratic officials. This leads us

**TABLE 9**

*NUMBER OF PARTISAN AND NONPARTISAN CITIES AND STATE PARTY PARTISANSHIP, VOTER LOYALTY, MANUFACTURING LEVELS AND RELIGIOUS COMPOSITION*

| State party partisanship | State voter loyalty | Manu- facturing levels | Proportion Catholic | Number of partisan cities | Number of nonpartisan cities | Total number cities |
|---|---|---|---|---|---|---|
| Democratic | High | High | High | 2 | 3 | 5 |
| | | Low | High | 7 | 9 | 16 |
| | | High | Low | 4 | 10 | 14 |
| | | Low | Low | 17 | 63 | 80 |
| Competitive | High | High | High | 37 | 36 | 73 |
| | | Low | High | 18 | 16 | 34 |
| | | High | Low | 21 | 20 | 41 |
| | | Low | Low | 9 | 21 | 30 |
| | Low | High | High | 15 | 5 | 20 |
| | | Low | High | 9 | 14 | 23 |
| | | High | Low | 8 | 11 | 19 |
| | | Low | Low | 7 | 33 | 40 |
| Republican | High | High | High | 7 | 15 | 22 |
| | | Low | High | 3 | 8 | 11 |
| | | High | Low | 1 | 3 | 4 |
| | | Low | Low | 0 | 5 | 5 |
| | Low | High | High | 0 | 13 | 13 |
| | | Low | High | 0 | 8 | 8 |
| | | High | Low | 1 | 6 | 7 |
| | | Low | Low | 0 | 15 | 15 |
| | | Totals | | 166 | 314 | 480 |

to an interesting though speculative point concerning the role of religious cleavage and manufacturing activity levels in aiding Republican one-party areas to return to two-party politics while Democratic one-party areas seem to be stuck in the one-party condition decade after decade. It would appear that states with cleavage attributes stand a better chance of maintaining two-party politics or returning to a two-party condition after voting heavily for one party for some period of time. States without these attributes are less likely to be able to return to the two-party condition. We believe that the key to an explanation (and to future research in this area) may be found in the social structures that are necessary for party organization to develop. Without party organization a minority party cannot become a majority party and without the social basis which is conducive to two-party organization a two-party system will have difficulty in maintaining itself in the long run.[12]

## Discussion

We have shown some of the political and social conditions under which pressures are likely to be generated so that a party system will be replaced by a non-party system, and we have, at the same time, located some of the structural attributes that are conducive to the maintenance of an on-going two-party system in which the major political parties continue to play a legal role in the selection of local government officials.

We have found that while state-wide two-party competition is of central importance to understanding the distribution of nonpartisan or partisan local elections rules, weak voter attachments to the major parties in one-party states also made a significant further contribution to the cause of the nonpartisan ballot. Within competitive areas (containing 58 per cent of the cities in our study) the social structure of the city discriminated between cities that adopted or failed to adopt nonpartisan elections. Cities that lack a manufacturing employment base are as likely to turn to nonpartisan elections as

---

[12] A failure to control variables properly may therefore account for the lack of comparability between investigations of attributes associated with two-party competition in different states. For example, an index of urbanization is associated with party competition in Ohio but not in Iowa. This suggests that religion might be introduced as a third variable. See David Gold and John Schmidhauser, "Urbanization and Party Competition: The Case of Iowa," *Midwest Journal of Political Science*, IV (February, 1960), pp. 67–72, and Heinz Eulau, "The Ecological Basis of Party Systems: The Case of Ohio," *Midwest Journal of Political Science*, I (August, 1957), pp. 125–135.

are cities that lack the basis for religious cleavage. The greatest difference in the effect of the community social structure was between cities that were high on both indicators of community cleavage and cities that were low on both. Each of these cleavage factors operates in the absence of the other as well as in combination with the other. A significant difference between cities which were high and cities which were low on religious cleavage was found only when these same cities were low on our indicator of class cleavage. Similarly, the effect of different levels of class cleavage was significant only when religious cleavage was low. (See Table 7).

We examined the distribution of community attributes among the different types of state political systems and offered a tentative statement of the relationship of urban social structures to the one party condition and to the two party condition. Other things being equal, it would appear that the one-party south has a less favorable social structure than several of the more important one-party Republican states. The same community structures that are associated with partisan political systems were found to be associated with the re-establishment of two party politics in several "traditional" one-party states.

We have found that nonpartisan elections are associated with several structural conditions: 1) overwhelming voter support to one party; 2) weak voter attachment to either party; 3) lack of an economic base which encourages class-based organizations and class alignment to political parties, and 4) lack of a religious base adequate for religious cleavage to effectively support political parties. Where these conditions occur, nonpartisan systems have won overwhelming support; in the absence of these conditions the tide of reform has had noticeably less effect. Further, where these conditions combine, a one-party system may become a relatively permanent feature on the political scene.

# Leadership and Decision-Making in Manager Cities

## CHARLES R. ADRIAN

This is a report on a continuing study of policy leadership in three middle-sized council-manager cities. All three cities are in the 50,000 to 80,000 population range, are in Michigan, and have been council-manager cities for over twenty-five years. The study covers the period of the calendar years 1953 through 1957. The manager in each city had been in office before the beginning of this period and remained in office throughout the period.[1]

None of the cities is within the six counties of the Detroit metropolitan area. Cities A and B are manufacturing cities with a fairly slow population growth; city C, also predominantly a manufacturing city, has grown somewhat more rapidly. All have nonpartisan elections. Labor is organized in the three cities but has been of little influence in the selection of the council in cities A and B. City C had one AFL and CIO endorsee elected to the council during the period studied; two other councilmen were given limited labor endorsement.

Tentative conclusions reached in this preliminary report indicate that the manager and his administration are the principal sources of policy innovation and leadership in council-manager cities, even though the manager seeks to avoid a public posture of policy leadership; that the manager has resources and techniques that enable him to withstand

Reprinted from *Public Administration Review*, Vol. 18 (Summer 1958), 208–13, by permission of the publisher.

[1] I wish to extend special thanks to William Cottrell, graduate Falk fellow at Michigan State University, for his able and considerable assistance in the collection of data for this paper. Concerning the research method used: council records and newspaper accounts were examined to determine the issues that were taken up by the city councils during the five-year period; newspaper stories were used to delineate the public roles played by the various individuals involved in the development of public policy toward each issue. Informants in each community helped to clarify the nonpublic roles played by these persons.

even strong attempts by some councilmen to take policy leadership away from him; that nonofficial groups provide a greater amount of leadership in council-manager cities than is allowed for in the theory of the plan; and that this leadership is a result of councilmanic leadership falling short of the idealized role assigned to it by the theory. Councilmen who do seek to lead place their political careers in greater jeopardy than do other councilmen. It was also found that there were few important issues confronting city councils in middle-sized cities and that even some of these were settled with little conflict, particularly those where few solutions seemed to be available.

## The Manager Plan

The basic idea of the council-manager plan is well known: an elective council of laymen is to make policy and a professional administration under a chief administrative officer selected by, and responsible to, the council is to carry out policy. It is not necessary to comment here on the fact that this approach to organization seems to imply the acceptance of the dichotomy which was held, some years ago, to exist between policy and administration. Practicing city managers quickly learned that they could not avoid taking leadership in policy-making. (The tempests created in academicians' teapots when the idea was presented that politics and administration cannot be separated were of little or no interest to managers and their subordinates who must have discovered the necessary interrelationships of the two about the time that the first manager was appointed in 1908.) Summarizing some studies which were made about twenty years ago, Stone, Price, and Stone noted that:

> It is generally impossible for a city manager to escape being a leader in matters of policy, for it is an essential part of his administrative job to make recommendations. The most important municipal policy is embodied in the budget, and the city manager, of course, must prepare and propose the budget. The city manager's recommendation on an important policy, even if he makes it in an executive session of the council, is usually a matter of common knowledge.[2]

Thus, while it was recognized no doubt almost at once that the manager would have to be a policy leader, he was also expected to do this in a discreet manner. The code of ethics of the International City Managers' Association enjoins each manager to further "positive de-

---

[2] Harold A. Stone, Don K. Price, and Kathryn H. Stone, *City Manager Government in the United States* (Public Administration Service, 1940), p. 243. See also, Steve Matthews, "Types of Managerial Leadership," 39 *Public Management* 50–53 (March, 1957).

cisions on policy by the council instead of passive acceptance of his recommendations," and to give formal credit for policy decisions to the council. (The code, with some modifications, dates from 1924.)

Thus, the role of the manager was conceived realistically decades ago and is well described in the study by Stone, Price, and Stone. On the other hand, neither that study nor other writings on the council-manager plan have paid very much attention to the role of other individuals and groups in the municipal policy-making process: the mayor, the council, and interest groups confronting the manager and the council between election campaigns. It is principally to these areas that this paper is addressed.

## Scarcity of Issues

A study of the role of various groups and actors in the making of municipal public policy is handicapped to some extent by the relative scarcity of issues that could be classified as important. Most of the work of the council appears to consist of routine approval of recommendations from the city manager or his staff; these actions are routine because they fit within general policy already well established.

Judged on the basis of the amount of controversy engendered, the time required to achieve a policy decision by the council, and the amount of space devoted to the issue by the local press, the number of important issues coming before the councils of the three cities averaged about two per year. There was little variation among the cities on this point. It should be noted, however, that an issue may be divided into a number of parts and take many forms. A major conflict between the manager and one of the councilmen in City C, for example, was raised as a background issue in connection with almost every other councilmanic discussion during the period of the controversy.

## The Role of the Manager

In all three cities studied, the manager played the social role expected of him by his professional organizations. In each case, he avoided taking a public role of policy innovator, except at the specific request of the council or in cases involving matters on which he could be considered a technical expert (e.g., on the effect of allowing a bank to install a drive-up window or of a proposed shuffling of administrative agencies).

If we assume, along with Herbert Simon,[3] that major decisions are almost always made through a "composite process" involving many

---

[3] *Administrative Behavior* (2d ed., Macmillan Co., 1957).

people, so that no single person is wholly responsible for the final product, it becomes advantageous to view the policy-making process as one in which individual roles are specialized. Since the leader, according to Simon, is a person "who is able to unite people in pursuit of a goal," alternating goals must first be perceived by someone. This is done through a precedent role of *policy innovation,* by which I mean the development of ideas, plans, or procedures that may be presented as alternative choices to the decision-makers. A decision might be said, for purposes of this article, to refer to the selection of an idea, plan, or procedure from among the perceived choices. Many decisions must be made in the development of a policy. To name only a few, the innovators of policy must decide whether their incipient suggestions are worthy of development and subsequent presentation for consideration by the leaders. Each leader must decide upon a policy from among what may be several proposals coming from a single individual or agency or from more than one agency. Once the manager or other leader has decided upon a proposal, he will seek to secure its acceptance. The governing body must then choose a proposal presented by one leader or must consolidate the proposals of two or more leaders. Final acceptance by the council gives the policy legitimacy. Of course, the council may veto all proposals, which would then force a reconsideration of the earlier decisions by other actors.

In the council-manager cities studied, the manager presented and sometimes strongly defended policy proposals that had originated largely from one of his own agencies (e.g., the police department on parking policies), from an advisory group (e.g., the planning commission which developed urban renewal plans), from study committees of lay citizens (e.g., citizens seeking to prevent the breakdown of public transportation), or private groups (e.g., downtown merchants interested in off-street parking).[4] There appeared to be a psychological advantage to the manager if he could place himself in the position of defending a policy developed by these individuals or groups.[5] He would take a strong stand, but would use the protective coloration of saying, "professional planners tell me. . . ." He would, in other words, take a public

---

[4] In City C, however, the manager was in the position of presenting an off-street parking plan that was strongly opposed by the downtown merchants and parking lot owners. The opponents were able to delay but not prevent the adoption of the plan developed by the manager and his staff.

[5] One manager (not from Cities A, B, or C) pointed out in an interview that his office is one from which "trial balloons" can be sent up. If a proposed policy is greeted with general disfavor, the council can reject "the manager's suggestion"—he takes the blame regardless of where the idea may have originated. If the proposal is well received, councilmen accept it as their own.

position of *leadership* in policy matters, but preferred to attribute policy *innovation* to technical experts or citizens groups.

Although managers in all cities appeared to exercise considerable skill in avoiding a public appearance of being the tail that wags the dog, in two cities they were accused of seeking to "control" the mayor or council. In City C, the manager had to overcome major opposition which, for a short while, actually held majority control of the council. The manager chose to wait out the opposition, almost succeeded in keeping from being quoted in the newspapers concerning his own views on the conflict, and eventually weaned the mayor from the opposition, thus making his supporters on the council a majority. In City B, two councilmen, elected to office late in the five-year period studied, accused the manager of policy domination and voted against proposals that had his blessings, but there appears to have been no support for the two from other councilmen. In an election toward the end of the period studied, a little-known candidate, seeking to join them, failed to secure nomination.

### The Role of the Mayor

What of the mayor as a leader? In two of the cities studied, the mayor did not play a special leadership role. In one, he was elected by the council; in the other he was directly elected. In the third city, the mayor was the councilman receiving the largest number of votes. An individual of high prestige both among the public and on the council was regularly elected mayor through the period studied. Because of his high status, he appears to have been deferred to by other councilmen and his views were respected. His leadership was rather inconspicuous, however, and he did not play the role of policy innovator, or of a chaperon of legislation through the council.[6]

In the thirty issues of importance during the five-year period, the mayor was a principal leader on only two, both of them in City B. The mayor in this case was an elderly man who had held his office for many years. He was chief spokesman on the council for an unsuccessful proposal for a metropolitan area hospital authority, although the plan had first been worked out by a citizen group which strongly supported it. A new city hall for the community was a matter close to his heart, but he was opposed by the chamber of commerce and the taxpayers groups which thought the plan extravagant and unnecessary. Although the

---

[6] In one of the cities, the office of city attorney was elective. The incumbent played a definite policy-making role independent of the manager. In the two cities where the attorney was appointed, his role was much less important.

mayor had the support of the manager and of the planning commission, the council finally accepted the plan of the economy groups.

It is impossible to conclude whether the manner by which the mayor was selected affected his role as a policy leader. In general, there was not much reason to believe that the office of mayor, as such, was prestigious enough to give the incumbent a significant advantage over other potential leaders.

## The Role of the Council

Members of the council did not emerge as either general policy innovators or as general policy leaders. The individual councilman, rather, was likely to assume leadership in connection with a specific issue or function of government. He developed pet interests or came to know one area of municipal activity especially well and concentrated upon that.

There was one exception: a councilman who acted as a leader both in the general development of policy and in seeking support for policies first presented by some other individual or group (Councilman n in City A). To this case might be added another, somewhat similar. In City C, one councilman definitely acted as the leader of the opposition to the manager, regardless of the particular policy issue under discussion. His leadership, with a few exceptions, was of a negative sort, however. Since the conflict over the manager began almost at the outset of the period covered by this study, it is impossible to say if this councilman could also have served as a constructive policy leader under other conditions.

While a councilman might concentrate upon a particular aspect of municipal policy, it was found to be dangerous for him to seek to make some specific issue a *cause celebre*. If he chose to do so, he immediately subjected himself to greater public attention and scrutiny than was the case for the typical councilman, and he risked a defeat on the issue which could in turn have disastrous political consequences for him. There is danger in leadership, relative safety in conformity and anonymity. The study indicated that councilmen were aware of this.

In the five-year period covered, there were two incidents in which councilmen chose to make major controversies out of particular issues, and in each case the councilman was defeated in his try for re-election. In City A, Councilman m, who had served continuously for a quarter of a century and who came from one of the city's high prestige families, chose to take the lead in a full defense of municipal ownership of the light plant. The plant, long owned by the city, competed with a private utility. It served relatively few customers and costs were higher than those of the private company. As a result, patronage was falling and unit cost rising. Shortly after a new councilman took office, he began a campaign for the sale of the light plant to the private utility. His proposal was immediately and vigorously opposed by Councilman m. The issue was carried along at council meetings, through referendums and into court before it was finally settled in favor of sale to the private company. When Councilman m ran for re-election, he was defeated. He lost again two years later. (The referendums on the issue indicated that he was on the unpopular side of the controversy.)

Another case, in City C, involved the leader of a group opposing the city manager and his policies. Councilman y in this case was hostile to the manager at the beginning of the period studied. It took him some time, however, to organize a bloc. After an election, he picked up two new council members. When the mayor joined with him on two important issues, involving the dismissal of two employees and wage and salary policies, Councilman y had a 4–3 majority on the council. The local newspaper speculated on the possible resignation of the manager. The manager apparently decided to wait for further developments and for public opinion to become crystallized. He neither fought back nor made plans for resignation. Later, he became ill and the mayor acted in his stead for a few weeks. Shortly after, the mayor began to support the pro-manager group under Councilman z's leadership. This switch produced a new one-vote majority in support of the administration and talk of the manager's resignation stopped. A hard fought election campaign followed in which the issues included the question of wage and salary policy, support for the principle of the council-manager plan (all groups claimed to support it, but Councilman y was accused of seeking to sabotage it), and support for the incumbent manager. Councilman y was defeated for re-election by one of the city's leading industrialists, a supporter of the manager.

## Leadership on Important Issues

Since in both policy innovation and leadership, the role of the councilmen was a relatively modest one, it is necessary to look elsewhere for the actors who played these parts. They were the manager, the members of his administration, and the leaders of interest groups.

Not all issues that were regarded in the community as being important involved intense controversy. In the case of some significant community problems, only one plausible solution was offered. In others, no councilman seemed to see any political advantage in presenting alternative solutions.

When the bus companies came to the councils from time to time asking for fare increases, each councilman would deplore the trend toward higher fares and poorer service, but since the only discernible alternative to refusing the rate increase was a discontinuance of service, almost all councilmen voted in favor of the request. In each of the cities, study committees of lay citizens were appointed to seek solutions to the bus problem. In two cities, they recommended that the city lease the lines and then hire the bus company to run them, thus avoiding certain taxes. In the third city, the committee found another bus company to operate in the city when the existing company sought to withdraw. In each case, the council gratefully, and with little discussion, accepted the proposed solutions. Although the operation of the bus lines was considered vital to each community, a crisis situation was solved in each of them with little or no conflict.

In cases where controversy did exist, as Table 1 indicates, leadership in favor of a proposal was most likely to come from the administration, with outside groups the second most likely source. In fact,

**TABLE 1**

LEADERSHIP ON MUNICIPAL ISSUES IN THREE
MICHIGAN CITIES

| Source of Leadership | In Favor | Opposed |
|---|---|---|
| Administration | 15 | — |
| Mayor | 2 | — |
| Councilmen | 7 | 15 |
| Outside Groups | 10 | 7 |

Note: The table covers the 30 important municipal issues discussed during the years 1953–57. Because leadership was shared in several and lacking in others, the totals do not equal 30.

nearly all the really significant issues derived their leadership from these two sources. (The cases are too few to attempt to correlate the types of issues with the sources of leadership.) Councilmanic leadership came in annexation proposals, in seeking to make suburbs "pay their own way," and in revolts against the manager. Only in the proposal to sell City A's light plant and in a water supply revenue bond plan in City B did a councilman provide the leadership. In the second case, he had strong administration backing. Issues involving sharp conflict were rarely resolved as the result of leadership coming from the governing body.

In contrast to the leadership *for* proposals, councilmen did lead in opposition to proposals more often than did persons in any other category. Most of the opposition was aimed either against the manager or against expanded services or capital outlay. A good bit of it was non-constructive and perfunctory. The picture of the council, in summary, was one of a largely passive body granting or withholding its approval in the name of the community when presented with proposals from a leadership outside itself.

Nonofficial leadership was important in the case of two types of issues in addition to those that were regarded as "hot potatoes" and so treated gingerly by elected officials. The first type included those submitted by both neighborhood and downtown businessmen seeking municipal assistance in solving their problems. The second included the public transportation problems which, in all three cities, were turned over to citizens committees to bring in recommendations. The first is the kind of interest group activity commonplace before legislative bodies at all levels of government. The second offers something of a puzzle, however. It would seem likely that the solution to the bus problem in each city was one that might have been pushed by almost any councilman, and to his political advantage. Yet, this was not the pattern. Possibly councilmen feared that any solution would also involve increased rates or the necessity of the city buying the transportation system—a solution that seemed unpopular in each city. Possibly controversy was anticipated that never materialized.

It might be noted that the important policy and leadership role of the manager, of his administration, and of leaders of nonofficial groups differs from the pattern intended in the original theory of the council-manager plan. That theory assumed that able, respected leaders of the community would be willing to serve on councils and would take responsibility for policy decisions in government as they did in their businesses. While the typical councilman in the three cities studied gave the impression of being a sufficiently competent person, it seems clear enough that he was not willing to assume a public leadership role under circumstances where he might thereby be plunged into controversy. The politician in the council-manager city, though he may be an amateur, thus follows the traditional practice of American politicians and seeks to avoid taking sides in closely matched battles.

## Suggested Areas for Further Study

A study covering a span of only five years in three cities is scarcely sufficient to serve as a basis for firm generalizations. It is, however, possible for certain tentative hypotheses to be offered from the work reported on here and these may properly provide a basis for further investigation. The following seven hypotheses appear to be most worthy of further inquiry:

1. There will be relatively few issues coming before the council that will be regarded by councilmen, the manager, or the press as involving important, nonroutine decisions.

2. A manager will avoid taking public positions as a policy innovator on items of major importance, but will serve as a leader in presenting and publicly defending policy recommendations developed within the administrative departments, the advisory boards and commissions, study committees of lay citizens, or private groups.

3. The mayor is not chosen on the basis of leadership ability or willingness to play a leadership role and he is, therefore, no more likely to serve as a policy leader than is any other councilman.

4. A councilman is likely to assume leadership in connection with a specific issue or a specific function of government, but not as a general policy leader.

5. A councilman who chooses to make some specific issue a *cause celebre* thereby becomes subject to greater public attention and scrutiny than is the case with the typical councilman and, if he fails in his objective, runs serious risk of defeat in the following election.

6. Important issues, measured by the consequences of failure to act, may involve little controversy if no alternative solutions are perceived, or if no political advantage is seen in the advancement of alternative solutions.

7. When issues are regarded as being important, but when possible solutions are controversial, or many plausible solutions are discernible, the alternative finally selected is likely to come from the administration or from a group outside of the local government structure.

Further inquiry into these hypotheses should help to expand our areas of knowledge about local government and the characteristics of the public policy-making process.

# Reformism and Public Policies
# in American Cities

## ROBERT L. LINEBERRY
## EDMUND P. FOWLER

A decade ago, political scientists were deploring the "lost world of municipal government" and calling for systematic studies of municipal life which emphasized the political, rather than the administrative, side of urban political life.[1] In recent years, this demand has been generously answered and urban politics is becoming one of the most richly plowed fields of political research. In terms originally introduced by David Easton,[2] political scientists have long been concerned with inputs, but more recently they have focused their attention on other system variables, particularly the political culture [3] and policy outputs of municipal governments.[4]

The present paper will treat two policy outputs, taxation and expenditure levels of cities, as dependent variables. We will relate these policy choices to socio-economic characteristics of cities and to struc-

Reprinted from *American Political Science Review,* Vol. LXI, No. 3 (September 1967), 701–16, by permission of the publisher and the authors.

[1] Lawrence J. R. Herson, "The Lost World of Municipal Government," this REVIEW, 51 (June, 1957), 330–345; Robert T. Daland, "Political Science and the Study of Urbanism," *ibid.,* 491–509.

[2] David Easton, "An Approach to the Analysis of Political Systems," *World Politics,* 9 (April, 1957), 383–400.

[3] Edward C. Banfield and James Q. Wilson, *City Politics* (Cambridge: Harvard University Press and the MIT Press, 1963); see also James Q. Wilson and Edward C. Banfield, "Public-Regardingness as a Value Premise in Voting Behavior," this REVIEW, 58 (December, 1964), 876–887.

[4] See, for example, Thomas R. Dye, "City-Suburban Social Distance and Public Policy," *Social Forces,* 4 (1965), 100–106; Raymond Wolfinger and John Osgood Field, "Political Ethos and the Structure of City Government," this REVIEW, 60 (June, 1966), 306–326; Edgar L. Sherbenou, "Class, Participation, and the Council-Manager Plan," *Public Administration Review,* 21 (Summer, 1961), 131–135; Lewis A. Froman, Jr., "An Analysis of Public Policies in Cities," *Journal of Politics,* 29 (February, 1967), 94–108.

tural characteristics of their governments. Our central research concern is to examine the impact of political structures, reformed and unreformed, on policy-making in American cities.

## Political Culture, Reformism
## and Political Institutions

The leaders of the Progressive movement in the United States left an enduring mark on the American political system, particularly at the state and municipal level. In the states, the primary election, the referendum, initiative and recall survive today. The residues of this *Age of Reform,*[5] as Richard Hofstadter called it, persist in municipal politics principally in the form of manager government and at-large and nonpartisan elections. The reformers were, to borrow Banfield and Wilson's phrase, the original embodiment of the "middle class ethos" in American politics. They were, by and large, White Anglo-Saxon Protestants reacting to the politics of the party machine, which operated by exchanging favors for votes.[6]

It is important that we understand the ideology of these reformers if we hope to be able to analyze the institutions which they created and their impact on political decisions. The reformers' goal was to "rationalize" and "democratize" city government by the substitution of "community oriented" leadership. To the reformers, the most pernicious characteristic of the machine was that it capitalized on socio-economic cleavages in the population, playing on class antagonisms and on racial and religious differences. Ernest S. Bradford, an early advocate of commission government with at-large elections, defended his plans for at-large representation on grounds that

> ...under the ward system of governmental representation, the ward receives the attention, not in proportion to its needs but to the ability of its representatives to 'trade' and arrange 'deals' with fellow members. ...Nearly every city under the aldermanic system offers flagrant examples of this vicious method of 'part representation.' The commission form changes this to representation of the city as a whole.[7]

---

[5] (New York: Alfred A. Knopf, 1955.)

[6] John Porter East, *Council Manager Government: The Political Thought of Its Founder, Richard S. Childs* (Chapel Hill: University of North Carolina Press, 1965), p. 18.

[7] Ernest S. Bradford, *Commission Government in American Cities* (New York: Macmillan, 1911), p. 165.

The principal tools which the reformers picked to maximize this "representation of the city as a whole" were the commission, and later the manager, form of government, the nonpartisan election and the election at-large. City manager government, it was argued, produced a no-nonsense, efficient and business-like regime, where decisions could be implemented by professional administrators rather than by victors in the battle over spoils. Nonpartisan elections meant to the reformer that state and national parties, whose issues were irrelevant to local politics anyway, would keep their divisive influences out of municipal decision-making. Nonpartisan elections, especially when combined with elections at-large, would also serve to reduce the impact of socio-economic cleavages and minority voting blocs in local politics. Once established, these institutions would serve as bastions against particularistic interests.

Banfield and Wilson have argued that the "middle class ethos" of the reformers has become a prevalent attitude in much of political life. The middle class stands for "public regarding" virtues rather than for "private regarding" values of the ethnic politics of machines and bosses. The middle class searches for the good of the "community as a whole" rather than for the benefit of particularistic interests.[8] Agger, Goldrich and Swanson, in their study of two western and two southern communities have documented the rise of a group they call the "community conservationists," who "see the values of community life maximized when political leadership is exercised by men representing the public at large, rather than 'special interests.' "[9] Robert Wood has taken up a similar theme in his penetrating analysis of American suburbia. The "no-party politics of suburbia" is characterized by "an outright reaction against partisan activity, a refusal to recognize that there may be persistent cleavages in the electorate and an ethical disapproval of permanent group collaboration as an appropriate means of settling disputes."[10] This ideological opposition to partisanship is a product of a tightly-knit and homogeneous community, for "nonpartisanship reflects a highly integrated community life with a powerful capacity to induce conformity."[11]

Considerable debate has ensued over both the existence and the consequences of these two political ethics in urban communities. Some

---

[8] Banfield and Wilson, *op. cit.,* p. 41.

[9] Robert Agger, Daniel Goldrich, and Bert E. Swanson, *The Rulers and the Ruled* (New York: John Wiley and Sons, 1964), p. 21.

[10] Robert C. Wood, *Suburbia: Its People and Their Politics* (Boston: Houghton Mifflin Co., 1959), p. 155.

[11] *Ibid.,* p. 154.

evidence has supported the view that reformed governments [12] are indeed found in cities with higher incomes, higher levels of education, greater proportions of Protestants and more white-collar job-holders. Schnore and Alford, for example, found that "the popular image of the manager city was verified; it does tend to be the natural habitat of the upper middle class." In addition, manager cities were "inhabited by a younger, more mobile population that is growing rapidly." [13]

More recently, Wolfinger and Field correlated socio-economic variables—particularly ethnicity and region—to political structures. They concluded that "the ethos theory is irrelevant to the South ... inapplicable to the West ... fares badly in the Northwest ..." and that support for the theory in the Midwest was "small and uneven." [14] Region proved to be a more important predictor of both government forms and of policy outputs like urban renewal expenditures than did the socio-economic composition of the population.

In our view, it is premature to carve a headstone for the ethos theory. It is our thesis that governments which are products of the reform movement behave differently from those which have unreformed institutions, even if the socio-economic composition of their population may be similar. Our central purpose is to determine the impact of both socio-economic variables and political institutions (structural variables) on outputs of city governments. By doing this, we hope to shed some additional illumination on the ethos theory.

## Research Design

### Variables

The independent variables used in this analysis, listed in Table 1, consist of relatively "hard" data, mostly drawn from the U.S. census.[15]

---

[12] We refer to cities characterized by commission or manager government, nonpartisan elections, and at-large constituencies as "reformed." Our use of the term is historical and no value position on reformism's merits is intended. To refer to reformed cities as "public regarding" or "middle class" is, it seems, to assume what needs to be proved.

[13] Leo Schnore and Robert Alford, "Forms of Government and Socio-Economic Characteristics of Suburbs," *Administrative Science Quarterly,* 8 (June, 1963), 1–17. See also the literature cited in Froman, *op. cit.*

[14] Wolfinger and Field, *op. cit.,* pp. 325–326.

[15] The source for the first nine variables is *The City and County Data Book* (Washington: United States Bureau of the Census, 1962). For the last three variables, the source is Orin F. Nolting and David S. Arnold (eds.), *The Municipal Yearbook 1965* (Chicago: International City Managers' Association, 1965), pp. 98 ff.

These variables were selected because they represent a variety of possible social cleavages which divide urban populations—rich vs. poor, Negro vs. White, ethnic vs. native, newcomers vs. old-timers, etc. We

**TABLE 1**

*INDEPENDENT VARIABLES*

1. Population, 1960
2. Per cent population increase or decrease, 1950–60
3. Per cent non-white
4. Per cent of native population with foreign born or mixed parentage
5. Median income
6. Per cent of population with incomes below $3000
7. Per cent of population with incomes above $10,000
8. Median school years completed by adult population
9. Per cent high school graduates among adult population
10. Per cent of population in white collar occupations
11. Per cent of elementary school children in private schools
12. Per cent of population in owner-occupied dwelling units

assume that such social and economic characteristics are important determinants of individual and group variations in political preferences. Data on each of these independent variables were gathered for each of the two hundred cities in the sample.[16]

Our principal theoretical concern is with the consequences of variations in the structural characteristics of form of government, type of constituency and partisanship of elections. The variable of government form is unambiguous. Except for a few small New England towns, all American cities have council-manager, mayor-council or commission government. There is, however, somewhat more ambiguity in the classification of election type. By definition, a "nonpartisan election is one in which no candidate is identified on the ballot by party affiliation." [17] The legal definition of nonpartisanship conceals the wide variation between Chicago's and Boston's nominal nonpartisanship and the more genuine variety in Minneapolis, Winnetka and Los Angeles.[18] We will quickly see, though, that formal nonpartisanship is not merely an empty

---

[16] We used a random sample of 200 of the 309 American cities with populations of 50,000 or more in 1960. All information on the forms of government and forms of election are drawn from *The Municipal Yearbook, 1965, op. cit.*

[17] Banfield and Wilson, *op. cit.,* p. 151.

[18] For Minneapolis, see Robert Morlan, "City Politics: Free Style," *National Municipal Review,* 48 (November, 1949), pp. 485–490; Winnetka, Banfield and Wilson, *op. cit.,* p. 140; Los Angeles, Charles G. Mayo, "The 1961 Mayorality Election in Los Angeles: The Political Party in a Nonpartisan Election," *Western Political Quarterly,* 17 (1964), 325–339.

legal nicety, but that there are very real differences in the political behavior of partisan and nonpartisan cities, even though we are defining them in legal terms only.[19]

Our classification of constituency types into only two groups also conceals some variation in the general pattern. While most cities use either the at-large or the ward pattern of constituencies exclusively, a handful use a combination of the two electoral methods. For our purposes, we classified these with district cities.

The dependent variables in this study are two measures of public policy outputs. A growing body of research on local politics has utilized policy measures as dependent variables.[20] The present research is intended to further this study of political outputs by relating socioeconomic variables to expenditure and taxation patterns in cities with varying political structures.

The dependent variables are computed by a simple formula. The between unreformed and reformed cities disappear when controls for measure for taxation was computed by dividing the total personal income of the city into the total tax of the city, giving us a tax/income ratio. Similarly, dividing expenditures by the city's aggregate personal income gave us an expenditure/income ratio as the measure for our second dependent variable. These measures, while admittedly imperfect,[21] permit us to ask how much of a city's income it is willing to commit for public taxation and expenditures.

---

[19] At least one other variable may produce a given institutional form in a city—the legal requirements of a state government, which vary from state to state and may even vary for different kinds of cities within the same state. We have not taken account of this variable because systematic information on comparative state requirements in this area was unavailable to us. However, Wolfinger and Field consulted several experts and eliminated cities which are not given free choice over their institutions. Nevertheless, a comparison of our figures with theirs revealed no important differences.

[20] See footnote 4, *supra*.

[21] We recognize that these are only rough indicators of city finance policies. Definitions of taxation vary from city to city and what may be financed from taxes in one city may be financed from fees in another. Expenditures present a more complex problem because the types and amounts of state transfer payments vary from state to state according to state laws, the division of governmental labor in a state, the incomes and sizes of cities, not to mention political factors at the state level. We think it important, however, that our independent variables explain a large proportion of the variation in municipal outputs as we measured them. No doubt one could explain an even larger proportion of the variation in measures which specify different functional responsibilities of cities. At least these measures constitute a starting point, and we hope others will improve on them.

The source of our output measures was the *County and City Data Book, op. cit.*

*Hypothesis*

Much of the research on city politics has treated reformed institutions as dependent variables. Although we shall briefly examine the social and economic differences between reformed and unreformed cities, our principal concern will be to explore the *consequences* for public policy of political institutions. From our earlier discussion of the political culture of cities we hypothesized that:

    *1*] The relationship between socio-economic cleavages and policy outputs is stronger in unreformed than in reformed cities.

This hypothesis focuses on the intention of the reformers to minimize the role of particularistic interests in policy making.

## Reformed and Unreformed
## Cities: A Comparison

The economic and social contrasts between reformed and unreformed cities have been the subject of much research,[22] and for our purposes we may be brief in our treatment. We divided the independent variables into three groups, one measuring population size and growth, a second containing social class indicators and a third including three measures of social homogeneity. The means and standard deviations for each variable by institutional category are found in Table 2.

It should initially be noted that population size and growth rate fairly clearly separate the reformed from the unreformed cities. As Alford and Scoble have amply documented,[23] the larger the city, the greater the likelihood of its being unreformed; the faster its growth rate, the more likely a city is to possess manager government, nonpartisan and at-large elections. These differences are largely accounted for by the fact that very large cities are most likely to (1) have unreformed institutions and (2) be stable or declining in population. Since neither of these variables emerged as particularly important predictors of our output variables, we relegated them to secondary importance in the rest of the analysis.

The data in Table 2 (on page 371) indicate that reformed cities (at least those over 50,000) do not appear to be "the natural habitat of the

---

[22] See, for example, Robert Alford and Harry Scoble, "Political and Socio-Economic Characteristics of American Cities," *The Municipal Yearbook 1965, op. cit.*, pp. 82–97; Sherbenou, *op. cit.*; John H. Kessel, "Governmental Structure and Political Environment," this REVIEW, 56 (September, 1962), 615–620.

[23] Alford and Scoble, *op. cit.*, The particularly large differences found between the populations of reformed and unreformed cities reflect the fact that New York City and several other urban giants are included in the sample.

upper middle class." While reformed cities have slightly more educated populations and slightly high proportions of white collar workers and home ownership, unreformed cities have generally high incomes. In any case, whatever their direction, the differences are not large. What is striking is not the differences between the cities but the similarities of their class composition.

Homogeneity is easily one of the most ambiguous terms in the ambiguous language of the social sciences. We have followed Alford and Scoble who used three measures of homogeneity: for ethnicity, the per cent of population native born of foreign born or mixed parentage; for race, the per cent nonwhite; and for religious homogeneity, the per cent of elementary school children in private schools. The last measure, while indirect, was the only one available, since data on religious affiliation are not collected by the Census Bureau.

With the exception of race, reformed cities appear somewhat more homogeneous than unreformed cities. While the differences in homogeneity are more clear-cut than class differences, this hardly indicates that reformed cities are the havens of a socially homogeneous population. Although the average nonpartisan city has 16.9 per cent of its children in private schools, this mean conceals a wide range—from 2 to 47 per cent.

Our findings about the insignificance of class differences between reformed and unreformed cities are at some variance with Alford and Scoble's conclusions. There is, however, some support for the argument that reformed cities are more homogeneous. While we used cities with populations of over 50,000, their sample included all cities over 25,000; and varying samples may produce varying conclusions. The only other study to analyze cities over 50,000 was Wolfinger and Field's and our conclusions are generally consistent with theirs. We differ with them, however, on two important questions.

First, Wolfinger and Field argued that what differences there are region are introduced: "The salient conclusion to be drawn from these data is that one can do a much better job of predicting a city's political form by knowing what part of the country it is in than by knowing anything about the composition of its population." [24] Since regions have had different historical experiences, controls for region are essentially controls for history, and more specifically, historical variation in settlement patterns. The problem with this reasoning, however, is that to "control" for "region" is to control not only for history, but for demography as well: to know what region a city is in *is* to know something

[24] *Op. cit.*, p. 320.

about the composition of its population. Geographical subdivisions are relevant subjects of political inquiry only because they are differentiated on the basis of attitudinal or socio-economic variables. The South is not a distinctive political region because two surveyors named Mason and

**TABLE 2**

COMPARISON OF THE MEANS (AND STANDARD DEVIATIONS) OF
SOCIO-ECONOMIC CHARACTERISTICS OF REFORMED AND
UNREFORMED CITIES

| Independent Variable | Mayor-Council | | Manager | | Commission | |
|---|---|---|---|---|---|---|
| | | | GOVERNMENT TYPE | | | |
| *Population:* | | | | | | |
| Population (10³) | 282.5 | (858.6) | 115.7 | (108.0) | 128.6 | (115.2) |
| % Change, 1950–60 | 36.4% | (118.8) | 64.1% | (130.4) | 18.5% | (36.7) |
| *Class:* | | | | | | |
| Median Income | $6199. | (1005.0) | $6131. | (999.6) | $5425. | (804.4) |
| % Under $3000 | 15.3% | (7.0) | 17.3% | (6.9) | 21.5% | (7.9) |
| % Over $10,000 | 16.9% | (7.2) | 17.5% | (6.7) | 12.5% | (3.7) |
| % High School | | | | | | |
| Graduates | 40.7% | (10.8) | 48.1% | (8.9) | 41.6% | (10.4) |
| Median Education | | | | | | |
| (yrs.) | 10.7 | (1.1) | 11.4 | (8.9) | 11.0 | (2.1) |
| % Owner-Occupied | | | | | | |
| Dwelling Units | 54.9% | (15.1) | 57.3% | (13.6) | 54.6% | (13.7) |
| % White Collar | 44.1% | (9.0) | 48.1% | (7.1) | 44.2% | (7.6) |
| *Homogeneity:* | | | | | | |
| % Nonwhite | 10.6% | (11.5) | 11.6% | (10.8) | 16.5% | (14.9) |
| % Native with For- | | | | | | |
| eign Born or | | | | | | |
| Mixed Parentage | 19.7% | (9.9) | 12.4% | (8.3) | 11.7% | (10.7) |
| % Private School | | | | | | |
| Attendance | 23.5% | (11.9) | 15.3% | (11.8) | 16.6% | (11.8) |
| | N = 85 | | N = 90 | | N = 25 | |

| Independent Variable | Partisan | | Nonpartisan | |
|---|---|---|---|---|
| | | ELECTION TYPE | | |
| *Population:* | | | | |
| Population (10³) | 270.8 | (1022.1) | 155.8 | (198.7) |
| % Population Increase 1950–1960 | 17.1 | (40.1) | 58.3% | (136.1) |
| *Class:* | | | | |
| Median Income | $5996 | (904.5) | $6074 | (1045.5) |
| % Under $3000 | 16.8% | (7.1) | 17.2% | (7.2) |
| % Over $10,000 | 16.1% | (6.1) | 16.7% | (7.0) |
| % High School Graduates | 40.5% | (9.2) | 45.3% | (10.6) |
| Median Education (yrs.) | 10.6 | (1.1) | 11.2 | (1.2) |
| % Owner-Occupied Dwelling Units | 51.5% | (14.4) | 57.7% | (13.8) |
| % White Collar | 43.5% | (7.5) | 46.7% | (8.3) |
| *Homogeneity:* | | | | |
| % Nonwhite | 13.0% | (11.9) | 11.5% | (11.8) |
| % Native with Foreign Born or | | | | |
| Mixed Parentage | 17.5% | (10.7) | 14.7% | (9.6) |
| % Private School Attendance | 24.1% | (13.6) | 16.9% | (11.3) |
| | N = 57 | | N = 143 | |

| Independent Variable | CONSTITUENCY TYPE | | | |
| --- | --- | --- | --- | --- |
| | District | | At-Large | |
| *Population:* | | | | |
| Population ($10^3$) | 246.9 | (909.8) | 153.6 | (191.2) |
| % Population Increase 1950–1960 | 23.1% | (36.4) | 59.1% | (143.7) |
| *Class:* | | | | |
| Median Income | $6297 | (965.2) | $5942 | (1031.9) |
| % Under $3000 | 14.7% | (6.5) | 18.2% | (7.6) |
| % Over $10,000 | 17.7% | (7.1) | 16.0% | (6.6) |
| % High School Graduates | 43.6% | (10.9) | 44.4% | (10.4) |
| Median Education (yrs.) | 10.9 | (1.1) | 11.2 | (1.2) |
| % Owner-Occupied Dwelling Units | 55.1% | (14.4) | 56.9% | (14.5) |
| % White Collar | 45.2% | (9.4) | 46.3% | (7.5) |
| *Homogeneity:* | | | | |
| % Nonwhite | 9.8% | (10.6) | 13.0% | (12.3) |
| % Native with Foreign Born or Mixed Parentage | 18.9% | (9.4) | 13.4% | (9.7) |
| % Private School Attendance | 23.2% | (12.5) | 16.6% | (11.7) |
| | N = 73 | | N = 127 | |

Dixon drew a famous line, but because the "composition of its population" differs from the rest of the country.

It is therefore difficult to unravel the meaning of "controlling" for "region" since regions are differentiated on precisely the kinds of demographic variables which we (and Wolfinger and Field) related to reformism. Cities in the Midwest, for example, have a much higher proportion of home ownership (64%) than cities in the Northeast (44%), while northeastern cities have more foreign stock in their population (27%) than the Midwest (16%). Hence, to relate ethnicity to political reformism and then to "control" for "region" is in part to relate ethnicity to reformism and then to control for ethnicity. Consequently, we have grave reservations that the substitution of the gross and unrefined variable of "region" for more refined demographic data adds much to our knowledge of American cities. "Controlling" for "region" is much more than controlling for historical experiences, because region as a variable is an undifferentiated *potpourri* of socio-economic, attitudinal, historical and cultural variations.[25]

We also differ with Wolfinger and Field in their assertion that their analysis constitutes a test of the ethos theory. As we understand it,

---

[25] In statistical parlance, the problem with "region" as an independent variable might be described as treating a complicated background variable as the first variable in a specific developmental sequence. But, as Blalock argues, "... *one should avoid complex indicators that are related in unknown ways to a given underlying variable*. Geographical region and certain background variables appear to have such undesirable properties": Hubert M. Blalock, *Causal Inferences in Nonexperimental Research* (Chapel Hill: University of North Carolina Press, 1964), p. 164 (italics in original).

Banfield and Wilson's theory posits that particular attitudes are held by persons with varying sociological characteristics (ethnic groups and middle class persons, in particular) and that these attitudes include preferences for one or another kind of political institution. But relating the proportion of middle class persons in a city's population to its form of government says nothing one way or another about middle class preferences. An important part of understanding, of course, is describing and it is certainly useful to know how reformed cities differ from unreformed cities.

In our view, however, such tests as Wolfinger and Field used cannot logically be called explanations, in any causal sense. The most obvious reason is that they violate some important assumptions about time—order: independent variables are measured with contemporary census data, which the dependent variables are results of decisions made ten to fifty years ago. Moreover, this problem is multiplied by the difficulty of inferring configurations of political power from demographic data. Presumably, their assumption is that there is a simple linear relationship between sheer numbers (or proportions) of, say, middle class persons and their political power: the larger the size of a group in the city's population, the easier it can enforce its choice of political forms. At least one prominent urban sociologist, however, has found empirical support for precisely the opposite proposition. Hawley concluded that the smaller the proportion of middle class persons in a city, the greater their power over urban renewal policies.[26] Similarly, it may also be dubious to assume that the size of an ethnic population is an accurate indicator of influence of ethnic groups. Although we recognize the importance of describing the socio-economic correlates of political forms, the logical problems involved suggest the need for a good deal of caution in interpreting these differences as explanations.[27]

In any case, the question of why the city adopts particular structures is of less interest to us than their consequences for public policy. It is to this analysis that we now turn.

## Policy Outputs and the Responsiveness of Cities

We are now in a position to take three additional steps. First, we can compare the differences in policy outputs between reformed and

---

[26] Amos Hawley, "Community Power and Urban Renewal Success," *American Journal of Sociology*, 68 (January, 1963), 422–431.

[27] See also the exchange between Banfield and Wilson and Wolfinger and Field in "Communications," this REVIEW, 60 (December, 1966), 998–1000.

unreformed cities. Second, we can assess the cumulative impact of socio-economic variables on these policy choices. Finally, we can specify what variables are related in what ways to these output variables. In essence, we can now treat political institutions, not as dependent variables, but as factors which influence the *level* of expenditures and taxation and the *relationship* between cleavage variables and these outputs.

## Differences Between Reformed and Unreformed Cities' Outputs

Contrary to Sherbenou's conclusions about Chicago suburbs,[28] our data indicate that reformed cities both spend and tax less than unreformed cities, with the exception of expenditures in partisan and nonpartisan cities. It appears that partisan, mayor-council and ward cities are less willing to commit their resources to public purposes than their reformed counterparts. What is of more importance than the difference in outputs, however, is the relative responsiveness of the two kinds of cities to social cleavages in their population.

## The Responsiveness of Cities

We have argued that one principal goal of the reform movement was to reduce the impact of partisan, socio-economic cleavages on governmental decision-making, to immunize city governments from "artificial" social cleavages—race, religion, ethnicity, and so on. As Banfield and Wilson put their argument, the reformers "assumed that there existed an interest ('the public interest') that pertained to the city 'as a whole' and that should always prevail over competing, partial (and usually private) interests." [29] The structural reforms of manager government, at-large, and nonpartisan elections would so insulate the business of governing from social cleavages that "private regarding" interests would count for little in making up the mind of the body politic. But amid the calls of the reformers for structural reforms to muffle the impact of socio-economic cleavages, a few hardy souls predicted precisely the opposite consequence of reform: instead of eliminating cleavages from political decision-making, the reforms, particularly the elimination of parties, would enhance the conflict. Nathan Matthews, Jr., a turn-of-the-century mayor of Boston, issued just such a warning:

> As a city is a political institution, the people in the end will divide into parties, and it would seem extremely doubtful whether the present system, however illogical its foundation be, does not in fact produce better

---

[28] Sherbenou, *op. cit.,* pp. 133–134.
[29] *Op. cit.,* p. 139.

results, at least in large cities, than if the voters divided into groups, separated by property, social or religious grounds.[30]

Matthews recognized implicitly what political scientists would now call the "interest aggregation" function of political parties.[31] Parties in a democracy manage conflict, structure it, and encapsulate social cleavages under the rubric of two or more broad social cleavages, the parties themselves. "Parties tend to crystallize opinion, they give skeletal articulation to a shapeless and jelly-like mass . . . they cause similar opinions to coagulate . . ." [32] The parties "reduce effectively the number of political opinions to manageable numbers, bring order and focus to the political struggle, simplify issues and frame alternatives, and compromise conflicting interests." [33] Since parties are the agencies of interest aggregation, so the argument goes, their elimination makes for greater, not lesser, impact of social cleavages on political decisions.

**TABLE 3**

MEAN VALUES OF TAX/INCOME AND EXPENDITURE/INCOME
RATIOS, BY STRUCTURAL CHARACTERISTICS

| Structural Variables | Taxes/ Income | Expenditures/ Income |
|---|---|---|
| *Election type:* | | |
| Partisan | .032 | .050 |
| Nonpartisan | .030 | .053 |
| *Government type:* | | |
| Mayor-Council | .037 | .058 |
| Manager | .024 | .045 |
| Commission | .031 | .057 |
| *Constituency type:* | | |
| Ward | .036 | .057 |
| At-large | .027 | .049 |

Political scientists have recently confirmed Matthews' fears, at least with regard to electoral behavior in partisan and nonpartisan elections. Evidence points to the increased impact of socio-economic cleavages on voting when a nonpartisan ballot is used than when the

---

[30] Quoted in Banfield and Wilson, *op. cit.*, p. 154.

[31] For a discussion of the concept of interest aggregation, see Gabriel Almond, "Introduction: A Functional Approach to Comparative Politics," in Gabriel Almond and James S. Coleman (eds.), *The Politics of Developing Areas* (Princeton: Princeton University Press, 1960), pp. 38–45.

[32] Maurice Duverger, *Political Parties* (New York: Science Editions, 1963), p. 378.

[33] Frank J. Sorauf, *Political Parties in the American System* (Boston: Little, Brown and Co., 1964), pp. 165–166.

**DIAGRAM 1**

*PROPORTION OF VARIATION EXPLAINED (R²) IN TAXATION POLICY WITH TWELVE SOCIO-ECONOMIC VARIABLES, BY INSTITUTIONAL CHARACTERISTICS* [a]

| Independent Variables | Structural Variables | Dependent Variable |
|---|---|---|
| | *Reformed Institution:* | |
| | Government: Commission | 62% |
| | Government: Council-Manager | 42% |
| | Election: Nonpartisan | 49% |
| | Constituency: At-Large | 49% |
| Twelve Socio-Economic | | Tax/Income Ratio |
| Variables | | |
| | *Unreformed Institution:* | |
| | Government: Mayor-Council | 52% |
| | Election: Partisan | 71% |
| | Constituency: Ward/Mixed | 59% |

[a] In the total sample, the twelve independent variables explained 52% of the variation in taxes.

**DIAGRAM 2**

*PROPORTION OF VARIATION EXPLAINED (R²) IN EXPENDITURE POLICY WITH TWELVE SOCIO-ECONOMIC VARIABLES, BY INSTITUTIONAL CHARACTERISTICS* [b]

| Independent Variables | Structural Variables | Dependent Variable |
|---|---|---|
| | *Reformed Institution:* | |
| | Government: Commission | 59% |
| | Government: Council-Manager | 30% |
| | Constituency: At-Large | 36% |
| | Elections: Nonpartisan | 41% |
| Twelve Socio-Economic | | Expenditure/Income |
| Variables | | Ratio |
| | *Unreformed Institution:* | |
| | Government: Mayor-Council | 42% |
| | Constituency: Ward/Mixed | 49% |
| | Elections: Partisan | 59% |

[b] In the total sample the twelve independent variables explained 36% of the variation in expenditures.

election is formally partisan. Gerald Pomper studied nonpartisan municipal elections and compared them with partisan elections for the New Jersey State Assembly in Newark. He concluded that the "goal of nonpartisanship is fulfilled, as party identification does not determine the outcome. In place of party, ethnic affiliation is emphasized and the result is 'to enhance the effect of basic social cleavages.' " [34] If (1) this

[34] Gerald Pomper, "Ethnic and Group Voting in Nonpartisan Municipal Elections," *Public Opinion Quarterly*, 30 (Spring, 1966), p. 90; see also, J. Leiper Freeman, "Local Party Systems: Theoretical Considerations and a Case Analysis," *American Journal of Sociology*, 64 (1958), 282–289.

is typical of other American cities and if (2) electoral cleavages can be translated effectively into demands on the government in the absence of aggregative parties, then we might assume that the reformed institutions would reflect cleavages more, rather than less, closely than unreformed ones.

Essentially, then, there are two contrasting views about the consequences of municipal reform. One, the reformers' ideal, holds that institutional reforms will mitigate the impact of social cleavages on public policy. The other argues that the elimination of political parties and the introduction of other reforms will make social cleavages more, rather than less, important in political decision-making.

## The Measurement of Responsiveness

We have hypothesized that socio-economic cleavages will have less impact on the policy choices of reformed than unreformed governments. Thus, one could do a better job of predicting a city's taxation and expenditure policy using socio-economic variables in partisan, mayor and ward cities than in nonpartisan, manager and at-large cities. Operationally, we will test this hypothesis by using multiple correlation coefficients. Squaring these coefficients, called "multiple R's," will give us a summary measure of the total amount of variation in our dependent variables explained by our twelve independent variables.[35] The results of the correlation analysis are summarized in Diagrams 1 and 2.

On the whole, the results of the correlation analysis strikingly support the hypothesis, with the exception of commission cities. Thus, we can say, for example, that our twelve socio-economic variables explain 71 per cent of the variations in taxation policy in partisan cities, and 49 per cent of the variation in nonpartisan cities. In commission cities, however, socio-economic variables predict substantially more variation in both taxes and expenditures than in the unreformed mayor-council cities.[36] The anomaly of commission governments is

---

[35] It is possible that the difference between two correlations may be a function of very different standard deviations of the independent variables. A quick look at Table 2, however, suggests that this is not likely to affect the relationships we find.

[36] Wolfinger and Field, op. cit., p. 312, ". . . omit the commission cities from consideration since this form does not figure in the ethos theory." Historically, however, commission government was the earliest of the structures advocated by the Progressives and is quite clearly a product of the reform era. While history tells us that commission cities can not legitimately be excluded from the fold of reformism, they appear to be its black sheep, characterized by low incomes, low population growth and large proportions of nonwhites. In fact, they present a marked contrast to both mayor-council and manager cities.

interesting, for they present, as we will see, marked exceptions to virtually every pattern of relationships we found. The substantial explanatory power of these socio-economic variables is not altered, but confirmed, by examining the variables independently. The rest of the correlations show a consistent pattern: reformed cities are less responsive to cleavages in their population than unreformed cities.

If one of the premises of the "political ethos" argument is that reformed institutions give less weight to the "private regarding" and "artificial" cleavages in the population, that premise receives striking support from our analysis. Our data suggest that when a city adopts reformed structures, it comes to be governed less on the basis of conflict and more on the basis of the rationalistic theory of administration. The making of public policy takes less count of the enduring differences between White and Negro, business and labor, Pole and WASP. The logic of the bureaucratic ethic demands an impersonal, apolitical settlement of issues, rather than the settlement of conflict in the arena of political battle.

## To Spend or Not to Spend

If efforts to expand or contract the scope of government stand at the core of municipal political life,[37] they are nowhere better reflected than in the taxation and expenditure patterns of cities. A generation ago, Charles Beard wrote, "In the purposes for which appropriations are made the policies of the city government are given concrete form—the culture of the city is reflected. Indeed, the history of urban civilization could be written in terms of appropriations, for they show what the citizens think is worth doing and worth paying for." [38] Pressures to expand and contract government regulations and services are almost always reflected one way or another in the municipal budget. Labor, ethnic groups, the poor and the liberal community may press for additional services and these must be paid for; the business community may demand municipal efforts to obtain new industry by paring city costs to create a "favorable business climate"; or businessmen may themelves demand municipal services for new or old business. In any case, few political conflicts arise which do not involve some conflict over the budget structure.

---

[37] Agger *et al.*, *op. cit.*, pp. 4–14.

[38] Charles A. Beard, *American Government and Politics* (New York: Macmillan, 1924, 4th edition), p. 727.

## Class Variables and Public Policies

Part of the political rhetoric associated with the demand for a decrease in the scope of the national government is the argument that the initiative for policy-making should rest more with the state and local governments. Opposition to high federal spending levels, as V. O. Key has demonstrated, is found more often among persons with middle class occupations than among the blue-collar workers.[39] It is not inconceivable that the middle class argument about state and local responsibility might be more than political rhetoric, and that at the local level, middle class voters are willing to undertake major programs of municipal services requiring large outlays of public capital. Wilson and Banfield have argued that the "public regarding" upper-middle class voters in metropolitan areas are often found voting for public policies at variance with their "self-interest narrowly conceived," and that "the higher the income of a ward or town, the more taste it has for public expenditures of various kinds." [40] Similarly a longitudinal study of voting patterns in metropolitan Cleveland found that an index of social rank was positively correlated with favorable votes on welfare referenda.[41] If these data reflect middle class willingness to spend on a local level, they might indicate that the "states' rights" argument was more than ideological camouflage: middle class voters stand foursquare behind public expenditures at the local level even when they oppose those expenditures from the national government. Therefore, we hypothesized that:

2a] The more middle class the city, measured by income, education and occupation, the higher the municipal taxes and expenditures.

In line with our general concern of testing the impact of political structures on municipal policies, we also hypothesized that:

2b] Unreformed cities reflect this relationship more strongly than reformed cities.

With respect to hypothesis 2a, the data in Table 4 on three middle class indicators are unambiguous and indicate a strong rejection of the hypothesis. However we measure social class, whether by income, education or occupation, class measures are negatively related to public taxes and expenditures.

---

[39] V. O. Key, *Public Opinion and American Democracy* (New York: Alfred A. Knopf, 1961), p. 124.

[40] Wilson and Banfield, *op. cit.*, p. 876. Footnote 5 in the same article conveniently summarized research supporting this proposition.

[41] Eugene S. Uyeki, "Patterns of Voting in a Metropolitan Area: 1938–1962," *Urban Affairs Quarterly,* 1 (June, 1966), 65–77.

It is possible, however, that income does not have a linear, but rather a curvilinear relationship with municipal outputs. Banfield and Wilson argue that "In the city, it is useful to think in terms of three income groups—low, middle, and high. Surprising as it may seem to Marxists, the conflict is generally between an alliance of low-income and high-income groups on one side and the middle-income groups on the other." [42] If the relationships between income and expenditure is curvilinear, then we should expect to find that proportions of both low and high income groups were positively correlated with outputs. Our data, however, lend no support to this notion of a "pro-expenditure" alliance. Rather, the proportion of the population with incomes below $3000 is positively correlated with expenditures in all city types (although the relationships are small) and the proportion of the population in the above $10,000 bracket is negatively correlated with ex-

**TABLE 4**

CORRELATIONS BETWEEN MIDDLE CLASS CHARACTERISTICS AND
OUTPUTS IN REFORMED AND UNREFORMED CITIES

| | GOVERNMENT TYPE | | | ELECTION TYPE | | CONSTITUENCY TYPE | |
| Correlations of | Mayor-Council | Man-ager | Com-mission | Par-tisan | Non-Partisan | Ward | At-large |
|---|---|---|---|---|---|---|---|
| *Taxes* with: | | | | | | | |
| Median Income | −.13 | −.24 | −.19 | .03 | −.19 | −.17 | −.22 |
| White Collar | −.23 | −.12 | −.62 | −.21 | −.33 | −.30 | −.32 |
| Median Education | −.36 | −.22 | −.08 | −.45 | −.24 | −.48 | −.18 |
| *Expenditures* with: | | | | | | | |
| Median Income | −.19 | −.32 | −.43 | −.04 | −.32 | −.23 | −.34 |
| White Collar | −.24 | −.23 | −.58 | −.18 | −.39 | −.32 | −.35 |
| Median Education | −.32 | −.36 | −.26 | −.36 | −.38 | −.44 | −.32 |

penditures. Summing the two measures and correlating the combined measure with outputs produced no correlation greater than .15 and the relationships were as likely to be negative as positive. Tests for nonlinearity also suggested that no such coalition exists in the cities in our analysis.

To be sure, aggregate data analysis using whole cities as units of analysis is no substitute for systematic survey data on middle class attitudes, but it is apparent that cities with larger middle class population have lower, not higher expenditures. As we emphasized earlier, the "ethos theory" deals with attitudes and the behavior of individuals, while our data deal with cities and their behavior. The coalition sug-

---

[42] Banfield and Wilson, *op. cit.,* p. 35.

gested by Banfield and Wilson, however, is not discernible at this level of aggregation in these cities.

Hypothesis 2b is not consistently borne out by the data. In fact, the relationships between middle class variables and outputs are, if anything, stronger in the reformed cities than in their unreformed counterparts. One would not want to make too much of the data, but a large body of literature on city politics, which we discuss below, suggests that reformed institutions maximize the power of the middle class.

We originally assumed that the proportion of owner-occupied dwelling units constituted another measure of middle class composition, but it soon became apparent that it was only weakly related to income, occupation and education measures. Nevertheless, it emerged as the strongest single predictor of both expenditure and taxation policy in our cities. We hypothesized that:

3a] Owner-occupancy and outputs are negatively correlated, and

3b] Unreformed cities reflect this relationship more strongly than reformed cities.

Hypothesis 3a is consistently borne out in the data presented in Table 5. These relationships were only slightly attenuated when we controlled for income, education and occupation. No doubt self-interest (perhaps "private regardingness") on the part of the home owner, whose property is intimately related to the tax structure of most local governments, may account for part of this relationship. Moreover, home ownership is correlated (almost by definition) with lower urban

**TABLE 5**

CORRELATIONS BETWEEN OWNER OCCUPANCY AND GOVERNMENT
OUTPUTS IN REFORMED AND UNREFORMED CITIES

| Correlations of Owner Occupancy with: | GOVERNMENT TYPE | | | ELECTION TYPE | | CONSTITUENCY TYPE | |
|---|---|---|---|---|---|---|---|
| | Mayor-Council | Man-ager | Com-mission | Par-tisan | Non-Partisan | Ward | At-large |
| Taxes | −.57 | −.31 | −.73 | −.64 | −.45 | −.56 | −.48 |
| Expenditures | −.51 | −.23 | −.62 | −.62 | −.40 | −.50 | −.40 |

population density. High density, bringing together all manner of men into the classic urban mosaic, may be itself correlated with factors which produce demands for higher expenditures—slums, increased needs for fire and police protection, and so on.

In confirmation of hypothesis 3a, the unmistakable pattern is for unreformed cities to reflect these negative relationships more strongly than the manager, nonpartisan and at-large cities, although commission cities show their usual remarkably high correlations.

## Homogeneity Variable and Public Policies

Dawson and Robinson, in their analysis of state welfare expenditures, found strong positive relationships between the ethnicity of a state's population and the level of its welfare expenditures.[43] If this is symptomatic of a generalized association of ethnic and religious minorities with higher expenditures, we might find support for the hypothesis that:

4a] The larger proportion of religious and ethnic minorities in the population, the higher the city's taxes and expenditures.

And, if our general hypothesis about the impact of political institutions is correct, then:

4b] Unreformed cities reflect this relationship more strongly than reformed cities.

The correlations between ethnicity, religious heterogeneity and outputs (see Table 6) are, with one exception, positive, as predicted

### TABLE 6

CORRELATIONS BETWEEN ETHNICITY AND RELIGIOUS HETEROGENEITY
AND OUTPUTS IN REFORMED AND UNREFORMED CITIES

| Correlations of | GOVERNMENT TYPE | | | ELECTION TYPE | | CONSTITUENCY TYPE | |
| | Mayor-Council | Man-ager | Com-mission | Par-tisan | Non-Partisan | Ward | At-large |
|---|---|---|---|---|---|---|---|
| *Taxes* with: | | | | | | | |
| Ethnicity | .49 | .26 | .57 | .61 | .43 | .56 | .40 |
| Private School Attendance | .38 | .15 | .37 | .33 | .37 | .41 | .25 |
| *Expenditures* with: | | | | | | | |
| Ethnicity | .36 | .02 | .21 | .48 | .21 | .44 | .13 |
| Private School Attendance | .34 | −.01 | .07 | .25 | .24 | .40 | .05 |

by hypothesis 4a. These associations may reflect the substantial participation by ethnic groups in municipal politics long after the tide of immigration has been reduced to a trickle.[44] The relatively intense politici-

---

[43] Richard E. Dawson and James A. Robinson, "The Politics of Welfare," in Herbert Jacob and Kenneth Vines (eds.), *Politics in the American States* (Boston: Little, Brown and Co., 1965), pp. 398–401.

[44] Raymond Wolfinger, "The Development and Persistence of Ethnic Voting," this REVIEW, 59 (December, 1965), 896–908.

zation of ethnic groups at the local level,[45] the appeals to nationality groups through "ticket balancing" and other means, and the resultant higher turnout of ethnic groups than other lower status groups,[46] may produce an influence on city government far out of proportion to their number.

We found when we related all twelve of our independent variables to outputs in various city types that the associations were much weaker in cities we have labeled reformed. The correlations for ethnicity and religious homogeneity show a generally similar pattern, with commission cities exhibiting their usual erratic behavior. The data, then, show fairly clear support for hypothesis 4b.

The third variable of our homogeneity indicators—per cent of population non-white—had almost no relationship to variation in outputs, regardless of city type. We found the same weak correlations for the poverty income variable, which was, of course, strongly related to the racial variable. An easy explanation suggests that this is a consequence of the political impotence of Negroes and the poor, but one should be cautious in inferring a lack of power from the lack of a statistical association.

We have dealt in this section with factors which are positively and negatively related to spending patterns in American cities. While social class variables are associated negatively with outputs, two measures of homogeneity, private school attendance and ethnicity are related to higher taxes and spending. Examining the strengths of these correlations in cities with differing forms, we found some support for our general hypothesis about the political consequences of institutions, especially for the homogeneity variables and the home ownership variable. Interestingly, however, this was not the case with class variables.

## Reformism as a Continuous Variable

The central thrust of our argument has been that reformed governments differ from their unreformed counterparts in their responsiveness to socio-economic cleavages in the population. Logically, if the presence of one feature of the "good government" syndrome had the impact of reducing responsiveness, the introduction of additional reformed institutions should have an additive effect and further reduce the impact of cleavages on decision-making. We therefore decided to treat "reform-

---

[45] Robert E. Lane, *Political Life* (Glencoe, Ill.: The Free Press, 1959), pp. 236–243.

[46] *Ibid.*

ism" as a continuous variable for analytic purposes and hypothesized that:

5] The higher the level of reformism in a city, the lower its responsiveness to socio-economic cleavages in the population.

We utilized a simple four-point index to test this hypothesis, ranging from the "least reformed" to the "most reformed." The sample cities were categorized as follows:

1] Cities with none of the reformed institutions (i.e., the government is mayor-council, elections are partisan and constituencies are wards).

2] Cities with any one of the reformed institutions.

3] Cities with two of the reformed institutions.

4] Cities with three reformed institutions (i.e., the government is either manager or commission, elections are nonpartisan and constituencies are at-large).

We can not overemphasize the crudity of this index as an operationalization of the complex and abstract concept of "reformism." Nonetheless, we think some of the relationships we found are strongly suggestive that reformism may in reality be a continuous variable.

To test this hypothesis, we took four variables which had moderate-to-strong correlations with our dependent variables and computed simple correlations in each reform category. If our hypothesis is correct, the strength of the correlations in Table 7 should decrease regularly with an increase in reform scores. While there are some clear exceptions to the predicted pattern of relationships, there is some fairly consistent support for the hypothesis. Even when the decreases in the strengths of

**TABLE 7**

CORRELATIONS BETWEEN SELECTED INDEPENDENT VARIABLES
AND OUTPUT VARIABLES BY FOUR CATEGORIES OF REFORMISM

| Correlations of | REFORM SCORES | | | |
| --- | --- | --- | --- | --- |
| | *1* *(least reformed)* | *2* | *3* | *4* *(most reformed)* |
| *Taxes* with: | | | | |
| Ethnicity | .62 | .41 | .50 | .34 |
| Private School Attendance | .40 | .32 | .28 | .25 |
| Owner-Occupancy | −.70 | .39 | −.54 | −.44 |
| Median Education | −.55 | −.27 | −.32 | −.13 |
| *Expenditures* with: | | | | |
| Ethnicity | .51 | .27 | .41 | .05 |
| Private School Attendance | .46 | .23 | .16 | .08 |
| Owner-Occupancy | −.67 | −.30 | −.54 | −.38 |
| Median Education | −.49 | −.19 | −.38 | −.37 |

the correlations are irregular, there is a clear difference between cities which we have labeled "most reformed" and "least reformed."

Again, we would not want to attach too much importance to the results of this rough-and-ready index. But, the patterns support our previous argument about the impact of reformism: the more reformed the city, the less responsive it is to socio-economic cleavages in its political decision-making.

## A Causal Model and an Interpretation

*A Causal Model*

The implicit, or at times explicit, causal model in much of the research on municipal reformism has been a simple one: socio-economic cleavages cause the adoption of particular political forms. A more sophisticated model would include political institutions as one of the factors which produce a given output structure in city politics. We hypothesize that a causal model would include four classes of variables: socio-economic cleavages, political variables (including party registration, structure of party systems, patterns of aggregation, strength of interest groups, voter turnout, etc.), political institutions (forms of government, type of elections and types of constituencies), and political outputs. Diagram 3 depicts one possible causal model.

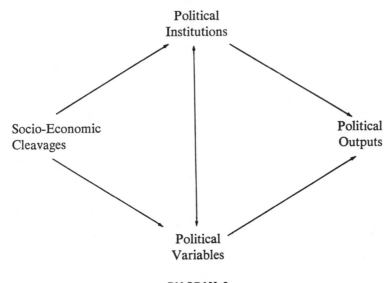

**DIAGRAM 3**

*A HYPOTHESIZED CAUSAL MODEL*

This study has of necessity been limited to exploring the linkages between socio-economic cleavages, political institutions and political outputs. We found that political institutions "filter" the process of converting inputs into outputs. Some structures, particularly partisan elections, ward constituencies, mayor-council governments and commission governments, operate to maximize the impact of cleavage indicators on public policies. We conclude by discussing some of the reasons why different structures have varying impacts on the conversion process.

## An Interpretation

Three principal conclusions may be derived from this analysis.

1. Cities with reformed and unreformed institutions are not markedly different in terms of demographic variables. Indeed, some variables, like income, ran counter to the popular hypothesis that reformed cities are havens of the middle class. Our data lent some support to the notion that reformed cities are more homogeneous in their ethnic and religious populations. Still, it is apparent that reformed cities are by no means free from the impact of these cleavages.

2. The more important difference between the two kinds of cities is in their behavior, rather than their demography. Using multiple correlation-coefficients, we were able to predict municipal outputs more exactly in unreformed than in reformed cities. The translation of social conflicts into public policy and the responsiveness of political systems to class, racial, and religious cleavages differs markedly with the kind of political structure. Thus, political institutions seem to play an important role in the political process—a role substantially independent of a city's demography.

3. Our analysis has also demonstrated that reformism may be viewed as a continuous variable and that the political structures of the reform syndrome have an additive effect: the greater the reformism, the lower the responsiveness.

Through these political institutions, the goal of the reformers has been substantially fulfilled, for nonpartisan elections, at-large constituencies and manager governments are associated with a lessened responsiveness of cities to the enduring conflicts of political life. Or, as Stone, Price and Stone argued in their study of changes produced by the adoption of manager governments, the council after the reform "tended to think more of the community as a whole and less of factional interests in making their decisions." [47]

---

[47] Harold Stone, Don K. Price and Kathryn Stone, *City Manager Government in the United States* (Chicago: Public Administration Service, 1940), p. 238.

The responsiveness of a political institution to political conflicts should not be confused with the "responsibility" of a political system as the latter term is used in the great debate over the relative "responsibility" of party systems.[48] In fact, the responsiveness of political forms to social cleavages may stand in sharp contrast to "responsible government" on the British model. Presumably, in American cities, partisan elections, ward constituencies, and mayor-council governments maximize minority rather than majority representation, assuring greater access to decision-makers than the reformed, bureaucratized and "depoliticized" administrations.

Partisan electoral systems, when combined with ward representation, increase the access of two kinds of minority groups: those which are residentially segregated, and which may as a consequence of the electoral system demand and obtain preferential consideration from their councilmen; and groups which constitute identifiable voting blocs to which parties and politicians may be beholden in the next election. The introduction of at-large, nonpartisan elections has at least five consequences for these groups. First, they remove an important cue-giving agency—the party—from the electoral scene, leaving the voter to make decisions less on the policy commitments (however vague) of the party, and more on irrelevancies such as ethnic identification and name familiarity.[49] Second, by removing the party from the ballot, the reforms eliminate the principal agency of interest aggregation from the political system. Hence, interests are articulated less clearly and are aggregated either by some other agency or not at all. Moreover, nonpartisanship has the effect of reducing the turnout in local elections by working class groups,[50] leaving officeholders freer from retaliation by these groups at the polls. Fourth, nonpartisanship may also serve to decrease the salience of "private regarding" demands by increasing the relative political power of "public regarding" agencies like the local press.[51] And when nonpartisanship is combined with election at-large,

---

[48] The standard argument for party responsibility is found in the works of E. E. Schattschneider, esp., *Party Government* (New York: Farrar and Rinehart, 1942) and in the report of the Committee on Political Parties of the American Political Science Association, *Toward a More Responsible Two-Party System* (New York: Rinehart, 1950).

[49] See Pomper, *op. cit.;* and Freeman, *op. cit.*

[50] Robert Salisbury and Gordon Black, "Class and Party in Partisan and Nonpartisan Elections: The Case of Des Moines," this REVIEW, 57 (September, 1963), 584–592.

[51] One newspaperman said of nonpartisan politics that "You can't tell the players without a scorecard, and we sell the scorecards": Banfield and Wilson, *op. cit.,* p. 157.

the impact of residentially segregated groups or groups which obtain their strength from voting as blocs in municipal elections is further reduced.[52] For these reasons, it is clear that political reforms may have a significant impact in minimizing the demands of private-regarding groups, the electoral institutions of reformed governments make public policy less responsive to the demands arising out of social conflicts in the population.

The structure of the government may serve further to modify the strength of minority groups over public policy. It is significant in this respect to note that commission governments, where social cleavages have the greatest impact on policy choices, are the most decentralized of the three governmental types and that manager governments are relatively the most centralized.[53] From the point of view of the reformer, commission government is a failure and their number has declined markedly in recent years.[54] This greater decentralization of commission and of mayor-council governments permits a multiplicity of access points for groups wishing to influence decision-makers.[55] It may also increase the possibilities for collaboration between groups and a bureaucratic agency, a relationship which has characterized administrative patterns in the federal government. As a result of this decentralization, group strength in local governments may be maximized.

It is important in any analysis of reformism to distinguish between the factors which produce the *adoption* of reformed institutions and the *impact* of the new political forms once they have been established. We can offer from out data no conclusions about the origins of reformed structures, for it is obviously impossible to impute causation, using contemporary census data, to events which occurred decades ago. Once a city has institutionalized the reformers' ideals, however, a diffused attitude structure may be less helpful in explaining the city's public policy than the characteristics of the institutions themselves. With the introduction of these reforms, a new political pattern may emerge in which disputes are settled outside the political system, or in which they may be settled by the crowd at the civic club at the periphery of the system.[56] If they do enter the political process, an impersonal, "non-po-

---

[52] Oliver P. Williams and Charles Adrian, *Four Cities* (Philadelphia: University of Pennsylvania Press, 1963), pp. 56–57.

[53] Alford and Scoble, *op. cit.,* p. 84.

[54] In our view, the failure of the commission government to achieve the intended reforms is more plausible as an explanation of its demise than its administrative unwieldiness—the conventional explanation.

[55] Williams and Adrian, *op. cit.,* pp. 30–31.

[56] Carol E. Thometz discusses the role of the "Civic Committee" in decision-making in Dallas: see *The Decision-Makers* (Dallas: Southern Methodist University Press, 1963).

litical" bureaucracy may take less account of the conflicting interests and pay more attention to the "correct" decision from the point of view of the municipal planner.

These conclusions are generally consistent with the ethos theory developed by Banfield and Wilson. If one of the components of the middle class reformer's ideal was "to seek the good of the community as a whole" and to minimize the impact of social cleavages on political decision-making, then their institutional reforms have served, by and large, to advance that goal.

# C. GOVERNING THE SUBURBS

## Republics in Miniature

### ROBERT C. WOOD

### The American Miniature

If a belief in small government and small society helps explain why the modern suburb exists in an age of bigness, the suburban renaissance should not be surprising. The conviction that provincial life is best has been with us for a long time and it has endured in the face of greater attacks than the ones contemporary America presents. We show our instinctive commitment to the ideology by the fact that we rarely examine its assumptions critically. We show our conscious allegiance by the oratorical homage we pay to the ideal of small neighborhoods, single homes, and political jurisdictions of limited size.

It is difficult to overestimate the vigor and pervasiveness of the belief. Three centuries stand behind the heritage—a full two hundred years of spectacular success and one hundred years of abject failure. The first period endowed the American cult of localism with its basic articles of faith: an assertion that local communities should maintain their own identity and manage their own affairs, and a justification for that assertion by the claim that the small society is the natural home of democracy. The last hundred years added endurance and stubbornness to the ideal by the very adversity which the reality of the urban world inflicted upon it. But whether made confident by success or contentious by disaster, the creed has remained to shape the American metropolis and make it what it is today.

Not the least of the reasons for the strength of the ideology is in its natural partiality to the American habitat. Grassroots life existed in fact in the United States long before the justification for its existence was ever articulated. The first settlements on the new continent were

Reprinted from *Suburbia: Its People and their Politics* (Boston: Houghton Mifflin, 1958), pp. 20–21, 66–69, 74–75, 83–87, by permission of the publisher.

by necessity small and relatively isolated, and the characteristics usually associated with small town life developed spontaneously. Colonial conditions led to a similarity of interests, and a sharing of customs, aims and ambitions. Some degree of economic inter-dependence and equality, a constant recognition of a vast unexplored land beyond the frontier outposts, close daily contact, bred early in conscious sense of community identity.

Under these social circumstances, nothing was more natural than the independence in fact, if not in legal theory, of local political institutions. Technically speaking, the first New England towns relied on grants of power from the Massachusetts Bay Company and later from the colonial legislature. Early settlements in the other colonies used the medieval corporation as the model for their authority. But in actual fact, colonial towns exercised independently the essential powers of police and taxation, and were, from the beginning, self-governing. They were independent because there was no other alternative; local authority stemmed from "the exercise of English common sense combined with the circumstance of the place."

## Crisis in Autonomy

The nostalgic image found a new frame then, in suburbia, and its popularity justified suburban independence. Faith in the ideology discouraged the creation of new political institutions to serve the entire metropolitan area and provided an appealing rationale for the preservation of local town halls and county court houses. It served to crystallize the new region into hundreds of small communities, each more or less conscious of its own identity.

But was suburbia a legitimate recipient of the legacy? Did it offer a genuine renaissance or only a pale counterfeit of the real article? The suburb, after all, was not an early New England town, a southern market center, or a western trading village. The United States was no longer rural, but urban and industrial, and destined to become more so. The pattern of large-scale organization, the values of togetherness, the political philosophy of positive government, all penetrated suburbia, made it something more and less than a replica of earlier times. There was an economic interdependence of the region as a whole, a new pattern of social intercourse throughout the area, and these developments had both direct and subtle influences on the reinvigorated jurisdictions. In the short run at least, the immediate answer to the question as to whether or not the suburb was the carrier of the grassroots faith depended upon the success of the local governments in maintaining their autonomy. If they went under and were absorbed by the metropolis, then no amount of imagery could re-establish the small community in its essential form.

In the beginning, this issue of genuineness and the critical role of suburban independence was scarcely recognized. The new environment was overlooked, and men took at face value the revival of the small-scale jurisdictions surrounding the large cities and the apparent renaissance of independent, healthy community life after one hundred years of somnolence. The issue in municipal reform throughout the last half of the nineteenth century had been so much the question of size—how to reduce urban congestion or manage it in accordance with historic values—and the solutions had been so tentative that its seemingly automatic resolution was accepted with delight, and with little critical examination.

For those who had emphasized the necessity of breaking up the mammoth city to guarantee a satisfactory local government, the suburb was an intimation of dreams about to come true. More pleasing still, their aspirations were turning into reality quite naturally, without the tremendous political and educational efforts that Geddes and Howard thought necessary. Writing at the turn of the century, Adna Weber could view the development of suburban towns even then as "the most encouraging feature of the whole situation." "The rise of the suburbs," he wrote, "is what furnishes the solid basis of a hope that the evils of city life, so far as they result from overcrowding, may be in large part removed . . . It will realize the wish and prediction of Kingsley, 'a complete interpenetration of city and country, a complete fusion of their different modes of life and a combination of the advantages of both, such as no country in the world has ever seen.' " And twenty-five years later, Harlan Douglass could speak of the suburban evangel, and after a biting indictment of the city, look to a new motivation for life in the satellite town of open land and cottage home. He could confidently predict, "A crowded world must be either suburban or savage." For the first planners, the trend was nothing awesome, but a movement devoutly prayed for and constantly encouraged.

Even the more pragmatic municipal reformers, those who believed they had solved the problem of size by political and administrative adjustments, never claimed that their program of reform was superior to the genuine article. Proportional representation, nonpartisanship, the short ballot, the small council had been offered as substitutes in a large city for the direct self-government possible in smaller places. Certainly these experts felt that the suburbs could profit by employing a city manager and business methods of organization and administration, but they did not believe that the suburban trend was contradicting their own efforts. Instead it appeared to reduce the size of their job, for now they could concentrate on the central cities of the metropolitan areas, secure in the knowledge that the surrounding towns could take care of themselves.

Of course, a nagging doubt as to what was happening to the metropolitan region as a whole tugged at the National Municipal League's conscience, and metropolitan problems were discussed spasmodically at annual meetings from 1917 to 1925. But the League did not publish its first report on the government of metropolitan areas until 1930, and although the study was hailed as "the first comprehensive survey of its kind," it arrived at no specific recommendations. Indeed, its conclusions were regarded as "so general in their scope that it is virtually impossible to disagree with them—a sure sign that they have little value." The perfection of the structural and procedural mechanisms of reform continued to hold the center of the stage, and though there were hints that suburbia might cause trouble, they received low priority on the agenda.

So the trend intensified, and far from vanishing, the number of governmental units within each metropolitan area multiplied at an astonishing rate. In 1900, the New York region had 127 minor civil divisions, by 1920, 204; in Cook County (Chicago) there were 55 in 1890 and 109 in 1920; around Pittsburgh, 107 units existed in 1920 where thirty years earlier only 91 were formally incorporated. For the seventeen largest cities, incorporations of new governments around the fringe of the city went on and on—most rapidly at the turn of the century, but steadily for the next fifty years. Between 1952 and 1957 alone, 170 new municipalities came into being in metropolitan areas and 519 new special districts were created. By 1957, there were over 3000 governments that could be said to possess more or less general municipal powers, and there was, of course, that awesome figure of 15,658 legally distinguishable local units. Village, hamlet, school district, city, county, town, they were each one equipped with the legal prerogatives of government, each claiming to speak for a separate constituency. They jostled one another in the crowded confines of the metropolitan backyard, jealous of their authority and suspicious of their neighbors.

From the organizational as well as the financial point of view then, the failure of the city to expand concurrently with the growing urban area seemed disastrous. The "crazy quilt hodge podge of local governmental agencies" could appear to H. G. Wells as far back as 1910, "like fifteenth century houses which have been continuously occupied by a succession of enterprising but short-sighted and close-fisted owners, and which have now been, with the very slightest use of lath and plaster partitions and geyser hot-water apparatus, converted into modern residential flats." To Victor Jones, thirty years later, the problem of metropolitan government remained much the same: "The need for servicing a large population scattered under the jurisdiction of many units of local government, most of which are crippled by limited powers over a restricted area, by inadequate tax resources and by such consequences of premature subdivision as heavy indebtedness and existence tax areas." And Betty Tableman, writing in 1951, insisted indignantly that "no governmental unit is an island. Sins of omission and commission of any one municipality affect not only its own citizens but all persons living in the metropolitan area." Criminals were escaping because no police jurisdiction had effective control; fires raged while unused equipment lay idle across artificial boundaries; sewage dumped in a river by one government contaminated the neighboring jurisdiction's lake; master highway plans could not be completed on an area-wide basis. The urban center was no longer, in Luther Gulick's words, "floating around in a great and green rural hinterland." Rather, "it is now elbow to elbow with other paved urban centers."

Suburbia was not, then, to slip smoothly into the modern world, as its first supporters had fondly imagined. It was causing trouble, real trouble, for the metropolis of which it was a part. The first tenet of its political ideology—independence for each locality—no longer had an economic or social base, and the justification for autonomy apparently collapsed. A collection of small governments, without financial self-sufficiency and some spatial isolation from each other, made for ineffective political structures, and the principle of autonomy no longer went hand in hand with its companion doctrine—democracy—to justify these small-scale reconstructions of an earlier culture. The two doctrines were turned against each other, and the close democracy a suburb promised almost guaranteed ineffective government for the region as a whole. The threat to American localism was not from Washington or the state capitals; the creed was doing itself in and its greatest virtue had been subverted into its greatest vice.

### Suburbia Triumphant

Annexation, consolidation, merger, country- city separation—suburbia considered all of them and concluded usually that it wanted none of them. It preferred legal autonomy and small town politics above all, and it continued to expand. The New York region by 1954 boasted 1071 separate jurisdictions; Chicago, 960; Philadelphia, 702; St. Louis, 420; until, all in all, 14 per cent of all local governments in the United States were in metropolitan areas. Against all appeals that this multiplicity fostered political irresponsibility and defeated "both the theory of popular control and the government's ability to provide services," the suburbs were adamant. They knew that what reform actually entailed was a reunion, at least in part, with the central city and its corrupt politics, its slums, immigrants, criminals, and the vicious elements from which they had only recently escaped. The reformers had demonstrated the expense of maintaining this isolation, but to most suburbanites, the figures merely proved that the price of liberty was always high.

In only one way did the suburbs adjust to modernity. When obvious breakdowns appeared in basic public utilities, metropolitan-wide institutions were permitted, so long as they were not governments. Public corporations, authorities, special districts were popular with suburbanites; they were self-supporting and businesslike in form. They were allowed to assume the money-making activities of local government—the building and operation of bridges, tunnels, terminals, and airports—and because they were run by state-appointed commissioners, aloof from the undignified ordeal of vote-getting, they were acceptable. By that curious *non sequitur* so appealing to Americans—that the authorities had "taken government out of politics"—the suburbs reasoned they had nothing to fear. These institutions could not be threats because they were not governments.

Thus the only way in which big organizations entered local government was by masquerade. The metropolitan agencies now at work are in the form of *ad hoc* special districts, in highways, sanitation, airports, mosquito control, water, garbage collection, hospitals, almost every conceivable local activity. The New York Port Authority, the Boston Metropolitan District Commission, the transit authorities, the Golden Gate Bridge and Highway District, these have been the novelties permitted. No period in American history saw more inventions in forms of pseudo government than the decades between 1920 and 1950, when the baffling array of "non-political" boards, commissions, and agencies sprang up across the country.

They were, of course, pseudo governments. Victor Jones was quite right when he wrote that their lack of direct accountability and numerical addition to the local governments already in existence "confuses the citizens and voters and makes it difficult to secure responsible local government in large urban communities." But the suburbs were satisfied; if the small town could not carry out a local function, then it was better to remove the program from government entirely. Grassroots democracy or big business—no other vehicle is trustworthy in the United States.

There was stubborn resistance, however, to all proposals for genuine government. The answer could be found in the words of Arthur E.

Morgan about Great Neck, Long Island, in the twenties: "All the people in that area moved in about the same time. They were young married couples with one or two children . . . the men have a volunteer fire department and have recently built a beautiful fire house which is equipped for recreational purposes as well . . . The women very often do the shopping cooperatively. If anyone is ill, everyone will do her bit to help . . . The church is a community church. The minister is young and has done much for all ages. A social is held once a month for the married couples. There are frequent dances for the young people. It seems that something is going on every week." Or it could come in the forthright declaration of the resident of Tarrytown that "I would feel that I had surrendered some of my manhood if I gave to the politicians in White Plains the legal right to control in the slightest degree the education of my children."

However presented, the suburban choice in the twentieth century had been to retain the form of government most closely resembling Jefferson's legacy—a choice, moreover, made in defiance of the compelling values of the modern world: large-scale organization, efficiency, economy and rationalization. Fortuitously supported by two decades of prosperity, the suburbanite has been able to brush aside the specter of municipal bankruptcy, ignore the obviously illusory nature of his legal autonomy, and retain his independent community. The nation's wealth for the moment supports his idol, and the Great Society, at least in the political sense, is excluded from his hearth and home.

This overwhelming victory implies, of course, some serious weaknesses in the doctrines of metropolitan reform. One tactical error seems clear immediately: for all their energy and ingenuity, for all their battle cries of annexation, merger and federation, the reformers have mounted only a limited offensive. They have challenged the feasibility of small government and small communities in the twentieth century, but they have never seriously questioned the desirability of small government whenever it can possibly be sustained. In the end, the reformers have offered only an alternative program for better metropolitan financial and administrative management; they have never promised a better brand of politics.

This reluctance to launch a full-scale attack on the ideology as well as the practicality of small government diminishes the prospects for reform's success. It allows the suburb the heroic role of defender of democracy, even though it remains the villain in the melodrama of metropolitan development. Thus the suburb possesses an almost impenetrable line of defense, for what citizen, faced with a choice of an ineffective government democratically controlled or an effective government less democratically controlled, will not wrap himself in high moral principle and choose the first?

By refusing to challenge the grassroots faith itself, reformers are forced back to a single argument: that the suburban claim to the status of a small community is necessarily counterfeit. Yet, even here, taking their stand as hard-bitten realists, they are on weak ground. They assume that the loss of financial self-sufficiency among suburban governments and the end of social isolation means inevitably the collapse of small town life and consciousness. On this assumption reformers conclude that the suburban commitment to the colonial legacy must be, of necessity, illusionary. And, on this assumption, they have constructed the best alternative structure they can devise in the belief that some day suburbanites will realize that their allegiance is nostalgia, a commitment to a shadow world which existed only in the past.

But it is a serious mistake to believe that an ideology simply reflects the social and political organization in a particular period of history, lingering for a while, but ultimately giving way to an expression of a new reality. When they are powerful enough, ideologies may shape—as well as mirror—the world about them. This fact metropolitan reformers are discovering today, for it is not the simple memory of the heritage which thwarts their efforts. It is the power of that heritage as a very real expression of the aspirations and values of the present generation which blocks the progress of reform.

In the final analysis, Wells and Mumford, as the early discoverers of the organization man, never challenged the suburban evangel to any real effect for a good reason: the more closely suburbs are studied, the more genuine their claim to provinciality appears. In many essential qualities many suburbs seem like the American small towns of the past, much more impervious to modern life than is commonly supposed.

# D. URBAN POWER STRUCTURES: ELITE AND PLURALIST MODELS

## The Structure of Power in Regional City

### FLOYD HUNTER

One of the first tasks in making a theoretical analysis of the community is that of delimiting and defining it as a structure.[1] The task of delimitation may take into account four basic elements, namely (1) personnel (members), (2) test(s) of admission and membership, (3) distinctive roles or functions of the members, and (4) norms regulating the conduct of the personnel.[2] The physical limits of the structure with which this study is concerned have been set, or at least an awareness of such limits has been indicated. We shall presently be concerned with all of the elements suggested here, and most particularly with the first three, but only in relation to a segment of the community—the power element. The fourth item, norms regulating conduct within the community of Regional City, presents problems with which the present study does not deal, except in a passing fashion. All of the norms of behavior of power personnel in Regional City are not known, but some specifications of men which may indicate norms will be outlined.

The personnel with which the current discussion is concerned represents but a minute fraction of the community in which it moves and functions. It does represent a definite group, however, and a very important one in Regional City. No pretense is made that the group to be discussed represents the totality of power leaders of the community, but it is felt that a representative case sample is presented, and that the men described come well within the range of the center of power in the community.

Reprinted from *Community Power Structure* (Chapel Hill: University of North Carolina Press, 1953), pp. 60–63, 82–95, 113, by permission of the publisher.

[1] E. T. Hiller, "The Community as a Social Group," *American Sociological Review*, VI (April 1941), 191–92.

[2] *Ibid.*, p. 189.

The leaders selected for study were secured from lists of leading civic, professional, and fraternal organizations, governmental personnel, business leaders, and "society" and "wealth" personnel suggested by various sources. These lists of more than 175 persons were rated by "judges" who selected by mutual choice the top forty persons in the total listings. These forty were the object of study and investigation in Regional City. Some data were collected about the total number. Twenty-seven members of the group were interviewed on the basis of a prepared schedule plus additional questions as the investigation proceeded. Any figures used in the study will need to be tied fairly rigidly to the twenty-seven members on whom there are comparable data. Thirty-four Negro citizens are included in the study, and this group will be discussed later. The fourteen under-structure professionals in civic and social work who were interviewed have also provided data which may be considered comparable.

The top leaders, the under-structure professionals, and the Negro community leaders represent community groups. They are identifiable groups. Since they are definitely groups, I shall rely to a considerable extent, in this portion of the discussion, upon George C. Homans for certain hypotheses he has put forward on group structure.[3]

The system of power groups which is being examined may not be called a closed system. The groups are links in a total pattern, which may offer suggestive clues to total power patterns in the operating system of Regional City. There are gaps in the power arc which investigation may not be able to close. Actually the discussion here is primarily concerned with the structuring of power on a policy-making level. Only a rudimentary "power pyramid" of Regional City will be presented. One may be content to do this because I doubt seriously that power forms a single pyramid with any nicety in a community the size of Regional City. There are *pyramids* of power in this community which seem more important to the present discussion than *a* pyramid. Let me illustrate this point.

In the interviews, Regional City leaders were asked to choose ten top leaders from the basic list of forty. The choices of the twenty-seven persons answering this question showed considerable unanimity of opinion. One leader received twenty-one votes out of a possible twenty-seven. Other leaders received nearly as many votes. Some received no votes at all. One could pyramid the forty leaders on the basis of the votes cast for them, as has been done in Table 1, but the pyramid is not a true expression of the existing relationships between the top leaders of the

---

[3] *The Human Group* (New York: Harcourt, Brace and Company, 1950).

**TABLE 1**

*REGIONAL CITY LEADERS RANKED ACCORDING TO NUMBER OF*
*VOTES RECEIVED FROM OTHER LEADERS IN LEADERSHIP POLL* *

| Leaders | Number of Votes |
|---|---|
| George Delbert | 21 |
| Cary Stokes | 19 |
| Ray Moster | 18 |
| Peter Barner | 17 |
| James Treat | 15 |
| Fargo Dunham | 14 |
| Charles Homer | 13 |
| Adam Graves, Joseph Hardy, Luke Street, Harry Parker, Jack Williams | 12 |
| Avery Spear | 11 |
| Elsworth Mines | 10 |
| Percy Latham | 9 |
| Mabel Gordon, Arthur Tarbell | 5 |
| Truman Worth, Edna Moore, Mark Parks | 4 |
| Harvey Aiken, Epworth Simpson, Bert Tidwell, Grover Smith, Edward Stokes | 3 |
| Phillip Gould, Harold Farmer, Brenda Howe, Gary Stone, Ralph Spade, Herman Schmidt | 2 |
| John Webster, Samuel Farris, Norman Trable, Claudia Mills, Horace Black, Howard Rake | 1 |
| Hetty Fairly, Gloria Stevens, Russell Gregory | 0 |

* Code numbers used in analyzing data and corresponding to fictional names of leaders are as follows:

| | | |
|---|---|---|
| 1. Latham | 14. Delbert | 28. Mills |
| 2. Graves | 15. Farris | 29. Spade |
| 3. Dunham | 16. Stevens | 30. Gregory |
| 4. Mines | 17. Trable | 31. Parker |
| 5. Smith | 18. Schmidt | 32. Williams |
| 6. Fairly | 19. Moore | 33. Black |
| 7. Webster | 20. Farmer | 34. Tidwell |
| 8. Worth | 21. Barner | 35. Tarbell |
| 9. C. Stokes | 22. Parks | 36. Moster |
| 10. Stone | 23. Gould | 37. Treat |
| 11. Simpson | 24. E. Stokes | 38. Street |
| 12. Aiken | 25. Gordon | 39. Rake |
| 13. Howe | 26. Spear | 40. Homer |
| | 27. Hardy | |

community. George Delbert, for example, was chosen eight times more than Charles Homer, and Homer is consequently six places down the scale from Delbert. Delbert is considered a "big man" in Regional City affairs, but he is not as big as Homer, according to most of the informants in answer to the simple question, "Who is the 'biggest' man in town?"

In the general social structure of community life social scientists are prone to look upon the institutions and formal associations as powerful forces, and it is easy to be in basic agreement with this view. Most institutions and associations are subordinate, however, to the interests of the policy-makers who operate in the economic sphere of community life in Regional City. The institutions of the family, church, state, education, and the like draw sustenance from economic institutional sources and are thereby subordinate to this particular institution more than any other. The associations stand in the same relationship to the economic interests as do the institutions. We see both the institutions and the formal associations playing a vital role in the execution of determined policy, but the formulation of policy often takes place outside these formalized groupings. Within the policy-forming groups the economic interests are dominant.

The economic institution in Regional City, in drawing around itself many of the other institutions in the community, provides from within itself much of the personnel which may be considered of primary influence in power relationships. A lengthy discussion on institutions per se is not proposed. Their existence as channels through which policy may be funneled up and down to broader groups of people than those represented by the top men of power is easily recognized. Some of the institutions would represent imperfect channels for power transmission, however. For example, the family as an institution is not a channel of itself for bringing about general community agreement on such a matter as the desirability of building a new bridge across Regional River. On the other hand, the church might represent a more potent force on this question. The preacher could preach a sermon on the matter in any given church, and the members could sign petitions, attend meetings at the behest of the church bureaucracy, and go through a whole series of activities motivated by the institution in question.

It may be noted here that none of the ministers of churches in Regional City were chosen as top leaders by the persons interviewed in the study. The idea was expressed several times by interviewees that some minister *ought* to be on the listing, but under the terms of power definitions used in the study they did not make "top billing." It is understood, however, that in order to get a project well under way it would be important to bring the churches in, but they are not, as institutions, considered crucial in the decision-making process. Their influence is crucial in restating settled policies from time to time and in interpreting new policies which have been formed or are in the process of formulation. Church leaders, however, whether they be prominent laymen or professional ministers, have relatively little influence with the larger economic interests.

One cannot, in Regional City at least, look to the organized institutions as policy-determining groupings, nor can one look to the formal associations which are part of these institutions.

Neither the institutional, associational, nor economic groupings comprise the totality of the power scheme in Regional City. The difference between policy-making and policy-execution has been stressed and it has been shown that the various organizations in the community may be very important in carrying out policy decisions. Segments of structure including individuals and cliques, particularly those related to the upper decision-making groups, have been identified. One more organizational component must be analyzed before tying together the units of the community structure. This component is what may be termed a fluid committee structure.

The committee is a phenomenon which is inescapable in organized community life in American hamlets, villages, small cities, and great metropolitan centers. Almost every activity of any importance in our culture must be preceded by committee work, carried on by committee work, and finally posthumously evaluated by a committee. Regional City is no exception to the general rule. Committees may have short lives or they may go on for years. An example of the latter is the Committee of 101. Committees may be quite formally organized, utilizing parliamentary rules of order, or they may be loosely organized and informal in their procedures. They may be accompanied by food and drink or they may be devoid of such amenities. They may have serious or light purposes, and consequently solemn or gay occasions as the case may be. Withal, each is accompanied by a certain degree of ritual befitting the occasion. Men used to committee work are sharp to detect poorly conducted meetings. No meeting, for example, can be said to have amounted to much if at least one motion is not put, passed, or put down—that is, in the more formally organized meetings. Men trained in conducting meetings are in demand, and such a person may display rare skills in ordering a group as it goes about its business.

Meetings are often a substitute for group action. As one Regional City professional phrased it, "There are those who believe in salvation by luncheon!" There is great faith manifest in certain quarters of our society that if people can just be got together in a meeting all problems will be solved. And there is some justification for this faith, since so many matters of community business, as well as private transactions, are brought to successful conclusions in meetings.

While it is important to stress the fluidity of committee structure, it must be pointed out that here is a stable base of personnel who are seen time and again in a variety of committee meetings. There are men in any community who devote large portions of their waking hours to attendance at one meeting or another. Public-relations men in industry and associational secretaries are paid to devote considerable of their time to meeting attendance. It becomes commonplace among this latter personnel group to see one another at committee meetings, and such personnel become familiar with community leaders who operate on a similar level with them. There is a tendency to judge the importance of these meetings by who is in attendance.

Most of the top personnel of the power group are rarely seen at meetings attended by the associational under-structure personnel in Regional City. The exception to this general statement may be found in those instances in which a project is broad enough so that the "whole community needs to be brought in on the matter." Such meetings as bring in the under-structure personnel are usually relatively large affairs, rather than the smaller, more personal meetings which characterize policy-determination sessions. The interaction patterns of the two groups discussed here have shown a much higher rate of interaction among the top group than between the top and lower groups.

In matters of power decision the committee structure assumes keystone importance. The committee as a structure is a vital part of community power relationships in Regional City. Let us illustrate graphically in Figure 1 the place of two hypothetical policy committees in relation to institutional, associational, and corporate groups.

Not all the institutions and associations in Regional City were identified as being related to the power leaders studied. For example, none of the leaders in a power relationship could be identified as representing the institution of the family or a cultural association. This does not mean that either of these groupings was unimportant for some of the top leaders, but in the specific power relations studied no identification could be made of persons within these groupings as such. Because of this, in Figure 1 the cultural association is indicated as a pyramid grouping for under-structure power personnel only. No family institutional pyramid is shown. On the other hand, some of the institutions and associations could be identified with both upper-limits and lower-limits power personnel, and these pyramids show this by contrasting shaded portions for the two types of power leaders. We have also indicated in the figure that some institutions and associations are more frequently drawn upon for power personnel than others. The dotted lines represent those groups that are potential contributors to the policy-making structure. The cultural association group has been so designated, for example, since policy is formulated around some cultural activities which may have bearing on power relations. As an illustration, the status factor operating when a leader becomes a patron of the arts may have some relation to his general power position.

A few generalized remarks may be made concerning Figure 1, using a hypothetical example, after which it will be illustrated concretely how the structure worked in relation to a specific community project in Regional City.

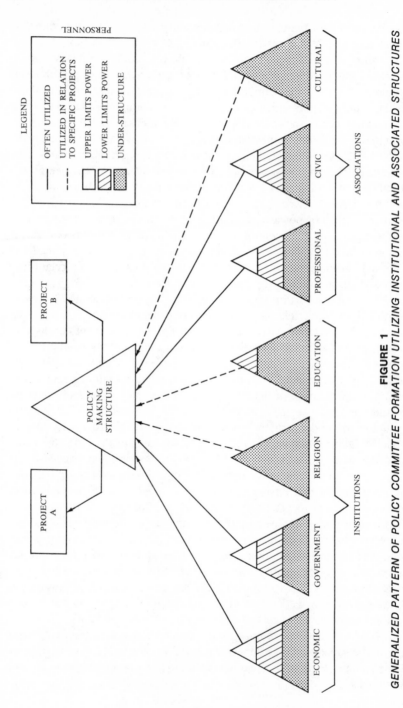

**FIGURE 1**

GENERALIZED PATTERN OF POLICY COMMITTEE FORMATION UTILIZING INSTITUTIONAL AND ASSOCIATED STRUCTURES

If a project of major proportions were before the community for consideration—let us say a project aimed at building a new municipal auditorium—a policy committee would be formed. This may be called Project Committee A. Such a policy committee would more than likely grow out of a series of informal meetings, and it might be related to a project that has been on the discussion agenda of many associations for months or even years. But the time has arrived for action. Money must be raised through private subscription or taxation, a site selected, and contracts let. The time for a policy committee is propitious. The selection of the policy committee will fall largely to the men of power in the community. They will likely be businessmen in one or more of the large business establishments. Mutual choices will be agreed upon for committee membership. In the early stages of policy formulation there will be a few men who make the basic decisions. As the project is trimmed, pared, and shaped into manageable proportions there will be a recognition that the committee should be enlarged. Top-ranking organizational and institutional personnel will then be selected by the original members to augment their numbers, i.e., the committee will be expanded. The civic associations and the formalized institutions will next be drawn into certain phases of planning and initiation of the project on a community-wide basis. The newspapers will finally carry stories of the proposals, the ministers will preach sermons, and the associational members will hear speeches regarding plans. This rather simply is the process, familiar to many, that goes on in getting any community project under way.

Project B might be related to changing the tax structure of the community. Much the same organizational procedure will be repeated, but different associations may be drawn into the planning and execution stages. The policy-making personnel will tend to be much the same as in Project A and this is an important point in the present discussion. There will be a hard core of policy leadership on Policy Committee B that was also present on Project Committee A. This relative stability of the top policy-making group is a pattern quite apparent in Regional City civic affairs. A similar pattern of stable committee membership exists in the under-structure of the associational and corporate bureaucracies in the community which interact in a chain of command with the top power leaders on given projects.

It must be stressed that the same policy leaders do not interact repeatedly with the same under-structure personnel in getting projects put over. The interaction is based entirely upon a given project that is under consideration at a given time. The under-structure personnel may be likened to a key-board over which the top structure personnel play, and the particular keys struck may vary from project to project. The players remain the same or nearly so, however.

A variation in the pattern of structuring a top-decision committee may be found in those policy committees in which the decision is made by individuals who are not to be out front on the project. In other words, the men of policy may wish to remain anonymous in relation to the action phases of the program in question. In such cases, the policy group remains informally intact, and "second-rate" or "third-rate" men are advertised as the sponsors of the particular project. This pattern may occur when a project is somewhat questionable as to its success. The policy-forming group is just as real, however, as if it were named publicly. The men upon whom falls the burden of carrying the project into its action stages are well aware of the persons who chose them.

Projects that are not originated in the policy-determining group are often allowed to proceed with a tentative blessing of a few of the men of decision if their interests and dominant values are not threatened by the proposed activity. If such a project goes sour, the men of decision cannot be blamed. This is another variation of structure and represents a real behavioral pattern in civic affairs in Regional City.

There is one more element in Regional City's power structure which must be discussed. It is the element of power residing in the Negro community of the city. The Negro community represents a sub-structure of power as well as a sub-community. As a community grouping it calls up many issues which tend to mobilize the total power structure. As a sub-community power structure it is inextricably interwoven with the elements discussed in the present chapter.

Two of the hypotheses of the study have been discussed in some measure in the preceding analysis. These hypotheses, restated, are as follows:

1. The exercise of power is limited and directed by the formulation and extension of social policy within a framework of socially sanctioned authority.

2. In a given power unit a smaller number of individuals will be found formulating and extending policy than those exercising power.

A corollary of the latter hypothesis was also touched upon: All policy-makers are men of power, but all men of power are not, per se, policy-makers.

The top group of the power hierarchy has been isolated and defined as comprised of policy-makers. These men are drawn largely from the businessmen's class in Regional City. They form cliques or crowds, as the term is more often used in the community, which formulate policy. Committees for formulation of policy are commonplace, and on community-wide issues policy is channeled by a "fluid committee structure" down to institutional, associational groupings through a lower-level bureaucracy which executes policy.

It has been pointed out that intra-community and extra-community policy matters are handled by essentially the same group of men in this city, but there is a differentiation of functional activity within this policy group. Some men operate on different levels of policy decision, particularly in matters concerning governmental action. Some structural weaknesses in the power structure have been touched upon but at no great length. Finally, it was found that the structure is held together by common interests, mutual obligations, money, habit, delegated responsibilities, and in some cases by coercion and force.

# Why American Cities are Pluralist

## AARON WILDAVSKY

We are talking about communities in which the rules of democracy are operative. There are free elections with universal adult suffrage, a secret ballot, some approximation of majority rule, and competition for office. Citizens are permitted, indeed encouraged, to organize themselves into what De Toqueville called free associations. Information is available for the interested participants and may be freely communicated. A community in which a substantial body of citizens are effectively disenfranchised or which is populated by migrant laborers without citizenship would be less likely to manifest a democratic structure or pattern.

We seek to explain the structure of leadership, power, influence, control (they are equivalent terms) over community decisions. In its most general aspect, we conceive of control over decisions within a democratic context as the result of low but (as among people) highly disparate amounts of interest in public affairs; the high costs and comparatively low returns from activity in public affairs; the unequal but dispersed distribution of resources; and the independent, conflicting relationships among leaders. Interest, activity, and access to effective resources are separately viewed as necessary and together as sufficient conditions of leadership. Conflicts among leaders supply the dynamics of the system. These variables, the factors affecting them, and their interrelationships, form the basis of our discussion.

Most people are not interested in most public issues most of the time. They simply do not care. Why should they? An individual in the United States can get a wonderful job, marry, have a happy family, and do creative work without ever taking an interest in the public realm.

Reprinted from *Leadership in a Small Town* (Totawa, N.J.: Bedminster Press, 1964), pp. 332–349, by permission of the publisher.

His primary satisfactions do not ordinarily lie in political life; basic needs are met or thwarted on the job, in the home, through friendship circles and the like.

Community affairs are remote. They are complex and usually unrelated to the individual. Before a person can understand them and relate himself to them, he needs a sensitive perceptual mechanism, a capacity for considerable abstract thought, equipment which most people do not have. This is especially true as one descends the educational ladder, for education not only indoctrinates one in the value of political participation, but also prepares one to make connections between apparently remote events. It is not easy to perceive that a new waterworks may attract more industry which will affect local merchants, and then consequently the service in stores and employment opportunities in town. It is difficult to maintain an interest in what one cannot understand.

And is it worth understanding? To take an interest means to spend some time which might bring greater returns on the job or through a hobby. The cost of interest is obvious, but the return is not, particularly if one does not believe that what the government does is important or that one can do anything about it. Study after study has shown that interest is related in a high and positive way to a sense of efficacy. The usual propaganda, of course, has it that every vote is crucial. But one vote out of millions or even thousands rarely changes anything and from the limited perspective of the individual he may rationally believe that nothing he would do could really be efficacious. This feeling may be overcome by a deep sense of civic obligation, but many people do not have this sense.

To be interested in some issues some of the time is one thing; to be interested in most of the issues most of the time is quite another. If time were free and unlimited, those with an inclination to be interested might gorge themselves. But this is not the case and even the most avid partisan of public affairs must be selective. What, then, can we say of the many who are not disposed to be interested when they are confronted with a vast and confusing array of subjects about which they might conceivably know something.

Let it not be thought that most people will remain disinterested under almost any provocation. Imagine a law which separated parents from children or which forbade citizens to watch television. Then one would really see what mass participation was like. There is no need to retreat into realms of fancy; policies adopted in the Soviet Union since World War II will serve to demonstrate the point. In 1946 the Soviet Government announced an exchange of currency—to fight inflation it said—which reduced the value of savings by about 90 percent. A decade or so later the regime, in effect, repudiated the national debt by announcing a moratorium on the payment of government bonds which workers had been compelled to buy to the amount of 20 percent of their salaries. Can anyone imagine a democratic government thinking of such a policy, let alone promulgating it? The participation engendered by it would be immense, but the experiment is hardly likely to be made.

There are a few people, a very few, who are continuously interested in a wide variety of issues. They usually are public officials, newspaper editors, academics, people whose occupations require this interest. There also are people who have specialized interests in specific policy areas. These may include public and private officials, members of civic organizations, and pressure groups, citizens who are directly affected, and a sprinkling of others who make a hobby out of being interested, including seekers after causes, club women, and people who like to get their names on letterheads.

The fact that individuals do vary enormously in their degree of interest has profound implications for political life. If interest is a necessary condition of leadership, then the disinterested remove themselves from consideration, and leadership is concentrated in the small population which does care. Yet the number of interested people, small though it is, is large compared to the number of active people. The factors which limit activity are of cardinal importance in understanding political affairs.

Activity is costly. It eats up time and energy at an astounding rate. To be active on strategic problems in nuclear politics or on the operations of a municipal electric plant is not a matter of a few moments of reflection; many hours must be spent. One must ordinarily attend meetings, listen to or participate in discussion, write letters, attempt to persuade or be persuaded by others, and engage in other time consuming labors. This means devoting less time to the job, to the children, and to hobbies. Yet these activities, rather than public affairs, are the primary concerns of most people, and so the cost of participation in public affairs seems greater than the return. Only a few issues, at best, induce most citizens to participate in politics.

Activity may be costly also in terms of ego involvement. The goal of the activity may not be achieved, leaving the participants with a sense of failure. If he is not especially skilled, his seemingly bumbling efforts may provoke ridicule, which is hard to bear. The hostilities incurred in controversies over policy may rebound in the form of personal invective.

The active person leaves himself open to social and financial retaliation, or thinks that he does. Hence some businessmen believe that

"politics is bad for business." All the more reason, then, for not following up an interest with dangerous overt activity.

Activity depends on the possession of certain skills which usually
are products of a middle and upper class subculture. People in academic
life, because these skills are part of their job, tend to underestimate the
extreme difficulty others have in speaking in public, in writing down
their ideas coherently, and in defending them in argument. Unless a
citizen is willing to confine himself to more routine operations, like
addressing envelopes, he finds that lack of these skills is a tremendous
handicap. Lower class individuals who are trained in these skills in labor
unions, churches, or social organizations provide an important source of
leadership in defense of their interests. But only a few take this path.

A sense of civic consciousness is more deeply ingrained in upper
class than in lower class mores. The explanation may rest in part upon
class-based experience of relative autonomy, of actually "making a difference" by one's actions. The result is that a person with higher income
and more advanced education is likely to feel more obliged to participate,
and to have this feeling reinforced by social pressure. These are statistical
tendencies, of course, and there are people on the "wrong" side of the
percentages.

Activity varies considerably with the nature of the issue. Some issues—an end to the Korean War, a tax increase, unemployment—have
a more obvious impact on large numbers of people than do others. Some
issues are selective of participation in that they bring out people with a
special concern who would not be active in other areas. Thus the relatively few people active on farm issues tend to be different from those
few concerned with labor, air pollution, or sewerage.

Participation is affected by the activities of leaders who have a stake
in decreasing or increasing it. Their ability to "make an issue," to
broaden the interested public, increases their bargaining power. The
task of the leader is to show the connection between the events he is
concerned about and the lives and fortunes of at least some segments of
the population. The general lack of public attention and inability to make
the desired connections turn issue-making into one of the most valuable
components of the art of leadership.

There are many types of activity and some are much less costly for
the individual than others. This is particularly true of voting, which is
done in secret and requires but little time and attention. Party labels and
factional alignments serve as a means of cutting information costs, enabling the voters to express a generalized preference without too great
attention to the issues.

The universally low participation in civic affairs does not mean that
the citizen who wishes to become active finds that others block his path.

Just the opposite is usually true. The demand for participants is almost always greater than the supply. Those who are or would be leaders require followers of all kinds to spread propaganda, ring doorbells, engage in research, and perform a multitude of other tasks. Entry into public affairs is so free and easy, in fact, that many individuals become participants by self-selection, by simply appearing and showing that they are willing to work.

With these comments in mind, we can proceed to classify political participation (interest plus activity) in a way which will prove useful for analytic purposes. We will distinguish between four types of participants according to the rate and scope of interest and activity:

1. The *apathetics* who neither vote nor participate in any other way.

2. The *meteors* who vote with some regularity, and engage in a few activities sporadically.

3. The *issue specialists* who vote regularly and who continuously participate in a particular issue area but are not active in other aspects of community affairs.

4. The *generalists* who vote regularly and participate extensively in many though not all issue areas.

The generalists compose an infinitesimal percent of any community, their number is easily counted on the fingers. The number of specialists is larger but is unlikely to include ten or even five percent of the people in most communities. The largest group of citizens is the meteors, with the apathetics making up from 20 to 60 percent of the population.

Routine issues, which do not involve innovation or challenge to established interests, may be decided by an administrator or a small number of specialists. Somewhat more controversial issues are likely to bring out a few meteors. Highly controversial issues increase the participation of meteors and may even arouse some of the normally apathetic. Elections bring out all but the apathetics and some meteors, depending on circumstances. Mass participation in which virtually everyone engages in a variety of activities other than voting is practically unknown.

One conclusion is obvious: the prizes in politics go to the interested and the active; people who do not try to influence decisions do not have a direct impact upon them. If the preferences of a large number of citizens are met, therefore, it is not because they ordinarily participate but because they might participate, because relationships between participants are arranged so as to secure this result, and because of the particular ways in which effective resources are distributed and used.

As everyone knows, resources which may be used to affect public decisions are unequally distributed. Some people have much more wealth, credit, control over jobs, information and social standing, than do others. But effective resources are also widely dispersed. No one has all of them and few have none. No single resource is dominant, so that use of it overwhelms attempts to wield others. The wealth of businessmen may be offset by soliciting small contributions from many workers. The popularity of a leader like Franklin Roosevelt may counter the hostility of the media of information. The skill of a Lyndon Johnson may smite enemies with higher social position. The bureaucratic positions of a Robert Moses may prove too much for elected leaders. And aroused citizens may overcome Moses by forming a barricade of carriages around a threatened playground in Central Park. There are, then, many different kinds of resources, not all tightly concentrated, nor useful for the same purposes, nor employed with similar effectiveness.

That resources exist does not mean that they will be used fully, skillfully, or at all. Most people use their resources sparingly, with varying degrees of effectiveness. The cost in terms of time, energy, money, and ego damage usually seems too great in comparison to the benefits which appear remote and uncertain. As a result, there is a vast reservoir of resources lying untapped by people who prefer not to use them. When and if they become conscious that things are going badly, and feel that participation in the community area may provide an answer, the meteors and (under great provocation) the apathetics may step-up their use of resources.

An exhaustive discussion of resources is literally out of the question. A few central points must suffice. Which resources might conceivably dominate over others in our society? Wealth comes readily to mind; its relative concentration is established, and there can be little doubt about its usefulness under many conditions. But it is not, as is commonly supposed, a universal solvent in the civic arena. It often cannot buy popularity with the electorate as many wealthy men have learned to their sorrow. A minimum sum for electoral purposes is a necessity, but a hundred times that sum may not bring additional returns and may actually bring resentment against the spender. Other resources may be converted into wealth; a politician may use patronage to fill the party coffers, or his continued tenure in office may demonstrate the advisability of contributing to his campaign fund. If an organization like the Cooperative Stores in Oberlin can raise funds by internal subscription or through outside sources, the local banks cannot effectively use against it their ability to withhold credit. It sometimes is said that politicians may be bought; but they are not worth buying unless they remain in office, and they may not be able to do that if they so consistently please the wealthy as to antagonize the more numerous citizens of moderate income. No doubt money may control some decisions in some issue areas just as superior information, skill, and even physical force may control in others. But money does not control in all decisions nor necessarily in any which are deemed vital by others who possess some wealth and other resources with which to engage in conflict.

Many who possess wealth do not in fact employ it to influence community decisions. If there was an X family in Middletown which sought to influence many decisions, there also was an extremely wealthy Y family which was not interested in most community decisions. Most large corporations are extremely wary of direct political participation, fearing adverse publicity. Since many who possess wealth do not attempt to employ it, and some who have but little do use what they have, it is not at all clear whether wealth *per se* confers an advantage. There is little point in arguing that the potential influence of the wealthy is great, should they care to employ their resources, for there are many individuals and groups who could employ more of the resources in their reservoir to considerable effect. Instead of the oversimplified notion of the billiard ball effect—asking how far can A influence B—we say that it depends on A's involvement, his willingness to use his resources to the limit, B's ability to expand his use of resources, the costs involved, and the activities of other participants.

While resources are subject diminishing returns, we would like to suggest that those which are capable of the most effective expansion are either widely diffused or most readily available to public officials who are subject to restraints of the electoral process. Time, energy and skill (to which least attention is paid) are among the most important resources. Merely by putting in a great deal of time, coupled with considerable energy and a modicum of skill, most participants can increase their influence over specific areas and, more important, increase their access to other resources. Politicians do this by devoting full time to public affairs, making friends, doing favors, and working with amazing energy, and it is not surprising that their experience increases their skill. The ensuing popularity can be converted into votes; public office can then be used to win more friends; this good will can be turned into contributions; increased wealth can be applied to buy expert advice; the knowledge gained thereby will provide advantages over opponents; this success can be used to recruit more followers. This process, which Dahl has called the pyramiding of resources, is not readily available to those who lack the legitimacy of public office, which carries with it a publicly recognized right to be active and the necessary time to do it.

It is conceivable that all the interested and active individuals might agree on most policies. They would then monopolize the resources which were being used to affect policies, thus reserving influence to themselves. If the rest of the population shared these preferences, the result would be an end to conflict and the millennium of total harmony spoken of in utopian novels but never seen on earth. If the participants used their resources to compel the obedience of nonparticipants, a ruling elite would result. But there is no ruling elite in Oberlin or any other city for which we have a full account. What is wrong here is the assumption of unity among the participants. How else can we explain the occurrence of conflict in our communities?

It is difficult to think of a community of any size which does not have its share of disagreements. This is true for many reasons. Issues have a differential impact. Different individuals and groups stand to lose or gain from a tax increase, from one type of service rather than another, and from a zoning ordinance. School issues may pit those with school children against those without. The "ins" versus the "outs" create another basis of rivalry as do personality conflicts. Members of different professions are likely to have somewhat different values. A category like businessmen has certain utilities as a statistical shorthand but it fails miserably as a predictor of unified interests and goals, as the Oberlin study should show to anyone's satisfaction. Those who stand to lose by industrial development may take different positions from those who stand to gain. When leadership depends on a few, the fact that some businessmen are opposed to others may assume critical importance.

Social class in the United States has not proved to be an efficient ground for organizing conflict, and we do not find monolithic alignments of the classes against the masses. We do find ethnic, religious, and racial grounds for conflict as well as liberal and conservative orientations and varieties of preferred political styles which cut across class lines. Our conclusion is that the interested and the active are not unified against the rest of society. Of course, they do agree on the "rules of the game," the procedural aspects of democracy; this places limits on their conflicts without doing away with the conflicts themselves. This has far-reaching implications for the problem of political change.

There are two simple answers to the question of how change takes place in the community. One is that a unified set of leaders is able to impose its will on all others. Either the elite decides and it is done or the elite is opposed and it is not done. Only a revolution can impose change against their will in the short run. Another easy answer invokes mass democracy; change occurs when a majority of citizens or voters decides that it is desirable. What can be said, then, of the infinitely more complex situation in which most people are uninterested and inactive; there are conflicts among the leaders; and no one of the leaders has sufficient resources to prevail most of the time?

To a limited extent a leader may introduce change into a community without encountering significant opposition. This is, in part, a consequence of the generally low interest, activity and use of resources. Most individuals and groups do not find it worthwhile to calculate precisely how they might be helped or hindered by a change. The leader's skill is important because issues may be so constructed and explained as to persuade some that they stand to gain. Indeed, it is sometimes possible to arrange things so that few in the community suffer and many gain as when funds are procured from other levels of government. Policies may be framed so that their impact is not immediately apparent —taxes may be hidden—or segmented in impact so that only limited numbers are adversely affected at any one time—enforcement may be selective. Because people do not always know what they want, the skillful leader may also create demands which he then fulfills. This is not possible when people are adversely affected in a recognizable way. There are strict limits to deception, especially when other would-be leaders are prepared to exploit it. The leader may use his popularity, support from those to whom benefits have been distributed, to weather storms which arise over objectionable innovations. But this fund of resources is not inexhaustible. He may be able to afford antagonizing some people part of the time but not most of the time. He has to pick and choose among policies with this in mind.

In his brilliant pamphlet, "What Is To Be Done," Lenin argues that revolution is not a task to be accomplished by amateurs devoting spare time and weekends but only by professionals devoting all their time to the job. We might phrase his argument in our own terms by saying that innovation in the community, like revolution in the nation, is most likely to be accomplished by interested and active participants who utilize their resources at a high rate and devote a great deal of time to the task. The most likely innovators, then, are participants who work full time at some aspect of community affairs—city managers, bureaucrats, elected officials, heads of private agencies and civic associations. Next, perhaps, are newspaper editors, businessmen, and attorneys who have "dispensable" occupations which permit them to devote considerable time to civic affairs or are especially related to them. The editors are more likely candidates because they are supposed to be concerned whereas only the occasional attorney or businessman has work which justifies his attention.

While innovation is possible it ordinarily does not go too far because there are persuasive reasons for leaders to minimize conflicts. The formal structure of government, with its emphasis upon free elections and separation of powers, frequently means that cooperation from others who cannot be coerced must be obtained. The chances are that the ordinary social division of labor in society also makes crucial individuals immune to pressure. Those who control jobs, for example, unless they are politicians, are engaged in different pursuits with different aims and rules. The leader who possesses resources dominant in one issue area often finds that they are not similarly effective in another. It soon becomes apparent that the opponent of today may be the indispensable ally of tomorrow, and that it is most unwise to alienate other leaders for the sake of one policy to the extent that agreement on other policies is precluded. Finally, competing sets of leaders have a stake in not pursuing policies which will lead to the entry of new participants who will make a bid for leadership that may upset prevailing patterns. The more extreme the policy, the greater the departure from the *status quo,* the more likely that interest will be created and potential leaders motivated to make their bid, thus threatening the powers that be.

Severe conflict is so costly that a multitude of techniques have evolved for avoiding or mitigating it. Perhaps the easiest way for a leader to avoid conflict is to limit his activities so that his goals and strategies are largely independent of those of other leaders. This appears to be the approach which is taken in most cities. Where this is not possible, his policies may be framed to accommodate values held by other leaders. Mutual agreement, granting rewards in one area to offset deprivations in another, compromise through bargaining, all are techniques leaders use to limit strife. They may narrow and segment conflict so that it does not become all pervasive. Issues may be blurred or ignored. They may confer symbolic rewards by designing an euphemistic cover for an unpalatable decision. Instead of "calling a spade a spade," so that losses and gains are immediately apparent to the contestants, leaders call it something entirely different. Only when the normal channels for limiting conflict have broken down, as in a bitter intra-party feud such as the one between the "reform" and "organization" Democrats in New York, are all the stops pulled out. Then the disputants fight for their political lives. At such times, it is necessary to have a commonly agreed arena—a primary, an election, or a convention—with clearly defined rules for waging the combat and registering the decisions considered legitimate.

We have now presented the four variables—interest, activity, resources, conflicts among participants—which we will use to explain the pluralist structure of power in most American communities. The time has come to draw the appropriate conclusions using these variables and the factors affecting them.

No one person or group is powerful in all or most of the significant areas of community life. Different individuals and small groups of participants typically make decisions in different issue areas. Specialists and generalists use resources more frequently and to a greater extent than others most of the time. It should come as no surprise, therefore, that they frequently prevail in their own domain, especially when the decisions they make are largely routine or do not interest others. (These people may not feel deprived because they are not influential; they just may not care.) When decisions are made which adversely affect others, or which alter established practices in which others have a stake, participation normally increases. Frequently, electoral sanction is necessary and this requires support or at least acquiescence from voters who may be mobilized by opponents. Other leaders must be pacified. Since this normally cannot be done by coercion (in the absence of dominant resources and in the presence of a reservoir of resources), it must be done by bargaining, or granting rewards in other areas, or recourse to the ballot. Leaders take care, under democratic conditions, not to systematically violate the preferences of the ever-present "others" who may challenge even their routine supremacy. This accounts for a great deal of the informal consultation, the formation of citizens' committees to secure widespread support, and the many compromises that take place. Leaders must ordinarily choose goals which permit coalitions with other leaders.

One type of pluralist system may be described as a multitude of independent centers manned by specialists whose goals and strategies are substantially nonconflicting. When conflict threatens it is settled by bargaining among leaders who find this method preferable to the risk of breaking up the system from which they all gain. Only small changes in policy are made so that the chances of severely depriving others by any one move are considerably reduced. When the policies pursued by one center adversely affect that of another, the difficulty is handled by "firetruck" tactics, that is by dealing with each small difficulty in turn in whatever center of decision it is. The city of Chicago may be described in these terms.

Another type of pluralist system, represented by New Haven and Oberlin, has central direction. Policy is effectively coordinated by a center of power. The leader or leaders are likely to be public officials with time, skill, energy, and ability to pyramid resources. While they are the only ones who are influential to some degree in most of the issue areas, they are not wholly influential in any area. They must share influence with specialists, meteors and other leaders who may threaten to or actually do mobilize against them. They are not equally effective. They are defeated now and then. They are compelled to husband their re-sources carefully lest they incur hostility which will deprive them of office. For the most part their success depends on the disinterest of others and their own skill in meeting the demands of the interested and active while serving their own purposes as well.

Conceivably there may be small communities in which a generalized elite, dominant on all or most issues, does exist. Perhaps there is a single employer who monopolizes wealth, jobs and credit to such a degree that no one can challenge him if he seeks to exert himself. Possibly there is a sharp educational difference between social classes so that a small, upper class group monopolizes political skills. Lower class members may wish to contest decisions, to make issues, but they do not know how. Never able to begin participating in the civic arena, they do not acquire the experience and confidence. Their sense of efficacy remains permanently low. Yet the ruling elite may not ignore them. There is still the possibility that the arrival of new citizens, defections from the elite, conflicts within it, or a bid for leadership by an exceptional lower class person might change the situation. Therefore the elite places self-imposed limits on actions which might disturb others. It seeks to maintain friendly contact with lower class individuals and goes so far as to seek approval from them before trying a new policy that might raise sufficient concern to upset the pattern of community power. Lower class persons do not lead, but neither are they led very far against their will.

Pluralist theory is supported not only by the Oberlin experience but also by a growing body of literature on American cities of various sizes and complexions. In *Governing New York City* (New York, 1960), Wallace Sayre and Herbert Kaufman conclude:

> No single elite dominates the political and governmental system of New York City. . . . Most individual decisions are shaped by a small percentage of the city's population—indeed, by a small percentage of those who engage actively in politics . . . the city government is most accurately visualized as a series of semi-autonomous little worlds each of which brings forth programs and policies through the interactions of its own inhabitants. . . . New York's huge and diverse system of government and politics is a loose-knit and multicentered network in which decisions are reached by ceaseless bargaining and fluctuating al-liances among the major categories of participants in each center, and in which the centers are partially but strikingly isolated from one an-other. (Pp. 709–16.)

Edward Banfield's description of Chicago politics in his *Political Influence* (New York, 1961), follows the pluralist lines of New York quite closely. He also describes an interesting political style that has evolved in Chicago which we may view as a result of the pluralist factors in the environment.

> Chicago is too big a city, and the interests in it far too diverse, to allow of quick and easy agreement on anything. By approaching an issue slowly, the political head gives opposing interests time to emerge to formulate their positions and to present their arguments. . . . According to the Chicago view, a policy ought to be framed by the interests affected. . . . The political head should see that all principally affected interests are represented, that residual interests (i.e., 'the general public') are not entirely disregarded, and that no interest suffers unduly in the outcome. (Pp. 270–71.)

Lorain, Ohio is a steel manufacturing city just a few miles away from Oberlin. James McKee, a sociologist, set out to study the community in order to test the hypothesis that management was the new ruling group in our society. He found that by organizing and mobilizing the votes of the previously conflicting ethnic groups in Lorain's polyglot population, CIO labor leaders forged a coalition with the Democratic party and the Catholic Church which controlled decisions in the city's educational system and government. McKee concludes that

> First, there is no single locus of decision-making, but rather a number of loci, each differently structured. . . . Second, a number of groups may have varying effects upon decision-making in any given locus. . . . Hence, the pyramidal model of the social order, with power and authority located at the apex, is inaccurate and misleading. Third, the organization of political power in the community provides a striking and contradictory contrast to the system of power and authority within the corporation. . . . In the community decision-making is more democratically structured. This is not to assert that what goes on in the community fully epitomizes democracy. But it is to assert that a share in decision-making in the community is now more easily attained by citizens of low status. (McKeen, *op. cit.,* pp. 369–71.)

In New Haven, reported in the studies by Dahl, Polsby and Wolfinger, the political style is quite different as the diverse centers have been unified under the forceful leadership of Mayor Richard Lee. The city's politics are unmistakably pluralist, however, for though Lee was the only participant who was influential in most of the issue areas studied, his degree of influence varied from area to area, and he was sometimes defeated. As Dahl puts it,

> The Mayor was not at the peak of a pyramid but at the center of intersecting circles. He rarely commanded. He negotiated, cajoled, exhorted, beguiled, charmed, pressed, appealed, reasoned, promised, insisted,

demanded, even threatened; but he most needed support and acquiescence from other leaders who simply could not be commanded. Because he could not command, he had to bargain. (Mimeo draft.)

The various reputation and stratification studies of community power do come up with different conclusions. But the evidence presented in them suggests that the communities they studied were probably pluralist. The Lynds report that power in Middletown (Muncie, Indiana) was held almost entirely by the X family through its control over jobs and finances. Yet we learn that an insurgent Mayor was elected over the opposition of the X family and that he successfully opposed a policy of relief payments which was desired by the X's. The Mayor also "forced the Chamber of Commerce [said to be dominated by the X family] to side with him in a WPA project favored by Middletown's working class before he would approve the pet project of the business class (opposed by the South side) for an interception sewer." (P. 329.) Coming closer to home, a river flowed through the upper class districts, right by the X house, which was so noxious that Mr. X had to close his windows in the summer time. The river did not, however, pass through the working class area in the South side. As a result, the workers' representatives on the City Council blocked the use of funds to clear up this nuisance because they did not want to tax themselves for the benefit of the wealthy. We also are given examples where the X family prevailed on public policies against opposition. Insofar as the limited evidence permits us to judge, there appear to be several centers of influence in town, no one of them uniformly successful in all areas.

Floyd Hunter studied Atlanta, Georgia and found it dominated by business leaders. It does not take long, nevertheless, to discover other participants who exercised leadership. There was Truman Worth, "The boss of a large suburban development," a reputed power in the state legislature, without whom, Hunter says, no move on a metropolitan wide basis was made. For years he successfully opposed a proposal favored by some businessmen to coordinate services on a metropolitan basis. There was Calvert Smith, a Negro leader, who used the substantial Negro vote to bargain for advantages for his people. "Everyone politically inclined," Hunter tells us, "is aware of the power of the Negro vote to swing elections within the city . . ." As our last example we have labor leaders. "In recent years public solicitations have reached down into the worker groups," Hunter reports, "and there is a growing tendency for some of the labor leaders to have a voice in the management of purely civic expenditures." The existence of several independent centers of leadership suggests that bargaining among leaders rather than coercion by businessmen is the order of the day.

Pluralist power structure is clearly visible in Harry Scoble's study of leaders and issues in Bennington, Vermont.

> The Bennington study, with its recognized limitations, indicated that no single power structure existed in the community. The data suggest that 'a community' is in fact to be characterized by a multiplicity of power structures to be empirically determined among different decisional areas. For example, the monolithic, flat-surfaced pyramid, with the empirical features: a small number of power-holders, acting in pre-determined concert, and with wealth as the dominant power-base, this seems appropriate to Bennington's hospital decision but not to the other, non-charity, public policies examined. For in the latter cases the data indicate consistent central factions which compete to control necessary public offices and/or to produce desired policy outcomes depending on the issue involved. Finally, lacking a formal governmental mechanism for coordination (which does exist in larger communities), we may infer from the data on office-holding that there was intent— somewhat self-limited and frequently unsuccessful—to achieve informal coordination through overlapping personnel and through controlling focusing of public attention. But in the last analysis coordination was achieved by the nonleaders. (Morris Janowitz, Editor, *Community Political Systems* [Glencoe, 1961], p. 141.)

In summing up the results of the massive inquiry into power in Syracuse, New York, Frank Munger writes as follows:

> Only three over-all conclusions seem warranted by the materials examined. First, the myth that significant decisions in Syracuse emanate from one source does not stand up under close scrutiny. Second, there tend to be as many decision centers as there are important decision areas, which means that the decision-making power is fragmented among the institutions, agencies, and individuals which cluster about these areas. Third, in reality there appear to be many kinds of community power, with one differing from another in so many fundamental ways as to make virtually impossible a meaningful comparison. (P. 311.)

It would be difficult to find a more direct description of a pluralist system than is found in *Decisions in Syracuse* (Bloomington, 1961).

Thus, evidence from cities as diverse as Lorain, Ohio, New Haven, Connecticut, Chicago, Illinois, and Atlanta, Georgia bears out our thesis that the contemporary city is likely to have a pluralist structure of power.

# Two Faces of Power[1]

## PETER BACHRACH
## MORTON S. BARATZ

The concept of power remains elusive despite the recent and prolific outpourings of case studies on community power. Its elusiveness is dramatically demonstrated by the regularity of disagreement as to the locus of community power between the sociologists and the political scientists. Sociologically oriented researchers have consistently found that power is highly centralized, while scholars trained in political science have just as regularly concluded that in "their" communities power is widely diffused.[2] Presumably, this explains why the latter group styles itself "pluralist," its counterpart "elitist."

There seems no room for doubt that the sharply divergent findings of the two groups are the product, not of sheer coincidence, but of fundamental differences in both their underlying assumptions and research methodology. The political scientists have contended that these differences in findings can be explained by the faulty approach and presuppositions of the sociologists. We contend in this paper that the pluralists

Reprinted from *American Political Science Review*, Vol. 58 (December 1962), 947–52, by permission of the publisher and the authors.

[1] This paper is an outgrowth of a seminar in Problems of Power in Contemporary Society, conducted jointly by the authors for graduate students and undergraduate majors in political science and economics.

[2] Compare, for example, the sociological studies of Floyd Hunter, *Community Power Structure* (Chapel Hill, 1953); Roland Pellegrini and Charles H. Coates, "Absentee-Owned Corporations and Community Power Structure," *American Journal of Sociology*, Vol. 61 (March 1956), pp. 413–19; and Robert O. Schulze, "Economic Dominants and Community Power Structure," *American Sociological Review*, Vol. 23 (February 1958), pp. 3–9; with political science studies of Wallace S. Sayre and Herbert Kaufman, *Governing New York City* (New York, 1960); Robert A. Dahl, *Who Governs?* (New Haven, 1961); and Norton E. Long and George Belknap, "A Research Program on Leadership and Decision-Making in Metropolitan Areas" (New York, Governmental Affairs Institute, 1956). See also Nelson W. Polsby, "How to Study Community Power: The Pluralist Alternative," *Journal of Politics*, Vol. 22 (August 1960), pp. 474–84.

themselves have not grasped the whole truth of the matter; that while their criticisms of the elitists are sound, they, like the elitists, utilize an approach and assumptions which predetermine their conclusions. Our argument is cast within the frame of our central thesis: that there are two faces of power, neither of which the sociologists see and only one of which the political scientists see.

## I

Against the elitist approach to power several criticisms may be, and have been levelled.[3] One has to do with its basic premise that in every human institution there is an ordered system of power, a "power structure" which is an integral part and the mirror image of the organization's stratification. This postulate the pluralists emphatically—and, to our mind, correctly—reject, on the ground that

> nothing categorical can be assumed about power in any community. . . . If anything, there seems to be an unspoken notion among pluralist researchers that at bottom *nobody* dominates in a town, so that their first question is not likely to be, "Who runs this community?," but rather, "Does anyone at all run this community?" The first query is somewhat like, "Have you stopped beating your wife?," in that virtually any response short of total unwillingness to answer will supply the researchers with a "power elite" along the lines presupposed by the stratification theory.[4]

Equally objectionable to the pluralists—and to us—is the sociologists' hypothesis that the power structure tends to be stable over time.

> Pluralists hold that power may be tied to issues, and issues can be fleeting or persistent, provoking coalitions among interested groups and citizens, ranging in their duration from momentary to semipermanent. . . . To presume that the set of coalitions which exists in the community at any given time is a timelessly stable aspect of social structure is to introduce systematic inaccuracies into one's description of social reality.[5]

A third criticism of the elitist model is that it wrongly equates reputed with actual power:

> If a man's major life work is banking, the pluralist presumes he will spend his time at the bank, and not in manipulating community deci-

---

[3] See especially N. W. Polsby, *op. cit.*, p. 475f.

[4] *Ibid.*, p. 476.

[5] *Ibid.*, pp. 478–79.

sions. This presumption holds until the banker's activities and participations indicate otherwise. . . . If we presume that the banker is really engaged in running the community, there is practically no way of disconfirming this notion, even if it is totally erroneous. On the other hand, it is easy to spot the banker who really *does* run community affairs when we presume he does not, because his activities will make this fact apparent.[6]

This is not an exhaustive bill of particulars; there are flaws other than these in the sociological model and methodology [7]—including some which the pluralists themselves have not noticed. But to go into this would not materially serve our current purposes. Suffice it simply to observe that whatever the merits of their own approach to power, the pluralists have effectively exposed the main weaknesses of the elitist model.

As the foregoing quotations make clear, the pluralists concentrate their attention, not upon the sources of power, but its exercise. Power to them means "participation in decision-making" [8] and can be analyzed only after "careful examination of a series of concrete decisions." [9] As a result, the pluralist researcher is uninterested in the reputedly powerful. His concerns instead are to (a) select for study a number of "key" as opposed to "routine" political decisions, (b) identify the people who took an active part in the decision-making process, (c) obtain a full account of their actual behavior while the policy conflict was being resolved, and (d) determine and analyze the specific outcome of the conflict.

The advantages of this approach, relative to the elitist alternative, need no further exposition. The same may not be said, however, about its defects—two of which seem to us to be of fundamental importance. One is that the model takes no account of the fact that power may be, and often is, exercised by confining the scope of decision-making to relatively "safe" issues. The other is that the model provides no *objective* criteria for distinguishing between "important" and "unimportant" issues arising in the political arena.

---

[6] *Ibid.*, pp. 480–81.

[7] See especially Robert A. Dahl, "A Critique of the Ruling-Elite Model," this REVIEW, Vol. 52 (June 1958), pp. 463–69; and Lawrence J. R. Herson, "In the Footsteps of Community Power," this REVIEW, Vol. 55 (December 1961), pp. 817–31.

[8] This definition originated with Harold D. Lasswell and Abraham Kaplan, *Power and Society* (New Haven, 1950), p. 75.

[9] Robert A. Dahl, "A Critique of the Ruling-Elite Model," *loc. cit.*, p. 466.

## II

There is no gainsaying that an analysis grounded entirely upon what is specific and visible to the outside observer is more "scientific" than one based upon pure speculation. To put it another way,

> If we can get our social life stated in terms of activity, and of nothing else, we have not indeed succeeded in measuring it, but we have at least reached a foundation upon which a coherent system of measurements can be built up. . . . We shall cease to be blocked by the intervention of unmeasurable elements, which claim to be themselves the real causes of all that is happening, and which by their spook-like arbitrariness make impossible any progress toward dependable knowledge.[10]

The question is, however, how can one be certain in any given situation that the "unmeasurable elements" are inconsequential, are not of decisive importance? Cast in slightly different terms, can a sound concept of power be predicated on the assumption that power is totally embodied and fully reflected in "concrete decisions" or in activity bearing directly upon their making?

We think not. Of course power is exercised when A participates in the making of decisions that affect B. But power is also exercised when A devotes his energies to creating or reinforcing social and political values and institutional practices that limit the scope of the political process to public consideration of only those issues which are comparatively innocuous to A. To the extent that A succeeds in doing this, B is prevented, for all practical purposes, from bringing to the fore any issues that might in their resolution be seriously detrimental to A's set of preferences.[11]

Situations of this kind are common. Consider, for example, the case —surely not unfamiliar to this audience—of the discontented faculty member in an academic institution headed by a tradition-bound executive. Aggrieved about a long-standing policy around which a strong vested interest has developed, the professor resolves in the privacy of his

---

[10] Arthur Bentley, *The Process of Government* (Chicago, 1908), p. 202, quoted in Polsby, *op. cit.*, p. 481n.

[11] As is perhaps self-evident, there are similarities in both faces of power. In each, A participates in decisions and thereby adversely effects B. But there is an important difference between the two: in the one case, A openly participates; in the other, he participates only in the sense that he works to sustain those values and rules of procedure that help him keep certain issues out of the public domain. True enough, participation of the second kind may at times be overt; that is the case, for instance, in cloture fights in the Congress. But the point is that it need not be. In fact, when the maneuver is most successfully executed, it neither involves nor can be identified with decisions arrived at on specific issues.

office to launch an attack upon the policy at the next faculty meeting. But, when the moment of truth is at hand, he sits frozen in silence. Why? Among the many possible reasons, one or more of these could have been of crucial importance: (a) the professor was fearful that his intended action would be interpreted as an expression of his disloyalty to the institution; or (b) he decided that, given the beliefs and attitudes of his colleagues on the faculty, he would almost certainly constitute on this issue a minority of one; or (c) he concluded that, given the nature of the law-making process in the institution, his proposed remedies would be pigeonholed permanently. But whatever the case, the central point to be made is the same: to the extent that a person or group—consciously or unconsciously—creates or reinforces barriers to the public airing of policy conflicts, that person or group has power. Or, as Professor Schattschneider has so admirably put it:

> All forms of political organization have a bias in favor of the exploitation of some kinds of conflict and the suppression of others because *organization is the mobilization of bias.* Some issues are organized into politics while others are organized out.[12]

Is such bias not relevant to the study of power? Should not the student be continuously alert to its possible existence in the human institution that he studies, and be ever prepared to examine the forces which brought it into being and sustain it? Can he safely ignore the possibility, for instance, that an individual or group in a community participates more vigorously in supporting the *non-decision-making* process than in participating in actual decisions within the process? Stated differently, can the researcher overlook the chance that some person or association could limit decision-making to relatively non-controversial matters, by influencing community values and political procedures and rituals, notwithstanding that there are in the community serious but latent power conflicts?[13] To do so is, in our judgment, to overlook the less apparent, but nonetheless extremely important, face of power.

---

[12] E. E. Schattschneider, *The Semi-Sovereign People* (New York, 1960), p. 71.

[13] Dahl *partially* concedes this point when he observes ("A Critique of the Ruling-Elite Model," pp. 468–69) that "one could argue that even in a society like ours a ruling elite might be so influential over ideas, attitudes, and opinions that a kind of false consensus will exist—not the phony consensus of a terroristic totalitarian dictatorship but the manipulated and superficially self-imposed adherence to the norms and goals of the elite by broad sections of a community.... This objection points to the need to be circumspect in interpreting the evidence." But that he largely misses our point is clear from the succeeding sentence: "Yet here, too, it seems to me that the hypothesis cannot be satisfactorily confirmed without something equivalent to the test I have proposed," and that is "by an examination of a series of concrete cases where key decisions are made...."

### III

In his critique of the "ruling-elite model," Professor Dahl argues that "the hypothesis of the existence of a ruling elite can be strictly tested only if . . . [t] here is a fair sample of cases involving key political decisions in which the preferences of the hypothetical ruling elite run counter to those of any other likely group that might be suggested." [14] With this assertion we have two complaints. One we have already discussed, viz., in erroneously assuming that power is solely reflected in concrete decisions, Dahl thereby excludes the possibility that in the community in question there is a group capable of preventing contests from arising on issues of importance to it. Beyond that, however, by ignoring the less apparent face of power Dahl and those who accept his pluralist approach are unable adequately to differentiate between a "key" and a "routine" political decision.

Nelson Polsby, for example, proposes that "by pre-selecting as issues for study those which are generally agreed to be significant, pluralist researchers can test stratification theory." [15] He is silent, however, on how the researcher is to determine *what* issues are "generally agreed to be significant," and on how the researcher is to appraise the reliability of the agreement. In fact, Polsby is guilty here of the same fault he himself has found with elitist methodology: by presupposing that in any community there are significant issues in the political arena, he takes for granted the very question which is in doubt. He accepts as issues what are reputed to be issues. As a result, his findings are fore-ordained. For even if there is no "truly" significant issue in the community under study, there is every likelihood that Polsby (or any like-minded researcher) will find one or some and, after careful study, research the appropriate pluralistic conclusions. [16]

Dahl's definition of "key political issues" in his essay on the ruling-elite model is open to the same criticism. He states that it is "a necessary although possibly not a sufficient condition that the [key] issue should involve actual disagreement in preferences among two or more groups." [17] In our view, this is an inadequate characterization of a "key political issue," simply because groups can have disagreements in preferences on unimportant as well as on important issues. Elite preferences which border on the indifferent are certainly not significant in determining

---

[14] *Op. cit.,* p. 466.

[15] *Op. cit.,* p. 478.

[16] As he points out, the expectations of the pluralist researchers "have seldom been disappointed." (*Ibid.,* p. 477)

[17] *Op. cit.,* p. 467.

whether a monolithic or polylithic distribution of power prevails in a given community. Using Dahl's definition of "key political issues," the researcher would have little difficulty in finding such in practically any community; and it would not be surprising then if he ultimately concluded that power in the community was widely diffused.

The distinction between important and unimportant issues, we believe, cannot be made intelligently in the absence of an analysis of the "mobilization of bias" in the community; of the dominant values and the political myths, rituals, and institutions which tend to favor the vested interests of one or more groups, relative to others. Armed with this knowledge, one could conclude that any challenge to the predominant values or to the established "rules of the game" would constitute an "important" issue; all else, unimportant. To be sure, judgments of this kind cannot be entirely objective. But to avoid making them in a study of power is both to neglect a highly significant aspect of power and thereby to undermine the only sound basis for discriminating between "key" and "routine" decisions. In effect, we contend, the pluralists have made each of these mistakes; that is to say, they have done just that for which Kaufman and Jones so severely taxed Floyd Hunter: they have begun "their structure at the mezzanine without showing us a lobby or foundation," [18] *i.e.,* they have begun by studying the issues rather than the values and biases that are built into the political system and that, for the student of power, give real meaning to those issues which do enter the political arena.

## IV

There is no better fulcrum for our critique of the pluralist model than Dahl's recent study of power in New Haven.[19]

At the outset it may be observed that Dahl does not attempt in this work to define his concept, "key political decision." In asking whether the "Notables" of New Haven are "influential overtly or covertly in the making of government decisions," he simply states that he will examine "three different 'issue-areas' in which important public decisions are made: nominations by the two political parties, urban redevelopment, and public education." These choices are justified on the grounds that "nominations determine which persons will hold public office. The New Haven redevelopment program measured by its cost—present and potential—is the largest in the country. Public education, aside from its

---

[18] Herbert Kaufman and Victor Jones, "The Mystery of Power," *Public Administration Review,* Vol. 14 (September 1954), p. 207.

[19] Robert A. Dahl, *Who Governs?* (New Haven, 1961).

intrinsic importance, is the costliest item in the city's budget." Therefore, Dahl concludes, "It is reasonable to expect . . . that the relative influence over public officials wielded by the . . . Notables would be revealed by an examination of their participation in these three areas of activity." [20]

The difficulty with this latter statement is that it is evident from Dahl's own account that the Notables are in fact uninterested in two of the three "key" decisions he has chosen. In regard to the public school issue, for example, Dahl points out that many of the Notables live in the suburbs and that those who do live in New Haven choose in the main to send their children to private schools. "As a consequence," he writes, "their interest in the public schools is ordinarily rather slight." [21] Nominations by the two political parties as an important "issue-area," is somewhat analogous to the public schools, in that the apparent lack of interest among the Notables in this issue is partially accounted for by their suburban residence—because of which they are disqualified from holding public office in New Haven. Indeed, Dahl himself concedes that with respect to both these issues the Notables are largely indifferent: "Business leaders might ignore the public schools or the political parties without any sharp awareness that their indifference would hurt their pocketbooks . . ." He goes on, however, to say that

> the prospect of profound changes [as a result of the urban-redevelopment program] in ownership, physical layout, and usage of property in the downtown area and the effects of these changes on the commercial and industrial prosperity of New Haven were all related in an obvious way to the daily concerns of businessmen.[22]

Thus, if one believes—as Professor Dahl did when he wrote his critique of the ruling-elite model—that an issue, to be considered as important, "should involve actual disagreement in preferences among two or more groups," [23] then clearly he has now for all practical purposes written off public education and party nominations as key "issue-areas." But this point aside, it appears somewhat dubious at best that "the relative influence over public officials wielded by the Social Notables" can be revealed by an examination of their nonparticipation in areas in which they were not interested.

Furthermore, we would not rule out the possibility that even on those issues to which they appear indifferent, the Notables may have a

---

[20] *Ibid.,* p. 64.

[21] *Ibid.,* p. 70.

[22] *Ibid.,* p. 71.

[23] *Op. cit.,* p. 467.

significant degree of *indirect* influence. We would suggest, for example, that although they send their children to private schools, the Notables do recognize that public school expenditures have a direct bearing upon their own tax liabilities. This being so, and given their strong representation on the New Haven Board of Finance,[24] the expectation must be that it is in their direct interest to play an active role in fiscal policy-making, in the establishment of the educational budget in particular. But as to this, Dahl is silent: he inquires not at all into either the decisions made by the Board of Finance with respect to education nor into their impact upon the public schools.[25] Let it be understood clearly that in making these points we are not attempting to refute Dahl's contention that the Notables lack power in New Haven. What we *are* saying, however, is that this conclusion is not adequately supported by his analysis of the "issue-areas" of public education and party nominations.

The same may not be said of redevelopment. This issue is by any reasonable standard important for purposes of determining whether New Haven is ruled by "the hidden hand of an economic elite." [26] For the Economic Notables have taken an active interest in the program and, beyond that, the socio-economic implications of it are not necessarily in harmony with the basic interests and values of businesses and businessmen.

In an effort to assure that the redevelopment program would be acceptable to what he dubbed "the biggest muscles" in New Haven, Mayor Lee created the Citizens Action Commission (CAC) and appointed to it primarily representatives of the economic elite. It was given the function of overseeing the work of the mayor and other officials involved in redevelopment, and, as well, the responsibility for organizing and encouraging citizens' participation in the program through an extensive committee system.

In order to weigh the relative influence of the mayor, other key officials, and the members of the CAC, Dahl reconstructs "all the *important*

---

[24] *Who Governs?*, p. 82. Dahl points out that "the main policy thrust of the Economic Notables is to oppose tax increases; this leads them to oppose expenditures for anything more than the minimal traditional city services. In this effort their two most effective weapons ordinarily are the mayor and the Board of Finance. The policies of the Notables are most easily achieved under a strong mayor if his policies coincide with theirs or under a weak mayor if they have the support of the Board of Finance. . . . New Haven mayors have continued to find it expedient to create confidence in their financial policies among businessmen by appointing them to the Board." (pp. 81–2)

[25] Dahl does discuss in general terms (pp. 79–84) changes in the level of tax rates and assessments in past years, but not actual decisions of the Board of Finance or their effects on the public school system.

[26] *Ibid.*, p. 124.

decisions on redevelopment and renewal between 1950–58 . . . [to] determine which individuals most often initiated the proposals that were finally adopted or most often successfully vetoed the proposals of the others." [27] The results of this test indicate that the mayor and his development administrator were by far the most influential, and that the "muscles" on the Commission, excepting in a few trivial instances, "never directly initiated, opposed, vetoed, or altered any proposal brought before them. . . ." [28]

The finding is, in our view, unreliable, not so much because Dahl was compelled to make a subjective selection of what constituted *important* decisions within what he felt to be an *important* "issue-area," as because the finding was based upon an excessively narrow test of influence. To measure relative influence solely in terms of the ability to initiate and veto proposals is to ignore the possible exercise of influence or power in limiting the scope of initiation. How, that is to say, can a judgment be made as to the relative influence of Mayor Lee and the CAC without knowing (through prior study of the political and social views of all concerned) the proposals that Lee did *not* make because he anticipated that they would provoke strenuous opposition and, perhaps, sanctions on the part of the CAC? [29]

In sum, since he does not recognize *both* faces of power, Dahl is in no position to evaluate the relative influence or power of the initiator and decision-maker, on the one hand, and of those persons, on the other, who may have been indirectly instrumental in preventing potentially dangerous issues from being raised. [30] As a result, he unduly emphasizes

---

[27] *Ibid.* "A rough test of a person's overt or covert influence," Dahl states in the first section of the book, "is the frequency with which he successfully initiates an important policy over the opposition of others, or vetoes policies initiated by others, or initiates a policy where no opposition appears." (*Ibid.*, p. 66)

[28] *Ibid.*, p. 131.

[29] Dahl is, of course, aware of the "law of anticipated reactions." In the case of the mayor's relationship with the CAC, Dahl notes that Lee was "particularly skillful in estimating what the CAC could be expected to support or reject." (p. 137). However, Dahl was not interested in analyzing or appraising to what extent the CAC limited Lee's freedom of action. Because of his restricted concept of power, Dahl did not consider that the CAC might in this respect have exercised power. That the CAC did not initiate or veto actual proposals by the mayor was to Dahl evidence enough that the CAC was virtually powerless; it might as plausibly be evidence that the CAC was (in itself or in what it represented) so powerful that Lee ventured nothing it would find worth quarreling with.

[30] The fact that the initiator of decisions also refrains—because he anticipates adverse reactions—from initiating other proposals does not obviously lessen the power of the agent who limited his initiative powers. Dahl missed this point: "It is," he writes, "all the more improbable, then, that a secret cabal of Notables dominates the public life of New Haven through means so clandestine that not one

the importance of initiating, deciding, and vetoing, and in the process casts the pluralist conclusions of his study into serious doubt.

## V

We have contended in this paper that a fresh approach to the study of power is called for, an approach based upon a recognition of the two faces of power. Under this approach the researcher would begin—not, as does the sociologist who asks, "Who rules?" nor as does the pluralist who asks, "Does anyone have power?"—but by investigating the particular "mobilization of bias" in the institution under scrutiny. Then, having analyzed the dominant values, the myths and the established political procedures and rules of the game, he would make a careful inquiry into which persons or groups, if any, gain from the existing bias and which, if any, are handicapped by it. Next, he would investigate the dynamics of *non-decision-making;* that is, he would examine the extent to which and the manner in which the *status quo* oriented persons and groups influence those community values and those political institutions (as, *e.g.,* the unanimity "rule" of New York City's Board of Estimate [31]) which tend to limit the scope of actual decision-making to "safe" issues. Finally, using his knowledge of the restrictive face of power as a foundation for analysis and as a standard for distinguishing between "key" and "routine" political decisions, the researcher would, after the manner of the pluralists, analyze participation in decision-making of concrete issues.

We reject in advance as unimpressive the possible criticism that this approach to the study of power is likely to prove fruitless because it goes beyond an investigation of what is objectively measurable. In reacting against the subjective aspects of the sociological model of power, the pluralists have, we believe, made the mistake of discarding "unmeasurable elements" as unreal. It is ironical that, by so doing, they have exposed themselves to the same fundamental criticism they have so forcefully levelled against the elitists: their approach to and assumption about power predetermine their findings and conclusions.

---

of the fifty prominent citizens interviewed in the course of this study—citizens who had participated extensively in various decisions—hinted at the existence of such a cabal . . ." (p. 185).

In conceiving of elite domination exclusively in the form of a conscious cabal exercising the power of decision-making and vetoing, he overlooks a more subtle form of domination; one in which those who actually dominate are not conscious of it themselves, simply because their position of dominance has never seriously been challenged.

[31] Sayre and Kaufman, *op. cit.,* p. 640. For perceptive study of the "mobilization of bias" in a rural American community, see Arthur Vidich and Joseph Bensman, *Small Town in Mass Society* (Princeton, 1958).

# E. URBAN ELECTORAL SYSTEMS

## Public-Regardingness as a Value Premise in Voting Behavior*

### JAMES Q. WILSON
### EDWARD C. BANFIELD

Our concern here is with the nature of the individual's attachment to the body politic and, more particularly, with the value premises underlying the choices made by certain classes of voters. Our hypothesis is that some classes of voters (provisionally defined as "subcultures" constituted on ethnic and income lines) are more disposed than others to rest their choices on some conception of "the public interest" or the "welfare of the community." To say the same thing in another way, the voting behavior of some classes tends to be more public-regarding and less private- (self- or family-) regarding than that of others. To test this hypothesis it is necessary to examine voting behavior in situations where one can say that a certain vote could not have been private-regarding. Local bond and other expenditure referenda present such situations: it is sometimes possible to say that a vote in favor of a particular expenditure proposal is incompatible with a certain voter's self-interest narrowly conceived. If the voter nevertheless casts such a vote and if there is evidence that his vote was not in some sense irrational or accidental, then it must be presumed that his action was based on some conception of "the public interest."

Our first step, accordingly, is to show how much of the behavior in question can, and cannot, be explained on grounds of self-interest alone,

Reprinted from *American Political Science Review,* Vol. 58 (December 1964), 876–87, by permission of the publisher and the authors.

\* This is a preliminary report of a study supported by the Joint Center for Urban Studies of M.I.T. and Harvard University and the Rockefeller Foundation. The writers wish to acknowledge assistance from Martha Derthick and Mark K. Adams and comments from James Beshers, Anthony Downs, Werner Hirsch, Hendrik Houthakker, H. Douglas Price, and Arthur Stinchcombe. This paper was originally presented at the Second Conference On Urban Public Expenditures, New York University, February 21–22, 1964.

narrowly conceived. If all of the data were consistent with the hypothesis that the voter acts as if he were trying to maximize his family income, the inquiry would end right there. In fact, it turns out that many of the data cannot be explained in this way. The question arises, therefore, whether the unexplained residue is purposive or "accidental." We suggest that for the most part it is purposive, and that the voters' purposes arise from their conceptions of "the public interest."

## I

We start, then, from the simple—and admittedly implausible— hypothesis that the voter tries to maximize his family income or (the same thing) self-interest narrowly conceived. We assume that the voter estimates in dollars both the benefits that will accrue to him and his family if the proposed public expenditure is made and the amount of the tax that will fall on him in consequence of the expenditure; if the esti- mated benefit is more than the estimated cost, he votes for the expen- diture; if it is less, he votes against it. We assume that all proposed ex- penditures will confer some benefits on all voters. The benefits conferred on a particular voter are "trivial," however, if the expenditure is for something that the particular voter (and his family) is not likely to use or enjoy. For example, improvement of sidewalks confers trivial benefits on those voters who are not likely to walk on them.

Insofar as behavior is consistent with these assumptions—*i.e.,* inso- far as the voter seems to act rationally in pursuit of self-interest nar- rowly conceived—we consider that no further "explanation" is required. It may be that other, entirely different hypotheses would account for the behavior just as well or better. That possibility is not of concern to us here, however.

No doubt, our assumptions lack realism. No doubt, relatively few voters make a conscious calculation of costs and benefits. Very often the voter has no way of knowing whether a public expenditure proposal will benefit him or not. In only one state which we have examined (Florida) do ballots in municipal referenda specify precisely *which* streets are to be paved or *where* a bridge is to be built. Even if a facility is to serve the whole city (*e.g.,* a zoo, civic center, or county hospital), in most cities the ballot proposition is usually so indefinite that the voter cannot ac- curately judge either the nature or the amount of the benefits that he would derive from the expenditure. Similarly, it is often difficult or im- possible for the voter to estimate even the approximate amount of the tax that will fall upon him in consequence of the expenditure. Some states (*e.g.,* Illinois and California) require that the anticipated cost of each undertaking be listed on the ballot (*e.g.,* "$12,800,000 for sewer improvements"). Of course, even when the total cost is given, the voter must depend on the newspapers to tell, or figure out for himself—if he can—how much it would increase the tax rate and how much the increased tax rate would add to his tax bill. Ohio is the only state we have studied where the voter is told on the ballot how the proposed expenditure will affect the tax rate.("17 cents per $100 valuation for each of two years"). Almost everywhere, most of the expenditure proposals are to be financed from the local property tax. Occasionally, however, a different tax (*e.g.,* the sales tax) or a different tax base (*e.g.,* the county or state rather than the city), is used. In these cases, the voter is likely to find it even harder to estimate how much he will have to pay.

We may be unrealistic also both in assuming that the voter takes only *money* costs into account (actually he may think that a proposed civic center would be an eyesore) and in assuming that the only money costs he takes into account are *taxes* levied upon him (actually, if he is a renter he may suppose—whether correctly or incorrectly is beside the point—that his landlord will pass a tax increase on to him in a higher rent).

The realism of the assumption does not really matter. What does matter is their usefulness in predicting the voters' behavior. It is possible that voters may act *as if* they are well informed and disposed to calculate even when in fact they are neither. If we can predict their behavior without going into the question of how much or how well they calculate, so much the better.

## II

On the assumptions we have made, one would expect voters who will have no tax levied upon them in consequence of the passage of an expenditure proposal to vote for it even if it will confer only trivial benefits on them. Having nothing to lose by the expenditure and something (however small) to gain, they will favor it. In the *very* low-income [1] wards and precincts of the larger cities a high proportion of the voters are in this position since most local public expenditures are financed from the property tax and the lowest-income people do not own property. We find that in these heavily non-home-owning districts the voters almost invariably support all expenditure proposals. We have examined returns on 35 expenditure proposals passed upon in 20 separate elections in seven cities and have not found a single instance in which this group

---

[1] Median family income under $3,000 per year. Needless to say, most voters in this category are Negroes.

failed to give a majority in favor of a proposal. Frequently the vote is 75 to 80 per cent in favor; sometimes it is over 90 per cent. The strength of voter support is about the same no matter what the character of the proposed expenditure.[2]

### TABLE 1

RELATIONSHIP BETWEEN PERCENTAGE OF WARD VOTING "YES" AND PERCENTAGE OF DWELLING UNITS OWNER OCCUPIED; VARIOUS ISSUES IN CLEVELAND AND CHICAGO

| Issue and Date | Simple Correlation Coefficient $(r)$ |
|---|---|
| *Cleveland (33 wards):* | |
| Administration Building (11/59) | −0.86 |
| County Hospital (11/59) | −0.77 |
| Tuberculosis Hospital (11/59) | −0.79 |
| Court House (11/59) | −0.85 |
| Juvenile Court (11/59) | −0.83 |
| Parks (11/59) | −0.67 |
| Welfare Levy (5/60) | −0.72 |
| Road and Bridges (11/60) | −0.77 |
| Zoo (11/60) | −0.81 |
| Parks (11/60) | −0.57 |
| | |
| *Chicago (50 wards):* | |
| County Hospital (1957) | −0.79 |
| Veterans' Bonus (1957) | −0.49 |
| Welfare Building (1958) | −0.67 |
| Street Lights (1959) | −0.83 |
| Municipal Building (1962) | −0.78 |
| Urban Renewal Bonds (1962) | −0.79 |
| Sewers (1962) | −0.79 |
| Street Lights (1962) | −0.81 |

In all of the elections we have examined, non-homeowners show more taste for public expenditures that are to be financed from property taxes than do homeowners. Table 1 shows by means of product-moment (Pearsonian $r$) coefficients of correlation the strength and consistency of this relationship over a wide variety of issues in several elections in Cleve-

---

[2] The cities and elections examined are:
Cleveland-Cuyahoga County: Nov., 1956; Nov., 1959; May, 1960; Nov., 1960.
Chicago-Cook County: June, 1957; Nov., 1958; Nov., 1959; April, 1962.
Detroit-Wayne County: August, 1960; Feb., 1961; April, 1961; April, 1963.
Kansas City: Nov., 1960; March, 1962.
Los Angeles: Nov., 1962.
Miami: Nov., 1956; May, 1960.
St. Louis: March, 1962; Nov., 1962; March, 1963.

land and Chicago.[3] As one would expect, when an expenditure is to be financed from a source other than the property tax the difference between homeowner and non-homeowner behavior is reduced. This is borne out in Table 2 in which we have compared wards typical of four major eco-

**TABLE 2**

*VOTING BEHAVIOR OF FOUR MAJOR ECONOMIC GROUPS*
*COMPARED IN COOK COUNTY*

| | Percent "Yes" Vote | |
| Group | County Hospital (1957) | State Welfare Building (1958) |
|---|---|---|
| *High Income Homeowners* * | (%) | (%) |
| Winnetka | 64 | 76 |
| Wilmette | 55 | 70 |
| Lincolnwood | 47 | 64 |
| *Middle Income Homeowners* † | | |
| Lansing | 30 | 54 |
| Bellwood | 21 | 55 |
| Brookfield | 22 | 51 |
| *Middle Income Renters* ‡ | | |
| Chicago Ward 44 | 65 | 71 |
| Chicago Ward 48 | 61 | 72 |
| Chicago Ward 49 | 64 | 74 |
| *Low Income Renters* § | | |
| Chicago Ward 2 | 88 | 73 |
| Chicago Ward 3 | 87 | 76 |
| Chicago Ward 27 | 87 | 78 |

* Three suburbs with the highest median family income ($13,200 to $23,000) among all suburbs with 85 percent or more home ownership.

† Three suburbs with lowest median family income ($8,000 to $8,300) among all suburbs with 85 percent or more home ownership.

‡ Three wards with highest median family income ($6,200 to $6,800) among all wards with less than 15 percent home ownership (none of the three wards is more than 4 percent Negro).

§ Three wards with lowest median family income ($3,100 to $4,100) among all wards with less than 15 percent home ownership (Negro population of wards ranges from 59 to 99 percent).

nomic groups in Cook County (Illinois) in their voting on two issues: first, a proposal to increase county hospital facilities and, second, a proposal to construct a state welfare building. The measures were alike in that they would benefit only indigents; they were different in that their costs would be assessed against different publics; the hospital was to be paid for from the local property tax, the welfare building from state

[3] The degree of association was also calculated using a nonparametric statistic (Kendall's *tau*). The relationship persists but at lower values. Since we are satisfied that the relationship found by *r* is not spurious, we have relied on it for the balance of the analysis because of its capacity to produce partial correlation coefficients.

sources, largely a sales tax. Middle-income homeowners showed themselves very sensitive to this difference; the percentage favoring the state-
financed measure was twice that favoring the property-tax-financed one.
Low-income renters, on the other hand, preferred the property-tax-
financed measure to the state-financed one.

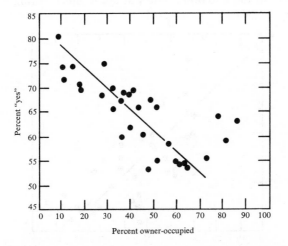

Source of housing data: U.S. Census of housing, 1960. Figure reprinted from Edward
C. Banfield and James Q. Wilson, *City Politics* (Cambridge: Harvard University Press,
1963), p. 238.

**FIGURE 1**

*RELATION BETWEEN PERCENTAGE VOTING "YES" ON PROPOSITION TO
PROVIDE INCREASED COUNTY HOSPITAL FACILITIES (NOVEMBER 1959)
AND PERCENTAGE OF DWELLING UNITS OWNER-OCCUPIED
IN THE 33 WARDS OF CLEVELAND*

Let us turn now to the behavior of voters who do own property and
whose taxes will therefore be increased in consequence of a public expenditure. One might suppose that the more property such a voter has,
the less likely it is that he will favor public expenditures. To be sure,
certain expenditures confer benefits roughly in proportion to the value
of property and some may even confer disproportionate benefits on the
more valuable properties; in such cases one would expect large property
owners to be as much in favor of expenditures as the small, or more so.
More expenditures, however, confer about the same benefits on large
properties as on small, whereas of course the taxes to pay for the expenditure are levied (in theory at least) strictly in proportion to the
value of property. The owner of a $30,000 home, for example, probably
gets no more benefit from the construction of a new city hall or the expansion of a zoo than does the owner of a $10,000 one; his share of the

tax increase is three times as much, however. Very often, indeed, there is an inverse relation between the value of a property and the benefits that accrue to its owner from a public expenditure. The probability is certainly greater that the owner of the $10,000 house will some day use the free county hospital (patronized chiefly by low-income Negroes) than that the owner of the $30,000 house will use it. Since normally the *ratio*

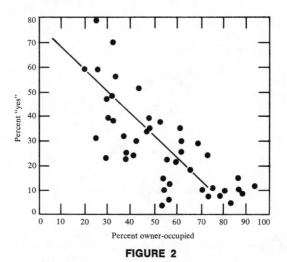

**FIGURE 2**

*RELATION BETWEEN PERCENTAGE VOTING "YES" ON PROPOSITION TO PROVIDE ADDITIONAL SEWER FACILITIES (1962) AND PERCENTAGE OF DWELLING UNITS OWNER-OCCUPIED IN WARDS OF CHICAGO*

of benefits to costs is less favorable the higher the value of the property, one might expect to find a positive correlation between the percentage of "No" votes in a neighborhood and the median value of homes there.

This expectation is not borne out by the facts, however. Table 3 gives partial correlation coefficients relating the per cent voting "Yes" in the wards of Cleveland and the suburban wards and towns of Cuyahoga County to the median family income in those wards and towns.[4] It shows

---

[4] Only two measures of tax liability can be got from the Census: median home value and median family income. We have used the latter for the most part. The Census classifies all homes valued at over $25,000 together, thereby collapsing distinctions that are important for us. We think, too, that people are more likely to know their incomes than to know the current market value of their homes, and that therefore the Census information on incomes is more reliable. Finally, in neighborhoods populated mostly by renters, median home values are likely to be unrepresentative of the class character of the neighborhood: this is so, for example, where a few owner-occupied slums exist in a district of luxury apartments.

## TABLE 3

PARTIAL CORRELATIONS BETWEEN MEDIAN FAMILY INCOME OF WARD
AND PERCENTAGE "YES" VOTE ON VARIOUS MEASURES,
CLEVELAND AND SUBURBS

| Area and Issue | Partial Correlation * |
|---|---|
| *Cleveland (33 wards)*: | |
| Administration Building | +0.49 |
| County Hospital | +0.64 |
| Tuberculosis Hospital | +0.57 |
| Court House | +0.49 |
| Juvenile Court | +0.66 |
| Parks | +0.48 |
| Welfare Levy | +0.70 |
| Roads and Bridges | +0.61 |
| Zoo | +0.59 |
| *Cuyahoga County Suburbs (90 wards and towns)*: | |
| Administration Building | +0.47 |
| County Hospital | +0.54 |
| Tuberculosis Hospital | +0.43 |
| Court House | +0.60 |
| Juvenile Court | +0.59 |
| Parks | +0.52 |
| Welfare Levy | +0.35 |
| Roads and Bridges | +0.60 |
| Zoo | +0.62 |

\* Controlling for proportion of dwelling units owner-occupied.

that the higher the income of a ward or town, the more taste it has for public expenditures of various kinds. That the ratio of benefits to costs declines as income goes up seems to make no difference.[5]

[5] Other studies which suggest that upper-income groups may have a greater preference for public expenditures than middle-income groups include Oliver P. Williams and Charles R. Adrian, *Four Cities: A Study in Comparative Policy Making* (Philadelphia: University of Pennsylvania Press, 1963), ch. v; Alvin Boskoff and Harmon Zeigler, *Voting Patterns in a Local Election* (Philadelphia: J. B. Lippincott Co., 1964), ch. iii; Richard A. Watson, *The Politics of Urban Change* (Kansas City, Mo.: Community Studies, Inc., 1963), ch. iv; and Robert H. Salisbury and Gordon Black, "Class and Party in Non-Partisan Elections: The Case of Des Moines," this REVIEW, Vol. 57 (September, 1963), p. 591. The Williams-Adrian and Salisbury-Black studies use electoral data; the Boskoff-Zeigler and Watson studies use survey data. See also Otto A. Davis, "Empirical Evidence of 'Political' Influences Upon the Expenditure and Taxation Policies of Public Schools," Graduate School of Industrial Administration of the Carnegie Institute of Technology, January, 1964 (mimeo), and William C. Birdsall, "Public Finance Allocation Decisions and the Preferences of Citizens: Some Theoretical and Empirical Considerations," unpublished Ph.D. thesis, Department of Economics, Johns Hopkins University, 1963. A difficulty with the Davis and Birdsall studies is the size (and thus the heterogeneity) of the units of analysis—entire school districts in one case, entire cities in the other.

The same pattern appears in a 1960 Flint, Michigan, vote on additional flood control facilities. This is shown graphically in Figure 3. Although there is a considerable dispersion around the line of regression, in general the higher the home value—and accordingly the more the expected tax—the greater the support for the expenditure.[6]

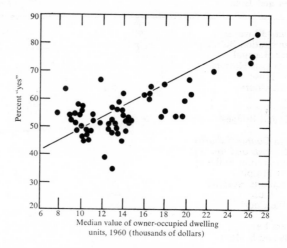

Note: Only property owners and their spouses could vote.
Source of housing data: U.S. Census of Housing, 1960.
Figure reprinted from Banfield and Wilson, *City Politics*, p. 239.

**FIGURE 3**

*RELATION BETWEEN PERCENTAGE VOTING "YES" ON PROPOSITION TO*
*PROVIDE ADDITIONAL FLOOD CONTROL FACILITIES (NOVEMBER, 1960)*
*AND MEDIAN VALUE OF OWNER-OCCUPIED DWELLING UNITS*
*IN THE PRECINCTS OF FLINT, MICHIGAN*

It may be argued that because of the phenomenon of the diminishing marginal utility of money these findings are not really anomalous. The richer a man is, perhaps, the smaller the sacrifice that an additional dollar of taxation represents to him. Thus, even though the well-to-do

---

[6] Michigan is one of the few states which restricts the right to vote on expenditures to property owners and their spouses. Because the Flint returns were tabulated on a precinct basis, demographic data had to be obtained from block rather than tract statistics; since median family income is given only for tracts, median value of owner-occupied homes had to be used.

Possibly the flood control benefits would be distributed roughly in proportion to the value of properties; about this we cannot say. However, it is worth noting that the vote in Flint on other expenditures which presumably would *not* distribute benefits in proportion to the value of the properties (*e.g., parks*) followed the same pattern.

voter may get no more benefit than the poor one gets and may have to pay a great deal more in taxes, an expenditure proposal may nevertheless be more attractive to him. He may be more willing to pay a dollar for certain benefits than his neighbor is to pay fifty cents because, having much more money than his neighbor, a dollar is worth only a quarter as much to him.

Differences in the value of the dollar to voters at different income levels account in part for the well-to-do voter's relatively strong taste for public expenditures. They can hardly account for it entirely, however. For one thing, they do not rationalize the behavior of those voters who support measures that would give them only trivial benefits while imposing substantial costs upon them. The suburbanite who favors a county hospital for the indigent which he and his family will certainly never use for which he will be heavily taxed is not acting according to self-interest narrowly conceived no matter how little a dollar is worth to him.

Moreover, if the well-to-do voter places a low value on the dollar when evaluating some expenditure proposals, one would expect him to place the same low value on it when evaluating all others. In fact, he does not seem to do so; indeed, he sometimes appears to place a *higher* value on it than does his less-well-off neighbor. Compare, for example, the behavior of the Cook County (Illinois) suburbanites who voted on a proposal to build a county hospital (an expenditure which would confer only trivial benefits on them and for which they would be taxed in proportion to the value of their property) with the behavior of the same suburbanites who voted on a proposal to give a bonus of $300 to Korean War veterans (an expenditure from which the well-to-do would benefit about as much as the less-well-to-do and for which they would not be taxed disproportionately, since the bonus was to be financed from state, not local, revenues, and the state had neither an income tax nor a corporate profits tax). As Figures 4 and 5 show, the higher the median family income of a voting district, the larger the percentage voting "Yes" on the welfare building (the rank-order correlation was $+0.57$), but the *smaller* the percentage voting "Yes" on the veterans' bonus (the rank-order correlation was $-0.71$).

In Cuyahoga County, Ohio, the same thing happened. There the higher the median family income, the larger the percentage voting for all the expenditure proposals except one—a bonus for Korean War veterans. On this one measure there was a correlation of $-0.65$ between median family income and percentage voting "Yes."

Thus, although it is undoubtedly true that the more dollars a voter has, the more he will pay for a given benefit, the principle does not ex-

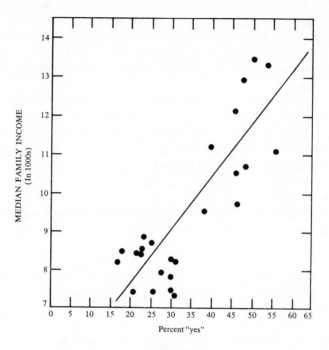

**FIGURE 4**

*RELATION BETWEEN PERCENTAGE VOTING "YES" ON PROPOSITION TO
PROVIDE INCREASED COUNTY HOSPITAL FACILITIES (1957) AND MEDIAN
FAMILY INCOME IN THE SUBURBAN CITIES AND TOWNS OF COOK COUNTY,
ILLINOIS, IN WHICH TWO-THIRDS OR MORE OF THE DWELLING
UNITS ARE OWNER-OCCUPIED*

plain all that needs explaining. When it comes to a veterans' bonus, for
example, the opposite principle seems to work: the more dollars the
voter has, the fewer he will spend for a given benefit of that sort.

That there is a positive correlation between amount of property
owned (or income) and tendency to vote "Yes" does not, of course, imply that a majority of property owners at *any* income level favors expenditures: the correlation would exist even if the highest income voters
opposed them, provided that at each lower level of income voters opposed them by ever-larger majorities. In fact, middle-income home-
owners often vote against proposals that are approved by both the very
poor (renters) and the very well-to-do (owners). Table 4 gives a rather
typical picture of the response of the various income groups to proposals
that are to be financed from the property tax in Cuyahoga County
(Ohio).

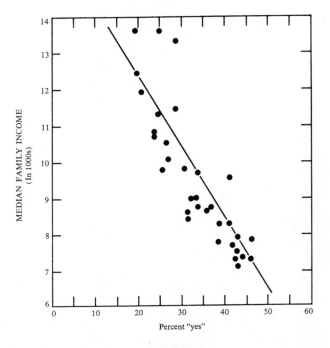

**FIGURE 5**

*RELATION BETWEEN PERCENTAGE VOTING "YES" ON PROPOSITION TO
APPROVE A $300 BONUS FOR VETERANS OF KOREAN WAR (1958) AND
MEDIAN FAMILY INCOME IN THE SUBURBAN CITIES AND TOWNS OF
COOK COUNTY, ILLINOIS, IN WHICH TWO-THIRDS OR MORE
OF THE DWELLING UNITS ARE OWNER-OCCUPIED*

Not infrequently the highest-income districts support expenditure
proposals by very large majorities—indeed, sometimes by majorities approaching those given in the property-less slums. Table 5 compares the
percentage voting "Yes" in the high-income, high-home-ownership precincts of three city-county areas with the percentage of all voters in these
areas who voted "Yes." [7] Except for Detroit and Dade County, where
only property owners and their spouses may vote on expenditures, the
city-county totals include large numbers of renters. Even so, the high-
income precincts are comparatively strong in their support of all expenditures.

---

[7] We isolated all precincts in Census tracts having median family incomes of
at least $10,000 a year, with at least 70 percent home ownership (the central city
of Chicago was excepted here), and at least 70 percent of the population third-
(or more) generation native born.

**TABLE 4**

*VOTING BEHAVIOR OF FOUR MAJOR ECONOMIC GROUPS COMPARED IN CUYAHOGA COUNTY*

| | Percent "Yes" Vote | |
|---|---|---|
| Group | County Hospital (1959) | County Court House (1959) |
| | (%) | (%) |
| *High-Income Homeowners* * | | |
| Pepper Pike | 69 | 47 |
| Beachwood | 72 | 47 |
| *Middle-Income Homeowners* † | | |
| Olmstead Township | 51 | 28 |
| Garfield Heights (Ward 4) | 48 | 29 |
| *Lower-Middle-Income Renters* ‡ | | |
| Cleveland Ward 31 | 76 | 66 |
| *Low-Income Renters* § | | |
| Cleveland Ward 11 | 73 | 63 |
| Cleveland Ward 17 | 74 | 62 |

* Two suburbs with highest median family income ($15,700 and $19,000) of all suburbs with 85 percent or more home ownership.

† Two suburbs with lowest median family income ($6,800 and $7,000) of all suburbs with 85 percent or more home ownership.

‡ The one ward with less than 15 percent home ownership and which is less than 10 percent Negro (median income: $4,700).

§ Two wards with lowest median family incomes ($3,400 and $3,600) of all wards with less than 15 percent home ownership (Negro population of wards was 90 and 97 percent).

**TABLE 5**

*PERCENTAGE VOTING "YES" ON EXPENDITURES IN HOME-OWNING, UPPER-INCOME "OLD-STOCK" PRECINCTS IN VARIOUS COUNTIES*

| County, Issue, and Date | Percent "Yes" Vote in Upper-Income Precincts | Percent "Yes" Vote in County As a Whole |
|---|---|---|
| | (%) | (%) |
| *Detroit-Wayne County* | | |
| Sewers (8/10) | 83.6 | 64.3 |
| Increase School tax limit | 52.0 | 39.0 |
| Build Schools (4/63) | 52.0 | 33.4 |
| Increase sales tax (11/60) | 78.6 | 47.8 |
| *Kansas City—Jefferson County* | | |
| Increase school taxes 11/60) | 68.6 | 54.9 |
| Build jails (3/62) | 86.3 | 78.0 |
| Sewage treatment plant (11/60) | 93.2 | 81.6 |
| *Miami-Dade County* | | |
| Highways (5/60) | 71.2 | 53.0 |
| Schools (1955) | 90.8 | 92.1 |

## III

When we hold constant the percentage of home ownership, percentage of nonwhites, and median family income, a negative correlation appears between the percentage of voters in the wards of Cleveland who are of foreign stock and the percentage of the total vote in those wards that is "Yes." This is shown in Column 1 of Table 6.[8] Of the many for-

**TABLE 6**

*PARTIAL CORRELATIONS BETWEEN SELECTED "ETHNIC" VARIABLES*
*AND PERCENTAGE VOTING "YES" ON EXPENDITURES IN CLEVELAND*
*AND CUYAHOGA COUNTY WARDS AND TOWNS \**

| Issue | Foreign Stock | | Polish-Czech | | Negro | |
|---|---|---|---|---|---|---|
| | City | Suburbs | City | Suburbs | City | Suburbs |
| Admin. Building | −0.40 | ns † | −0.54 | −0.17 | ns | ns |
| County Hospital | ns | ns | −0.79 | −0.40 | ns | ns |
| TB Hospital | ns | −0.22 | −0.74 | −0.46 | ns | ns |
| Court House | −0.47 | ns | −0.58 | −0.28 | ns | ns |
| Juvenile Court | −0.46 | ns | −0.74 | −0.40 | ns | ns |
| Parks (1959) | −0.41 | ns | −0.62 | −0.31 | −0.49 | ns |
| Welfare Levy | −0.58 | ns | −0.71 | −0.49 | ns | ns |
| Roads and Bridges | −0.48 | ns | −0.66 | −0.40 | ns | ns |
| Zoo | −0.62 | ns | −0.71 | −0.40 | ns | ns |
| Parks (1960) | ns | ns | ns | −0.50 | ns | ns |

\* These are partial correlation coefficients derived from a regression analysis in which home ownership, median family income, and two "ethnic" variables have been held constant.

† If the correlations were not significant at the .05 level (Student's $t$), "ns" is entered in the table. The critical values were based on 27 degrees of freedom for the city data and 84 degrees of freedom for the suburban data.

eign stocks in Cleveland, the Poles and Czechs have the strongest distaste for expenditures. Column 2 of Table 6 shows how markedly the presence of Poles and Czechs in a voting district affects the "Yes" vote.[9] In the

---

[8] A person is of "foreign stock" if he was born abroad or if one or both of his parents was born abroad. We believe that the reason why a significant relationship does not appear for the suburbs is that there is a considerable number of Jews among the foreign stock of the suburbs. In the central city, there are practically no Jews. Like other Jews, Jews of Eastern European origin tend to favor expenditure proposals of all kinds. Their presence in the suburbs, therefore, offsets the "No" vote of the non-Jews of foreign stock.

[9] Since no home-owning ward or town in Cuyahoga County is more than 25 per cent Polish-Czech according to the 1960 Census, it may be that no inferences can be drawn from the voting data about Polish-Czech behavior. Three considerations increase our confidence in the possibility of drawing inferences, however. (1) Only first- and second-generation Poles and Czechs are counted as such by the Census, but third- and fourth-generation Poles and Czechs tend to live in the

suburbs the correlation is only slightly weaker, but significant at the
.001 level in all but two cases and in these at the .01 level. The complete correlation table shows that in all but three cases the percentage
of Poles and Czechs is a more important influence on voting than median
family income, and is second in influence only to home ownership. In
two of the three exceptional cases, indeed, it was *more* important than
home ownership.

The findings in Column 3 of Table 6 are surprising. We expected
a positive correlation between percentage of Negroes and the strength
of the "Yes" vote. Deficiencies in the data may possibly account for
the absence of any correlation: there are not enough home-owning
Negroes or enough very low-income whites in Cleveland to make a
really satisfactory matching of wards possible.

In order to get a closer view of ethnic voting it is necessary to
forego general correlations and instead to examine individual precincts
known to be predominantly of a single ethnic group. In Tables 7 and 8
we show how selected "ethnic" precincts belonging to two income and
home-ownership classes voted in several elections in the Chicago and
Cleveland areas.[10] There is a remarkable degree of consistency in the
influence of both ethnicity and income or home-ownership, whether
viewed on an intra- or inter-city basis. In Chicago, for example, the
low-income renters in *every* case voted more favorably for expenditures
than did the middle-income home-owners of the same ethnic group.
Within the same economic class, however, ethnicity makes a striking
difference. Low-income Negro renters are in *every* case more enthusiastic by a wide margin about public expenditures than low-income Irish
or Polish renters. Middle-income Negro home-owners are in *every* case
more enthusiastic about the same proposals than middle-income Irish

---

same wards and towns; thus the proportion of the electorate sharing Polish-Czech
cultural values (the relevant thing from our standpoint) is considerably larger
than the Census figures suggest. (2) When other factors are held constant, even
small increases in the number of Poles and Czechs are accompanied by increases
in the "No" vote; nothing "explains" this except the hypothesis that the Poles and
Czechs make the difference. (3) When we take as the unit for analysis not wards
but precincts of a few hundred persons that are known to contain very high proportions of Poles and Czechs, we get the same results. Because we are using
ecological, not individual, data, we are perforce analyzing the behavior of ethnic
"ghettos" where ethnic identification and attitudes are probably reinforced. Poles
in non-Polish wards, for example, may behave quite differently.

[10] The method by which these precincts were selected is given in the Appendix.
Unfortunately, it proved impossible to identify relatively homogeneous precincts
typical of other ethnic groups at various income levels and degrees of home-
ownership. For example, middle-income Jews tend to be renters, not home owners,
and there are practically no low-income Jewish precincts in either city. A complete
list of these precincts is available from the authors.

## TABLE 7

*PERCENTAGE OF VARIOUS "ETHNIC" PRECINCTS VOTING "YES" ON
SELECTED EXPENDITURES IN CHICAGO*

| Ethnic Group and Number of Precincts | Percent Voting "Yes" on: | | | | |
|---|---|---|---|---|---|
| | Co. Hosp. (6/57) | Vet's Bonus (11/58) | Urban Renewal (4/62) | City Hall (5/62) | School (4/59) |
| *Low Income Renters** | (%) | (%) | (%) | (%) | (%) |
| Negro (22) | 84.9 | 80.2 | 88.6 | 82.3 | 97.8 |
| Irish (6) | 61.3 | 55.3 | 45.7 | 46.3 | 79.4 |
| Polish (26) | 60.1 | 54.6 | 57.1 | 53.8 | 81.8 |
| *Middle Income Home-Owners †* | | | | | |
| Negro (13) | 66.8 | 54.9 | 69.6 | 49.8 | 88.9 |
| Irish (6) | 54.6 | 44.1 | 22.0 | 27.2 | 64.2 |
| Polish (38) | 47.4 | 40.0 | 14.6 | 15.2 | 58.3 |

* Average median family income under $6,000 per year; at least two-thirds of all dwelling units renter-occupied.

† Average median family income between $7,500 and $10,000 a year for whites; over $6,000 a year for Negroes. At least 80 percent of all dwelling units owner-occupied.

## TABLE 8

*PERCENTAGE OF VARIOUS "ETHNIC" PRECINCTS VOTING "YES" ON
SELECTED EXPENDITURES IN CLEVELAND AND CUYAHOGA COUNTY*

| Ethnic Group and Number of Precincts | Percent Voting "Yes" on: | | | | |
|---|---|---|---|---|---|
| | Co. Hosp. (11/59) | Court House (11/59) | Parks (11/59) | Welfare Levy (5/60) | Vet's Bonus (11/59) |
| *Low-Income Renters** | (%) | (%) | (%) | (%) | (%) |
| Negro (16) | 78.6 | 67.3 | 52.6 | 85.9 | 89.9 |
| Italian (10) | 68.8 | 53.3 | 43.5 | 49.9 | 74.8 |
| Polish (6) | 54.9 | 39.9 | 28.1 | 33.7 | 71.6 |
| *Middle-Income Home-Owners †* | | | | | |
| Negro (8) | 68.1 | 54.0 | 39.6 | 73.2 | 79.2 |
| Italian (7) | 59.3 | 49.7 | 41.1 | 56.8 | 66.8 |
| Polish (12) | 52.9 | 35.8 | 34.3 | 46.4 | 61.7 |
| *Upper-Income Home-Owners ‡* | | | | | |
| Anglo-Saxon (11) | 70.6 | 51.4 | 57.2 | 64.8 | 53.7 |
| Jewish (7) | 71.7 | 47.1 | 48.4 | 64.5 | 56.8 |

* Average median family income less than $6,000 per year; at least two-thirds of all dwelling units renter-occupied.

† Average median family income between $7,000 and $9,000 a year for whites; over $6,000 a year for Negroes. At least 75 percent of all dwelling units owner-occupied.

‡ Average median family income over $10,000 per year; over 85 percent of all dwelling units owner-occupied.

or Polish home-owners. (In passing it is worth noting that Negroes are two or three times more favorable toward urban renewal—despite the fact that they are commonly the chief victims of land clearance programs—than Irish or Polish voters.)

Essentially the same relationships appear in Table 8 for Cleveland-Cuyahoga County. With one exception (Italians voting on the welfare levy), low-income renters in an ethnic group are more favorable to expenditures than middle-income home-owners in the same ethnic group. Low-income Negro renters are the most favorable to all proposals and middle-income Negro home-owners are more favorable to them than are the other middle-income ethnic groups. Aside from the veterans' bonus (a special case), both the "Anglo-Saxon" and the Jewish upper-income home-owners are more favorable to expenditures than any middle-income groups except the Negro.

## IV

We have shown both that a considerable proportion of voters, especially in the upper income groups, vote against their self-interest narrowly conceived and that a marked ethnic influence appears in the vote. Now we would like to bring these two findings together under a single explanatory principle.

One such principle—but one we reject—is that the voters in question have acted irrationally (either in not calculating benefits and costs at all or else by making mistakes in their calculations) and that their irrationality is a function of their ethnic status. According to this theory, the low-income Polish renter who votes against expenditures proposals that would cost him nothing and would confer benefits upon him and the high-income Anglo-Saxon or Jewish home-owner who favors expenditures proposals that will cost him heavily without benefitting him would both behave differently if they thought about the matter more or if their information were better.

A more tenable hypothesis, we think, is that voters in some income and ethnic groups are more likely than voters in others to take a public-regarding rather than a narrowly self-interested view of things—*i.e.,* to take the welfare of others, especially that of "the community" into account as an aspect of their own welfare.[11] We offer the additional hypothesis that both the tendency of a voter to take a public-regarding view and the content of that view (*e.g.,* whether or not he thinks a Korean war veterans' bonus is in the public interest) are largely func-

---

[11] *Cf.* Anthony Downs, "The Public Interest: Its Meaning in a Democracy," *Social Research,* Vol. 29 (Spring 1962), pp. 28–29.

tions of his participation in a subculture that is definable in ethnic and income terms. Each subcultural group, we think, has a more or less distinctive notion of how much a citizen ought to sacrifice for the sake of the community as well as of what the welfare of the community is constituted; in a word, each has its own idea of what justice requires and of the importance of acting justly. According to this hypothesis, the voter is presumed to act rationally; the ends he seeks are not always narrowly self-interested ones, however. On the contrary, depending upon his income and ethnic status they are more or less public-regarding.[12]

That his income status does not by itself determine how public-regarding he is, or what content he gives to the public interest, can be shown from the voting data. As we explained above, generally the higher a home-owner's income the more likely he is to favor expenditures. This is partly—but only partly—because the value of the dollar is usually less to people who have many of them than to people who have few of them. We suggest that it is also because upper-income people tend to be more public-regarding than lower-income people. We do not think that income *per se* has this effect; rather it is the ethnic attributes, or culture, empirically associated with it. It happens that most upper-income voters belong, if not by inheritance then by adoption, to an ethnic group (especially the Anglo-Saxon and the Jewish) that is relatively public-regarding in its outlook; hence ethnic influence on voting is hard to distinguish from income influence.

In the three scatter diagrams which comprise Figure 6 we have tried to distinguish the two kinds of influence. For this figure, we divided all wards and towns of Cleveland and Cuyahoga County in which 85 or more percent of the dwelling units were owner-occupied into three classes according to median home value. Diagram 6a shows the voting where that value was more than $27,000; diagram 6b shows it where it was $19,000–27,000, and diagram 6c shows it where it was less than $19,000. The horizontal and vertical axes are the same for all diagrams; each diagram shows the relationship between the percentage of voters in the ward or town who are Polish-Czech (vertical axis) and the percentage of "Yes" vote on a proposal to expand the zoo (horizontal axis). In the group of wards and towns having the lowest median home value (diagram 6c) the presence of Polish-Czech voters made little difference; these wards and towns were about 65 percent against the proposal no matter how many Poles and Czechs lived in them. In both groups of

---

[12] The proposition that "subculture" can be defined in ethnic and income terms is highly provisional. We are looking for other and better criteria and we think we may find some. But so far as the present data are concerned, ethnic and income status are all we have.

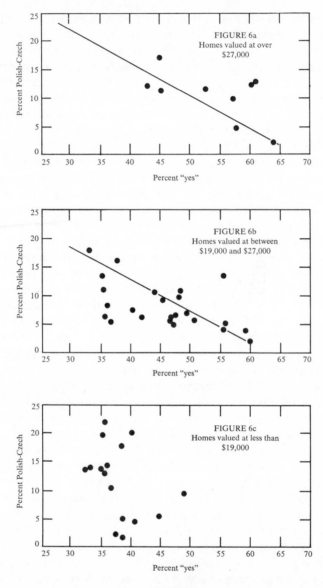

**FIGURE 6**

*RELATION BETWEEN PERCENTAGE VOTING "YES" ON PROPOSITION TO
PROVIDE ADDITIONAL ZOO FACILITIES (1960) AND PROPORTION OF
WARD OR TOWN POPULATION WHICH IS OF POLISH OR CZECH FOREIGN
STOCK IN CUYAHOGA COUNTY, OHIO; AT THREE MEDIAN HOME VALUE
LEVELS (ONLY WARDS AND TOWNS WITH 85 PERCENT OR MORE
OWNER-OCCUPIED DWELLINGS USED).*

higher home-value wards and towns, however, Poles and Czechs were conspicuously less favorable to the proposal than were the rest of the voters. Among the non-Polish-Czech voters in these higher home-value wards and towns, Anglo-Saxons and Jews were heavily represented; therefore it seems plausible to conclude that, as compared to Poles and Czechs in these two income groups, the Anglo-Saxons and Jews were decidedly public-regarding.

Another interpretation of the behavior of the Poles and Czechs is possible, however. It may be that they had the welfare of the community in view also but defined it differently than did the Anglo-Saxons and the Jews. They may have thought that the particular expenditure proposed, or for that matter all public expenditures, would do the community more harm than good. (This would rationalize the behavior of those low-income renters—see Table 8—who voted against proposals giving them benefits without any costs.) [13] Whatever may be true of the Poles and Czechs, it seems clear that upper-income Anglo-Saxons, and to a somewhat lesser degree Jews, tend to vote on public-regarding grounds *against* some proposals (notably those, like veterans' bonuses and city employees' pension benefits and pay increases) that they regard as serving "special interests" rather than "the community as a whole."

When we know more about each of the various subcultures—especially about the nature of the individual's attachment to the society, his conception of what is just, and the extent of the obligation he feels to subordinate his interest to that of various others (*e.g.,* the community)—we should doubtless be able to make and test more refined hypotheses about voting behavior.

## Appendix

We chose the "ethnic" precincts for Tables 7 and 8 by inspecting census tract data and then visiting the precincts that appeared to be predominantly of one ethnic group to get confirmatory evidence from well-informed persons and from a view of the neighborhoods. We could

---

[13] Two other explanations are possible and, in our opinion, plausible. One is that the low income renters may have taken into account costs to them other than taxes—*e.g.,* the cost, (perhaps monetary) of changes in the neighborhood that would ensue from expenditures. (Irish objections to urban renewal in Chicago may have been due, not to a fear of higher taxes, but to fear of neighborhood "invasion" by Negroes displaced from land clearance projects.) The other is that in these precincts a much higher proportion of renters than of home-owners may have stayed away from the polls. In Cleveland (though not, interestingly, in Chicago) voter turnout is highly correlated with home ownership and almost all white renter precincts have at least a few homeowners in them. Conceivably—we think it unlikely—all those who voted in some "renter" precincts were actually owners.

have used a less impressionistic method (*e.g.,* counting the proportion of ethnic names on voter registration lists), but since we wanted only to identify precincts that are predominantly of one ethnic group, not to place them on a scale of ethnicity, this did not appear necessary.

Having identified the "ethnic" precincts, we divided them into two (sometimes three) income groups on the basis of census data. As we indicate on the tables, with one exception we used the same cutting points to separate the income levels of all ethnic groups. The exception was the Negro. The income distribution among Negroes is so skewed to the low end of the scale that "middle-income" has to be defined differently for Negroes than for whites. We identified "middle-income Negro" precincts by selecting from among all precincts that were at least 85 percent Negro and had an owner-occupancy rate of at least 80 percent those few with the highest median family incomes. Some of these precincts turned out to have median incomes as low as $6,000 a year, which is about $1,000 less than any of the "middle-income white" precincts had. If we had made the cutting point higher, however, we would not have had enough middle-income Negro precincts to work with. In our opinion, Negroes with incomes of $6,000 are about as likely to "feel" middle-income as are whites with incomes of $7,000.

# The Making of the Negro Mayors 1967

## JEFFREY K. HADDEN
## LOUIS H. MASOTTI
## VICTOR THIESSEN

Throughout most of 1967, black power and Vietnam kept this nation in an almost continual state of crisis. The summer months were the longest and hottest in modern U.S. history—many political analysts even felt that the nation was entering its most serious domestic conflict since the Civil War. Over a hundred cities were rocked with violence.

As the summer gave way to autumn, the interest of the nation shifted a little from the summer's riots to the elections on the first Tuesday of November. An unprecedented number of Negroes were running for office, but public attention focused on three elections. In Cleveland, Carl B. Stokes, a lawyer who in 1962 had become the first Democratic Negro legislator in Ohio, was now seeking to become the first Negro mayor of a large American city. In Gary, Ind., another young Negro lawyer, Richard D. Hatcher, was battling the Republican Party's candidate—as well as his own Democratic Party—to become the first Negro mayor of a "medium-sized" city. And in Boston, Louise Day Hicks, a symbol of white backlash, was conducting a "You know where I stand" campaign to capture the mayorality.

Normally, the nation couldn't care less about who would become the next mayors of Cleveland, Gary, and Boston. But the tenseness of the summer months gave these elections enormous significance. If Stokes and Hatcher lost and Hicks won, could Negroes be persuaded to use the power of the ballot box rather than the power of fire bombs?

Fortunately, November 7 proved to be a triumphant day for racial peace. Stokes and Hatcher won squeaker victories, both by margins of only about 1500 votes; in Boston, Kevin H. White defeated Mrs. Hicks by a 12,000 plurality. Labor leader George Meany was exultant—

Reprinted from *Transaction* (January/February 1968), pp. 21–30, by permission of the publisher. Copyright © by *Transaction* magazine, New Brunswick, New Jersey.

"American voters have rejected racism as a political issue." Negroes in the three cities were also jubilant. In Gary, the most tense of the cities, Richard Hatcher urged the mostly Negro crowd at his headquarters to "cool it." "I urge that the outcome of this election be unmarred by any incident of any kind. . . . If we spoil this victory with any kind of occurrence here tonight, or anywhere in the city, it will be a hollow victory." The evening *was* cool: Joyous Negroes danced and sang in the streets.

But beyond the exultation of victory remain many hard questions. Now that Cleveland and Gary have Negro mayors, just how much difference will it make in solving the many grave problems that these cities face? Will these victories cool militancy in urban ghettos next summer, or will the momentum of frustration prove too great to put on the brakes? A careful analysis of *how* these candidates won office may help provide the answers.

The focus of this report is on Cleveland because:

As residents of Cleveland, we are more familiar with the campaign and the election.

Cleveland is unique because, in 1965, it had a special census. By matching voting wards with census tracts, we can draw a clearer picture of voting behavior than we could in the other cities, where rapid neighborhood transitions have made 1960 census data quite unreliable in assessing voting patterns. Having examined Cleveland in some detail, we will draw some comparisons with the Gary and Boston elections, then speculate about their significance and implications.

## Cleveland—City in Decline

Cleveland has something less than 2,000,000 residents. Among metropolitan areas in America, it ranks eleventh in size. Like many other American cities, the central city of Cleveland is experiencing an absolute decline in population—residents are fleeing from the decaying core to the surrounding suburbs. The city certainly ranks high both in terms of absolute and proportional decline in the central-city population.

Between 1950 and 1960, the population of the central city declined from 914,808 to 876,050, a loss of almost 39,000. By 1965 the population had sunk to 810,858, an additional loss of 65,000. But these figures are only a partial reflection of the changing composition of the population, since new Negro residents coming into the central city helped offset the white exodus. *Between 1950 and 1960, nearly 142,000 white residents left the central city, and an additional 94,000 left between 1960 and 1965—nearly a quarter of a million in just 15 years.*

During the same period the number of Negro residents of Cleveland rose from 147,847 to 279,352—an increase of 16.1 percent to 34.4

percent of the city's population. There is no evidence that this dramatic population redistribution has changed since the special 1965 census. Some suburbanization of Negroes is beginning on the east and southeast side of the city, but the pace is not nearly so dramatic as for whites. In 1960, approximately 97 percent of the Negroes in the metropolitan area lived in the central city. This percentage has probably declined somewhat since then—16,000 Negro residents have moved to East Cleveland. But the basic pattern of segregation in the metropolitan area remains. The development in East Cleveland is little more than an eastward extension of the ghetto, and the older, decaying residential units the Negroes have moved to are hardly "suburban" in character.

While the population composition of Cleveland is changing rapidly, whites are still a significant majority—about 62 percent. Again like many other central cities, a significant percentage of the white population comprises nationality groups that live in segregated sections, with a strong sense of ethnic identity and a deep fear of Negro encroachment. (In 1964, the bussing of Negro students into Murray Hill, an Italian neighborhood, resulted in rioting.)

In 1960, the census classified 43 percent of the central city's white residents as "foreign stock." In that year, five groups—Germans, Poles, Czechs, Hungarians, and Italians—had populations of 25,000 or greater; at least 20 other nationality groups were large enough to have to be contended with in the political arena. But today these ethnic groups—although unwilling to admit it—have become less than the controlling majority they constituted before 1960.

The Cuyahoga River divides Cleveland, physically as well as socially. When Negroes first began to move into the city, during World War I, they occupied the decaying section to the south and east of the central business district. As their numbers grew, they continued pushing in this direction and now occupy the larger part of the eastside (except for some ethnic strongholds). There are no stable, integrated neighborhoods in the central city—only areas in transition from white to black. To the west, the Cuyahoga River constitutes a barrier to Negro penetration.

Ever since 1941, when Frank Lausche was elected, Cleveland has had a succession of basically honest but unimaginative Democratic mayors. These mayors have kept their hold on City Hall by means of a relatively weak coalition of nationality groups. At no point in this 26-year Lausche dynasty did a mayor gather enough power to seriously confront the long-range needs and problems of the city.

By early 1967, the city had seemingly hit rock bottom. A long procession of reporters began arriving to write about its many problems.

The racial unrest of the past several years had, during the summer of 1966, culminated in the worst rioting in Cleveland's history. This unrest was continuing to grow as several militant groups were organizing. Urban renewal was a dismal failure; in January, the Department of Housing and Urban Development even cut off the city's urban-renewal funds, the first such action by the Federal Government. The exodus of whites, along with business, shoved the city to the brink of financial disaster. In February, the Moody Bond Survey reduced the city's credit rating. In May, the Federal Government cut off several million dollars of construction funds—because the construction industry had failed to assure equal job opportunities for minority groups. In short, the city was, and remains, in deep trouble. And while most ethnic groups probably continued to believe that Cleveland was the "Best Location in the Nation," the Negro community—and a growing number of whites— were beginning to feel that Cleveland was the "Mistake on the Lake," and that it was time for a change.

Carl Stokes's campaign for mayor was his second try. In 1965, while serving in the state House of Representatives, he came within 2100 votes of defeating Mayor Ralph S. Locher. Stokes had taken advantage of a city-charter provision that lets a candidate file as an independent, and bypass the partisan primaries. Ralph McAllister, then president of the Cleveland School Board, did the same. For his hard line on *de facto* school segregation, however, McAllister had earned the enmity of the Negro community. The Republican candidate was Ralph Perk, the first Republican elected to a county-wide position (auditor) in many years. A second generation Czech-Bohemian, Perk hoped to win by combining his ethnic appeal with his program for the city (Perk's Plan). He had no opposition for his party's nomination. The fourth candidate was Mayor Locher, who had defeated Mark McElroy, county recorder and perennial candidate for something, in the Democratic primary.

It was in the 1965 Democratic primary that the first signs of a "black bloc" vote emerged. The Negroes, who had previously supported incumbent Democratic mayoral candidates, if not enthusiastically at least consistently, made a concerted effort to dump Locher in favor of McElroy. There were two reasons.

Locher had supported his police chief after the latter had made some tactless remarks about Negroes. Incensed Negro leaders demanded an audience with the mayor, and when he refused, his office was the scene of demonstrations, sit-ins, and arrests. At that point, as one of the local reporters put it, "Ralph Locher became a dirty name in the ghetto."

Stokes, as an independent, and his supporters hoped that the Democratic primary would eliminate the *stronger* candidate, Locher. For then a black bloc would have a good chance of deciding the general election because of an even split in the white vote.

Despite the Negro community's efforts, Locher won the primary and went on to narrowly defeat Stokes. Locher received 37 percent of the vote, Stokes 36 percent, Perk 17 percent, and McAllister 9 percent. Some observers reported that a last-minute whispering campaign in Republican precincts—to the effect that "A vote for Perk is a vote for Stokes"—may have given Locher enough Republican votes to win. The evidence: the popular Perk received only a 17 percent vote in a city where a Republican could have expected something closer to 25 percent. Had Perk gotten anything close to 25 percent, Stokes would have probably been elected two years earlier.

Although he made a strong showing in defeat, Carl Stokes's political future looked bleak. No one expected the Democratic leaders to give Stokes another opportunity to win by means of a split vote. Nor were there other desirable elected offices Stokes could seek. Cleveland has no Negro Congressman—largely because the heavy Negro concentration in the city has been "conveniently" gerrymandered. The only district where Stokes might have had a chance has been represented by Charles Vanik, a popular and liberal white, and as long as Vanik remained in Congress Stokes was locked out. Stokes's state Senate district was predominantly white; and a county or state office seemed politically unrealistic because of his race. So, in 1966, Stokes sought re-election to the state House unopposed.

Between 1965 and 1967, Cleveland went from bad to worse, physically, socially, and financially. With no other immediate possibilities, Stokes began to think about running for mayor again. The big question was whether to risk taking on Locher in the primary—or to file as an independent again.

### The Primary Race

In effect, Stokes's decision was made for him. Seth Taft, slated to be the Republican candidate, told Stokes he would withdraw from the election entirely if Stokes filed as an independent in order to gain the advantage of a three-man general election. Taft had concluded that his best strategy was to face a Negro, *alone,* or a faltering incumbent, *alone,* in the general election. But not both. In a three-man race with Locher and Stokes, Taft correctly assumed that he would be the man in the middle with no chance for victory. (Taft would have preferred to run as an independent—to gain Democratic votes—but the county Republican leader threatened to file *another* Republican candidate unless Taft ran as a Republican.)

Meanwhile, Locher committed blunder after blunder—and Democratic party leaders began to question whether he could actually win another election. In the weeks before filing for the primary, Democratic leaders even pressured Locher to accept a Federal judgeship and clear the way for the president of the city council to run. But the Democratic leaders in Cleveland are not noted for their strength or effectiveness, as is evidenced by the fact that none of the Democratic mayors since 1941 were endorsed by the party when they were first elected. When Locher refused to withdraw, the party reluctantly rallied behind him.

Another Democratic candidate was Frank P. Celeste, former mayor of the Republican westside suburb of Lakewood. Celeste established residency in the city, announced his candidacy early, and—despite pressure from the Democratic Party—remained in the primary race.

There was always the possibility that Celeste would withdraw from the primary, which would leave Stokes facing Locher alone. But the threat of Taft's withdrawal from the general election left Stokes with little choice but to face Locher head-on in the primary. A primary race against Locher and a strong Democrat was more appealing than a general election against Locher and a weak Republican.

Now, in 1965 Stokes had received only about 6000 white votes in the city in a 239,000 voter turnout. To win in the primary, he had to enlarge and consolidate the Negro vote—and increase his white support on the westside and in the eastside ethnic wards.

The first part of his strategy was a massive voter-registration drive in the Negro wards—to reinstate the potential Stokes voters dropped from the rolls for failing to vote since the 1964 Presidential election. The Stokes organization—aided by Martin Luther King Jr. and the Southern Christian Leadership Conference, as well as by a grant (in part earmarked for voter registration) from the Ford Foundation to the Cleveland chapter of CORE—did succeed in registering many Negroes. But there was a similar drive mounted by the Democratic Party on behalf of Locher. (Registration figures are not available by race.)

The second part of the Stokes strategy took him across the polluted Cuyahoga River into the white wards that had given him a mere 3 percent of the vote in 1965. He spoke wherever he would be received —to small groups in private homes, in churches, and in public and private halls. While he was not always received enthusiastically, he did not confront many hostile crowds. He faced the race issue squarely and encouraged his audience to judge him on his ability.

**TABLE I**

| | City Totals | | | Negro Wards | | |
|---|---|---|---|---|---|---|
| | 1965 General | 1967 Primary | 1967 General | 1965 General | 1967 Primary | 1967 General |
| Registered Voters | 337,803 | 326,003 | 326,003 | 103,123 | 99,885 | 99,885 |
| Turnout | 239,479 | 210,926 | 257,157 | 74,396 | 73,360 | 79,591 |
| % Turnout | 70.9 | 64.7 | 78.9 | 72.1 | 73.4 | 79.7 |
| Stokes Votes | 85,716 | 110,769 | 129,829 | 63,550 | 70,575 | 75,586 |
| % Stokes Votes | 35.8 | 52.5 | 50.5 | 85.4 | 96.2 | 95.0 |

| | White Wards | | | Mixed Wards | | |
|---|---|---|---|---|---|---|
| | 1965 General | 1967 Primary | 1967 General | 1965 General | 1967 Primary | 1967 General |
| Registered Voters | 159,419 | 152,737 | 152,737 | 75,261 | 73,421 | 73,421 |
| Turnout | 111,129 | 88,525 | 119,883 | 53,962 | 49,105 | 57,113 |
| % Turnout | 69.7 | 58.0 | 78.5 | 71.7 | 66.9 | 77.8 |
| Stokes Votes | 3,300 | 13,495 | 23,158 | 18,866 | 26,699 | 30,872 |
| % Stokes Votes | 3.0 | 15.2 | 19.3 | 35.0 | 54.4 | 54.1 |

Stokes's campaign received a big boost when the *Plain Dealer,* the largest daily in Ohio, endorsed him. Next, the *Cleveland Press* called for a change in City Hall, but declined to endorse either Stokes or Celeste. But since the polls indicated that Celeste was doing very badly, this amounted to an endorsement of Stokes.

More people voted in this primary than in any other in Cleveland's history. When the ballots were counted, Stokes had 52.5 percent of the votes—he had defeated Locher by a plurality of 18,000 votes. Celeste was the man in the middle, getting only 4 percent of the votes, the lowest of any mayoral candidate in recent Cleveland history.

What produced Stokes's clear victory? Table I (above) reveals the answer. The decisive factor was the size of the Negro turnout. While Negroes constituted only about 40 percent of the voters, 73.4 percent of them turned out, compared with only 58.4 percent of the whites. Predominantly Negro wards cast 96.2 percent of their votes for Stokes. (Actually this figure underrepresents the Negro vote for Stokes, since some of the non-Stokes votes in these wards were cast by whites. Similarly, the 15.4 percent vote for Stokes in the predominantly white wards slightly overestimates the white vote because of the Negro minority.)

Newspaper and magazine reports of the primary election proclaimed that Stokes could not have won without the white vote. Our own estimate—based on matching wards with census tracts, and allowing for only slight shifts in racial composition in some wards since the 1965 special census—is that Stokes received 16,000 white votes. His margin of victory was 18,000. How would the voting have gone if the third man, Celeste, had not been in the race? Many white voters, feeling that Stokes could not win in a two-man race, might not have bothered to vote at all, so perhaps Stokes would have won by an even larger margin. Thus Stokes's inroad into the white vote was not the decisive factor in his primary victory, although it was important.

Stokes emerged from the primary as the odds-on favorite to win— five weeks later—in the general election. And in the first few days of the campaign, it seemed that Stokes had everything going for him.

Stokes was bright, handsome, and articulate. His opponent, Seth Taft, while bright, had never won an election, and his family name, associated with the Taft-Hartley Act, could hardly be an advantage among union members. In addition, he was shy and seemingly uncomfortable in a crowd.

Both the *Plain Dealer* and the *Cleveland Press* endorsed Stokes in the general election.

The wounds of the primary were quickly (if perhaps superficially) healed, and the Democratic candidate was endorsed by both the Democratic Party and Mayor Locher.

Labor—both the A.F.L.-C.I.O. and the Teamsters—also endorsed Stokes.

He had a partisan advantage. Of the 326,003 registered voters, only 34,000 (10 percent) were Republican. The closest any Republican mayoral candidate had come to winning was in 1951, when—in a small turnout—William J. McDermott received 45 percent of the vote.

Stokes had 90,000 or more Negro votes virtually assured, with little possibility that Taft would make more than slight inroads.

Perhaps most important, voting-behavior studies over the years have demonstrated that voters who are confronted by a dilemma react by staying home from the polls. Large numbers of life-long Democrats, faced with voting for a Negro or a Republican by the name of Taft, were likely to stay home.

Had this been a normal election, Democrat Carl Stokes would have won handily. But this was not destined to be a normal election. During the final days of the campaign, Stokes knew he was in a fight for his political life. Those who predicted that the cross-pressures would keep many voters away from the polls forgot that the variable "Negro" had never been involved in an election of this importance.

On Election Day, an estimated 90 percent of those who voted for Locher or Celeste in the Democratic primary shifted to Taft—many pulling a Republican lever for the first time in their life. Was this clearly and unequivocally bigoted backlash? To be sure, bigotry *did* play a major role in the election. But to dismiss the campaign and the election as pure overt bigotry is to miss the significance of what happened in Cleveland and the emerging subtle nature of prejudice in American society.

### The Non-Issue of Race

A closer look at the personal characteristics and campaign strategy of Seth Taft, the Republican candidate, reveals the complexity and subtlety of the race issue.

In the final days of the Democratic primary campaign, Taft repeatedly told reporters that he would rather run against Locher and his record than against Carl Stokes. On the evening of the primary, Taft appeared at Stokes's headquarters to congratulate him. As far as he was concerned, Taft said, the campaign issue was, Who could present the most constructive program for change in Cleveland? Further, he said he didn't want people voting for him simply because he was white. A few days later, Taft even presented a strongly-worded statement to his campaign workers:

"The Cuyahoga Democratic party has issued a number of vicious statements concerning the candidacy of Carl Stokes, and others have conducted whisper campaigns. We cannot tolerate injection of race into this campaign. . . . Many people will vote for Carl Stokes because he is a Negro. Many people will vote for me because I am white. I regret this fact. I will work hard to convince people they should not vote on a racial basis."

Seth Taft's programs to solve racial tensions may have been paternalistic, not really perceptive of emerging moods of the ghetto. But one thing is clear—he was not a bigot. Every indication is that he remained uncomfortable about being in a race in which his chances to win depended, in large part, upon a backlash vote.

Whether Taft's attempt to silence the race issue was a deliberate strategy or a reflection of deep personal feelings, it probably enhanced his chances of winning. He knew that he had the hard-core bigot vote.

His task was to convince those in the middle that they could vote for him and *not* be bigots.

Stokes, on the other hand, had another kind of problem. While he had to draw more white votes, he also had to retain and, if possible, increase the 73 percent Negro turnout that had delivered him 96 percent of the Negro votes in the primary. Stokes's campaign leaders feared a fall-off in the voter turnout from Negro wards—with good reason. The entire primary campaign had pushed the October 3 date so hard that some Negroes could not understand why Carl Stokes was not mayor on October 4. Full-page newspaper ads paid for by CORE had stated, *"If you don't vote Oct. 3rd, forget it. The man who wins will be the next mayor of Cleveland!"* So Stokes felt he had to remobilize the Negro vote.

The moment came during the question-and-answer period of the second of four debates with Taft in the all-white westside. Stokes said:

> "The personal analysis of Seth Taft—and the analysis of the many competent political analysts—is that Seth Taft may win the November 7 election, but for only one reason. That reason is that his skin happens to be white."

The predominantly white crowd booed loudly and angrily for several minutes, and throughout the rest of the evening repeatedly interrupted him. Later, Stokes's campaign manager revealed that his candidate's remark was a calculated risk to arouse Negro interest. Stokes probably succeeded, but he also gave Taft supporters an excuse to bring the race issue into the open. And they could claim that it was *Stokes,* not Taft, who was trying to exploit the race issue.

To be sure, *both* candidates exploited the race issue. But, for the most part, it was done rather subtly. Stokes's campaign posters stated, "Let's do Cleveland Proud"—another way of saying, "Let's show the world that Cleveland is capable of rising above racial bigotry." A full-page ad for Stokes stated in bold print, "Vote for Seth Taft. It Would Be Easy, Wouldn't It?" After the debate, Taft was free to accuse Stokes of using the race issue—itself a subtle way of exploiting the issue. Then there was the letter, signed by the leaders of 22 nationality clubs, that was mailed to 40,000 members in the city. It didn't mention race, but comments such as "protecting our way of life," "safeguard our liberty," and "false charges of police brutality" were blatant in their implications. Taft sidestepped comment on the letter.

No matter how much the candidates may have wanted to keep race out of the picture, race turned out to be the most important issue. Both Taft and Stokes could benefit from the issue if they played it right, and both did use it. And although the Stokes's remark at the second debate gave white voters an excuse to vote for Taft without feeling that they were bigots, many whites probably would have found another excuse.

## Taft as a Strategist

The fact is that Taft, for all his lackluster qualities, emerged as a strong candidate. He was able to turn many of his liabilities into assets.

Taft was able to insulate himself against his Republican identity. He successfully dissociated himself from his uncle's position on labor by pointing to his own active role, as a student, against "right to work" laws. At the same time, he hit hard at Stokes's record as an off again-on again Democrat. This strategy neutralized, at least in part, Taft's first political disadvantage—running as a Republican in a Democratic city.

A second liability was that he came from a wealthy family. Taft was an Ivy League intellectual, cast in the role of a "do-gooder." He lived in an exclusive suburb, Pepper Pike, and had bought a modest home in Cleveland only a few weeks before declaring his candidacy. How, it was frequently asked, could such a man understand the problems of the inner-city and of the poor? Almost invariably the answer was: "Did John F. Kennedy, Franklin D. Roosevelt, and Nelson Rockefeller have to be poor in order to understand and respond to the problems of the poor?" Taft's campaign posters were a side profile that bore a striking resemblance to President Kennedy. Whether he was consciously exploiting the Kennedy image is an open question. But there can be little doubt that when Taft mentioned his Republican heritage, he tried to project an image of the new breed of Republican—John Lindsay and Charles Percy. This image didn't come across very well at first, but as he became a seasoned campaigner it became clearer.

Another liability was that Taft had never held an elected office. His opponent tried to exploit this—unsuccessfully. Taft could point to 20 years of active civic service, including the fact that he was one of the authors of the Ohio fair-housing law. Then too, the charge gave Taft an opportunity to point out that Stokes had the worst absentee record of anyone in the state legislature. Stokes never successfully answered this charge until the last of their four debates, when he produced a pre-campaign letter from Taft commending him on his legislative service. But this came moments *after* the TV cameras had gone off the air.

Still another liability emerged during the campaign. Taft's strategy of discussing programs, not personalities, was seemingly getting him nowhere. He presented specific proposals; Stokes, a skilled debater, succeeded in picking them apart. Stokes himself discussed programs only at a general level and contended that he was best-qualified to "cut the red tape" in Washington. His frequent trips to Washington to confer with top Government officials, before and during the campaign, indicated that he had the inside track.

Taft, realizing at this point that his campaign was not gaining much momentum, suddenly switched gears and began attacking Stokes's record (not Stokes personally). Stokes had claimed he would crack-down on slumlords. Taft discovered that Stokes owned a piece of rental property with several code violations—and that it had not been repaired despite an order from the city. He hit hard at Stokes's absenteeism and his record as a "good" Democrat. He put a "bird-dog" on Stokes and, if Stokes told one group one thing and another group something else, the public heard about it.

The upshot was that in the final days of the campaign Taft captured the momentum. Stokes was easily the more flashy debater and projected a superior image; but Taft emerged as the better strategist.

### Should Taft Have Withdrawn?

One may ask whether all of this discussion is really relevant, since the final vote was sharply divided along racial lines. In one sense it *is* irrelevant, since it is possible that a weaker candidate than Taft might have run just as well. It is also possible that a white racist might actually have won. Still, this discussion has buttressed two important points.

Taft was not all black, and Stokes was not all white. Taft proved a strong candidate, and—had he been running against Locher instead of Stokes—he might have amassed strong support from Negroes and defeated Locher.

By being a strong candidate, Taft made it much easier for many white Democrats, who might otherwise have been cross-pressured into staying home, to come out and vote for him.

Some people felt that Taft should have withdrawn and let Stokes run uncontested. But many of the same people also decried white liberals who, at recent conferences to form coalitions between black-power advocates and the New Left, let black militants castrate them. It is not traditional in American politics that candidates enter a race to lose. Taft was in to win, and he fought a hard and relatively clean campaign—as high a compliment as can be paid to any candidate.

Yet all of this doesn't change the basic nature of the voting. This is clear from the evidence in Table II. Stokes won by holding his black bloc, and increasing his white vote from 15 percent in the primary to

**TABLE II**

*PERCENT STOKES VOTE BY WARD*

| WHITE WARDS | %<br>Negro | 1965<br>General | 1967<br>Primary | 1967<br>General |
|---|---|---|---|---|
| 1 | .6 | 3.2 | 17.2 | 20.5 |
| 2 | .3 | 1.9 | 12.8 | 17.4 |
| 3 | .9 | 2.5 | 13.6 | 22.1 |
| 4 | .3 | 3.0 | 18.2 | 20.9 |
| 5 | .6 | 1.7 | 11.8 | 17.8 |
| 6 | .8 | 2.3 | 15.1 | 16.7 |
| 7 | .6 | 3.4 | 16.5 | 23.7 |
| 8 | 3.0 | 6.1 | 24.7 | 29.3 |
| 9 | .2 | 1.9 | 12.4 | 16.4 |
| 14 | 1.4 | 1.1 | 12.7 | 13.0 |
| 15 | 1.4 | 1.2 | 9.2 | 14.1 |
| 22 | 5.7 | 8.1 | 22.5 | 26.3 |
| 26 | 1.1 | 2.8 | 16.3 | 19.9 |
| 32 | 2.4 | 2.9 | 10.0 | 15.3 |
| 33 | .3 | 2.5 | 17.7 | 21.4 |
| Average | | 3.0 | 15.2 | 19.3 |

| NEGRO WARDS | | | | |
|---|---|---|---|---|
| 10 | 91.3 | 88.7 | 97.3 | 96.7 |
| 11 | 91.8 | 86.3 | 95.9 | 96.0 |
| 12 | 82.7 | 76.9 | 90.4 | 90.5 |
| 13 | 75.2 | 75.8 | 90.7 | 88.4 |
| 17 | 99.0 | 86.6 | 98.1 | 97.9 |
| 18 | 89.3 | 84.0 | 96.0 | 95.7 |
| 20 | 91.0 | 83.0 | 95.0 | 92.8 |
| 24 | 92.6 | 90.6 | 98.1 | 98.1 |
| 25 | 90.9 | 91.3 | 98.4 | 98.2 |
| 27 | 85.7 | 85.2 | 95.6 | 94.0 |
| Average | | 85.4 | 96.2 | 95.0 |

| MIXED WARDS | | | | |
|---|---|---|---|---|
| 16 | 56.6 | 50.7 | 69.9 | 70.1 |
| 19 | 25.3 | 29.2 | 48.0 | 39.9 |
| 21 | 61.1 | 55.2 | 66.3 | 68.9 |
| 23 | 20.3 | 9.8 | 18.2 | 23.2 |
| 28 | 28.5 | 26.5 | 54.8 | 57.3 |
| 29 | 24.4 | 26.8 | 43.2 | 42.3 |
| 30 | 51.7 | 51.5 | 75.3 | 71.4 |
| 31 | 21.8 | 16.9 | 31.8 | 39.0 |
| Average | | 35.0 | 54.4 | 54.1 |

almost 20 percent in the general. An enormous amount of the white vote was, whether covert or overt, anti-Negro. It is hard to believe that Catholics, ethnic groups, and laborers who never voted for anyone but a Democrat should suddenly decide to evaluate candidates on their qualifications and programs, and—in overwhelming numbers—decide that the Republican candidate was better qualified. The implication is that they were prejudiced. But to assume that such people perceive themselves as bigots is to oversimplify the nature of prejudice. And to call such people bigots is to make their responses even more rigid—as Carl Stokes discovered after his remark in the second debate with Taft.

This, then, is perhaps an important lesson of the Cleveland election: Bigotry cannot be defeated directly, by telling bigots that they are bigoted. For the most part Stokes learned this lesson well, accumulating as many as 30,000 white votes, nearly five times the number he received in 1965. But another slip like the one in the second debate might have cost him the election.

A few words on the voting for Stokes ward by ward, as shown in the table. Wards 9, 14, and 15—which gave Stokes a comparatively low vote—have the highest concentration of ethnic groups in the city. Not only is there the historical element of prejudice in these areas, but there is the ever-present fear among the residents that Negroes will invade their neighborhoods. (This fear is less a factor in ward 9, which is across the river.)

Wards 26 and 32 also gave Stokes a low percentage of votes, and these wards are also the ones most likely to have Negro migration. They are just to the north of East Cleveland, which is currently undergoing heavy transition, and to the east of ward 27, which in the past few years has changed from white to black. In these two wards, then, high ethnic composition and a fear of Negro migration would seem to account for Stokes's 19.9 and 15.3 percentages.

The highest percentage *for* Stokes in predominantly white areas was in wards 8 and 22. Ward 8 has a growing concentration of Puerto Ricans, and—according to newspaper polls—they voted heavily for Stokes. Ward 22 has a very large automobile-assembly plant that employs many Negroes. Now, in 1965 the ward was 5.7 percent Negro—a large increase from 1960. Since 1965, this percentage has probably grown another 2 or 3 percent. Therefore, if one subtracts the Negro vote that Stokes received in this ward, the size of the white vote is about the same as in other wards.

## 'Imminent Danger' in Gary

The race for mayor in Gary, Ind., was not overtly racist. Still, the racial issue was much less subtle than it was in Cleveland. When Democratic chairman John G. Krupa refused to support Richard D. Hatcher, the Democratic candidate, it was clear that the reason was race. When the Gary newspaper failed to give similar coverage to both candidates and sometimes failed to print news releases from Hatcher headquarters (ostensibly because press deadlines had not been met), it was clear that race was a factor.

Even though race was rarely mentioned openly, the city polarized. While Stokes had the support of the white-owned newspapers and many white campaign workers, many of Hatcher's white supporters preferred to remain in the background—in part, at least, because they feared reprisals from white racists. Hatcher didn't use the black-power slogan, but to the community the election was a contest between black and white. And when the Justice Department supported Hatcher's claim that the election board had illegally removed some 5000 Negro voters from the registration lists and added nonexistent whites, the tension in the city became so great that the Governor, feeling that there was "imminent danger" of violence on election night, called up 4000 National Guardsmen.

Negroes constitute an estimated 55 percent of Gary's 180,000 residents, but white voter registration outnumbers Negroes by 2000 or 3000. Like Stokes, Hatcher—in order to win—had to pull some white votes, or have a significantly higher Negro turnout.

The voter turnout and voting patterns in Cleveland and Gary were very similar. In both cities, almost 80 percent of the registered voters turned out at the polls. In the Glen Park and Miller areas, predominantly white neighborhoods, Joseph B. Radigan—Hatcher's opponent—received more than 90 percent of the votes. In the predominantly Negro areas, Hatcher received an estimated 93 percent of the votes. In all, Hatcher received about 4000 white votes, while losing probably 1000 Negro votes, at most, to Radigan. This relatively small white vote was enough to give him victory. If Stokes's miscalculation in bringing race into the Cleveland campaign gave prejudiced whites an excuse to vote for Taft, the glaring way the Democratic Party in Gary tried to defeat Hatcher probably tipped the scales and gave Hatcher some white votes he wouldn't have received otherwise.

### The School Issue in Boston

The Boston election, unlike the Cleveland and Gary elections, didn't pose a Negro against a white, but a lackluster candidate—Kevin White—against a 48-year-old grandmother who had gained national attention over the past several years for her stand against school integration. On the surface, Mrs. Hicks seems to be an obvious racial bigot. But she herself has repeatedly denied charges that she is a racist, and many who have followed her closely claim that this description is too simple.

Mrs. Hicks, perhaps more than any other public figure to emerge in recent years, reflects the complex and subtle nature of prejudice in America. Her public denial of bigotry is, in all probability, an honest expression of her self-image. But she is basically unaware of, and unwilling to become informed about, the way her views maintain the barriers of segregation and discrimination in American society. In 1963, when the N.A.A.C.P. asked the Boston School Committee to acknowledge the *de facto* segregation in the schools, she refused to review the evidence. Meeting with the N.A.A.C.P., she abruptly ended the discussion by proclaiming: "There is no *de facto* segregation in Boston's schools. Kindly proceed to educational matters." Later, when the State Board of Education presented a 132-page report on racial imbalance in Massachusetts schools, she lashed out at the report's recommendations without bothering to read it.

Mrs. Hicks, like millions of Americans, holds views on race that are born out of and perpetuated by ignorance. John Spiegel, director of Brandeis University's Lemberg Center for the Study of Violence, has summed up the preliminary report of its study of six cities:

> ". . . the attitude of whites seems to be based on ignorance of or indifference to the factual basis of Negro resentment and bitterness. . . . If white populations generally had a fuller appreciation of the just grievances and overwhelming problems of Negroes in the ghetto, they would give stronger support to their city governments to promote change and to correct the circumstances which give rise to strong feelings of resentment now characteristic of ghetto populations."

Prejudice is born not only out of ignorance, but also out of fear. There is much about the Negro ghettos of poverty that causes whites, lacking objective knowledge, to be afraid, and their fear in turn reinforces their prejudice and their inability to hear out and understand the plight of the Negro in America.

In Boston, the voter turnout was heavy (71 percent) but below the turnouts in Cleveland and Gary. White accumulated 53 percent of the vote and a 12,000 plurality. Compared with Stokes and Hatcher, he had an easy victory. But considering Mrs. Hicks's lack of qualifications and the racial overtones of her campaign, Boston also experienced a massive backlash vote. Had it not been for the final days of the campaign—when she pledged, unrealistically, to raise police and firemen's salaries to $10,000 without raising taxes, and came back from Washington with "positive assurance" that nonexistent Federal monies would cover the raises—she might even have won. But throughout the campaign Mrs. Hicks repeatedly revealed her ignorance of fiscal and political matters. Mrs. Hicks had another handicap: She is a woman. The incredible fact that she ran a close race demonstrated again the hard core of prejudice and ignorance in American society.

Now let us consider the broader implications these elections will have on the racial crisis in America. To be sure, the immediate implications are quite different from what they would have been if Stokes and Hatcher had lost and Mrs. Hicks had won. If the elections had gone the other way, Summer '68 might well have begun November 8. As Thomas Pettigrew of Harvard put it a few days before the election, "If Stokes and Hatcher lose and Mrs. Hicks wins, then I just wonder how a white man in this country could ever look a Negro in the eye and say, 'Why don't you make it the way we did, through the political system, rather than burning us down?' "

## The Meaning of the Elections

But do these victories really alter the basic nature of the racial crisis? There is, true, some reason for hope. But to assume that anything has been fundamentally altered would be disastrous. First of all, it is by no means clear that these elections will pacify militant Negroes—including those in Cleveland, Gary, and Boston. In Boston, some militants were even encouraging people to vote for Mrs. Hicks—because they felt that her victory would help unify the Negro community against a well-defined foe. In Cleveland, most militants remained less than enthusiastic about the possibility of a Stokes victory. Of the militant groups, only CORE worked hard for him. In Gary alone did the candidate have the solid support of militants—probably because Hatcher refused to explicitly rebuke Stokely Carmichael and H. Rap Brown, and because his opponents repeatedly claimed that Hatcher was a black-power advocate.

If the Stokes and Hatcher victories are to represent a turning point in the racial crisis, they must deliver results. Unfortunately, Hatcher faces an unsympathetic Democratic Party and city council. Stokes has gone a long way toward healing the wounds of the bitter primary, but it remains to be seen whether he will receive eager support for his programs. Some councilmen from ethnic wards will almost certainly buck his programs for fear of alienating their constituencies.

Stokes and Hatcher themselves face a difficult and delicate situation.

Their margins of victory were so narrow that they, like Kennedy in 1960, must proceed with great caution.

Enthusiasm and promises of change are not the same as the power to implement change. And the two mayors must share power with whites.

They must demonstrate to Negroes that their presence in City Hall has made a difference. But if their programs seem too preferential toward Negroes, they run the risk of massive white resistance.

This delicate situation was clearly seen in the early days of the Stokes administration. Of his first ten appointments, only two were Negroes. Although relations with the police have been one of the most sensitive issues in the Negro ghetto, Stokes's choice for a new police chief was Michael Blackwell, a 67-year-old "hardliner." This appointment was intended to east anxieties in the ethnic neighborhoods, but it was not popular in the Negro ghetto. Blackwell, in his first public address after being sworn in, lashed out at the Supreme Court, state laws, and "publicity-seeking clergy and beatniks" for "crippling law enforcement." Cleveland's Negroes are already beginning to wonder whether a Negro in City Hall is going to make any difference.

Some observers believe that Stokes is basically quite conservative, and point to his sponsorship of anti-riot legislation. To be sure, Stokes's position on many issues remains uncertain, but what does seem fairly clear from his early days in office is that his efforts to gain support in white communities is going to lead to disaffection among Negroes. How much and how quickly is a difficult question.

Race relations is only one of many problems that these two new mayors must face. Stokes has inherited all of the problems that brought national attention to Cleveland last spring—poverty, urban renewal, finance, transportation, air and water pollution, and so on. Hatcher faces similar problems in Gary, and must also cope with one of the nation's worst strongholds of organized crime. If they fail, the responsibility will fall heavier on them than had a white man failed. Some whites will generalize the failures to all Negro politicians, and some Negroes will generalize the failures to the "bankruptcy" of the American political system.

Almost certainly, Washington will be a key factor in determining if these two men succeed. The national Democratic Party has a strong interest in making Stokes and Hatcher look good, for it desperately needs to recapture the disaffected Negro voters before the 1968 national election. But how much can the party deliver? The war in Vietnam is draining enormous national resources and Congress is threatening to slash poverty programs. Even if Federal monies were no problem, there is the question whether *any* of Washington's existing programs are directed at the roots of ghetto unrest. Many informed administrators, scientists, and political analysts feel they are not. And the chances for creative Federal programs seem, at this moment, fairly dim.

Another clear implication of these elections is that white resistance to change remains large and widespread. More than 90 percent of the Democrats in Cleveland who voted for a Democrat in the primary switched, in the general election, to the Republican candidate. Now, not many American cities are currently composed of as many as 35 percent Negroes; the possibility of coalitions to elect other Negro candidates appears, except in a handful of cities, remote. Additional Negro mayoral candidates are almost certain to arise, and many will go down to bitter defeat.

Stokes and Hatcher won because black-voter power coalesced with a relatively small minority of liberal whites. It was not a victory of acceptance or even tolerance of Negroes, but a numerical failure of the powers of discrimination, a failure that resulted in large part because of the massive exodus of whites from the central city. The election of Stokes and Hatcher may break down white resistance to voting for a Negro, but this is, at best, problematical. Also problematical is how bigoted whites will react to the election of a Negro mayor. Their organized efforts to resist change may intensify. As we have already indicated, the pace of white exodus from the central city of Cleveland is already alarming. And an acceleration of this pace could push the city into financial bankruptcy.

## America Has Bought a Little Time

In short, while the implications of the November 7 elections are ambiguous, it does seem that the victories of Stokes and Hatcher, and the defeat of Mrs. Hicks, have kept the door open on the growing racial crisis. America has, at best, bought a little time.

On the other hand, we do not find much cause for optimism in those elections—unlike George Meany, and unlike the *New York Times,* which, five days after the election, published a glowing editorial about "the willingness of most voters today to choose men solely on personal quality and impersonal issues." To us, it would seem that the elections have only accelerated the pace of ever-rising expectations among Negroes. And if results don't follow, and rather rapidly, then we believe that the Negro community's frustration with the American political system will almost certainly heighten.

The hard task of demonstrating that Negroes can actually achieve justice and equality in America still lies ahead.

# PART FIVE

# Metropolitan Governmental Integration: Reform and Reality

The discipline of political science does not speak with one voice about governing the metropolis. Some political scientists are in the front ranks of the "metropolitan reform" movement and hope to centralize (or integrate) metropolitan area governments. Their ultimate goal is the integration of all services—of governments—not just those services that help maintain life-style decentralization. To that end they support various integrative and cooperative devices—"solutions to the metropolitan problem." Other political scientists, whom we shall call "realists," question the need of centralization, point out the political and social values that centralization threatens, and criticize much of the writing of their reform-oriented colleagues.

The reformist approach is much the older of the two. It goes back at least to Studenski's *Government of Metropolitan Areas* (1930), which was sponsored by the National Municipal League. Skepticism toward reform, on the other hand, is a fairly new phenomenon, although there have been criticisms of the reformist approach for years. As a distinct school in the field of metropolitan politics, "realism" first appeared in the late 1950's and early 1960's.

Realists suggest that reform-oriented political scientists start their research with prior assumptions about the desirability of metropolitan integration. They see differentiation but ignore separatist values. Realists suggest that reformers tend to define good government as technically proficient administration and to overlook the fact that many voters see good government in terms of small governmental units, increased citizen participation, social or racial separatism, and access to policy makers. Indeed, some realists contend that the values of the voters are often ignored in the reformers' eagerness to advance their own values.

Finally, many realists complain that reform literature is prematurely prescriptive, that there has been little systematic research into the conditions of centralization, and that we have little reliable knowledge of centralization's consequences for policy.

"Government Adaptation to Metropolitan Growth," by Roscoe Martin, offers a description and a classification of the many reforms that have been proposed for achieving metropolitan governmental centralization. Some of the reforms, the reader will note, contemplate major changes in existing governmental arrangements; some only minor changes.

"Metropolitan 'Fragmentation': A Research Note" focuses on three tasks that have been largely ignored by both reformers and their critics: (1) measuring fragmentation in metropolitan areas, (2) identifying conditions associated with fragmentation, and (3) examining fragmentation's service consequences. Data from 212 metropolitan areas indicate that fragmentation does not affect per capita spending in any significant way. On the other hand, income and other status characteristics of the metropolitan population do seem to affect spending. This suggests that a better way to raise service levels than reducing 'fragmentation' is to increase opportunities for community economic growth, individual education and training, and upward social mobility. Despite assumptions that reduced fragmentation is of great value and in the interest of people who do not value it, fragmentation is not importantly related to metropolitan governmental spending.

The remaining selections suggest how the metropolitan reform movement has fared in its encounter with reality. On the whole, the picture is a bleak one for reformers. It is difficult to resist the conclusion that metropolitan governmental centralization, although perhaps recommended by the fact of sub-area interdependence, flies in the face of the very social heterogeneity that is natural to the process of urbanization. The differentiated sub-areas produced by urbanization seem very much inclined to defend their separateness, which is based on actual differences. They tend to verbalize their effort, moreover, in terms of "grass roots government" and "government close to the people," and in so doing lay claim to a great American tradition.

When one considers the growing demands for decentralization and neighborhood autonomy it is difficult to see how centralization is likely to bear much fruit in the future. It appears that most of the nation's metropolitan residents will have to accustom themselves to living with recurrent conflict and managing it within the present fragmented governmental structure. Conflict management and cooperative action are by no means impossible within the existing framework, of course, but they require cooperation *between* or *among* different polities rather than within one metropolitan-wide polity.

"Urban Political Integration: Conditions Associated with Annexation in American Cities" concerns annexation as a device for metropolitan integration. Approximately three-quarters of the nation's 213 largest central cities annexed some territory between 1950 and 1960. Using census data from all United States metropolitan areas, Dye shows that annexation is likely to be accomplished under certain socioeconomic and political conditions but not under others. Favorable conditions include the manager form of government in the annexing city and social class similarities between city and suburbs.

"Public Opinion and Metropolitan Reorganization in Nashville" tests some hypotheses found in the literature and analyzes voter attitudes in the successful, and celebrated, 1962 consolidation of Nashville and Davidson County, Tennessee. Whereas many surveys of voter attitudes in the metropolis focus on suburban voters only (because suburbanites have so often blocked integration proposals), the Nashville data are from both suburban and central city voters. The author's conclusions offer little encouragement to those who would like to "find out how it's done" from the Nashville story. The final selection, "Public Attitudes and Metropolitan Decision-Making" by Charles R. Adrian, summarizes much of the thinking of "realist" political scientists.

# Government Adaptation
# to Metropolitan Growth

## ROSCOE C. MARTIN

Modifications in the practice and structure of local government normally result not from considerations of logic but from demonstration of need. Most of the time the need will be related to a deficiency in quality or quantity of service: To a function ill performed or performed at an inadequate level, or to one for which government has not yet acknowledged responsibility. The need must be of a type or character and it must be felt by a sufficient number of people to command attention. These conditions are met most readily if the need can be described in terms of emergency. Signs of crisis and near crisis in local government generally appear first in the metropolitan areas. That is where a large and increasing proportion of the people live: Almost 63 percent of the total, according to the census of 1960. That is where the problems occasioned by urban growth have their sharpest impact, where public services experience their severest strains, where governments exist in wildest profusion.[1]

This is a study of local government adaptation to changing metropolitan needs. Its bounds are suggested by two features of the kind of action to be examined. First, it must be taken by local governments. This properly rules out adaptive measures required by superior law—by State statutes, for example—though of course it does

---

Reprinted from *Metropolis in Transition* (Housing and Home Finance Agency, Washington, D.C., 1963), pp. 1–11.

[1] W. Brooke Graves, Senior Specialist in American Government and Public Administration in the Legislative Reference Service of the Library of Congress, is the author of an exhaustive study entitled "American Intergovernmental Relations," (New York: Charles Scribner's Sons, 1964). Dr. Graves not only permitted me to read the relevant portions of his study in manuscript but spent considerable time discussing my own work with me. His careful and thorough bibliographies in the field, likewise made available to me, proved highly useful. I am pleased to acknowledge his assistance with these words of appreciation.

not exclude action taken under cover of State enabling legislation. It would be a mistake, however, to place a restrictive meaning on the word "local," for a situation may arise in which effective steps toward the solution of a metropolitan problem may be taken only through the State acting in behalf of its local governments. The point is that the voice of local government must be paramount in any decision made.

A second feature is that the action taken must be voluntary. This is a corollary of the first point, but it is worthy of explicit statement. Here again care must be taken not to abuse the idea of volitional action through restrictive interpretation. If the law authorizes such-and-such a measure to be taken by, say, 75 percent of the governments concerned with a problem, or by governments representing 75 percent of the people of the areas involved, a decision so approved may be said to have been taken voluntarily notwithstanding opposition by one or two governments or by a minority of the populace. Neither the concept of voluntary action nor that of democratic procedure calls for unanimous agreement.

Attention will be focused, then, on voluntary local action whose purpose is to make the procedure or structure of local government more nearly adequate to metropolitan needs. The exercise by the definition of its purpose is centered on the current scene, for the needs which occasion governmental adaptation grow from contemporary developments. There is merit in examining the history of the metropolis, but its problems are the problems of today.

## Methods of Local Adaptation

There is a considerable and growing literature on the subject of local government adaptation to changing needs, but it is for the most part discrete and of fairly recent vintage. It follows that, while many scholars have dealt casually with the subject in the past, few have attempted systematic analyses. There is therefore no established pattern of treatment and no generally accepted classification of the devices or techniques available for adaptive action among local governments. A few words on this subject will prove useful by way of orientation.

Four distinct approaches to the problem of classifying the methods of local adaptation may be discerned. The first emphasizes the existing pattern of local government. Holding the light firm on the local units—counties, cities, towns and townships, villages and boroughs, school and other districts—it examines adaptive measures in terms of their significance for traditional governments. This may be called the "jurisdictional" approach.

The second approach concentrates upon the needs and purposes of a particular activity, such as health, education, or recreation. It tends to minimize, sometimes (as in the case of education) even to ignore, traditional governments. The emphasis on the job to be done in a special program area to the virtual exclusion of all other considerations warrants our designating this the "functional" approach.

When stress is placed on the problems of the metropolitan area as a whole, the tendency is to minimize both traditional governments and individual functions in favor of the governmental needs of the entire region. Existing general governments are likely to be regarded as obstacles to progress, special districts as evidence of schismatic tendencies. Both general and special-district local governments arouse the ire of the devotee of an areawide general government, whose approach may be said to be "regional."

Finally, attention may be focused not on the existing pattern of government, nor on the individual functions to be performed, nor on the needs of the region as a whole, but rather on the "methods" available for employment in adapting local government to changing needs. This approach is avowedly pragmatic. It accepts two basic propositions: First, there are some 18,500 units of local government in the Nation's metropolitan areas; second, opportunities for the dramatic rationalization of the pattern of metropolitan government are few and far between. Then it proceeds to the final, starkly simple question: Given the structure of government which prevails in the metropolitan areas, what devices are available for making the system operate more effectively? If we cannot have the metropolitan governments recommended by the experts almost unanimously three decades ago, what can we have? What in fact is possible by way of governmental adaptation within the metropolitan areas? These are the questions to be examined, and insofar as possible answered, in this study.

Table 1 proposes a classification of the methods of local government adaptation to changing needs. Let it be said quickly that another classifier—any other classifier—would have come up with a different list. The table reveals, indeed, that five authorities over the course of more than two decades have adopted varying systems. All employed a few of the better known concepts. Several used terms without much apparent striving for precision: Lepawsky, for example, seems to have used the words "district" and "authority" interchangeably. No previous classification fits the terminology employed here perfectly, and most rest on concepts which make comparisons difficult and which defy pigeonholing into any preconceived set of categories. So far as the literature of the subject is concerned, therefore, the table's principal value is suggestive.

It may be employed with more assurance in relation to the study at hand, for it indicates the methods of local adaptation which have been identified by the author of this study. These number 16, and they run from the simplest (informal cooperation) to the most complex (metropolitan government and the regional agency), from that which has little or no effect on the structure of local government to

## TABLE 1

### METHODS OF LOCAL ADAPTATION

|  | Lepaw-sky 1939[1] | Jones 1942[2] | Jones 1953[3] | Shefel-man 1960[4] | Adrian 1961[5] | ACIR 1962[6] |
|---|---|---|---|---|---|---|
| 1. Informal cooperation | x | x |  | x |  |  |
| 2. The service contract | x |  |  | x |  |  |
| 3. Parallel action |  |  |  |  |  |  |
| 4. The conference approach |  |  |  |  |  | x |
| 5. The compact | x | x | x |  |  | x |
| 6. Transfer of functions |  |  |  |  |  | x |
| 7. Extraterritorial jurisdiction | x | x | x |  | x | x |
| 8. Incorporation |  |  |  | x |  |  |
| 9. Annexation | x | x | x | x | x | x |
| 10. City-county separation |  | x | x |  | x | x |
| 11. Geographical consolidation | x | x | x | x | x | x |
| 12. Functional consolidation |  | x |  | x |  |  |
| 13. The special district | x |  | x | x | x | x |
| 14. The authority | x | x |  |  |  |  |
| 15. Metropolitan government | x | x | x | x | x | x |
| 16. The regional agency |  |  |  |  |  |  |
| Total | 9 | 9 | 7 | 8 | 6 | 9 |

[1] Albert Lepawsky, "Development of Urban Government," in "Urban Government" (vol. I of the Supplementary Report of the Urbanism Committee to the Natural Resources Committee; Washington, 1939), pp. 30–35.

[2] Victor Jones, "Metropolitan Government" Chicago: University of Chicago Press, 1942), p. 87.

[3] Victor Jones, "Local Government Organization in Metropolitan Areas: Its Relation to Urban Redevelopment," in Coleman Woodbury (ed.), "The Future of Our Cities and Urban Redevelopment" (Chicago: University of Chicago Press, 1953), pp. 529–530.

[4] Harold S. Shefelman, "Local Intergovernmental Relations," in Local Government Workshop, "Proceedings, 1960" (Albany: Office for Local Government, 1960), pp. 62–63.

[5] Charles R. Adrian, "Governing Urban America" (New York: McGraw-Hill, 1961), p. 276.

[6] Advisory Commission on Intergovernmental Relations, "Alternative Approaches to Governmental Reorganization in Metropolitan Areas" (Washington, 1962, ch. IV).

that which has (or may have) considerable effect. The methods are arranged, indeed, in order of complexity and severity of impact on local governments from 1 through 15–16, although the rank order is not to be regarded as fixed. Annexation might well constitute a greater trauma than, say, the establishment of a special district. Nevertheless each succeeding method in normal circumstances would appear to edge a little nearer to an outright metropolitan solution to the area's problems of government.

Close examination of the table will suggest that the first several methods can be achieved without notable effect on the structure of local government. These may be called methods of "procedural" adaptation. The purpose may be nothing more than to exchange information, or to secure the advantages of mutual aid. Sometimes it may extend to the improvement of service, or even to the provision of a new service. In general, such changes seek to adapt local procedures to new needs without significant structural modifications. They may be pursued constructively, in a positive effort to achieve improved government. On the other hand the purpose may be essentially a negative one, for the action taken may be a defensive maneuver against more drastic measures.

The methods listed in the bottom half of the table generally look toward "structural" modifications. They seek to adapt local government to changing needs through areal adjustment, either by enlarging an existing unit of government or by creating a new one to deal with new or changing requirements. Methods 1 through 5 generally can be accommodated without basic structural change and therefore without significant threat to existing local governments; methods 6 through 9 may or may not have an adverse effect on existing governments, depending on local circumstances; methods 10 through 16 are likely to have an identifiable effect on the pattern of local government, either overtly through the establishment of new governments or indirectly through significant functional shifts.

It is a safe presumption that the local governments of virtually every metropolitan area have employed one or more of these methods in their efforts to adapt at least minimally to changing needs, while many areas have experimented with several mechanisms.

## Procedural Adaptation [2]

One major category of devices for local adaptation, it will be recalled, emphasizes procedure. Procedural adaptation may in fact

---

[2] In connection with the next two sections, the report of the Advisory Commission on Intergovernmental Relations titled "Alternative Approaches to Governmental Reorganization in Metropolitan Areas" (Washington, 1962) will prove useful as parallel reading. As noted above (table 1), the classification of approaches employed there differs from that used here, but the differences relate largely to nomenclature. Anyone whose interest may be piqued by the following thumbnail sketches will find extended discussions of most of the methods treated in ch. IV of the ACIR study.

entail structural modification as well, but that is not its central focus. Its primary concern is with the manner in which the public's business is conducted rather than with the organization of government.

1. *Informal cooperation.*—The earliest agreements for procedural adaptation were wholly informal. Neither authorized nor prohibited by law, such agreements in the past grew normally from the simple desire on the part of the spokesmen of two or more local units to improve service. The exchange of information is one of the oldest and still most effective forms of cooperation among governments. The sharing of police teletype intelligence is an excellent example of this kind of cooperation. This suggests mutual aid of a somewhat more formal type, such as that found where neighboring governments agree to the reciprocal use of firefighting equipment in case of emergency. Street or other equipment may be exchanged as well, and there are instances of the joint sharing of technical personnel. Sometimes such arrangements are of long standing, sometimes they are "ad hoc"; sometimes the safety or other advantage enjoyed is deemed to be adequate compensation, sometimes there is payment for services rendered. The variations are many, but the central feature remains fixed: The arrangement for procedural adjustment rests on informal agreement.

2. *The service contract.*—One step removed from informal cooperation is the provision of a specified service (or, sometimes, a list of services) by contract. This involves a legal undertaking on the part of one government to supply and on the part of another to receive (and usually to pay for) the service or services named. There are literally thousands of local service contracts in effect throughout the country; indeed it would be a safe presumption that a large majority of all local governments are involved in selling or buying services under contract. Cities and counties are the units most actively engaged in this practice; they buy and sell water, sewage disposal, library service, hospital and other health services, garbage and refuse removal, fire protection, building inspection, planning assistance, and many other services. In Los Angeles County service by contract has been carried to the point where a city may make a "package deal" with the county for the purchase of all municipal services. The service contract is one of the principal devices for easing the pains of metropolitan growth.[3]

---

[3] The service contract is discussed with care in ch. II in *Metropolis in Transition.*

3. *Parallel action.*—When two or more governments agree to pursue a common course, the result may be called parallel action. The decisions are agreed upon jointly, but their implementation requires individual action by the governments involved. The end product nevertheless is, in effect, common action. The agreement may be informal (personal) or contractual; more commonly it is the former. A number of states, California, Indiana, Minnesota, and Wisconsin among them, have adopted "joint powers" legislation which authorizes a local government to enter into agreement with another unit (or units) for the joint performance of any function which the cooperating governments have the power to undertake individually. Joint powers statutes provide for a variation on parallel action, and the two usually receive separate treatment. Because of their common requirement of joint agreement, they are considered as one for present purposes. Parallel action, and more especially joint powers action, appears to be spreading as a device for interlocal adaptation.

4. *The conference approach.*—A regional conference (or council) as conceived here may be defined as a device for bringing together, at regular intervals, representatives (including—and often limited to —the chief elected officials) of the local governments within a given metropolitan area for the discussion of common problems, the exchange of information, and the development of agreement on policy questions of mutual interest. Since there is no sanction by which to compel either participation in the beginning or acquiescence in policy decisions in the end, the metropolitan council rests explicitly on the voluntary cooperation of the member governments. The conference movement began in Detroit in 1954; by 1962 it numbered about eight recognized adherents and appeared to be gaining momentum.[4]

5. *The compact.*—A compact may be described as a formal agreement under which two or more governments undertake certain mutual obligations. In a sense it resembles, and indeed is sometimes considered to be, a contract. There is a significant distinction, however, in the fact that a compact normally binds the signatory governments to a course of reciprocal action, whereas a contract usually covers a simple "business" transaction, for example sale of a service by one government and purchase by another. A compact may exist between or among local governments in the same State, between local governments in different States, or between States. A current

---

[4] The metropolitan regional council, as it developed in two quite different settings, is discussed in chs. III IV in *Metropolis in Transition.*

example of the first is found in an agreement between Campbell and Kenton Counties, Ky., to form the Northern Kentucky Area Planning Commission.[5] With respect to interlocal, interstate cooperation, New York in 1957, Connecticut in 1961, and New Jersey in 1962 passed laws authorizing local governments to enter into agreements across State lines.[6] In point of fact these authorizations serve mainly to give legal recognition to existing practice, for there has been cooperative action between local governments in neighboring States for many years. There are examples, too, of action to deal with what were essentially metropolitan problems by interstate compact.[7]

6. *Transfer of functions.*—Adaptation may be sought through the transfer of one or more functions from one government to another more nearly adequate in jurisdiction and resources—as from a village or city to the county, or from a city or county to the State. This indeed is one of the principal means by which a government limited in geographical scope, powers, or resources seeks to deal with expanding needs, or with demands for more service. Thus in the Syracuse, N.Y., area a sewage problem was placed in the hands of a metropolitan agency, and a suburban water problem that had got out of hand was bucked up to the county. A governmental unit of adequate size which benefits from a series of such transfers over the years may wake up one day to find itself a metropolitan government, whether by intent or no. Onondaga County, N.Y., appears to be in a fair way to answer this description at some not-distant date.[8]

---

[5] The authorization for such action as contained in a law passed by the Kentucky legislature in its 1960 session. Letter, D. Reid Ross, chief, advance planning section, NKAPC, to Morton J. Schussheim, Assistant Administrator for Program Policy, HHFA, Sept. 19, 1962.

[6] New York State Department of Audit and Control, "Interlocal Cooperation in New York State" (Albany, 1958), p. 8; "State Government News," January 1962; and "National Civic Review," September 1962, p. 438. See also Frederick L. Zimmermann and Mitchell Wendell, "Bridging State Lines," "National Municipal Review," February 1957, pp. 71–76.

[7] Ch. X in *Metropolis in Transition* treats of a regional approach to a suprametropolitan problem by interstate compact.

[8] See ch. VIII in *Metropolis in Transition* for a discussion of a "forward pass" to the county. Among its alternative approaches to governmental reorganization in metropolitan areas, the Advisory Commission on Intergovernmental Relations (*op. cit.*) lists the urban county. This study, while accepting the urban county as the most logical solution to the problem of government in many metropolitan areas, adopts the view that the county is most likely to emerge as a metropolitan government through a buildup of functions over a period of years. One of the principal elements in such a buildup is the gradual transfer of functions from local governments to the urban county. It is obvious that such transfers over the course of time may so transform the county as to make of it in effect a new unit of

7. *Extraterritorial jurisdiction.*—If the concept of a city limited in its power to act to a fixed and definite territory is an ancient one, so also is the practice of engaging in certain activities "beyond the wall." Extraterritorial jurisdiction for the city must be granted by the State either explicitly or by implication, but it has been granted generally in certain fields of action. Thus cities go outside their legal limits, some of them great distances, for their water supply. Thus also do they establish sewage disposal plants, acquire and operate extramural forests and parks, and sell services to neighboring communities. The service areas thus established are far from uniform; on the contrary, they vary according to the nature and needs of a particular activity. The grant of extraterritorial jurisdiction thus has the effect of creating a series of flexible and variable city limits so that the city may, within reasonable bounds, do what it needs to do and what is expected of it without undertaking the arduous task of modifying either the boundaries or the powers of neighboring governmental units. Such an arrangement works to the benefit of both the central-city dwellers and the residents of the urban fringe. It is one of the major methods by which the needs of urban areas may be taken into account without substantial change in the structure of local government.[9]

8. *Incorporation.*—The role of incorporation in the metropolitan area is a vital one, for incorporation is the step by which an urban population prepares itself to take effective governmental action. In setting its original limits in terms both of area and of legal powers, the municipality will determine in good part its competence to deal with the problems it will confront. It will also make ready, by the act of incorporation, to take a constructive part in or to resist attempts to solve the metropolitan problem; for a particular move to incorporate may stem from either positive or negative motives. Metropolitan area municipalities increased in number 8 percent from 1957 to 1962.[10] Some of the new incorporations were of course bona fide; but some cities were created to hold services at a minimum (that is, to keep taxes down), to thwart annexation, to serve the cause

---

government. In this event, the transfer of functions might well be regarded as a device for structural rather than for procedural adaptations, or indeed for both simultaneously.

[9] See Frank S. Sengstock, "Extraterritorial Powers in the Metropolitan Area" (Ann Arbor: Legislative Research Center, University of Michigan Law School, 1962).

[10] 1962 Census of Govenments, *op. cit.,* p. 11.

of suburban pride, or otherwise to further local interests. Some, that is, were established for defensive purposes. From such, few contributions toward the solution of metropolitan problems can be expected.[11]

## Structural Adaptation

The methods of adaptation examined to this point have procedural change as their distinguishing feature, though some may produce significant secondary effects on organization. At the other end of the balance are several adjustive devices whose principal emphasis is on structural change. Like the methods of the first category they may produce side results, in their case procedural modifications. Their principal effect, however, is to change the organization of local government. They are rightly regarded as being both more direct and more severe in their impact on the pattern of local government than are adaptive measures of a more purely procedural nature.

9. *Annexation.*—Through the simple device of expanding boundaries to incorporate additional territory, the municipal service area may be enlarged to permit the city to take care of increasing needs. Because needs continue to grow, annexation does not solve the metropolitan government problem; it may, however, ameliorate it by dulling its sharp edges for a period. Many cities have enlarged their limits through annexation in the past—indeed growth by annexation was the normal thing in earlier years. With the coming of the metropolitan era, however, all that changed; for the typical pattern now features a central city surrounded by a number of incorporated suburbs. The expansion of boundaries to take in unincorporated fringe areas was relatively simple. The annexation of an incorporated suburb—that is, the absorption of one city by another —is quite a different matter. In some States—Missouri, New Mexico, Ohio, Texas, and Virginia chief among them—annexation remains a relatively simple process. In most, however, an annexation move becomes effective only on popular approval by referendum vote in each affected governmental unit. This requirement, which gives the incorporated suburb a built-in veto, has slowed the annexation movement to a walk in most parts of the country. Annexation, there-

---

[11] Amos Hawley, "The Incorporation Trend in Metropolitan Areas, 1900–1950" (Ann Arbor: Department of Sociology and Institute of Public Administration, University of Michigan, 1959); Henry J. Schmandt, "The Municipal Incorporation Trend, 1950–1960" (Madison: Bureau of Government, University of Wisconsin, 1961).

fore, whatever its virtues and its weaknesses, has lost much of its effectiveness as a means of areal adaptation to changing local needs.[12]

10. *City-county separation.*—The basic purpose of city-county separation is to divide urban and rural populations so that each may have the kind and level of service it desires and is willing to pay for. Four major cities—Baltimore, Denver, St. Louis, and San Francisco—were separated from their respective counties and set up as cities-counties before 1902. Since that time, however, the city-county separation movement has been active only in Virginia, where in 1962 there were 33 "independent" cities with the functions of both cities and counties. As in the case of annexation, rapid metropolitan growth would appear largely to have destroyed any lasting promise the device may have had for the amelioration of metropolitan problems. In an earlier day it was (or appeared) easy enough to separate urban and rural populations and to design for each an appropriate unit of government. In an era when the total population is preponderantly urban and when the urban population is increasing explosively from decade to decade, such a simple division is no longer possible except in rare circumstances. City-county separation was essentially a product of a bygone rural age.

11. *Geographical consolidation.*—The potential range for the merger of two or more governments into one is very wide. Consolidations involving a city and a county, two or more cities, two or more counties, a special district with either a city or a county, and two or more special districts come readily to mind as possibilities. There were four major city-county consolidations—hinging on Boston, Philadelphia, New Orleans, and New York—during the 19th century, but only two or three of moment since. An apparent reawakening of interest in the plan in 1962 justifies the question whether city-county consolidation may not yet emerge as a live option in the adaptation of local governments to metropolitan needs.[13] At another level, there are instances of inter-

---

[12] The subject of annexation is examined with care in Robert G. Dixon, Jr., and John R. Kerstetter, "Adjusting Municipal Boundaries: The Law and Practice in 48 States" (Chicago and Washington: American Municipal Association, 1959), and in Frank S. Sengstock, "Annexation: A Solution to the Municipal Area Problem" (Ann Arbor: Legislative Research Center, University of Michigan Law School, 1960).

[13] Because it involves governments of different kinds in respect of traditional usage, scope of powers and functions, and relations to the State, city-county consolidation is usually accorded separate treatment. The purpose here was to identify a generic class which would embrace all forms of geographical combinations. Such a class logically would include city-county consolidation.

A recent consolidation involving Nashville and Davidson County, Tenn., is discussed in ch. IX in *Metropolis in Transition.*

municipal consolidation—the annexation of one city to another is of this character. Consolidation is most active with respect to school districts, which decreased 20 percent in the metropolitan areas from 1957 to 1962.[14] In actuality, therefore, geographical consolidation is confined largely to school districts, though its potential for constructive use on a broader front remains high.

12. *Functional consolidation.*—Whereas the consolidation of governmental units involves modification of existing boundaries, functional consolidation most often rests upon cooperative action taken by existing governments. It arises from recognition of the simple fact that it is often more economical to perform common functions jointly, or to lodge responsibility for a service in a larger and stronger unit. The most elementary functional consolidation occurs when two or more governments agree to take common action with respect to a particular activity. An example is found in the joint purchase of supplies, a practice which has enjoyed wide acceptance over a long period. An illustration of a more far-reaching functional consolidation is that provided by Campbell and Kenton Counties, Ky., in their agreement (cited earlier) to entrust their planning interests to the intercounty Northern Kentucky Area Planning Commission. Here the effect of joint action was to establish a new unit of local government possessed of the power to tax and to enter into contracts with other governments and with private corporations.[15] Functional consolidation, then, may run the gamut from a simple agreement to take joint action to the creation of a new government to administer the function (or functions) consolidated. The whole range of action would appear to be useful as means for adapting local government to changing needs.

13. *The special district.*—A special district is a unit of government established to administer one or more designated functions. The "one or more" suggests that such districts may be either single-purpose or multi-purpose in character. The best known and most widely used special district is the local school district, which in truth is so firmly rooted in tradition that it has, so to speak, gained "separate billing:" that is, it is widely regarded as being *sui generis,* and therefore neither local government nor special district. It is well to recognize that it is both. Other special districts deal with a wide spectrum of activities, among which water supply, sewage disposal, and fire protection are illustrative. Virtually all such districts are single purpose. Some are so small as to suggest nothing more than a groping

---

[14] 1962 Census of Governments, *loc. cit.*
[15] See footnote 5, above.

toward local functional adjustment; others by contrast are of broader reach and reflect an effort to adapt boundaries to metropolitan requirements. The latter may be called metropolitan special districts. The Metropolitan Water District of Southern California provides a well-known example.

In 1962 there were 5,411 special districts (apart from school districts) in the 212 standard metropolitan statistical areas, and their number had increased 45 percent in the preceding 5 years.[16] By no means all of these districts, either existing or new, were of a metropolitan character, but many were. The very establishment of a new government is *prima facie* evidence that there is a function (or functions) to be administered which no existing unit is able or willing to undertake. The growth of metropolitan special districts demonstrates both that the number of such functions is increasing and that the special district has proved its worth as a method of attack on the metropolitan problem.[17]

14. *The authority.*—A device which commends itself increasingly to those who seek on-the-ground solutions to metropolitan problems is the authority. In many respects the authority resembles the special district, yet there are points of difference which warrant separate listing for the two. Chief among these is the fact that (normally) the special district has the power to tax but not to issue revenue bonds, while in the case of the authority the situation (again normally) is exactly reversed. There are special districts, as there are also authorities, which possess both powers, hence the distinction cannot be pressed too far. Nevertheless the principal feature attributed to the authority is considered a vital one. The bond market likes to see a unit which proposes to float bonds organized on a "businesslike" basis; an authority, which as a public corporation can be represented as being immune to the politics of local government, has greater appeal in the investment market than does an ordinary special district.

Public authorities, though of long lineage, have come into their own only in the last two decades, during which they have increased rapidly in popularity. There is no count on authorities which purports to be complete—the Bureau of the Census, which ordinarily would supply such a count, lists them along with special districts; but a

---

[16] 1962 Census of Governments, *loc. cit.* This increase was accounted for in part by a redefinition of the term "special district."

[17] See John C. Bollens, "Special District Governments in the United States" (Berkeley and Los Angeles: University of California Press, 1957).

For a discussion of one of the most recent metropolitan special districts, see ch. VII in *Metropolis in Transition.*

recent unpublished study uncovered some 800 authorities in the Northeastern States alone. Like special districts, authorities may be either purely local or metropolitan in their scope. They have been used extensively in the fields of housing, education, mass transit, and port development and management. The New York Port Authority is the classic example of the public authority. There is no discernible limit to the employment of the authority save that set by the revenue potential of its operations and the willingness of the people to exempt a public undertaking from control by elected officials. The public authority would appear to be equally available with the special district as a device for functional administration over a metropolitan area.[18]

15. *Metropolitan government.*—In the sense that every device considered to this point has for its purpose, implicit or avowed, the rationalization of local government in the metropolitan area, each is related, though in some instances tenuously, to metropolitan government. Some methods, however, attack that problem frontally. The elevation of the urban county to a position of dominance as a unit of general government is one measure—the word "trend" may indeed be justified—which presages the emergence of a metropolitan government in some areas. Geographical consolidation is another device which points in the same direction. So is the proposal to establish a general government with jurisdiction over the whole of the metropolitan area, a proposal which at times in the past has gone to the extreme of advocating creation of a number of city-States for the largest urbanized areas. So, finally, is the federated (or borough) plan, which currently enjoys wide support. Notwithstanding the case which can be made in logic for metropolitan government, only two or three of the numerous proposals which have [been] made looking to that end have found favor in adoption.[19]

---

[18] There is considerable interest in the authority device and a good deal of literature on the subject. See, for example, Temporary State Commission on Coordination of State Activities, "Staff Report on Public Authorities Under New York State," Legislative Document (1956) No. 46 (Albany, 1956); Frederick L. Bird, "Local Special Districts and Authorities in Rhode Island" (Kingston, R.I.: Bureau of Government Research, University of Rhode Island, 1962); and George G. Sause, "Municipal Authorities: The Pennsylvania Experience (Harrisburg: Pennsylvania Department of Internal Affairs, 1962).

[19] Actually, in each of the three cases of metropolitan government usually cited (Baton Rouge, Miami, Nashville) the county has played a dominant role. See Mark B. Feldman and Everett L. Jassy, "The Urban County: A Study of New Approaches to Local Government in Metropolitan Areas," "Harvard Law Review," January 1960, pp. 526–582. For an analysis of the Dade County experience, see Edward Sofen, "The Miami Metropolitan Experiment" (Bloomington: Indiana University Press, 1963). For an account of recent events in Nashville and Davidson County, see ch. IX in *Metropolis in Transition*.

16. *The regional agency.*—Now and again a need appears which cannot be satisfied through utilization of any of the devices examined above. Under certain conditions water supply is such a need, as are control of air and water pollution and development of transportation. In this circumstance adaptive action may require creation of a regional organization. The agencies which represent a regional approach to suprametropolitan problems are not large in number, but they are significant in their import. The Interstate Sanitation Commission, which deals with pollution problems generated by the New York City complex, is such an agency. A somewhat similar instrument, with responsibility for water-resources administration extending over half a dozen metropolitan areas, is the newly created Delaware River Basin Commission . . .

# Metropolitan "Fragmentation":
# A Research Note

## BRETT W. HAWKINS
## THOMAS R. DYE

For many years the metropolitan reform movement devoted itself, among other things, to ridding the nation's metropolitan areas of "fragmented government" with its "ineffective, multiple local jurisdictions" and "inefficiencies and duplication of services." Centralization of governmental activity in metropolitan areas was given high priority in the recommendations of metropolitan reformers. "A metropolitan area is a single unit in an economic and social sense, and it should be a single unit governmentally." [1]

Recent research has challenged many of the assumptions of the metropolitan reform movement, however. The political and social values that are threatened by centralization have been identified.[2] Much of the metropolitan reform literature now appears naive in light of recent demands to *de*centralize urban bureaucracies and establish local community control.

Reprinted from *The American Behavioral Scientist*, Vol. 5 (May 1962), p. 11, by permission of the publisher.

This research was made possible by grants from the office of General Research, University of Georgia. The authors are also grateful to Andrew T. Cowart and Carolyn Beatie for aiding in the analysis. A special debt is owed to Alfred K. Barr for collecting the data and helping in the initial stages of analysis.

[1] An interesting review of this and related arguments can be found in Anwar Syed, *The Political Theory of American Local Government* (New York: Random House, 1966).

[2] See Charles R. Adrian, "Public Attitudes and Metropolitan Decision Making," Institute of Local Government, University of Pittsburgh, 1962; Brett W. Hawkins, "Public Opinion and Metropolitan Reorganization in Nashville," *Journal of Politics* (May, 1966), 408–418; Thomas R. Dye, "The Local-Cosmopolitan Dimension and the Study of Urban Politics," *Social Forces* (March, 1963), 239–246; Basil G. Zimmer and Amos H. Hawley, "Local Government as Viewed by Fringe Residents," *Rural Sociology* (December, 1958), 363–370; and G. R. Boynton and Marion Roth, "Communal Ideology and Political Support," *Journal of Politics* (February, 1969), 167–185.

Yet to date neither reformers nor their critics have made much effort to measure comparatively the extent of "fragmentation" in each of the nation's metropolitan areas (although the Bureau of the Census has). Also there has been little systematic, comparative analysis of the conditions associated with fragmentation, or the consequences of fragmentation.[3] The purpose of this note is to measure fragmentation in all 212 (1962) metropolitan areas and observe some of fragmentation's environmental correlates and policy consequences. We assume that fragmentation will not be significantly reduced in the near future, much less eliminated, and that therefore it is important to measure it, discover its correlates, and study comparatively its policy consequences.

## Measuring Metropolitan Fragmentation

The concept of metropolitan fragmentation can be operationalized in terms of the number of governmental units in a metropolitan area (an absolute measure of fragmentation), and the number of governmental units *per person* in a metropolitan area (a relative measure of fragmentation). In 1967 there were a total of 20,703 governments operating in the nation's 227 metropolitan areas. This was twenty-five percent of all local governments in the nation. The total figure for governmental units was composed of 5,018 school districts, 4,977 municipalities, 3,255 townships, 404 counties, and 7,049 special districts. In 1967 there was approximately one governmental unit for every 5,600 persons living in metropolitan areas, and one governmental unit for every 940 persons living in non-metropolitan areas. On a relative basis, that is (governments in relation to the number of people) metropolitan areas are *less* fragmented than non-metropolitan areas. Maybe this fact has something to do with demands for decentralized and increased citizen participation in the nation's metropolitan areas.

Individual metropolitan areas differ widely in the complexity of their governmental structure. According to the 1967 census of governments, the Chicago metropolitan area has the most fragmented governmental system in the nation. A total of 1,113 local governments operate in the Chicago metropolitan area, including 327 school districts, 6 counties, 250 municipalities, 113 townships, and 417 special districts. Other metropolitan areas with complex governmental structures include Phil-

---

[3] In a study of data from a sample (N-36) of the nation's metropolitan areas, Campbell and Sacks find measures of fragmentation—population per government and area per government—not closely related to levels of spending and taxing. Alan K. Campbell and Seymour Sacks, *Metropolitan America: Fiscal Patterns and Governmental Systems* (New York: Free Press, 1967), p. 179.

adelphia with 876 governmental units, Pittsburgh with 704, New York with 551, St. Louis with 474, Portland with 385, San Francisco with 312, and Los Angeles with 233. In contrast there are several single county metropolitan areas (mainly in the South) with fewer than ten governmental units. For example, the Richmond, Virginia metropolitan area has 2 municipalities, 3 county governments, and 2 special districts, for a total of 7 governmental units.

### Environmental Correlates of Fragmentation

Governmental fragmentation in metropolitan areas is a function of size: the larger the metropolitan area, the more fragmented the governmental structure. The simple coefficients in Table 1 indicate that 50 percent of the variation in the numbers of governments in metropolitan areas can be attributed to size. Fragmentation is also related to the age of settlement and to income levels in the metropolis, although these factors are less influential than size. Apparently the older a metropolitan area, the more complex its governmental structure becomes; and the more affluent its citizens are, the more complexity in the form of separate, relatively small units of government can be afforded. Partial coefficients (not shown) indicate that age and income are independently though weakly related to fragmentation; these relationships are not a product of the intervening effect of size.

**TABLE 1**

*CONDITIONS ASSOCIATED WITH*
*METROPOLITAN GOVERNMENTAL FRAGMENTATION*

|  | Numbers of Governments | | | Governments per 100,000 | | |
|  | Total | School Districts | Munici- palities | Total | School Districts | Munici- palities |
|---|---|---|---|---|---|---|
| Size of Metropolitan Area | .71 | .67 | .74 | −.15 | −.11 | .00 |
| Age in Decades | .48 | .40 | .49 | −.19 | −.14 | .00 |
| Percent Nonwhite, Central City | .06 | .00 | −.04 | −.37 | −.31 | −.03 |
| Metropolitan-wide SES |  |  |  |  |  |  |
|   Median Family Income | .28 | .29 | .24 | .00 | .00 | −.05 |
|   White Collar Occup. | .15 | .14 | .15 | .03 | −.07 | .07 |
|   High School Grad. | .06 | .08 | .01 | .12 | .06 | .08 |
| City-Suburban SES Differences |  |  |  |  |  |  |
|   Non-white | .05 | .01 | .17 | −.22 | −.17 | −.03 |
|   Median Family Income | .15 | .07 | .24 | −.16 | −.21 | .00 |
|   White Collar Occup. | .17 | .11 | .26 | −.26 | −.25 | −.04 |
|   High School Grad. | .22 | .16 | .27 | −.11 | −.17 | .00 |
| Central City Population as Percent SMSA Pop. | −.23 | −.19 | −.27 | .14 | .09 | .05 |

NOTE: Figures are simple correlation coefficients for 212 Metropolitan areas.

Contrary to expectation, the racial composition of the central city does not correlate with fragmentation. One might expect that increases in central city non-white population would be associated with "white flight" to the suburbs, the development and incorporation of independent suburbs, and thus with fragmentation. But the data do not support such an explanation of fragmentation. We also expected that city-suburban differences in socio-economic levels would be related to fragmentation. Again, this expectation was based on a belief that middle class whites seeking to escape from the problems of less affluent central city populations would develop and incorporate independent suburbs, and thereby contribute to fragmentation. But the relationships between city-suburban social differences and fragmentation are generally so weak (the coefficients so low), that this does not appear to be an explanation of fragmentation.

Finally, it might be noted that central city dominance of the metropolitan area, as indexed by the percent of the metropolitan area population living in the central city, is inversely related to fragmentation. Governmental fragmentation is less where central cities have managed to hold onto a substantial proportion of the metropolitan population.

If fragmentation is measured in *relative* terms (governments per 100,000 population), it is much more difficult to observe environmental correlates. Governmental complexity in relative terms is *not* associated with size. In fact, there is a slight tendency for larger, older and racially heterogeneous metropolitan areas to have *fewer* governments *per capita*.

## Fragmentation and Special District Government

One of the "solutions" to the "problem" of metropolitan governmental fragmentation which is frequently encountered in the reform literature is special district government. Special districts or authorities charged with administering a particular service on a metropolitan-wide or inter-municipal level—such as park, sewerage, water, parking, airport, planning, etc. districts—are found in most metropolitan areas. They provide a means of overcoming fragmentation and providing metropolitan-wide or inter-municipal governmental service.

Table 2 suggests that indeed one of the concommitants of governmental fragmentation is the growth of special district government. Special districts proliferate where municipalities and school districts proliferate.

However, *reliance* on counties and special districts, as measured by county and special district revenues and expenditures as a percent of all government expenditures, is *not* associated with fragmentation. Thus,

**TABLE 2**

METROPOLITAN GOVERNMENTAL FRAGMENTATION
AND RELIANCE ON SPECIAL DISTRICT GOVERNMENT

| | Numbers of Governments | | | Governments per 100,000 | | |
| | Total | School Districts | Munici- palities | Total | School Districts | Munici- palities |
|---|---|---|---|---|---|---|
| Special Districts, Number | .89 | .79 | .72 | .14 | .01 | .03 |
| Special Districts, Per 100,000 | .30 | .24 | .22 | .26 | .14 | −.03 |
| County and Special District Expenditures as % SMSA Exp. | .06 | .05 | .06 | −.01 | −.06 | .09 |
| County and Special District Revenues as % SMSA Rev. | −.03 | −.02 | −.03 | −.02 | .00 | .11 |

NOTE: Figures are simple correlation coefficients for 212 metropolitan areas.

special districts and authorities proliferate in a fragmented governmental structure, but there is no observable tendency to rely more heavily on these units for the provision of governmental services.

## Fragmentation and Public Policy

It is not easy to assess all of the policy consequences of fragmentation. We have made a preliminary effort to assess the impact of fragmentation on levels of governmental spending in metropolitan areas for particular services. However, it is quite possible that fragmentation affects policy outcomes in urban government in ways which do not lend themselves to measurement in aggregate financial statistics. Fragmentation may be a very significant factor in policy outcomes concerning fair housing, de facto school segregation, inequality in municipal tax burdens, action by higher levels of government to compensate for inequality in municipal tax burdens, or resources, and a host of other important policy areas. These outcomes are not reflected in aggregate figures on governmental spending, and their relationship to fragmentation must await further analysis.

However, one of the assumptions of the reform literature on metropolitan "problems" is that fragmentation adversely affects the level of governmental service. Fragmentation is said to increase the costs of municipal services and lower the quality and/or quantity of services provided. Such an assumption *does* lend itself to investigation with aggregate figures.

Before turning to an assessment of the impact of fragmentation on levels of government spending, it is important to note that environmental variables play an important role in determining spending levels. Table 3 indicates that income levels in metropolitan areas explain about 28 percent of the variation of total per capita governmental expenditures in metropolitan areas. In other words, governments in metropolitan areas spend more money per capita when their citizens make more money per capita. Government spending levels in metropolitan areas are also related to the size of the metropolis and other socio-economic characteristics of the population. Governments in larger metropolitan areas spend more *per capita* than those in smaller areas; and governments spend more per capita in areas with well-educated, prestigeously employed populations. There is also a slight tendency for governments to spend *less* per capita where there is a larger non-white population.

Certain kinds of government expenditures are more closely associated with environmental variables than other kinds of expenditures. For example, a glance at Table 3 suggests that police expenditures are particularly influenced by size and income levels of metropolitan areas. Certain other expenditures—highways, health, financial administration, utilities—appear relatively uninfluenced by environmental factors.

What is the relationship between fragmentation and government spending in metropolitan areas? Compared to the influence of environmental variables on public spending, the influence of fragmentation appears very weak. Table 4 fails to reveal any close relationships between any measure of fragmentation and any measure of public spending.

**TABLE 3**

**CONDITIONS ASSOCIATED WITH SPENDING
FOR PUBLIC SERVICES IN METROPOLITAN AREAS**

| Per Capita Expenditures | Size | Age | Non-white | Income | Occupation | Education |
|---|---|---|---|---|---|---|
| Total | .33 | .16 | −.20 | .55 | .28 | .35 |
| Education | .12 | −.07 | −.35 | .48 | .26 | .43 |
| Highways | .10 | −.05 | −.11 | .20 | .14 | .16 |
| Welfare | .21 | .26 | −.24 | .30 | −.04 | .00 |
| Health & Hosp. | .22 | .06 | .13 | .12 | .09 | .08 |
| Police | .57 | .39 | .01 | .51 | .30 | .20 |
| Fire | .21 | .32 | −.20 | .45 | .16 | .12 |
| Sewage | .04 | .02 | −.10 | .31 | .28 | .35 |
| Sanitation | .38 | .20 | .23 | .21 | .26 | .10 |
| Housing and Urban Renewal | .21 | .33 | .11 | .23 | .03 | −.12 |
| Libraries | .17 | .19 | −.17 | .34 | .29 | .30 |
| Financial Adm. | .08 | .03 | −.14 | .16 | .23 | .32 |
| Utilities | .13 | −.01 | .04 | −.04 | .26 | .24 |

NOTE: Figures are simple correlation coefficients for 212 metropolitan areas.

**TABLE 4**

*METROPOLITAN GOVERNMENTAL FRAGMENTATION*
*AND SPENDING FOR PUBLIC SERVICES*

| Per Capita Expenditures | Numbers of Governments | | | Governments per 100,000 | | |
|---|---|---|---|---|---|---|
| | Total | School Districts | Munici-palities | Total | School Districts | Munici-palities |
| Total | .23 | .25 | .16 | −.00 | .02 | .02 |
| Education | .18 | .20 | .06 | .16 | .10 | .03 |
| Highways | .11 | .16 | .07 | .21 | .20 | .03 |
| Welfare | .15 | .15 | .05 | .01 | .09 | −.05 |
| Health & Hosp. | .05 | .05 | .08 | −.18 | −.14 | .11 |
| Police | .31 | .29 | .35 | −.29 | −.18 | −.01 |
| Fire | .00 | .00 | −.04 | −.24 | −.10 | −.01 |
| Sewage | .07 | .09 | .06 | .04 | .05 | .00 |
| Sanitation | .09 | .08 | .18 | −.26 | −.24 | .04 |
| Housing and Urban Renewal | .11 | .08 | .11 | −.19 | −.16 | −.09 |
| Libraries | .12 | .14 | .08 | .06 | .13 | .00 |
| Financial Adm. | .09 | .12 | .06 | .07 | .13 | −.01 |
| Utilities | .04 | .02 | .03 | −.10 | −.11 | .13 |

NOTE: Figures are simple correlation coefficients for 212 metropolitan areas.

Fragmentation does *not* appear to increase or decrease government spending for municipal services. Partial and multiple-partial coefficients (not shown) confirm that fragmentation has little association with per capita spending even when environmental influences are controlled. In other words, a metropolitan political system characteristic, the importance of which has often been insisted upon, is not closely related to spending in metropolitan areas.

## Some Thoughts on "Fragmentation"

The dollar consequences of metropolitan governmental fragmentation have probably been over-emphasized in the reform literature. Neither fragmentation nor centralization are likely to affect per capita levels of government spending in any significant way. Of course, one might still argue that a per capita dollar spent by a centralized governmental structure is more "efficiently" spent than a per capita dollar by a fragmented structure. But "efficiency" is as much a value judgment as anything else.

Our point is that metropolitan "fragmentation," as well as reorganization and centralization, must be examined primarily in terms of the socio-political values involved, rather than their public service or spending consequences. Evidently the service argument against fragmentation has been used in error.

# Urban Political Integration:
# Conditions Associated with
# Annexation in American Cities

## THOMAS R. DYE

Metropolitan political integration has long been a concern of the municipal reform movement. However, much of the early literature on metropolitan government was prescriptive in character and did little to advance
our understanding of the politics of metropolitan integration. Advocacy
of metropolitan integration too often rested upon a penchant for organizational neatness and little recognition was shown for the social and
political values affected by integrative proposals. Only recently have
there been any systematic attempts to identify the divisive influences in
metropolitan politics,[1] or to state the conditions requisite for effective
political integration in metropolitan areas.[2] The research reported here

Reprinted from *Midwest Journal of Political Science,* Vol. 8 (November
1964), 430–46, by permission of the Wayne State University Press.

This study was sponsored by the Bureau of Government, The University of
Wisconsin, and the Wisconsin Urban Program under a grant from the Ford
Foundation. I am grateful to Rajal Rathee and the Numerical Analysis Laboratory
of The University of Wisconsin for aid in statistical analysis, Harold Herman and
Oliver P. Williams of the University of Pennsylvania for helpful criticism, and
Sandra Sciacchitano, The University of Wisconsin, and William Matuzeski, Harvard
Law School, for general assistance.

[1] See in particular Edward C. Banfield, "The Politics of Metropolitan Organization," *Midwest Journal of Political Science,* Volume I (May 1957), 77–91;
Henry J. Schmandt, "The City and the Ring," *American Behavioral Scientist,*
Volume 3 (November, 1960), 17–19; Robert Wood, "Metropolitan Government
1975: An Exploration of Trends," *American Political Science Review,* Volume 52
(March, 1958), 108–122; Scott Greer, *Governing The Metropolis,* John Wiley,
1962; Robert Wood, *1400 Governments,* Harvard University Press, 1961.

[2] See Vincent Ostron, Charles Tiebout and Robert Wamen, "The Organization
of Government in Metropolitan Areas: A Theoretical Inquiry," *American Political Science Review,* Volume 55 (December, 1961), 831–842; Charles S. Liebman
*et al.,* "Social Status, Tax Resources, and Metropolitan Cooperation," *National
Tax Journal,* Volume 16 (March, 1963), 56–62; Thomas R. Dye *et al.,* "Differentiation and Cooperation in a Metropolitan Area," *Midwest Journal of Political
Science,* Volume 7 (May, 1963), 145–155; Edward Sofen, "Problems in Metropolitan Leadership: The Miami Experience," *Midwest Journal of Political Science,*
Volume 5 (February, 1961), 18–38.

focuses on the annexation device as a means to political integration and endeavors to set forth the conditions associated with its employment.

Political integration at the municipal level may take a variety of forms. These include metropolitan federation, city-county consolidation, municipal jointure, inter-jurisdictional agreements and contracts, and joint authorities or boards. But perhaps the most salient expression of political integration in municipal government is annexation. While many students of urban government have expressed doubts about annexation as an effective approach to metropolitan integration, annexation continues to win widespread acceptance as an integrative device in the nation's urban areas. Between 1950 and 1960 over six million persons were annexed to central cities in 213 urbanized areas, more than the combined populations of a dozen states. Approximately three quarters of the nation's 213· largest central cities succeeded in annexing some territory and people in the same ten year period; half of these major cities annexed more than ten percent of their 1960 populations. The *Municipal Yearbook* reports that annexation activity has increased markedly in the last few years; in 1962 alone, 754 cities with populations over 5,000 (one out of every five municipalities of this size) annexed a total of 968 square miles of territory, an area almost the size of Rhode Island. In short, annexation remains an important political phenomenon in urban areas and invites systematic investigation.

Several conditions were originally hypothesized to be relevant to the pattern of annexation activity in the nation's urban areas. One of these was age of settlement. The boundaries of older cities were thought to be less subject to pressures for change than the boundaries of newer and growing cities. Another hypothesis centered about the relationship between annexation success and the size of metropolitan areas. Suburban resistance to annexation was expected to be more intense and more effective in larger metropolitan areas. It was also suggested that annexation was less likely to occur in urban areas where the city and its surrounding suburbs were socially differentiated from one another. Suburbanites were expected to resist integration with the central city where there was a significant status differential between the city and its suburbs.

In addition to the hypotheses that annexation success is related to the age and size of urban areas and the social distance between city and suburb, several other conditions thought to be associated with incidence of annexation were also examined. These were: the legal difficulty of annexation under controlling statutes, the form of organization of the government of the central city, and the educational, occupational, income and racial characteristics of the central city.

The incidence of annexation was examined in the 213 urbanized areas of the united States delineated by the Census Bureau.[3] The measure of annexation activity is the percent of the 1960 central city population which was annexed to it between 1950 and 1960. The assumption underlying this procedure is that cities of different sizes which annex equal percentages of their population are undergoing "comparable political experiences." While this assumption may be open to question in many instances, it seemed less objectionable than the use of absolute numbers of persons annexed which would disfavor small urbanized areas. Each urbanized area in the United States was assigned an "annexation score." These scores ranged from zero in 60 of the 213 urbanized areas (indicating that no one had been annexed to the central cities in these areas in ten years), to highs of 76 and 78 in Phoenix and Tucson (indicating that 76 and 78 percent of the 1960 populations of these cities had been annexed to them in the last decade). Twenty-seven central cities had annexed 30 percent or more of their 1960 populations, twenty-eight had annexed between 20 and 30 percent, forty had annexed between 10 and 20 percent, fifty-eight had annexed less than 10 percent, and sixty had no annexations. The mean annexation score for all 213 urbanized areas was 11.7 with a standard deviation of 15.0. In the analysis to follow, these scores are treated as the dependent variable.[4]

## Legal Restraints on Annexation

From a legal standpoint one could argue that the statutes of each state are the determining factors in the success of annexation. But to offer controlling statutes as an explanation is, in a sense, to beg the question. The statutes themselves are reflections of widely held values within a political system. The controlling statutes under which any city must implement its annexation policies are likely to be a product of the social

---

[3] An urbanized area contains at least one city of 50,000 inhabitants or more with contiguous densely settled areas constituting its urban fringe. There were 213 such areas in 1960. The figures on numbers of people annexed by each central city from 1950 to 1960 are found in the U.S. Census Bureau's PC(1) series of reports, "Number of Inhabitants," for each state. *See U.S. Census of Population: 1960,* "Number of Inhabitants," "United States Summary," PC(1)–1A, 1960. In those cases where an urbanized area had two or more central cities, they were combined and treated as one city for analytical purposes.

[4] In the tabular presentation of some of the findings below, *mean* annexation scores are given for various groupings of urban areas. The technical objection to the use of means which are based upon percentage figures is avoided if we think of the annexation score as a discrete concept rather than a proportion. A mean annexation score refers to the average success in annexing people experienced by a particular grouping of cities. It is not weighed in favor of larger cities.

conditions and attitudes prevailing in that city and its surrounding suburbs. It is to these underlying conditions that our attention is primarily directed.

However, some analysis of the relationship between the stringency of annexation law and success of annexation was undertaken. In general this analysis confirmed the judgment that controlling statutes do not in themselves provide a satisfactory explanation for the success of annexation. Statutes vary a great deal from state to state with regard to the ease or difficulty of annexation; even within states separate statutes may govern different cities.[5] Statutes are not easily ranked in terms of the ease or difficulty of a procedure which they authorize, such as annexation. Nonetheless an attempt was made to rank each of 213 central cities in the U.S. on a scale of 1 to 10 according to the ease of difficulty of annexation under prevailing statutes. Cities which could not annex land without a special act of the state legislature or some equally laborious procedure received a rating of 1. Cities which could annex incorporated and unincorporated areas unilaterally by vote of the city council alone were given a rating of 10. A vast majority of cities, 174 of 213, were rated between these extreme scores depending upon certain key provisions affecting ease of annexation. Of course, such a ranking is necessarily subjective.[6]

Table 1 indicates that mean annexation scores increased with increasing statutory permissiveness, but not consistently so.

## Metropolitan Area Size and Incidence of Annexation

It was expected that suburban opposition to central city annexation would be more intense in larger metropolitan areas. Suburban resistance

---

[5] Providence for example is governed by a statute which froze all boundaries in the state 35 years ago. At the other end of the spectrum Chattanooga may annex any "suitable adjoining territory," with "suitable" usually judged liberally by Tennessee courts. Action is unilateral on the part of the City Council and the only recourse for those affected is a court review of "reasonableness." Of course most cities fell between these two extremes.

[6] In these operations the following summary of annexation laws proved invaluable: Robert G. Dixon, Jr. and John R. Kerstetter, *Adjusting Municipal Boundaries: Law and Practice in 48 States,* Mimeograph edition. Public Administration Service, Chicago, 1962. Key provisions upon which categorization depended were: whether annexation could be accomplished by unilateral action by the city council or only by referenda in the area to be annexed, whether it could be accomplished under general law rather than special act of the legislature, whether petitioning by citizens in the area to be annexed is required, what are the criteria for appeal and the role of the courts, what is the extent of city home rule, and how liberal are court interpretations of reasonableness and adjacency in annexation cases.

**TABLE 1**

ANNEXATION LAW AND THE INCIDENCE OF ANNEXATION

| | Categories of Difficulty in Annexing Procedures | | | | | | | | |
| | Most Difficult | | | | | | | | Least Difficult |
| | 1 | 2 | 3 | 4 | 5 | 6 | 7 | 8 | 9 | 10 |
|---|---|---|---|---|---|---|---|---|---|---|
| Mean Annexation Score | 00.0 | 05.8 | 12.8 | 09.2 | 15.6 | 15.2 | 16.2 | 22.8 | 22.6 | 10.9 |
| Number of Cities | 29 | 25 | 8 | 33 | 22 | 23 | 18 | 19 | 26 | 10 |

to integration was thought to be based partly upon the suburbanite's desire to reduce his scale of social experience. The individual feels personally more effective in the small community; he feels a greater sense of manageability over its public affairs; he feels that his vote and his opinion count for more in the small community. Hence, the bigger the metropolis, the more ardently one would expect its suburbanites to defend themselves against being "swallowed" or "submerged" by the city.

Yet Table 2 indicates that there was little discernable association between size of metropolitan area and annexation activity in the ten year period under study. The mean annexation score for urbanized areas over 500,000 population was 11.1, only slightly lower than the 15.0 mean for the smallest urbanized areas.

The size of an urbanized area is a degree-variable which lends itself readily to regression analysis. The zero order correlation coefficient (product moment) for the relationship between size of urbanized area and annexation activity was $-.15$. This would indicate a slight inverse relationship. But the low coefficient suggests that this relationship may be a spurious one, that is, one which depends upon some other relation-

**TABLE 2**

SIZE OF URBANIZED AREA AND INCIDENCE OF ANNEXATION

| Mean Annexation Scores | Size of Urbanized Area in Thousands | | | | | |
| | 50–80 | 81–115 | 116–160 | 161–240 | 241–500 | over 500 |
|---|---|---|---|---|---|---|
| All Cities | 15.0 | 9.4 | 13.8 | 13.0 | 9.0 | 11.1 |
| (Number) | (33) | (39) | (35) | (35) | (33) | (38) |
| Manager Cities | 16.6 | 21.6 | 18.1 | 19.4 | 8.9 | 21.4 |
| (Number) | (14) | (19) | (18) | (17) | (14) | (12) |
| Non-Manager Cities | 13.8 | 4.3 | 9.1 | 7.1 | 9.8 | 9.9 |
| (Number) | (19) | (20) | (17) | (18) | (19) | (26) |

ship. For example, larger metropolitan areas tend to be older; annexation success may really be related to the age of settlement and the relationship between size and annexation may depend upon this latter relationship. Or it may be that annexation success is really a function of social distance between city and suburb; size and annexation success may correlate only because city-suburban social distance is greater in the larger metropolitan areas. Both of these possibilities are explored below.

## Form of Government and the
## Incidence of Annexation

The possibility was also explored that the form of organization of a city's government facilitates or discourages annexation. The manager form of government is predicated on the belief that city government can and should be managed "scientifically, efficiently and nonpolitically." Commentators on suburban politics have detected a surburban preference for "antiseptic" "no-party" style of politics at the municipal level.[7] Given the popular belief that city manager government is honest, efficient, and devoid of the stigma of "politics," it was hypothesized that the annexation of suburban areas might be more readily accomplished by a manager city than by a city with an acknowledged "partisan" government.

According to the *Municipal Yearbook,* 94 of the nation's 213 central cities operate under the manager form of government. The mean annexation score during the period under study for all manager cities was 17.4 compared to a mean score of 8.4 for all non-manager cities. Table 2 shows that in most categories of metropolitan area size manager cities were more likely to annex more people than non-manager cities. In addition to controlling for size, the relationship between form of government and annexation was also observed while controlling for age of settlement, status of central city population, and city-suburban social distance. (See Tables 3, 4, and 6 below.) In short, form of government appears independently associated with annexation activity.

## Age of Settlement and
## Incidence of Annexation

The "age" of urbanized areas was measured by counting the number of decades which have passed since their central cities first contained

---

[7] See Robert Wood, *Suburbia: Its People and Their Politics,* Houghton Mifflin, 1958, pp. 158–166.

50,000 inhabitants.[8] City boundary lines in "older" urbanized areas were expected to be relatively more fixed than in "newer" areas. Table 3 indicates that in general this is the case. The 35 cities which attained 50,000 inhabitants since 1950 possessed a mean annexation score of 22.3; the 49 cities which have had 50,000 people for 70 years or more possessed a mean annexation score of only 4.2. The simple correlation coefficient for the relationship between age of settlement and incidence of annexation is −.39.

**TABLE 3**

*AGE OF CENTRAL CITY AND INCIDENCE OF ANNEXATION*

| Mean Annexation Score | Age: Number of Decades Since City Population Surpassed 50,000 | | | | |
|---|---|---|---|---|---|
| | 0 | 1–2 | 3–4 | 5–7 | Over 7 |
| All Cities | 22.3 | 13.1 | 14.3 | 7.8 | 4.2 |
| (Number) | (35) | (25) | (49) | (40) | (49) |
| Manager Cities | 26.6 | 18.0 | 15.7 | 14.4 | 2.9 |
| (Number) | (21) | (12) | (28) | (13) | (13) |
| Non-Manager Cities | 15.8 | 8.5 | 12.5 | 4.6 | 4.6 |
| (Number) | (14) | (13) | (21) | (27) | (36) |

What is it about age of settlement which might explain the differences in the annexation records of older and newer cities? It may be that the immobility of boundaries is a product of sheer age. Over time persons and organizations adjust themselves to circumstances as they find them. The longer these adjustments have been in existence, the greater the discomfiture, expense, and fear of unanticipated consequences associated with change. Or it may be that some other condition associated with age is responsible for the correlation between age and annexation. As Table 3 indicates, the manager form of government is more popular in newer than in older cities. Yet manager government can not explain the success of younger cities in annexation, because even younger cities *without* managers annex more than older cities. In short, both age and form of government appear in Table 3 to be independently related to incidence of annexation.

Age of settlement also correlates with city-suburban social differential. Older urbanized areas tend to possess peripheral populations of

---

[8] See Donald J. Bogue and Dorothy L. Harris, *Comparative Population and Urban Research via Multiple Regression and Covariance Analysis,* Chicago: Scripps Foundation for Research in Population Problems, 1954.

higher socio-economic standing than the populations of their central cities. In contrast newer cities tend to contain populations with socio-economic attributes similar to, or even higher than, the populations of their suburbs.[9] The housing stock of the central cities in older areas is obsolescent. These areas come to be occupied by the lowest socio-economic groups. In older areas new housing development is concentrated in suburban areas, where they come to be occupied by persons who can afford new home ownership and the added transportation charges of peripheral residence. In newer urbanized areas housing stock of the central city is neither so old or so run down as to be unattractive to middle class home buyers. Thus the spatial distribution of social classes in older urbanized areas may help explain the relative inability of their cities to annex surrounding territory.

## Annexation Activity and the Status Characteristics of Central Cities

Several recent studies have examined the linkages between the social composition of municipalities and their governmental structure.[10] These studies suggested the importance of socio-economic characteristics in the political environment and provided the grounds for examining the relationship between status characteristics of central cities and their record in annexation activity. The hypothesis was that central cities with higher proportions of well educated, white collar, middle income persons would be more successful in annexing their suburbs than cities with smaller proportions of persons with these "middle class" attributes. This hypothesis assumes that suburban populations, and particularly annexed populations, are generally more "middle class" than central city populations (an assumption that will be examined in detail below), and that suburbanites will put up less resistance to incorporation by cities with larger proportions of "middle class" residents, i.e., residents who are like themselves.

Three common measures of the status of population aggregates were employed in testing this hypothesis: the education measure was the median school years completed by persons 25 years of age and over;

---

[9] This finding is reported by Leo Schnore, "The Socio-economic Status of Cities and Suburbs," *American Sociological Review*, Vol. 28 (February, 1963), 76–85.

[10] For example, John H. Kessel, "Governmental Structure and Political Environment: A Statistical Note About American Cities," *American Political Science Review*, Vol. 56 (September, 1962), 615–620; Leo Schnore and Robert Alford, "Forms of Government and Socio-Economic Characteristics of Suburbs," *Administrative Science Quarterly*, Vol. 8 (June, 1963), 1–17.

the occupation measure was the percent of the male labor force engaged in white collar occupations (professional, managerial, clerical, and sales); and the income measure was the median family income expressed in dollars. All data was derived from the 1960 Census of Population.

The zero order correlation coefficients for the relationship between annexation activity and the three status measures of central city populations for 213 cities were as follows: education r = .37; occupation r = .36; and income r = .04. The coefficients for the education and occupation relationships possessed high levels of significance. Table 4 shows mean annexation scores by categories on the education measure, the most influential of the three status variables. The mean annexation

**TABLE 4**

EDUCATIONAL CHARACTER OF CENTRAL CITY POPULATION
AND INCIDENCE OF ANNEXATION

| Mean Annexation Scores | Median School Years Completed | | | | | |
|---|---|---|---|---|---|---|
| | Less than 9.8 | 9.8–10.2 | 10.2–10.8 | 10.8–11.4 | 11.4–12.0 | More than 12.0 |
| All Cities | 3.8 | 6.4 | 11.8 | 12.2 | 18.9 | 20.1 |
| (Number) | (36) | (33) | (35) | (34) | (35) | (40) |
| Manager Cities | 12.6 | 9.7 | 10.8 | 13.0 | 25.1 | 24.0 |
| (Number) | (7) | (10) | (26) | (16) | (20) | (24) |
| Non-Manager Cities | 1.6 | 5.0 | 12.3 | 11.6 | 10.7 | 16.4 |
| (Number) | (29) | (23) | (15) | (18) | (15) | (16) |

score of the highest status group of cities on the education measure was 20.1 compared to a mean score of 3.8 for the lowest status group of cities. Manager governments appear slightly more popular among cities with "middle class" populations. Yet manager government does not explain their propensity to annex, since even "middle class" cities *without* managers annex more than non "middle class" cities.

Thus, analysis reveals that cities with higher status populations tend to annex more people than cities with lower status populations. But before we can explain this fact in terms of the social proximity of higher status populations to their suburban populations, it is necessary to perform additional operations. Social proximity or distance between city and suburb is a relative concept; it is not measured by the status attributes of central cities *in themselves* but by these attributes *in relation* to the attributes of surrounding suburbs. The social differential between city and suburb is smaller in urbanized areas with high status cities. The

next problem, then, was one of observing the relationship between annexation activity and the status *differential* between city and suburb,
rather than the status characteristics of cities themselves.

## City-Suburban Social Distance and the
## Incidence of Annexation

Students of international politics have suggested that viable political
integration is in part a function of cultural distance. Culturally similar
societies are more likely to share enough values and to enjoy sufficient
facility of communication so as to provide the necessary policy consensus for political integration. Culturally dissimilar societies are less likely
to achieve the consensus necessary for integration.[11] The related hypothesis explored in this paper is that political integration at the municipal
level is in part a function of social class distance. The literature on class
in America is replete with attitudinal and valuational differences associated with class. Persons at separate status levels bring to political life
separate sets of internalized values which cause them to perceive, to
experience, and to behave toward social and political issues in separate
and characteristic fashions. This leads us to suggest that policy consensus is less likely to be found, and political integration less likely to
occur, among socially dissimilar municipalities in urban areas.[12]

Four measures of social distance were employed. Social distance
was operationally defined as the *difference* on each of these three measures between the central city and its suburbs. The status measures were
in terms of education (the median school years completed by persons
25 years of age and over); occupation (the percent of the male labor

---

[11] Professor Karl Deutsch includes in his description of the "background conditions" for political integration: compatibility of the values of the "relevant
strata" of the political systems involved. He reasons that common culture facilitates
communication and that communication and community are closely related. In
addition to cultural similarity, political integration is viewed as a function of common expectation of reward or increase in capabilities; mobility of persons among
the communities involved; communications and transactions on a wide range of
topics; and mutual predictability of behavior (understanding). These conditions
would also make interesting hypotheses for investigation at the municipal level.
See Karl Deutsch et al., *Political Community and the North Atlantic Area,*
Princeton: Princeton University Press, 1957.

[12] The hypothesis that inter-municipal cooperation in a metropolitan area is a
function of social distance was tested in an earlier study of inter-jurisdictional
agreements and joint activities. Operations performed with data derived from
the Philadelphia Metropolitan Area indicated that what cooperation did occur
among urban municipalities tended to occur significantly more often among communities which were socially similar rather than dissimilar. See Thomas R. Dye,
*et al.,* "Differentiation and Cooperation in a Metropolitan Area," *Midwest Journal
of Political Science,* Volume 7 (May, 1963), 145–155.

force in "white collar" occupations); median family income; and non-white population percentages. The difference between the city and its surrounding suburbs (social distance) on each of these measures was derived for 198 urbanized areas.[13]

Social distance is commonly supposed to run in favor of the suburbs, that is, suburbs are usually thought to contain higher socio-economic status populations than the cities they surround. But data on city-suburban social differential derived from the 1960 census indicated that in many urbanized areas this was not the case. While social differentials favor the suburbs in the larger and older urban areas, smaller and newer cities tend to rank higher in education, occupation, and income than their suburbs.[14] However, since social differentials only favored the city in smaller urbanized areas, the popular generalizations regarding city-suburban social differences are still accurate descriptions of the vast majority of persons living in urbanized areas in the nation.

First let us examine, then, the impact of the *direction* of social distance on the success of annexation. Table 5 contrasts the mean annexa-

**TABLE 5**

INCIDENCE OF ANNEXATION AND THE
DIRECTION OF SOCIAL DISTANCE

| | Mean Annexation Scores | | | |
|---|---|---|---|---|
| | Social Distance: Education | Social Distance: Occupation | Social Distance: Income | Social Distance: Race |
| Social Differential Favors Suburb Over City | 9.0 (N = 139) | 8.3 (N = 101) | 10.1 (N = 159) | 10.7 (N – 176) |
| Social Differential Favors City Over Suburb | 18.4 (N = 58) | 14.2 (N = 96) | 17.4 (N = 38) | 19.9 (N = 21) |

tion scores of those areas in which the social differential favored the city over the suburb with mean scores of those areas in which the social differential favored the suburbs over the city. The differences in the scores of the two types of urbanized areas are very large and possess a high level of statistical significance. Annexation is much more frequent

---

[13] There were fifteen urbanized areas for which city-suburban comparisons (social distance) were unavailable: Amarillo, Austin, Beaumont, El Paso, Laredo, Lawton, Lewiston, Lubbock, Meriden, Midland, Raleigh, San Angelo, Topeka, Tyler, and Wichita Falls.

[14] Schnore first made this observation; see Leo F. Schnore, *op. cit.*

in urbanized areas where social differentials favor the city over the suburbs.

Status differentials were next considered on a continuum from largest-differential-favoring-city to largest-differential-favoring-suburb. The incidence of annexation was associated with each of the four measures of social distance in the following manner: education $r = -.39$; occupation $r = -.38$; income $r = -.22$; and race $r = -.14$. Each of these zero order coefficients was significant at the .05 level; each indicated that annexation activity decreased as status differentials favoring the suburbs increased. Since these four measures of social differential were themselves closely correlated, the multiple coefficient for the relationship between annexation activity and all four measures was not much higher than the coefficient for the most influential single variable, $R1.2345 = -.40$.

Mean annexation scores for several categories on the social differential scale for education are shown in Table 6. Annexation activity declines consistently with increases in social differential favoring the suburbs. It also appears from Table 6 that even though there are more

**TABLE 6**

*CITY-SUBURBAN SOCIAL DISTANCE AND THE INCIDENCE OF ANNEXATION*

| Mean Annexation Scores | City-Suburban Differences on Education Index [15] | | | | | |
|---|---|---|---|---|---|---|
| | favors city | | | | | favors suburbs |
| | more than | $-0.5-0$ | $0-.5$ | $0.5-0.8$ | $0.8-1.8$ | more than 1.8 |
| All Cities | 21.7 | 14.6 | 12.7 | 10.2 | 4.7 | 5.9 |
| (Number) | (36) | (32) | (31) | (32) | (36) | (31) |
| Manager Cities | 26.6 | 21.1 | 14.6 | 16.9 | 3.9 | 6.9 |
| (Number) | (20) | (19) | (17) | (10) | (12) | (8) |
| Non-Manager Cities | 15.5 | 5.4 | 10.6 | 7.2 | 5.2 | 5.6 |
| (Number) | (16) | (11) | (16) | (22) | (23) | (23) |

[15] Categories expressed in absolute differences between city and suburbs in median school years completed by population over 25.

manager cities in socially non-differentiated urbanized areas, this fact does not explain the relationship between social differential and annexation activity. Declines in annexation activity occurred with increasing social distance for both manager and non-manager cities. And in most categories of social distance manager cities were more successful in annexing people than non-manager cities.

## Further Analysis: A Multivariate Approach

In the preceding analysis it was observed that higher status groups tended to concentrate on the periphery of older and larger urban areas and that the manager form of government was more common in younger and smaller urban areas. Thus, age of settlement, size, form of government, and city-suburban social distance are all related, and each correlated in some measure with annexation activity. The next analytical problem became one of assigning "weight" to these several relationships and determining how much of the total variation in annexation activity could be attributed to these conditions.

The multiple correlation coefficient for the relationship between annexation activity and size, age, form of government, and social distance in 198 urbanized areas was $R1.2345 = .48$. Although these three conditions explain only about 23 percent of the total variation in annexation activity, the relationships obtain at a high level of significance; and F test showed the value of this coefficient to be significant at the .05 level. Beta weights were obtained for the age, size, form of government, and social distance variables in order to ascertain how much change in annexation activity is produced by a standardized change in each of these independent variables when the others are controlled. Beta weights were as follows: size of urbanized area $B12.345 = .06$; age of settlement $B13.245 = .23$; city-suburban social distance $B14.235 = .29$; and form of government $B15.234 = .15$. Test statistics on beta values (beta divided by the standard error) indicated that the explanatory value of age, social distance, and form of government in the regression equation was significant at the .05 level, but the size variable was not significant at that level in the equation. In short, age of settlement and social distance were independently influential in annexation activity and possessed approximately the same relative importance. Form of government was independently related to annexation activity but somewhat less influential. Size of urbanized area was related to annexation but much less important than age, form of government or social distance.

## Summary

Annexation is an increasingly popular integrative device in urban areas. Several hypotheses about urban political integration were suggested by a series of operations performed on data which reflected annexation activity over a ten year period in the nation's urbanized areas.

First of all, the ease or difficulty of annexation procedures under controlling statutes does not appear to be predictive of annexation activity. The permissiveness of annexation law was not closely associated with success in annexation. On the other hand, the form of organization of the government of the central city proved to be an important variable: manager governments were significantly more successful in annexing people than non-manager governments. Size of urbanized area was not particularly influential in explaining annexation activity; central cities in smaller urbanized areas had only slightly more success in annexing people than cities in larger urbanized areas.

The spatial distribution of persons with differing status attributes in urbanized areas appeared to be an important condition influencing annexation activity. Central cities with larger proportions of persons with "middle class" educational and occupational attributes were more successful in annexation than less "middle class" central cities. Higher status cities were more similar in social composition to their suburbs than lower status cities. The important sociological variable appeared to be the *differential* in status between the city and its surrounding suburbs. Social class distance favoring the suburbs appeared as a distinct barrier to urban political integration. City-suburban status differentials emerged as an independent predictor of success in annexation, even when controlling for the effects of age and size of urbanized area. Part of the demand for political independence from the central city is probably an attempt by suburbanites to insulate themselves from those whose standards and way of life they do not share. Persons who have striven to place physical distance between themselves and those with different status attributes are unlikely to look with favor upon attempts to remove identifiable boundaries between their communities and a socially dissimilar central city. Where city and suburb are socially undifferentiated, this barrier to political integration is missing.

Age of settlement also emerged as an important independent variable. Although status differentials are greater in older urbanized areas, this does not explain the relationship between age and annexation activity. Holding constant for the effect of social distance, sheer age of settlement has an important influence on annexation success. Separate from the crystallization of social differential which accompanies age of settlement, cities appear to experience a certain inertia or "immobilisme" over time which operates to maintain existing city boundaries.

The demand for effective organization of metropolitan areas is likely to continue. Pressures toward political integration in one form or another stem from the functional interdependence of the various sectors of a metropolis. Highway location, sewage systems, mass transit, recreation facilities, law enforcement, and land use control will be among the particular areas which will generate demand for metropolitan coordination. How will these integrative demands be accommodated? This analysis of the conditions associated with one form of urban political integration suggests that integrative demands will be accommodated through separate patterns of activity depending upon certain characteristics of urbanized areas. Annexation is a likely integrative device in younger urbanized areas and those in which social differentials between city and suburb have not crystallized. It is also more likely to be the device employed by central cities with manager governments. On the other hand, in older urbanized areas and in urbanized areas where the suburbs have become socially differentiated from the central city, integrative demands will have to be met through devices other than annexation. In these areas successful integrative efforts will probably have to take the form of specialized agencies, interjurisdictional agreements and contracts, joint activities or boards, or informal cooperation.

# Public Opinion and Metropolitan Reorganization in Nashville

## BRETT W. HAWKINS

Recent years have witnessed an enormous outpouring of literature on the nation's metropolitan areas, much of it designed to offer solutions to the problems of governing such areas. In spite of extensive interest in reform, however, few major structural changes have occurred when a vote was required. From 1950 to 1961, for example, there were six failures in seven attempts that contemplated the consolidation of two previously independent governments.[1]

Why have metropolitan area workers been so reluctant to approve reorganization proposals? What kinds of voter attitudes underlie opposition and support? These are the fundamental questions of this study. Its focus is on voter attitudes toward metropolitan reorganization; and the author's purpose is to contribute to an understanding of the conditions under which major reorganizations are probable and the conditions under which they are improbable. It is also hoped that the following analysis will help to meet the objections of those students of metropolitics who are critical of reform-oriented research, and who complain that there has been little systematic research into voter attitudes for and against reorganization.[2]

On June 28, 1962, the voters of Nashville and Davidson County, Tennessee attracted nationwide attention by approving a consolidation charter. In 1958 they had rejected a similar charter despite the heavy

---

Reprinted from *Journal of Politics,* Vol. 28 (May 1966), 408–18, by permission of the publisher.

[1] Advisory Commission on Intergovernmental Relations, *Factors Affecting Voter Reactions to Governmental Reorganization in Metropolitan Areas* (Washington, 1962), pp. 7, 26.

See for example Scott Greer, "Dilemmas of Action Research on the 'Metropolitan Problem,'" *Community Political Systems,* ed. Morris Janowitz (Glencoe, Illinois: The Free Press, 1961), p. 188.

support of the area's civic and business leaders.[3] Following this defeat the City of Nashville annexed some 85,000 county residents. The Nashville *Tennessean,* long a foe of Mayor West, portrayed the annexation as an assault on country residents and began a crusade for another vote on consolidation. Supported by the *Tennessean* and a well-organized (though heterogeneous and unstable) citizens' committee, the proponents of "Metro" soon succeeded in placing a second consolidation charter before the voters.

The campaign that followed was marked by the efforts of Metro's proponents to stigmatize the governmental status quo and to personalize the issue by attacking Mayor West. The proponents also conducted a block-by-block canvas for votes. Metro's opponents, on the other hand, hoped to use the reputedly well-oiled West organization to obtain a "no" vote in the city. (West himself believed that the adoption of Metro would spell the end of his tenure as Mayor, as indeed it did.) The opponents also expected a heavy "no" vote from city Negroes who feared the dilution of their influence in a consolidated city-county.

Subsequently the city voters approved the charter by 57 percent and the county voters by 56 percent.

### Voter Attitude Hypotheses

In the present section four voter attitude hypotheses gleaned from the relevant literature are compared with data from 181 interviews in the Nashville area. Only the data from the 181 interviews are considered. "Don't know" and "no answer" responses are discarded in all cases, and for purposes of this paper null hypotheses are rejected when the probability value for chi square is less than .05.[4] It is also important to understand that the present research was conducted *after* the 1962 consolidation vote. Consequently, in addition to any sampling error that might be present, the *ex post facto* nature of the research was likely to introduce a bias in favor of the actual outcome of the referendum (in this case on the pro-Metro side). Such discrepancies are common in *ex post facto research.*[5]

---

[3] See David A. Booth (ed.) *Metropolitics: The Nashville Consolidation* (East Lansing, Michigan: Institute for Community Development and Services, 1963).

[4] The interview schedule used in this study was pre-coded for punch card tabulation and included both open and fixed alternative questions. The sample was drawn randomly from the official list of registered voters in Davidson County. Inasmuch as the hypotheses tested relate to the attitudes of voters, only those registrants whose cards indicated that they had actually voted in the referendum were chosen. (If the choice happened to fall on a non-voter, the next card was chosen, and so on.)

[5] Herbert Hyman, *Survey Design and Analysis* (Free Press of Glencoe, Illinois, 1955), p. 151. See also F. Mosteller *et al., The Pre-Election Polls of 1948* (New York: Social Science Research Bulletin #6, 1949), p. 213.

*(1) Dissatisfaction with Public Service under Fragmented Structure*

"It is frequently assumed that the impetus for governmental change in metropolitan areas is generated by widespread dissatisfaction with services." [6]

In St. Louis a large proportion indicated some dissatisfaction (approximately 80 percent had some suggestion for change) but there was very little consensus as to changes desired and there was no significant criticism of most major services.[7]

One hypothesis implied by findings of dissatisfaction is that *voters who are dissatisfied with services are more likely to support reorganization than voters who are satisfied.* This is perhaps the most common hypothesis and is the one tested here.

Each Nashville area respondent was first asked what he thought of his services at the present time. The question was intentionally left open-ended in order to provide a measure of the saliency of this issue among respondents. Fifty-four per cent answered "inadequate." [8] These results were then compared with answers to the question on how the respondents voted. Table 1 shows the relationship.

**TABLE 1**

*RELATIONSHIP BETWEEN DISSATISFACTION WITH SERVICES AND SUPPORT FOR REORGANIZATION IN NASHVILLE, 1962*

| | Percent | |
| --- | --- | --- |
| Vote | Satisfied with Services | Not Satisfied with Services |
| For reorganization | 52.6 | 81.1 |
| Against reorganization | 47.4 | 18.9 |
| N(=100%) | 76 | 90 |
| $X^2 = 14.09$, df$=1$, p$<.001$ | | |

These data show much greater support for reorganization among voters not satisfied with their services than among satisfied voters, and thus the data confirm the hypothesis as stated. It is worth emphasizing, however, that even among those expressing satisfaction more than half voted for consolidation.

---

[6] Henry J. Schmandt *et al., Metropolitan Reform in St. Louis: A Case Study* (New York: Holt, Rinehart and Winston, 1961), p. 63.

[7] Scott Greer, *op. cit.,* pp. 197, 198.

[8] Sewage disposal and street and road maintenance were most often mentioned as needing improvement.

*(2) Anticipation of Higher Taxes with Reorganization*

It seems likely that voters will oppose reorganization when they feel that higher taxes will follow. Other attitudes are possible, however, including the belief that reorganization will save money by ending duplication and waste. It is nonetheless generally assumed in the literature that voter anticipation of higher taxes is associated with opposition to reorganization. Thus the hypothesis tested here is that *voters who anticipate higher taxes with reorganization are more likely to oppose it than those who do not anticipate higher taxes.*

To discover something of the saliency of this issue compared to others, all Nashville area respondents were asked to state the most important reason causing them to vote either for or against Metro. Among those voting against it, 23.7 percent said that their decision was based on the belief that consolidation would cost them more in taxes. Although this percentage is not large (76.3 percent expressed other reasons), it was the modal reason.

Each respondent was also asked to say what he thought would happen to taxes "as a result of Metro." In Table 2 these responses are compared with those from the question on how the respondents voted.

**TABLE 2**

RELATIONSHIP BETWEEN ANTICIPATION OF HIGHER TAXES
WITH REORGANIZATION AND OPPOSITION TO
REORGANIZATION—NASHVILLE, 1962

|  | Percent | |
| --- | --- | --- |
| Vote | Anticipating Higher Taxes | Not Anticipating Higher Taxes |
| For reorganization | 41.4 | 85.7 |
| Against reorganization | 58.6 | 14.3 |
| N(=100%) | 70 | 98 |
| $X^2 = 34.38$, df $= 1$, p$<.001$ | | |

It is clear from Table 2 that a majority of those who indicated that they anticipated higher taxes with reorganization voted "no," whereas those who did not anticipate higher taxes voted heavily for reorganization. The sample data therefore support the hypothesis.

The author also considered the possibility that this correlation represents as much the satisfaction or dissatisfaction with services variable as the anticipation or nonanticipation of higher taxes. If this were true it would suggest that opposition to metropolitan reorganization can be explained equally well with either variable.

The data in Table 3 lend some support to this hunch. Thus 92.7 percent of those both dissatisfied with their services and *not* anticipating higher taxes were "yes" voters, whereas only 26.3 percent of those both satisfied with their services and anticipating higher taxes were "yes" voters. In the latter group more than 7 out of 10 were "no" voters.

**TABLE 3**

RELATIONSHIP OF SATISFACTION WITH SERVICES TO ANTICIPATION
OF HIGHER TAXES IN NASHVILLE, 1962

| | Percent | | | | | |
|---|---|---|---|---|---|---|
| | *Satisfied with Services* | | | *Dissatisfied with Services* | | |
| Vote | Antici-pating Higher Taxes | Not Antici-pating Higher Taxes | TOTAL | Antici-pating Higher Taxes | Not Antici-pating Higher Taxes | TOTAL |
| For reorganization | 26.3 | 87.5 | 52.6 | 63.3 | 92.7 | 81.1 |
| Against reorganization | 73.7 | 12.5 | 47.4 | 36.7 | 7.3 | 18.9 |
| N( =100% ) | 38 | 32 | 76 | 30 | 55 | 90 |
| | $X^2=23.80$, df=1, p<.001 | | | $X^2=9.61$, df=1, p<.01 | | |

On the other hand, it appears that the anticipation of higher taxes variable *is still relevant* when the satisfaction with services variable is held constant, because among all voters dissatisfied with their services a much higher percentage of those *not* anticipating higher taxes (NAT) were for reorganization than those anticipating higher taxes (AT). Furthermore, among all satisfied voters a much higher percentage of NAT's were "yes" voters than of AT's. Thus given the wording of the hypothesis, it is not required that the hypothesis be rejected from these data.

In any case, the Nashville data do suggest that more research is needed into these relationships.

*(3) Rural and Suburban Suspicion of the City*

It is frequently assumed that fringe distaste for the central city is fairly widespread, thus providing a base for anti-reorganization sentiment where reorganization can be viewed as a device for enabling the city to reach out and swallow up the fringe. The survey research undertaken in this area suggests that such distaste is in fact widespread. It turned up in Flint, Michigan, for example.[9]

[9] Amos H. Hawley and Basil G. Zimmer, "Resistance to Unification in a Metropolitan Community," *Community Political Systems,* ed. Morris Janowitz (Glencoe, Illinois: the Free Press, 1961), pp. 170, 182.

The hypothesis inferred from such findings is that where there is suspicion there will be resistance to reorganization. The hypothesis tested here therefore is that *fringe voters who are suspicious of the central city are more likely to oppose reorganization than those who are not.* (This hypothesis uses the word "suspicious" only to convey the anti-city attitudes widely attributed in the literature to fringe residents.)

All respondents outside the City of Nashville were asked to indicate whether they agreed or disagreed with the following statements printed on a card:

(1) This community (or area) is really a separate community from Nashville and should have a separate government.
(2) On the whole, big city politics are more corrupt than smaller city politics.
(3) As a rule, it is better to live in small communities with small governments than large communities with large governments.

Responses of agreement were regarded as indicating some degree of suspicion. These data were then compared with those from the question on how respondents voted. Space prohibits a complete presentation of results, but they were very similar from all three measures of suspicion. Table 4 presents the results using measure number 3.

### TABLE 4

RELATIONSHIP BETWEEN SUSPICION OF THE CENTRAL CITY
AMONG FRINGE VOTERS AND OPPOSITION TO
REORGANIZATION IN NASHVILLE, 1962

|  | Percent | |
|---|---|---|
| Vote | Suspicious | Not Suspicious |
| For reorganization | 37.5 | 75.0 |
| Against reorganization | 62.5 | 25.0 |
| N(=100%) | 32 | 40 |

$X^2 = 8.80$, df $= 1$, p $< .01$

If our measures of suspicion are valid there is clearly a higher incidence of opposition to reorganization among those who expressed suspicion than among those who did not. These data therefore support the hypothesis.

### (4) *Voter Ignorance and Unfamiliarity with Local Government*

In the literature there is strong documentation for the conclusion that many voters are woefully ignorant about government. In Flint, Hawley and Zimmer were brought to the tentative conclusion that resistance to unification rested largely in ignorance of government and what to expect from it.[10] The proposition inferred from such findings is that voter ignorance is associated with resistance to reorganization. The hypothesis tested here is that *less knowledgeable voters are more likely to oppose reorganization than more knowledgeable voters.*

Among the measures of knowledgeability used in Nashville were two fixed alternative questions designed to test the respondents' familiarity with the proposed consolidation charter.

The data from these two questions, compared to those on how the respondents voted, were in conflict as to their support for the hypothesis. In the first case the less knowledgeable voters (LKV's), 26 in all, split evenly in their support for the charter, whereas the more knowledgeable voters (MKV), 104 in all, supported it. Thus although the LKV's did not oppose reorganization they did vote against it proportionately more than the knowledgeable voters. In the second case, however, the LKV's heavily supported the proposal and the MKV's split evenly. The data from the second measure, therefore, offer nothing in the way of confirmation of the hypothesis.

A third measure of voter ignorance was an open-ended question asking the respondents what other courses of action, beside Metro, might metropolitan areas take to deal with some of their problems.[11] Of those whose answers were knowledgeable (only 29 in all) an overwhelming 86.2 percent supported reorganization. The "unknowledgeable" also supported it, however, although in less striking fashion.

A final test of the hypothesis was to compare education (measured by last grade in school) to voting. The results are presented in Table 5.

Except for those in the grade school category, all groups supported Metro in a clear pattern of increasing support with increasing education and decreasing support with decreasing education. Clearly this is some support for the hypothesis, although the measure used (years in school) is not a measure of knowledge about government.

The author also considered the possibility that this correlation is as much "income" as "education." If this were true the poorly educated voters (anti-Metro) would be predominantly the same persons as those in the very low income brackets. Table 6 shows the support for Metro at each intersection of the two stratified populations.

---

[10] *Ibid.,* p. 182.

[11] Answers coded by the author as "knowledgeable" included annexation by the central city, partial consolidation, and intergovernmental co-operation. "Unknowledgeable" answers included "make studies," more civic spirit by the citizenry, better leadership, and the levying of higher city taxes.

**TABLE 5**

RELATIONSHIP BETWEEN VOTER EDUCATION LEVEL AND
OPPOSITION TO REORGANIZATION IN NASHVILLE, 1962

| | Percent | | | | |
|---|---|---|---|---|---|
| Vote | Grades 1–8 | Grades 9–11 | High School Graduate | Some College | College Graduate |
| For reorganization | 33.3 | 57.7 | 71.4 | 80.8 | 95.7 |
| Against reorganization | 66.7 | 42.3 | 28.6 | 19.2 | 4.3 |
| N ( = 100% ) | 30 | 26 | 63 | 26 | 23 |
| $X^2 = 27.87$, df $= 4$, p $< .001$ | | | | | |

Since the pro-Metro percentages generally increase across the rows and not down the columns—that is, the percentages increase with increasing education—these data suggest that education was a more relevant variable than income. Even so the income categories used in this study were probably too broad to permit any very meaningful conclusions as to whether it is "really" low income or low education that is primarily correlated with opposition to metropolitan reorganization.

No consistent pattern emerges from all these data on voter knowledgeability and attitude toward reorganization. It therefore seems possible to conclude that voter ignorance (at least of government) and opposition are not significantly associated, perhaps because ignorance

**TABLE 6**

RELATIONSHIP OF INCOME TO EDUCATION LEVEL AND
SUPPORT FOR METRO IN NASHVILLE, 1962

| Reported Annual Income | Percent Support for Metro | | | | |
|---|---|---|---|---|---|
| | Grades 1–8 | Grades 9–11 | High School Graduate | Some College | College Graduate |
| Under $3,000 | (n=13) 38.5 | (n=3) 66.7 | (n=1) 100 | (n=2) 100 | (n=1) 100 |
| 3,000– 5,999 | (n=9) 33.3 | (n=10) 60.0 | (n=20) 70.0 | (n=3) 66.7 | (n=5) 100 |
| 6,000– 9,999 | (n=3) 66.7 | (n=10) 50.0 | (n=23) 60.9 | (n=12) 75.0 | (n=7) 100 |
| 10,000– 14,999 | (n=4) 0.0 | (n=3) 66.7 | (n=7) 57.1 | (n=6) 83.3 | (n=6) 83.3 |
| 15,000 and over | (n=1) 0.0 | (n=0) ..... | (n=4) 100 | (n=3) 100 | (n=4) 100 |

is manipulatable and can go either way. On the other hand the sample data do suggest that voter support is associated with greater knowledge about local government and higher education.

## Aggregate Voting Behavior

A breakdown of the aggregate voting figures reveals some important geographical variations. Thus when the central city is broken down into old city (7 wards) and annexed area (3 wards) the results are striking. And when the county outside (15 civil districts) is then broken down into unincorporated suburban areas, rural areas, and incorporated cities further important variations appear. See Table 7.

**TABLE 7**

RELATIONSHIP BETWEEN GEOGRAPHIC AREA, BY GROUPS OF
PRECINCTS, AND 1962 METRO VOTE

| | Percent | | | | | | |
|---|---|---|---|---|---|---|---|
| | *Within City* | | | *Outside City* | | | |
| | Old City | Annexed Area | Total | Unincorporated Suburban Area | Rural Area | Incorporated Suburban Cities | Total |
| Number of precincts | 42 | 27 | 69 | 53 | 20 | 6 | 79 |
| Vote | | | | | | | |
| For reorganization | 45.2 | 72.2 | 57.4 | 62.6 | 34.0 | 47.3 | 56.0 |
| Against reorganization | 54.8 | 27.8 | 42.6 | 37.4 | 66.0 | 52.7 | 44.0 |
| Number of voters ( = 100% ) | 19,960 | 16,726 | 36,686 | 19,706 | 4,040 | 4,662 | 28,408 |

There are a number of plausible explanations for these figures. In the old city it appears that West's political organization carried the day, with an assist from most Negro voters (the 13 city precincts with a non-white majority voted "no" by 56.8 percent in aggregate). Of course the whites in the city also voted "no," and by a very similar margin (55.6 percent in 29 precincts). Thus while the data provide little evidence that the racial factor was of great importance, it is quite possible that whites and Negroes voted similarly for different reasons; the whites in support of West and the Negroes in fear of losing their voting power.

In the recently annexed areas it is possible that anti-city and anti-West sentiments, whether clearly separated by the voters or not, resulted in the 72 percent "yes" vote. In *the county* it appears that the unincorporated suburban areas, which may have felt threatened by further annexations, played a part comparable to that of the annexed areas in the city; that is, they pushed the entire area into the "yes" column. Annexation, one can argue, made it possible for the proponents of change to stigmatize successfully the status quo and to champion Metro as a device for eliminating not only future annexations but also the fomentor of such evils—namely, Mayor West. In a word, most county residents perhaps voted for consolidation to fend off being annexed involuntarily.

The reader will recall, however, that the sample data presented above showed not support but opposition from fringe area residents who were suspicious of the central city. Possible explanations for this are that the sample may have been off and that the questionnaire measures of suspicion may have uncovered only the extraordinarily "suspicious" who would not vote for governmental integration under any circumstances.

Turning to incorporated cities, it is interesting to note that the three high income cities voted "yes" whereas the three lower income cities voted "no." Two of the latter, however, were several miles from the central city. It is therefore possible that the higher education or income levels in the former, plus their perhaps less locally oriented populations, were the deciding factors.

## Conclusions

The outcome in Nashville of a proposed reorganization was not the usual one. Therefore voter attitudes underlying support for metropolitan reorganization are perhaps the most important findings of this study. The interview data suggest that such support is associated with (1) voter dissatisfaction with services (2) the nonanticipation by voters of higher taxes stemming from reorganization (3) voter education levels higher than grade school, and (4) voter understanding of "metropolitan problems."

A common sense conclusion from the aggregate voting data, in addition, is that annexation transformed the usual "no" vote of fringe residents (an anti-city vote) into a "yes" vote. The relevant interview data contradict this conclusion, however. Doubtless more research is required into the character and correlates of fringe "suspicion."

Scott Greer has suggested that the available alternatives for bringing about metropolitan reform are (1) to manipulate the electorate through redefining (or misdefining) the issue and (2) to bring about change through *fiat*. The former course, he finds, was taken in Dade County, the latter in Toronto.[12]

The Nashville experience perhaps falls into the Dade County category. Certainly the annexation of 85,000 county residents helped Metro's proponents to put the issue on a personal, barely relevant, non-rational basis—namely, for or against Mayor West. The insertion of a "devil," moreover, simplified the task of selling a highly complicated governmental reorganization. It is certainly true, in any case, that the circumstances which pertained to Nashville from 1958 to 1962 have not been common to proposals for governmental reorganization in metropolitan areas. This in turn lends some support to Robert C. Wood's proposition that "program expansion of urban governments" not initiated from without the system, nor by highly mobilized elite groups, is random —"the result of accident, not design." [13]

---

[12] Scott Greer, *Metropolitics: A Study of Political Culture* (New York: John Wiley and Sons, 1963), p. 199.

[13] Robert C. Wood, "The Contributions of Political Science to Urban Form," *Urban Life and Form,* ed. Werner Z. Hirsch (New York: Holt, Rinehart and Winston, 1963), p. 113.

# Public Attitudes and
# Metropolitan Decision Making

## CHARLES R. ADRIAN

The study of individual metropolitan areas in the United States has become a ritualistic activity to be repeated every few years. The folk rite is engaged in with deadly seriousness by a handful of persons who are told by the local newspaper that they are "civic leaders." With but a few exceptions, most of them very recent, the studies that have resulted have been highly predictable as to the way in which the operation is structured, the method of study used, the kinds of people who participate, the findings that are made, the recommendations that follow upon them—and the fate of the action proposals. The fate they suffer is, of course, nearly always to be greeted by an enormous citizen yawn, followed by rejection of any proposal which dares to present itself at the polling booth. Without attempting to decide whether or not these proposals are deserving of acceptance, or even of serious consideration, we can wonder at the almost unbelievably low batting average of the players. If the civic leaders were major league ballplayers, they would quickly be sent down to the minors for so inept a series of performances. There is little reason to believe that they will suffer an equivalent fate, however, or that they are considering a change in their batting styles. Although there was a successful metro reform during the present year— in Nashville—this points to no trend. The usual pattern is for metro proposals to be defeated almost before the game begins. One wonders why the effort is even made. In 1962, the people of St. Louis and St. Louis County voted on a so-called "borough" plan. It got a majority of the votes in only four city wards and failed to carry in a single township. This year, too, in Memphis, a county charter plan was rejected in a majority of precincts in both the city and the county. Many other

Reprinted from Charles R. Adrian, "Public Attitudes and Metropolitan Decision Making," Institute of Local Government, University of Pittsburgh, 1962, pp. 3–16, with the permission of the publisher.

cases of rejection by the voters, sometimes even by those of the core city, have been reported by the staff of the Commission on Intergovernmental Relations.[1]

Clearly, proposed structural changes in metropolitan areas are unpopular with rank-and-file voters. But why are they unpopular? The usual lame excuse that the plan was opposed by "selfish" interests explains little, if anything. The world is made up of selfish people—selfish, if their interests are viewed from the perspectives of others. The fact is that although most metropolitan-area studies and resulting action programs have been carried on in the Age of the Opinion Poll, when techniques have existed for determining the limits of tolerance within which people will accept proposals and for determining what people consider to be their problems, almost no use has been made of these tools in the development of substantive plans and the strategies to be used in putting them into effect.

We might first look at the question of why leaders of metropolitan government reform have paid so little attention to citizen attitudes and the political environment within which metro leaders must do their politicking. The subject, like almost any subject, has not been completely ignored in the past, of course. Among others who have been concerned with it, Luther Gulick has long had an interest in fundamental American values and their relevance to metropolitan decision making.[2] Victor Jones, the leading pioneer in seeking to relate the political environment to the metropolitan "problem," wrote an insightful article as long ago as 1940, an article that never received the attention it deserved.[3] Robert Wood, in constructing a process model for suburban decision making, dealt extensively with attitudes.[4] But each of these gentlemen found little empirical evidence upon which to write and their words have not had much impact upon the way metropolitan studies have been conducted. As a result, few of their prescriptive statements have been subjected to empirical test—at least that has been the picture until very recently. There is reason to believe that those who will study

---

[1] Allen D. Manvel and Sally O. Shames, *Factors Affecting Voter Reactions to Governmental Reorganization in Metropolitan Areas* (Advisory Commission on Intergovernmental Relations, Washington, 1962, Number M-15).

[2] Most recently in Luther H. Gulick, *The Metropolitan Problem and American Ideas* (Alfred A. Knopf, New York, 1962).

[3] Victor Jones, "The Politics of Integration in Metropolitan Areas," *Annals*, 207:161–167, January, 1940.

[4] Robert C. Wood, *Suburbia* (Houghton Mifflin Company, Boston, 1959). Some empirical evidence is cited below; see also Scott Greer, "Citizen Participation and Attitudes," in John C. Bollens, *Exploring the Metropolitan Community* (University of California Press, Los Angeles, 1961), Part III.

the metropolis in the future will approach the subject with more of the open mind of academic inquisitiveness than has been the case in the past.

Why have citizen attitudes received so little attention and why has so little been done to integrate them into a theory of decision making in the metropolitan area? Probably because of the attitudes and values of the upper-middle-class citizens who have been the prime movers and financers of metropolitan-area studies—for most of them, I hesitate to use the word "research," for the frame of reference within which the researchers have had to operate for the most part has been such that research within the social scientific meaning has been discouraged. Often, the researcher is expected only to lend his good name and status to conclusions that the civic leader regards as "self-evident," and therefore beyond question. With most areas of inquiry foreclosed, there has been no reason to look at attitudes.

What have been the principal values and attitudes of the civic leader-reformer? They have been those of the efficiency and economy movement, in which he was also in the van, and through which he brought about many changes in municipal government. The typical reformer has brought to the metropolitan problem a strong middle-class bias: he has favored honesty over expediency, efficiency over representativeness, order over convenience. Most importantly, he subscribed to two major fallacies which stem from his beliefs: the Efficiency and Economy Fallacy, and the Rational Man Fallacy. The former, I have already discussed elsewhere.[5] In brief, it is the view that the typical citizen shares with the upper-middle-class community leader a concern for efficiency and economy, however defined, and that these twin objectives are highly valued by the *hoi polloi*. I think there is ample, if unsystematic, evidence to show that these are not goals for many citizens, indeed that the citizen is cynical about efficiency if it interests him at all, and that he therefore concentrates on what is, in any case, a higher order of values to him—access to decision makers, and a sense of having councils and boards that are representative.

The Rational Man Fallacy, of course, has roots dating from the eighteenth century and before. The metro leader, probably in part by projecting his values upon the typical citizen when doing his planning, has seen metropolitan man much as John Locke saw the middle-class Englishman of his day. The voter is assumed to be a rational person who believes in his capacity to control his own destiny. The reformer has assumed that if you "give people the facts," they will act in favor of

---

[5] Charles R. Adrian, "Metropology: Folklore and Field Research," *Public Administration Review*, 21:148–157, Summer, 1961.

metropolitan-wide government and other objectives of the reformer. Of course, there is no reason why he should have ensnared himself with this delusion. The writings on the nature of the voter and how he makes up his mind have been outlined by a series of scholars, such as Paul Lazarsfeld and Angus Campbell, and they date from before World War II. Furthermore, the community leader, or his father, has spent many years fighting political machines and he well knows that the ordinary citizen, even after decades of universal public education, has a reaction to things political that is overwhelmingly visceral in character. Closely reasoned logic stemming from a normative or ideal model cannot compete, they should have known, with the symbols which trigger emotions when effectively used by the professional politicians who often oppose their action programs. Similarly, the assumption that the ordinary metropolitan man believes that he is the master of his fate has for many years been under suspicion, if it is not outrightly repudiated by psychological studies on alienation—on the widespread feeling among ordinary citizens that whatever they may do, they cannot much affect the forces that control government, especially large governments.

The metropolitan reform leader, then, has typically spent his years in constructing models which are unconcerned with belief systems other than his own, and he has built into his models assumptions about psychological motivation and rationality that are as unrealistic as were those of John Locke, Jean Jacques Rousseau, or Adam Smith. No wonder that he has so often gone around the day after an election muttering about "selfish, narrow-minded voters" and "self-seeking politicians."

## The Ingredients of a Political System

The model builders might well have started with the work of a man who had considerable success at the craft: Aristotle. As interpreted by Norton Long, the Aristotelian mode would be to seek metropolitan government through finding "a potential metropolitan governing class, the institutions through which it can function and a set of ideal goals which it can embody and which will render its leadership legitimate in the eyes of the people." [6] Here we see why it is that models to date have not provided the basis for a viable political system: The metropolitan area is a complex of persons pursuing a variety of economic and social goals. There is no image of the "good metropolitan life" outside of the writings of reformers and planners, none that stems from the grass

---

[6] Norton E. Long, *The Polity* (Rand, McNally & Company, Chicago, 1962), pp. 174–175.

roots, a latter-day Jacksonianism as a foundation upon which to build a political system. To the typical citizen, the metropolitan area is a place where his work is. It is not a community, but an aggregate of persons and places.

In addition to the absence of a metropolitan community with a collective set of goals, there is also no governing class which is viewed as the source of legitimate leadership, as is the case with the middle class of England. Furthermore, the metropolitan leaders are handicapped by the present patterns of business and industrial administration. The Mellons of Pittsburgh and the Upjohns of Kalamazoo are still on the scene, but in most communities, their ilk has been replaced by the essentially rootless organization man who moves from job to job, but is generally viewed neither as the law-giver—a function that belongs to the mayor or manager—or the job-giver—a function that belongs to the Chamber of Commerce secretary and the state employment service or state industrial development department. Organization man leads, if he leads the community at all, because he chooses to do so, not because it is an obligation of his class. It need hardly be added that Aristotle's third requirement, the necessary institutions, do not exist.

In addition to being accorded legitimacy and a set of consensual goals, a political system must, if it is to be democratic, be one in which people feel secure in the possession of a psychological sense of having access to the decision makers and of having decision makers who are representative of their interests and protective of their preferred life styles. I emphasize that this is a psychological matter—the question of whether the person does have access and whether his interests are, in fact, protected is largely irrelevant. We need only recall the old-fashioned political machines in which the function of the block worker was, among other things, to shortstop citizen complaints before they got to city hall by promises that the matter "will be looked into." Similarly, the machine leaders sometimes took enormous advantage of the trust placed in them by the *hoi polloi* by stealing their money and selling out their interests in some agreement convenient to the boss. Many an indignant reformer could not understand that these *de facto* breaches of trust were often unimportant to the ordinary slum dweller if his confidence in this leadership class remained undimmed and his feeling of security was unchallenged. The facts, in politics, are never as important in determining loyalty and legitimacy as is the perception of reality—the picture in men's minds that Walter Lippman long ago talked about.

If we so clearly lack the ingredients of a political system which can serve as the principal decision-making arena for the metropolis, how do we manage to get along? Had we taken literally the somber warnings concerning the consequences of our alleged folly as they have appeared over several decades, we would long ago have created metropolitan governments, believing it a necessary step for survival. And if the warnings had been accurate, the nation's population centers would today be in shambles. But they have not done so. Despite our resistance to advance planning, to the rational use of land, to the assumption of responsibility for preserving water supplies and keeping them unpolluted, and to dozens of other matters that are important to professional administrators in many fields of activity, the metropolis does not quite collapse of its own weight, or choke in its traffic or its non-abated smoke, or poison itself with its own sewage. Why not?

The present system of Balkanization never ceases to amaze observers who believe that it ought not to work, but somehow seems to fit surprisingly well American values, life styles, and aesthetics. It does this because of elaborate procedures and rituals for consultation and negotiation. In fact, some of the more imaginative work in the conceptualization of metropolitan areas has been through the use of analogies with the biological concept of ecology,[7] the international relations concepts involved in diplomatic negotiations,[8] and the economic concept of the market.[9] Just as independence-interdependence, confusion, and occasionally terror and violence are a part of a natural ecology, yet it is a system that "works," so the metropolitan area is not ideal, yet to a degree it "works." Diplomacy is not the most efficient decision-making process, but most of the time it makes possible compromise agreements upon critical issues. Some person's sense of equity will sometimes be violated, but seldom to the extent that he would prefer no negotiation to negotiation. The market place possesses a mechanism that is functional, though its results again strain the values of those who feel that its laws favor those who are already privileged.

In addition to negotiation, compromise, and exchange among the many units of the metropolis—the present system of muddling through—state governments are available as institutions for metropolitan government. Although state boundaries are arbitrarily drawn and sometimes divide in two a metropolitan area, state government is often a viable decision-making unit and is certainly more appropriate than are the

---

[7] *Ibid.*, Chapter 10, "The Local Community as an Ecology of Games," pp. 139–155.

[8] Matthew Holden, Jr., "The Metropolitan Area as a Problem in Diplomacy." A paper presented at the 1962 meeting of the American Political Science Association.

[9] Vincent Ostrom and others, "The Organization of Government in Metropolitan Areas," *American Political Science Review*, 55:831–842, December, 1961.

strip cities and continuous urban areas extending for hundreds of miles that seem to be the metropolitan areas of the future.

## Citizen Attitudes and Metropolitan Models

Let us turn to the information we have concerning citizen attitudes and see how it fits or may be fitted into a model for metropolitan government. We shall see at once that many of the items in popular belief systems are not what thóse who have in the past assumed responsibility for model building want. Furthermore, in spite of their implicit assumption that goals are shared, we shall see that there is much conflict among the values relevant to the building of a metropolitan model.

*Legitimacy: The Proper Function of Local Government*

There is, first of all, no agreement among urban residents as to why local governments exist at all. Some want these governments to serve primarily in order to provide for life's amenities; others see them as something of an arm of the local Chamber of Commerce, with the task of doing what is necessary in order to attract more business and industry to the area; a third group wants to keep down the cost of government at all levels and wants local government to restrict its activities to that which has been traditionally regarded as necessary; a fourth group, often consisting of self-conscious minorities, sees local government as an arbiter among many forces and a device whereby each minority gets at least some slice of the pie.[10] These four images of local government contain within themselves many conflicts. Even the concept of amenities varies by class: the notion is quite different in the mind's eye of the middle-class suburbanite and of the welfare-oriented marginal worker in the slum. Furthermore, there is a considerable difference between the parochial or localite views of most members of the working class and the area-wide or cosmopolite views of the upper-middle-class.[11] The laborer, preoccupied with a chronically tight family budget and hopeful of accumulating a few "luxuries" during his years of gainful employment, has neither the inclination nor the indoctrination which would cause him to be concerned about boosterism, the city beautiful, or the future of Zilchville. He has, as it were, a culturally imposed trained incapacity to react to generalities or to considerations that are unrelated to pocket-

---

[10] See Oliver P. Williams, "A Typology for Comparative Local Government," *Midwest Journal of Political Science,* 2:150–164, May, 1961.

[11] Robert K. Merton, "Patterns of Influence: A Study of Interpersonal Influence and of Communications Behavior in a Local Community," in Paul F. Lazarsfeld and F. N. Stanton (eds.), *Communication Research in 1948–49* (Harper & Bros., New York, 1949), pp. 180–219; Daniel Elazar, *A Case Study of Failure in Attempted Metropolitan Integration* (National Opinion Research Center, University of Chicago, Chicago, 1961); and other studies.

book or stomach. Personally, I do not blame him or expect much else from him. But the model builders have expected much more from him, and they have expected it without asking the question: how can people be led to believe that there is a causal relationship between an integrated governmental structure and their *personal* hopes for the future?

*Legitimacy: That Government that Governs Most Blandly Governs Best*

Between the working man and his concerns with neighborhood and family and the upper-middle-class do-gooder lies the vast area of the more typical middle-class—the white-collar organization man and conformist *par excellence*. To him, the model of the reformer is unacceptable because it seeks to engulf him in political conflict. The reformer, of course, has no such intent, but there is little doubt in the mind of the $10,000 a year junior executive what an integrated government will mean. Has not the core city government been conflict ridden for years? Would not such conflict be transferred to a metropolitan government? Did he not move to the suburbs to gain what Robert Wood has called "fraternity" and to escape the duties and battles imposed by democracy as a mediating force? [12] He, in other words, rejects the idea of government as arbiter. Indeed, in his problem-filled life at the office and home, he has enough of conflict. His government in his suburb can give him some peace by operating on the basis of consensus, just as did grandfather's small town. The middle-class suburbanite wants his politics bland. Even in state and national politics, he deplores conflict,[13] and his image of the ideal is to take the politics out of politics.

The typical middle-class metropolitanite probably wants a government that has a minimal anxiety-producing potential. One that threatens, by area-wide control, to break down class, ethnic, and racial barriers is not a government that furthers his goals. Furthermore, a government is least anxiety-producing when its actions are highly predictable. The more consensus that exists within the governmental unit, the more predictable it is, the more conflict, the less predictable—another reason for the middle-class suburbanite to oppose metro government. From the suburbanite's point of view, the functions of government that are most important to him and that he therefore most wants to keep local control over, are those of land-use controls and public school policy. The former represent the only effective devices by which to shape the life styles of the suburb and to exclude those who do not fit it; the latter is important either because the bulk of those in a given suburban area do not use the

---

[12] Robert C. Wood, *Suburbia* (Houghton Mifflin & Co., Boston, 1959), Chap. 7.

[13] Samuel Lubell, *Revolt of the Moderates* (Harper & Bros., New York, 1956).

public schools, or because they do want them and consider them important in establishing the image of the community and in preparing the children for preferred social roles.

## Legitimacy: Access and Representativeness

The high-status model builders have never seemed to be concerned about access or representation as considerations in a model. This has probably been the case because these prestigeful persons have had no doubts about their personal ability to influence government at the metropolitan level. They had, of course, once been cognizant of the problem —they had strongly supported municipal home rule and opposed "interference" by the state legislature back in the salad days of the reform movement. In those days, they had been aware of the unpredictability of state decision-makers and the sense of lack of control over the situation that this had produced. As a result, they argued strongly for the independence of the local community in matters of local concern. But, once they had passed this phase, they forgot, apparently, that others might also be concerned about having a governmental structure over which they could have control.

Today, the upper-middle-class still has no doubt of its ability to secure a hearing and to influence the governing board or the executives of either local or metropolitan governments. But other metropolitan citizens are by no means so confident that they can preserve access once the established—and predictable—pattern has been abandoned. The core-city dweller, with his concern for a voice through his ward alderman, and the suburbanite, with his confidence in councilmen who share his income level and life style, see only a threat in any new and untried method of representation.

One of the greatest fears of the metropolitanite today is that he will lose access to, or influence over, government at all levels. He is confronted with a sense of alienation, or the feeling that no matter what he does, his actions will not influence decisions which are important to him.[14] Proposals for metropolitan-wide government add fuel to his anxieties. Incipient alienation is to be seen, in addition to attitudes toward core city governments, in the belief that the suburbanite fight is

---

[14] E. L. McDill and Jean C. Ridley, "Status, Anomia, Political Alienation, and Political Participation," *American Journal of Sociology,* 68:205–213, Sept., 1962; Murray B. Levin, *The Alienated Voter* (Holt, Rinehart and Winston, New York, 1960); Jerome S. Bruner, "The Boss and the Vote," *Public Opinion Quarterly,* 10:1–23, Spring, 1946; John E. Horton and Wayne E. Thompson, "Powerlessness and Political Negativism," *American Journal of Sociology,* 47:485–493, March 1962; other studies are cited in Charles Press, *Main Street Politics* (Institute for Community Development, Michigan State University, East Lansing, 1962), pp. 75–92.

a losing one—that eventually their area will become part of the core city or of a metropolitan super-government. In at least two empirical studies, these attitudes have been uncovered.[15]

Despite this feeling of pessimism, the suburbanite wants to continue to have a separate local government. Some critics have argued that suburbanites do not value independence. The argument is that if they really valued it, they would be better informed about the identity of their leaders and about policy issues and conflicts than are residents of the core city. Several studies have shown that they are not, however.[16] Yet, this criticism is almost certainly invalid, for what the suburbanite is interested in is a psychological sense of access to be used *when he needs it,* not something to be availed of every day of the year. He also wants to have the feeling that those who sit on the governing body think and act as he does. If he believes that they do so, and if government is through consensus rather than compromise, it is not necessary to know the actual names of the actors; indeed, it is a waste of time to learn them —they are interchangeable parts, any combination of which will produce essentially the same policies. The figures which show that suburbanites commonly cannot identify their local officials and that core city residents can do so more readily, probably do nothing more than demonstrate that core city officials and area-wide "civic leaders" get better publicity than do suburban officials.

*Functionality*

Despite frenetic insistence by reformers that the Balkanized approach to the metropolis leads only to chaos, there is evidence that the typical citizen of the area does not consider the problem to be serious. Indeed, he is likely to see the present arrangement as generally adequate. He does not even deign to take notice of metropolitan area studies—in Dayton, less than a majority even of the well-informed, or politically active citizens, knew that a major study of the area was being conducted.[17] And in St. Louis, only one person in ten among the politically

---

[15] Charles Press, "Concepts of Access and Representation in Metropolitan Area Studies," summarized in Charles Press, *Main Street Politics* (Institute for Community Development, Michigan State University, East Lansing, 1962), pp. 84–85; Basil G. Zimmer and Amos Hawley, "Local Government as Viewed by Fringe Area Residents," *Rural Sociology,* 23:363–370, December, 1958.

[16] John C. Bollens and others, *Metropolitan Challenge* (Metropolitan Community Studies, Inc., Dayton, Ohio, 1959), pp. 234–235, 238–239; and the studies cited in footnote 15.

[17] Bollens, *op. cit.,* p. 240. On satisfaction with existing levels see *ibid.;* also David A. Booth, *Metropolitics: The Nashville Consolidation* (Institute for Community Development, Michigan State University, East Lansing, 1963), which seems to show that the metro plan there was adopted on the second try more for negative reasons than as a revolt against existing conditions.

active could explain the three major provisions of the so-called borough plan that was voted upon in that area. But 20 percent could not even name one provision—and these were not among the typical, apathetic, apolitical citizens, but among the supposed leading citizens of the suburbs.[18] As Scott Greer has noted, "the ordinary voters were not even voting on the plan: nobody knows what they *were* voting on." [19] In many other circumstances, the voter turnout level has been very low, and this despite generous publicity by local newspapers and a frenetic effort by leaders of the cause.[20]

Apathy is not the only indication of satisfaction with the status quo, or alternatively, of the lack of awareness on the part of the typical citizen. A study of farmers on the outer fringe of the Lansing metropolitan area indicated not only that most of them did not understand that they were farming directly in the path of future urban expansion, but did not even understand who were their political supporters or enemies.[21] Not only does the typical American citizen grossly discount the future, he is incurably optimistic concerning the possibility of solving his problems—whenever he feels the time has come to face up to them.

### Manageable Area

Each year the old idea of the reformers that a single metropolitan area should have a single government becomes less realistic. With strip cities and metropolises blending into metropolises, the prospects for a single government for such areas is about as likely as having a Rorschach blot come up as a rectangle. In addition, the typical citizen almost certainly does not view the metropolis as a manageable area for *local* government. No matter what reformers may argue, the citizen does not see metropolitan-wide structures as forms of local government. Furthermore, suburbanites tend to reject any conflict-ridden structure as being unacceptable—and all metropolitan-wide governments are institutions for the management of conflict. We need look only at the history of the Miami-Dade County plan to see that the ordinary citizen is realistic in

---

[18] Scott Greer, *Governing the Metropolis* (John Wiley and Sons, Inc., New York, 1962), p. 125.

[19] *Ibid.*

[20] For a summary of voting on several proposals, see Allen D. Manvel, and Sally O. Shames, *Factors Affecting Voter Reactions to Government Reorganization in Metropolitan Areas* (Advisory Commission on Intergovernmental Relations, Washington, 1962, Number M-15).

[21] Charles Press and Clarence J. Hein, *Farmers and Urban Expansion* (U.S. Department of Agriculture, Washington, 1962, publication ERS-59).

his assumption that area-wide government is conflict-ridden.[22] Robert Wood has made the point that such conflict is a part of democracy, but the ordinary citizen would rather avoid this part of his social responsibility whenever he can.

## Effective Machinery

What of the views of the ordinary citizen as to the acceptable way of handling critical issues? He no doubt does recognize some issues as of importance from time to time. There is as yet no study that I know of, which has asked a sample of metropolitanites how serious problems should be handled, but there is evidence to indicate that most citizens either overtly prefer or tacitly accept three kinds of solutions, only one of them of the sort carried in the medicine bag of conventional reform. The three are: (1) use of the special district; (2) use of the county; and (3) reliance on the state government to one degree or another.

The special district has been discussed so much I will not attempt to comment further on it here. The criticisms of it are well known, as are the reasons why both ordinary citizens and many professional and technical personnel favor it. The county has some serious built-in limitations as to its effectiveness. These are greater in some states than in others, but in all, urban counties are increasingly being turned to for the performance of municipal functions. Since about 75 per cent of all Standard Metropolitan Statistical Areas are contained within a single county, this approach often makes sense, though not necessarily to the farmers in the distant corners of the county. But this unit of government is well known to all except the most apolitical of citizens, it is deeply imbedded in the traditions of America, and hence its proposed use for new functions creates much less uncertainty in the minds of voters than do proposals involving untried and unknown federated, district, or borough plans, or even city-county consolidation which, for all the innocence of its title, sounds like a new breed of animals to the uneasy, confused citizen.

The state has the same advantages as the county: familiarity and legitimacy. Despite ideological lessons about self-reliance and doing for ourselves at home whatever we can, the fact is that the typical metropolitanite probably does not see state government as any more distant or less responsive than a metropolitan-wide government. Furthermore, the state enjoys the advantage of being familiar and traditional, of having a substantial tax base, a sounder one than any local govern-

---

[22] Edward Sofen, "Problems of Metropolitan Leadership," *Midwest Journal of Political Science*, 5:18–38, February, 1961.

ment, and probably sounder than any metropolitan government that might be created. In addition, the state has the legal powers to cope with the problems of most metropolitan areas.

Both state and Federal governments possess a sense of legitimacy when they enter a new metropolitan functional area that cannot be claimed by any new forms of government or even by the county. Furthermore, people turn to these levels of government because the marginal sacrifice in raising additional dollars is less there than at other levels, and the burden is less visible. To this is added the great psychological advantage to the local politician of being able to step off the airplane from Harrisburg or Washington and announce to assembled reporters that Zilchville has just been qualified for a new grant-in-aid, or for a special one for a sewage-disposal plant, or that the state is about to adopt a new shared tax system. All of these allow him to say that he is bringing money into the community and relieving the "overburdened" local property tax—a task that is quite a bit easier for him than to have to say, "Well, folks, in order to provide the urban services you want, we will have to increase the property tax rate again next year; there just is no other way out." Today, there is, in fact, another way out. Furthermore, the state is increasingly assuming responsibility as an umpire among local units of government, and as the agency that applies sanctions on behalf of society when local units do not assume responsibility or cannot work out their differences. People object to "bureaucracy" or "red tape," to be sure, but they generally accept the increasingly good job that state governments are doing in such areas as pollution control and the planning and routing of freeways.

What of the Future? Despite evidence of pessimism by suburbanites concerning the future viability of their independent municipalities, prospects for the future would appear to imply conservatism in the making of readjustments. The projection of current trends a decade or two into the future indicates that both the size and number of metropolitan areas will increase. These areas will not usually be governed by area-wide governments, except for a few adoptions of city-county consolidation plans, and for the expanded function of the traditional county—whose boundaries will in only rare cases be changed to fit the urbanizing pattern.

In the meanwhile, the social service state will grow by slow evolution with additional domestic policy responsibilities being assumed by the Federal government and greater concern being shown for metropolitan public policy matters by the state. The consequences of having the courts assume jurisdiction over the determination of fair representation in state legislatures will almost surely have the eventual effect of making state governments more responsive to the wants of urban areas. The very fact of greater state awareness will diminish the demand for metropolitan-wide governments and with the greater weighting of urban areas in the legislatures, the confidence of urbanites in state government will probably increase. I think it a good guess, therefore, that the state will play an increasing role in the future, not just in connection with such high-expense items as highways, public schools, welfare, renewal, and pollution control, but also in the somewhat less expensive areas of physical planning, capital-outlay planning, and land-use controls. The economic and psychological advantages that ride with greater use of state and Federal financing will add to the pressures for making these units, and perhaps especially the state government, the true metropolitan-wide governments of the future. This is not to say that there will not continue to be financial problems in metropolitan areas. State and Federal grants will only soften the impact of increasing urbanization accompanied by increasing service level expectations. Yet, the projected expansion of the gross national product leads us to believe that the financial strain on the citizen will probably not be much greater in the future than it has been in the last decade.[23] Probably no system for governing the metropolis could do much about reducing these costs or to prevent service supply from lagging somewhat behind demand. The rapid growth of our urban areas will keep "metropolitan area problems" constantly on the pages of the newspapers. Even if the rate of family formation declines, the professionals in various service areas will keep right on raising standards—there is no likelihood that we will ever catch them.

Problems will face the metropolis in the future, of course. Henrik Ibsen once noted that "life is cruel, life is earnest." And so it is, even in the affluent society. In addition to the ideological conflicts that will accompany the increasing role of the state and Federal governments, and in addition to the financial questions, here are a few items we will have to concern ourselves with:

1. The reluctance to face up to democratic responsibilities at the local level. The ghettoization of the suburbs has made it possible to put aside temporarily an issue that eventually must be faced.[24] It is slowly being faced, however, it seems to me. Current trends, I think, will within a generation put our most successful Negro lawyers and physicians into homes in the most fashionable suburbs not as an occasional exception

---

[23] Robert C. Wood, *1400 Governments* (Harvard University Press, Cambridge, Mass., 1961), pp. 182–184.

[24] Edward C. Banfield and Morton Grodzins, *Government and Housing in Metropolitan Areas* (McGraw-Hill Book Co., New York, 1958).

but as a matter of course. The rough cutting edge of status striving will hurt the lower middle class much more than the well-to-do, of course; this group will continue to see all kinds of threats to itself—and it will be the last to be reconciled to policies of open occupancy, desegregation of recreational facilities, and equal job opportunities. But the problems do not appear to be insurmountable.

2. Alienation. We today know too little about the sense of alienation in the urbanite. Some studies of the phenomenon have been made, however, and there is at least some reason to be concerned that the increasing size of urban places is correlated with increasing feelings of alienation.[25] There are probably several ways by which this sense, which appears to be a side effect or withdrawal symptom related to the disappearance of grass-roots government, may be managed. Some possibly effective methods may not even have been conceived, as yet. But alienation probably can be reduced if we can find ways of creating in the typical citizen a sense of legitimacy for a leadership group. To some extent this sense is appearing in the form of deference to or at least acceptance of professional administrators in the crucial policy innovation and decision making roles. It could also be reduced if we modified the traditional American belief in the cult of the common man, the notion that any man can be a decision maker. A return to the traditional concept of democracy would help; if we could relearn the ancient lesson that democracy is a system of government in which the *hoi polloi* chooses the rulers but does not itself rule. If we could get some acceptance of this idea—a common one in Great Britain—we would see fewer parochial vetoes of bond issues and tax levies, and we could get greater acceptance of the role of the state as the guardian which steps in to the decision-making process when local governments do not do what is generally expected of them by the prevailing values of society. We might also seek to increase the sense of legitimacy and representativeness of state governments—but as this sense increases for members of the working classes, it may decline for members of the lower middle classes. There is also some doubt as to what would happen to the confidence levels of upper-middle-class reformers if state legislatures are drastically reapportioned, even though these are the persons who have been in the forefront of the campaign for stronger urban representation at the state capitals.

3. The Reuse of Urban Land. As a frontier nation, Americans found it convenient to despoil the land and then move on; clearing urban structures for rebuilding has long been viewed as uneconomic. The prob-

---

[25] See footnote 14.

lems of the declining core-city tax base, the expansion of suburban slums, the increasing differences between the low-status core-city residents and the suburbanites, the penalizing effects of the property tax when land owners seek to improve their properties, are all too well known for me to discuss here. But if we ever do decide to take seriously the planned reuse of land—and this seems to be something I see in my crystal ball—it will probably be done largely with state and Federal subsidies and with direct state and Federal administrative participation. I see this as the trend despite the fact that actual experiences in cities such as Pittsburgh indicate that it need not be the case. Of course, America has the wealth which would permit us to clean away all slums within a few years, if our citizens saw that as a truly worthwhile objective. So far, there is little evidence that attitudes of apathy and acceptance are changing. But the problem cannot be ignored, and to the extent action is demanded, the high cost makes it seem natural for the typical citizen to accept the expanding state and Federal role in the usual pattern of cooperative federalism.

4. Rational Land Use. I once described the metropolitan-area planner as a kind of group therapist, a community hand holder, and verbalizer of our ideals.[26] Most Americans do not want those ideals denounced, but to date they do not want them acted upon with vigor, either. My interpretation of the planner does not imply that his task is futile or unimportant, of course. To the contrary, a psychiatrist is one with whom we often develop a dependency relationship—he becomes enormously important to us. He will become even more important in future years, for both economic and social pressures will demand a more rational approach to land use than has been the case in the past. In some instances, metropolitan planning agencies will be given effective powers to carry out planning decisions, but there is reason to believe that in many states this metropolitan task will be shared by the local units and the state government. In matters of great urgency involving area-wide services, we already turn to the state, as in connection with highway and water matters, for example. We will probably do so even more in the future. The state is a viable unit of government. It possesses effective jurisdiction and an adequate degree of legitimacy. The practical-minded American will turn to it. He will turn to it only when he thinks the time has come, however, and when he feels that he can no longer avoid doing so.

---

[26] Charles R. Adrian, "Metropology and the Planner," *Planning 1962* (American Society of Planning Officials, Chicago, 1962); also Charles R. Adrian, "Metropology: Folklore and Field Research," *Public Administration Review,* 21:148–157, Summer, 1961.

Closing note. My effort in this paper has been to show that activists and many writers and scholars in the area of metropolitan-area problems have followed a line of endeavor that has borne relatively little fruit over a couple of generations and that this has been so because the implicit assumptions concerning the nature of the political process or the ingredients of a political system, have been unreal. I have also noted that plans for metropolitan-area government have often been made with no consideration for the values, goals, and limits of believability possessed by the ordinary citizen. I have tried to compare the requirements of a political system for the metropolis with what is popularly acceptable and I have suggested that the future metropolis will probably be governed through the process of cooperative federalism which has become so typical a part of the American political system. In particular, I have indicated that suburban governments will survive and urban counties will expand their functions somewhat, but that the greatest future changes will be in the increased financial and administrative role of the state and Federal governments. Finally, I have indicated that the greatest future changes in role will take place at the state level. As legislatures become more representative, citizen acceptance of the role of the state as a legitimate one will expand. Its already ample legal powers and reasonably adequate financial powers will, in the future, make it the closest facsimile of a metropolitan-wide government in most urban areas. Whether the trend I anticipate is desirable or not, I would not be so arrogant as to claim to know. But I will say that democratic policy-making, like a biological infection, tends to follow the path of least resistance. And so far as I can tell, what I have been describing is that path. Persons interested in the problems of the metropolis might well give appropriate consideration as they make their plans for future action.[27]

---

[27] For a related conclusion that has received relatively little attention, perhaps because it defies conventional wisdom, see Robert C. Wood, *Suburbia,* pp. 225–242.

THOMAS R. DYE (Ph.D. University of Pennsylvania) is Professor and Chairman of the Department of Government at Florida State University. He is the author of *Politics in States and Communities; American Public Policy; Politics, Economics, and the Public;* and *American Government: Theory Structure and Process.*

BRETT W. HAWKINS (Ph.D. Vanderbilt University) is Associate Professor of the Department of Political Science at The University of Wisconsin. He is the author of *Nashville Metro: The Politics of City-County Consolidation; The Ethnic Factor in American Politics;* and *Politics and Urban Policy* (forthcoming).